Volume Two of *A Traveller's Story of Vietnam's Past*
From 2nd century BCE to 10th century CE
One Thousand Years
The Stories of Giao Châu, the Kingdoms of Linyi, Funan and Zhenla

© 2022 Tan Pham

All rights reserved. No part of this book may be reproduced or modified in any form, including photocopying, recording, or by any information storage and retrieval system, without permission in writing from the publisher, 315Kio Publishing.

First edition 2022
For inquiries, please email: NXB315KIO@GMAIL.COM

Edited by Paul Litterick   Designed by Son La Pham and Holly Zeng
Typeset in Fournier with Vietnamese language support provided by Seb McLauchlan

Published by 315Kio Publishing

ISBN: 978-0-473-63527-5

ONE THOUSAND YEARS

The Stories of Giao Châu, the Kingdoms of Linyi, Funan and Zhenla

Volume Two of *A Traveller's Story of Vietnam's Past*
FROM 2ND CENTURY BCE TO 10TH CENTURY CE

TAN PHAM

Contents

List of Tables	15
List of Figures	17
Preface	21
Acknowledgements	29
Chapter 1 – A summary of this book	31
1.1 – Three regions and four polities	32
Giao Châu	34
Linyi	35
Funan/Zhenla	36
Conclusions	36
1.2 – Story timeline	36
1.3 – Mountains in Southern China	37
Chapter 2 – Under the Han (III BCE – 220 CE) - Giao Châu I	43
2.1 – Circuit, provinces, and commanderies	45
2.2 – The Trưng sisters - *"as easy as turning over their hands"* (Years 40-43)	47
The event	47
The causes	49
The scale of the revolt	51
The aftermath	53
Ma Yuan's bronze pillars	54
The Zhuang people (Zhuangzu)	55
2.3 – The ancient citadel of Luy Lâu (*Thành cổ Luy Lâu*, first century to the sixth)	56
A discovery	56
Luy Lâu today	58
An archaeology story of Luy Lâu	61
Chapter 3 – Shi Xie and the beginning of Buddhism in Vietnam - Lady Triệu rebellion - Giao Châu II	63
3.1 – Shi Xie (136-226)	65
The early years	65
Sĩ Vương or King Sĩ - a Vietnamese king	66

The Shi clan	68
The peaceful and majestic years	70
A bloody end	73
3.2 – Men of Hu and the oldest pagodas in Vietnam - the coming of Buddhism (second to third centuries)	77
The tale of Man Nương - a pregnant orphan and the four statues	77
The belief of four Pháp	78
The four statues - Cloud, Rain, Thunder and Lightning	79
Vietnamese Buddhism and monks from Southern India	82
3.3 – Lady Triệu rebellion (third century)	87
Cửu Chân - A rebellious prefecture	88
Chapter 4 – A forest town - the kingdom of Linyi (Lâm Ấp) and the Fans - A Generation of Raiders - Linyi I	**93**
4.1 – Southern rebellions	95
Year 100	96
Year 137	96
Years 144, 157	97
Years 178, 184	98
4.2 – A new kingdom in the south	98
Year 192	98
The name of Linyi	99
4.3 – Where was Linyi?	99
4.4 – "The people of that country are aggressive."	101
The Fans	101
Sources of information	102
Austronesian and Mon-Khmer languages	102
4.5 – Fan Xiong (Phạm Hùng, 270-280) and Fan Yi (Phạm Dật, 280-336)	103
Tao Huang - "a stubborn and cowardly horse"	103
Year 248	105
Fan Yi	105
4.6 – The slave king	105
Fan Wen (Phạm Văn, 336-349) - A royal usurper	106
The battle of Cửa Lô Dung	107
In remembrance of Fan Wen	108
4.7 – Khu Túc - The elusive capital	109
4.8 – Cao Lao Hạ - A citadel in a paddy field	110
4.9 – The citadel of Thành Lồi	112
Chapter 5 – One hundred years of raids and plunders (336 – 446) - Linyi II	**117**
5.1 – Fan Fo (or Fu, Phạm Phật, 349-380) - Like father like son	119

Year 351 campaign - against Yang Ping/Deng Zhun - Version 1	119
Year 351 campaign - against Guan Cui/Deng Zhun - Version 2	119
Year 351 campaign - against Yang Ping/Guan Cui/Deng Zhun - Version 3	119
Year 353 campaign - against Yuan Fu	120
Year 359 campaign - against Wen Fangzhi	120
5.2 – Fan Huda or Houta (Phạm Hồ Đạt, 380-413) - The man who laid siege to Long Biên	121
Year 399 campaign	121
Year 407 campaign	122
Year 420 invasion of Linyi	122
5.3 – Fan Yangmai (or Yan Mah, Phạm Dương Mại, c. 425-446) - The Golden Prince	123
The Golden Prince	123
Year 431 campaigns	123
River fighting in the dark	124
5.4 – The destruction of Linyi's capital in 446	125
Tan Hezhi and Zong Que	125
An attempt to negotiate	125
First battle at Khu Túc	126
Second battle at Điển Xung	126
They all died	127
5.5 – Điển Xung – "catches the winds"	129
5.6 – Trà Kiệu - An ancient ruin of sandstone dancers	129
5.7 – Of gold and fragrant wood	132
Chapter 6 – The End of Linyi - Linyi III	**135**
6.1 – Fan Fanzhi (Phạm Phan Chí) - Southern pillage	137
A shameful event	137
The campaign	137
A heavy price	139
War elephants	139
Three new names	139
6.2 – Fan Touli (Phạm Đầu Lê) - A beautiful king and a talking parrot	140
6.3 – Fan Zhenlong (Phạm Trấn Long) - End of the line	140
6.4 – The kingdom of Huanwang (757-859)	141
Chapter 7 – The inscriptions and the Varman's - Linyi IV	**143**
7.1 – C.40 - Võ Cạnh - the oldest Sanskrit inscription in Vietnam.	146
The location	146
The content	146
The debate	147
7.2 – A valley of kings - Mỹ Sơn	149
The discovery	149

The three deities	150
C. 72 - The donation of lands	150
7.3 – C. 96 - A genealogy of kings	152
7.4 – C. 111 - A mutilated stele	153
7.5 – The Varman's and the Fans	155
Who is king Bhadravarman?	155
C. 105 - Carved in rocks	156
Gone to India	156
The return of an exile from Zhenla	157
7.6 – The coming of Champa	158
Campapura	158
Zhanbulao, Zhanpo and Zhancheng (Chiêm Thành)	159
Chapter 8 – The Roman medals and the Óc Eo culture - Funan/Zhenla I	**161**
8.1 – The monsoon trader	162
8.2 – Óc Eo - A trading and jewellery manufacturing hub	163
The location	163
The discovery	164
The excavation	165
A traveller's destination	166
8.3 – The Óc Eo culture and archaeological sites	167
Buddha statues	169
Hindu statues	172
Chapter 9 – The Kingdoms of Funan and Zhenla - Funan/Zhenla II	**175**
9.1 – Funan - the Chinese records	178
9.2 – The founding legend	179
9.3 – The Huns and the Fans - Interfamily killings	180
Fan Shiman – the great king (early third century)	180
Fan Zhan - West to India (c.230-c.243?)	181
Fan Xun - North to China (245/250-287)	182
Chu Zhantan	182
Liutuobamo - the last recorded king of Funan	183
9.4 – Funan - A widely spread South-East Asia kingdom	183
9.5 – The people of Funan - "the men are all ugly and black with curly hair."	184
9.6 – Funan and Linyi	185
9.7 – The end of Funan - the coming of Zhenla	186
Sui shu	186
Jiu Tang shu and the two Zhenlas	187
Xin Tang shu and the two Zhenlas	188
Location of two Zhenlas	188

Zhenla and Giao Châu	189
Chapter 10 – Pre-Angkor Inscriptions and three Khmer towers - Funan/Zhenla III	**191**
10.1 – Geographical distribution	192
10.2 – Funan - the inscriptions	194
K. 5 - A noble and intelligent prince	194
K. 40 - An inscription on the door lintel	195
10.3 – Zhenla - the inscriptions	196
K. 53 - The list of kings	196
K. 213 and K. 978 - Bhavavarman	196
K. 363 - The mount of the kingdom	197
K. 604 and K. 438 - Sambor Prei Kuk	197
10.4 – The pre-Angkor inscriptions found in southern Vietnam	198
K. 1 - Vat ThLen, or Vat Thling	198
K. 3 - Linh Sơn Tự, also known as Phnom Bathê.	198
K. 5 - Tháp Mười, Prasat Pram Loveng	199
K. 6, K. 7, K. 8 - Tháp Mười, Prasat Pram Loveng	199
K. 9 - Phú Hựu	199
Other pre-Angkor inscriptions	199
10.5 – Three oldest towers in southern Vietnam	200
The tower of Chóp Mạt	200
The tower of Bình Thạnh	200
The tower of Vĩnh Hưng	202
10.6 – The Angkor-period inscriptions in southern Vietnam	203
Chapter 11 – Ten thousand springs or Vạn Xuân (542-602) - Giao Châu III	**205**
11.1 – The Former Lý Nam Đế (Lý, Emperor of the South)	208
Early life	209
The revolt	209
Fought off a two-prong attack by imperial troops	210
Helped by a disease that decimated the second imperial campaign	210
Successfully fought off a southern raid by Linyi	211
Ten Thousand Life Spans	211
Up against a future emperor, 546-548	213
11.2 – King of the Night Marsh	216
The marsh of Dạ Trạch - The first guerrilla	217
The betrayal	219
11.3 – The Later Lý Nam Đế - facing the wrong way	220
A peaceful reign	220
The empire came south	221
Coming from the rear	221

The legacy	222

Chapter 12 – The Black Emperor - The Great Father and Mother King or Bố Cái Đại Vương (seventh and eighth centuries) - Giao Châu IV — 225

12.1 – The Black Emperor - Mai Thúc Loan and the Hoan Châu Uprising	227
Early life	227
The alliance	228
12.2 – The Imperial Consort, the lychees and other historical revisions	229
The lychees	229
Size of the rebellion	229
Duration	230
12.3 – A mound of dead bodies	230
12.4 – The Great Father and Mother King or *Bố Cái Đại Vương*	231
Đường Lâm commune	232
Vietnamese Atlas	232
Death from acute anxiety	233
A seven-year reign	233
A peaceful transfer of power	233

Chapter 13 – Surrounded by rivers - A city of lakes: Hanoi, a nation capital - Giao Châu V — 237

13.1 – Đông Kinh - a 15th-century capital	239
Tô Lịch river	239
Kim Ngưu river	239
A city of lakes	242
13.2 – Hanoi citadel - a 19th-century Vauban-designed fortress	243
13.3 – Of *Thành* and *Zheng*	244
13.4 – Tử Thành citadel	245
13.5 – The "mountains" or Núi of Hanoi	246
Núi Sưa	246
Núi Nùng	246
Núi Vạn Bảo, Núi Cung, Núi Thái Hòa, Núi Voi, Núi Khán Sơn	247
13.6 – La Thành citadel	247
13.7 – Đại La Thành - a citadel with 6.5-metre-tall walls	248
13.8 – A headquarters north of the river	248
13.9 – Gao Pian's La Thành - back to where it all started	249
An ancient dyke	249

Chapter 14 – The Nanzhao-An Nam war - Giao Châu VI — 253

14.1 – Nanzhao – "a country of cunning and dangerous people"	255
14.2 – Prelude to a war - A greedy and violent *duhu*	256
A river route to the north-west	256

One speck of salt for one horse	257
The Peach-Flower people	257
14.3 – The killing Đỗ Tồn Thành.	258
14.4 – Wang Shi and the thorny bamboos	259
14.5 – The first sacking of La Thành (Hanoi) in 860.	259
Li Hu - an ambitious duhu	260
14.6 – The second sacking of La Thành - the war of 862-863	260
Wang Kuang - appeasement to buy time	260
The attack	261
The elite forces - Luojuzi	261
14.7 – The empire struck back - The arrival of Gao Pian, a prince general	262
Government in exile	263
The first victory	263
Reinforcements and the reverse of roles	264
An escape and the final victory	265
14.8 – The aftermath - a dying empire	265
A Peaceful Sea Military District	265
Another invasion	265
The burning of the imperial capital of Chang'an	266
The Kingdom of Dachannghe	266
14.9 – A historical footnote on the Đỗ	267
Chapter 15 – Prelude to independence - Giao Châu VII	269
15.1 – The Khúc family (906-930) - the first native *jiedushi*	271
Khúc Thừa Dụ - the founder	271
The family village	272
Khúc Hạo – the reformer	272
Khúc Thừa Mỹ - died in exile	273
15.2 – Dương Đình Nghệ - A general from Ái.	273
Victory in 931	274
The pattern was broken	274
Temples	274
Chapter 16 – The Dawn of Independence - Giao Châu VIII	277
16.1 – The betrayal	279
16.2 – The revenge	279
16.3 – Battle of the Bạch Đằng river	280
The tides	281
The trap	281
The battle	282
The painting	283

The archaeological evidence	284
An amazing feat	285
16.4 – Aftermath of the battle	286
Declaration as king	286
The killing of brothers	287
Chapter 17 – Conclusions	289
17.1 – The river trips	290
In the north	290
In the north-central	290
In the Mekong Delta	291
17.2 – The inscriptions and monuments	291
17.3 – The independence question	292
Corrupted officials	292
Historians' views	293
A contemporary historian	295
A contribution	296

Appendices

1.	Sources of Vietnamese history in the Chinese language used in this book	299
2.	Sources of Vietnamese history by Vietnamese authors written before the 19th century	303
3.	Names in Pinyin Chinese, English, and Vietnamese	306
4.	Polities under the Northern Rule period	318
5.	Giao Chỉ, Giao Châu, Luy Lâu and Long Biên	320
6.	List of Governors, Prefects, Protectorate Generals, Governor Generals, Military Commissioners during the Northern Rule period	328
7.	In Search of ancient Hanoi	341
8.	Ma Yuan's expeditions (41-44)	349
9.	The Kings of Linyi	356
10.	The Kings of Funan and Zhenla	364
11.	The land that was Linyi	369
12.	Citadels of blood and gold - Khu Túc (Qusu), Điển Xung (Dian Chong) and other battlefields	395
13.	An eyewitness account of the Nanzhao-An Nam war	410
14.	The population question	417
15.	Of *li, bu, chi, liang, and jin* – Chinese units of measurements	423
16.	Museums in southern Vietnam with exhibits of the Óc Eo civilisation	425

Endnotes 430
Bibliography 511

List of Tables

Table 1 – A timeline of Vietnamese history from 111 BCE to the fourth century CE.	39
Table 2 – A timeline of Vietnamese history from the fifth to the 10th centuries.	40
Table 3 – Four statues and their locations.	81
Table 4 – A timeline of Funan, Zhenla and Kambuja.	177
Table 5 – Comparisons between citadels in the vicinity of Hanoi from the sixth to the 19th centuries.	250
Table 6 – A timeline of the Nanzhao-An Nam war.	254
Table 7 – Polities in three regions of Vietnam from the first to the 10th centuries.	319
Table 8 – A summary of Giao Chỉ, Giao Châu, Luy Lâu, and Long Biên.	327
Table 9 – Cishis and taishous of Giao Châu under the Han dynasty.	330
Table 10 – Cishis and taishous of Giao Châu under the Eastern Wu and Shu Han kingdoms.	331
Table 11 – Cishis and taishous of Giao Châu under the Jin dynasty.	333
Table 12 – Cishis and taishous of Giao Châu under the Southern Dynasties.	335
Table 13 – List A of cishis, taishous of Giao Châu under the Tang dynasty.	337
Table 14 – List B of cishis, taishous of Giao Châu under the Tang dynasty.	339
Table 15 – Cishis and taishous of Giao Châu under the Tang dynasty and Southern Han.	340
Table 16 – The kings of Linyi from the second to the fifth centuries.	357
Table 17 – The kings of Linyi from the sixth to the eighth centuries.	358
Table 18 – The kings, based on inscriptions from the fourth to the eighth centuries.	360
Table 19 – The kings of Funan based on Chinese records.	366
Table 20 – The kings, based on pre-Angkor inscriptions.	367
Table 21 – The list of the main rivers in north-central Vietnam.	371
Table 22 – Northern Champa prefectures.	375
Table 23 – Gnomon measurements.	378
Table 24 – Latitudes of places in Vietnam checked against historical gnomon measurements.	379
Table 25 – The distribution of five prefectures in Nhật Nam from different sources (from north to south).	381
Table 26 – Routes taken in the 1069 campaign by Đại Việt against Champa.	385
Table 27 – Details of Jia Dan's trip in the eighth century.	387
Table 28 – The number of mouths (or heads) in the commanderies (and zhou).	419

Table 29 – The number of households (or hearths) in the commanderies (and zhou). 420
Table 30 – The number of registered taxpayers and population of some of the provinces in Central Vietnam. 422
Table 31 – The Chinese unit of measurements (length). 424
Table 32 – The Chinese unit of measurements (weight). 424
Table 33 – Museums in 13 provinces in the Mekong Delta. 427
Table 34 – Museums in six provinces around Ho Chi Minh City. 428

List of Figures

Figure 1 – Timeline showing the eight periods of Vietnamese history.	22-23
Figure 2 – Indicative positions of Giao Châu, Linyi, and Funan on the map of Vietnam.	33
Figure 3 – Contemporary China, showing the features associated with Vietnamese history.	38
Figure 4 – Commanderies under the Former Han dynasty as of 108 BCE.	45
Figure 5 – Đông Hồ painting of the Trưng sisters' rebellion.	48
Figure 6 – The annual remembrance on the 6th day of Tết, Vietnamese Lunar New Year of the Trưng sisters at Mê Linh, Hanoi.	54
Figure 7 – The ancient citadel of Luy Lâu.	58
Figure 8 – View toward the corner between the northern and eastern ramparts of Luy Lâu.	59
Figure 9 – The base of the northern outer rampart of Luy Lâu.	60
Figure 10 – Shi Xie's temple (formerly residence) at Luy Lâu.	60
Figure 11 – The gateway to the temple and tomb of Shi Xie at Tam Á.	67
Figure 12 – A stone sheep in front of Shi Xie's tomb.	68
Figure 13 – Warlords at the end of the Later Han, circa 195.	70
Figure 14 – The Shi family tree - circa 140-230.	76
Figure 15 – Lady Dàn (Lightning, Pháp Lôi) without the ceremonial costume.	80
Figure 16 – The statue of Lady Dâu at the Dâu pagoda.	80
Figure 17 – Dâu pagoda, also known as Pháp Vân (cloud) or Diên Ứng.	86
Figure 18 – Hòa Phong tower at Dâu pagoda.	87
Figure 19 – The statue of Lady Triệu at her temple.	90
Figure 20 – Lady Triệu temple at Triệu Lộc commune, Hậu Lộc district, Thanh Hóa province.	90
Figure 21 – Ba Đồn town (1), Thọ Linh (2), Cao Lao Hạ citadel (3), and the Gianh river (4).	111
Figure 22 – Thành Lồi in Huế.	113
Figure 23 – The southern rampart, inside the citadel, off Huyền Trân Công Chúa street, Huế.	114
Figure 24 – View of the western rampart, from outside the citadel on Long Thọ street.	114
Figure 25 – A sketch of Điển Xung based on TKCS.	128
Figure 26 – The Linyi and Champa citadel of Trà Kiệu.	129
Figure 27 – The Asparas, Trà Kiệu style, 10th century, sandstone, Museum of Cham Sculpture.	131
Figure 28 – Dancer, Trà Kiệu, 10th century, sandstone, Museum of Vietnamese History.	131
Figure 29 – The Võ Cạnh stele (or block).	148

Figure 30 – The stone stele inscription of C.96 (dated 657) by Mỹ Sơn B6. 152

Figure 31 – The stele of Dinh Thị, C. 111, Huế. 154

Figure 32 – View of Ba Thê mountain from Gò Cây Thị road. 164

Figure 33 – Some archaeological sites of the Óc Eo civilisation and the three towers. 169

Figure 34 – A statue of Tháp Mười wooden Buddha (Museum code BTLS 1615). 170

Figure 35 – A Buddha in Meditation, sandstone. 171

Figure 36 – A statue of Brahma (sixth/seventh century), found in 1981 at Giồng Xoài. 172

Figure 37 – A statue of Vishnu - Trung Điền - Vĩnh Long - Museum of History - Ho Chi Minh City. 173

Figure 38 – Locations related to the stories of Funan. 189

Figure 39 – The distribution of pre-Angkor (before 802) inscriptions. 193

Figure 40 – The Four-arm Buddha at Linh Sơn Ba Thê pagoda. 198

Figure 41 – The tower of Chóp Mạt (seventh/eighth century), Tây Ninh province, Vietnam. 201

Figure 42 – The tower of Bình Thạnh, (seventh/eighth century), Tây Ninh province, Vietnam. 201

Figure 43 – The tower of Vĩnh Hưng (seventh century), Bạc Liêu province, Vietnam. 202

Figure 44 – A painting of the Former Lý Nam Đế and his Queen. 212

Figure 45 – Trấn Quốc Pagoda – Hanoi. 213

Figure 46 – Key locations during the reign of Lý Bí. 214

Figure 47 – A very small area in the vicinity of the Dạ Trạch marsh. 218

Figure 48 – Buildings at the Dạ Trạch temple for Chử Đồng Tử. 218

Figure 49 – Key locations under the reign of Lý Phật Tử, not including 2, 4, and 8. 223

Figure 50 – The temple and tomb of the Black Emperor Mai Hắc Đế. 229

Figure 51 – The temple of Phùng Hưng. 234

Figure 52 – The map of Đông Kinh (or Trung Đô – the Middle Capital) – 1490. 240

Figure 53 – Details of the Đông Kinh map showing the Inner Wall. 241

Figure 54 – Outline of the Đông Kinh map imposed on the map of contemporary Hanoi. 242

Figure 55 – The map of Hanoi circa 1873. 244

Figure 56 – Núi Sưa in Hanoi Botanic Garden. 246

Figure 57 – A photo of the Yi minority in Shilin (Kunming, Yunnan, China). 255

Figure 58 – Key locations related to Nanzhao. 258

Figure 59 – A painting of the bare-footed soldiers – possibly the Luojuzi. 262

Figure 60 – The Thanh Mai bronze bell. 267

Figure 61 – A map of China around 926, Dachanghe is the successor of the Nanzhao kingdom. 270

Figure 62 – Battle of the Bạch Đằng river, National Museum of Vietnamese History, Hanoi. 283

Figure 63 – Locations where stakes were found at the Bạch Đằng river. 285

Figure 64 – Mobilisation of the Later Han armies under Ma Yuan to Hepu and the sea routes to Mê Linh. 350

Figure 65 – Possible routes of Ma Yuan expedition into Cửu Chân (43-44). 354

Figure 66 – Family tree of the kings of Linyi from the middle of the sixth century to the middle of the seventh based on Chinese annals. 361

Figure 67 – Family tree of the kings of Linyi, based on C.96 inscriptions. 362

Figure 68 – The map of some of the main rivers in north-central Vietnam. 370

Figure 69 – A 15th-century map of Thuận Hóa (contemporary Thừa Thiên-Huế and Quảng Trị provinces). 373

Figure 70 – Locations of Linyi and Champa citadels. 376

Figure 71 – An illustration of the gnomon latitude during the summer solstice. 378

Figure 72 – Estimated positions of Jia Dan's trip. 388

Figure 73 – The Lô Dung river as described in TKCS. 397

PREFACE

This volume is the second in a number of books on Vietnamese history that I am writing. As a methodology, I have selected and approached the stories from a traveller's perspective, which explains the series title, *"A Traveller's Story of Vietnam's Past"*. My aim is simply to fix a historical site in time, to the period of history this place belongs, and in space; where it is located, why it is there and how it is connected to other historical locations. However, my books are not travel guides; readers will not find standard details, such as where to stay, or travel particulars, but where appropriate I include notes of my visits to the sites as mentioned in the books. In time, barring ongoing pandemic restrictions, I plan to visit these sites for a deeper appreciation of their stories.

My primary objective is to seek an understanding of the stories, their meanings and the interconnections between the historical events and the historical sites I have visited in Vietnam. Such information exists, but is dispersed in many different books at varying levels of complexity, and in different languages. My work attempts to gather the stories in one place by making geography the common thread.

PERIOD I — AUTONOMY (~500 YEARS: 630-111 BCE) ANCIENT TIMES TO PRE-HÙNG KINGS, HÙNG KINGS TO NAN-YUE	PERIOD II — NORTHERN RULE [NOTE 1] (~1000 YEARS: 111 BCE-938 CE)

Figure 1 – Timeline showing eight periods of Vietnamese history.

Note 1: The thousand-year period mainly addresses the land north of Ngang pass. Immediately south, the territory became autonomous from around the third century. The southern border marks the extent of Northern Rule, which kept changing from Ngang to Hải Vân passes; from the fifth century, it settled at Ngang pass.[4,5] The kingdoms to the south, Linyi/Champa and Funan/Zhenla, ruled themselves.

PERIOD VII — DIVISION AND WAR
(21 YEARS: 1954-1975 CE)

PERIOD IV — DIVISION
(~200 YEARS: 1558-1802 CE)

| PERIOD III — INDEPENDENCE (~600 YEARS: 938-1558 CE) | IV | V | VI | VIII |

PERIOD V — ONE COUNTRY
(~60 YEARS: 1802-1858 CE)

PERIOD VI — FRENCH RULE
(~100 YEARS)

PERIOD VIII — UNITED VIETNAM
(47 YEARS: 1975–)

Eight periods of history

I have divided the history of Vietnam into eight periods, based on the major events that marked key turning points in the story of Vietnam, and altered the course of its history. The selection of these eight periods is mine and not necessarily based on the historical timeline I was taught at school, where I had to memorise the story of one king and one battle following another king and another battle, often against foreign invaders; it was difficult to remember them all.

In broad terms, Period I covers the ancient times to 111 BCE (BCE=Before Common Era, same as BC=Before Christ) when the people of present-day Vietnam ruled themselves. My first published volume, Volume One, entitled *"The Bronze Drums and The Earrings"* deals with this period.[1] In the following millennium, Period II, the land of northern and north-central Vietnam was ruled by various Chinese dynasties barring a few years of Vietnamese autonomy. The country gained independence in 938 at the beginning of the second millennium in the 10th century CE (CE=Common Era, same as AD=Anno Domini, the year of our Lord); hence the title of my Volume Two, *"One Thousand Years - The Stories of Giao Châu, the Kingdoms of Linyi, Funan and Zhenla"*. The names refer to different political entities which existed in the land of present-day Vietnam over that time.

From 938 until the present time – barring a few episodes of foreign rule, divisions and shedding of much blood – the country was once again autonomous, with its land area more than double that of the previous millennium. I have divided this second millennium into periods III, IV, V, VI, VII and VIII.

Period III lasted for around 600 years from the 10th to 16th centuries, when there were three polities in Vietnam: Đại Việt (formerly Giao Châu) in the north, Champa (formerly Linyi) in the central, and part of the Khmer Empire in the south.[2] This southern region was called Zhenla and Funan before that.

Period IV followed period III when Champa lost most of its land to Đại Việt, but Đại Việt itself was divided; and ruled by two different lords for around 200 years from the early 17th century until the end of the 18th century.

Following a thirty-year civil war at the end of the 18th century, Đại Việt was united, expanded its territory south and west, absorbed Champa and southern Vietnam to become what is Vietnam. This is Period V, a brief time of around 60 years in the first half of the 19th century.

The expansion ended when the French arrived in the middle of the 19th century until they were driven out nearly a century later. This is Period VI.

In Period VII, Vietnam was once again divided and at war for another 21 years until its unification in 1975.

Period VIII covers Vietnam from 1975 to the present time.

The eight periods are summarised in Figure 1.

My volumes to come cover the following four periods, III, IV, V and VI, until 1954, when the French finally departed from the country after first bombarding and landing in Touraine (Đà Nẵng) in 1858. I will limit my contribution up to the year 1954, as there are already many history books covering Period VII, and Period VIII is too recent to be of interest to a historical traveller.

To avoid repeating my introduction from Volume One, I have simplified both the introduction and description of the eight periods of history, but the content of Volume Two is unique to this book.

Reading this book

Since there are many stories to tell, readers may find this book a little overwhelming, so to help make it easier to read, I have included a summary at the beginning of each chapter. Readers may choose to read these summaries on their first read and dwell on the details at a later date. Similarly, I have labelled each chapter with the name of the polities the chapter is about, such as Linyi I, Linyi II, etc. While there are some links between the stories of the polities, in general, these polities are relatively independent of each other, so readers may choose to read the stories of each polity separately. Each chapter also has a list of locations of interest relevant to the chapter so that a traveller can work out an itinerary for the visits.

Convention and references

As a matter of convention, I use the local spelling for names of people and locations in their respective countries. Vietnamese names and places are written with accents; Pinyin Chinese is used rather than Wade-Giles Chinese. For example: Giao Chỉ instead of Jiaozhi, Guangdong instead of Quảng Đông, Shi Xie and not Sĩ Nhiếp. I have applied this convention where possible, but there are exceptions, such as Vietnam instead of Việt Nam and Hanoi instead of Hà Nội since these names are very familiar to readers in either language. Similarly, I use Linyi instead of Lâm Ấp and Champa instead of Chiêm Thành, as these are terms English readers more familiar with. However, to assist those readers more familiar with the names in Vietnamese, I have included a translation list in Appendix 3. As to official titles, to avoid confusion, given there are several English translations of the Chinese originals, I have opted to keep Pinyin Chinese where applicable, e.g. *cishi* and *taishou* instead of Inspector and Governor.

The written language of Linyi, Funan, and Zhenla is Sanskrit – as well as Chamic and Khmer – so where possible, I have reproduced the names with the Sanskrit alphabet as given in the references.[3] For example, Mahārāja instead of Maharaja.

Similarly, these kingdoms adopted the Indian Śaka calendar when year 0 in this calendar was year 78 in CE (Common Era). We can thus derive the CE year by adding 78 to the Śaka year when the latter is clearly stated on the artefact. However, when it is not, and an estimate has to be made of the age, it can be problematic. This is because a fifth century Śaka could be a fifth or sixth century CE depending on whether the estimate is in the early or late of the Śaka century. To avoid confusion, I have not made the conversion in such cases.

The dates mentioned in Chinese and early Vietnamese texts are based on the lunar calendar, which is 11 to 12 days shorter than the solar year. To avoid any inaccuracy in the conversion, I have used the lunar dates as noted in the original texts. However, as a rough estimate, a lunar month is one month behind; for example, March 2022 is the second lunar month of the same year.

As to references, I have included both English and Vietnamese sources, acknowledging that the latter would mean little to those who do not read the language, but I would be remiss not to include them as there are readers who may and do find these helpful.

The Appendixes and End Notes provide many details and reference sources I have used to construct the stories. Such information may not appeal to the average reader, but others may wish to look them up for their research.

ACKNOWLEDGEMENTS

I wish to thank my wife, Mỹ Thành, my son, Sonla Pham, and my daughter Mai-Linh Pham, who have each given me much encouragement and support for this book. I am grateful to Biện Công Danh, Nguyễn Minh Long, Nguyễn Lê Việt Dũng, Võ Phú Thanh and Chris Hawley who have taken time out of their busy lives to read and comment on my draft. I am also grateful for the editing by Paul Litterick and the encouragement of Phạm Phan Long and Dương Vân Tuyết. My thanks also go to Nguyễn Hải Yến, Nguyễn Văn Thăng and Nguyễn Phạm Phúc Nhân for their help with the site visits. My appreciation also to Google Maps for their permission to use.

CHAPTER 1

A SUMMARY OF THIS BOOK

Volume One, *"The Bronze Drums and The Earrings"*, of this book series tells the stories of the ancient Vietnamese: the Lạc people in the northern part of the country and the Sa Huỳnh people in the central region. They were independent people until the Lạc fell under the rule of the Han dynasty in 111 BCE. Meanwhile, the Sa Huỳnh people went on to establish Linyi at the end of the second century.[1] This book, Volume Two, continues the stories of how both people evolved over the following one thousand years to the 10th century until the Lạc were able to rule themselves again; Linyi then became Huanwang in the eighth century and Champa from the ninth century. It also tells the stories of the people who lived in southern Vietnam around the Mekong Delta and how their history developed over this period.

For centuries, the people of these kingdoms inhabited the land south of Ngang pass, around 60 per cent of the area of Vietnam, but most people either have not heard or only possessed a vague idea about them.[2] I hope my contribution to the subject will aid in filling a vacuum that a prominent 20th-century Vietnamese historian, Phan Huy Lê, lamented regarding the number of people who asked him when the history of southern Vietnam began, who resided there before the Vietnamese migrated south, and how such histories relate to the history of Vietnam.[3]

1.1 – Three regions and four polities

During the thousand-year period covered in this volume, modern Vietnam existed in three/four separate polities: that north of Ngang pass was ruled by different Chinese dynasties; the land south of Ngang pass, from at least the third century to possibly Nha Trang, belonged to Linyi and its successors. Further south, from Ho Chi Minh City (Saigon), the region was under the successive rule of Funan and Zhenla kingdoms. Zhenla then fell under the control of the Khmer (or Angkorian) empire from the ninth to the 15th centuries. Since the stories of Funan, Zhenla and Khmer are also parts of the history of Cambodia, to keep them within the scope of this book, I will limit my narrative to locations within the Vietnamese border with Cambodia.

The approximate locations of these kingdoms are marked in Figure 2. I have not included Zhenla in this figure as it did not exist at the same time as Funan. However, Zhenla was where Funan is shown but also extended to most of eastern Cambodia, including southern Laos. Similarly, I have not shown the extent of Funan, which reaches south Cambodia and the Malay Peninsula.

This book is about the stories, historic locations and associated polities in these three regions. Over the thousand years, the region north of Ngang pass had several names at different times covered by this book: Giao Chỉ, Giao Châu, and An Nam. In this book, for simplicity, I have used Giao Châu in the title to represent both Giao Chỉ and An Nam, acknowledging it is not strictly correct: the names were different at different times, as discussed in Appendix 4. I should also point out that the name An Nam (or Annan in Pinyin Chinese which means Pacified South) used in the following chapters is not the same as Annam, used during the French colonial period to designate central Vietnam.

Until I began research for this volume, my knowledge of the polities south of Ngang pass was sketchy; in my school history lessons, these polities were treated as foreign countries with minimal impact on Vietnam. Now that I have had the opportunity to study the subject more closely, it has become clear to me that these kingdoms are as important to the understanding of Vietnamese history as the battle of the Bạch Đằng river in 938, where Ngô Quyền defeated an armada from Southern Han and established an independent nation. I have therefore devoted a few chapters to these kingdoms, which were roughly located in central and south Vietnam.

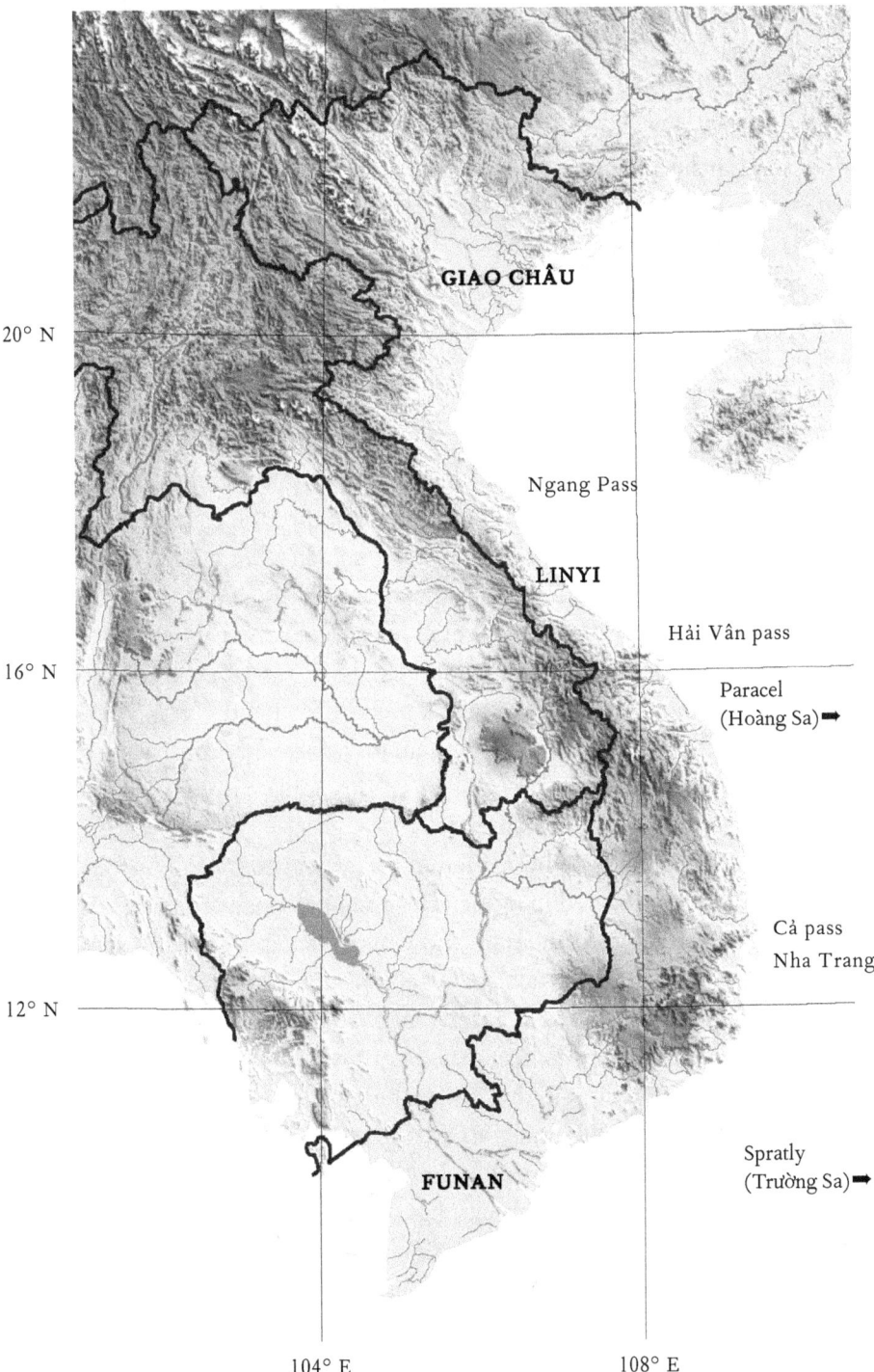

Figure 2 – Indicative positions of Giao Châu, Linyi, and Funan on the map of Vietnam (offshore islands not shown).[4]

I have set out this book – broadly in chronological order – from the first century to the 10th, beginning with the fall of Nan-yue to the Former Han dynasty in 111 BCE to the battle of the Bạch Đằng river by the coastal city of Hải Phòng in 938. Nan-yue was a kingdom that once included southern China, and northern Vietnam, extending as far south as Hải Vân pass. Its story is discussed in my Volume One.

GIAO CHÂU

Over the thousand-year period, there were a number of rebellions against the northern rulers. The major revolts were the Trưng sisters in the first century, Lady Triệu in the third, the Lý in the sixth, the Black Emperor in the eighth, the Great Father and Mother King also in the eighth, and culminating in Ngô Quyền's victorious naval battle in the 10th century. Historians have mentioned two other rebellions of Lý Tự Tiên - Đinh Kiến (687) and Dương Thanh (819-820) in the official list of revolts against Northern Rule, but I have not described them in detail as they were relatively obscure and not related to any significant landmarks.[5,6]

These rebellions are discussed in Chapters 2, 3, 11 and 12.

Buddhism came from India to Vietnam in the second century at a place named Luy Lâu east of Hanoi. The story of Luy Lâu or Long Biên and the early monks is recounted in Chapter 3.

In the ninth century, northern Vietnam was invaded by troops from Nanzhao, a kingdom located in modern Yunnan province of China, northwest of the border between Vietnam and China – an event that, to some historians, prompted an avalanche of rebellions that brought down the Tang dynasty (618-906) in China, and accelerated Vietnam's independence. Like Linyi and Funan, this war has been cursorily covered by Vietnamese historians, but I found it fascinating, so I have therefore allocated a few pages in Chapter 14 to discuss it, including an eyewitness account.

Between stories of rebellions, I include older maps of Hanoi, the current capital, within the narrative. This city has occupied a significant role in the historical development of Vietnam, beginning in the middle of the sixth century, and a discussion of its evolution aids us in gaining a deeper understanding of Vietnamese history. I have devoted significant time tracing the city's development through the use of maps so that a traveller can explore its history, from at least the sixth to the 10th centuries. The story of this city, which I term a 'City of Lakes', is told in Chapter 13.

Events that led the Lạc people to move out of the Northern Rule and ushered in an independent Vietnam are described in Chapters 15 and 16, including the battle of the Bạch Đằng river in 938.

LINYI

South of Ngang pass, the stories of the kingdom of Linyi – founded at the end of the second century – and its kings, the Fans, particularly the bloodthirsty Fan Wen, are described in some detail in Chapter 4. Places associated with Linyi such as Thành Lồi, Cao Lao Hạ, Trà Kiệu and Mỹ Sơn are also included. Sadly, one of the most famous cities in Linyi history, Khu Túc, remained elusive to historians despite their best attempts to unearth traces of the past. The results of my attempt, using the mathematics of gnomon measurements recorded in Chinese annals related to Khu Túc, are explained in Appendix 11.

The Fans lineage ended in the middle of the seventh century, and Linyi was no longer cited in Chinese annals from the middle of the eighth century. By that time, another kingdom, Huanwang, had taken its place. The decline of Linyi and the story of Huanwang is told in Chapter 6.

After the year 938, the Vietnamese (the Lạc) began to move beyond Ngang pass and pushed the successors of Linyi, by then called Champa, south. During the fourth and fifth centuries, the Linyi kings and their army of raiders were the aggressors against those living in the northern region beyond Ngang pass. There was also cooperation between Linyi, Zhenla, and the Vietnamese Black Emperor in the revolt against the local Tang's administration in the eighth century.

Most historians believe Linyi became Indianised around the fourth century when Hindu gods were worshipped and Indian scripts were used; this is demonstrated by a letter from Fan Wen, a Linyi king, to imperial court written in a south Indian script. The names of Linyi, Huanwang, and associated stories only appeared in Chinese dynastic annals. Inscriptions, in both Chamic and Sanskrit languages, engraved on stone steles and rocks found in what is believed to be Linyi territory, do not mention these names, nor those of the Fans.

In effect, we have two sources of information on Linyi: Chinese annals and the inscriptions. The name of Huanwang was recorded in Chinese annals for around 100 years, but from the ninth century, another kingdom appeared in the annals, called Champa. This name was first mentioned in inscriptions made in the seventh century.

The content and location of some of these inscriptions are discussed in Chapter 7.

FUNAN/ZHENLA

Further south, just beyond Ho Chi Minh City, Chinese envoys first reported a kingdom called Funan around the third century. This kingdom left behind many artefacts found in the 20th century. It was overtaken by Zhenla, which in turn was absorbed into the Khmer Empire in the ninth century. The stories of Funan and the associated civilisation, named Óc Eo, are told in Chapters 8 and 9.

Like Linyi and Champa, Funan was Hinduised in the fourth century; like the Chams, the people of Funan and Zhenla left behind inscriptions in Khmer and Sanskrit languages. The stories of these pre-Angkor inscriptions (made before 802 when the Khmer or Angkorian empire began) are told in Chapter 10.

To help those readers who want to take a more in-depth interest in the stories, I have included the names of the governors appointed by the northern dynasties, the kings of Linyi, Funan, and Zhenla in Appendixes 6, 9, and 10.

CONCLUSIONS

One can draw different conclusions from the stories told in this volume, and I have settled on three topics. The first is about the river trips I wish to take, the second is about the inscriptions, and the third is about the question of how the Vietnamese managed to emerge from the Northern Rule and gain independence after one thousand years. The conclusions are in Chapter 17.

1.2 – Story timeline

The 15th-century historian Ngô Sĩ Liên commented on the surrender of the Vietnamese king, Lý Phật Tử, in 602 to the Sui general as follows:[7]

> "South-North, strong and weak, there are moments. When the North is weak, we are strong; the North is strong, we become weak. The great world is like that."

"North" refers to the northern dynasties, and "South" refers to Đại Việt.

From 111 BCE to 938 CE, one thousand and forty-nine years, is a long time in human history. Given that a millennium holds a substantial trove of stories, I have generally followed four-time spans based on the timeline of Chinese history to make sense of this vast period. This choice has been inspired by Ngô Sĩ Liên's remark, as many major events in Vietnam during the Northern Rule generally occurred during a period of major upheaval in China.⁸ The four-time spans are:⁹

- DYNASTIC UNITY: Former (or Western) Han (202 BCE-8 CE), Xin (9-23), and Later (or Eastern) Han (25 -220).

- DYNASTIC BREAK-UP: Six Dynasties (220-589).¹⁰

- DYNASTIC UNITY: Sui (581-618) and Tang (618-906).

- DYNASTIC BREAK-UP: Five Dynasties and Ten Kingdoms (907-960).¹¹

However, it is worth noting that Vietnamese historians typically use the brief years of Vietnamese independence as milestones and thus divide these 1,000 years into three eras of *"Bắc thuộc"*; first (111 BCE-39 CE), second (43-544) and third (602-939). *Bắc thuộc* is loosely translated as "A colony of the north or belonging to the north".¹² My equivalent term for this period is *"Northern Rule"*.

While I have no issue with such a division as a framework to study Vietnamese history from the first to the 10th century, I have opted for the above dynastic timeline instead. Further, while the stories in this volume include key characters from the rebellions, in my view, the dynastic timeline provides a more useful framework to examine the nature of such events as rebellions and so forth and their impacts on Vietnamese history overall.

Tables 1 and 2 show a summary of this book based on these periods. However, I will limit my stories of Linyi, Funan, Zhenla to the beginning of Champa and the Khmer Empire. The history of Champa will be told in Volume Three of this book series.

1.3 – Mountains in Southern China

Interactions between Vietnam and its neighbour to the north, China, have significantly shaped the history of Vietnam. Many stories in early Vietnamese history refer to locations in China, so it is helpful to briefly address the geography of China to identify these sites. Figure 3 shows the topography of China where the three major rivers flow from its hinterland in the west to the sea in the east; the Yellow (Huang He) river in the north; the Yangtze (or Yangzi) river in the centre; and the Pearl (Zhu Jiang or Xujiang or Xi) river in the south.

Figure 3 – Contemporary China, showing the features associated with Vietnamese history.[13] Keys: 1. Wuling, 2. Wuyi.

The relevant locations to Vietnamese history are mostly located south of the Yangtze river. Those of interest are along the south-eastern coast of China and immediately north of the current border, as shown in Figure 3.

The map shows the border of the two southern provinces of Guangxi, Guangdong; the immediate northern neighbours of Hunan, and Jiangxi. This border is where a mountain range called Nanling (also known as Wuling), literally translates as "Southern (or Five) Mountains".[14] This mountain range, stretching some 1,400 kilometres from west to east, separates the Pearl River Basin from the Yangtze Valley, and serves as the dividing line between the south and central subtropical zones.[15]

Similarly, the border between Jiangxi and Fujian provinces is formed by another mountain range, Wuyi or Wuyishan, south of Shanghai, which runs approximately in the north-south direction. It also extends in the north-east direction into Zhejiang province. Knowledge of these ranges aids in understanding the stories within this volume.

TIMELINES	CHINESE DYNASTIES	POLITIES	EVENTS
111-1 BCE	Former Han	Giao Chỉ	Former Han's conquest of Nan-yue and absorbed the north and north-central Vietnam into its empire.
1-99 CE	Former/Later Han	Giao Chỉ	The Trưng sisters' rebellion.
	Former/Later Han	Funan	Funan kingdom founded.
100-199 CE	Later Han	Giao Chỉ	Buddhism came to Vietnam. Shi Xie clan established.
	Later Han	Funan Linyi	Southern rebellions. Linyi founded.
	Later Han/ Six Dynasties	Linyi	Linyi raids of provinces north of Ngang pass.
200-299 CE	Six Dynasties	Funan Giao Châu	Destruction of Shi Xie clan. Chinese envoys to Funan and Linyi. Lady Triệu rebellion.
	Six Dynasties	Funan	Óc Eo settlement date. Expansion of the Funan kingdom from the Mekong Delta to the Malay Peninsula. Arrival of two Chinese envoys at the Funan court. Funan envoys arrived in India. Funan sent envoys to China.
300-399 CE	Six Dynasties	Funan	End of the lineage of the Fans of Funan. A Chu Zhantan appeared as the king of Funan. Funan Hinduised.
	Six Dynasties	Funan Linyi	Plunders and raids of provinces north of Ngang pass.

Table 1 – A timeline of Vietnamese history from 111 BCE to the fourth century CE.

TIMELINES	CHINESE DYNASTIES	POLITIES	EVENTS
400-499 CE	Six Dynasties	Funan Linyi	Plunders and raids of provinces north of Ngang pass. Destruction of Linyi capital in 446.
500-599 CE	Six Dynasties (Liang-Chen)	Funan	Last recorded king of Funan by Chinese annals.
	Six Dynasties (Liang-Chen)	Funan Linyi Giao Châu	Lý Bí's rebellion. Construction of a fort near modern Hanoi.
600-699 CE	Sui-Tang	Zhenla Linyi	Destruction of another Linyi capital in 605. End of the lineage of the Fans of Linyi.
	Sui-Tang	Zhenla	Envoys from Zhenla to the Chinese court.
	Sui-Tang	Zhenla Linyi An Nam	Construction of Tử Thành (modern Hanoi)
700-799 CE	Tang	Zhenla Linyi An Nam	Rebellions of the Black Emperor, the Great Father and Mother King. Construction of La Thành (modern Hanoi).
	Tang	Water Zhenla, Land Zhenla Huanwang	Appearance of the name Huanwang in 757, in place of Linyi, in Chinese annals.
800-899 CE	Tang	Khmer Empire Huanwang An Nam	Construction of Đại La (modern Hanoi). Nanzhao – An Nam War.
	Tang	Khmer Empire	Establishment of the Khmer Empire from 802.
	Tang	Khmer Empire Champa	Appearance of the name Zhancheng (Champa) in 877, in place of Huanwang, in Chinese annals.
900-999 CE	Tang-Five Dynasties and Ten Kingdoms	Khmer Empire Champa An Nam	First native *Jiedushi* (Imperial Commissioner). The battle of Bạch Đằng river in 938. An Nam gained independence, free from the Northern Rule.

Table 2 – A timeline of Vietnamese history from the fifth to the 10th centuries.

CHAPTER 2

UNDER THE HAN (III BCE – 220 CE)

GIAO CHÂU I

STORY TIMELINE: Second century BCE to second century CE.
STORY LOCATION: North Vietnam.
KEY CHARACTERS: *The Trưng sisters:* led the rebellion against Su Ding and the Han rulers, *Su Ding:* Han's governor of Giao Châu, *Ma Yuan:* Han's general, suppressed the rebellion.
LOCATIONS OF INTEREST: Trưng sisters' temple. Luy Lâu citadel.

Chapter Summary

Our stories begin in the first three centuries following the conquest of Nan-yue by the Han empire and its absorption into contemporary north and north-central Vietnam. The region is shown in Figure 4.

For the first 150 years or so, the Han generally left the local people to be governed by their chieftains, which had been local practice for centuries. However, at the beginning of the first century, the first Han dynasty (known as the Former Han: 202 BCE-8 CE) was overthrown by a major rebellion.[1]

The upheaval created many refugees who escaped to the Red River Delta. This pattern was repeated many times in the history of Vietnam until the 18th century. Red River Delta is furthest from the imperial capital, but is accessible by boat using coastal and river routes. During a time of crisis, one might imagine it made more sense for former members of the ruling regime or wealthy elites from the imperial capital to escape by boats to the sea and head south, rather than take the land route to other areas of the empire. This was arguably safer and quicker, with little risk of capture en route.

In any case, historians have suggested the large number of northern refugees combined with the change in policy—the new regime sought more direct control—severely strained the relationship between imperial officials and local chieftains. In 40 CE, the actions of a greedy *cishi* (Inspector) who sought to make local chieftains comply with new legislation sparked a widespread rebellion led by two sisters, Trưng Trắc and Trưng Nhị, or Vietnamese Hai Bà Trưng. Today, a traveller to Vietnam will likely find streets and temples named Hai Bà Trưng in most cities. Other than the legendary Hùng kings, the first kings of Vietnam before the Han arrived, the Trưng sisters are the nation's foremost Vietnamese heroes.

But the Trưng sisters' reign was not to last. A Han general named Ma Yuan led a force of 10,000 (or 20,000 as per Appendix 8) who marched down from southern China in 41 and ended their rule. Ma Yuan decimated the local ruling class, taking 300 chieftains as prisoners to China, melting the bronze drums– a symbol of local power – to cast a horse and instigating changes to local laws in alignment with Han laws. Further, he is said to have erected two bronze pillars to mark the southernmost border of the empire. Their whereabouts are unknown, but my research has found that their original location is probably at Chân Mây bay, north of Hải Vân pass (Appendix 11).

There were three administrative centres or provincial capitals in north Vietnam during Han rule. Luy Lâu – also known as Long Biên – remained a provincial capital for nearly five centuries until the middle of the sixth century. It then disappeared from history until it was located on the eastern side of Hanoi by a French resident in 1933. Today, one can spend a day or two wandering its remaining ramparts and visiting nearby pagodas and temples. The two other provincial centres were to the west of contemporary Hanoi: one was at Mê Linh, while the other remains a mystery.

Luy Lâu was a major centre of Buddhism in the northern empire. This story, and that of the Shi family who ruled northern Vietnam and southern China for nearly 90 years, is discussed in Chapter 3. In the same chapter, the rebellion of Lady Triệu in the middle of the third century is also told.

2.1 – Circuit, provinces, and commanderies

One night in the winter of 111 BCE, the Former Han army surrounded and burned Panyu, the capital of Nan-yue, near modern-day Guangzhou, 140 kilometres inland from Hong Kong. By the early morning, Nan-yue surrendered; its chancellor and king fled and were captured.[2]

Nan-yue was one of several independent kingdoms in the south of China that the Former Han dynasty eventually absorbed into its empire, including today's Hainan Island. The region was divided into nine commanderies. Four were in southern China: Nan-hai (Guangzhou), Yulin (Guilin), Cangwu (near Wuzhou) and Hepu (near Beihai). Three were in northern Vietnam: Giao Chỉ (Jiaozhi), Cửu Chân (Jiuzhen) and Nhật Nam (Rinan). Hainan island also became part of the Han empire and was divided into two counties: Zhuya and Dan'er.

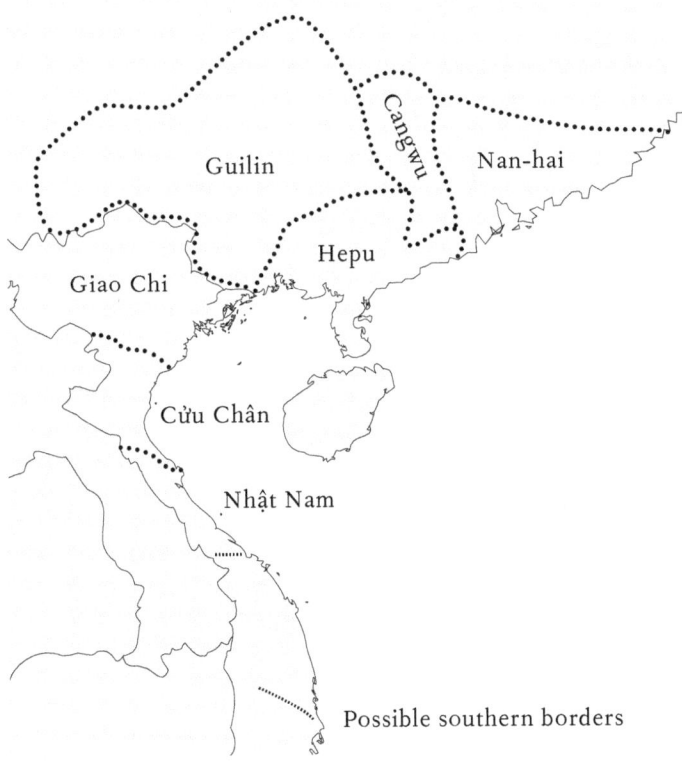

Figure 4 – Commanderies under the Former Han dynasty as of 108 BCE.[3,4]

In the dying days of Nan-yue, two envoys from Giao Chỉ and Cửu Chân, which once belonged to Nan-yue, submitted to the Former Han general, Lu Bode, and were awarded the *taishou* (Governor or Administrator) positions of their commanderies.[5] By all accounts, these officials continued the tradition set during the Nan-yue time, whereby they acted as imperial representatives and left the day-to-day governing of the people to the local indigenous chiefs or Lạc Tướng (Lạc, or Luo, general).[6]

During this time, until around year 106 or over two centuries from the first year of Han rule, the administrative centre of the Giao Chỉ circuit, which included all seven commanderies, resided at a place called Luy Lâu (O).[7] In this book, I suggest there are two places named Luy Lâu: Luy Lâu (O), where O is the abbreviation for "original", and Luy Lâu itself. The former is west of Hanoi, and the latter is east of it, both at a distance of approximately 30 kilometres from Hanoi. A detailed discussion of the two is given in Appendix 5.

In year 106, the administrative centre was moved to present-day Wuzhou in the Cangwu prefecture of Guangxi province, China.

The Former Han had a military garrison at Mê Linh, approximately 60 kilometres northwest of Hanoi on the northern side of the Red river, downstream from Phú Thọ, the land of the legendary Hùng kings.[8] It was built as a frontier camp, presumably to keep watch over hostile forces travelling down the Red river to attack the main settlement around Luy Lâu (O). In year 40, that was precisely what happened.

Until then, around 150 years after the first year of Han rule, it appears the three commanderies of Giao Chỉ, Cửu Chân and Nhật Nam were relatively uneventful; history books have not recorded significant events from this period. However, the apparent peace was shattered. The Trưng sisters rose against the cruel *taishou* of Giao Chỉ; the population of 65 towns of three other commanderies, and Hepu (Figure 4), joined them in their campaign.

Down the centuries, this event has been remembered by all Vietnamese and is celebrated each year. Like the legendary Hùng kings in the first millennium, which I examined in Volume One, the Trưng sisters are the most revered heroines within the second millennium in the history of the Vietnamese. I now turn to their story.

2.2 – The Trưng sisters - "as easy as turning over their hands" (Year 40-43)

THE EVENT

The uprising led by the sisters is described in a Chinese dynastic annal, Hou Han shu (Book of the Later Han), which was compiled in the fifth century, and reads as follows: [9]

> "*During the 16th year (year 40), there was a woman from Giao Chỉ called Trưng Trắc and her younger sister, Trưng Nhị, rebelled and attacked the commandery. Trưng Trắc was a daughter of a Lạc Tướng from Mê Linh prefecture. She married Thi Sách, a man from Chu Diên. She was very heroic and brave. The taishou of Giao Chỉ, Su Ding used laws to constrain her; outraged, she rebelled. So, the Man Lái* [Lái barbarians] *of Cửu Chân, Nhật Nam and Hepu commanderies responded and joined her 65 towns were taken, she established herself as king. The taishou of Giao Chỉ and all other taishous could only be on the defensive. The Guangwu Emperor* [Later Han dynasty, 25-57] *ordered* [officials of] *Changsha, Hepu and Giao Chỉ* [commanderies] *to prepare carts and ships, to repair all roads and bridges, to make sure all ravines can be crossed, and to hoard food and grain. In the 18th year* [year 42]*, he ordered the Wave-Calming General, Ma Yuan, along with the General of the Towered Ships, Duan Zhi, to assemble troops from Changsha, Guiyang, Lingling and Cangwu, a total of over 10,000 soldiers, to attack the rebels.*[10] *The next summer, in the fourth month of the following year* [43]*, Ma Yuan broke Giao Chỉ, beheaded Trưng Trắc and Trưng Nhị, the rest surrendered and scattered. He then advanced to attack the rebels from Cửu Chân, Đô Dương and his followers, also defeated them and secured their surrender.* [Ma Yuan] *then sent over 300 local chieftains to exile in Lingling* [at contemporary Yongzhou, Hunan, province, China]. *Thereupon, Liangbiao* [Lingnan] *region was pacified."*

The story of the uprising is also relayed in two later Vietnamese books from the 14th and 15th centuries: "Compilation of the Departed Spirits in the Realm of Viet" (or *Việt Điện U Linh* – abbreviated as VDUL) and "A Collection of Strange Stories from Linh Nam (or *Lĩnh Nam Chích Quái* – abbreviated as LNCQ).[11,12] In essence, the stories in each of these books resemble those of Hou Han shu but for a few differences. Firstly, in both books, the sisters come from the lineage of the legendary Hùng kings from the seventh century BCE, and adopt the name Trưng once they become kings. Secondly, Su Ding escaped Giao Chỉ back to China and was banished to Dan'er (Hainan Island); finally, both sisters were killed during the battle.

In a Vietnamese 19th-century work – The Imperially Ordered Annotated Text Completely Reflecting the History of Viet (*Khâm Định Việt Sử Thông Giám Cương Mục* – abbreviated as CM) – the sisters died in battle.[13] In another account, they committed suicide by jumping into Hát Giang, near where Đáy and Red rivers meet.[14] Presently, the commonly accepted version is the sisters committed suicide. The description of being brave and heroic is also not clear; in VDUL, it refers to Thi Sách, the husband, but in LNCQ, it is Trưng Trắc who was brave and courageous.

There is now a temple in their honour at Hát Môn nearby.[15,16] These locations are shown in Figure 49 of Chapter 11.

Figure 5 – *Đông Hồ* painting of the Trưng sisters' rebellion.[17]

Đông Hồ is a form of traditional Vietnamese woodcut painting, which originated in a village of the same name around 30 kilometres east of Hanoi. In this picture (Figure 5), the lower left depicts Su Ding on the run. The sisters, sitting on elephants, wave their swords and direct their troops forwards, trampling over fleeing enemy soldiers. The sisters riding elephants is the image that often appears during the annual celebration of their rebellion. It is fitting to have the sisters sitting majestically on elephants, but it could have been horses. In VDUL, the two sisters appeared in a dream of a Vietnamese king, Lý Anh Tông (1138-1175), to help end a severe drought, they

"*have the face of a flower, eyebrows like a willow, wear a blue dress, a red skirt with a red cap and belt, ride on an iron horse and follow the rain to visit the king*".[18]

As a matter of interest, elephants appeared in Chinese annals at a later date as gifts from Funan, and as war animals in battles between Linyi and the generals of the Sui dynasty in the seventh century.

THE CAUSES

Policy change

Until the sisters' revolt, life appeared peaceful in Giao Chỉ and other southern commanderies. The governing policy of the Former Han was said to be based on the three Ts: trade, tribute and tax, and the governing of the local people was at the behest of the Lạc Tướng. Such an arrangement appears to have worked smoothly, other than the fact that little tax, if any, was collected.[19,20,21] One can speculate and propose that the indigenous ruling class, the Lạc generals or chieftains who existed before the Former Han arrived, may have decided that using trade and tributes to maintain peace and their power was preferable to conflict. After all, there had been a precedent where the legates (or envoys) of these commanderies made a similar arrangement when they offered the Former Han general Lu Bode gifts and household records to achieve a comparable aim in 111 BCE.

Northern refugees

However, times were changing, and by the beginning of the first century, the Former Han dynasty was coming to an end when, in 9 CE, the regent Wang Mang, the nephew of the dowager empress, refused to relinquish control when the heir to the throne came of age. Wang Mang declared a new dynasty for himself, the Xin dynasty (9–23) and initiated major reforms that were ultimately unsuccessful. Chaos followed; rebellions combined with two massive floods sealed his fate. The Later Han dynasty followed in the year 25, but for this brief period of Wang Mang, a large number of Former Han ruling class people fled to Giao Chỉ to find refuge. The violent transition of power from the Former Han to Wang Mang and then to Later Han dynasties set up a chain of events that sparked the revolt, as explained by different historians and summarised below:[22,23,24]

Wang Mang's usurpation led to a civil war in the north, creating refugees who fled to southern commanderies, including Giao Chỉ and Cửu Chân. The influx of refugees increased the demand for land to accommodate and feed these new settlers. Attempts to sinicise local people caused social tension between the northern immigrants and the indigenous population. The efforts of local authorities to reinforce new Chinese rules regarding marriage undermined the indigenous tradition of women's rights to own, inherit land and precipitated resentment. The aggressive application of Chinese laws by a greedy and brutal *taishou* finally broke the "peaceful coexistence, live-and-let-live" policy between the Lạc elites and the northern rulers that had endured for nearly 150 years since the Han first arrived. Massive revolt was the result.

Sinicisation

The sinicisation began with two Han officials: Xi Guang (Tích Quang), *taishou* of Giao Chỉ in the early years of the second millennium, who used rites and ceremonies to teach the local people.[25,26,27] Ren Yan (Nhâm Diên), *taishou* of Cửu Chân in the years 25 to 29 taught local people to cast agricultural implements, to reclaim land, and to plant annually in order to feed hundreds of families. Prior to Ren Yan's arrival, these folk survived off fishing and hunting and did not know about farming. He also instructed the village chiefs to reduce their personal benefits to pay for the marriages of the poor; many named their children Nhâm as a result.[28,29] Ren Yan was known as a "Young Sage" for his mastery of the classics.[30]

The author of a 15th-century work – Complete Book of the Historical Records of Great Việt (*Đại Việt Sử Ký Toàn Thư* (abbreviated as SKTT) – borrowing from Hou Han shu, suggests the civilised customs of the land Lĩnh Nam (or Lingnan, south of Nanling mountains) were initiated by these two Han officials.[31] However, some later Vietnamese historians have questioned these stories, instead suggesting that under Nan-yue, Zhao Tuo (207–111 BCE) was an educated king; therefore he surely possessed the knowledge to teach the local people farming and marriage years earlier. In short, such expertise developed before the arrival of these two *taishous*.[32]

I support this claim, not because of Zhao Tuo, but because the local Lạc people already had their customs and marriage rites. Those in the Red River Delta already knew about agriculture and practised wet-rice culture many centuries earlier.[33] However, it is possible there were places in Cửu Chân commandery that did not practice farming and that the land there required cultivation in order to feed the growing population.

Key characters

Xi Guang was replaced in 34 as the *cishi* of Giao Chỉ by Su Ding, who was described as "*Greedy and brutal, so Trưng Trắc killed him*".[34,35] SKTT puts it differently whereby Su Ding used the law to bind Trưng Trắc and killed her husband, so she revolted, and Su Ding escaped to China.[36] Su Ding was described as follows: "*When seeing money, [his] eyes shine, but when seeing enemies, [his] eyes darken with fear*".[37]

Other Chinese sources note that Trưng Trắc's husband, Thi Sách, was fighting alongside her and was not killed by Su Ding; but most Vietnamese textbooks, based on SKTT, attribute revenge of her husband's killing as the key cause of the revolt.[38,39] The personal nature of the rebellion is also suggested by historian Đào Duy Anh who speculates their marriage, a union between two powerful Lạc families, posed such a political threat to Su Ding that he decided to arrest them.[40] Sinologist Henri Maspero cites the inability of Thi Sách to comply with Chinese laws due to his violent and haughty character as a major contributing factor to the revolt.[41] While I do not disagree with these explanations, I tend to support the underlying social and political roots of the revolt.

According to local folklore, 20 female generals fought alongside the sisters.[42] There are temples for these women; many can be found around Phú Thọ – the land of the legendary Hùng kings – but if one visits Hải Phòng near Hạ Long bay, one will see a giant statue of Lady Lê Chân, one of the sisters' most able generals, in the city centre.

THE SCALE OF THE REVOLT

The revolt was a significant event at the time, judging by the simultaneous uprisings from three other commanderies and the extensive mobilisation of resources by the empire in its efforts to suppress it.[43] Trưng Trắc and Thi Sách were both children of the Lạc Tướng of two of the largest prefectures among 10 in Giao Chỉ commandery.[44] Mê Linh was located northwest of Hanoi and roughly occupied today's Vĩnh Phúc, Phú Thọ and possibly part of Tuyên Quang. It extended to the mountainous regions at Hòa Bình and Sơn La provinces east of Đà river; Chu Diên lay in the relatively flat area between Đáy and Red rivers south of Hanoi towards Hà Nam as far as Hưng Yên and Phủ Lý.[45] The combination of these two prefectures on the western side of Hanoi effectively split the commandery in two, with the remaining eight prefectures on the eastern side.

The revolt started in the second lunar month of 40. The sisters and their forces marched to Luy Lâu (O), drove out the *taishou* and returned to Mê Linh to declare themselves king (*Vương*) at Mê Linh, which they decreed their capital.[46,47,48] The revolt spread rapidly; three commanderies joined their call, and 65 towns fell in succession. Chinese annals record 27 prefectures in four commanderies for a region from southern Guangxi province of China to the middle of Central Vietnam. If each had two towns, some three, then the total of 65 is not an unreasonable estimate.[49] It is arguable that the speed and extent of the revolt support claims of widespread resentment against the northern rulers by local people in these commanderies, as outlined above, rather than purely a reaction prompted by revenge.

Around a year later, in the spring of 41, Emperor Guangwu, the founder of the Later Han dynasty, ordered the mobilisation of an expedition force to retake the lost territory, which held a sizeable population. As of 2 CE, the population of these four commanderies totalled approximately one million, with over 75 per cent living in Giao Chỉ in 160,000 households. These figures emphasise just how remarkable the revolt was, and the reaction from the empire was not surprising.[50]

From the description in Hou Han shu as quoted above, it appears the *taishous* were driven inside their forts. However, they managed to hold out and retained controls as officials of both Giao Chỉ and Hepu commanderies were instructed to prepare for war, even if all 65 towns in all the commanderies fell to the rebels.

The empire prepared for the coming war for around a year, and in February 42, taking advantage of the seasonal winds, Ma Yuan (14 BCE-49 CE) – a seasoned general and a comrade-in-arms of the Emperor himself – led a 10,000 army south. There were no reports of resistance along the route until the soldiers reached Giao Chỉ commandery. The major battles occurred in 43 in Mê Linh and Cửu Chân, but the sisters and their followers were no match for the Later Han army, and they were killed together, along with many others; 300 local chieftains were captured and taken to the north (at Lingling).

Ma Yuan was a preeminently talented and successful general of his time. Following his successful southern expedition, he returned to Luoyang in triumph in September 43 and continued to serve the empire. In 49 CE, aged 65, he died from illness while on another expedition. His biography has provided historians with great insight into his campaign against the sisters' rebellion. A detailed description of his campaign is given in Appendix 8.

THE AFTERMATH

Historians generally agree that the revolt was a major turning point in Vietnamese history. Before 40, the northern emperors ruled by proxy via the Lạc Tướng. After 43, this local nobility class was nearly eradicated. Most were killed during the fighting against Han troops, and those who survived fled to the mountains or were captured and taken to China. They were replaced by others who were more compliant with imperial edicts.

Many rebellions following the sisters' revolt, but it took some 500 years before another figure, Lý Bí, rose against the northern emperor and declared himself king. However, the story of the Trưng sisters' rebellion lived on among the people. The sisters are among the first in the pantheon of Vietnamese national heroes, with hundreds of temples and shrines dedicated to their memory, together with numerous street names across Vietnam. Today, one can visit the main shrine at Hà Lôi hamlet, some 25 kilometres north-east of Hanoi on the northern side of the Red river (Figure 49).[51] Excavations in 1960 and 1970 unearthed evidence of the ancient fort of Mê Linh, where two parallel walls covered by bamboo form a path between what the locals call a "tube-shaped wall".[52,53]

While the reign of the Trưng sisters was brief, from just 40 – 43, they occupy a special place in the consciousness of the Vietnamese. The sisters are heralded as a heroic example against foreign invaders over the centuries. Lê Văn Hưu, a 13th-century historian, summarises it thus:

> "*Trưng Trắc and Trưng Nhị were women: they let out one shout and all the prefectures of Cửu Chân, Nhật Nam, and Hepu, along with 65 towns beyond [south of] the Wuling [or Nanling] mountains, responded to them. Founding a nation, proclaiming themselves kings was as easy as turning over their hands, which shows our land of Việt is able to establish a tradition of hundred kings. What a pity that, after the Triệu [Zhao Tuo] and before the Ngô [Ngô Quyền] for around one thousand years, the men of our land bowed their heads, folded their arms, and served the northerners; how shameful this was in comparison with the two Trưng sisters, who were women! Oh, it is as if one wants to abandon oneself [no self-respect]!*"[54]

While I appreciate the sentiment, I find the comment rather harsh, given there were a number of rebellions following the Trưng sisters, before the country gained independence, as discussed in the following chapters.

Figure 6 – The annual remembrance on the 6th day of Tết, Vietnamese Lunar New Year of the Trưng sisters at Mê Linh, Hanoi.[55]

MA YUAN'S BRONZE PILLARS

Following the brutal suppression of the sisters' rebellion, Ma Yuan took a number of actions to cement imperial rule. He divided one of the prefectures of Giao Chỉ commandery, Tây Vu with 32,000 households, into two: Vọng Hải (Wanghai) and Phong Khê (Fengxi). Tây Vu itself includes parts of the present-day provinces of Bắc Ninh, Thái Nguyên and Vĩnh Yên, north of the Đuống and Red rivers. The two new prefectures, Phong Khê include Bắc Ninh, possibly part of Hanoi, and the land north is Vọng Hải.[56,57]

Ma Yuan established additional prefectures and districts to govern walled towns; ditches were dug to irrigate the fields in order to benefit those living in these places. He found ten discrepancies between Việt and Han statues and explained the old regulations to bind the Việt people henceforth the people of Lạc Việt followed what had thus been established by General Ma.[58]

In effect, Ma Yuan established new imperial governance by removing the local elites of the ruling class and setting up new administrative institutions and statues for Giao Chỉ. Another act attributed to Ma Yuan was the marking of the empire's border in the south by erecting bronze pillars. However, historians have debated whether these exist at all, given they did not appear in Chinese historical texts until around the fourth century.[59]

It is known that boundary markers of stone or pillars had already been used in China at the time of Ma Yuan. In 1999, a boundary stone was discovered in Jiangsu province dated back to 12 CE.[60] Ma Yuan was not unfamiliar with bronze; he ordered the melting of a number of Đông Sơn bronze drums to make a bronze horse which stood outside the Luban gate (later named Golden Horse Gate) at the capital Luoyang, believed to be Weiyang Palace in modern-day Xi'an.[61] It is not a full-sized horse, measuring three Chinese feet, five inches tall (84 centimetres) and four Chinese feet five inches (96 centimetres) in circumference (or 30 centimetres in diameter).[62]

Based on the above examples, it is reasonable to expect Ma Yuan to mark the border with bronze pillars. In any case, *"Ma Yuan bronze pillars"* appears to have been a generic term applied to boundary markers. In the eighth century, a *Duhu* (Protectorate General) of Annam, He Li-guang, erected *"Ma Yuan bronze pillars"* to mark the north-western border near Kunming, Yunnan.[63] Another *Duhu* of An Nam, Ma Zong, also constructed these to prove his lineage traced back to Ma Yuan.[64] In the following centuries, rulers of the Yuan dynasty (1279-1368) made repeated requests to locate these pillars, presumably as a justification to claim the territory in subsequent invasions.[65]

Where are these pillars?

Theories abound as to their precise locations, ranging from sites within the present border between Vietnam and China at Lạng Sơn or Quảng Yên; Mount Hùng Sơn, Nghệ An, to Hải Vân pass and Phú Yên.[66]

While it seems certain that the debate around these bronze pillars and their locations will continue, it is my view that they were indeed erected but are now lost. Over the centuries, it is arguable they were melted down, buried, or sunken to the river bottom or sea bed. Their location is likely to be found at a natural border, such as a river bank or mountain top.

My research indicates two likely locations for the pillars: one by Thanh Hóa and the other at Huế. However, as discussed in Appendix 11, I believe the original Ma Yuan pillars recorded in Chinese texts were erected at Bu Lu river estuary, Chân Mây bay, just north of Hải Vân pass in Thừa Thiên - Huế province.

THE ZHUANG PEOPLE (ZHUANGZU)

Hou Han shu noted that the Man (barbarians) of Hepu also joined the Trưng sisters in the rebellion of 40 CE. Who were these barbarians? I believe they were likely the ancestors of today's Zhuangzu, a large ethnic group who live in Guangxi Zhuang Autonomous Region of Southern China, once occupied by Hepu. During the Former Han, they were recorded as *Wuhu (Ô Hử)*, which became *Li* under the Later Han, *Lao or Liao* during the Three Kingdoms and *Lang* under the Jin dynasty. Their close relatives on the Vietnamese border are the Tày, and the Nùng, who live around Lạng Sơn, Cao Bằng and Hà Giang provinces.[67]

Based on the names and location, it is likely that the Zhuangzu was involved in several major rebellions with the Vietnamese. For example, Hou Han shu records Ma Yuan and his soldiers marching through the *Wuhu* territory on their way south. Vietnamese historians in CM, presumably copied from Hou Han shu, cited the *Man*, *Lý*, who joined the sisters, and *Lý* is the Vietnamese of *Li*.[68] Furthermore, in 178, the *Wuhu* joined with the people of Giao Chỉ and persuaded Cửu Chân, Nhật Nam to mobilise tens of thousands to attack the commanderies and prefectures. The rebellion was not recorded in great detail, but geographically it was as large as the rebellion of 40 CE.[69] Again, in 411, the *Lý* and *Lạo* joined with rebels from Cửu Chân to fight against the *cishi* of Giao Châu, Đỗ Tuệ Độ.[70] The *Lạo* people also appear in the story of Nanzhao in 858 (see Chapter 13).

2.3 – The ancient citadel of Luy Lâu (Thành cổ Luy Lâu, first century to the sixth)

Taishou Su Ding likely escaped from an ancient capital called Luy Lâu (O) during the Trưng sisters' uprisings, but we do not know its location. On the other hand, a traveller can visit Luy Lâu, given its close proximity to Hanoi.

After Cổ Loa – the 2,200-year-old bronze-age fort built between 300 and 100 BCE – Luy Lâu (Figure 7) is the second oldest capital in Vietnam. Sadly, not much remains. It seems the Vietnamese lost sight of its location until it was found by the French in 1933. Cổ Loa citadel is around 20 kilometres north of Hanoi, and its story is told in Volume One of this book series.[71]

A DISCOVERY

In 1933, Henry Wintrebert, a resident of Bắc Ninh province, wrote to Claudius Madrolle (1870-1949), a French explorer and travel writer, of his discovery of an ancient place he believed to be Luy Lâu or Liên Lâu. From the study of a 1:25,000 map, Wintrebert noted that there are two lines which intersect and form a boundary around an area with a number of ancient structures. The locals informed him that the first line or route is known as the "invaders' route", dating back to the Chinese rule of northern Vietnam, centuries earlier.[72]

They also told him that the location was once a very large centre, but they were unsure whether it was a capital. However, they did confirm that the building, 200-300 metres north of the bridge, was the residence of a man named Sĩ Vương (or king Sĩ, 137-226) – the *taishou* of Giao Chỉ commandery – at the end of the Later Han rule. In that building was a stone stele, one in particular among a few, dated to 1687, with an inscription stating that the villagers of contemporary Khương Tự, Lũng Khê and Tư Thế were exempted from corvees. According to Wintrebert,

> "One can access Sĩ Vương's house by a paved bridge, entirely in stone, including the uprights. Suspended on the *lim* [wooden] columns are ancient panels in red lacquer, several of which bear Chinese characters, indicating that it is "the capital of the ancient king of An Nam"."[73]

These wooden columns are used to support the roof and are made from *lim* (Erythrophleum fordii) trees.

Wintrebert noted the building faced west and was located in the centre of a quadrilateral with brick gatehouses/watch posts at the four corners. The dimensions of the entrenchment are approximately 300 metres, in the north-south direction, by 1,000 metres, in the east-west.[74]

Alongside the residence, Wintrebert also located the tomb of Sĩ Vương just off the invaders' route and noted a place called *Đống Biền* at Tam Á commune nearby on the route. He speculated that *Đống Biền* could be the deformation of *Long Biên*, another ancient capital, the site of which historians, up to the present time, are yet to agree. However, I believe that Luy Lâu is Long Biên, as discussed in Appendix 5.

Wintrebert reasoned that the emperors of China and the kings of Annam often prepared their tombs beside their capital, so the existence of both the resident and tomb of Sĩ Vương would indicate the vicinity of the capital.[75] Close to Sĩ Vương's residence, Wintrebert also noticed in the courtyard of the monastery of Khương Tự, a ruined tower with three floors of an ancient stupa, which he speculates was once nine storeys high.[76]

From the map, he also spotted the tomb of King Dương Vương, whom he identified as a descendant of Đế Minh, at the village of Á Lũ, on the southern bank of the Đuống river. According to Vietnamese folklore, Kinh Dương Vương (or Lộc Tục) is the father of the legendary Lạc Long Quân, who married Âu Cơ and gave birth to the first of the Hùng kings, who founded a kingdom in the seventh century BCE as the first Vietnamese sovereign.[77] These discoveries confirmed to Wintrebert the special significance of the region in Vietnamese history.

LUY LÂU TODAY

The majority of the names of the locations as identified in Wintrebert's letter have not changed since 1933. He notes the invaders' route passed through Đông Triều and Sept-Pagodes (Phả Lại). Today, it is the national highway QL17.

The bridge connecting the villages of Khương Tự and Tư Thế, which Wintrebert thought once had a tiled roof, is now a modern bridge across the Dâu river with a rather obvious name of Dâu bridge. However, I am unable to locate the monastery of Khương Tự, but the three floors of the ancient stupa could be the tower at Dâu pagoda. This tower also had nine floors, but only three remain.

The Pinyin Chinese name of Sĩ Vương is Shi Xie. His residence is now a temple with a stone bridge leading to a courtyard (Figure 10), likely the bridge Wintrebert mentioned in his letter.

Historians now agree that Luy Lâu was indeed the capital of the Giao Chỉ circuit when Vietnam was under Han rule. It is around 30 kilometres east of Hanoi and 3.3 kilometres south of the Đuống river.[78] Today, one can spend an hour or so at Luy Lâu following the remains of the outer ramparts where the trees are (Figures 8 and 9) and visit the former residence (now a temple) of Shi Xie.

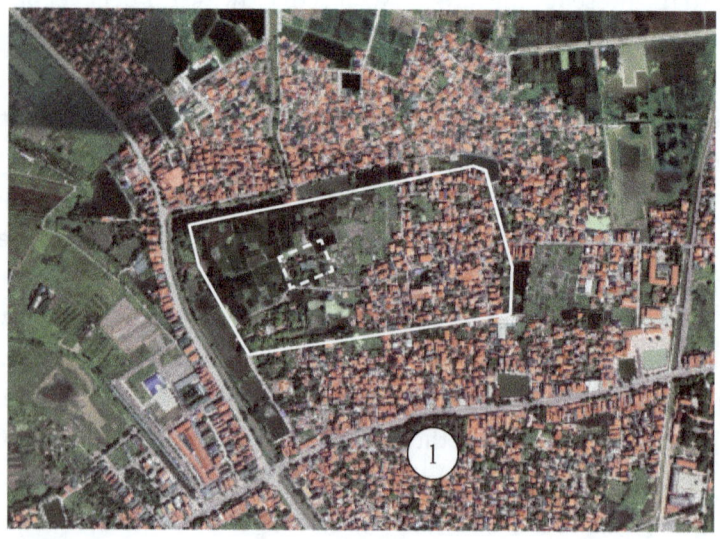

Figure 7 – The ancient citadel of Luy Lâu. Dâu pagoda is at (1).

The white line in Figure 7 follows the ramparts (or the outer wall) and it is measured to match the dimensions given by archaeologists of 603 metres north, 512 metres south, 290 metres west and 268 metres east – a perimeter of 1,678 metres.[79] The width of the enclosure in the north-south direction seems to match Wintrebert's estimate of 300 metres. However, the length in the east-west direction is shorter than his estimate of 1,000 metres.

Parts of the northern and western ramparts are easily visible (see Figures 8 and 9). The dotted line is the assumed position of the inner compound by archaeologists as 115 metres north, 117 metres south, 110 metres west and 112 metres east; the temple of Shi Xie is approximately at the centre of this inner compound.

Moats surrounding the outer walls can be seen in Figure 7. There is no sign of the brick gatehouse/watch towers at the four corners noted by Wintrebert. The main entrance to the citadel, also recorded by Wintrebert, is from the west.[80] A western entrance makes sense given the moat at this side is believed to be the ancient Dâu river that linked with Đuống and Thái Bình rivers thus providing a continuous river route from Luy Lâu all the way to the Gulf of Tonkin. The Dâu river has dried up over the years, and there are now only patches of short canals left.[81]

Figure 8 – View toward the corner between the northern and eastern ramparts of Luy Lâu.[82]

The description on the white billboard in the centre of the photograph reads *"Korea University ICHC-Vietnam Association of -Co-excavation project of the Luy Lau Site – January 2019"*.

Figure 9 – The base of the northern outer rampart of Luy Lâu.

Figure 10 – Shi Xie's temple (formerly residence) at Luy Lâu; note the stone bridge at the forefront.[83]

AN ARCHAEOLOGY STORY OF LUY LÂU

Several excavations were undertaken inside the ramparts of Luy Lâu citadel from 1968 to 2014. Based on the artefacts, archaeologists believe the citadel was built in the second century and continuously occupied until the fifth or early sixth century.[84] This project, together with a number of other excavation projects undertaken in the same period, found a number of artefacts including bricks, tiles, bowls, plates, and coins of the Han and Tang eras. They also discovered kilns and moulds used for making Đông Sơn bronze drums.[85,86] Of particular interest are the roof-tile ends with face mask and lotus petal motifs, table-shape stone mortar (*pesani*), and kendi vessels which show cultural affinity to those found in Trà Kiệu and Óc Eo.[87] The Indian origin of these vessels matches the description of the Indian monks at Luy Lâu, as discussed in Chapter 3.

CHAPTER 3

SHI XIE AND THE BEGINNING OF BUDDHISM IN VIETNAM - LADY TRIỆU REBELLION

GIAO CHÂU II

STORY TIMELINE: Second to third centuries.
STORY LOCATION: Southern China and Northern Vietnam.
KEY CHARACTERS: *Shi Xie and the Shi clan:* warlords of southern China and northern Vietnam, *Sun Quan:* Eastern Wu's emperor, *Lu Dai:* Eastern Wu's general who decimated the Shi clan, *Man Nương:* the orphan girl who became an idol, the monks of South India, *Lady Triệu:* led the rebellion against Eastern Wu.
LOCATIONS OF INTEREST: Dâu pagoda and other pagodas in Bắc Ninh province. Lady Triệu temple, Thanh Hóa province.

Chapter Summary

For around 150 years after the rebellion of the Trưng sisters, north Vietnam was relatively uneventful. The second Han dynasty, known as the Later Han (25-220), began to decay toward the end of the second century. At the turn of the third century, China was broken up into smaller dynasties and kingdoms ruled by self-proclaimed emperors, kings and warlords, a state of affairs that lasted for three centuries (220-589) until the end of the sixth century.
One of those warlords was a highly educated man, Shi Xie (Vietnamese Sĩ Nhiếp), considered by 15th-century Vietnamese historians as one of their kings and the founder of Vietnamese education. Shi Xie negotiated his way through the maze of court intrigues and powerful warlords to ensure that his family, including three of his brothers, stayed at the head of the provinces once part of Nan-yue (Figure 13).

He also attracted many educated men as refugees from the north, as well as Buddhist monks from India. During his reign, Luy Lâu was the oasis among the chaos that engulfed China. The monks brought with them Buddhist texts; some of the most important books on Buddhism were translated from Sanskrit into Chinese, or written at Luy Lâu. Some wonderful tales related to these monks were passed on down the centuries; pagodas and temples were built on sites that were originally their schools and places of worship. One of these is Dâu pagoda, reported to be the oldest pagoda in Vietnam. At this pagoda and others nearby, one finds the wonderful statues of the women associated with the tales of Man Nương (Figures 15 and 16).

Tragically, Shi Xie's golden years soon came to an end. One of his sons, who inherited his mantle, made a fatal decision of picking a fight with the family of Shi Xie's clerk and defying the most powerful warlord at the time. The end was inevitable, and the Shi clan was brutally exterminated, the brothers beheaded, possibly just outside Luy Lâu; their heads were sent to the northern capital as proof.

The new ruler of north and north-central Vietnam was the dynasty of Eastern Wu (220-280). However, not everyone complied, and in the middle of the third century, a woman in contemporary Thanh Hóa rose up against the local officials. She and her followers, once again, were brutally suppressed. The people built a temple for her at a restful place on a hillside off Highway 1A, where one can stop to light an incense stick and offer a prayer to this wonderful lady, Lady Triệu, who died some 18 centuries ago (Figures 19 and 20).

3.1 – Shi Xie (136-226)

THE EARLY YEARS

Among the refugees who came to Giao Châu at the beginning of the first century during the Wang Mang rebellion were the ancestors of Shi Xie.¹ They came from Weyang, a small town near Tai'an, in the ancient state of Lu (1042-249 BCE), in modern-day Shandong province, China.² Lu was also the home state of Confucius and Zuo Qiuming, the author of Zuo Zhuan, (or The Commentary of Zuo), a Chinese classic completed in 300 BCE which was used for centuries to teach the Chinese about their history. Shi Xie studied it and became known as an expert of the text.

In the middle of the second century, his father, Shi Ci, was appointed as the *taishou* of Nhật Nam commandery –present-day north-central Vietnam –during the reign of Emperor Huan (146-168). Shi Xie was born in 137 and recorded as a native of Guangxin (modern Wuzhou) in Cangwu prefecture of Guangxi province, the administrative centre of the Giao Chỉ circuit. Since he came from there before his father was appointed as the *taishou* of Nhật Nam, I assume his family was at Guangxin before they moved south for his father to take up the new post. I do not know when his family went south, but there is a strong possibility that he may have stayed behind for his education. Nhật Nam was the southernmost commandery of the empire, a back-of-beyond place and no place for a young man to obtain his education.

Shi Xie eventually travelled to Luoyang, the capital of the Later Han dynasty, for an education. There, he studied the Zuo Zhuan, under the tutelage of Liu Tao. He went on to be nominated for a Candidate of Probity and Piety (*xiaolian*) and served as a Gentleman of Writing (*Shangshu lang*) in the government – but was dismissed for "official reasons".³ After his father's death, he was nominated as a Candidate of Accomplished Talent (*maocai*) and appointed as the Prefect of Wu prefecture. During his time, obtaining the status of *xiaolian* and/or *maocai* was the prerequisite to be appointed as an imperial official.⁴ I have no information on how long he spent at Wu prefecture, but apparently, it was the present-day Wushan prefecture – a remote place in Chongqing province.⁵ I suspect he did not stay there long since he was promoted to become the *taishou* of Giao Chỉ commandery in 187 when he was 50 years old.

History recorded that he spent the next 40 years in Luy Lâu until he died in 226. During that time, Shi Xie and his family were the top political clan of

Giao Châu. Shi Xie was revered and given a title of king by the Vietnamese, his presence is still felt by his residence and tomb.

SĨ VƯƠNG OR KING SĨ - A VIETNAMESE KING

Over 12 centuries after his death, Ngô Sĩ Liên, wrote the following tribute to Shi Xie:

> "*Our country's knowledge of Shi and Shu* [two of five Confucian Classics], *music and rituals, and turning into a civilised country, is to begin with Sĩ Vương, and that merit is not only present at the time but also passed on to the next generation, isn't it great.*" [6,7]

Historian Stephen O'Harrow went further "*Yet it can be argued that, be he Chinese or not, it is with Sĩ Nhiếp that the "Vietnamese" nature of Việt-Nam per se really begins.*" [8] However, contemporary scholars such as archaeologist Hà Văn Tấn are more dismissive:

> "*During the time of Shi Xie, Confucianism became more widespread. He was a Chinese-born Việt scholar who made "Chunqiu" his special subject and governed Jiaozhi* [Giao Chỉ] *late in the second century and early in the third century. Shi Xie himself contributed much to its propagation .....Later day Việt scholars all thought very highly of Shi Xie. They went so far as calling him "the founder of education in Vietnam". In truth, Confucianism had been taught in Jiaozhou* [Giao Châu] *long before his time.*" [9]

Hà went on to comment:

> "*Generally speaking, the only purpose of the Han in teaching Chinese and Confucianism was to train administrative personnel at lower echelons. The fact was that very few people had access to education, and fewer still were employed after graduation.*" [10]

Hà is correct: as mentioned earlier, both *taishous*, Xi Guang and Ren Yan, embarked on the teaching of Confucianism at the beginning of the first century. Similarly, not many locally educated persons made it to imperial rank of higher officials. During Tang times in 845, over 600 years after Shi Xe's death, it was reported that there were only eight imperial officials and not more than 10 senior graduates from An Nam (previously Giao Chỉ).[11]

Scholars will go on to debate the role of Shi Xie in Vietnamese history but my study to date has indicated that the story of the three regions, North, Central and South, and their people that eventually make up Vietnam is diverse and complex. It would be difficult to generalise the impact of any individual to its evolution.

Figure 11 – The gateway to the temple and tomb of Shi Xie at Tam Á.[12]

It is not clear when the complex (Figure 11) was built, but there are three 17th-century steles at the temple, 1763 and 1801. The Chinese scripts on the gate say, "The Founder of Education of the South (*Nam Giao Học Tổ*, reading from right to left). The design of a gateway with three separate entrances is typical of temples, pagodas and citadels in Vietnam. The three entrances are provided so that important people, like the king, would enter the central gate without having to mix with his officials; the generals who would enter through the right gate and the civilians through the left gate. The three entrances are also based on the Buddhist concept of Three Marks of Existence: Anicca, Dukkha, and Anatta – impermanence, suffering and non-self. Another explanation is the passing of the Three Doors of Liberation, or three dharma seals, of Buddha's teaching: Shunyata, Animitta, and Apranihita – emptiness, signlessness, aimlessness.[13] I prefer the first explanation, which seems practical and suits the hierarchical structure at the time.

Figure 12 – A stone sheep in front of Shi Xie's tomb.

It is unusual to see the statue of a sheep (Figure 12) at Vietnamese temples; generally, horses, elephants, turtles, lions and oxen are the common ones. The local explanation is that the stone sheep was a gift from Indian monks who came to Luy Lâu: they brought live sheep with them and decided to leave their mark by presenting to Shi Xie the stone sheep. A second sheep is at the Dâu pagoda.

THE SHI CLAN

Shi Xie has three younger brothers, Shi Yi, Shi Wei and Shi Wu. During the reign of Emperor Huan, the *cishi* of Giao Châu was Ting Kung. At the time, Shi Yi was working as an inspector at the commandery; when Ting Kung was recalled to the capital, Yi escorted him. The record does not say where Shi Yi was working, but, since the administrative centre of Giao Châu was at Guangxin, it is reasonable to assume Ting Kung was stationed at Cangwu commandery with Shi Yi.

Ting Kung was recalled to take up an important position as the Minister of the Masses (*Situ*), one of three Ducal Ministers advising the emperor. Since Shi Yi served him diligently as an escort on the return to the capital, Ting Kung promised Shi Yi a post in his ministry; but when Shi Yi arrived, Ting Kung had been replaced. The new *Situ* treated Shi Yi well, but when Dong Zhuo rebelled, Shi Yi fled home.[14] Dong Zhuo, a general, politician, and warlord, seized Luoyang in 189, likely the year when Shi Yi returned home.

The record does not say where he had his home but it could be Guangxin.[15]

The decline of the Later Han dynasty started after the death of Emperor Huan in 168, when the next emperor, Ling, was 11 or 12 years old. His reign was marked by rebellions and protests, the most dangerous being the Yellow Turban peasant revolt of 184. Emperor Ling died in 189 without an heir. Dong Zhuo stepped into the power vacuum, seized power and moved the capital from Luoyang to Chang'an (Xi'an) in 190. The new Emperor Xian was eight years old when he was put on the throne by Dong Zhuo.

Within two years, Dong Zhuo was killed, and all his affiliates were put to death. Even though officially, the Later Han dynasty did not end until 220, by 193, it was effectively over. The empire was in continuous turmoil, and it seems Shi Yi made the right decision to return home.

The Shi family lived during a turbulent time in Chinese history, and Shi Xie proved to be adept at surviving and taking advantage of the situation to secure power for himself and his clan. After Ting Kung left, there were six more *cishis* of Giao Châu, but the sixth one, Zhu Fu, was killed by bandits in 200, and the province fell into chaos. Shi Xie saw the opportunity and submitted to the court for the appointment of his brother Shi Yi as the *taishou* of Hepu commandery, his second brother Shi Wei, formerly the Prefect of Xuwen prefecture (at the southern tip of Leizhou Peninsula) as the *taishou* of Cửu Chân commandery, and Shi Wu as the *taishou* of Nan-hai commandery.

Meanwhile, the court sent Zhang Jin as the new *cishi to* replace Zhu Fu. It was Zhang Jin who made a joint submission to the court to change the Giao Chỉ circuit to Giao Châu in 203; tragically, Zhang Jin was assassinated by one of his generals. Meanwhile, the *zhou mu* (equivalent to *a cishi*), or governor of the nearby Jingzhou province (contemporary Hunan and part of Hubei provinces), by the name of Liu Biao, had figured out what Shi Xie was up to and decided to send his own man, Lai Kung to be the new *cishi* of Giao Châu. On hearing the news, the court of the Later Han sent an imperial edict to grant Shi Xie the power over all seven commanderies but still maintain his position as the *taishou* of Giao Chỉ commandery. The court was worried about Liu Biao's ambition; they were right as Liu Biao had already replaced the *taishou* of Cangwu with his own man and became one of the southern warlords as the Later Han dynasty finally disintegrated. Liu Biao died of illness in 208, and by 223, his domain was taken and split between Shu Han and Eastern Wu kingdoms as China entered a period known as the Three Kingdoms.

The Shi clan now controlled the whole of Giao Châu, which covered territory similar to Nan-yue under Zhao Tuo nearly four hundred years earlier (Figures 4 and 13). Shi Xie consolidated the family position by keeping up with tributes to the court despite the difficult conditions during the period of revolts, with many roads cut off. The court returned the favour by granting him the title of The Marquis of Long Độ Đình. I do not know where Long Độ Đình is, but it could be another name for Long Biên, where Shi Xie resided.

Figure 13 – Warlords at the end of the Later Han, circa 195.[16]

THE PEACEFUL AND MAJESTIC YEARS

For around 30 years, from 193 to 229, when the Eastern Wu ruler, Sun Quan, declared himself an emperor, China was in a total upheaval, with civil wars raging across the continent between the warlords. During this time, Shi Xie managed to keep Giao Chỉ very much out of the conflict and while offering sheltering for many refugees fleeing the wars from the north. He did this by showering his superiors with expensive, rare gifts, offering his son as a hostage and generally taking a submissive, obedient position in dealing with the power of the day.

Shi Xie was a scholar, a diplomat and a shrewd political operator but not a warrior. He did try to suppress a revolt in Cửu Chân commandery sometime at the beginning of his time as a *taishou* without much success.[17]

He was described in the Records of the Three Kingdoms (Sanguo zhi), a Chinese work written in the third century, as:

> "*Xie was a man of generous capacity and broad forbearance, and he treated his subordinates with humility and open-mindedness. As for the Chinese literati who fled to him from the troubles, they numbered in the hundreds.* [A contemporary of him wrote] "*This gentleman and official of Jiaozhi named Shi is not only highly learned in literary matters but also very able in the affairs of government. Amid the great rebellions, he was able to preserve and protect the whole of the commandery; for more than 20 years, there were no incidents within his borders. The people are not without employment; those who sojourn in their travels all receive his blessings. …. he is incisive and profound, particularly on the Zuo Zhuan commentaries to the Spring and Autumn Chronicles* [or Chunqiu]." [18]

It should be noted that Shi Xie was never made *cishi* of Giao Châu even though he was given the command of all seven commanderies of the province, a decision which was likely deliberate by the court to keep Shi Xie's power in check. In 210, Later Han was on its deathbed and the fast-rising warlord in south-eastern China, Sun Quan, appointed Bu Zhi as the new *cishi* of Giao Châu. Despite the fact that the emperor was still in Chang'an, Shi Xie, wisely recognised where actual power lay, led his brothers to receive Bu Zhi and accepted his authority. Bu Zhi rewarded him with the title of General on the Left.[19]

Towards the end of the Later Han, in 220, Sun Quan, who was the brother of Sun Ce (Figure 13), had extended his territory south and west and had already reached the northern border of Shi Xie's domain. Shi Xie, an astute politician, demonstrated his loyalty to Sun Quan further by sending his son Shi Xin to the court of Eastern Wu as a hostage. In return, Sun Quan appointed Shi Xin as the Prefect of Wuchang (present-day Ezhou, Hubei province) and granted all the sons of Shi Xie and Shi Yi in the south the title Generals of the Gentlemen of the Household (*Zhonglang Jiang*).

Shi Xie then persuaded the powerful clans in Yizhou to submit to the court of Sun Quan, where Yizhou was a western province occupied by present-day Sichuan and Chongqing with a capital at Chengdu. Shi Xie was able to accomplish that, possibly because of the relationship with the clan leaders he established during his time as the Prefect in Chongqing province. Not surprisingly, Sun Quan was delighted; his archenemy was the Shu Han kingdom on his western flank and having an ally further west at Yizhou, effectively wedging Shu Han in between, was strategically important to him.

Sun Quan was grateful and granted Shi Xie the Marquis of Lung-pien (Long Biên) title, his brother Shi Yi, the Marquis of Du Xiang. Since Shi Yi was the *taishou* of Hepu, Du Xiang could be a location in the commandery. By now, Shi Wu was already dead from illness, and I do not have information on Shi Wei; he may have died or retired, as by 220, Nan-hai had already fallen to Sun Quan.

The brothers showered Sun Quan with gifts, which according to Sanguo zhi, included

> "*Spices, finest grass cloth and always by the thousand-fold, glossy pearls and great conches, liu-li pottery, emerald kingfisher feathers, shells of tortoise and horn of rhinoceros, elephant tusks and various valuables and strange fruits: bananas, coconuts, longans and such like. And in no year did these things not come. Now and again, Yi would send horses in tribute, hundreds of heads at a time. Quan would always send letters increasing royal favours to assuage them in reciprocation.*"[20]

The *liu-li* pottery may refer to

> "*anything from glass vessels, ceramic coatings, coloured stones, or could simply mean 'radiance' or shining. The term liuli is a variant of a number of words transcribing the Sanskrit word vaiḍūrya, a gemstone*".[21]

Given Shi Xie's connection with India, as discussed earlier; it could explain why he had access to gemstones and fine cloth to present to Sun Quan. The pearls were likely to come from Hepu; as for the horses, they could have come from the region upstream of the Red river (Chapter 14).[22,23] Horses were highly prized in Han times for use in military, transportation, recreation and sport purposes.[24]

The other items on the list were native to Shi Xie region and were commonly used as gifts to northern courts. Shi Xie and his brothers lived a majestic life, Sanguo zhi describes it thus:

> "*The Xie brothers oversaw the commanderies,* [acted as] *the chief of a province, thousands of miles away, and no one else could be more prestigious. When coming and going, the bell and stone chimes rang, full of majesty with the sound of flutes and pipes. The road was packed with horse-drawn carriages while there were often dozens of men of Hu burning incense riding on either side of* [his] *coach. The wives and concubines sat in carriages with canopy and curtains;*

the children had an entourage, the esteem now subdued even hundreds of Man [barbarians]. *The old Commandant Tuo* [Zhao Tuo of Nan-yue] *could not get any better than that."* [25]

Men of Hu in this passage refers to those who came from southern or central Asia, such as Sogdians and Indians.[26] The comparison to Zhao Tuo is interesting; it acknowledges the extent of Shi Xie's power over the domain that was once under Zhao Tuo, in the second century BCE.

Today, because of the noise and the people, it is not easy, but with a little imagination, one could visualise the scene of Shi Xie, and his family returning to his residence at Luy Lâu, along the "invaders route" from the Dâu pagoda, turning right just before Dâu bridge, some 1,800 years earlier.

A BLOODY END

In 222, Sun Quan declared an independent kingdom, and became the King of Wu; he proclaimed himself emperor in 229, and in the fifth year of his reign, in 226, Shi Xie died. He was 90 years old. At his death, Sun Quan thought the Giao Chỉ commandery was too remote, so he divided Giao Châu and gave Hepu, hitherto part of Giao Châu, to Guangzhou with Lu Dai as its *cishi*. Giao Châu was reduced in size and included only the three commanderies of Giao Chỉ, Cửu Chân and Nhật Nam. He also appointed Dai Liang as the *cishi* of Giao Châu with Chen Shi as the *taishou* of Giao Chỉ commandery. [27]

Lu Dai remained in Nan-hai, but Dai Liang and Chen Shi, en route to taking up their new posts, got as far as Hepu. It was a critical time for the Shi clan; they had lost control of both Nan-hai and Hepu commanderies and Shi Hui, the son of Shi Xie, tragically made a fatal mistake by defying Sun Quan. He proclaimed himself the *taishou* of Giao Chỉ commandery in the meantime.

His decision went against what his father would have done, and not surprisingly, his father's clerk, Huan Ling, opposed the idea. Hui had him whipped to death with terrible consequences. Ling's brother, in revenge, raised various clan armies and attacked Hui, who took refuge in the citadel, which presumably was Luy Lâu.

Meanwhile, Lu Dai (161-256) received an imperial order to kill Sun Hui. At 65 years old, Lu Dai was a seasoned general involved in the suppression of several revolts and had thousands killed on his order.[28] The Shi clan was no match for such a ruthless warrior. Lu Dai accomplished his deeds by taking with him 3,000 troops and quickly marching them south, collecting Dai Liang at Hepu. He also recruited an old friend Shi Kuang, a son of Shi

Yi and thus a cousin of Shi Hui. At the time, Kuang served as a General of the Gentlemen of the Household, presumably at Sun Quan's court.

Lu Dai sent Kuang in advance with a letter and offered a deal that if Shi Wei stepped down from the *taishou* position, he would be guaranteed safety. Shi Wei was in no position to negotiate; the fight against the clan of his father's clerk had weakened his forces and the fact that Lu Dai's troops arrived so quickly shocked him. Furthermore, the messenger was his cousin, which helped him trust Lu Dai. As events turned out, his trust was fatally misplaced.

Lu Dai arrived soon after Kuang, Shi Hui and his five brothers welcomed Dai with bare shoulders as a sign of submission, Dai thanked them and told them all to dress. They then all proceeded to the capital, presumably at Luy Lâu. The following morning; Dai invited them into his tent one by one. Guests were already seated. Dai stood up and read the imperial proclamation accusing them; guards then bound the brothers, took them outside and beheaded them. Their heads were sent on to Wuchang (modern Erzhou, near contemporary Wuhan), the capital of Eastern Wu. When one visits Luy Lâu, one may wish to remember the headless bodies of the Shi brothers, who could have been buried nearby.

Shi Xi's remaining brothers, Shi Wei, Shi Yi, and Yi's son, Shi Kuang, came forth, and Sun Quan forgave them for their mistakes. They, together with Shi Xie's hostage son, Shi Xin, were reduced to commoner status. The forgiveness did not last very long; after several years, both Shi Wei and Shi Yi were executed for breaking the law. I do not know which laws they broke, but it would come as no surprise if they were executed on some trumped-up charges by Lu Dai. As for Shi Xin, he died of illness without children; the court ordered the local government to provide his widow with the monthly rice allocation and 400,000 coins. Sun Quan or someone at court must have felt bad after what they did to Shi Xin's brothers!

Two of the officers serving Shi Hui rallied forces to attack Lu Dai, but to no avail; they were quickly defeated. Lu Dai continued the campaign to Cửu Chân, Shi Wei's domain, and killed or captured tens of thousands opposing him.[29]

Having destroyed the Shi clan, Sun Quan merged Guangzhou with Giao Châu and returned the seven commanderies under the same command of a *zhou mu* under Lu Dai. Lu Dai left Giao Chỉ commandery in 231 and died in 256 at 96. Sun Quan died four years earlier in 252, and the Eastern Wu kingdom fell into internal fighting among his descendants until 280, it succumbed to the new dynasty, Jin (266-420). Later historians were scathing of Lu Dai's action, considered it an act of bad faith and committed murder for his profit and accomplishment against the Shi brothers. They bared their breasts as a sign of sincerity, thinking they would not be harmed when they entered Lu Dai's tent on that fatal morning.[30]

It would be easy for us to be critical of Shi Hui 18 centuries later, judging him naïve, reckless and spoiled. We will never know what debates went on among the Shi clan in 226, but Shi Wei's decision led to the decimation of the whole clan, which Shi Xie and his father had built up over at least four generations. Worse still, the control of the southern commanderies was taken from the local people for the next 300 years until the middle of the sixth century, when it was recaptured briefly by Lý Bí, as discussed in Chapter 11.

If Shi Hui were to taken the actions following his father Shi Xie's policy of appeasement, he might have saved his life, his family and thousands of others, but given the ambition of Sun Quan, it would be a matter of time before Eastern Wu took control of the southern commanderies. The Shi clan was never powerful enough to stop Sun Quan's army.

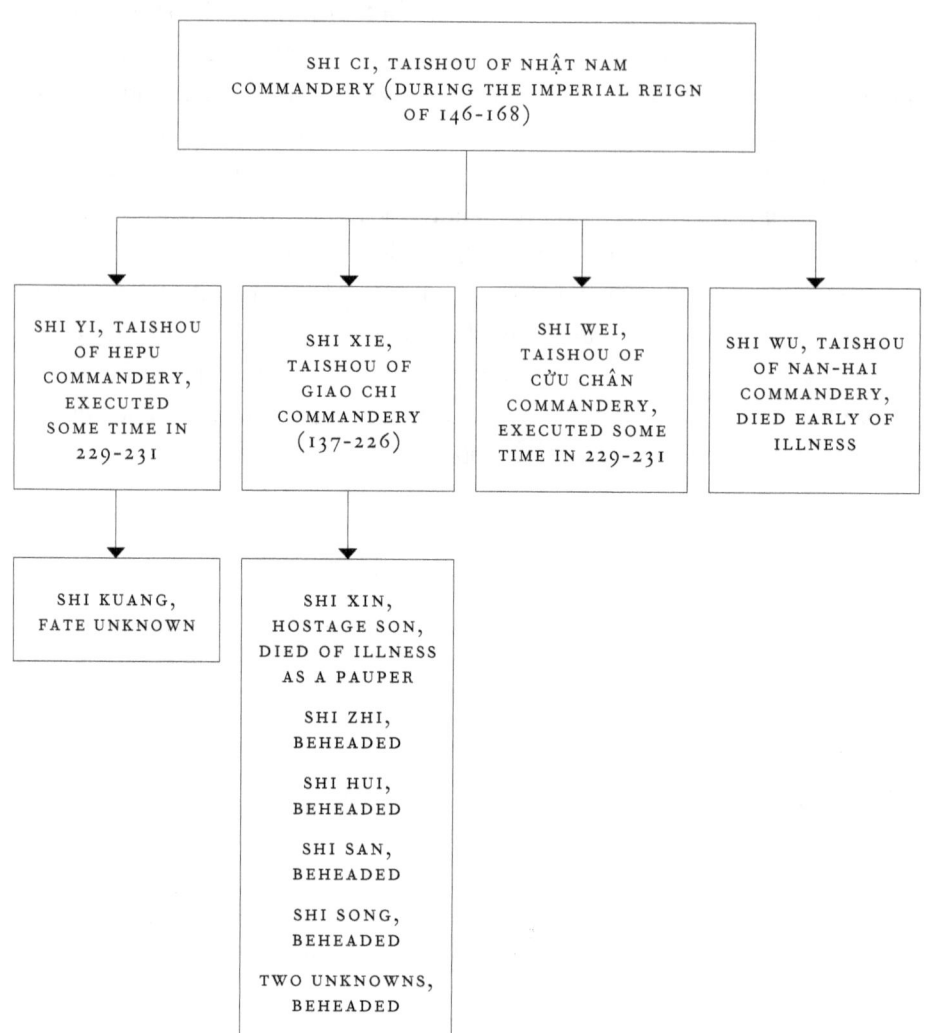

Figure 14 – The Shi family tree - circa 140-230.

3.2 – Men of Hu and the oldest pagodas in Vietnam - the coming of Buddhism (second to third centuries)

The Shi clan was wiped out soon after Shi Xie's death by a ruthless, duplicitous general from Eastern Wu, but his legacy has lived on for centuries. While the title of "Founder of Southern Education" may not be acceptable to all, there is no doubt the pagodas and the teaching of Buddhism started under his reign left a lasting impact on Vietnamese history.

The term Hu in the Men of Hu, who accompanied Shi Xie's carriage, was used by Chinese writers to refer to barbarians from Central Asia (the Sogdians) and India.[31] Among such men, there was an Indian of Brahma caste named Ksudra (Khâu Đà La) who came in 189. His story was told in a number of Vietnamese sources, but in this book, I use the tale in "A Collection of Strange Stories from Linh Nam (or *Lĩnh Nam Chích Quái* –abbreviated as LNCQ) since it is easily accessible compared with other more obscured sources. In LNCQ, he was known as Già La Đồ Lê – or Kalacarya, which means "black doctor" or "black sage" – instead of Ksudra.[32,33]

THE TALE OF MAN NƯƠNG – A PREGNANT ORPHAN AND THE FOUR STATUES.

This tale introduces Kalacarya as follows: during the reign of the Emperor Xian of Han (189-220), *taishou* Shi Xie had his capital located south of Bình Giang (modern Đuống river, Luy Lâu). South of the capital was a pagoda run by a monk from the west, Kalacarya.

At the pagoda, there was a girl named Man Nương. She was a poor, wretched orphan who wanted to learn the Buddha's teachings but suffered from stuttering so could not join other monks in praying. She spent her time in the kitchen, cooking for the monks and other visitors. One short night in the fifth lunar month, the monks did not finish their prayers until the early hours; Man Nương was tired and fell asleep by the door to the kitchen. On his way to his room, Kalacarya had to step over her, and after that, Man Nương found out she was pregnant. Three or four months later, Man Nương, feeling ashamed, left the pagoda and found refuge in another pagoda at a river junction. Kalacarya, embarrassed, also left.

In time, Man Nương gave birth to a baby girl; she found the monk Kalacarya and handed the baby over to him. That night, Kalacarya carried the baby to a crossroad where he found a clean hollow at the base of a bushy confederate rose tree.[34] He placed the baby there and said: "*I entrust you with this Buddha's child, look after her and you will become a Buddhist disciple*".

Kalacarya and Man Nương departed, but before that, Kalacarya gave her a stick and told her to plant it in the ground during drought to save the people. She did so in a drought year; water burst forth from the planted staff, and the people were grateful.³⁵

When Man Nương was over 90 years old, the tree fell and floated down the river but was stuck by the ferry near the pagoda. The villagers wanted to retrieve it for firewood, but all their axes broke when they tried to cut up the tree. Three hundred people from the village failed to move the tree, yet when Man Nương came to wash her hands, and she tried to pull it for fun, the tree moved. The villagers were amazed and asked her to bring the tree ashore so carpenters could make statues of Buddha. But when they got to where the baby girl was placed, it had turned into a stone slab. They struck it with their axes, but chipped it instead so they threw the slab into the river; as it hit the water, a bright light appeared for some time before it sank. They were all killed by the light. The villagers were terrified, so they asked Man Nương to make an offering and then hired the fishermen to dive and bring back the stone.

The stone was taken to the pagoda and placed inside a statue of Buddha; immediately it took on the look of a gold-plated figure. Kalacarya gave the four statues carved from the tree Buddhist names: *Pháp Vân* (Cloud), *Pháp Vũ* (Rain), *Pháp Lôi* (Thunder) and *Pháp Điện* (Lightning).³⁶

The villagers named Mān Nương Mother Buddha (*Phật Mẫu*), and on the fourth day of the fourth lunar month, she died. From that time, people gather at the pagoda every year for singing and entertainment, a day known as the Buddha Bathing Festival (now the eighth).

THE BELIEF OF FOUR PHÁP

I am taking a little detour here to briefly explain the Buddhist concept of *Pháp* since it has a direct bearing on the statues a traveller can see at the pagodas around Luy Lâu.

Pháp is the Vietnamese translation of a Sanskrit word, Dhamma or Dharma, which fundamentally means the teachings of Buddha. It is one of Triratna or Three Jewels or Treasures of Buddhism: Buddha-Dharma-Sangha (*Phật-Pháp-Tăng*), where Sangha means the monastic order or community. Besides "teachings of Buddha", *Pháp* has many religious meanings well outside the scope of this book and my understanding to explain. However, *Pháp* is of interest to us since they belong to the *Tứ Pháp* (or Four *Pháp*s), a common system of belief of the people in the Red river

Delta for centuries, which has continued to the present day.³⁷

The *Tứ Pháp* belief has a deep root in the wet-rice practice of the Red River Delta. A common proverb among the Vietnamese in the countryside is "*First the water, second, the fertiliser, third hard work and fourth the seeds.*"³⁸ Water is most important – but to have water, one must have rain which comes from clouds – preceded by thunder and lightning. The Vietnamese thus worshipped these elements as gods critical for their survival. Kalacarya may have been astute enough to graft the Buddhism concept of Dharma to the local set of beliefs as he named the four statues.

This explanation is not the only narrative; for other scholars, the four names begin with *Pháp* are purely Buddhist in nature:

> "*Pháp Vân (Dharmmegha, Buddhism as a fertilising cloud)*, "*Pháp Vũ*" *(the rain of Buddha-truth which fertilises all beings)*, "*Pháp Lôi*" *(the thunder of dharma, awakening man from stupor and stimulating the growth of virtue, the awful voice of Buddha-truth)* and "*Pháp Điện*" *(the lightning of the truth).*" ³⁹

I prefer the Vietnamese proverb explanation: it seems down to earth, easy to understand and less esoteric.

THE FOUR STATUES - CLOUD, RAIN, THUNDER AND LIGHTNING

In 2017, the Vietnamese government declared four statues worshipped at four different Bắc Ninh pagodas as national treasures. These were made in the 18th century, carved from wood and painted. All were females with curly hair, wearing sarongs, bare-chested, sitting in a Buddha position, and known as Lady Dâu, Lady Đậu, Lady Tướng and Lady Dàn, the eldest is Lady Dâu, and the youngest is Lady Dàn. The statues of Lady Dàn and Lady Dâu are shown in Figure 15 and Figure 16. Today, one can view them at the pagodas listed in Table 3.

As the youngest, Lady Dàn is shown with a playful smile; she holds a pearl on each palm. Note the traditional curls of the Buddha statue and the Indian feature of the *bindi* (dot) in the centre of the forehead. The statue is around 1.7 metres tall.

The statue of Lay Dâu is fully dressed in ceremonial clothes. Note the two statues of the female attendants in more traditional Vietnamese dresses and hats (Figure 16). They have different skin colours and no *bindi* on their forehead.

Figure 15 – Lady Dàn (Lightning, Pháp Lôi) without the ceremonial costume.⁴⁰

Figure 16 – The statue of Lady Dâu at the Dâu pagoda.⁴¹

One will never know if these statues were modelled on the legendary ones in Man Nương's story or even if the legendary statues existed. However, every year, on the eighth day of the fourth lunar month, the local people would organise a Dâu festival to bring the four statues from the pagodas to unite with their mother, Man Nương at Mẫu Tứ Pháp pagoda at Mãn Xá, Hà Mãn, Thuận Thành, Bắc Ninh.

Unfortunately, the original Đậu pagoda was destroyed during the war against the French (1945-1954), so the statue of Lady Đậu was sent to the Dâu pagoda for safe keeping, but it has not been returned despite repeated attempts. One of the main reasons is that there are two Đậu pagodas, both claimed to be the original owner.[42] Because of the controversy, Lady Đậu, the Lady Rain, stays behind at Dâu pagoda for fear of getting stolen en route and only three statues are included in the procession.

STATUES	FORMAL TITLES	KEPT AT	PAGODA LOCATIONS
Lady Dâu	Pháp Vân (cloud)	Dâu (or Diên Ứng, Pháp Vân, Cổ Châu) pagoda	Chùa Dâu, Lạc Long Quân, Thanh Khương, Thuận Thành, Bắc Ninh.
Lady Đậu	Pháp Vũ (rain)	Dâu pagoda	Chùa Đậu Thành Đạo Tự, Thôn Đại Tự, Thuận Thành, Bắc Ninh. Chùa Đậu (Pháp Vũ), Đại Tự, Thuận Thành, Bắc Ninh.
Lady Tướng	Pháp Lôi (thunder)	Tướng (or Phi Tướng) pagoda	Chùa Phi Tướng, Trí Quả, Thuận Thành, Bắc Ninh.
Lady Dàn	Pháp Điện (lightning)	Dàn (or Trí Quả tự, Dàn Phương Quan, Dàn Câu) pagoda	Chùa Dàn, Phương Quan, Trí Quả, Thuận Thành, Bắc Ninh.

Table 3 – Four statues and their locations

VIETNAMESE BUDDHISM AND MONKS FROM SOUTHERN INDIA

Mahajivaka (Ma-la-kỳ-vực)

The name Kalacarya suggested he was a Dravidian from Southern India.[43] He did not come alone; other sources mentioned another Indian, Mahajivaka, (Ma-la-kỳ-thành or Ma-la-kỳ-vực) came with him to Luy Lâu. Both of them met a lay devotee (or Upāśś), named Tu Định, who invited them to stay. Tu Định had a 12 years old daughter named A Man who lit the candles and cooked for Kalacarya.[44] The story unfolded from there as already told above in the legend of Man Nương and the four statues.

Mahajivaka did not stay in Luy Lâu long but continued his journey to China. The description of him suggested a wandering monk. He travelled from India to Funan, to Giao Châu (Luy Lâu) and Guangzhou towards the end of the reign of Emperor Hui of the Jin dynasty (290-307), other sources stated explicitly 294. He came to Luoyang and returned to India after unrest started there.[45] The unrest was caused by civil wars (291-306) among the princes and kings competing for the throne.

His story seems consistent with the arrival of Indian traders at Óc Eo in the early days of Funan and may have taken the same coastal route described in Chapter 8. The Indian merchants were looking for gold because the Roman emperor stopped the illegal export of gold coins.[46] On such long journeys, the merchants often had monks on the boats to serve as doctors, chaplains and sorcerers.[47] Interestingly, it was also the gold and the Indian monk that appeared in the story of the legendary Chử Đồng Tử, one of four Vietnamese immortals.[48]

Mahajivaka came to Giao Châu in 294, and Kalacarya arrived at Luy Lâu in 189, nearly a century earlier, so they could not have met. It should be noted that, by 294, the Shi clan had already been dead for almost 70 years, and Giao Châu was firmly in the Jin empire.

Whatever the case, Mahajivaka has been included as one of five monks who introduced Buddhism to Vietnam; the others are Mouzi (Mou Bo or Mâu Tử, Mâu Bác), Kang Shenghui (Khương or Khang Tăng Hội) and Kalasivi (Chi Cương Lương (or Tiếp, Lâu, Chỉ) or Zhi Gangliang). I will discuss each of these monks briefly since they are related to Luy Lâu, but it is not my intention to dwell deeply in the history of Buddhism in Vietnam. Readers can find a number of excellent books and papers which deal with this subject; one such book is by Dinh et al.[49]

Kang Shenghui (Khương Tăng Hội)

The ancestors of Kang Shenghui are Sogdians (a region covering parts of modern Uzbekistan, Tajikistan, Kazakhstan, and Kyrgyzstan) but settled in India for several generations. His father took the family, including Kang Shenghui, to Giao Châu to trade. When he was 10 years old, his parents died, and after a period of mourning, he decided to become a monk and devoted his time to studying. He is recorded as a distinguished man, highly educated with an open mind and well-versed in Sanskrit and Chinese; he could explain the Buddhist scriptures (Tripiṭaka or Three Baskets) clearly.[50] He also studied astronomical texts and non-canonical works. He knew about the machinery of government and was also gifted with a great literary talent.[51]

When Kang Shenghui lived in Giao Châu (presumably at Luy Lâu), the capital of Eastern Wu had moved to Jianye or Jiankang (modern Nanjing, west of Shanghai, around 550 kilometres downstream from the previous capital of Wuchang on the Yangtze river). At that time, Buddhism had spread to Eastern Wu territory, but apparently, effective conversion had yet to be completed. Kang Shenghui wanted to strengthen Buddha's wisdom and establish a number of stupas and temples there in Jiangdong (or Jiangnan region, encompassing the region south of the lower reaches of the Yangtze river), the heart of the Eastern Wu dynasty.

In 247, Kang Shenghui arrived at Jianye and built a thatched hut (a parnasala or *thảo am*) with a number of Buddha statues. When he accomplished the miracle of the appearance of the relic of the Buddha, Sun Quan, the emperor of Eastern Wu, admitted defeat and immediately raised a stupa for the relic, named Jian Chu (*Kiến Sơ*), meaning the first temple.

The relic is a bone relic (śarīra) of the Buddha which miraculously appeared in a copper jar after 21 days of praying.[52] Today, this first temple is believed to be relocated to Jing'an temple (Temple of Peace and Tranquillity) in Jing'an district of Shanghai.[53,54] During his time in Giao Châu and Jianye, Kang Shenghui translated 14 sets of sutras (ancient Indian texts) but only five survived to this day.[55] Among those is the well-known Liudu ji jing (Six perfection sutras or Lục Độ Tập Kinh).[56] He died in 280.[57]

Kalasivi (Chi Cương Lương)

There are several names for this monk; scholars have suggested he is an Indo-Scythian from north-west India and came to Giao Châu in the middle of the third century. One source mentions a Chi Cương Cương Chí translated a number of sutras in Guangzhou in 266, the other cites a Chi Cương Cương Tiếp (or Lâu) also translated sutras in Giao Châu in 255, 256. They were likely the same persons and, according to sinologist Paul Pelliot, should be referred to by his real name of Kâlaruci.[58] Based on these dates, he would be a contemporary of Kang Shenghui.

Mouzi (Mou Bo, Mâu Tử, Mâu Bác)

Mouzi was born sometime between 165 and 170 in modern Wuzhou, Cangwu prefecture, by the Xunjiang river in Guangxi province. With his mother, he took refuge in Giao Châu some years before 189 but returned to Wuzhou when he turned 26 to get married.[59,60] After the death of Emperor Ling in 189, China was plunged into chaos and wars, many northern refugees came to Luy Lâu of Giao Châu because it was a place of safety. Among them were many people who believed in and practised the doctrine of abstaining from eating in order to reach immortality, as advocated by Taoism. Mouzi used the Confucian Five Classics to argue with those people who were unable to answer his questions.[61,62]

Shi Xie knew about him and offered him a position; Mouzi wrote:

> "Taishou Shi Xie heard that I had a little education and invited me to accept a position. At that time, I was young; my heart was dedicated to studying, I also saw that life was full of chaos. I did not plan to become an official so I refused to come."[63]

He was asked by a *zhou mu* (provincial governor) to go to Lingling and Guiyang (south of modern Hunan province in China) to seek permission for *zhou mu*'s troops to take revenge for the death of his brother.[64] Despite his misgivings, Mouzi was prepared to go, but his mother died, and that provided him with a reason to stay. I am unable to identify this *zhou mu*, but his brother was a Chu Hạo, scholar Lê Mạnh Thát places this event at 195 and Mouzi decided to become a Buddhist monk soon after.[65,66]

Mouzi mentioned these events in a preface of his book, named Lihou lun (*Lý Hoặc Luận*), which has been variously translated as Mou-tzu's Treatise on Alleviating Doubt or Mou-tzu's Disposing of Error.[67,68] "Li" means to treat or settle, "Huo" denotes things that mislead people, puzzles, or errors and finally, "Lun" is an opinion, view, or statement.[69]

While there are different opinions about when Mouzi wrote this book, the reference to Shi Xie and the death of Emperor Ling would indicate he wrote it towards the end of the *taishou*'s reign. Lê suggests Mouzi wrote this book in 198.[70] Mouzi wrote this book because, as he put it in the third person:

> "*Then* [I] *committed to following Buddhism, studied together with Lao Tzu* [Dao De Jing], *took the mysticism as a good wine, took the Five Classics as a flute... Most secular people didn't know that* [they] *thought Mouzi had betrayed the Five Classics and followed the heretical religion. If you open your mouth to argue with them, it is also unethical, but if you stay silent, you will appear helpless, so you use pen and ink to quote the sages to prove what you think. That's why it is called Mouzi's Lihou.*"[71]

Lihou lun contains 37 questions and answers, chiefly challenges to Buddhism by Confucianists, the last nine by Taoists.[72] The philosophical discussion of the three religions is way beyond the scope of this volume and my understanding, but I note two things of interest, one is that there were many Buddhists prayer books in Luy Lâu during Mouzi's time, confirming Luy Lâu as a major Buddhism centre. Secondly, the Buddhist monks there wore red robes like the Indian monks at the time, validating the proposition that the Indians introduced Buddhism to Luy Lâu.[73]

Luy Lâu – a major Buddhist and commercial centre in the second and third century

The five monks above were named in a classic book about the Vietnamese Zen Masters (*Thiền Sư*) from the sixth to the 13th century. It is the oldest book on Vietnamese history of Buddhism that is currently in existence, compiled before 1134 and completed in the 13th century. The current version is based on a 1715 copy.[74] It is called "Collection of Outstanding Figures of the Zen Garden" or *Thiền Uyển Tập Anh*.[75]

This book quotes a story of a Buddhist monk (*Pháp Sư*) Tan Tian (*Đàm Thiên*, 542-607), who explained to the first Sui emperor Wendi (581-604) that there was no need to send monks to Giao Châu to spread the words of Buddha as the emperor suggested. Tan Tian said:

> "*Giao Châu is on the road through Thiền Trúc* [India], *and when Buddhism first arrived, Giang Đông* [Jiangdong or Jiangnan] *had not had anything, but Luy Lâu had already built more than 20 temples, with more than 500 monks and translated 15 sutras because it* [Buddhism] *got there first. At that time, there were Khâu Đà La* [Kalacarya], *Ma-La Kỳ Vực* [Mahajivaka], *Khương Tăng Hội* [Kang Shenghui], *Chi Cường Lương* [Kâlaruci], *Mâu Bác* [Mouzi] *living*

there. Now, there is Pháp Hiền (?-626), grand master, having reached enlightenment with Vinitaruci (Tỳ Ni Đa Lưu Chi) [?-591] propagated the Three Founders principles, who is among the Bodhisattvas [enlightened being]. *He is living at the temple of Chúng Thiện, teaching students. In that classroom, there are no less than 300 people, no different from China. Your Majesty is the good father of the world, wanting to donate to charity equally, just get a messenger to bring the relics [to Luy Lâu], but because there are already teachers there, there is no need to* [send monks] *to teach."* [76]

Figure 17 – Dâu pagoda, also known as Pháp Vân (cloud) or Diên Ứng.[77]

Dâu pagoda (Figure 17) was built on the site of the oldest Buddhist pagoda in Vietnam during the reign of Shi Xie in the second/third century. The pagoda was rebuilt and extended several times with the design attributed to First Doctoral Candidate (Trạng Nguyên) Mạc Đĩnh Chi in the 14th century. There is a statue of him at the pagoda.

The two monks: Vinitaruci (Tỳ Ni Đa Lưu Chi) and Pháp Hiền cited in the above text, were the resident monks at the Dâu pagoda, and there is a statue of Vinitaruci sitting on a lion and a lotus flower inside the pagoda.

The tower (Figure 18) is believed to be built by Mạc Đĩnh Chi in the 14th century, but the original nine storeys now are reduced to three. Inside there is a large 18th-century bronze bell. Note the stone sheep, believed to be carved in the second century and brought to Luy Lâu by the Indian monks.

Figure 18 – Hòa Phong tower at Dâu pagoda.

3.3 – Lady Triệu rebellion (third century)

I am now leaving Luy Lâu and heading south to Thanh Hóa when in 248, a Lady Triệu and her followers in Cửu Chân revolted against the Jin administration. Today, there is a temple for her (Figure 20) around 20 kilometres north of Thanh Hóa city. Tragically, her rebellion only lasted for five to six months, but she is revered as one of Vietnamese greatest heroes, second only or even comparable to the Trưng sisters.[78]

There are a number of stories about her, including one in which the *cishi* of Giao Châu, Liu Yin, exposed his soldiers completely naked in the final battle against her; she was so embarrassed and abandoned the fight.[79] However, in this book, I refer to a passage in SKTT, quoted "The annals of Giao Chỉ (or Giao Chỉ Chí)", since it is the earliest source:

> "*In the mountain of Cửu Chân prefecture, there is a girl with a family name of Triệu, with breasts of three "thước"* [nearly one metre] *long, unmarried, gathered a gang to plunder the prefecture and district, often wearing a short yellow tunic, shoes with curved toes, sitting on the head of an elephant and fight, after death, [she] became a divinity.*" [80,81]

The mountain that the passage refers to is Núi Nưa (Mount Nưa), a narrow range of around 16 kilometres long with an elevation of approximately 500 metres, some 25 kilometres south-west of Thanh Hóa city. According to legends, that was where Lady Triệu trained her soldiers. There is lovely folk poetry about her:

> "*Lull your baby to sleep well,*
> *Let the mother carry water to wash the elephant's seat* [howdah],
> *If you want to watch, go up to the mountain,*
> *Watch General Lady Triệu riding the elephant and beat the gong,*
> *Brocade bags and pink bags,*
> *Embedding betel nuts with phoenix wings for the husband to join the march.*" [82]

The reference to her as a general who beats the gong to exhort the husband to go to war does not seem to match a person who was unmarried and wanted to ride the waves. Besides, elephant-riding generals do not normally beat the gong to drive the troops forward; they would leave that task to a private or a drummer boy. In any case, I include the poem here as it is a lovely lullaby.

CỬU CHÂN - A REBELLIOUS PREFECTURE

Before Lady Triệu led the charge with the elephants, around 90 years earlier, in 157, Chu Đại (or Châu Đạt) attacked and killed the magistrate, who was greedy and violent. Over 100 years before that, Ma Yuan defeated the followers of the Trưng sisters in the same prefecture. In 226, Lu Dai, after beheaded the Shi brothers in Luy Lâu, came through, killed and captured thousands in Cửu Chân. So, the people of Cửu Chân would hardly be expected to be loyal to the empire and in 248, they and the people of Giao Chỉ attacked and seized control of cities, causing great unrest throughout the province.

Sanguo zhi records the revolt and the appointment of a new *cishi*, Lu Yin, by Sun Quan to quell it. Among the rebels is a chieftain, a Huang Wu from Gaoliang county (believed to be present-day Yangjiang, Guangdong). Lu Yin adopted a diplomatic approach and succeeded in getting Huang Wu to surrender with over 3,000 households. Lu Yin then continued south with Wu's forces using the same strategy. He paid a large sum of money to the local tribes and was successful in getting more than 100 of them with over 50,000 households from the hills to surrender to him; with that accomplishment, he managed to restore peace and stability in Giao Châu.[83,84]

Sanguo zhi does not mention anything about Lady Triệu, but its record provided a background for her story because it was Lu Yin who eventually defeated her. Perhaps she was considered one of 100 local tribes paid off, so not worth mentioning as these tribes were small hill tribes with an average of 500 households each compared to Huang Wu's tribe of 3,000 households.

In any case, the household of Lady Triệu was not among those who surrendered to Lu Yin and in 248, she led her followers, presumably down Núi Nưa, and attacked the administrative centre of Cửu Chân of Tư Phố (now believed to be at Thiệu Khánh, Thiệu Dương communes) where the Chu and Mã rivers meet at Ngã Ba Đầu, before flowing to the sea. SKTT reports very briefly that Lu Yin defeated her. Other historians tell of a very lengthy and detailed campaign with the Eastern Wu forces losing thirty battles to Lady Triệu.[85]

She died young at 23 at the base of Núi Tùng (Mount Tùng); her temple is at Triệu Lộc commune, Hậu Lộc district, Thanh Hóa province.[86] Her temple is just north of Tư Phố so perhaps that was where they fought the last pitch battle with Lu Yin forces as they marched down from the north. Lu Yin stayed as a cishi of Giao Châu for 10 years until he was assigned to another commanding position in Hubei.

The statue shows her sitting with her right hand raised and facing outwards – a Buddhism *vitarka mudra* (teaching gesture). Note the long earlobes, typical of Buddha-like statues, but there is no yellow tunic nor metre-long breasts as described in SKTT.

At the temple (Figure 20), there is a famous quote attributed to her reply to her brother at the tender age of 20 when he admonished her who, as a woman, should not be so extravagant:

"I want to ride the wind and trample the waves, cut down the great whale in the Eastern Sea, sweep the land [of the enemy], *save the people from drowning* [in misery]. *Why should I imitate the common people, bowing their heads to become the concubines of others, willing to serve inside the house* [as a servant]*?"* [89]

Figure 19 – The statue of Lady Triệu at her temple.[87]

Figure 20 – Lady Triệu temple at Triệu Lộc commune, Hậu Lộc district, Thanh Hóa province.[88]

CHAPTER 4

A FOREST TOWN - THE KINGDOM OF LINYI (LÂM ẤP) AND THE FANS

A GENERATION OF RAIDERS
LINYI I

STORY TIMELINE: Second to fourth centuries.
STORY LOCATION: North-central Vietnam.
KEY CHARACTERS: *Khu Liên:* led the rebellion which led to the establishment of Linyi, *Tao Huang:* the governor of Giao Châu, *Fan Xiong:* king of Linyi, *Fan Yi:* king of Linyi, *Fan Wen:* king of Linyi, an usurper.
LOCATIONS OF INTEREST: The ruin of Thành Lồi in Huế. The ruin of Cao Lao Hạ in Quảng Bình province. Linyi ramparts in Quảng Bình province (yet to be located).

Chapter Summary

The tragic end of Shi Xie's family marked a watershed in Vietnamese history. The Former and Later Han dynasties had come to an end and paved the way for the Six Dynasties period (220-589), including the three kingdoms (Cao Wei, Shu Han and Eastern Wu) between 220 and 280.

In this chapter, we are entering the third century, and these three kingdoms were replaced by the southern dynasty of Jin (265-420), who became the new ruler of Vietnam, at least north of Ngang pass. For the next 300 years, major events in Vietnamese history tended to happen around the southern provinces, so for my stories, I will travel south to embark on the story of a kingdom called Linyi and its rulers, the Fans.

The southernmost provinces of the northern empire – from north to south: modern Thanh Hóa, Nghệ An, Hà Tĩnh, Quảng Bình, Quảng Trị, Thừa Thiên-Huế, and Quảng Nam – had never been fully submitted to the Northern Rule, particularly those south of Ngang pass. One rebellion after another, the people pushed back. South of Ngang pass was the empire's backwater; it was where northern courts sent their convicts and political prisoners. In fact, in 102, the family of a Later Han empress was exiled to Tỷ Ảnh prefecture, now around Đồng Hới city in Quảng Bình province.

It came as no surprise that eventually, during the dying days of the Later Han dynasty, in 192, a group of rebels successfully staged a revolution and founded a kingdom which history comes to know as Linyi (Vietnamese Lâm Ấp).

The story of Linyi is complex, and many issues which have vexed historians since Linyi first came to their attention and I will touch upon them in the text.

Historians have different views as to who the people of Linyi were. Some suggest they are direct descendants of the Sa Huỳnh people who came from Borneo and spoke Chamic languages; others believe the primary language of the Linyi people is Mon-Khmer, native to the region. In either case, the languages would be incomprehensible to an average Vietnamese speaker, then and now.

In the early third century, Lu Dai, who vanquished the Shi clan, sent envoys to Linyi and another kingdom further south, Funan. That was when Linyi first appeared in Chinese annals. According to these annals, Linyi kings were aggressive. They seemed to have decided that the best economic policy for their kingdom was to undertake raids, capture slaves as well as food, and other manufactured goods from the imperial territory, mainly north of Ngang pass. The land between Ngang and Hải Vân passes never been very fertile and has never been able to support a large number of people even to this day (Appendix 14). Perhaps a raid and plunder policy would be most appropriate for their survival at the time.

In any case, Linyi kings caused the Eastern Wu and the following Jin dynasties endless headaches. The most formidable king was Fan Wen, recorded as an enslaved person from a place near modern Shanghai, who seized the throne once his benefactor king died. Fan Wen assembled a vast army; among them were descendants of the prisoners from the three-kingdom periods (220-280). In the early days of his reign, he continued to send tributes to the court of the Jin dynasty, but as soon he conquered the small states in the region, he crossed Ngang pass, killed the *taishou* of Cửu Chân and burned the body as an offering.

Fan Wen built a number of citadels and ramparts, but to this date, their whereabouts are still unknown. The two citadels often mentioned in Chinese text are Khu Túc and Điển Xung. The exact location of Khu Túc remains a mystery; the most likely candidates are Cao Lao Hạ in Quảng Bình (Figure 21) and Thành Lồi in Huế (Figure 22). Cao Lao Hạ is on flat ground, and the remains of a rectangular rampart may be built later on the site of a Linyi citadel. Compared with Thành Lồi, it is not an exciting place to visit other than for historical interest.

Thành Lồi is now overgrown with vegetation, but one can get a feel for the place. The Linyi kings who built it had chosen an excellent defensive position on the high ground but easily accessible from the river which connects it to the coast.

Historians generally agree that Điển Xung was built at contemporary Trà Kiệu in Quảng Nam province (Figure 26, Chapter 5). As for the northern ramparts which the kings of Linyi built, while there are traces of them just north of the Gianh river according to the local newspapers, I have not been able to locate them on the map.

For a traveller visiting "Champa" ruins and artefacts found between Hải Vân and Ngang passes, given the difficulty around the distinction between when Linyi ended, and Champa began, I would suggest anything from the second to the seventh centuries would belong to Linyi.

4.1 – Southern rebellions

After a long and brutal campaign to crush the rebellion of the Trưng sisters in 43 CE, Ma Yuan returned to China; things appeared quiet in the southern commanderies of the Later Han empire for around 60 years until a major revolt in 100. This was followed by other rebellions in 137, 144, 157, 178, 184 and culminated in the emergence of the kingdom of Linyi in 192 towards the end of the Later Han dynasty.

YEAR 100

It all started in 100 when more than 2,000 inhabitants of Tượng Lâm – the southernmost prefecture of the Later Han empire – attacked, plundered and burned the administrative centre in their prefecture. It was quickly suppressed, and their leaders beheaded.[1]

YEAR 137

Over 30 years later, in 137, Chinese annals report that a group of barbarians of the same prefecture, Tượng Lâm, called Khu Liên rebelled, ransacked the prefecture and killed the magistrate. Khu Liên is the Vietnamese translation of Chinese "Qu Lian", believed to be the transcription of the local Kunlun (or Kurung or Kuruï) meaning "people of the south of black colour and crinkled hair" or could mean "chief or king".[2]

At the news of the revolt, the *cishi* of the Giao Chỉ circuit, Fan Ye, took an army of 10,000 from the commanderies of Giao Chỉ and Cửu Chân to Nhật Nam, but the soldiers did not want to go to the far frontier and in the autumn of 137, they also rebelled, and occupied these two commanderies.[3] In 138, it happened that an Attendant Censor (*Shi Yushi*) named Jia Zhang (Giả Xương) was in Nhật Nam; he assembled forces from other prefectures to fight the Khu Liên rebels but ended up getting completely surrounded for over a year with not enough food to eat.[4] I do not have information as to where he was surrounded, but the situation had become desperate for imperial troops. The news must have been so bad for the court to plan to send 40,000 men from regions around its capital, Luoyang – some 3,000 kilometres north of Hanoi – south to break the siege.

A court official named Lu Gu advised against the expedition. He explained: [5,6,7]

> "*The climate* [water and land] *in the southern land, humid and* [susceptible to] *epidemics, will cause four or five deaths out of 10 people; that's the third reason not to proceed. The road is many miles long, the soldiers will get tired and have no strength to fight the enemy just to get to the outside of the Lĩnh region.*[8] *That is the fourth reason not to proceed. A soldier's capacity to march is 30 li* [13.5 kilometres] *per day, but from Duyện and Dư circuits to Nhật Nam is 9,000 li* [3,870 kilometres], *so it*

*would take 300 days to arrive.*⁹ *Each person would consume five sheng* [1 litre or roughly 0.8 kg] *of rice per day so it would require 600,000 dan* [or 9,600 tons approximately] *not to mention vegetation* [grass, hay] *for the horses and donkeys, that would be the cost to send an army and the fifth reason not to proceed."* ¹⁰

Duyên and Dư circuits are near Henan and Shandong provinces in China. The distance given by Google Maps from Jinan in Shandong province (Duyên) to Huế (Nhật Nam) by road is around 3,038 kilometres, so 3,900 kilometres is not a bad estimate of distance at the time. ¹¹

0.8 kg of rice per day does not seem too high based on the normal field ration for Japanese soldiers in WWII of 23.3 ounces (0.65 kg) of rice.¹²

Instead, he recommended to the court to appoint a new *cishi* of Giao Châu, Zhang Qiao, and a new *taishou* of Cửu Chân, Zhu Liang, with the instructions to evacuate local people from Nhật Nam to Giao Chỉ, to recruit the Khu Liên barbarians, to encourage them to fight each other and to reward them with silk and goods; those were persuaded to surrender would be provided with land. The strategy worked; Zhu Liang rode to Cửu Chân by himself to demonstrate imperial confidence and prestige, after that, thousands of rebels surrendered.¹³

YEARS 144, 157

But peace did not last long; in the winter of 144, the people of Nhật Nam rose again and burned the central buildings; again the local *taishou* managed to persuade them to surrender. It got worse in 157 when a person from Cư Phong prefecture in Cửu Chân – where Ma Yuan defeated the remnants of the Trưng sisters' rebellion over 100 years earlier – named Chu Đại (or Châu Đạt) attacked, and killed the magistrate, who was greedy and violent. ¹⁴,¹⁵ He then marched with a rebel army of between four and five thousand against the *taishou* of Cửu Chân, Ni Shi, who was killed in the ensuing battles. Fortunately for the Later Han, the military overseer of Cửu Chân, Wei Lang, was able to defend Cửu Chân and went on to capture and beheaded over 2,000 rebels.¹⁶ Wei Lang went on to Nhật Nam and used the "enticing and soothing" policy to get the rest of the rebels to surrender, but it took nearly three years to 160 before the southern frontier was pacified.

Back in 43, one of the leaders during the Trưng sisters rebellion was Chu Bá, who was hunted down and killed by a Later Han general, Ma Yuan, in Cư Phong prefecture, as discussed in Appendix 8. Chu Đạt could be his descendant.

YEARS 178, 184

Not long after, in 178, another major revolt broke out that included not only Cửu Chân and Nhật Nam but also Giao Chỉ and Hepu, covering a similar geographical area to that of the Trưng sisters' rebellion, over 120 years earlier, as discussed in Chapter 2. It took three years before the revolt was suppressed, but then, in 184, it flared up again in Giao Chỉ and was only calmed down by peaceful means a year later.[17]

4.2 – A new kingdom in the south

YEAR 192

But at the frontier prefecture of Tượng Lâm, unrest remained. According to a Chinese dynastic annal, toward the end of the Later Han dynasty, a local administrator (or *Gongcao*) with a surname Khu (Qu) had a son called Liên (Lian) who killed the magistrate of the prefecture and declared himself king.[18,19] This annal – compiled in the seventh century – is Jin shu, or the Book of Jin, which I will rely upon as a source of reference in my story of Linyi.

This event happened in 192, and that is the year that most historians used to date as the beginning of the kingdom of Linyi.[20,21] However, other historians suggest it should be 137 when Khu Liên barbarians revolted against the Later Han, one reason cited is that the name of Khu Liên appeared in both events.[22,23] It should be noted that early Vietnamese historical works such as Abridged Annals of An Nam (An Nam Chí Lược, abbreviated as ANCL), SKTT or CM, all recorded the 137 events but nothing of 192.

The revolt in 137, as noted earlier, was sufficiently major to trigger a proposal from the Later Han court to send 40,000 relief troops, but there was no equivalent response for 192 events. So perhaps this is a good reason to support 137 as the start of Linyi.

However, since Jin shu described the event as *"towards the end of the Later Han dynasty"* which started after the death of Emperor Ling in 189, I would support the year of 192 as the beginning of Linyi.

The founding of Linyi is such a major event in Vietnamese history. Sadly, it is barely noted by early Vietnamese historians in ANCL, SKTT or CM; similarly, contemporary Vietnamese historians have not paid much attention to it either.[24] Linyi effectively created a bulwark against northern expansion from the third century until the people north of Ngang pass obtained their independence in the 10th century. Without Linyi, the history of Vietnam may have taken a completely different path.

THE NAME OF LINYI

While the event that gave rise to the new kingdom took place in 192, the name of Linyi did not appear in Chinese annals until after 226 in the biography of Lu Dai (161-256), the *cishi* of Giao Châu. One of the actions Lu Dai took after he killed and completely wiped the Shi clan out of history in 226 was to send envoys to Linyi, Funan and Tangming kingdoms, each sending ambassadors with tributes in return.[25,26]

At the time of Lu Dai, northern Vietnam was part of the Eastern Wu dynasty (222-280) that occupied most of the southern and eastern provinces south of the Yangtze. On the west of Eastern Wu, however, the land was occupied by its adversary, the kingdom of Shu Han, effectively blocking its trade route to the west thus Eastern Wu was keen to explore an alternative route via the southern sea route.[27] In fact until Lu Dai established contacts with Linyi and Funan, the Chinese appeared to know little about the land this far south.

Some historians suggest Lin means forest and Yi means town. It is apparently derived from the name of the southernmost prefecture of the Former Han dynasty, Tượng Lâm (Xianglin), which means the forest of elephants. Writers of Chinese annals simply dropped the term Xiang in Xianglin and referred to the new kingdom as Linyi.[28] In another context, there is a city named Linyi in the Shandong province of China, north of Shanghai. The city is by the river Yihe (or Yi), but I have not been able to find any connection between this Linyi, the city and Linyi, the kingdom.

4.3 – Where was Linyi?

As shown in Figure 4, the southernmost commandery of the Han empire is Nhật Nam, which extended beyond Ngang to Hải Vân passes, according to one source, and to Cả pass, according to another.[29] Under the Han, Nhật Nam was divided into five prefectures, four of them covering present-day provinces of Quảng Bình, Quảng Trị, Thừa Thiên-Huế located north of Hải Vân pass.[30] The fifth prefecture, in the region south of this pass also the southernmost prefecture of the Han empire, was called Tượng Lâm, in the vicinity of Quảng Nam province.[31,32] According to Maspero, during Ma

Yuan's expedition in 41-44, he did not go beyond contemporary Thanh Hóa province of Cửu Chân and did not set foot in Nhật Nam, so while he may have decimated the Trưng sisters' rebellion in Cửu Chân in 43, the people there rose again with Nhật Nam, and the latter finally broke away from the Later Han dynasty to become independent as the kingdom of Linyi.[33]

At one time, Linyi stretched from Ngang pass in the north to at least Quảng Nam province in the south. Linyi lasted for around 550 years, from 192 to 749, when the name disappeared from Chinese annals, and a new name Huanwang was cited for over 100 years to 859. Huanwang then disappeared, and the name of Champa appeared in Chinese annals from the ninth century onwards, as discussed in Chapter 7.

As to where Linyi first started, my analysis in Appendixes 11 and 12 has indicated that it began in Quảng Nam province. My view is in line with an article on the website of the Vietnam National Museum of History, which summarised different views by archaeologists as follows:[34]

Linyi began:

a. North of Hải Vân pass, centred around Huế and expanded from there, or

b. South of Hải Vân pass — where Tượng Lâm was — i.e. present-day Quảng Nam province and moved north from there, or

c. Further south in Bình Định province.

Based on the archaeological evidence, the article supports b), and dismisses c) for lack of archaeological proof. It suggests the artefacts for a) are very thinly distributed for such a major settlement and favoured b) where a large number of Sa Huỳnh sites (pre-Linyi) was found in Quảng Nam as compared with that north of Hải Vân pass. Most other historians agree that Linyi began at Tượng Lâm.[35,36]

4.4 – "The people of that country are aggressive."

Below is a description of the people of Linyi in Nan Qi shu (or The Book of Southern Qi), a Chinese dynastic annal compiled sometime in the fifth/sixth century.[37]

> "The king wears a heavenly hat like a Buddha's hat, [also] wears a necklace of fragrant pearls. The people of that country are aggressive, accustomed to the mountains and water, good at fighting, and use sea shells as blowing horns. Everyone is half-naked, the four seasons are warm and sunny, there is no frost and snow. They respect women and despise men, calling monks [religious men] brahmins. People of the same tribe marry each other; the bride's family brings wedding presents to ask the groom first. Girl marries husband, wearing a blue robe [áo Già Lam], wrapping a cloth around her back like the wall of a well, and wearing precious flowers on her head. The brahmin leads the groom to his wife to hold his hand and then prays auspicious words. When mourning, they cut their hair for filial piety. Burning a corpse in the middle of a field is burial. In the distance, there is a species of bird called Linh Thứu (a vulture) that know a person is about to die, immediately gathers at the house, eats the dead person's flesh, and flies away. The people collect the bones, burn them to ashes, and throw them into the sea for burial. [As for] the skin colour, black is valuable; all southern countries are like that."

THE FANS

Among the forebears of the people described by Nan Qi shu, is the son of the district administrator who began the rebellion in 192, established Linyi and started a kingdom ruled by over 20 kings, all with Fan (Vietnamese Phạm) as a surname. The meaning of Fan has been debated among scholars. The debate is between Fan as a transliteration of the Sanskrit *"varman"*, meaning "shield, royal or honorific title"; Fan as a family name denoting *Brahma*, as in the Hindu god of creation; or Fan as a transcription of *pha, phô, phò* meaning headman or leader.[38,39,40] I prefer the last interpretation as the first two require knowledge of Indian culture whereas calling the chieftain of the tribe by a term which means headman seems a lot simpler and thus makes a lot more sense, at least in the early years of Linyi's formation.

The Fans lasted for nearly 450 years from the third to the seventh centuries until the last one and his immediate family were all killed by someone with a long name of Ma Ha Mạn Đa Gia Độc (Mahamanduka) in 645 and replaced by his brother-in-law.⁴¹ Around 100 years later, the kingdom then appeared in Chinese annals as Huanwang (Vietnamese Hoàn Vương).

SOURCES OF INFORMATION

The bulk of the information related to Linyi is recorded in the books of various Chinese dynasties and kingdoms; they provide, albeit a one-sided view, vivid scenes of cities, people and the personalities of its kings.

Over four centuries, Chinese records painted a picture of exotic tributes from Linyi to its court and the various battles between imperial troops and those of Linyi. The annals also mention the raids by soldiers led by different Fans across the border of southern imperial territories, the plunders and killing across the length of central Vietnam from Quảng Nam all the way to Ngang pass and beyond to Cửu Chân, Giao Chỉ (or contemporary Thanh Hóa and Hanoi). Finally, the annals record different military campaigns and the burning, looting of Linyi citadels by imperial soldiers.

In parallel to the annals, there are inscriptions on rocks and steles in Sanskrit and "old or proto-Cham" language which have also been used to study Linyi and Champa history.⁴²,⁴³ Archaeologist/historian Southworth points out that the bulk of the inscriptions found from the fifth to the eighth centuries are located within Quảng Nam province (19 in Quảng Nam and one each at Thừa Thiên-Huế, Phú Yên and Khánh Hòa. The last two provinces are south of Quảng Nam). Of those 19, 12 are from Mỹ Sơn near Trà Kiệu.⁴⁴

AUSTRONESIAN AND MON-KHMER LANGUAGES

The consensus among scholars is that the "barbarians" of Khu Liên are not aboriginal but Austronesian navigators who landed on the coast of central Vietnam and inserted themselves into the mainland Mon-Khmer linguistic culture.⁴⁵ These people were descendants of the Sa Huỳnh settlement from Borneo who spoke Chamic languages, a Malayo-Polynesian subgroup of the Austronesian language family and closely related to the Malaysian language of western Borneo, Sumatra and the Malay Peninsula.⁴⁶ However, historian Michael Vickery suggests the main ethnolinguistic group of Linyi was Mon-Khmer and that Linyi was not Champa (except from the early seventh century).⁴⁷

Mon-Khmer belongs to the Austro-Asiatic language family that includes Vietnamese and Khmer; this is a different language family from Austronesian; thus, the Fan rulers of Linyi who spoke Chamic would not be able to understand a person who spoke Vietnamese whom he came across during his campaign north.[48,49] The situation exists presently; the Cham people in modern Vietnam speak their language, which Vietnamese speakers do not understand.

The transition from Linyi to Champa is subject to a number of scholarly debates, and I will return to this subject in Chapter 7 but for now, let us continue with the story of the Fans.

The Fans embarked on many northern campaigns starting from Tượng Lâm and fought against imperial generals over many generations. Once the northern rulers were driven out in the 10th century, the fighting continued between the kingdoms of Đại Việt (formerly Giao Châu) in the north and Champa (formerly Linyi) in the south. The region that is north-central Vietnam between Ngang and Hải Vân passes did not achieve a lasting peace until the 14th century, when it became part of Đại Việt.

Jin shu tells us the Linyi kings wanted the land of Nhật Nam because they did not have enough rice paddies. It is borne out by the topography map of Vietnam (Figure 2), which shows clearly there is only some flat land between Ngang and Hải Vân passes with the red earth of Gio Linh in Quảng Trị, and the plain of the Gianh river in Quảng Bình provinces are the most fertile.[50,51,52] The low population density of Nhật Nam and easy access from the sea via many rivers may have also encouraged Linyi kings to go north.[53]

4.5 – Fan Xiong (Phạm Hùng, 270-280) and Fan Yi (Phạm Dật, 280-336)

TAO HUANG - "A STUBBORN AND COWARDLY HORSE"

Around two decades after Linyi came into existence, the Han dynasty, which had unified China for over 400 years, came to an end; China was broken up and entered the Three Kingdoms (220-280) of the Six Dynasties period when China was divided among three kingdoms: Cao Wei, Shu Han and Eastern Wu. Giao Châu, which included Vietnam north of Hải Vân pass, was part of the Eastern Wu kingdom, but the three-kingdom period did not last long, and by 280, China was united again under Sima Yan, the son of an official in the Cao Wei kingdom, north of the Yangtze, who founded the Jin dynasty and became its first emperor.[54]

Around 280, Tao Huang, the *cishi* of Giao Châu, wrote to Sima Yan to explain why the army in Giao Châu should not be demobilised. His official dispatch provides a fascinating glimpse of the political and geographical relationships between Giao Châu and Linyi at the time. It appears Tao Huang was sufficiently persuasive as the emperor, listened to him and reappointed him as the *cishi* even though he was an official of Eastern Wu, a state that Jin finally defeated in the spring of 280. I have translated the relevant passage as shown below:

> "*Giao Châu is a strip of land that has not yet developed at a remote distance and requires two to three levels of translation to understand. Externally, only several thousand li distances* [there is] *the kingdom of Linyi,* [there] *a barbarian general name of Fan Xiong hidden in a dangerous place,* [who] *has been a rebel for several generations, proclaimed himself king and violated the people.*[55] *Their border is next to Funan, there are many races divided into many factions, relying on each other to occupy dangerous places, not submitted* [to the imperial rule]. *Before they belonged to the Wu dynasty, they used to plunder the honest people, killing the chief officials. I am a stubborn and cowardly horse, employed by the* [Eastern] *Wu in the past to defend the south. It has been over 10 years, and over that time, there were many times of fighting, eliminating a few chiefs, but some were still hidden in the depths of remote areas, unable to eradicate. Originally, the number of soldiers that I led was 8,000 men, but the land of the south is humid with a lot of poisonous gas; moreover, the yearly fights against the enemy caused many soldiers to die, considerable worn out currently; there are only 2,400.*
>
> *Now, the four seas have been unified, and there are no places that have not submitted; the military should be disarmed. But I see that the people of this region like to rebel, so* [we] *should not reduce the arm forces to weaken ourselves. In the lull* [who knows] *when the unexpected events happen, but I am a survivor of the* [Eastern] *Wu, so the discussion would not mean much.*" [56,57]

Tao Huang served the Jin emperor, but his loyalty may have remained with the bygone Eastern Wu as he stayed in Giao Châu for 30 years and died in 290. Like the Shi clan before him, Tao Huang, his father, his sons and his grandson all became *cishis* of Giao Châu. Other than the nepotism nature of such an arrangement, it may reflect the political instability of China at the time, so there was little attention by the imperial court to the appointments of new *cishis* in Giao Châu.

A FOREST TOWN - THE KINGDOM OF LINYI (LÂM ẤP) AND THE FANS

YEAR 248

In 248, troops from Linyi had fought their way to Thọ Linh (Shouling) river for a major battle with Giao Châu at the bay.[58,59] This was named *vụng Cố Chiến* (same as *vịnh* or *vũng* meaning a small bay) and historian Đào believes it is the same as *Vũng Chùa*, just south of Ngang pass by *Yến* island.[60] A 19th-century book, "Additional explanation of the Commentary on the Water Classic" (Shui Jing Zhu Shu or Thủy kinh chú sớ – abbreviated as TKCS), notes Thọ Linh is a sub-prefecture of Tây Quyển, a prefecture located south of a citadel named Khu Túc (Qusu).

There is no mention of the name of the Linyi leader in the 248 event, but it could have been Fan Xiong, to whom Tao Huang referred in his official correspondence, or his father (given the long years between 248 and 280). 248 is also the year Lady Triệu revolted; Linyi could have taken advantage of the unrest north of Ngang pass to carry out the raid.

FAN YI

In 282, Tao Huang managed to push back Linyi forces and reoccupied Khu Túc at Ba Đồn.[61] The son of Fan Xiong by the name of Fan Yi succeeded him and ruled for over 50 years (284-336). Fan Yi continued the practice of paying tribute to the imperial court of the Jin dynasty in 280 and 289, which had stopped since Eastern Wu times. By all accounts, Fan Yi's reign was relatively peaceful, but after his death, war broke out again between Linyi and the Jin armies, and the next 20 years plunged the regions on either side of Ngang pass into death and destruction.

4.6 – *The slave king*

Jin shu describes the campaign in 347 of the king of Linyi, Fan Wen, nearly 100 years after Linyi forces occupied the region around the Gianh river as:

> "*In 347, Wen brought the army to attack Nhật Nam, killed the taishou Xia Houlan (Hà Hầu Lãm), murdered five to six thousand people and the remainders fled to Cửu Chân. Wen sacrificed Xia Houlan dead body to heaven and razed Tây Quyển to the ground. [He] then occupied Nhật Nam, informed the cishi of Giao Châu, Zhu Fan (Chu Phiên) and requested that Hoành Sơn mountain range [where Ngang pass is] be the northern border [between Linyi and Giao Châu].*"[62,63]

FAN WEN (PHẠM VĂN, 336-349) - A ROYAL USURPER

The bloodshed started with a slave, an adventurer and a royal usurper that history knows as Fan Wen, who, according to TKCS, was born in Anhui province, east of Shanghai. As a child, he was sold into slavery in Giao Châu, and, at the age of around 15, scared of being beaten for an offence, he escaped and joined a merchant in Linyi where he became a levy payment to the king, Fan Yi.

TKCS tells us Wen firmly believed it was his fate to become king. His job was to graze oxen; one day at a ravine with the oxen, he caught two snake-head fish he wanted to keep to eat later, but his master found out. Scared and embarrassed, he lied, saying there was no fish but only two stones. The master saw the stones where the fish were and believed him; Wen thought it was strange that the fish disappeared to be replaced by two stones. However, he knew these rocks had iron, so he took them to the forest, melted them down and made two swords out of them. Wen then raised the sword over a large rock and prayed that since fish turned into stones and stones made swords, if there were a spirit in the swords, it would cut through the rock, and he would become a king; if not, there was no spirit. As the blade hit the rock, it cut through it like through a bale of hay. Wen was amazed, but the story became a legend, and local people gradually submitted to him.

In time, Wen gained the king's confidence and was dearly loved by him.[64] Ten years later, the king died. Wen immediately enacted his deadly plan by poisoning the crown prince, killing the marquises and the generals. With rivals out of the way, he declared himself king. In another part of TKCS, the story is told slightly different, whereby Wen was a slave of Phạm Trĩ (or Phạm Trùy), a barbarian chief at Tây Quyền prefecture. Phạm Trĩ often sent Wen on long-distance business trips, as far as China in the north, where he learned many things. During the reign of Min Emperor Jianxing (313-316), Fan Wen travelled south to Linyi and taught its king, Fan Yi, how to build forts, manufacture tools and weapons and town planning. The king loved, trusted Wen and appointed him a general.[65]

Wen ingratiated himself with everyone but disparaged the king's children; they then left or fled. The king became isolated, and once he died in 336, Wen seized the opportunity killed the king's son on his return from overseas by offering him a drink of coconut milk full of poison. He intimidated other people in court and proclaimed himself king. The wives and concubines of the dead king were kept on the upper floors. Wen took those who submitted to him; those who did not were not given food and drink and died from starvation.⁶⁶,⁶⁷ Based on TKCS, if he travelled to Linyi at the age of 15 in 316 then he would be 35 years old by the time he became the king of Linyi, an ambitious, treacherous and brutal man at his peak.

THE BATTLE OF CỬA LÔ DUNG

Wen wasted no time in conquering seven small neighbouring states which Southworth suggests to be interior states and described by TKCS as all barbarians who ate through the mouth but drank through the nose, with facial incisions and tattooed bodies like the naked people of Lang Hoang.⁶⁸,⁶⁹,⁷⁰ Wen also employed all the red-dressed prisoners (or their descendants) from Shu Han and Cao Wei kingdoms who were exiled to Nhật Nam by Eastern Wu. Exiling prisoners was a common policy by the northern rulers, back to the Qin dynasty (221-206 BCE).

By now, he had an army of between forty to fifty thousand: very large, given that Tao Huang, some 50 years earlier, could only muster 8,000, reduced to 2,400 troops by deaths and sickness.⁷¹ However, Fan Wen did not move against Giao Châu until 344, but continued paying tributes to the Jin court. In 340, court annals record Linyi gifted an elephant with a letter written entirely in barbarian characters, which later scholars believe to be a south Indian Brahmi script.⁷²,⁷³,⁷⁴ Fan Wen is recorded as a slave from China, but his court's written language was Indian, which confirms the consensus that, by the fourth century, Linyi was Indianized.

At the time of Fan Wen, Jin shu reports a number of greedy *cishis* and *taishous* of Giao Châu and Nhật Nam who set the price of goods sold to China at less than half of the market price, bullied merchants, confiscated their wares and only returned two or three out 10 items.⁷⁵,⁷⁶ Such practices must have been galling to Wen, himself a trader, and in 344, his forces attacked Nhật Nam and crossed Ngang pass to invade Cửu Đức (Hà Tĩnh and Nghệ An provinces) and Cửu Chân (Thanh Hóa province) prefectures. Hundreds of families fled, and lands were empty of people, then Wen returned to Linyi.⁷⁷,⁷⁸ Jin shu does not mention the event but cites the attack in 347 with the sacrifice of the prefect of Cửu Chân, Xia Houlan. Wen's northern invasion was timely as Xia Houlan was a drunkard who lost control of the prefecture and caused widespread resentment among the populace.⁷⁹

Wen razed Tây Quyển, where he was kept as a slave in his youth, to the ground. He then occupied the whole of Nhật Nam prefecture, informed the *cishi* of Giao Châu, Zhu Fan, and requested that Hoành Sơn mountain range be the northern border between Linyi and Giao Châu. He returned to Linyi, which in this context, could be Huế or Quảng Nam. My study of Linyi geography in Appendix 11 indicates that Tây Quyển is in the vicinity of the Gianh river, just south of Ngang pass over the Hoành Sơn mountain range.

One could imagine how Zhu Fan reacted to this request from a barbarian who burned the dead body of his local representative, killed thousands of his soldiers and razed a prefecture of the empire into the ground. Zhu Fan immediately sent a high-ranking officer, Liu Xiong, to Nhật Nam, but Wen attacked him and went on to make a surprise assault on Cửu Chân on the northern side of Ngang pass, killing 80 to 90 per cent of Jin soldiers, a disaster for Zhu Fan.[80]

Stung into action, in 349, the Jin emperor sent soldiers from Giao Châu and Guangzhou under Deng Zhun, who had the same official title as Liu Xiong, and the new *cishi* of Giao Châu, Yang Ping, to attack Wen. The combined forces arrived by ships, and the battle took place at the mouth of Lô Dung river.[81] Wen defeated them, and Deng Zhun withdrew to Cửu Chân; but that year, Wen died from wounds suffered during the battle, and his son Fan Fo (or Fan Fu) became the next king of Linyi and remained in Nhật Nam.[82,83,84]

Historical records only have a few lines to describe this event, but the invasion by Fan Wen must have threatened the Jin court sufficiently for the emperor to order the mobilisation of the resources of both Giao Châu and Guangzhou to crush him. However, unlike the rebellion of the Trưng sisters, the emperor did not send one of his top generals from his court but left local officials and commanders to lead the campaign, and they failed.

As discussed in Appendix 12, I believe this battle took place at Cửa Tư Hiền in modern Thừa Thiên-Huế province.

IN REMEMBRANCE OF FAN WEN

From the time Fan Wen poisoned the king's son around 336 until his death from battle wounds in 348, he led a number of successful raids across Ngang pass into the southern counties of Cửu Chân. Wen also fought and won a naval battle against the might of the Jin empire at the mouth of the Lô Dung river.

He also razed and left a "no-man-land", the buffer zone between Linyi and the border across the Hoành Sơn mountain range, where he reportedly built stone ramparts along the side of the mountain all the way to the sea. A 19th-century geography work described it:

> "*On Ngang pass to the north of Bình Chính district, [there is] a series of stone ramparts running along the mountain to the sea. It is said to have been built by the king of Linyi, Fan Wen, as the dividing line for the border.*" [85]

Bình Chính district is north of contemporary Quảng Trạch district in Quảng Bình province.

Wen's death marked the end of a remarkable man, but he has no place in the Vietnamese pantheon of heroes; there is no street named after him and no temple for him even though he defeated imperial armies led by generals appointed by the northern dynasties a number of times. Vietnamese historians barely mentioned him, and when they did, he was seen as a foreign barbarian whose regular raids caused untold miseries to the people of Giao Châu.[86,87]

The work also mentioned another rampart built at a later date in the same vicinity:

> "*At Trung Ái commune, Bình Chính district, there is a rampart from Thành Thang mountain extending to the Tô Xá, Vân Tập, Phù Lưu communes, crossing the passes and gullies, each section has a mound and a platform. According to legend, it is the ancient rampart of Hoàn Vương. Today there are still traces of it.*" [88]

The same work records Thành Thang mountain as 4.8 kilometres north-east of the Bình Chính district. In Google Maps, there is a Tô Xá commune and a Phù Lưu hamlet in the Quảng Lưu district; both are north of the Gianh river and in the contemporary district of Quảng Trạch. Unfortunately, so far, I have not been able to identify any traces of these ramparts even though they had survived, at least to the 19th century.

4.7 – Khu Túc - *The elusive capital*

Khu Túc is described with some details in TKCS, and it must have been an impressive sight for the people who lived there and the invaders who came from the north.[89] The citadel is of a rectangular shape with an approximate dimension of 975 by 502 metres, not very large when compared with the 19th-century Imperial City at Huế of around 2,300 square metres, but its walls at 5.1 metres are of a significant height. Above these walls were 2.55-metre brick walls with square holes, and above the walls, there was a wooden floor; above the floor, there was a level with five floors with a roof. Above the roof were upper stories with various heights from 12 metres to a dizzy height of 20 metres.

There are 13 gates to the citadel, and the palaces within it all face south. Looking up from the river surrounding it, a traveller could see several wooden buildings with five floors soaring to the sky at various heights from 20 to 28 metres. It is equivalent to modern seven to nine-story buildings; in the fourth or fifth century, it must have been a spectacular sight and proof of a great achievement of its kings.

Khu Túc is situated between two rivers, surrounded by high rocky mountains, rugged land where the Linyi army kept all their weapons and other materiel. Its perimeter is estimated at 3 kilometres, comparable to Thành Lồi in Huế at 2.6-3.0 kilometres. Around the citadel were markets and 2,100 houses.

TKCS attributes the founding of Khu Túc to the Linyi's king, Fan Huda, grandson or great-grandson of Fan Wen. Judging from the description of the citadel, its builders were certainly not poor; their wealth (built from locally produced gold, commercial trades and booty collected from raids) was there for all to see and, as historical events unfolded, to be looted – its wooden buildings burned and inhabitants massacred.

Exactly where Khu Túc is located is still a mystery. However, it could be at one or both places a traveller can visit: Cao Lao Hạ and Thành Lồi.

4.8 – Cao Lao Hạ - A citadel in a paddy field

Figure 23 also shows the village of Thọ Linh, which shares its name with the sub-prefecture Linyi troops occupied in 248. On the east of this village and south of the Gianh river, there are remains of a citadel named Cao Lao Hạ, and for a number of years, scholars believed it to be Khu Túc. However, recent studies have indicated that it is too small (250 by 180 m) to be the citadel mentioned in TKCS and not many early artefacts were found there.[90,91] Most were dated between the 17th and 18th centuries with some from the 13th and 14th centuries, which would fall under the Đại Việt period. However, the presence of some Champa artefacts led to an observation that the people of Đại Việt may have built the citadel upon a foundation established by Champa.[92]

The width at the base of the ramparts at Cao Lao Hạ varies from 8.6 to 12.5 metres; the top of the ramparts is between 0.8 and 5 metres wide and is covered with trees. The ramparts vary in height from 0.8 to 2.0 metres. There is also a moat on the east wall. The citadel is rectangular in shape, measured at 250 metres in length and 180 metres in width adding up to a perimeter of 860 metres which matches the distances taken from Google Maps.[93,94]

Archaeologist Ngô Văn Doanh, from his site visit in 2000, suggests Cao Lao Hạ, as it stands now, could be the inner citadel of the original Khu Túc, which is much larger.[95] While this is a possible explanation, I have some doubts as my inspection of the surrounding area on Google Maps has not indicated any feature, such as trees-lined ramparts, that would resemble outer walls.

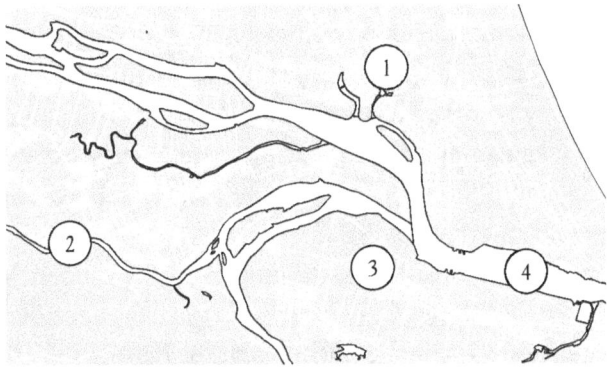

Figure 21 – Ba Đồn town (1), Thọ Linh (2), Cao Lao Hạ citadel (3), and the Gianh river (4).

TKCS reports that on the summer solstice, the shadow of a gnomon of 8 *chi* (Chinese foot) height planted at Khu Túc was 8 *cun* (Chinese inch).[96,97] On this basis and as analysed in Appendix 11, the latitude works out to be 17° 43' 33", a position around 2.5 kilometres due south of the building of the Ba Đồn Town People's Committee on the northern side of Gianh river in contemporary Quảng Bình province. This is in line with Sinologist Rolf Stein's calculation of 170 40' latitude which he equates to the location of Ba Đồn town and concludes Khu Túc is at Ba Đồn.[98,99]

Khu Túc citadel featured significantly in Linyi history and for many years, scholars have debated its location; some suggested it is not at Ba Đồn but by Hương or Ô Lâu rivers in Huế.[100,101,102] As discussed in Appendix 12, I believe there is more than one Khu Túc citadel cited in TKCS. The one where the gnomon measurements were taken, is not the large Khu Túc citadel where the Linyi army kept their materiel. This Khu Túc is most likely at Thành Lồi in Huế, as the other possible locations are generally on flat terrain close to river estuaries and could be easily overwhelmed by enemies coming from the sea. They are not ideal locations for an armoury.

4.9 – The citadel of Thành Lồi

Located around 230 kilometres south of Ngang pass, the old capital of the Nguyễn dynasty was built in the early 19th century of Huế. The capital is on the northern bank of the Hương (or Perfume) river and if one travels around 5 kilometres upstream of this capital, one arrives at a tourist spot called Tiger Arena (Hổ Quyền), where the Nguyễn kings used to have elephant fighting against tigers. But over 1,500 years earlier, this was the centre of an ancient Champa citadel. Whether this citadel (Figure 22) —currently named Thành Lồi – is Khu Túc, which in TKCS is positioned between two rivers, is still debated among historians and archaeologists. However, its existence as a Linyi and Champa citadel has been known for some time. Historians under the Nguyễn dynasty recorded its location, and French, Vietnamese archaeologists have undertaken a number of excavations since the early 20th century.[103]

Based on my studies in Appendix 12, I believe Thành Lồi is the Linyi citadel of Khu Túc described by TKCS.

The tracing of the ramparts is based on the map by scholar Nguyễn Văn Quảng; the broken line shows where the ramparts have been demolished. The circles mark the approximate positions of the flatmounds external to the wall.[104]

Today, there is not much left except for the remains of the ramparts and brick walls. The citadel is generally rectangular with an estimated perimeter of 2 kilometres and a continuous rampart, but I have not been able to locate entrance gates through it. The southern rampart (Figure 23), measured at 474 metres, is the most intact, with an average height of 4 metres. The width at the top of the wall, at its widest, is 17.9 metres.[105] Outside this rampart is a canal, still visible, of around five metres wide which would have been a moat. Around the middle of its length is a flatmound (no. 2 in Figure 22) extended beyond the wall, measured at 25 by 15 metres.[106] There are two other mounds (nos. 3 and 4 in Figure 22), and from there, one can have an expansive view of the surroundings. Archaeologists have speculated that these were used for guard posts or defensive towers.[107]

The citadel gently slopes from south to north as the land reaches the river; the eastern rampart is shorter at around 370 metres with a dogleg and measured at 2.5 to 3.0 metres in height. The northern rampart is around the same length as the southern rampart at 530 metres and follows Bùi Thị Xuân street on the southern side. The western rampart (Figure 24) is short at 288 metres, with the tallest section at seven metres and the widest at 15.6 metres on top of the rampart.[108] It should be noted that other than the southern

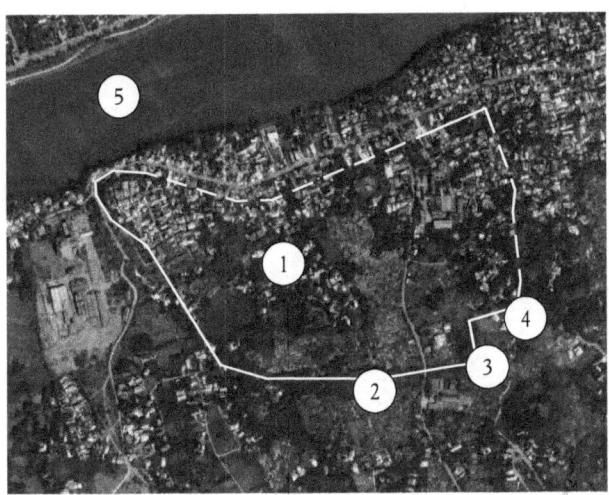

Figure 22 – Thành Lồi in Huế. 1. Tiger Arena; mounds at 2, 3, and 4; 5. The Hương river.

rampart, the ramparts as reported appear too short when checked against measurements by Google Maps.[109]

Inside the southern rampart, at around 100 metres north within Dương Biểu cemetery and next to the statue of Địa Tạng (Dizang) buddha, there are three large sandstone slabs without any inscription that archaeologists believed to be the artefacts left behind by Champa cited in the record of the Nguyễn dynasty mentioned earlier.[110] The perimeter of the citadel, as measured by Google Maps, is around 2.6 to 3.0 kilometres.

Excavations have found some pottery, tiles and bricks. Based on these artefacts and construction method, archaeologists have dated this citadel to the fourth/fifth century – around the time of Fan Wen, his son and grandson.[111]

Historians generally agree that the citadel was well-built and well-positioned, taking advantage of the river on the northern side with high mountains on the west. The ramparts were surrounded by a moat that appeared as the canals on all three sides. It was built on an elevated location with a panoramic view across the relatively flat terrain in the north and east.[112] This enables the citadel defenders to see the enemies from afar if they were coming by ships on the Hương river or on foot along the flat ground along the river. Furthermore, as it is located around 20 kilometres from the coast, it would give the defenders time to prepare against invaders from the sea.

Figure 23 – The southern rampart, viewed from inside the citadel, off Huyền Trân Công Chúa street, Huế.[113]

Figure 24 – View of the western rampart, from outside the citadel on Long Thọ street.[114]

CHAPTER 5

ONE HUNDRED YEARS OF RAIDS AND PLUNDERS (336 – 446)

LINYI II

STORY TIMELINE: Fourth to fifth centuries.
STORY LOCATION: Central Vietnam.
KEY CHARACTERS: *Fan Fo:* king of Linyi, *Fan Huda:* king of Linyi who surrounded Luy Lâu, *The Đỗ family:* who successfully repelled several Linyi's invasion, *Fan Yangmai:* king of Linyi who gambled and lost heavily to Tan Hezhi, *Tan Hezhi:* general of the Liu Song dynasty who ransacked Linyi's capital.
LOCATIONS OF INTEREST: Điển Xung/Trà Kiệu in Quảng Nam province.

Chapter Summary

Fan Wen died from battle wounds in 349, but for the next hundred years or so, his descendants continued the policy of raids and plunders against the region north of Ngang pass. Many battles took place on both sides of the pass in modern Hà Tĩnh and Quảng Bình provinces. A number of the battles took place at the river estuaries or bays, some on open ground and others against fortified citadels.

Other than the usual weapons of swords, halberds and spears, Linyi troops often had war elephants, and imperial troops had horses and crossbows.

Linyi forces got as far as Luy Lâu (Long Biên) but were pushed back, and imperial soldiers ransacked Linyi capitals (both in Huế and Quảng Nam) twice, in 446 and 605. The war, while intermittent, was intense and violent, with thousands killed on both sides over 100 years.

In the early years of the conflict, the imperial court ordered the evacuation of the population in the southern provinces to a safe area around Thanh Hóa. Fan Wen laid waste to the region immediately south of Ngang pass to create a no man's land as part of his strategy and possibly avenge his days there as a slave.

Fan Wen's immediate successors were not as successful as him in battles, but his great-grandson (or grandson) Fan Huda made a significant stride in pushing Linyi's northern border when his troops arrived outside the walls of Luy Lâu citadel itself. Fan Huda also built the magnificent capital of Điển Xung in contemporary Trà Kiệu of Quảng Nam province. Today, there is not much left, but a traveller can spend a few hours there visiting Trà Kiệu Marian Shrine, walking along the edge of the ancient ramparts and stopping at Café Champa for a nice cup of Vietnamese coffee. Within the vicinity, one can visit the sanctuary of Mỹ Sơn and climb up Núi Răng Mèo (Cat's Tooth mountain) close by.

Unlike his forbear, Fan Wen, who was enslaved, Fan Huda's son, Fan Yangmai, was born as the golden prince of Linyi. Chinese records portray him as an impetuous young man eager for a fight. In 446, the northern dynasty, now the Liu Song (420-479), had had enough and ordered an expedition to punish the kingdom once and for all. The northern troops marched and sailed south, defeated Linyi defensive lines at Khu Túc and entered Điển Xung. They thoroughly ransacked the capital, seized countless gold and gems, melted down golden statues and took over three tons of gold back to China. Yangmai managed to escape but died as a broken man as he witnessed the devastation of his capital.

5.1 – Fan Fo (or Fu, Phạm Phật, 349-380) - Like father like son

YEAR 351 CAMPAIGN - AGAINST YANG PING/DENG ZHUN - VERSION 1

Two years after Fan Wen's death, in 351, Fan Fo, son of Fan Wen, and the new king of Linyi invaded and surrounded *taishou* Guan Cui in the capital of the prefecture of Cửu Chân, but his forces were driven back by a relief column by Yang Ping and Deng Zhun.[1]

YEAR 351 CAMPAIGN - AGAINST GUAN CUI/DENG ZHUN - VERSION 2

In this version, there is no mention of Fan Fo invading Cửu Chân. The pacifying general, Huan Wen, ordered *đốc hộ* Deng Zhun and Guan Cui to attack Fan Fo, who took a defensive position inside a citadel and closed the gates. Guan Cui then divided his force into two; Deng Zhun made the frontal attack with the bulk of Jin troops, while Cui led a small force of 700 muscular soldiers to break through the fortification and attack from behind. Fan Fo's troops panicked and fled. It was a decisive victory for Jin commanders. Guan Cui chased Fan Fo to Linyi, where he surrendered.[2]

YEAR 351 CAMPAIGN - AGAINST YANG PING/GUAN CUI/DENG ZHUN - VERSION 3

In this account, Jin forces, under Deng Zhun, having recovered in Cửu Chân after the defeat by Fan Wen, went on the offensive together with the *cishi* of Giao Châu, Yang Ping. This time, there was no mention of a naval battle, but Jin commanders took the route to the Thọ Linh river; they camped at lake Lang and attacked Fan Fo at the old administrative centre of Nhật Nam. Fo's troops, "*as many as ants*", took a defensive position behind 50 *li* (22 kilometres) of ramparts. However, their line was broken and smashed by Jin troops.[3] Fan Fo escaped to a lagoon area, asked his commander to tie his hands behind his back, went to the camp of the Jin commanders and surrendered. Deng Zhun asked his guard to comfort Fan Fo and let him go after he took a pledge.[4]

It was an unusual practice at the time when the beheading of the captured enemies tended to be the rule. It was even more uncommon as one of the commanders, Guan Cui, was a replacement for the *taishou* killed by Fan Wen. This is not to mention thousands of Jin soldiers slaughtered by Fan Wen barely a few years earlier. One possible explanation is that Fan Fo paid a ransom for his freedom, as was the common practice by Linyi kings at the time.

It is interesting to note that 22 kilometres is around the distance between the mountains on the west to the sea on the east in the vicinity of the Gianh river.

Irrespective of which versions, I believe the battles in 351 likely occurred in the area around the Giang river.

YEAR 353 CAMPAIGN - AGAINST YUAN FU

Fan Fo lived to fight another day and, in all likelihood, continued to conduct raids across Ngang pass. Two years later, in 353, Jin troops, under the command of Yuan Fu, the *cishi* of Giao Châu, attacked Fan Fo and defeated him. Yuan Fu destroyed 15 ramparts and encampments which TKCS believes are linked to the 50 *li* of ramparts cited earlier.[5]

As discussed in Appendix 12, I believe the 353 battles likely occurred near the Nhật Lệ river.

YEAR 359 CAMPAIGN - AGAINST WEN FANGZHI

These losses did not deter Fan Fo, who kept up the raids across the northern border. By then, Jin high command must have had enough, so in 359, ten years after the war began, they again marched south. The forces were under the command of Wen Fangzhi (Ôn Phóng Chi), the *cishi* of Giao Châu, who proved himself a strict disciplinarian by putting to death two senior officials, named Đỗ Bảo and Nguyễn Lạng, who refused to join him. Wen Fangzhi marched south and engaged Fan Fo continuously in a series of battles on water and land. Fan Fo was driven into his citadel, where he asked for the truce a number of times and eventually surrendered.[6] At 5 *li* to the east side of Fan Fo's citadel were two stone walls named Ôn Công (Wen Kong) and a branch of a river also named Ôn Công; both were believed to be named after Wen Fangzhi, for he built the walls in the campaign and travelled by this river branch to attack Fan Fo.[7]

It appears the war strategy of the Jin army had changed over 10 years. The first expedition against Fan Wen was by the sea route, where Jin forces lost heavily at Cửa Lô Dung, a long way south of Ngang pass. Subsequent expeditions were mainly on foot across Ngang pass when Jin forces destroyed many sections of ramparts south of the pass. Wen Fangzhi's expedition appeared to have employed both sea and land routes and had gone further than his predecessors.

As discussed in Appendix 12, the battle against Wen Fangzhi likely took place near the Thạch Hãn river.

Either from war exhaustion or an acknowledgement that he could never live up to his father's reputation, Fan Fo decided to call it a day and in the following years, sent three missions to the Jin court in 372, 373-374 and 377.[8] The southern frontier appeared to remain peaceful until Fan Fo died in 380.

5.2 – Fan Huda or Houta (Phạm Hồ Đạt, 380-413) - The man who laid siege to Long Biên

YEAR 399 CAMPAIGN

Chinese annals do not record any unrest in the southern frontier for 19 years after the death of Fan Fo, but in 399, it erupted again, just as violent and bloody. The grandson (or son) of Fan Fo by the name of Fan Huda, continued the family tradition of raiding the prefectures north of Linyi frontier. This time, he captured the *taishous* of Nhật Nam and Cửu Đức, named Qúy Nguyên and Tào Bình respectively, and got as far as the administrative centre of Giao Châu at Long Biên but was driven back.[9] Fan Huda's troops went a lot further than his predecessors to get into the heart of Giao Châu, a feat not repeated until nearly 1,000 years later when the king of Champa, Chế Bồng Nga, ransacked and burned Đại Việt's capital of Thăng Long (Hanoi) in 1371.

It was to Fan Huda's misfortune (and Giao Châu's luck) that his reign coincided with the time when Giao Chỉ was led by a competent family of the Đỗ, born and bred in Chu Diên prefecture, some 60 kilometres east of Hanoi.[10] Unlike previous battles led by those who were sent from China to take up positions in the south, the Đỗ were locals even if their grandfather was originally from southern China. History records Đỗ Viện, the one-time *taishou* of Nhật Nam, Cửu Đức and Giao Chỉ and his third son, Huyền Chi, put up a vigorous fight as Huda's troops surrounded the provincial capital at Long Biên:

> "The king of Linyi, Fan Huda, attacked Nhật Nam, Cửu Đức, and Cửu Chân, then surrounded the provincial capital. At that time, General Đen Dunji [Độn Chi], was away, Viện and his third son, Huyền Chi, employed all their resources to defend, hatched many schemes and ruses, repeatedly fought then able to make a great breakthrough. They then chased and fought [Linyi forces] at Cửu Chân, Nhật Nam; they won continuously and forced Huda to flee back to Linyi."[11]

Đỗ Viện was then appointed as the *cishi* of Giao Châu, overseeing all six prefectures of Giao Chỉ, Tân Xương, Vũ Bình, Cửu Chân, Cửu Đức and Nhật Nam.[12]

YEAR 407 CAMPAIGN

Less than 10 years later, in 407, Fan Huda tried again. He attacked and killed the magistrate of Nhật Nam but was beaten back with heavy losses. In 413, his raid into Cửu Chân ended as a complete disaster. His forces were up against one of Đỗ Viện's sons, Đỗ Tuệ Kỳ, the *taishou* of Cửu Chân, who killed Huda's son and heir, Giao Long Vương Chân Tri, and general Phạm Kiện. Đỗ Tuệ Kỳ also captured Huda's other son, Na Năng, and over 100 prisoners.[13]

These setbacks did not deter Linyi, and after Đỗ Viện's death in 410 at 84 years of age, Linyi troops continued to raid Nhật Nam, Cửu Đức and weakened the whole province of Giao Châu as a result. Meanwhile, the Jin dynasty was coming to an end, China was broken up again into what is known as the Northern and Southern Dynasties period (420-589), and Giao Châu came under the rule of the Liu Song (Southern Song or Former Song) dynasty (420-479).

YEAR 420 INVASION OF LINYI

Đỗ Viện's fifth son, Đỗ Tuệ Độ, replaced him in 411. In 420, Tuệ Độ must have had enough of Linyi raids. Under the new dynasty, he assembled a force 10,000 strong, including military personnel and civilian officials, to invade Linyi.[14] The invasion caused devastation to Linyi, killing over half of its population and recapturing all the plundered goods and territories. Linyi surrendered and submitted cattle, large elephants, gold, silver and kapok to Tuệ Độ, who granted amnesty to Linyi prisoners. Afterwards, peace reigned in the southern prefectures for a few years.[15] In 423, Tuệ Độ, at the age of 50 and was awarded the posthumous title of Left General by the Liu Song emperor; his father was also awarded a similar title of Right General at his death.

I have not been able to establish where this battle took place, it could be around the same place that Fan Fo surrendered in 359, or it could be at Thành Lồi in Huế.

5.3 – Fan Yangmai (or Yan Mah, Phạm Dương Mại, c. 425-446) - The Golden Prince

THE GOLDEN PRINCE

After Fan Huda died sometime in the early fifth century, his death threw the Linyi court into disarray with a number of successors; the transition from Fan Huda to the subsequent kings is a confusing period of Linyi history. One character who stood out is a person named Di Zhen (Địch Chân), the son of Huda who succeeded him and then relinquished his throne and went to India.[16]

In 421, the Liu Song court received an envoy from Linyi's king by the name of Fan Yangmai. Yangmai is a transcription of the Cham honorific "Yah Mah" or "Golden Prince."[17] Unlike his forebear, Fan Wen, who was born into slavery, Yangmai was born into royalty. TKCS records:

> *"His mother, while pregnant, saw in her dream a person spreading out a golden straw mat, she laid her baby on the mat, and the gold began to shine brightly"*, and that is how Fan Yangmai got his name.[18]

After his death, his 19-year-old son, Đốt, became king, calling himself after his father's name, and history also knows him as Fan Yangmai.[19]

While the early childhoods of Fan Wen and both Yangmai's were different, their foreign policy as kings was similar; Yangmai followed the family tradition of raids and plunders while making tributes and sending envoys to the Liu Song court every three to fourth years from 430 to 441.[20] Despite the massive defeat in 420 by Đỗ Tuệ Độ, less than 10 years later, early in the reign of Liu Song Emperor Wen (Yuanjia, 424-453), Yangmai continued to raid Nhật Nam and Cửu Đức. Tuệ Độ's eldest son, Đỗ Hoàng Văn, now a *cishi* of Giao Châu, reacted by preparing to invade Linyi, but upon hearing he was to be replaced, the plan was cancelled.[21,22] Hoàng Văn was summoned to the Liu Song court to take on another position, but he died en route at Guangzhou in 427, thus ending the three generations of the Đỗ family's dominance of Giao Châu politics.

YEAR 431 CAMPAIGNS

In 431, Yangmai raided Cửu Đức again with 100 tower ships; they got to the entrance of Tứ Hội river but were driven back.[23,24] Once again, a similar story played out whereby the *cishi* of Giao Châu, not one of the Đỗ but an official appointed by the northern court named Yuan Miji (Nguyễn Di Chi), assembled an expeditionary force for a southern counterattack against Linyi. It appears two separate expeditions took place at two different times. The first, 3,000 strong, was led by Tương Đạo Sinh, attacked the citadel but was unsuccessful and withdrew.[25] The second, a naval force 7,000 strong including those from the first expedition a year earlier, was led by general Yuan Qianji (Nguyễn Khiêm Chi), who is different from Yuan Miji. They left the river mouth of Tứ Hội and spent three days and three nights sailing to get to Khu Túc. There, while the sea was calm, a storm brewed up, hit the armada and sank a number of ships, leaving Yuan Qianji with a few.

As mentioned previously, Cửu Đức is north of Ngang pass in Hà Tĩnh, Nghệ An region so Tứ Hội river must also be north of Ngang pass, which I believe it to be the entrance to Hà Tĩnh by Hạ Vàng river. It is also known as Cửa Sót or Cửa Nam Giới, a key port for any southern expedition, as discussed in Appendix 11.[26]

RIVER FIGHTING IN THE DARK

At the time, Fan Yangmai was away from Linyi to get married but he came back to rescue Linyi with his father-in-law in 300 ships. The battle took place at night in the river branch of Thọ Linh. Yuan Qianji was lucky: in the dark, he shot the helmsman of Fan Yangmai's boat, which was damaged and drifted; fortunately, Fan Yangmai was rescued by one of his larger ships. With the enemy in disarray, Qian Ji decided that with only a few surviving ships after the storm, it would be difficult to defeat Yangmai, so he withdrew, sailed back up the Thọ Linh river to the Ôn Công river branch and returned to Giao Châu.

This battle could have taken place at the Ô Lâu river, as discussed in Appendix 12.

Fan Yangmai, in his thirties, recently married and having repulsed attacks by the Liu Song armies, must have felt very confident and cocky. In 433, barely two years later, he sent an envoy to the court of Liu Song and requested that Giao Châu be placed under his authority. As expected, the emperor politely refused, and in the following years, Fan Yangmai continued to plague the southern counties of Nhật Nam, Cửu Đức and Cửu Chân. He still paid tributes, but these were increasingly crude and meagre.[27]

Unbeknown to him, the empire was slowly waking up, and over a decade later, he was to pay a terrible price for his actions.

5.4 – The destruction of Linyi's capital in 446

TAN HEZHI AND ZONG QUE

"In the year 456, he [Tan Hezhi] was appointed the cishi of Yanzhou (Duyện Châu) in northern China but was dismissed on charges of intoxication and corruption of public assets. In his sick bed, he was haunted and tortured by the Hồ demons and died." [28,29,30]

Ten years earlier, Tan Hezhi (Đàn Hòa Chi), the *cishi* of Giao Châu, had assembled a major expedition against Linyi under the order of Liu Song's Emperor Wen who became angry at Linyi over its arrogance.[31] From the time he ascended the throne in 424, Linyi had regularly raided the southern counties of his domain and their last raid in 433 was the last straw, he became enraged and ordered Tan Hezhi to mobilise.

The forces Tan Hezhi assembled included a man who loved wars and chose to have a military career during peacetime even though he came from a scholarly family in the modern Henan province of northern China. Zong Que (Tông Xác or Khác) reputedly said he *"wanted to ride the big wind and break miles of waves"*.[32] He had his chance when the Linyi campaign came up and was most enthusiastic about getting a transfer to Tan Hezhi's command. He was appointed as the "Shaking Martial Arts General" and joined forces with the cavalry commander Xiao Jing Xian (Tiêu Cảnh Hiến), who led the frontline troops.[33,34]

AN ATTEMPT TO NEGOTIATE

Upon hearing the news of the invasion, Fan Yangmai became frightened and sent an envoy to the emperor with an offer to return the captured families from Nhật Nam and to pay 10,000 *jin* of gold (around 2,200 kg), 10,000 *jin* of silver, 30,000 *jin* of bronze.[35] At today's price, 2,200 kilograms of gold would be valued at around $131 million USD.[36] Over two tonnes of gold is a lot of gold for Linyi, about the same as the gold reserves of Iceland or Hong Kong or Luxembourg. So it is no surprise, as events unfolded, Yangmai had no intention of following it through; besides, it would be unlikely that he could assemble that much gold.[37] In any case, Emperor Wen was agreeable and instructed Tan Hezhi to negotiate. Hezhi's forces arrived at Chu Ngô in the second lunar month of 446, where a gnomon measure was taken. As analysed in Appendix 11, this location was near Cửa Việt, the entrance to Thạch Hãn river in Quảng Trị province.

Hezhi sent a delegation of 28 people, including the *taishou* of Nhật Nam, to Linyi capital to meet with Yangmai, who immediately detained all but one, who was sent back to Hezhi's camp.[38] Hezhi sent this person back north to report that Fan Yangmai while appearing submissive, was taking defensive measures so Hezhi decided to act by attacking Khu Túc citadel. Meanwhile, Fan Yangmai sent his generalissimo Fan Fulong (Phạm Phù Long) to defend Khu Túc and reinforcements, taking the land and sea routes to the front line.

FIRST BATTLE AT KHU TÚC

Hezhi's Cavalry Commander Xiao Jing Xian defeated the reinforcements and concentrated his force around Khu Túc; his troops crossed over the moat, mounted ladders against the walls of the citadel, which measured over 5 metres tall.[39] With the strong winds fanning the flame, they overwhelmed the citadel defence, beheaded Fan Fulong and everyone inside over the age of 15: "*upper floors were awash with blood, and dead bodies formed a small hill*", the victors completely ransacked the citadel and took countless gold and silver objects.[40]

As discussed in Appendix 12, the Khu Túc citadel in this campaign is likely Thành Lồi in Huế.

SECOND BATTLE AT ĐIỂN XUNG

With the momentum of victory behind him, Tan Hezhi proceeded to attack the Linyi capital at Điển Xung,

> "*After the destruction of Khu Túc,* [Tan Hezhi] *headed straight to Điển Xung,* [his ships] *with flags filling up the whole sea, fought a fierce battle near the Tower of Demons at the bay of Bành Long, after that they proceeded to Điển Xung.*[41] *Linyi troops entered the estuary, under order to hold* [the line] *and defend* [it at all cost]. *West of the estuary was the capital of Linyi- Điển Xung, located at 40 li* [around 17 kilometres] *from the coast*".[42]

Fan Yangmai threw everything into the battle with countless rows of war elephants. Now Zong Que rose to the occasion and declared he "*heard that in foreign countries, there is a type of lion that can command hundreds of different animal species*"; he then deployed mock lions which alarmed the elephants so much that they fled, causing panic among Linyi troops, leading to a rout.

Fortunately, Fan Yangmai and his son managed to escape. Tan Hezhi entered Điển Xung victoriously, seized countless gold and gems, melted down golden statues and took a few of ten thousand *jin* of gold.[43,44] This seems to be a considerable amount of gold, well over three tons. Zong Que did not take anything and appeared very dreary when he returned to his hometown in China. Song shu does not offer an explanation for his behaviour.

THEY ALL DIED

Tan Hezhi's forces then withdrew and returned to Giao Châu. Fan Yangmai came back to Điển Xung, saw the devastation of his city with most of his people gone, and became very disoriented, distressed and angry. He fainted and recovered but died a year later in 447, a broken man at 50.

Tan Hezhi returned to northern China and died in disgrace, on charges of corruption, in 456, haunted by ghosts of the Linyi people whom his troops massacred in the southern campaigns. A few years earlier, in 453, Emperor Wen was killed by an assassin sent by one of his sons. After his death, the decay of Liu Song began, and the dynasty finally disappeared from history in 479, paving the way to the reunification of China under another short-lived dynasty, the Sui (581-618).

Linyi went through a period of change after the death of Fan Yangmai, but it slowly recovered; history does not record any more northern raids nor bloody retribution from the north until around 150 years later, when the dynasty of Sui embarked on another invasion in 605.

5.5 – Điển Xung – "catches the winds"

The architecture of Điển Xung (Figure 25) – the capital of Linyi – which Tan Hezhi ransacked, perhaps unsurprisingly, was similar to Khu Túc. TKCS describes brick walls and wooden storeys, albeit a little shorter at between 10 and 18 metres.[45] It also had a rectangular shape with the east-west side longer than the north-east side and a broken curve at the north-west corner. The perimeter of the citadel was 3.825 kilometres, so it was a little larger than Khu Túc. The palaces were very tall with an eagle-tail shape at the end that *"catches the winds and touches the clouds"*.

There was an inner citadel 490 metres in perimeter, equivalent to a square of 22 metres in length. The buildings inside were all palaces, built in a long rectangular shape with the tiled roof running along the north-south direction and no openings on the south wall. The palaces opened to the east; the roofs had the eagle-tail shape and the doors coloured blue with red floors. The walls were plastered with cow manure, and the Queen's room had purple-coloured windows, like those of other wives and concubines. The king's living and working spaces and those of his wives and concubines were on the upper floors. They squatted on the veranda on the east side and conversed with people below; their siblings, children, officials or servants were not allowed to come up. There were more than 50 groups of houses, eight temples, and demon towers, small and large; at the top of these were wooden buildings that resembled Buddhist shrines.

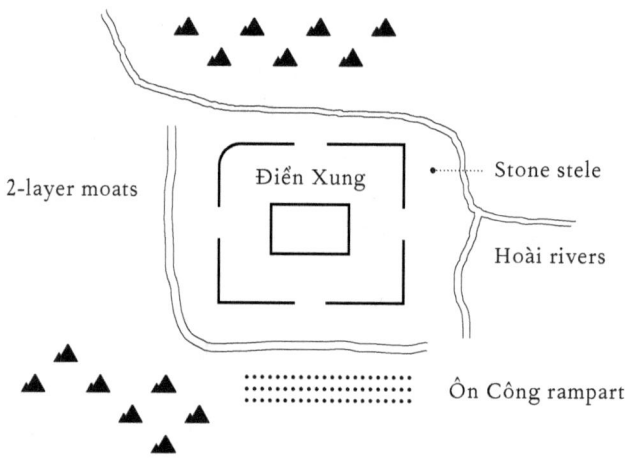

Figure 25 – A sketch of Điển Xung based on TKCS; jagged black shapes denote mountains.

In contrast to Khu Túc, there were no markets, villages or hamlets outside the citadel. The surrounding area was dreary, not a place where many people could live. TKCS asks how the leaders of the realm managed to live peacefully and maintain their kingdom for 10 generations.[46] That was until Tan Hezhi completely ransacked it and drove Fan Yangmai and his entourage to the mountains. Fan Yangmai died as a broken man on his return sometime in 446. By this time, Linyi had existed for 254 years, counting from the first rebellion in 192, so 10 generations as in TKCS, 25 years per generation on average, is not too far off. This passage also indicated that until 446, Điển Xung had been saved from the ravages of war.

As discussed in Appendix 12, most historians agree that Điển Xung was built at the Champa ruin of Trà Kiệu, as described below.

5.6 – Trà Kiệu - An ancient ruin of sandstone dancers[47]

Today, one of Vietnam's most popular tourist towns is Hội An. It is located at the estuary of the Thu Bồn river, the first major river south of Hải Vân pass; if one travels west from there for around 20 kilometres, one arrives at a small hill on the southern bank of a tributary of Thu Bồn river called Bửu Châu. On top of the hill is Trà Kiệu Marian Shrine (or Centre), a Roman Catholic shrine built in 1898. From the hill, looking south, one can see a straight line of trees and houses standing out among the paddy fields, the base of the ancient rampart of Trà Kiệu citadel.[48]

Figure 26 – The Linyi and Champa citadel of Trà Kiệu. The circle marks the Trà Kiệu Marian Shrine.

The southern and eastern ramparts (marked in white) are visible (Figure 26). The dotted white lines show the approximate position of the northern and western ramparts as depicted by archaeologist Jean-Yves Claeys. The white circle marks the Bửu Châu hill.[49]

The citadel is almost rectangular, with the southern rampart measured around 1,500 metres in the east-west direction and the width, in the north-south direction, around 550 metres.[50] The base of the ramparts is around 33 metres wide and the ramparts themselves rise above the paddy fields by 2 to 3 metres. In 1927-28, the French archaeologist, Jean-Yves Claeys, carried out extensive excavations near Bửu Châu hill, where he uncovered large-scale foundations, altar bases, lingam and yoni stones, large quantities of stone sculptures and other items. Many of these are now on display at the Museum of Cham Sculpture in Đà Nẵng, just over 30 kilometres north of Trà Kiệu, and at the Museum of Vietnamese History in Ho Chi Minh City. Examples of such finds are shown in Figures 27 and 28. Claeys believed that Trà Kiệu was the capital of Linyi but subsequent work indicated that most of these artefacts are dated to a much later period from the ninth century to the 11th, when Linyi is no longer mentioned in Chinese annals, replaced by Champa.[51] Trà Kiệu is also known as Simhapura or Lion City, the capital of Champa during this period.

Since Claeys' dig, local and international archaeologists have excavated Trà Kiệu nine more times at locations around Bửu Châu hill; between the hill and the southern rampart, as well as places at the ramparts themselves. They suggest: [55]

a. Trà Kiệu had been occupied continuously from the first century during Linyi, Champa and well into Đại Việt periods (17th century).

b. The construction of the ramparts started at the end of the third century and the beginning of the fourth.

c. Timber buildings with roof tiles (with textile impressions on the concave surfaces) were built from the second century.

d. Brick buildings with roof tiles (but no textile impressions) and eaves tiles were built after the third century.[56]

e. Brick temple towers and stone sculptures were from the seventh century.

They also noted that the eaves tiles with a human face found at Trà Kiệu are similar to those found in Nanjing, Jiangsu province in China, dated back to the Eastern Wu kingdom and at the Lũng Khê site near the ancient citadel of Luy Lâu. They also found similarities in the rampart construction methods, using rammed infill clay layers between two brick walls at Trà Kiệu and Lũng Khê.[57]

Figure 27 – The Asparas, Trà Kiệu style, 10th century, sandstone, Museum of Cham Sculpture.[52,53]

Figure 28 – Dancer, Trà Kiệu, 10th century, sandstone, Museum of Vietnamese History.[54]

5.7 – Of gold and fragrant wood

Ma Duanlin (1245-1322), a Chinese historical writer and encyclopaedist, describes Linyi as [58,59]

> "This country has mountains which contain gold mines, of which the ore is red. The gold generated in these mines produces, during the night, fires that resemble those of glowworms. In Linyi, we collect turtle scales, shells that serve as currency, the perfume called tchin-choui [made from agarwood] *and the flower of ki-pei. When ripe, the flowers of the ki-pei tree produce filaments as fine and as white as goose down. They are spun and made into very beautiful fabrics, which can be dyed in any colour".*

> *"The inhabitants build the walls of their houses with fired bricks, coated with a layer of lime. The houses are all topped by a platform or terrace, called kan-lan.*[60] *The openings are generally placed on the north side; sometimes on the east or west side, without a fixed rule".*

> *"For writing, the inhabitants of this kingdom use tree leaves which serve as paper; as mats, they use coconut leaves".*

Ma Duanlin wrote the description in the 13th century, long after Linyi ceased to exist as an entity; it would be reasonable to assume he relied on the various passages from older Chinese works such as Tongdian, Jin shu, Liang shu, Sui shu and Shui Jing Zhu and so on.[61] One common story that ran through these works is that Linyi had plenty of gold. They were not wrong, not if we go by the fact that the two largest and long-known gold mines in Vietnam are at Bồng Miêu and Phước Sơn in Quảng Nam province.[62,63,64] Both are within 100 kilometres from Trà Kiệu.

Ma Duanlin also mentions the production of floating and sinking agarwood in Linyi.[65,66] Such aromatic woods, used for making incense, perfume and small carvings are well-known in central Vietnam, including Quảng Nam and Khánh Hòa provinces.[67] The latter is known as the agarwood region of Vietnam – where the popular beach resort of Nha Trang is located – at around 520 kilometres south of Trà Kiệu.[68] According to historian Tana Li, trades in aromatics with China were thought to form the basis for Linyi's prosperity.[69] Further down the years, in the 15th century, Chinese traders offered to pay for the product with its weight in silver, and during the 17th century, Europeans wrote that they could sell the product for

15 times its cost in Champa.⁷⁰ In other words, Linyi and successive Champa kingdoms are inherently wealthy from the gold and scented wood.

Based on the locations of the gold mines and agarwood, the above description of Ma Duanlin would most likely refer to the land at Quảng Nam province and not north of it.

Ma Duanlin also reported that the climate at Linyi was warm all year round. It would be difficult to extrapolate temperature backward to when this observation was made, but Đà Nẵng, a city south of Hải Vân pass, has always been known to have a warmer weather than Huế, a city north of the pass.

CHAPTER 6

THE END OF LINYI

LINYI III

STORY TIMELINE: Seventh to eighth centuries.
STORY LOCATION: Central Vietnam
KEY CHARACTERS: *Fan Fanzhi:* king of Linyi, presided over the destruction of Linyi's capital a second time, *Fan Touli:* king of Linyi, *Fan Zhenlong:* king of Linyi, last of the Fan lineage, *Liu Fang:* general of the Sui dynasty who ransacked Linyi's capital of Điển Xung in 606.
LOCATIONS OF INTEREST: Điển Xung/Trà Kiệu in Quảng Nam province. The ramparts of Fan Wen and Huanwang in Quảng Bình province.

Chapter Summary

The wealth plundered from Điển Xung in 446, and subsequent rich tributes from Linyi to the imperial court encouraged its officials to convince one of the early emperors of the Sui dynasty (618-906) to order another pillaging expedition. In 605, fresh from the victory over another independent aspiration of the Vietnamese (Chapter 11), imperial troops marched south again in two columns, taking the land and sea route. Linyi's king, Fan Fanzhi, put up a fierce resistance, but their elephants proved no match against northern crossbows. Sui troops entered the capital of Điển Xung and took 18 gold statues representing 18 generations of the Fan Fanzhi family, among other spoils.

This time, the Linyi's gods may have answered their king's prayer: most of the Sui troops, including their commander, died on their way back north. Their feet became swollen, and most died soon after. The Sui dynasty ended over the following decade and the emperor, who benefited from the plundered gold, met his end when one of his generals killed him.

After the sacking of their capital in 605, Fan Fanzhi decided to bide his time, and as the Sui dynasty disintegrated, he regained the territory lost between Hải Vân and Ngang passes. The Tang dynasty (618-906) followed Sui but Linyi appeared content with staying on the south side of Ngang pass. Perhaps Linyi kings were too occupied with internal infighting to carry out more northern raids. Similarly, while having the names of the provinces south of the pass on their records, the Tang dynasty effectively abandoned any effort to recapture the territory. The region between these two passes was occupied continuously by Linyi, their Champa descendants and under the rule of their kings for the next four centuries until the 11th century.

After Fan Fanzhi, there were two more Fans in the family, but the last, Fan Zhenlong, was killed with all his family members, and the Fan lineage died around 645. Linyi's name disappeared from Chinese annals until a new name, Huanwang, was cited in 757.

The king of Huanwang, whose name is not recorded in Chinese annals, may have forgotten the lesson of his predecessors: he decided to invade the provinces north of Ngang pass and may have held them for a time but was driven out in the early ninth century. Vietnamese historians record a series of ramparts built by the king of Huanwang, also north of the Gianh river, which I have not been able to locate.

6.1 – Fan Fanzhi (Phạm Phan Chí) - Southern pillage

A SHAMEFUL EVENT

The sacking of Linyi in 605 is probably one of the most shameful events of the Northern Rule period. It was simply an act of greed and piracy by the empire against one of its vassals. Linyi presented no strategic threat, provoked no war, and undertook no raid across the southern frontier to attract such a vicious attack. In fact, it sent envoys with tributes to the Sui court before the invasion.

The tributes were precious, and attracted the attention of officials at the court, who informed the emperor that Linyi had many exotic objects.[1] Having absorbed the Chen dynasty (557-789), Sui was in a relatively peaceful period. Liu Fang had just defeated Lý Phật Tử in Giao Châu (Chapter 11), so it would seem an excellent opportunity for the Sui emperor to send him further south to rob and pillage Linyi.

The memory of the booty taken in the 446 expeditions by Tan Hezhi may have been still fresh at court in 604 when Emperor Wendi ordered Commander-in-Chief (*da jiangjun*), Liu Fang to assemble a substantial force in two divisions to invade Linyi. The first was a combination of infantry and cavalry under the *cishi* of Quinzhou (a coastal prefecture in Guangxi province), Ning Changzhen; the *cishi* of Hoan Châu (Hà Tĩnh, Nghệ An), Li Yun; and *kai fu* (Commander or Establishment Official) Qin Xiong. They started from the land of Việt Thường (Hà Tĩnh), reportedly more than 10,000 strong plus several thousand convicts.[2] Liu Fang, together with *da jiangjun* Zhang Xun and *sima* (commander of horses) Li Gang took the coastal route by ships to the prefecture of Tỷ Ảnh.

Emperor Wendi died while the expedition was in transit; in the first lunar month of 605, Liu Fang arrived at a sea gate (a river entrance) with a new emperor at court, Emperor Yangdi. As a matter of interest, this is the same emperor who embarked on a disastrous invasion of present-day North Korea that spelt the end of the Sui dynasty.

THE CAMPAIGN

The biography of Liu Fang describes the campaign as a series of battles (at least four) in colourful and callous terms:

"*In the first lunar month of the first year of the Daye era (605), the army arrived at a sea gate. The king of Linyi, Fan Fanzhi, sent troops to hold the vital places, but Fang was able to repel them* [first battle]. *The army then went to the Đồ Lê river; the enemy was on the southern bank of the river and set up camp. Fang unfurled an array of flags; troops beat up drums and gongs; the enemy was frightened and broken. Crossing the river and going another 30 li* [13.5 kilometres], *the enemy mounted great elephants and approached from all four sides.*

Fang gave orders for troops armed with crossbows to shoot the elephants. Injured elephants ran in panic and stepped on the enemy formation. Imperial troops fought hard and the enemy fled into the camp, but Fang was able to break through and took prisoners of tens of thousands [second battle]. *Thus, they overcame Khu Túc, passed Lục Lí, met the enemy and the front and rear but fought and captured them all* [third battle].

They advanced to the Đại Duyên river, the enemy occupied a dangerous, difficult-to-approach place and set up camp, but Fang was able to attack and destroy it again [fourth battle]. *Passing through the bronze pillars of Ma Yuan, going south for eight days, one would reach the capital of that country. The king of Linyi, Fan Zhi, fled the city and escaped to the sea. Fang took the golden statue of the master god in the temple, disgraced the palace, carved a stone to record his accomplishment and left."*

As analysed in Appendix 12, I believe the first battle took place just south of Ngang pass, Đồ Lê river is the Ròn river; the second battle took place near the Gianh river, and Khu Túc citadel cited would be in the vicinity of Ba Đồn. The Đại Duyên river is the Nhật Lệ river, the scene of the fourth battle. It would seem that Fan Zhi fled his capital, and Liu Fang entered unopposed. Linyi's capital in this expedition is likely at Điển Xung/Trà Kiệu.

Sui shu (or the Book of Sui) described the battle against the elephants differently, whereby Liu Fang dug a number of small pits just behind the front line, covered them with grass and provoked a fight with Linyi troops. In a feint, they retreated with Fanzhi and his elephants in hot pursuit. The elephants fell into the pits and were decimated by the bulk of Fang's forces. The booty was substantial, including 18 gold statues representing 18 generations of the Fanzhi family.[3] As shown in Appendix 9, if Qu Lian is excluded, there are indeed 18 kings before Fan Fanzhi.

Among the items which Liu Fang took were 1,350 Buddhist books in Kunlun language written in a South Indian script.[4] Much has been said about these books as evidence of Buddhism practised at the Linyi court in the sixth and seventh centuries, but I am unable to find the original reference in any of the dynastic annals.

A HEAVY PRICE

Liu Fang and his troops paid a heavy price for the invasion; four or five of ten died on the return trip from swelling feet, including Fang. They may have suffered from beriberi or elephantiasis disease.[5] The former is caused by a vitamin B-1 deficiency, also known as thiamine deficiency – a diet-related disorder. The latter can be caused by a parasitic disease from three species of worms. The larval form of the worms is introduced into the human body through the bite of infected mosquitoes.[6] I would suggest the second is the most feasible cause as victorious northern troops were unlikely to lack food to have a deficiency of vitamin B-1, found in meat and fish.

The Sui dynasty fared little better; its massive invasion of Goguryeo, one of the kingdoms in modern Korea, between 598 and 614 ended up in failure. The campaign assembled up to 1.15 million infantry, stretching over 410 kilometres, and 3,000 warships; its cost spelt the end of the dynasty four years later in 618.[7]

Emperor Yangdi of Sui led the ill-fated expedition, and a few years later in 617, his first cousin Li Yuan rose in rebellion and deposed him. On hearing the emperor had been killed by one of his generals, Li Yuan declared himself the emperor of the new dynasty, the Tang (618-906).

WAR ELEPHANTS

In a minor footnote, Lady Triệu (Chapter 3) had elephants in her army, Linyi kings used them in other battles, and Đại Việt kings also employed them. The sight of massive elephants charging against a line of soldiers would be so frightening to break any opposition. However, elephants can easily panic and, once wounded, would run amok, similarly, the loss of the elephant rider (or mahout) would cause the elephants to charge about indiscriminately. So, wounding them with powerful crossbows or trapping their feet in small pits were successful strategies for Liu Fang.

THREE NEW NAMES

The Sui dynasty named three new provinces in the region that Liu Fang had conquered, from north to south: Đảng Châu (Dangzhou), Nông Châu and Xung Châu from Ngang to Hải Vân pass. Sui shu cites Đảng Châu as Tỷ Ảnh or contemporary southern Quảng Bình province.[8] Historians locate Nông Châu at Quảng Trị and Xung Châu at Thừa Thiên-Huế.[9] In 607, they were changed to Tỷ Ảnh, Hải Âm and Lâm Ấp (Linyi) but as the Sui dynasty disintegrated in 618, Fan Fanzhi simply reoccupied the territory.[10]

6.2 – Fan Touli (Phạm Đầu Lê) - *A beautiful king and a talking parrot*

After the terrible destruction of the Linyi capital in 605, Fan Touli, the son of Fan Fanzhi, must have decided to take a peaceful approach to his reign. He sent envoys to the Tang court with rare and rich tributes; in 630, he sent a "fire globe pearl (or fire orb)": a crystal globe as big as a chicken egg that could light up the surroundings as far as several *chi* (up to one metre) and can set fire to a herb (sagebrush or mugwort) if pointed towards the sun at midday. In 631, he sent a parakeet with five colours and then a talking white parrot which was intelligent, knowledgeable and good at answering questions. However, Emperor Taizong (626-649) felt sorry for the parrot and ordered the envoy to return it to the woods.[11] In the dynastic annal, Xin Tang shu (or the New Book of Tang), compiled in the 11th century, the parrot complained of being cold, so it was sent back.[12] The rich tributes of Fan Touli must have pleased the emperor so much that, after his death, there was an edict that a statue of Fan Touli be made and positioned by a gate to the emperor's tomb.[13]

Fan Touli's reign lasted around 12 years, from 629 to c.640.[14] While he may have been a virtuous sovereign doing his best to protect his subjects, he was not able to protect his son, Fan Zhelong (c.640-645) who was killed not long after Fan Touli's death.

6.3 – Fan Zhenlong (Phạm Trấn Long) - *End of the line*

Another annal of the Tang dynasty, Jiu Tang shu, or the Old Book of Tang, compiled in the 10th century, tells us Fan Touli's father, Fan Fanzhi, continued paying tributes to the Tang court in 623 and 625. Touli sent envoys in 630 and 631, followed by his son, Fan Zhenlong, who was killed with his kinsmen in 645 by his Minister Mahamanduka (Ma Ha Mạn Đa Già Độc), so the Fan clan came to an end.[15,16]

Fan Touli's son-in-law, a Brahman (court priest), was installed as the new king, but the great ministers abandoned him, and installed the daughter of Touli, Zhenlong's sister, as the next king.[17]

The daughter was not able to pacify the country and the great ministers recalled the son of Touli's aunt named Zhuge Di (Chư Cát Địa), who was an exile in Zhenla because of his father's sin, to become the next king and marry the daughter. From 650 to 756, Linyi sent tributes three times, but they stopped during 756-758, and after that, Chinese annals no longer cite Linyi but record another kingdom, Huanwang.[18,19]

However, Masperos quoted other Chinese works such as Tang Huiyao (Institutional History of Tang, complied in 961), which mentions at least 15 tributes.[20,21,22] The name of the king associated with the tributes in 713 was Kien To Ta Mo. The list of Linyi kings is shown in Appendix 9.

6.4 – The kingdom of Huanwang (757-859)

During the era of Yuanhe of Tang Emperor Xianzong (806-820), Huanwang did not send their envoys but continued to raid across the Ngang pass and apparently captured the forts there. In 808, the new *duhu* of An Nam, Zhang Zhou, employed 250,000 workers to build Đại La citadel (Hanoi); the perimeter was increased to 2000 bu (3,000 metres, Appendix 7). He also built thirty-two "*đồng mông*", long narrow boats designed for fast speed during attacks. He was planning a southern expedition to attack Huanwang and recapture the two southern provinces of Ái and Hoan (Thanh Hóa, Nghệ An, Hà Tĩnh), which fell to Huanwang. The expedition was a success; Zhang Zhou arrested the leaders, decapitated some 30,000 heads, took 59 children of the king prisoners, a number of war elephants, fast boats and cuirasses.[23]

It must have been an enormous campaign, given the number beheaded. Capturing the princes and princesses may indicate that Zhang Zhou's army had entered the capital of Linyi, where the king's children likely lived. The capital, either at Huế or Quảng Nam, is a long way south from Ái and Hoan provinces and thus may explain the construction of the boats. But all these comments are just speculation; unfortunately, I do not have more information about this campaign than what is recorded in Xin Tang shu.

A Vietnamese 19th-century geographical work entitled "A Unification Record of Đại Nam" or Đại Nam Nhất Thống Chí mentions an ancient citadel of Hoàn Vương (Huanwang) at Thăng Bình commune, Diên Phước district of Quảng Nam province that used to be called Vệ Thành. I have not been able to locate this citadel. The text describes:

> "*Legend has it that in the past, Huanwang built its capital here but the walls in three sides: front, left and right of the citadel were widely eroded, only the northwest corner remains.*"[24]

CHAPTER 7

THE INSCRIPTIONS AND THE VARMAN'S

LINYI IV

STORY TIMELINE: Third to seventh centuries.
STORY LOCATION: Central Vietnam
KEY CHARACTERS: *Bhadravarman:* the king who donated land to establish the Mỹ Sơn sanctuary in Quảng Nam province, *Rudravarman:* the king who started a lineage of kings in Quảng Nam province, *Śambhuvarman:* the king who rebuilt the burned temples at Mỹ Sơn, *Jagaddharma:* the king who married a royal from the kingdom of Zhenla, *Prakāśadharma-Vikrānta-varman:* the king who authored at least 12 of 24 inscriptions in this period.
LOCATIONS OF INTEREST: Điền Xung/Trà Kiệu in Quảng Nam province. Mỹ Sơn sanctuary. Võ Cạnh inscription at the National History Museum in Hanoi. The rock of Thạch Bích.

Chapter Summary

Up to this point, my stories about Linyi have been primarily based on Chinese works, but over six centuries, the kings of Linyi carved into stone steles and rocks their own stories. Sadly, there are not many. To date, 24 inscriptions have been found in Cham and Sanskrit languages for this period, mostly from the fifth, sixth and seventh centuries. These inscriptions are coded as, for example, C. 72, where C is an abbreviation for Cham (as different from K for Khmer (Chapter 10)), and the number is the order by which the inscription is found.[1]

The content of most of these inscriptions is the donation of lands, temples or offerings from the king to the gods, primarily Shiva, the glorification of the king and his relationship with previous kings. The last verses often contain a threat of hell or other punishments to those who dare to destroy the king's offerings.

Most of the inscriptions were found in Quảng Nam province (19 in total, with 12 of those from the sanctuary of Mỹ Sơn near Trà Kiệu). The northernmost inscription was found in Huế (1), some 130 kilometres north of Quảng Nam, and the southernmost was in Phú Yên (1), around 400 kilometres south of Quảng Nam.[2] The figure in brackets is the number of inscriptions found.

The oldest inscription found is C.40 (Võ Cạnh) considered the oldest in Southeast Asia in Sanskrit. The inscription describes a celebration event in Nha Trang, sometime in the third/fourth century. The second oldest inscription, C.72 (Mỹ Sơn A1), records the donation of land to create the Mỹ Sơn sanctuary in Quảng Nam province – the largest Cham archaeological site in Vietnam (and the world). C. 72 is dated to the fifth century Śaka.

One of the most important inscriptions is C.96, which has given us the genealogy of the kings from the fifth to the eighth century. As engraved on the inscriptions, the names of kings are very long and not easy to remember. For ease of recall, the names consist of two words, the first, such as *"Rudra"*, is named after a Hindu god, and the second, *"varman"*, in Sanskrit, means "shield, royal or honorific title"; sometimes the word "Śri" which means "Sir" is added to the names.[3] What makes it further confusing is that Cham kings sometimes shared the same name but did not distinguish them on the inscriptions, so historians have added a number after the name to separate them, for example, Rudravarman I and Rudravarman II but the inscriptions only mention Rudravarman.

The important kings are:

- Bhadravarman, who donated the land and established Mỹ Sơn sanctuary,

- Rudravarman, who began a lineage of kings as recorded on the inscriptions,

- Śambhuvarman, his son, who restored the temple at Mỹ Sơn and first mentioned the name of Champa,

- Prakāśadharma-Vikrāntavarman, a fifth-generation removed king from Rudravarman, has a Cham father, and a Zhenla mother. Prakāśadharma is his name and Vikrāntavarman is his reign title.

Prakāśadharma-Vikrāntavarman must have ruled for a long time and over a peaceful period of Linyi. His name appears on 12 inscriptions, and he was the author of most, if not all, of them.

Historians have attempted to align the names of the kings on these inscriptions and those mentioned in Chinese annals. Generally, most traditional historical accounts of Linyi and Champa would link these kings – for example, Śambhuvarman with Fan Fanzhi – but while there is evidence to support the links, I have struggled to explain some of the discrepancies.

For example, both inscribed stories and annal writings mention the abdication of a king who travelled to India. Both also mention a king who went to Zhenla and a female king who ruled the kingdom. On the other hand, the inscriptions do not mention the battles against the northern generals, the destruction of Linyi capitals in 446 and 605 nor any of the Fans as discussed previously. I do not have an adequate explanation for such omissions; perhaps the kings did not want to make "reports of failures" to the gods, noting that inscriptions in the 10th century mentioned Cham's victories against Kamboja (Cambodia).

Similarly, the name of Linyi appears nowhere on the inscriptions, but Champa does. Champa appears on the inscription as early as the seventh century, but not until the middle of the ninth century that it is cited in Chinese annals.

One explanation is that the stories of Linyi as reported by Chinese annals have nothing to do with the kings named on the inscriptions. Some historians consider the Linyi stories in these annals to only relate to the region between Ngang and Hải Vân passes, whereas the stories on the inscription are to do with the kings of a separate kingdom based in Quảng Nam province, south of Hải Vân pass. I am not so sure about such a definite conclusion.

Based on historical evidence, I am reasonably confident that Fan Huda and Fan Yangmai ruled from Trà Kiệu in Quảng Nam province. However, neither have Sanskrit names; if they did, Chinese annalists would most likely transcribe them into Chinese – for example, Rudravarman is Lūtuoluobamo – which would make life easier to historians and people like me trying to make sense of historical events.

The debate will continue, but in this book, unlike most other books about Linyi, I will keep the two lines of kings, those recorded on the dynastic annals, separate from those carved on stone. A list of these kings is shown in Appendix 9.

A traveller can view examples of some of the inscriptions at the National Museum of History in Hanoi or at Mỹ Sơn itself.

7.1 – C.40 - Võ Cạnh - the oldest Sanskrit inscription in Vietnam.

THE LOCATION

As a traveller interested in Linyi and Champa history, sooner or later, one will come across this large and famous block of stone found in 1885 at the village of Võ Cạnh, Vĩnh Trung commune, Nha Trang, Khánh Hòa province in central Vietnam. The village itself is by the bank of the Cái river, some 10 kilometres from the coast. It is currently on display at the National History Museum in Hanoi (Figure 29)

When found, it was lying flat at the base of an old *duối* tree (a kind of toothbrush tree or streblus asper) with half of it buried in the mud, the other half protruding above the ground, and nobody took any notice of it.[4] Given the enormous size of the block, scholars believe it was erected there and not transported from elsewhere.

THE CONTENT

The inscription is catalogued as C.40. In brief, the block was erected to celebrate the occasion when a king donated his wealth to his family members during a clear day of the full moon by the bank of the Cái river. The assembly included priests and relatives – all drinking ambrosia, a kind of nectar or milk honey drink – and was witnessed by his minister, Vira.

THE DEBATE

The block lay anonymously for centuries, but its discovery sparked a fierce debate among researchers, which has continued until this day. The debate has centred around:

- The origin of the characters of the inscription (North or South India),

- The identification of king Śrīmāra (Sri Mara) cited in the inscription (Qu Lian of Linyi, or Fan Shiman of Funan, or a local or a foreign king),

- The age of the stele (second, third or fourth century),

- Whether the text reflects Buddhist or Hindu tradition.

I am no specialist in the subject, but from what I have researched to date, I agree that Śri Mara is not Qu Lian nor Fan Shiman for reasons of geography and archaeological finds. Nha Trang is some 550 kilometres south of Hải Vân pass, and there is no record that Qu Lian or the early kings had been this far south. Similarly, no archaeological artefacts related to Óc Eo civilisation and Funan have been found north of Vũng Tàu, some 400 kilometres south of Nha Trang.

I also support the Hindu tradition of the inscription from South India. Buddhist monks travelled to Luy Lâu in the second century as it was the centre of learning; there is no mention of them stopping in Nha Trang.[5]

I also prefer the interpretation of Indologist and linguist Jean Filliozat that the author of the inscription is not king Śrīmāra but is the "joy of the family" of his great-granddaughter, four generations removed or around 60 to 90 years down the line. Filliozat also speculates that Śri Mara never reigned but his name is in reference to a king of Pandya – a kingdom in the south of India – since the Tamil translation of Mara is Maran. There were Nanmaran and Maran Vazhudhi kings of Pandya during the period from the sixth century BCE to the third century CE, but I do not have enough information to make the linkage between these kings and Śri Mara.[6]

Given the importance of Nha Trang in the subsequent development of the Champa location of Kauṭhāra in the eighth century, I am inclined to support the position that Śri Mara is a local king. As for the age of the stele, I would adopt the commonly accepted date of the third to fourth centuries.[7]

Figure 29 – The Võ Cạnh stele (or block).[8]

My English translation of the text, as translated by Indologist and Linguist Jean Filliozat, with the additional explanation in brackets, is as follows:[9]

> LINES 1 TO 5: *deleted*. Only a few isolated aksara [symbols in the Brahmic scripts] are readable.
>
> LINE 6: *...compassion for creatures...*
>
> LINE 7: *...place... for the first triumph...*
>
> LINE 8: *.... clear day of the fortnight... at the Full Moon, ordered in assembly by the best of kings...*
>
> LINE 9: *.... with his priests, certainly, we drink the ambrosia of the hundred words of the king. Family and lineage of King Śrīmāra...*
>
> LINE 10: *.... by ornament... by him who is the joy of the family of the daughter of King Śrīmāra's grandson... was ordained.. engendered his kinship..*

LINE 11: ....*in the middle... the letter that does good for creatures, for the best of both Karin* [both elephants and the king are Karin]... *the coming and going of this world...*

LINE 12: .... *those who sit on the throne... by the desire for equalisation properties* [wealth?] *affecting the son, the brother, the posterity* [future generation]...

LINE 13: *all that there is silver or even gold, what is alive with what is material* [in] *the treasure...*

LINE 14: .... *all this is delivered by me in a pleasant and helpful* [way]. *This is what is granted by me. Even by the kings of the future...*

LINE 15: .... *is to be approved... and let it be known from my minister Vira.*

7.2 – A valley of kings - Mỹ Sơn

THE DISCOVERY

In 1885-1886, the parish priest of the Trà Kiệu Marian Shrine, Père Bruyère, led a French detachment to reconnoitre this sacred site of Mỹ Sơn, located around 20 kilometres south-west of Trà Kiệu in Quảng Nam province.[10,11] The first clearing was conducted by a colonial official, Camille Pâris, in 1897-98. An inventory of the inscriptions, found scattered at the site, was compiled by archaeologists Louis Finot and Étienne Edmond Lunet de Lajonquière in 1899.[12] A few years later, for 12 months from 11 March 1903 to 3 February 1904, architect Henri Parmentier and photographer Charles Carpeaux led an archaeological excavation of Mỹ Sơn.[13,14] There, they found the largest Cham archaeological site in Vietnam with traces of 68 buildings or temples made of bricks and 25 of them appeared to withstand the test of time.[15] The earliest building was built of wood around the late fourth, early fifth century but they were destroyed by fire. The earliest brick building was built at around the seventh/eighth century, and the last, five centuries later, in the 13th century.[16,17]

Mỹ Sơn is a beautiful historical site to visit, but its story is closely linked with Champa, so I will not go into details here but will cover its story in Volume Three of this series. In this book, I will only discuss the kings shown on the inscriptions made during the Linyi period, from the second to the eighth century. One is the second oldest found to date after Võ Cạnh and is known as the Mỹ Sơn A1 or inscription C.72. The inscriptions were engraved on both sides of a large slab 2 metres tall and one metre wide which was found buried in the ground in front of tower A1 at Mỹ Sơn.[18] The stele is now kept at the National History Museum in Hanoi.

Tower A1, at 24 metres tall and 10 metres wide, built around the early 10th century, is considered a masterpiece of Southeast Asian architecture.[19] However, in August 1969, during Operation Durham Peak of the Vietnam War, together with other monuments in Group A, it was utterly demolished by B-52 bombing.[20,21]

THE THREE DEITIES

The inscription was translated by Finot in his paper published in 1902. It records the donation of lands to the god Bhadreśvara by King Bhadravarman. The gods worshipped by the Linyi/Chams-Funan/Zhenla people are Hindu gods which the Indian merchants brought with them to Vietnam in the second and third centuries; by the fourth and fifth centuries, the kingdoms of Linyi and Funan south of Ngang pass had been completely Hinduised.[22]

The most potent Hindu gods are the three deities (Trimurti or three forms) representing the three fundamental forces in the creation, upkeep and destruction of the universe in cyclic successions. They are Brahma, the creator, Vishnu, the preserver, and Shiva, the destroyer.[23] The Linyi/Chams appeared to have adopted Shiva as their primary god whereas, the Funanese of the Mekong Delta settled on Vishnu, as reflected by the number of statues of these gods found over the years. Brahma was not popular among the Chams. In modern times, he is not worshipped by many Hindus around the world.[24,25]

Bhadreśvara is an epithet of Shiva and, as an idol, is represented by a linga but occasionally as a human figure.[26]

C. 72 - THE DONATION OF LANDS

The inscription of C.72 (Mỹ Sơn A1) is dated around the 5th century Śaka. Its lines were translated from Sanskrit by historian Ramesh Chandra Majumdar as below: [27]

LINE 1: *"Perfection has been attained. Reverence to Maheśvara and to Umā.....*

LINE 2: *to Brahma and to Viṣṇu. Reverence to the Earth, Wind, Sky, Water*

LINE 3: *and fifthly, the Fire. Having saluted them, I wish all eminent people to note the following: That with a view to*

LINE 4: *atone for all evil deeds, and to perform good and virtuous work, and having realised the destiny of human life. a perpetual endowment has been given to Bhadreśvara by our king Bhadravarman, who is devoted to the feet of Bhadreśvarasvāmi: To wit,*

LINES 6-7: *the land within (the boundaries viz.) Sulaha mountain in the east, the great mountain in the south, the Kucaka mountain in the west and the Great River in the north, together with its inhabitants, has been given.*

LINE 8: *The (royal share of the) revenue consisting of a sixth of the produce, but reduced, through the favour of the Lord (king ? or the owner of the temple to which land is given ?) to one-tenth, is to be given to the God. If what is written above is not done for the God by anybody,*

LINE 9: *the fruit of merits, acquired by him since his very birth, belongs to Bhadravarman. But if somebody plunders, or destroys it by force, then*

LINE 10: *the people are exempt from guilt which falls upon that man alone. To the king, versed in the four Vedas, and to his*

LINE 11: *officers and other people, I declare: Out of compassion for me, don't destroy my gifts."*

The Great River is the present-day Thu Bồn river which flows by Trà Kiệu and Hội An to the sea at Cửa Đại. A quick review of the topographic map of Quảng Nam province shows very clearly that the Thu Bồn river flows between two high mountain ranges: on the east, it forms the border between Duy Sơn and Duy Xuyên districts with an elevation of around 880 metres; the mountain on the west is almost of the same distance from the river and of a similar elevation.[28] These are Sulaha and Kucaka mountains named some 15 centuries ago. The great mountain (or Mahāparvata in Sanskrit) in the south is likely Núi Răng Mèo (Cat's Tooth mountain), with an elevation of around 711 metres.

7.3 – C. 96 - *A genealogy of kings*

At 200 metres north of tower Group A at Mỹ Sơn is tower Group E and by a small tower of this group, designated as E6, a stele was found. This greyish sandstone stele, measured at 1.25 metres high by 0.75 metres wide, turns out to be one of the most valuable records of the early history of Linyi and Champa. Not only does it record the exact year it was erected (579 Śaka, a Hindu calendar or 657 CE by adding 78), but the inscription, C. 96 (Mỹ Sơn E6) also lists a detailed genealogy of kings in its 55 lines of writing in Sanskrit.[29,30] It is still there at Mỹ Sơn (Figure 30) and together with other inscriptions, archaeologists have managed to put together a detailed genealogy of the Linyi and Champa kings during the sixth and seventh century.[31]

Figure 30 – The stone stele inscription of C.96 (dated 657) by Mỹ Sơn B6.[32]

Other than the definite date of 657 on C.96, erected by a king of the long name, Prakāśadharma-Vikrāntavarman, the other date is related to the reign of the father of his great-grandmother (grandfather's mother), king Rudravarman, recorded on C.73 A (Mỹ Sơn A1), found next to C.72, as having ruled sometime between the 401 and 499 Śaka.[33] C.73 A was erected by a king by the name of Śambhuvarman, the son of Rudravarman.

Inscription C.137 (Trà Kiệu) records this relationship between these two kings across a span of between 80 and 180 years and five generations, which generally makes sense as each generation would be between 25 to 30 years.

The inscription of C.96 described Kandarpadharma as follows:

VERSE 6: *"Of that Śambhuvarman, renowned for his prowess, who re-established on this earth this Śambhubhadreśa.*

VERSE 7: *Was born a son of mighty fame, called Kandarpadharma, endowed with beauty, and like an incarnation of Dharma.*

VERSE 8: *"I have nothing to expect from a king who, free from passion, dutifully protects his subjects like his own sons," with this melancholy reflection, Kali* [a hindu goddess], *chased by the splendour of the king, sadly moved away, nobody knows where, even as the army of darkness flies before the Sun, leaving its unbearable rays behind."* [34]

Translated from verses 6 to 8 of Mỹ Sơn stele C.96, 657.[35]

7.4 – C. 111 - A mutilated stele

At the eastern corner of the imperial city of Huế is the Gia Hội bridge. On the north side of the bridge is Chi Lăng street, a tree-lined street along the bank of the beautiful Hương river with some old Chinese temples. One of those, at no. 321, is Phúc Kiến Temple.[36] South of that temple, in 1911, apparently was the location of a pagoda, and there, someone found a roughly square block with strange letters on it. It was used as a support for the pagoda column, the base of which left behind a blank ring with the letters all erased. Fortunately, some writings are still visible inside and outside the ring (Figure 31).

This block found its way to M. Eberhardt, the tutor of His Majesty Duy Tân, the King of Annam, who was 11 years old at the time. Eberhardt, in his wisdom, handed the block over to a Swiss language scholar and researcher, Edouard Huber. It turns out the block is an ancient stele; the writing is Sanskrit, and Huber had just found the oldest Cham epigraphic document north of Hải Vân pass.

So, what does it say on this ancient stele? I have translated Huber's French translation of the seven lines as follows:

LINES 1-3: *"If natives or foreigners (destroy what has been given) by the King... varma (or dharma) to the god... Lord of the city of Kandarpapura, those with their parents... be unhappy always."*

LINES 4-7: *"Those who destroy (this foundation) of H.M. the king of Campa, fall into the most terrible hell,...but may those who protect her enjoy infinite happiness with the women of Heaven."* [37]

Huber puts the date of this stele at around the first half of the sixth century (it could be a misspelt as it should read seventh based on the genealogy from another inscription).

This stele is known as Dinh Thị, named after a village nearby.[38] It is coded C. 111 and is presently in the National Museum of History in Hanoi. It is the only stele north of Hải Vân pass, of 24 Sanskrit and Cam (Champa) inscriptions from central Vietnam dating from the third/fourth century to the eighth century as listed by Southworth, who dated it in the seventh century.[39]

So, who is this king of Campa (Champa) cited on the stele and how does he fit into the lineage of the Linyi kings? From the name of the city, Kandarpapura, Huber believes the king is Kandarpadharma, who was the grandson of Rudravarman.

Figure 31 – The stele of Dinh Thị, C. 111, Huế.[40]

7.5 – The Varman's and the Fans

WHO IS KING BHADRAVARMAN?

So who is this king Bhadravarman who donated the piece of land at Mỹ Sơn where, over the next nine centuries, successive Linyi/Cham kings built beautiful temples dedicated to the gods, so a remote corner of central Vietnam is now the oldest man-made UNESCO World Heritage site in the country? [41]

Maspero suggests he is the same as Fan Huda (380-413), and Ngô explains he is Fan Fo (349-380), the father of Fan Huda.[42,43] On the other hand, Southworth believes he is a king of a separate kingdom in the Thu Bồn valley, different from Linyi and according to historian Anne-Valérie Schweyer, he seems to have come from Funan in the south.[44,45]

Bhadravarman must have been a remarkable king; other than C.72, his name appears on three other inscriptions: C.105 (Hòn Cụt), C.147 (Chiêm Sơn) and C.41 (Chợ Dinh), all around the fifth century Śaka. The first three were all found in Quảng Nam province, but C.41 was a surprise. It was found carved on a rock at Phú Yên, some 400 kilometres south, just north of Cả pass and dated to approximately 400.[46,47] The writing, in Sanskrit, is about a sacrifice offered to Shiva under the name of Bhadreśvarasvāmi. The inscriptions were translated by historian Majumdar as follows:

> "*Reverence [homage] to God ! By the favour of the feet of the Bhadreśvarasvāmi, I shall make thee agreeable to fire (sacrifice thee). So long as the Sun and the Moon endure, he (Agni)* [the fire god of Hinduism] *will save the sons and grandsons of Dharma- Mahārāja Śri* [Great King Sir] *Bhadravarman. May the work (sacrifice) be successful through the grace of the earth.*"

> "*Siva, the slave, is bound (to the post)*".[48,49]

The last line implies a human sacrifice, but the practice is not associated with Brahmanical rituals in this period, and archaeologist Bishnupriya Basak suggests it was a local practice.[50]

Most historians agree that the territory of Linyi extended from Quảng Nam or Thừa Thiên-Huế to Quảng Bình, just south of Ngang pass. The discovery of C.41 changes that if Bhadravarman is indeed a Linyi king, it would mean his rule extended further south, or he is a king of a different kingdom.

While I can see the logic in this alternative, I am reluctant to support it, as Chinese annals do not mention such a kingdom, which would have been substantial in terms of its size not to have been recorded. A description of the ancient citadel of Điển Xung, including an inscription in TKCS, reinforces Maspero's suggestion that Bhadravarman is Fan Huda. As for the Fan Fo suggestion, we know he and his son Fan Huda ruled for over 30 years in the fourth and fifth centuries, which would have been sufficiently long for either of them to construct temples, citadels and make a lasting impact on their subjects. However, based on the dating of C.41 of 400, I would support the proposition that Fan Huda (380-413) is king Bhadravarman.

C. 105 - CARVED IN ROCKS

As previously discussed, one citadel which features prominently in the history of Linyi is Điển Xung (now Trà Kiệu, Quảng Nam province, see Figure 25). TKCS describes it:

> "*The custom of the Di* [barbarian] *people is that the city has four gates. The eastern one is the front gate, on the same level as the banks of the two Hoài rivers. At a bend on the path, there is an ancient stele,* [on which] *the Di people wrote in a barbaric script, praising the virtue of the king of the country of Huda (Hồ Đạt). The western gate goes straight to the 2-layer moat* [double ditch]; *turning to the north would lead to the mountain and the west of the mountain is the Hoài river. The south gate goes through the 2-layer moat opposite to the Ôn Công rampart.*" [51]

Historian Leonard Aurousseau suggests the ancient stele cited above is the same as the inscription found on a rock, known as Hòn Cục (also Hòn Cúc, Hòn Cụp – coded C. 105 and dated at the fifth century) by the bank of Thu Bồn river.[52] The letters are large, 11 centimetres, and translated by archaeologist Louis Finot as: "*Homage to the august Mahādeva Bhadreśvarasvāmin, head bowed*".[53]

GONE TO INDIA

As mentioned earlier, after Fan Huda died, his son Di Zhen became the new king but acting out of guilt for not accommodating his brother and son, Di Zhen abdicated his throne and travelled to India. We know this because Liang shu records the story.

In C.96, a king named Gaṅgārāja abandoned his throne to enjoy "*the joy of arising from a view of Ganga*", he went to the Jāhanavī (Ganges).[54] Historians make the connection and align these two kings, which would place Gaṅgārāja at the early fifth century.[55] However, this alignment is not agreed to by all scholars, some suggest the motives of the two kings are different, Di Zhen went to India out of guilt. In contrast, Gaṅgārāja went on a pilgrimage, so they are not the same man.

It is all speculative, but I am inclined to believe the stories refer to the same king for the reason that the abandonment of the throne to travel to India would have been such a significant and rare event to occur twice by two different kings, irrespective of the motives.

THE RETURN OF AN EXILE FROM ZHENLA

In the previous chapter, we learned that Fan Zhenlong was killed, and his sister became king. She was not able to rule the kingdom by herself, so the nobles recalled her cousin, Zhugedi from Zhenla, who returned to the capital, married her and became the next king. Some historians had speculated that the father of Zhugedi killed Zhenlong and that Zhenlong's sister and Zhugendi were already married before he escaped to Zhenla, but I do not have any evidence to support this.[56]

Inscription C.96 records Prabhāsadharma has a sister who was "*the source of welfare and prosperity of the whole world*"; a king has a husband named Satyakauśikasvāmi, also a king. By comparing this line in the inscription with the story above, historians connect Prabhāsadharma to Fan Zhenlong and his father, Kandarpadharma to Fan Touli, which would make Śambhuvarman as Fan Fanzhi.[57]

The same inscription also mentions Śrī Jagaddharma went to Bhava "*on account of certain circumstances*". Bhava is short for Bhavapura, the capital of Zhenla in the seventh century – believed to be the present-day Sambor Prei Kuk, the city of Zhenla's king Īśānavarman (616-637) 200 kilometres north of Phnom Penh, Cambodia.[58,59]

Based on the connection with Zhenla, historians identify Śrī Jagaddharma with Zhugedi.

What about Rudravarman? Liang shu tells us in 530, a Linyi king named Gaoshi Liutuobamo (Cao Thức Luật Đà La Bạt Ma, according to Southworth, Gaoshi is the Chinese transcription of Sanskrit Ku Śrī, and Bamo is for Varman but Southworth refers to him as Lūtuoluobamo) sent tributes to the court of Liang.[60, 61] The date seems to match as it fits between 479 and 577 when Rudravarman ruled. However, in contrast to other historians, Southworth identifies Kandarpadharma, the son of Śambhuvarman, with Fan Fanzhi.[62]

In 534, Lūtuoluobamo sent other tributes; in 605, Điển Xung, the capital of his successor, Fan Fanzhi was ransacked. Between these 71 years, no tributes from Linyi were recorded, not until nearly 20 years later in 623. The long years between these two kings, father and son, mean either Lūtuoluobamo ruled for a very long time or there was another king in between but not recorded by the annals.

So, while I can see some historical connections, given these confusions, I am hesitant to accept all the links between the Fans and the Varmans as commonly described. For now, I prefer to keep them separate in my reading of Linyi and Champa stories.

7.6 – The coming of Champa

Linyi and Huanwang are named in Chinese annals, but the Cham kings never mention them in any inscriptions. However, they did record the name of Campapura in the seventh century.

CAMPAPURA

Inscription C.96, dated 657, is also the first to mention "the city of Champa" or Campāpura or Campānagara.[63] The opening line reads:

> LINES 1-7: *"Perfection has been attained............ another family............... the town of Brahma...............consecrated image of God Śri Śambhu-Bhadreśvara......... in the prosperous city of Champa."* [64,65]

The honorific Śri Campeśvara or "H.M King of Campa or Lord of Campa" also appears on Dinh Thị stele (C.111) as mentioned above. It also appears on Thạch Bích (stone wall, C.135) rock inscription by the bank of Thu Bồn river as:

> "Śri *Prakāśadharma, H.M King of Champā, always victorious, master of the land,...................has installed here the God Śiva (Amareśa)."* [66,67]

Prakāśadharma is the great-grandson of Kandarpadharma who appears on Dinh Thị stele found in Huế, as introduced previously. The rock is in a lovely spot; Huber described it in 1911:

> *"The rock of Thach-bich, "the Stone Wall", is around four hours of sampan upstream from Nông Sơn on the Thu Bồn river, at the limit of the "moï"* [Montagnard] *country, in a site of wild beauty. At this place, high slopes, rocky lines surround the river on both sides and take away half of its width.*
>
> *From the right bank stands a rock which still blocks part of the bed of the torrent. The inscription is drawn flush with the current on the face of the rock which looks downstream. It only emerges from the water during the dry season, from July to December. Every year on the full moon day of the eighth month, it receives offerings of flowers, bananas and rice wine from the boatmen passing by this place."* [68]

It is still there, half-submerged in water near Hòn Kẽm-Đá Dừng, Thạch Bích hamlet, Quế Lâm commune, Nông Sơn district, Quảng Nam province.[69]

ZHANBULAO, ZHANPO AND ZHANCHENG (CHIÊM THÀNH)

In Chinese texts, Champa appears as Zhanbulao, Zhanpo in Xin Tang shu, and Zhancheng (or the city of the Chams) in Song shi (History of Song, not to be confused with The Book of Song or Song shu), Volume 489.[70,71] The Vietnamese refer to the kingdom as Chiêm Thành. The name Zhancheng appears after 859 the Biography of Wang Shi (Xin Tang shu, Volume 167).

Some authors refer to Champa as Campā or Čampa but I prefer the more common English usage of Champa. The story of Champa will be covered in Volume III so I will not go into its discussion in this book.

CHAPTER 8

THE ROMAN MEDALS AND THE ÓC EO CULTURE

FUNAN/ZHENLA I

STORY TIMELINE: First to seventh centuries
STORY LOCATION: Southern Vietnam
KEY CHARACTER: *Louis Malleret:* French archaeologist who excavated Óc Eo.
LOCATIONS OF INTEREST: Ba Thê mountain in An Giang province, Museum History in Ho Chi Minh City, Provincial museums and archaeological sites of southern provinces.

Chapter summary

In this chapter, I will explore the region roughly south of Phan Rang-Tháp Chàm to the Mekong Delta and begin our stories from there. In the north of Vietnam, I have told the stories of the Trưng sisters, Shi Xie's family and the Buddhist monks. In north-central Vietnam, I have discussed the kings of Linyi, the Fans and years of almost continuous warfare. I will now discuss the people in the south who left behind wonderful gold ornaments, stone statues, magnificent brick towers (temples), worshipped the Hindu gods and Buddha in what has become known as the Óc Eo culture.

Unlike the people of Linyi and Champa, who are either Cham or Mon-Khmer in origin, the people of Óc Eo culture are most likely Khmer, the ethnic group of present-day Cambodia.

The site of Óc Eo, located inland from contemporary Rạch Giá city, north of the southern tip of Vietnam, was excavated by a French archaeologist, Louis Malleret, in the middle of World War II. The excavation was a tale in itself. Afterwards, Malleret wrote a masterpiece on the archaeology of the Mekong Delta which has become a classic on the subject.

Today, one can see many of the artefacts he recovered and those found by other archaeologists at almost all the provincial museums in the Mekong Delta. A list of these museums is shown in Appendix 16.

To begin my stories, I am going back in time to the first century with the story of an imaginary trader from India who was looking for gold and ended up bringing Buddhism and Hinduism to Vietnam.

8.1 – *The monsoon trader*

For an imaginary trader in the first millennium, to travel from India to China and return by the sea route, he would sail east across the Bay of Bengal, through one of the channels between the Andaman and Nicobar Islands to the Andaman Sea. From there, he would take a shortcut by sailing upstream the Kra Buri river, along the border of Myanmar and Thailand, then travelling overland to the eastern side of the Malay Peninsula, coming out around Chumphon north of the Thai tourist island of Koh Samui. The overland part is relatively short, around 50 kilometres as the crow flies.[1]

Once on the other side, he would get into another boat and pick up the journey by sailing across the Gulf of Thailand, stopping en route at Óc Eo in southern Vietnam for a rest, make a few trades and continue along the coast of central Vietnam. He may decide to stop at modern Hội An before sailing north-east towards Hongkong and entering Guangzhou.

Alternatively, later in the millennium, as ship technology improves and he carries more cargo, he would continue down the Malacca strait to Singapore, or further to Jakarta, and stop there instead. He may then bypass Óc Eo, sail up the coast of central Vietnam, stop at Hội An (or Nha Trang, Quy Nhơn) and eventually reach Guangzhou. The distance between Ranong (Kra Buri estuary) to Singapore by modern road is around 1,400 kilometres, so one can understand the value of taking the shortcut.

He would follow the monsoon rhythm and leave from a port in India during the south-west monsoon of summer (May-August) and return from China during the northeast monsoon of winter (November-February) to catch the prevailing winds; a round trip that would take between 12 to 18 months. It was observed that all sailing vessels arrived in China from the end of the fourth moon (around May) to the sixth moon (around July) and left outwards from the end of the 10th moon (around November) to the 12th moons (around January).[2] Most southern expeditions by the Chinese dynasties against southern territories as discussed in this book generally occurred during the winter months for this reason.

Our trader would likely leave from a southern port in eastern India, say Chennai or from the mouth of the Ganges, from Ceylon or other ports in the west.[3] He would be taking beads, textiles, religious icons, coins and other things he could trade; in return, he would want gold, spices, aromatic woods and other goods manufactured in China or Southeast Asia. However, it would be the gold that attracts him to make the long journey.[4]

As a matter of interest, in the eighth century, a trip recorded by Jia Dan (730-805) by ship from Guangzhou to the strait of Malacca took an estimated 20 days.[5,6]

8.2 – Óc Eo - A trading and jewellery manufacturing hub

THE LOCATION

Around 40 kilometres as the crow flies, north of the coastal city of Rạch Giá in south Vietnam is Óc Eo. This is where our trader would likely stop as it was the major port in the first to the seventh centuries for the kingdom of Funan. Óc Eo is not by the coast, but inland, and access would be by a canal. Why it is there and not by the coast could be explained by the fact that the site is near Ba Thê mountain (221 metres in elevation), one of the few high grounds in a flat region subject to regular flooding during the rainy season (Figure 32). The mountain offered a place of refuge during floods, so its surrounding area became a major settlement and was turned into a port for sea-going merchants. However, sand samples from the site do not indicate that Óc Eo was an old beach.

THE DISCOVERY

Óc Eo and its buried treasures lay dormant for centuries until some gold jewel pieces turned up in the Saigon market and attracted a large number of artisanal miners to the area. On 11 April 1942, Louis Malleret came to Óc Eo for the first time and walked the ground. He was 41 years old, having come to Saigon sometime in the thirties as a teacher; then, he became a librarian, finally an archaeologist and curator, working for the French School of the Far East (l'École française d'Extrême-Orient).[7] Two years later, in early 1944, the Director of the school, George Coedès sent a mission led by Malleret to Óc Eo. Malleret would eventually replace George Coedès as the Director of the school, but in 1944, he had a lot more to worry about.

Figure 32 – View of Ba Thê mountain from Gò Cây Thị Road (approximately NW direction).[8] Note: the canal running parallel to the road. The whole region is crisscrossed with these canals of different widths.

THE EXCAVATION

Vietnam in 1944 had been under Japanese occupation for nearly four years, but the Japanese left the French colonial government very much intact. The country now had two masters: French and Japanese. How the Vietnamese managed under such conditions is another story to be told in another volume. For our story, in 1944, Malleret had to contend with the Japanese authority, keep the artisan miners from digging up the ground, and prevent his people from getting sick from malaria and water-related diseases. He also needed the funds to buy back a large number of artefacts from the illegal diggers. Malleret assembled a team including M. Manikus, Head of the Photographic Service, M. Trần buy (huy?) Bá, a designer, a secretary from the Blanchard de la Brosse Museum, M. Đặng văn Minh, a modeller from the Art School of Biên Hoà, M. Nguyễn Văn Yên, and 20 young people serving as supervisors recruited a month earlier. He also had a nurse permanently seconded from the nearest towns of Long Xuyên and Rạch Giá; just as well he did, as they had six cases of amoebic dysentery. He also hired ten guards to provide security to the site.[9]

The general opinion among his contemporaries was that the Mekong Delta, with its land of recent alluvium (deposit of silt, clay, sand and gravel) would not be where great civilisations were established. However, Malleret thought that since the Khmer Empire, which built the famous Angkor Wat temple, extended to this region, other civilisations might have occupied the same land at an earlier date.

As events turned out, he was right, and much of our knowledge about Óc Eo civilisation is due to Malleret and his team. The excavation took place over the dry season from February to April 1944. They found plenty of gold jewellery, jewellery-making tools, moulds, several thousand rock crystals, carnelians, onyx-threading beads, seals with characters in Sanskrit, gold coins, a few bronze objects, objects in pewter and lead, terracotta objects, pottery, some Chinese artefacts including what appeared a mirror of the Later Han, natural-looking linga in sandstone and granite, Indian hip torso, a bust, and Visnu sandstone statues.

Of particular interest was an incuse medal of the bracteate type (thin, single-sided gold medal) with a laureate effigy, Antoninus Pius (Roman emperor 138-161), and the indication of his 15th tribunician power of 152. The second one of less readable imprint seemed to be assigned to Marcus Aurelius (Roman emperor 161-180).[10]

On 9 March 1945, the Japanese abruptly ended French rule and seized direct control of Vietnam, but that did not last. On 30 November 1945, Japan's Southern Expeditionary Army Commander, Hisaichi Terauchi, surrendered to the Supreme Allied Commander, Lord Louis Mountbatten, in Saigon. Malleret was unable to return to the site until April 1946; to his horror, the site looked like a lunar landscape riddled with craters resembling a WWI battlefield after a heavy artillery bombardment.[11] The looters and treasure hunters had obviously been there in his absence.

The French colonial government regained their control of Vietnam in 1945 but was finally driven out in 1954 as Vietnam regained independence. Malleret continued his official work until he retired in 1956 and returned to France after 1957. He died in 1970. It is reported that he told one of his friends that *"it is in full labour that I will disappear"*, and that he did.[12] He left behind a masterpiece, "*L'archéologie du delta du Mékong*", in four volumes printed as seven books between 1959 and 1963. The volumes are:

T. 1. *L'exploration archéologique et les fouilles D'oc-èo*
T. 2. *La civilisation matérielle d'oc-èo*
T. 3. *La culture du Fou-nan*
T. 4. *Le Cisbassac*

These volumes have remained a key reference for anyone interested in the archaeology of the region south of Ho Chi Minh City. Besides Óc Eo, Volume 1 covers a total of 138 sites as far west as Hà Tiên and to the east at Sóc Trăng plus two sites on the island of Côn Đảo (Poulo Condore).[13]

The artefacts found by Malleret (including those he purchased) were taken to the Museum of Vietnamese History in Ho Chi Minh city, and one can view most of them on display. The mix of the artefacts confirms Óc Eo as a trading and jewellery manufacturing hub; 1311 gold pieces were found there.[14] Our monsoon trader was on the right route after all.

A TRAVELLER'S DESTINATION

Today, one can walk over Óc Eo and adjacent sites, and see some of the gold pieces, including the Roman coins at The Management Board of Oc Eo Cultural Relics (*Ban quản lý Di tích Văn hóa Óc Eo*) in An Giang province.[15] While there, one can climb Ba Thê mountain, and visit the Óc Eo Culture of An Giang (*Văn Hóa An Giang*) building, built in the shape of a giant linga (or lingam) with a stylised phallus design. The design is to reflect the linga artefacts found at a number of sites in the region. In Hinduism, the linga symbolises the god Shiva and stands for fertility and regeneration. According to the legend, Brahma was unable to create mortals, so he told Shiva to do the work for him. Furious, Shiva castrated himself and threw his phallus to the ground; in another version, he turned himself into a post.[16] Linga is often found with the associated Yoni, representing the female genitalia.

8.3 – The Óc Eo culture and archaeological sites

Since 1979, Vietnamese archaeologists began to explore and undertake a number of excavations across the whole region of southern Vietnam as far north as Tây Ninh to the west and Đồng Nai province to the east. In 1997, they cooperated with the school where Malleret had been director to undertake a programme of research focusing on sites at two western provinces near the Gulf of Thailand: An Giang (Óc Eo/Ba Thê) and Kiên Giang (Nền Chùa/Cạnh Đền) provinces.[17] Many artefacts found from these excavations are now on display, not only at the History Museum in Ho Chi Minh City but also at the An Giang Museum including a rare and beautiful Brahma sculpture (sixth to seventh century) made from sandstone (Figure 36). Kiên Giang Museum also has a number of artefacts.

The spread of artefacts found over this region indicates the existence of a civilisation archaeologists refer to as the Óc Eo culture, dating between the first and the sixth or seventh centuries. Other than Óc Eo, as a trading port, there is another site at Gò Tháp (also known as Prasat Pram Loveng) which archaeologists have suggested was the religious centre for this culture, based on the number of Hindu stone and wooden Buddha statues found there, including temple bases. Eight stone steles were found here from the sixth and seventh centuries.[18] Some of these statues are kept at the History Museum in Ho Chi Minh City, and at the Đồng Tháp Provincial Museum. The Gò Tháp site itself is in a complex at around 40 kilometres northeast of the museum, where one can visit the Relics Gò Tháp (*Di Tích Quốc Gia Đặt Biệt Gò Tháp*) including Gò Tháp Mười (Vishnu temple, where two Vishu statues were found), Gò Minh Sư (where a Shiva temple was believed to be located) and Gò Bà Chúa Xứ (where a Sungod (Surya) temple was believed to be located).

The complex is in Đồng Tháp province, which, together with Long An and Tiền Giang provinces, form the Plain of Reeds (*Đồng Tháp Mười or Plaine des Joncs*), a vast swampy wetland. It is thus no accident that the artefacts were found at these high grounds called *Gò* or the mounds where people lived and stored valuables or religious statues.

Around 30 kilometres west of Ho Chi Minh City is a ruin of another site of Óc Eo civilisation, named Bình Tả, which includes Gò Đồn and Gò Xoài sites. Unfortunately, there is not much to see beyond the overgrowth vegetation covering ancient rock walls and a square brick temple base measuring 15.4 metres at Gò Xoài. The artefacts found in this structure included a thin-inscribed gold leaf text; inlaid jewels; gold repoussé tortoise, snake, eight elephants; and a number of lotuses.[19] These are kept at Long An provincial museum. The complex itself is at Bình Tả hamlet, Đức Hòa Hạ commune, Đức Hòa district, some 45 kilometres north of the museum. At the museum, there is also a statue of the Hindu goddess of Pavarti, consort of Shiva and mother of the elephant-headed god Ganesha.

The archaeological sites of Óc Eo civilisation spread across southern Vietnam, especially those in the Mekong Delta, covering all thirteen provinces. Artefacts found at these sites are displayed in the provincial museums where one can view them; some museums have more items, such as An Giang, Kiên Giang and Đồng Tháp, but most of the others have some displays. The addresses of these museums are shown in Appendix 16; some of the sites are shown in Figure 33.

From a traveller's perspective, the artwork of Óc Eo civilisation is a treasure to discover. It includes statues of Buddha, Hindu gods, carvings on wood, stones, precious gems, gold pieces, bricks, tiles and lintels. However, it would be beyond the scope of this book to discuss this subject in detail. Here, I only summarise a few key findings from an excellent book by archaeologist Lê Thị Liên on the Arts of Buddhism and Hinduism in the Mekong Delta as described below.

Lê divided the development of the Óc Eo artwork into four periods: Period I was from the first/second century BCE to about the fourth century CE when many sculptures were imported. Period II is from the fifth to the seventh centuries, with the art of the Mekong Delta reaching its peak in the late half of the sixth to the seventh centuries. Period III is from the late seventh to the eighth centuries; the artwork then declined from the ninth to the 10th centuries with a decline in quantity and quality.[20]

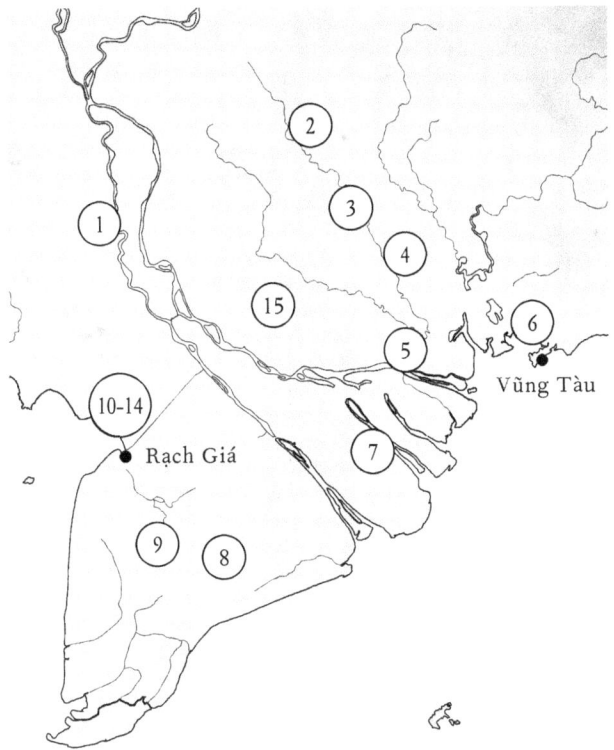

Figure 33 – Some archaeological sites of the Óc Eo civilisation and the three towers.
1. Angkor Borei, 2. The tower of Chóp Mạt, 3. The tower of Bình Thạnh, 4. Di tích khảo cổ học Bình Tả, 5. Gò Thành, 6. Long Sơn island, 7. Bờ Lũy-Gò Gạch, 8. The tower of Vĩnh Hưng, 9. Cạnh đền, 10. Núi Ba Thê, 11. Óc Eo, 12. Di Tích Nền Chùa, 13. Di Tích Gò Cây Thị, 14. Rạch Giá, 15. Di Tích Quốc Gia Đặc Biệt (Gò Tháp).

BUDDHA STATUES

A number of wooden statues of Buddha were found over the years of excavation. They are classified by different standing poses in Indian art: Tribhanga, Abhanga and Smabhanga, where bhanga means the inflexion of the body. Tribhanga is where the body is in an "S" shape with three bends: at the knees, hips, shoulders and neck. However, in Lê's classification, it is more about the bend at the hip and that the statue was carved in three different portions.[21] Wooden Buddha statues in this position (8) are mostly from the second to the fourth centuries of the first period.[22] The largest of these statues is nearly 268 centimetres tall, as shown in Figure 34.

Figure 34 – A statue of Tháp Mười wooden Buddha (Museum code BTLS 1615).

This statue is fourth century and 268 centimetres tall. It was found at Sa Đéc, Tháp Mười and carved from Hopea (Dipterocarpaceae family) wood (Gỗ Sao).[23,24] The wood comes from trees commonly found in Sri Lanka, Southern India, the region west of the Mekong Delta, and the provinces of Kontum, Gia Lai in the Vietnamese central highland. One can find them among the tall trees in Ho Chi Minh City.[25]

Abhanga is another standing pose in which

"the plumbline or the centre line from the crown of the head to a point midway between the heels passes slightly to the right of the navel." [26]

In Lê's classification, these statues (10) have a slight bend at the hip with the upper body straight and carved in two separate sections. These were carved a little later than the Tribhanga pose during the fifth and seventh centuries. Smabhanga pose means a straight pose where the left and right side of the body is symmetrical. Most of these statues (6) were dated later between the sixth and seventh centuries. The number in bracket is the quantity found.

Buddha statues carved from stone, bronze and terracotta were also found. There are standing statues (6) carved from sandstone, from the fifth to eighth centuries. The sitting Buddha statues (13) are dated over a long period from the middle of the second to the eighth century. Most were carved from sandstones. There are not many bronze (4) or terracotta Buddha statues (1).

There are also a number of Bodhisattva statues (9) from the middle of the sixth to the eighth centuries. These are the most revered Avalokitesvara, Lokesvara and Maitrya. Bodhisattva means a person who is on the path towards Buddhahood, who saves others and accepts all sufferings but dedicates merits to others.

Figure 35 – A Buddha in Meditation, sandstone.[27] Dimensions: 46.5 cm (H), 32.8 cm (W), 18 cm (D), 20 kg weight. Found at Phnom Cangek in 1920-21, transferred to Wat Trapan Ven in Trà Vinh province and moved to the current museum in 1938. I have not been able to identify the name of these locations, but they should be around Trà Vinh province by the river mouth of the Mekong Delta (Cổ Chiên river).

"*The open robe, with the right shoulder exposed, and the layered rather than interlocking legs point to southern Indian or, more likely, Sri Lankan influences.*"[28,29]

Most Buddha statues found in Southeast Asia are characterised by a bare right shoulder – but not all, some have garments covering both shoulders.[30]

HINDU STATUES

Hindu statues were later, between the fifth and the eighth centuries. Many are the gods of Vishnu (around 35), the others are Siva, Harihara, Brahma and Surya at two, two, four and four in numbers, respectively. A Vishnu statue is shown in Figure 37.

There are statues of other Hindu deities like Ganesha, Lakshmi, and Mahishasuramardini. Many linga and yoni pedestals were found from the second to the 10th centuries.[31]

Brahma is one of the gods in the three deities (or Trimurti) of Hinduism, representing the three fundamental forces in the creation, upkeep and destruction of the universe in cyclic succession. The three gods are Brahma, creation; Vishnu, the preservation; and Shiva, the destruction.

The sculpture (45 centimetres high, 20 centimetres wide and deep) shows three of Brahma's four heads visible; the hair is matted with the braids neatly secured with two coils of locks. It is believed the four Vedas (the most ancient religious texts for Hindus) came from these heads.

Figure 36 – A statue of Brahma (sixth/seventh century), found in 1981 at Giồng Xoài.[32]

Figure 37 – A statue of Vishnu - Trung Điền - Vĩnh Long - Museum of History - Ho Chi Minh City.[33]

This 85 centimetres tall, seventh/eighth-century statue of Vishnu (Figure 37) shows him holding a conch shell (*shankha*) in the back right hand, a discus (*chakra*) in the back left side (half of it is missing), the lotus flower (*padma*) in the front right hand and a mace (*gada*) in the front left hand; it appears the head of the mace by his feet (normally represented by a sphere in shape) is missing. He is wearing a decorative mitred hat and a long plated sampot (or sompot), but the tie at the front, just below his navel, is broken.

There are differences in the interpretation of these items but broadly, the conch shell produces the sound of creation, the discus is the weapon against evils, the lotus (sometimes a globe) represents the beauty of life, and the mace represents strength.

A statue of the Hindu god of the Sun, Surya, was found at Gò Bà Chúa Xứ. He was once ranked with Vishnu, but his worship declined, and he was seen as absorbed into Vishnu. The statue in the History Museum, Ho Chi Minh City, shows him holding two lotuses with heavy clothing, which attests to his ties to the solar gods of northern countries.[34]

CHAPTER 9

THE KINGDOMS OF FUNAN AND ZHENLA

FUNAN/ZHENLA II

STORY TIMELINE: First to sixth centuries.
STORY LOCATION: Southern Vietnam.
KEY CHARACTERS: *Lu Dai:* general of Eastern Wu who sent envoys to Funan, *Hun-houei:* mythical first king of Funan, *Fan Shiman:* the king who expanded Funan, *Fan Zhan:* king of Funan, who sent envoys to India, *Fan Xun:* king of Funan, who sent envoys to China, *Chu Zhantan:* king of Funan, *Rudravarman:* last king of Funan.
LOCATIONS OF INTEREST: Ta Prohm temple, Cambodia. Angkor Borei, Cambodia. Ba Phnum, Cambodia. Sambor Prei Kuk, Cambodia, Thakhek of Central Laos.

Chapter summary

Óc Eo civilisation existed at the time and in the territory that the Chinese referred to in their annals as the kingdom of Funan. To put Óc Eo in context, we need to learn about Funan, which historians agree existed between the first and seventh century (or the middle of the sixth century according to historian Lawrence Palmer Briggs), generally in southern Cambodia, Vietnam and extending from the Gulf of Thailand to the Malay Peninsula.[1]

The emperor of Eastern Wu (220-280) not only wanted the Shi clan destroyed, he also apparently ordered his local representative to find a southern trade route. Accordingly, envoys were sent to Linyi, and a southern kingdom the Chinese named Funan.

More envoys followed, including two officials in the middle of the third century who wrote a report of their trip. Their report, probably the first book by the Chinese on the region, was lost, but parts of it were reproduced in other dynastic records which have survived.[2] They tell of a kingdom established by a woman who gave up her power to a man from overseas sometime in the first or second century. Upon his death, the crown was passed onto his son, his grandson, and after that to a general named Fan Shiman. Historians do not believe there is a family relationship between this Fan and other Fans of the Linyi kings; some suggest Fan is simply a Chinese transcription of a local term which means leader.

Fan Shiman became king in the early third century, began to build large ships, conquered other small kingdoms, and expanded his reign from the Mekong Delta westwards as far as Myanmar. His successor continued with the ambitious growth plan and sent envoys to India who reached the mouth of the Ganges sometime in the middle of the third century. The next king sent envoys to China, and it was this king, Fan Xun, to whom the two envoys from Eastern Wu presented themselves in 245-250.

Funan and Linyi were founded roughly at around the same time, but Funan took a much more peaceful path in the next few centuries. Certainly, there was plenty of family infighting and local squabbles, but no major and continuing warfare on the same scale as Linyi. As far as I can tell, there is no record of soldiers of the northern dynasties beyond Quảng Nam or Quảng Ngãi province in Central Vietnam, let alone the Mekong Delta, some 900 kilometres south.

The two kingdoms sent their tributes to the northern court, and they certainly knew of each other but were not exactly allies. Linyi pirates regularly raided Funan coastal towns and the son of a Funan's king murdered the king of Linyi to claim the throne. He was, in turn, killed by a Linyi general. In the fifth century, Linyi asked Funan's help to defend against the Liu Song dynasty but was refused.

Historians believe Funan is mainly in the coastal region of southern Vietnam, Cambodia extending to the Malay Peninsula. It was eventually overtaken by a polity that the Chinese annals refer to as Zhenla in the sixth/seventh century. Zhenla joined with Linyi to participate in a rebellion by the Black Emperor in the Hà Tĩnh Nghệ An region in the middle of the eighth century (Chapter 12).

Funan and Zhenla kingdoms existed centuries before the famous Angkor Wat in Cambodia were constructed in the 12th century, during the golden age of the Khmer Empire (802-1431). However, there is a continuity of the people, culture and language between these kingdoms which set them apart from those of Giao Châu. Funan and Zhenla people are Khmer, the people of Giao Châu are Vietnamese, and those of Linyi are Chams. They spoke different languages even though Linyi shared similar political and religious practices to Funan and Zhenla.

The territory of Funan and Zhenla included the southern region of south Vietnam, at least around the provinces near the present-day border between Vietnam, Cambodia and the Mekong Delta near the coast.[3] Thus, for us to know about the history of Vietnam, we need to explore the stories of these kingdoms in some detail. However, I will limit the discussion of the Funan/Zhenla historical sites to those found in Vietnam. A full discussion of the other sites in Cambodia and Laos in this period would be outside the scope of this book.

In brief, the chronological timeline of the kingdoms which, during their time, occupied the southern region of present-day Vietnam is shown in Table 4 as follows:

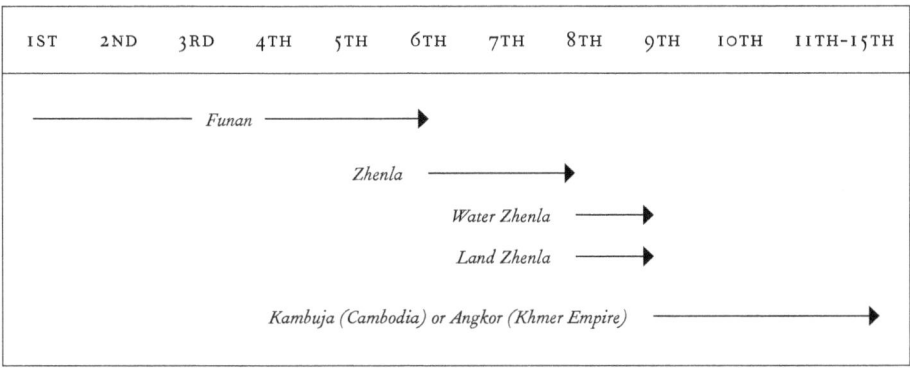

Table 4 – A timeline of Funan, Zhenla and Kambuja.[4,5]

In this chapter, I will first tell the stories of Funan and Zhenla based on Chinese dynastic annals. In the next chapter, I will follow up with the epigraphical records found during the period. The towers of Bình Thạnh, Chót Mạt in Tây Ninh and Vĩnh Hưng in Bạc Liêu provinces will also be described.

9.1 – *Funan - the Chinese records*

Jin shu (The Book of Jin), compiled in 648, describes Funan as:[6]

> *"The kingdom of Funan is over 3,000 li* [1,350 kilometres] *west of Linyi, in a large bay by the sea* [believed to be the Gulf of Thailand]. *Its territory extends into a width of over 3,000 li. There are walled cities, palaces and houses dwelling. The men are ugly and black; their hair is curly; they go naked and barefoot. Their nature is simple, and they are not at all thieves. They are engaged in agriculture. They sow once a year and reap in three. In addition, they like to engrave ornaments and chisel. A lot of utensils they use to eat are silver. Tax is paid in gold, silver, pearls and perfumes. They have books, archives and other things. Their writing characters resemble those of the Hou* [or Hu, the people of India and Central Asia]. *Their funerals and weddings are the same as the people of Linyi."*

Funan is first mentioned in the Records of the Three Kingdoms (Sanguo zhi), written in the third century, in the biography of Lu Dai (161-256). After he became the cishi of Giao Châu between 225-230, Lu Dai sent envoys to the kingdoms of Linyi and Funan. Following them were a pair of Chinese envoys, Kang Tai and Chou Ying, who arrived in Funan in the years 245-250.[7] They wrote a report about Funan, known as Records of Funan (Funan Ji) or Funan Nation (Funan Zuan) now lost, but the stories from these texts were copied by other historians down the centuries and reached us.

After this first appearance in historical records, Funan is again mentioned in other Chinese dynastic annals from Song shu (the Book of Song, 492), Nan Qi shu (the Book of Southern Qi, compiled around 537), and Liang shu (the Book of Liang, 635).[8] However, other later works such as Sui shu (The Book of Sui, 636) and Jiu Tang shu (The Old Book of Tang, 941) no longer set aside a special section on Funan but mention the kingdom of Zhenla, as a successor to Funan, except for Xin Tang shu (The New Book of Tang, 1060) which has a section on Funan as well as Zhenla.[9]

9.2 – The founding legend

One of such stories is the founding legend of Funan. There are several versions with different names and details, but all have the same thread of a woman ruler giving up her power to a man from overseas.[10] The one that I reproduce here comes from Jin shu, which continues from the passage quoted above:

> Their [Funanese] *ruler was originally a woman called Ye-liu. There was then a foreigner, called Hun-houei, who practised the cult of genie* [spirit worshipping]; *he dreamed that the genie gave him a bow and ordered him to get on merchant junk and go to sea. In the morning, Hun-houei went to the temple of the genie; he found a bow there, then, following merchants, embarked at sea. He arrived outside the town of Funan. Ye-liu brought troops to resist him. Hun-houei raised his bow. Ye-liu was frightened and submitted to him. Hun-houei took her for his wife and seized the kingdom. His descendants weakened, and his posterity ceased to reign. General Fan Siun started the hereditary lineage of kings of Fu-nan again.*[11]

Historians have generally agreed that Hun-houei (or Hun-tian), the first king of Funan came either from India, the Malay Peninsula or the southern islands.[12] However, they have different views on who he was. Without going into the details of the discussion, I adopt Vickery's view that:

> "There is no evidence that the initial foreign conqueror came from India, nor is it clear that he was a Brahman and his name, as given to the Chinese, was not Kauṇḍinya [a Sanskrit name]".[13]

My reasoning runs as follows: firstly, there is no evidence of Indianisation anywhere in Southeast Asia in the first century.[14] Secondly, this legendary event could not have occurred later than the first century because, in the following century, historians find other Funanese historical figures documented by epigraphy and by Chinese historians.[15] Thirdly, Hun-houei worshipped a genie unrelated to any Hindu gods.[16]

However, Chinese annals do mention the name of Qiaochenru (Vietnamese Kiều Trần Như) as a transcription of Kauṇḍinya, who appears as two individuals. Qiaochenru first appeared in the fifth century.[17] This king changed all the rules to the Indian ways.

In any case, the arrival of Kang Tai and Chou Ying at Funan in the middle of the third century marked a significant milestone in Funan history and, for that matter, the Chinese-Southeast Asia-India trades. In their report, they wrote down what the Funanese told them about its past; fragments of this past, such as the above legend, found their way into subsequent Chinese annals. When Kang Tai and Chou Ying were long gone, the dynastic annals continued to record actual events related to Funan and these formed the historical records of the kingdom.[18]

9.3 – The Huns and the Fans - Interfamily killings

FAN SHIMAN – THE GREAT KING (EARLY THIRD CENTURY)

After Hun-houei, power was passed on to his son (Hun Pan-huang), who probably lived in the second century and died in old age at 90; the throne was then inherited by his young son (Pan-Pan), who died after three years.[19] After his death, the people elected the great general Fan-man or Fan Shiman as the next king, who proclaimed himself as the "Great Funanese King". Fan Shiman was indeed a great king, who built large ships, conquered ten other small kingdoms, including Ju-du-kun, Jiu-jin, Dian-sun (or Tun-sun), and expanded Funan by 5-6,000 *li* (2,250 to 2,700 kilometres).[20,21]

There is not much information about the first two kingdoms, but most scholars have placed Tun-sun on the Malay Peninsula by the Kra isthmus.[22] Tragically, on one of these expeditions, Fan Shiman died from illness; he was on his way to Chin-lin or the "Land of Gold" which Pelliot placed at Martaban or Mottama in Myanmar on the coast of Gulf of Martaban, north of the Kra isthmus.[23] Coincidentally, located just north of Martaban, almost on a straight line by Mandalay to Myitkynia near the northern border of Myanmar is a series of at least 24 primary gold deposits.[24] Further south on the Malay Peninsula, there are also four gold belts running approximately in the north-south direction for the whole length of Malaysia.[25] So it seems the Chinese writers would simply use the term Chin-lin to refer to the region around southern Myanmar and the Malay Peninsula where gold was found.

The ships Fan Shiman built were likely thin planks bound with cords made with coconut husk and caulked with tree resin. It is now common knowledge that Southeast Asians were great navigators at the time, not Indian nor Chinese.[26] These ships were described as:

> "*Twelve hsin (eight Chinese feet [2.4 m]) long and six feet [1.8 m] broad, with their bows and sterns like fishes ... the large ones carry a hundred men, each man carrying a long or short oar, or a boat-pole ...*" [27]

Fan Shiman ruled in the early years of the third century, and his surname, Fan or Phạm in Vietnamese, is the same as Linyi rulers (Fan Xiong, Fan Yi) at a later time period, but there is no evidence that they were related as Fan could simply mean a chief or leader. After his death, estimated around 205 or 210, one of his commanders, general Fan Zhan, tricked his son, Fan Jinsheng (or Kin-cheng), the heir to the throne and killed him. Fan Zhan was the son of his older sister and a commander of 2,000 troops, so he had at least some military might behind him.[28]

FAN ZHAN - WEST TO INDIA (C.230-C.243?)

Fan Zhan became the new king, and sometime in the third century, he received a visitor from the country of Tan Yang, apparently in the west of India. The visitor had travelled to India on his way to Funan, he told Fan Zhan about the wonders of the country, and it could be based on this information that Fan Zhan decided to send an envoy to India.[29] This event marked a significant turning point in Funan history as it was the first time that a king of Funan and a prince of India established an official relationship. The envoy, Sou-wou, embarked at Teou-kiu-li – likely the ancient port of Takkola by Trang, Mueang Trang District, Thailand.[30] Trang is on one of several routes across the Malay Peninsula from the Andaman Sea to the Gulf of Thailand that ancient travellers could take, the other ones are at Ranong (Kra Buri) further north or at Kedah further south.[31]

From Trang, Sou-wou and the delegation sailed north along the coast of Myanmar, and after more than a year, reached the mouth of the Ganges; they travelled up the river for several thousand *li* (2000 li is 900 kilometres). At that time, the eastern part of India, including the Indian states of Bihar, Orissa, and Jharkland was under the reign of the Murunda dynasty.[32] A major city by the bank of the Ganges in the state of Bihar is Pataliputra or Patna, some 900 kilometres from the mouth of the river, perhaps where they disembarked.[33]

In any event, it was likely a ruler of the Muranda family, a Muranda-raja, to whom Sou-wou eventually presented himself with gifts from Fan Zhan. According to the Chinese annals, the king of India was astonished and said:

"On the far shore of the ocean, there are still these men", then he ordered that they visit [his] kingdom. In addition, he delegated two people, including Chen-song to thank Fan Zhan for the donation of four horses (from the country) of Yue-che; and he sent Sou-wou and the others away.[34] *After four years of absence, they arrived* [came back to Funan]. *At this time, (the emperor of the dynasty) Wu had sent on ʒhong-lang Kang Tai as the ambassador to Funan. He saw Chen-song and the others and asked them in detail about the country and the customs of India..."* [35]

By the time Sou-wou got back to Funan, events had overtaken him. His king, Fan Zhan, no longer ruled: he had been assassinated by his cousin, Fan Chang, the younger brother of Fan Jinsheng. We can reasonably assume that Fan Zhan did not know about Fan Chang, who was a baby when his brother was killed. Fan Chang was brought up by the common people, and at the age of 20, he gathered a team of strong men to ambush Fan Zhan, stabbing him with a knife, and said *"years ago, you killed my brother; now I kill you in revenge for my father and brother"*. This time, Fan Chang's team of strong men was no match for the army, for a general of Fan Zhan, Fan Xun, promptly killed him and became the next king of Funan.[36] It was to Fan Xun the Chinese envoys, Kang Tai and Chou Ying presented themselves.[37]

FAN XUN - NORTH TO CHINA (245/250-287)

We do not know what became of Kang Tai and Chou Ying when they returned to China; they may have died of old age. As by then, their master had already lost the Eastern Wu dynasty to the Jin emperor. Fortunately, Liang shu continues their story and tells us in the era of Taikang (280-289) of the Western Jin dynasty (266-316), Funan sent an envoy to the Jin court.[38]

CHU ZHANTAN

For the next 70 years or so, little was reported on Funan in Chinese annals until 357, when a Chu Zhantan from Funan offered a tame elephant to the court of Eastern Jin (318-420) but the court politely declined.
There is a lot of discussion among scholars about this character as to whether Chu Zhantan was a Hindu from India or had a local Malayo-Polynesian title, but most agree that by the fourth century onwards, Funan was completely Hinduised. The Fans had gone by then, and we have no idea what happened to the family lineage.

LIUTUOBAMO - THE LAST RECORDED KING OF FUNAN[39]

Following Chu Zhantan was a Qiaochenru (Vietnamese Kiều Trần Như or Sanskrit Kauṇḍinya) who was a Brahmin, a member of the priestly or teaching class in Hinduism; under him, according to Liang shu, the kingdom changed their regime to the Indian customs. Qiaochenru died and was succeeded by Chilituobamo (Trì Lê Đà Bạt Ma), followed by a king with a combined name, Qiaochenru Shesiebamo (Sheyebamo?, Kiều Trần Như Xà Da Bạt Ma).[40]

Over the hundred years, during the fifth and sixth centuries, Funan continued to pay tributes to dynastic China, as the Chinese annals studiously recorded the events.[41] The centuries may have gone by, but the tradition of killing family members to gain the throne had not. Liutuobamo (the Chinese transcription of Rudravarman as mentioned earlier), son of the second wife (or a concubine) of Qiaochenru Shesiebamo, put to death the younger son of the first wife of his father, who was to inherit the throne legitimately. Liutuobamo was the last recorded king of Funan.[42] However, Xin Tang shu records during the eras of Wude (618-626) and Zhenguang (627-649), Funan sent two more tributes, including two "White Heads" (a tribe of people with white hair and creamy skin who lived in caves at the south-west of Funan), but no names are mentioned.[43] However, the reference to Funan could have been a mistake as the Jiu Tang shu records in 623, Zhenla, not Funan, sent their envoy to the Tang court and in 628, they came again with an envoy from Linyi.[44, 45]

Qiaochenru Shesiebamo was conferred the title "General of the Pacified South, king of Funan" in 503 by the Liang emperor.

9.4 – Funan - A widely spread South-East Asia kingdom

Most historians agree that Funan was mainly in southern Vietnam and Cambodia with extensions by conquest into the Malay Peninsula (Figure 38). That is, its expansion was from east to west. The map of Funan is often shown extending as far east as contemporary Nha Trang in central Vietnam, as far west as southern Thailand, and southern Myanmar on the Malay Peninsula. The northern border of the kingdom is shown as encompassing southern Laos, the whole of Cambodia, and central Thailand including Bangkok.

Having studied the history of Funan and reviewing the map, I doubt Funan would be that large. On the eastern side, it may go as far as Vũng Tàu but not to Nha Trang, reflecting archaeological sites that have been found to date.[46] Similarly, the northern border is unlikely to extend far into the hinterland of southern Laos, and northern Cambodia. Funan was likely to include southern Vietnam, coastal settlements along the Gulf of Thailand, including southern Myanmar, and Thailand on the Malay Peninsula.[47]

Tonle Bati is around 60 kilometres north of Angkor Borei, both west of the Mekong river. On the east side of the river, there is a place called Ba Phnum (Phnom); historians have suggested either could be the capital of Funan.[48] Both are within 100 kilometres as the crow flies from Óc Eo and are easily accessible from there by canals and the Mekong river. The Funan power centre was likely around this region. Archaeological records appear to support Angkor Borei.[49]

9.5 – The people of Funan - "the men are all ugly and black with curly hair."

What we know about the people of Funan and their society has come down to us via Chinese annals and archaeological artefacts.

We learn that the people lived in elevated houses built of wood; they had plenty of gold and silver. The king and people rode elephants, and there were plenty of crocodiles. They did not dig wells for water and did not have prisons. They kept slaves; the women wore sarongs, and men went half-naked. The dead were buried, thrown into the river, cremated or left out in the field to the birds and rot.

They worshipped the heavenly spirit and made bronze images; those with two faces have four arms; those with four faces have eight arms. The people of Funan were intelligent and clever; they were also honest and did not like to fight.[50]

As for the ethnicity of the Funanese, scholars have had different theories, but it is likely to be Khmer, the ethnicity of the Cambodians.[51,52] According to the Vietnamese 2019 census, there are 1,319,652 people of Khmer ethnicity in a total population of 96 million. Eighty-six per cent of these Khmer people live in the Mekong Delta in the region that was once the Óc Eo civilisation.

9.6 – Funan and Linyi

Funan, from the first to the seventh centuries, and Linyi, from the second to the eighth centuries, occupied the land south of Ngang pass to the Mekong Delta. Linyi was north of Funan, but the border between the two kingdoms was not defined. Since travelling between the two kingdoms was predominantly by ships from one river estuary to the next, the idea of having a land border does not have any meaning. There was likely a swath of empty land between the two kingdoms.

Tao Huang, the *cishi* of Giao Châu, referred to both kingdoms in 280 as barbarians beyond imperial control (Chapter 4). In his view, both actively cooperated to resist Northern Rule. While some of their kings had the same surname as Fan and some were possibly relatives, as events developed, there was no indication of any formal alliance against a common foe.

As mentioned earlier, after the death of Fan Huda in the early fifth century, the king of Linyi was killed by a son of the king of Funan, who was in turn killed by the father of Fan Yangmai.[53] It was thus no surprise that when Fan Yangmai asked for help from Funan around 431 in his fight against the Liu Song dynasty, Funan's king refused.[54]

Chinese annals report that Funan people are honest and do not like fighting, but the kingdom was often raided by Linyi, which prevented it from travelling to Giao Chỉ, and hence their envoys seldom came.[55] In 484, the king of Funan, Qiaochenru Sheseibamo, wrote to the court of the Southern Qi (479–502) protesting the seizure and confiscation of his ship, when it was blown off course to the coast of Linyi. He requested that the court send a military expedition against Linyi. The tone of his letter made it clear that there was no love lost between the two kingdoms:

> *"That country* [Linyi] *belongs to Your Majesty* [as a vassal], *so I respectfully report it. I learned that Linyi, for several years, has made modest tributes, reduced to almost nothing; they also want to leave the court completely. There is no way a lion sitting still and letting the rats in peace? I sincerely hope that Your Majesty sends his generals to conquer the rebels; I will also give a little help to the court to defeat them so that all coastal countries will submit* [to your Majesty]. *If Your Majesty does not want to mobilise the soldiers and punish Linyi, please grant permission to Your Majesty's local officials to send a small number of troops to help us, with Your Majesty divine, to exterminate this small bandit, to punish evil and follow goodness. On the day of peace, I would like to dedicate five po lo of gold,* [between 30 to 50 million USD in today's value]*."* [56,57]

Apart from the expected, prostrating, submissive tone, this letter shows Qiaochenru Sheseibamo's diplomatic skills in trying to convince the emperor of Southern Qi by appealing to his vanity and pride, giving him options, and even offering him the promise of a reward which amounts to a bribe.

In the same letter, Qiaochenru Sheseibamo mentions one of his servants, Jiu Chouluo (Cửu Thù La), had conquered Linyi and proclaimed himself king. Historians suggest Jiu Chouluo could be the same as Fan Danggenchun (Appendix 9).

Fortunately for Linyi, the court of Southern Qi was in no mood for a military expedition. It barely survived a number of internal revolts at the time. If anything, it welcomed an envoy from Linyi in 491 and rewarded the usurper Fan Danggenchun with the title of "General of the Pacified South, Commander-In-chief of all Military on the Sea-coast, King of Linyi".[58]

On a separate note, I have found it difficult to reconcile the tone of the above correspondence by a Funan king and that carved into a stone stele (e.g. K. 40). The former is generally full of hidden meanings, and the latter is direct with many superlatives. I do not have any explanation for such discrepancy, which has encouraged me not to align the kings by two sources as mentioned elsewhere.

9.7 – The end of Funan - the coming of Zhenla

The last envoy sent by Funan was in 539; following that year, Chinese annals did not record any more news from Funan until the early seventh century. By then, the annals no longer mention Funan but cite a new kingdom called Zhenla.

Zhenla is mentioned in Sui shu (The Book of Sui, 636), Bei shi (The Book of Northern Dynasties (643-659), Jiu Tang shu (The Old Book of Tang, 941), Xin Tang shu (The New Book of Tang, 1060), and Song shi (The History of Song, 1346).[59]

SUI SHU

The earliest source, Sui shu, extensively described Zhenla:

> "*The kingdom of Zhenla is south-west of Linyi. It was originally a vassal of Funan. It bordered Chequ on the south, the kingdom of Zhu Jiang on the west, and took 60 days' travel by sea from Rinan* [Nhật Nam]. *The family name*

of the king was Chali [or Kṣatriya], *his personal name was She-to-ssu-na* [or Citrasena], *and from the time of [his] grandfathers, it had gradually become wealthy and powerful.* [when it came to his reign] *She-to-ssu-na seized Funan and subdued it. She-to-ssu-na died and his son, Y-che-na-sien-tai or Yishenaxiandai (Vietnamese Y Xa Na Tiên) succeeded him as king in the city of Y-che-na or Y Xa Na* [Īśānapura in Sanskrit], *the outer of the city has more than 20,000 households."* [60,61,62]

Sui shu explains that near the capital, there is a mountain called Ling-jia-bo-po (or Lingapavarta in Sanskrit), which some historians suggest it is Mt Phu Kao near Vat Phu (Phou) in southern Laos but not all agree.[63] However, most historians agree that Īśānapura is present-day Sambor Prei Kuk in Kompong Thom province, over 430 kilometres south of Vat Phu.[64]

Sui shu also mentions two more kingdoms: Tham Bán and Chitu, while Zhu Jiang means red river, Chitu means red earth. I have not researched the location of these kingdoms in depth, but I note that with the red earth, Chitu shows the presence of iron oxides. In Cambodia, Phnom Dek of Kompong Thom province is known as an ancient iron mining area, so Chitu could be in the vicinity.[65] It is about 64 kilometres north of Sambor Prei Kuk.

The record of several small kingdoms in Shi shu could indicate that Funan was broken into a number of minor vassals before they became part of Zhenla, as Zhenla's king subdued Funan. However, Vickey suggests no conquest was necessary as by the sixth century, Funan was in irreversible economic and political decline.[66] One of the reasons is the coastal trades Funan had relied on were replaced by a direct sailing route between Indonesia and China, bypassing places such as Óc Eo.[67]

The transition from Funan to Zhenla is also recorded by Xin Tang shu as *"The capital (of Funan) is Temu (Đặc Mục), but not long after, it was subjugated by Zhenla and moved to the city of Na-fu-na (Na-Phất-Na) in the south."*[68] These places could be Ba Phnum (Phnom) and Angkor Borei respectively.[69]

JIU TANG SHU AND THE TWO ZHENLAS

Jiu Tang shu records that in 623, Zhenla sent their envoys to the Tang court, and in 628, they came again with envoys from Linyi. It also cites the name of Khmer (Cát Miệt in Vietnamese) as another name for Zhenla. From the reign of Chen-long (705-707), Jiu Tang shu refers to a Water Zhenla in the south, near the seas with lakes and waterways and a Land Zhenla in the north with mountains and hills, also called Wen Tan. During the reigns of Gao Zong

(649-683), (Wu) Zhou dynasty (690-705) and Xuanzong (712-756), Zhenla also sent tributes.

Jiu Tang shu continues to record that Water Zhenla, measured from the east, west, north to south directions, is about 800 *li* (360 kilometres). To the west is the kingdom of Trụy La Bát Đế, to the south is a small sea, and to the north is Land Zhenla. Its capital is called Bà La Đề Bạt; to the east, there are small forts, all called kingdoms. Water Zhenla has many elephants; in the year of 813, it sent a party of Lý Ma Na to attend the imperial court.[70]

XIN TANG SHU AND THE TWO ZHENLAS

Xin Tang shu records that during the era under the Zhou dynasty (690-705), Zhenla sent tributes four times. Xin Tang shu also cites the same information about Land and Water Zhenlas but includes that Land Zhenla is 700 *li* (315 kilometres) wide. It is also called Wendan or Polou, its king is called "Thạ Khuất". During the eras of Kaiyuan (713-741) and Tianbao (742-756), the Crown Prince of Land Zhenla came to the Tang court with 26 attendants. Around 10 years later, during the era of Dali (766-779), the Viceroy, named Pho-Mi came to the Tang court with his wife and 11 trained elephants but the next emperor, Dezong (780-805), having just ascended the throne, released them – up to that time were kept in a garden – to the wild. Water Zhenla also sent their envoy during the era of Yuanhe (806-820).[71]

LOCATION OF TWO ZHENLAS

Historians have different views on the locations of both Zhenlas; some suggest that Water Zhenla covered roughly southern Cambodia and southern Vietnam; Land Zhenla included northern Cambodia, southern, and central Laos. Others argued that both Zhenlas was located entirely within the boundary of Cambodia.[72]

Based on the records of where the pre-Angkor (before 802) inscriptions were found, I would suggest Water Zhenla includes southern Cambodia and the provinces in Southern Vietnam near the present-day border with Cambodia. It is interesting to note that the distance between the provinces of Kratié in the north-east and Kampot in the south-west is around 360 kilometres as the crow flies. If I consider that as a diagonal of a square, then the equivalent square would be 254 kilometres measured in the east, west, north, and south directions, not much less than the estimate in Jiu Tang shu of 360 kilometres.

As for the Land Zhenla, I would suggest it covers the region north of Tonlé Sap and may include southern Laos and possibly some provinces in Thailand, just north of Cambodia. As an estimate, the distance between the provinces of Battambang in the west and Krong Stung Streng in the east is around 329 kilometres as the crow flies, which appears consistent with the estimate of 315 kilometres in Xin Tang shu.

ZHENLA AND GIAO CHÂU

In the story of the Black Emperor (Chapter 11), Zhenla is mentioned by Chinese annals as a member of the alliances that joined in the revolt. While the records do not state whether it was Water or Land Zhenla, it would seem to me, based on the geography and the invasion of Nghê An by Zhenla in the 12th century, that Land Zhenla would be the most likely. Land Zhenla would be much closer to the northern parts of central Vietnam than Water Zhenla. From Thakhek of Central Laos, believed to be the capital of Land Zhenla, to Vinh of Nghê An province, where the revolt started, is around 300 kilometres, but it would be nearly 1,600 kilometres from Sambor Prei Kuk, thought to be the capital of Water Zhenla.[73]

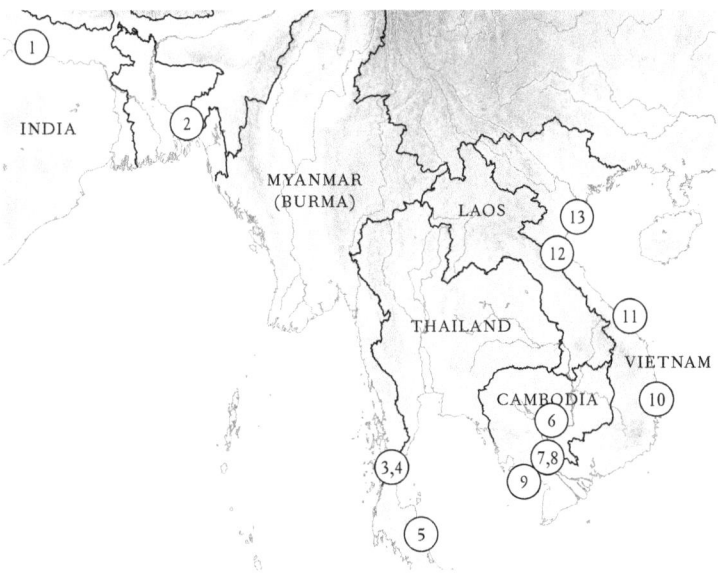

Figure 38 – Locations related to the stories of Funan. 1. Patna, 2. Chattogram, 3. Ranong, 4. Chumphon, 5. Trang, 6. Sambor Prei Kuk, 7. Ba Phnum, 8. Angkor Borei, 9. Óc Eo, 10. Nha Trang, 11. Hội An, 12. Thakhek, 13. Vinh.

CHAPTER 10

PRE-ANGKOR INSCRIPTIONS AND THREE KHMER TOWERS

FUNAN/ZHENLA III

STORY TIMELINE: Seventh to eighth centuries.
STORY LOCATION: Cambodia, Thailand and Laos provinces north of Cambodia, Southern Vietnam.
KEY CHARACTERS: *Rudravarman, Bhavavarman, Mahendravarman, Īśānavarman* and *Jayavarman*.
LOCATIONS OF INTEREST: Linh Sơn Tự, An Giang province, Vietnam. Chóp Mạt, Bình Thạnh, Vĩnh Hưng towers.

Chapter summary

The Chinese, Vietnamese court officials and historians compiled annals, but the Khmer, like the Chams, left behind inscriptions on stone, rock and metal surfaces written in Sanskrit and Khmer. As of 2017, 1,360 such inscriptions have been found in Cambodia, Thailand, Laos and Vietnam, reflecting the geographical extent of the Khmer Empire.[1,2]

Historians agree that the year 802 is the start of the Khmer (Angkor) empire (802-1432). Of 1,360 inscriptions, around 111 are pre-Angkor, with the bulk belonging to the times of Zhenla. For this book, I will focus on those pre-Angkor inscriptions, particularly those found in Vietnam, since coverage of Angkor history would be outside the scope of this book.

I am trying to find some links between the information recorded on the inscriptions with that written down in Chinese annals related to Zhenla. In the process, I have also located temples and ancient Khmer towers in Vietnam, which a traveller can visit.

I should point out that except for Kambuja (Cambodia), the names of Zhenla, Funan and other kingdoms, cited earlier by the Chinese annals, were never registered on any of the inscriptions.[3] Similarly, the term Kambuja appears on many of them, but none is found on the pre-Angkor inscriptions.[4]

To write this chapter, the primary source of information came from the monumental work of eight volumes by the French Professor George Cœdès (1886-1969): *Inscriptions du Cambodge*, (1937- 1966). Without his work, I would not be able to write this chapter with inscription stories related to Funan and Zhenla.[5]

10.1 – Geographical distribution

While the media are different, the Chinese annals and inscriptions follow a certain format generally consistent from one to the next, down the centuries. The format of the inscription varies a little depending on whether the language used is Sanskrit or Khmer. The Khmer inscriptions generally have more details, but they both include praise to a god, glory to a king, the purpose of the inscription, the name of the donor, the date, prices paid for the land and complete with a warning of punishment to those who wish to cause damages.[6]

Of the 111 pre-Angkor inscriptions, 37 have dates carved on them, with the earliest (K. 600, Angkor Borei) at 533 Śaka or 611 CE and the latest (K.

134, Lobok Srot Jams, Kratié) at 781, over a span of about two centuries.[7,8] Of the 74 undated inscriptions, the earliest (K. 499, Si T'ep in Thailand) is fifth or sixth century and the latest around the eighth century Śaka.[9,10]

With the exception of the inscriptions during the Funanese period, to be discussed further (K. 5, K. 40, K. 875), the other pre-Angkor inscriptions belong to the time of Zhenla. The distribution of these inscriptions is interesting to me since it would give me an indication of their territory.

In the centre of present-day Cambodia is Tonlé Sap, or the Great Lake, the largest freshwater lake in Southeast Asia.[11] The lake provides a helpful reference landmark to discuss the distribution of the pre-Angkor inscriptions. In broad terms, there is a group of inscriptions found at the northern end of the lake around the provinces of Battambang, Siem Reap, Preah Vihear, Stung Treng in Cambodia, Prachin-Buri, Nakhon-Ratchasima and Surin in Thailand, and Muang Champasak in southern Laos, also across the northern border of Cambodia.[12]

The second group of inscriptions is at the southern end of the lake in the provinces of Takeo, Kandal, Kompong Speu, Prey Veng, Svay Rieng, Kompong Cham and further to the east at Kratié.[13] While there is no obvious landmark like a mountain range or a large river to separate the two

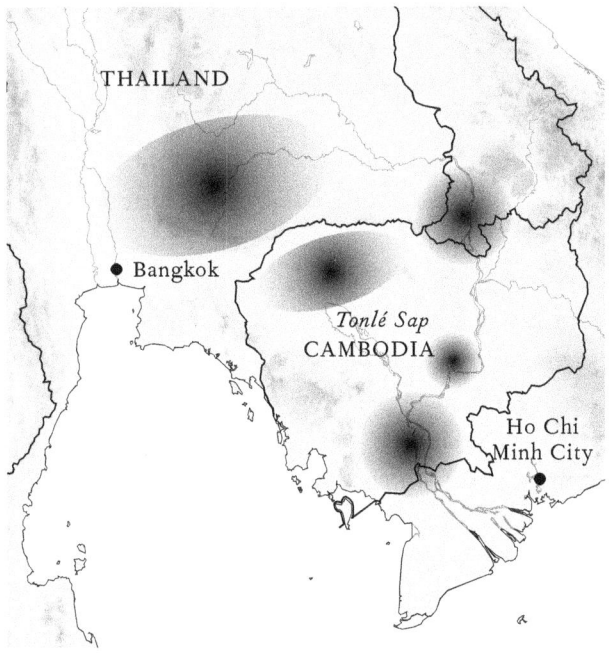

Figure 39 – The distribution of pre-Angkor (before 802) inscriptions.

regions, such distribution appears to lend credence to the Water and Land Zhenlas as discussed in Chinese annals. Generally speaking, inscriptions in the southern region are older indicating an earlier settlement as it is closer to the coast and Óc Eo. It would also support the proposition of an east-to-west expansion of Funan.

An outline of the provinces where pre-Angkor inscriptions were found is shown in Figure 39. For clarity, I have not included K. 499 (fourth to fifth centuries Śaka) found in Phitsanulok and K. 1102 (sixth century Śaka) found in Khon Kaen, in northern Thailand. Also, I have not included K. 419 found in Cần Thơ and K. 884 found in Trà Vinh, in the deep south of Vietnam.[14]

10.2 – Funan - the inscriptions

We have two Chinese-transcribed Sanskrit names, Lutuoluobamo for Rudravarman and Qiaochenru for Kauṇḍinya, but to check if these kings exist, we need to turn to epigraphy. Fortunately, like the kings of Linyi, the Funanese also left behind their stories on inscriptions carved in stone. Among those found so far, two inscriptions have provided historians with interesting information. These are K. 40 (Vat Bati) and K. 5 (also known as Prasat Pram Loveng or Gò Tháp) in the fifth century Śaka.[15,16] Their details are described below.

K. 5 - A NOBLE AND INTELLIGENT PRINCE

Among the ruins of the monument at Gò Tháp in southern Vietnam (Prasat Pram Loveng) as cited earlier, archaeologists found an inscription engraved on a schist pedestal. The text referred to a certain Gunavarman who is described as the "son of the king", and the father king is of the race of Kauṇḍinya and that he had appointed his son to head of a domain "conquered on the mud", which Cœdès links to the Plain of Reeds (*Đồng Tháp Mười or Plaine des Joncs*). The inscription is no later than the second half of the fifth century Śaka.[17]

Some historians suggest Gunavarman could be the prince Rudravarman killed.[18] Majumdar suggests Gunavarman is the son of Jayavarman and queen Kulaprabhāvati mentioned in K. 875 below.[19] However the dates may not match; K. 40 is dated in the fifth century Śaka whereas Jayavarman and Rudravarman were rulers of Funan in the late fifth and early sixth centuries.[20] In any event, the two lines from the inscription, reproduced below, do provide a feel for the sentiment of the day:

> LINE VI: *"This king who had taken for wife a lovely woman with a gait... and a beautiful belt, had (a son) named Gunavarman, of whom the soul was noble and intelligent (!)...*
>
> LINE VII: *By the fortunate king who took the victorious step (?) of Vikramin and who is the moon of the line of Kauṇḍinya, this king's son, although young, was, because he unites in himself virtue and value, designated, as the head of a religious domain, conquered on the mud."* [21]

K. 40 - AN INSCRIPTION ON THE DOOR LINTEL

At the exterior lintel above the southern side door of the easter entrance, inside the Ta Prohm monument, Cambodia, French archaeologists found an inscription written in Sanskrit. The lintel, a slab of schist, must have been originally used as a pedestal. It is now at the National Museum of Cambodia in Phnom Penh.

The first two lines of the inscription are in honour of Buddha, the next two lines are to the glory of king Rudravarman, and the fifth line mentions his father, Jayavarman:

> LINE III: *"(The king) who, despite his superiority, does not regard any virtue as insignificant, which like a jewel adorning the head... stand on the heads of creatures, and strives to observe all the royal virtues combined, this Śri Rudravarman was truly created unique on earth by the Creator.*
>
> LINE V: *The father of this (king), king Jayavarman, appointed the son of a religious leader of the Brahmins as an inspector of goods...".* [22]

The lintel is dated to the fifth century Śaka. Ta Prohm temple is near lake Tonle Bati, some 30 kilometres south of Phnom Penh, and the names of two kings recorded on the inscription Jayavarman, and his son Rudravarman, match those recorded in Chinese annals as mentioned earlier.[23]

At around 55 kilometres south of Ta Prohm temple, the name of Jayavarman is also found engraved on a slab of sandstone at Neak Ta Dambang Dêk in the province of Treang, Takeo (K. 875).[24,25] This is believed to be the same Jayavarman, king of Funan. Treang province is around 20 kilometres west of Angkor Borei, which would tend to confirm the important role of the region in the history of Funan.[26]

10.3 – Zhenla - the inscriptions

There are more Zhenla inscriptions than Funans, but to make a full study of them would be outside the scope of this book. Below is a list of some relevant Zhenla-era inscriptions which gives some links to the records in Chinese annals and indicates the extent of the territory of Zhenla.

K. 53 - THE LIST OF KINGS

A list of kings is always a good place to start; a list of Zhenla kings is recorded on inscription K. 53 (Kdei Ang, also known as Ang Chumnik), found at a temple in Prey Veng province in Cambodia.[27] It is written on a stele now held at the Musée Guimet in Paris.

The inscription records the erection of a linga and the foundation of a temple and is dated 589 Śaka or 667 CE. It also has a list of the kings Rudravarman, Bhavavarman, Mahendravarman, Īśānavarman and Jayavarman.[28] While the Chinese annals have recorded that Rudravarman is the last king of Funan, the list does not show such a transition between him and the next king, Bhavavarman. However, the next inscription, K. 363, tends to support the account in Chinese annals (see below).

The inscription also discusses the taking of power by Bhavavarman *"with energy"*, which could imply a conquest.[29]

K. 213 AND K. 978 - BHAVAVARMAN

There are two inscriptions related to Bhavavarman; one is K. 213 (Phnom Banteay Neang), found in Battambang province, north-west of Tonlé Sap, dated in the fifth century Śaka and K. 978 (Si Thep), found at Phetchabun province, north of Bangkok, Thailand. K. 978 is also dated to the fifth century Śaka.[30]

Both locations are north of Tonlé Sap which indicates the reach of Bhavavarman's territory. The capital under Bhavavarman's reign is Bhavapura which has been identified as Ampil Rolum near Sambor Prei Kuk, Thala Borivat in Stung Treng, further south in Ta Keo, and Sambor Prei Kuk itself.[31] I would hazard a guess at the location near or at Sambor Prei Kuk.

K. 363 - THE MOUNT OF THE KINGDOM

A few kilometres upstream from the confluence between the Mun and the Mekong rivers, on the left bank of the Mekong, is a sandstone mound called Phou Lokhon or "the mount of the kingdom", a square pillar of sandstone where an inscription was found.[32] It is now known as K. 363 (Phou Hlak Khon (or Can Nakhon) in the Champasak province of Laos. It is dated to the fifth century Śaka and apparently is still there, but I have not been able to locate it on the map.[33]

What is interesting about this inscription is that copies were made and found in southern provinces of Thailand, which indicate the extent of king Mahendravarman's rule.[34] It records the installation of a Śiva-linga by him, formerly known as Citrasena, younger brother (or cousin) of Bhavavarman, son of Vīravarman and grandson of Sārvabhauma. The Śiva-linga was established as a sign of his victory.[35,36]

So now we have a record of a king, by Sui shu as She-to-ssu-na, a Chinese transcription of Citrasena whose capital, based on the location of K. 363, could be in southern Laos and matches the description of a mountain, Ling-jia-bo-po, found there. The inscription confirms Citrasena/Mahendravarman's victory, which could be related to the subjugation of Funan as recorded by Sui shu.

K. 604 AND K. 438 - SAMBOR PREI KUK

After the death of She-to-ssu-na, his son Y-che-na-sien-tai succeeded him. Y-che-na-sien-tai is the transcription of Īśānavarman, and the inscriptions found show him as a remarkable king. His capital at Īśānapura is believed to be present-day Sambor Prei Kuk. Several inscriptions were found there citing his name; of these K. 604 stands out.[37] It is dated 549 Śaka or 627 and provides a eulogy to him:

> *"There was a king named Śrī- Īśānavarman, who, having conquered by his valour the circle of the earth".*[38]

K. 438 commemorates the marriage of one of Īśānavarman's daughters and religious dedications made by her husband. It mentions both Īśānavarman and Īśānapura.[39]

10.4 – The pre-Angkor inscriptions found in southern Vietnam

The current border between Cambodia and Vietnam was only drawn in the 19th century, so it is no surprise that a number of pre-Angkor inscriptions were found in the Vietnamese provinces close to the Cambodian provinces, where inscriptions of a similar age were found.[40] These provinces are Đồng Tháp and An Giang, across the border from Takeo and Prey Veng. The inscriptions are discussed briefly as follows:

K. 1 - VAT THLEN, OR VAT THLING

I am unable to locate precisely where this inscription was found. Apparently, it is still there on a stele/masonry at a pagoda in Châu Đốc city of An Giang province.[41] It is dated between the sixth and seventh centuries Śaka which would be Zhenla or possibly late Funan. The inscription records the granting of lands and slaves by the local governors.[42]

K. 3 - LINH SƠN TỰ, ALSO KNOWN AS PHNOM BATHÊ.

The inscription is embedded in the altar of Linh Sơn Tự, in a pagoda named Chùa Linh Sơn Ba Thê or Four-arm Buddha pagoda (Chùa Phật Bốn Tay) next to the Óc Eo relic - Linh Sơn Tự (Nam Linh Sơn Tự-Khu Di Tích Óc Eo), An Giang province. It is dated between the sixth and seventh centuries Śaka and records the construction of a brick temple for a god.[43]

Figure 40 – The Four-arm Buddha at Linh Sơn Ba Thê pagoda.[44]

The Four-arm Buddha pagoda is so-called because of a statue the local people found in 1913 of Vishnu resting on a Shesha (or Sesanaga), a Hindu mythical serpent (*naga*) with seven heads. The statue has been painted as shown in Figure 40.[45] The right hand of the statue holds what looks like a prayer bead, which I find intriguing as my research so far has not shown any Vishnu statue holding a prayer bead usually, Vishnu would hold a discus instead.[46] There is an inscription on a stele built into the left side of the statue pedestal which has the same number of verses, eleven, as those on K. 3. However, the stele on the right side shown in the photograph, does not have any inscription.

K. 5 - THÁP MƯỜI, PRASAT PRAM LOVENG

This is the oldest inscription of the group. It is dated to the fifth century Śaka and is one of a few Funanese inscriptions. I will discuss them separately, but K. 6, K. 7 and K. 8 are dated between the sixth to the seventh centuries Śaka which fall under the Zhenla period. These inscriptions were found at Gò Tháp in southern Vietnam (also known as Prasat Pram Loveng).

K. 6, K. 7, K. 8 - THÁP MƯỜI, PRASAT PRAM LOVENG

K. 6 records the donation of slaves, lands, and nut trees to the gods, K. 7 also records a donation by a Zhenla king, Sambhuvarman (eighth century).[47] K. 8 provides names of the servants and cites the name of a Zhenla king, Jayavarman I (seventh century).[48,49]

K. 9 - PHÚ HỰU

This inscription was seen at Cái Tàu Hạ pagoda at Phú Hựu, Đồng Tháp province.[50] It could have come to the pagoda from Gò Tháp where K. 5, K. 6, K. 7 and K. 8 inscriptions were found. K. 9 lists the names and gifts by various people and date of 561 Śaka or 639 CE, now in the Vietnam History Museum of Ho Chi Minh City.[51]

OTHER PRE-ANGKOR INSCRIPTIONS

The inscriptions described above were found in the early years of inscriptions work; for example, K.1 was the first to be recorded. But in the following decades, more inscriptions were found. For completeness, I have included those found in the Mekong Delta, as listed below:[52]

K. 419 *Hòa Thịnh, Cần Thơ*, dated sixth/seventh century Śaka

K. 884 *Nhị Trường, Trà Vinh*, dated sixth/seventh century Śaka

K. 918 *Thoại Sơn, An Giang*, dated sixth century Śaka

K. 924 *Hòa Bình Thạnh, An Giang*, fifth century Śaka

10.5 – Three oldest towers in southern Vietnam

THE TOWER OF CHÓP MẠT

At around 90 kilometres north-west of Ho Chi Minh city is the province of Tây Ninh, which borders Cambodia. In this province, there are two old brick towers: Chót Mạt and Bình Thạnh. Both are well over 1,000 years old and well worth a visit.

The French came across the tower of Chóp Mạt in 1886; the photo taken then showed a ruin, deeply buried in the jungle and almost collapsed.[53] Today, it has been restored, the ground is cleared; the tower is basking in the sun with the beautiful colour of orange/black of the new and old bricks as shown on Figure 41.

The local sign indicates the tower was built between the seventh and early eighth centuries, which would be at the time of the two Zhenlas. Parmentier compares this tower to Prasat Preah Srei (present Prasat Srey at Kampong Chhnang province in Cambodia, 240 km north-west of Chóp Mạt).[54] In his paper, he is very clear that the tower is Khmer and not Champa in origin.[55] I am inclined to agree, partly because of the similarity of the design in these two towers and partly because of the geography. The closest Chams towers of a similar age are at Mỹ Sơn, some 850 kilometres north of Chóp Mạt. The other nearest Chams tower, Hòa Lai, built at a later date, late eighth to early ninth centuries, is around 450 kilometres east of Chóp Mạt, and there is no record of the Chams ever settled around Tây Ninh in the eighth century.

THE TOWER OF BÌNH THẠNH

At some 60 kilometres south of Chóp Mạt, not very far from the border between Vietnam and Cambodia, one finds another tower of a similar age to Chóp Mạt. It has also been restored, and the information from the Tây Ninh Provincial Museum shows it was built around the seventh to the eighth centuries. Excavation at the sites found fragments of a Vishnu statue (dated around the seventh century) and other artefacts of a similar age; given its

Figure 41 – The tower of Chóp Mạt (seventh/eighth century), Tây Ninh province, Vietnam.[56]

Figure 42 – The tower of Bình Thạnh, (seventh/eighth century), Tây Ninh province, Vietnam.[59]

similar design to Chóp Mạt, it is likely to be Khmer in origin.⁵⁷

The two towers are not the only historical sites of the same period in Tây Ninh. Étienne Lunet de Lajonquière in the third volume of his monumental *Inventaire descriptif des monuments du Cambodge*, shows a number of sites along the bank of Vàm Cỏ Đông river which flows through Tây Ninh province. However, he did not record Bình Thạnh. Henri Parmentier did not mention it either, but he drew the plan of a tower called Teai-ho in Svay Rieng, Cambodia, which I have not been able to locate.⁵⁸

Figure 43 – The tower of Vĩnh Hưng (seventh century), Bạc Liêu province, Vietnam.⁶¹

THE TOWER OF VĨNH HƯNG

Some 350 kilometres south of Chóp Mạt in the province of Tây Ninh is the third late Zhenla or early Kambuja tower, Vĩnh Hưng. The site was excavated in 1911, 1960, 2002, and 2011, and a number of artefacts was found, including a stele, bronze heads, bronze arms, a stone statue of goddess Laksmi (Lakṣmī), a linga-yoni plus a number of other items (Laksmi, being the wife of Vishnu, is the Hindu goddess of wealth and fortune). Information on the stele at the site indicates the site was occupied as early as the fourth century, the period of the Funan and Óc Eo civilisation. It also mentions the tower was built during the seventh century and repaired during the eighth and 13th centuries. The linga-yoni at the site is a copy of the original, currently held at the Bạc Liêu Provincial Museum. The artefacts are exhibited at the exhibition hall at the site.

The inscription on the stele mentions the name of Yasodhara, the personal name of the Khmer (Angkor) king, Yasovarman (889-910) and the date on the stele, K. 492 (Vĩnh Hưng), of 814 Śaka or 892 CE confirms it.[60] Vĩnh Hưng tower is an amazing monument to visit. Firstly because of its location, it is a long way east of the Vietnam-Cambodia border and, as far as I can find, the southernmost tower in Vietnam worshipping Hindu gods. Secondly, it has been wonderfully restored from the original tower, which has lost half of its body, as shown in Figure 43. The tower is also called Trà Long (by de Lajonquière) and Lục Hiền (by Parmentier).

10.6 – The Angkor-period inscriptions in southern Vietnam

Angkor-period inscriptions (post 802) belong to the Kambuja period and are thus related to the history of Cambodia and outside the scope of this book. However, during this period, most of southern Vietnam came under the Khmer Empire, so I have included here the inscriptions found there to give a geographical indication of the Khmer settlements. These are:

K. 516 *Mỹ Hưng or Mỹ Lộc, Vĩnh Long*, dated 11th to 12th centuries.
K. 912 *Vat Sway (Chùa Xòa?), My Trung (?), Trà Vinh*, dated 1108.
K. 1212 *Wath Som Rong Ék, Trà Vinh*, dated 1851.[62]

CHAPTER 11

TEN THOUSAND SPRINGS OR VẠN XUÂN (542-602)

GIAO CHÂU III

STORY TIMELINE: Sixth to seventh centuries.
STORY LOCATION: Northern Vietnam.
KEY CHARACTERS: *Lý Bí or the Former Lý Nam Đế:* first emperor of an independent kingdom, Vạn Xuân, *Chen Baxian:* Emperor of the Chen dynasty, the man who defeated Lý Bí, Triệu Quang Phục: king of Vạn Xuân, *Lý Phật Tử or the Later Lý Nam Đế:* the last emperor of Vạn Xuân, *Liu Fang:* general of the Sui dynasty who defeated Lý Bí.
LOCATIONS OF INTEREST: Trấn Quốc pagoda, Hanoi. Lý Bí temple, Phú Thọ. Lake Điển Triệt, Vĩnh Phúc province. The marsh of Dạ Trạch, Hưng Yên province. The temple of Triệu Việt Vương/Triệu Quang Phục, Hưng Yên province. Ô Diên (Hạ Mỗ), Hanoi.

Chapter summary

In the previous chapters, I have covered the story of Linyi in central Vietnam, and in the south of the country now I am heading back to the north of Ngang pass to see what was happening there during the 250 years from the last major revolt by Lady Triệu in 248.

The end of the Jin dynasty (266-420) brought about a period historians term the Northern and Southern Dynasties (420-589). In the north, they include the Northern Wei (386-535), Eastern Wei (534-550), and Western Wei (535-557). In the south, the southern dynasties are Liu Song (420-479), Southern Qi (479-502), Liang (502-559) and Chen (557-589).

All these dynasties can get very confusing, but for my purposes, I am only interested in the southern dynasties of Liu Song and Liang, the former because of its destruction of Linyi's citadels of Khu Túc and Điển Xung, the latter because it terminated the independence aspirations of the Vietnamese people during the second half of the sixth century, and pushed it out for another three centuries.

This chapter covers a remarkable period of Vietnamese history which historians refer to as the Former Lý dynasty (542-602). For over 60 years in the second half of the sixth century, the people of the north and north-central Vietnam were free from Northern Rule, and it had taken nearly five centuries since the Trưng sisters' rebellion for them to gain independence.

There are three characters in this story: Lý Bí (or Lý Bôn), Triệu Quang Phục, and Lý Phật Tử. Triệu Quang Phục is the son of Lý Bí's Great Master and Lý Phật Tử is one of Lý Bí's relatives. It began with Lý Bí, an educated man from a village north of Hanoi who worked for a time at the imperial capital, Jianye (modern Nanjing). There he may have met another compatriot who was also erudite. Both apparently could not attain their ambition as they came from a remote region of the empire and thus were not considered to have the right lineage. Disappointed, they returned to Giao Châu and plotted a rebellion.

Their timing was perfect as the *cishsi* at the time was a deeply unpopular character who alienated the local population with extortion and cruelty. They were joined by forces of a local chieftain, the father of Triệu Quang Phục, and successfully drove out this *cishsi*. They entered Long Biên (Luy Lâu) in 542. In 544, Lý Bí proclaimed himself as Lý Nam Đế (Lý, Emperor of the South); historians have no consensus as to the location of this event.

My research has indicated that Lý Bí's capital is in modern Hanoi. Its location was likely the reason for the Sui dynasty (581-618) to move the provincial capital there from Luy Lâu once they returned to Giao Châu in the early seventh century (Chapter 13).

The exiled *cishsi* wanted revenge, and he returned with strong expeditionary forces led by the man destined to become the emperor of the next dynasty – the Chen dynasty (557-589). Lý Bí and his men fought hard for nearly a year as they were forced further upstream of the Red river. Faced with a determined foe, Lý Bí eventually succumbed at the final battle at a lake in the heartland of the legendary Hùng kings, lake Điển Triệt by the Lô river bridge.

The resistance continued with Triệu Quang Phục, who successfully waged a guerrilla campaign against imperial troops from a marshland south of Hanoi. He eventually drove them out and entered Long Biên to become the next king (crowned as Triệu Việt Vương or Triệu, King of the Việt). Tragically he was betrayed by one of Lý Bí's relatives, Lý Phật Tử, and committed suicide.

Lý Phật Tử also declared himself as emperor and is known by history as the Later Lý Nam Đế to distinguish him from Lý Bí. He ruled for around 30 relatively peaceful years, but little is known about him. Thirty years is rather long time but Lý Phật Tử did not leave behind many traces to be found; there were no court annals, no monuments, and no tragic tales.

On the other hand, his kinsman, Lý Bí, who ruled for a much shorter period, most of it involved fighting against imperial forces to survive, is believed to have built a beautiful pagoda by the West Lake. Lý Bí arguably could be considered the founder of Hanoi. Historians are not kind to Lý Phật Tử, who quickly surrendered to a Sui general, Liu Fang in the early seventh century. Perhaps this is the difference between the two men. To be fair, Liu Fang caught Lý Phật Tử by surprise as his forces attacked the latter's strongholds, effectively from behind, as he came down from Yunnan in the north-west direction whereas Lý Phật Tử was expected the Sui soldiers to come from the south-east.

Liu Fang went on to plunder the capital of Linyi but died en route on the way back (Chapter 6).

Today, a traveller can visit Trấn Quốc pagoda, spend a few hours at the marsh of Dạ Trạch, visit the new temple of Triệu Quang Phục nearby, perhaps take a long ride to sit by lake Điển Triệt and visit Lý Bí temple near Phú Thọ. Their stories are told below in more detail.

11.1 – The Former Lý Nam Đế (Lý, Emperor of the South)

Ngô Sĩ Liên, a 15th-century Vietnamese historian, explains: [1]

> *"The Former Lý Nam Đế raised an army to fight against tyranny in harmony with the teaching of heaven, but in the end, he was defeated. Is it because heaven did not want our country to be peaceful? Alas, not only because he met Bá Tiên* [Chen Baxian], *who was good at deploying troops, but he also faced the sudden surge of the river* [water level] *supporting the enemy, was it not caused by heaven?"*

By the middle of the sixth century, Vietnam, at least north of Ngang pass, had been a part of the Chinese empire for over 600 years. Over these centuries, while dynasties came and went, there are a few patterns that had shaped the path to the independence of Vietnam in the 10th century.

As discussed previously, the suppression of the rebellion by the Trưng sisters in 43 almost wiped out the indigenous ruling class and replaced them with those appointed by the northern courts. Some of these came, stayed and built up a family ruling class over generations, such as the Shi brothers in the second, and third centuries[2], the Tao family in the third, and fourth centuries[3], and the Đỗ family in the fourth, fifth centuries.[4] Others took the opportunity to enrich themselves and returned north as soon as their tenure was over. For those who stayed behind, as the dynasties changed, there were plenty of power struggles among the local rulers to keep their positions.

Among the changes, whoever was in charge still had to collect taxes and pay annual levies to the imperial court, not to mention gifts of various types.[5] There were many different types of taxes ranging from "household", "grass-cutting" to "field" taxes, and other forms of exploitation such as drafting of master craftsmen to working in the imperial capital.[6] Campaigns against Linyi, fighting among each other or against armies sent by the empire during episodes of power struggles, all required foot soldiers. The people who under took these tasks were a mixture of indigenous people and immigrants whose forefathers came to settle many years earlier.[7] Most immigrants were refugees from the north, escaping the rebellions and civil wars; some were exiled, banished from the imperial court for getting on the wrong side of the emperors.[8] A number of refugees came up from the south driven by the raids of Linyi, others were economic refugees driven by hardship.[9] Many of the immigrants had been "Vietnamised", their loyalty was likely to rest with their families, the land that they now inhabited, and not necessarily to the empire, whose dynasties kept changing which must have been a challenge to their allegiance.

EARLY LIFE

Among those in the immigrant group was a man by the name of Lý Bí (or Lý Bôn), who revolted and drove out the *cishi* of Giao Châu in 541. Lý Bí's ancestors fled to Giao Châu during the usurpation of the Wang Mang rebellion (9-23) at the end of the Former Han dynasty. By the sixth century, Lý Bí was a seventh-generation immigrant and had become a local southern man.[10,11] Contemporary Chinese works refer to him as a native of Giao Châu.

Lý Bí was born in 499 and died in 548; the place of his birth has been subjected to many studies, but the current consensus is that Lý Bí grew up at Cổ Tháp hamlet, Tiên Phong commune, Phổ Yên district of Thái Nguyên province. It is some 70 kilometres north of Hanoi, with a small pagoda called Hương Ấp, where Lý Bí is believed to have spent his youth. The hamlet itself is not very far from Long Biên, and Lý Bí could have easily travelled there by boat on the Cầu river.[12,13]

He may have done so to obtain an education; according to historical records, he was a man of talents, well-versed in literature and military affairs. In any event, Lý Bí joined the imperial rank and worked at the Liang court for a time before returning home to become a military overseer at Cửu Đức prefecture in Hà Tĩnh province, just north of Ngang pass. Apparently, he was *"unable to attain his ambition"*; at any rate, the move must have been a disappointment for him; it was more likely caused by a demotion or resulted from a vindictive act by his rivals at court.[14] Cửu Đức was a back-of-beyond, southernmost frontier where Linyi kings carried out repeatedly raids years earlier and was not a place for an ambitious man such as Lý Bí who wanted to get ahead at the imperial capital some 2,000 kilometres north.

THE REVOLT

Whatever the case, the move did not stop his ambition; in due course, he joined with *"Heroes from other prefectures"* and rebelled.[15] One of these was Tinh Thiều, a man of some literary talents who also travelled to the Liang court to seek an official position, but the president of the Board of Civil Service decided that, since Thiều's family had not produced any scholar, he was not worthy of a desk role but appointed him as an overseer of one of the gates in the city walls.[16,17] Thiều was insulted and, full of resentment, he returned to Giao Châu and plotted with Lý Bí, who was at Cửu Đức at the time, for a rebellion.[18,19]

The other person was a tribal leader from Chu Diên prefecture, Triệu Túc, who came to join Lý Bí with his army. Historical records do not tell us how the rebellion spread but the addition of Triệu Túc's army may have tipped the balance; after hearing the news, the *cishi* of Giao Châu, Xiao Zi, ceased any resistance, paid a bribe and escaped to Guangzhou. Xiao Zi, a nephew of the Liang emperor alienated the population with acts of extortion and cruelty.[20,21] With Xiao Zi gone, in 541, Lý Bí and his army entered Long Biên.

FOUGHT OFF A TWO-PRONG ATTACK BY IMPERIAL TROOPS

The Liang emperor reacted quickly and in April 542, he ordered the *cishi* of Việt Châu, Chen Hou, the *cishi* of La Châu, Luo Ning, the *cishi* of An Châu, Li Zhi and the *taishou* of Ái Châu, Nguyễn Hán to march against Lý Bí.[22] Việt Châu was a newly formed province that includes Hepu, and most of southern Guangxi, south-west Guangdong provinces. Ái Châu is the name for Cửu Chân commandery under the Han, and located at Thanh Hóa province, south of Long Biên. The others came from southern China in the north, so Lý Bí was faced with a two-prong attack in both directions, but he appeared to fight them off. Unfortunately, there is nothing in the record to tell us what became of the campaign.[23,24]

HELPED BY A DISEASE THAT DECIMATED THE SECOND IMPERIAL CAMPAIGN

Later that year, the emperor mobilised again; this time, he sent Lu Zi Xiong, the *cishi* of Gaozhou and Sun Qiong, the *cishi* of Xinzhou – both in Guangdong province – with their armies south. Both men were reluctant to go, citing the risk of malaria and other tropical diseases during the spring and summer, and would rather depart in the autumn of 543 once the risk of disease was reduced.[25] However, their objection was overridden by the *cishi* of Guangzhou, Xiao Yong, and the disgraced Xiao Zi. This is the same Xiao Zi who bribed his way out of Giao Châu and was eager for revenge. Reluctantly, the armies marched out in January 543 and got as far as Hepu. They may have planned to take the same route as Ma Yuan in his expedition against the Trưng sisters in 41/42, where the troops took both land and sea routes (Appendix 8). As events turned out, the worst fears of both *cishis* were realised; between 60 and 70 per cent of the soldiers died at Hepu, and the rest scattered and returned to Guangzhou. They were likely struck down by an epidemic, possibly malaria. On the other hand, others have attributed the deaths to an ambush by Lý Bí's forces.[26,27,28]

The scheming Xiao Zi reported to the emperor that the two men cooperated with the rebels, hesitant to move, and that was the cause of the disaster; consequently, both were forced to commit suicide by imperial order.[29]

Their deaths provoked a violent reaction from their family members, including Lu Zi Xiong's brothers and relatives.[30] They marched to Guangzhou with the intention of killing Xiao Zi and his cousin Xiao Yong. Fortunately for both Xiao, their lives were saved by the arrival of a future Chinese emperor, Chen Baxian (Trần Bá Tiên), who came with 3,000 hand-picked soldiers and restored order. Xiao Yong died soon after, but the fate of Xiao Zi is unknown.[31]

SUCCESSFULLY FOUGHT OFF A SOUTHERN RAID BY LINYI

Meanwhile, in the summer of 543, the king of Linyi (believed to be Rudravarman I, a descendant of Fan Yangmai) raided Cửu Đức but was defeated by Lí Bí's general Phạm Tu (Fan Xiu).[32] The clash was the first of many in the centuries to come between two independent kingdoms, Đại Việt in the north and Champa in the south across Ngang pass – until the border slowly pushed further south to Hải Vân pass in the 15th century, and eventually in the 19th century to the border of Vietnam as we know today.

TEN THOUSAND LIFE SPANS

In the spring of 544, around February, a victorious Lý Bí, having fought off the aggression from the north, and the south declared himself the Nam Việt Đế (The Emperor of Southern Việt), named his realm as Vạn Xuân (Ten Thousand Springs), took the title as Thiện Đức (Heavenly Virtue), and built a palace named Vạn Thọ (Ten Thousand Life Spans).[33,34] As a matter of historical interest, Nam Việt or Nan-yue is the name of a second century BCE kingdom under Zhao Tuo that includes both Giao Châu, Guangxi, and Guangdong provinces.[35]

Lý Bí then appointed Phạm Tu as his chief military official, Tinh Thiều as his chief civil official and Triệu Túc as the "Great Master" or "*Thái Phố*", a position akin to a royal mentor.[36]

Vietnamese historians interpret these names as an expression of Lý Bí's wish to have his kingdom continue for generations.[37] Sadly, Lý Bí did not rule very long; his reign lasted barely four years, and history does not mention any heirs.

Today, there is little physical evidence of where his Vạn Xuân capital was, but I agree with some historians that it was built near the Tô Lịch river mouth in central Hanoi and not at Long Biên or Thanh Trì as suggested by others.[38,39]

To look for Vạn Xuân, I refer to a 15th-century map that shows Tô Lịch river connecting the West Lake in Hanoi to the Red river, but that branch was drained and filled.[40] The river inlet was somewhere between Long Biên and Chương Dương bridges near Bạch Mã temple. The land-filled branch is around Phan Đình Phùng street, so Vạn Thọ palace could be in the vicinity (see Chapter 13 and Appendix 7).[41] He also built a Buddhist pagoda named Khai Quốc (National Founding) which was relocated to its current position at West Lake (Hồ Tây) as Trấn Quốc pagoda in the early 17th century as shown in Figure 45. The pagoda is less than 3 kilometres from the Long Biên bridge, which makes sense if the Vạn Thọ palace is nearby.

Figure 44 – A painting of the Former Lý Nam Đế and his Queen.[42]

Figure 44 shows a 19th-century painting on wood. Note the beautiful horses in the lower corners and the musicians on the right lower corner playing the Đàn Đáy (a plucked lute with three strings) and Sáo (flute).

Figure 45 – Trấn Quốc Pagoda – Hanoi.

Trấn Quốc Pagoda has been voted by Team Wanderlust as the most beautiful pagoda in the world.[43,44]

UP AGAINST A FUTURE EMPEROR, 546-548

It would be another decade before the Liang dynasty came to an end, to be replaced by the man who the Liang emperor sent to challenge Lý Bí, Chen Baxian. Meanwhile, the Liang emperor was not about to accept a setback in his endeavour to eliminate the threat posed by a southern barbarian who had the audacity to declare himself emperor. As with the case of Zhao Tuo of Nan-yue in the second century BCE, there was only one emperor in imperial China; the others, at best, could call themselves kings and paid tributes to the imperial court but certainly not an emperor. It would be an open challenge to the empire and not to be tolerated.

A year after Lý Bí's declaration of independence, at the beginning of 545, Chen Baxian was ordered south together with the newly appointed *cishi* of Giao Châu, Yang Piao (Dương Phiêu), as the military commander. They met with the cishi of Dingzhou (in Guangxi province), Xiao Bo, at Xijiang (or Xi river) in the vicinity of Guangzhou. Xiao Bo was reluctant to participate in the campaign, but at the urging of Chen Baxian, the army proceeded.[45,46] The record shows the army was to go to Panyu, so it is likely that they sailed from there following the coastal route that Ma Yuan took in 41.[47]

Route of battles – First clash

Figure 46 shows the locations of the battles showing the route that the Liang army took to get to Lý Bí's capital near Hanoi, their final destination. Once arriving at the east coast of north Vietnam in the Gulf of Tonkin, Liang ships would sail up the Red river estuaries, or across from the Luộc or perhaps the Trà Lý river. All three routes meet at a river intersection near Chu Diên (Hưng Yên), and that is the most likely place where Lý Bí decided to face them.

In July of 545, they arrived and met Lý Bí's forces of 30,000 at Chu Diên.[48] There is not much information about the battle, but it must have been a major clash of arms; typical forces employed against Linyi at the time which counted only to around 10,000. Lý Bí lost the battle and was forced to retreat upstream.

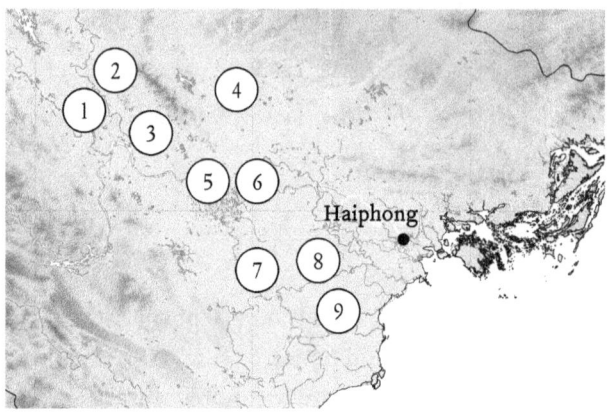

Figure 46 – Key locations during the reign of Lý Bí.
1. Văn Lương, 2. Tứ Yên, 3. Yên Lạc, 4. Tiên Phong, 5. Trấn Quốc pagoda,
6. Luy Lâu, 7. Hưng Yên, 8. Luộc river, 9. Trà Lý river. Haiphong (Hải Phòng).

The second and third battle

Lý Bí retreated to the mouth of the Tô Lịch river, where he built a wooden boom, a line of floating timbers across the river, to stop Chen's ships.[49] His forces still numbered thousands, but they were unable to slow down the advance of Chen's army and were driven towards Gia Ninh near where three rivers – Đà, Lô and Thao (Hồng) – meet.[50]

According to local history, general Phạm Tu died at the battle of Tô Lịch river mouth, but the Gia Ninh fort proved a more difficult obstacle for the

Liang army.⁵¹ They surrounded it and with a combined assault from Chen Baxian and Yang Piao forces, captured it in February 546, nine months after their ships arrived at the estuary of the Red river.

Lý Bí proved himself a survivor; he and others escaped to the cave at Khuất Lão, at Văn Lương commune, Tam Nông district in Phú Thọ province, further upstream.⁵²

Battle at lake Điển Triệt

From the cave, he sought support from the Lao tribesmen, gathered his scattered forces and raised an army of 20,000 men. Seven months later, in the autumn of 546, they moved from Khuất Lão, presumably by an overland route, to camp at lake Điển Triệt in Tứ Yên commune by the east bank of Lô river, some 125 kilometres northeast of Hanoi. They built a large number of boats which almost filled the whole lake. The stage was set for a final showdown with Liang troops, who had moved up the Red and Lô rivers from Gia Ninh citadel, which they captured early in the year, to face Lý Bí.

Liang troops occupied the lake entrance and watched the construction of the boats with dread; by then they had already campaigned for nearly 16 months of hard fighting and were exhausted. However, Chen Baxian had none of it; he told them in blunt terms that they were fighting deep in the heart of enemy territory without any support, and if they did not win, they could not hope to survive. Besides, Lý Bí's forces repeatedly fled, local support of his cause was not strong, and the tribesmen were ill-disciplined and unreliable, so they must fight to the death and take their chances.⁵³

His generals were silent, and did not respond but that night, the rain fell heavily, and the river level rose by seven *chi* (around 2.1 m), water was pouring into the lake. At Chen's command, Liang ships rushed into it along with the flow; his troops yelled, beat the drums and generally made a lot of threatening noises. Lý Bí's forces were caught unprepared in the commotion and scattered; Tinh Thiều, the chief civil official, died during the battle.⁵⁴

Lý Bí escaped once again to Khuất Lão but was killed by Lao tribesmen. His head was sent to the capital, according to Chinese sources.⁵⁵ However, Vietnamese sources record that he died from illness two years after the disaster at lake Điển Triệt.⁵⁶ In any event, the war continued until the Liang army was driven out in 550.

Some Vietnamese historians suggest it was bad luck that Lý Bí lost; others believe he should have been more aggressive. Some suggest he was fighting a clever war by a tactical withdrawal up the Red river to draw the

Liang army deeper into the hinterland.⁵⁷,⁵⁸ After Lý Bí died, his successor, Triệu Quang Phục, adopted a hit-and-run, war prolonging strategy, so perhaps Lý Bí did make a tactical withdrawal after all.

Despite his defeat, in Vietnamese history, Lý Bí is considered the second sovereign after the Trưng sisters and much revered. Unlike the sisters' rebellion, the reign of Lý Bí and his successors lasted nearly 60 years, from 544 to 602. It was long enough to leave behind an impression on the local people of what is possible despite centuries under imperial rule.

Today there are at least 20 temples dedicated to Lý Bí in north Vietnam, one near Khuất Lão.⁵⁹

11.2 – King of the Night Marsh

Two of Lý Bí's three original comrades died during the battles in 545/546, but there is no information on the fate of the third, Great Master Triệu Túc, who was instrumental in the success of the rebellion. History records that before he died in 548, Lý Bí handed over the military command to Triệu Túc's son, Triệu Quang Phục, who went on to prove his family's military prowess by driving out the Liang, and recaptured the provincial capital at Long Biên in 550.

Chinese works do not mention Triệu Quang Phục, and what we know about him is from Vietnamese sources.⁶⁰ We learn Lý Bí died in Khuất Lão cave but the war against the Liang continued, from a marsh named Dạ Trạch, some 120 kilometres downstream in Chu Diên district on the eastern bank of the Red river (Figure 49).⁶¹ Quang Phục was a native of the area, from where he gathered the remains of Lý Bí's soldiers and assembled an army 20,000 strong. He took full advantage of the inaccessibility of the marsh, adopted what we now know as guerrilla warfare tactics, and avoided any frontal confrontation which proved disastrous in previous years.

During the day, Triệu Quang Phục's soldiers left no sign of smoke nor fires from the marsh, but at night, they would come out in small boats, kill and capture many Liang troops, and take food. Chen Baxian attacked Quang Phục several times at the marsh but did not get very far; he was recorded to lament: *"In the past, this place was a one-night marsh to fly to heaven, now it is a one-night marsh to rob people"*.⁶²,⁶³ In 548, on hearing the news of Lý Bí's death, Quang Phục declared himself Triệu Việt Vương (Triệu, King of the Việt) in 549. At the time, China was in turmoil with the Hou Jing rebellion; the Liang dynasty was in disarray, so Chen Baxian was recalled to the north sometime around 548 to rescue the emperor. He left the command to a general, Yang Zhan, who could be a relative of Yang Piao. Quang Phục seized the opportunity, moved out of the marsh, smashed Liang camps, killed Zhan and entered the provincial capital of Long Biên in 550; the remnants of the Liang army escaped back north.[64,65]

The kingdom of Vạn Xuân survived under Triệu Quang Phục at least for another 20 years.

THE MARSH OF DẠ TRẠCH – THE FIRST GUERRILLA

The marsh of Dạ Trạch occupies a special place in Vietnamese history; up to that time, battles between opposing armies in the country had been set pieces on water or land. The prolonged, hit-and-run, attritionary guerrilla warfare from inaccessible locations was a new development. In the centuries to come, the Vietnamese learned from this experience and applied the tactic again and again against overwhelming foes.[66]

The marsh was an unforgiving place, described in SKTT as follows:

"The marsh was at Chu Diên prefecture; it is not known how many miles its perimeter was, the trees were overgrown, the land covered with thick bushes. There was a high habitable ground in the centre surrounded by the four swampy sides; it was difficult for people and horses to get to except by small canoes pushed along by poles over the water [thick with] grass. But if one did not know the way, one would not know where to go, and if one fell into the water, one would be bitten by poisonous snakes."[67]

Legend has it that the marsh was created by one of the Vietnamese four immortals: the husband and wife of Chử Đồng Tử and Tiên Dung as they ascended to heaven.[68] Chử Đồng Tử returned in the form of a golden dragon, and helped Triệu Quang Phục by giving him a claw, told him to wear it on his helmet; and with that; he could defeat the enemy.[69,70] The comment related to *"fly to heaven"* is a reference to this story.

Sadly, the marsh has been mostly drained, replaced by small chicken farms, vegetable plots, and commercial and residential areas. There is not much to see (Figure 47) except for the recently constructed temple for Triệu Quang Phục and the Dạ Trạch temple for Chử Đồng Tử (Figure 48).

Figure 47 – A very small area in the vicinity of the Dạ Trạch marsh.[71]

Figure 48 – Buildings at the Dạ Trạch temple for Chử Đồng Tử.[72]

THE BETRAYAL

The authors of SKTT are scornful of Lý Phật Tử, the third character in this story: [73]

> *"The king* [Lý Phật Tử] *used deceitful techniques to seize the kingdom but surrendered readily at the shadow of the enemy, these acts, before and after, were not righteous."*

Đào Lang Vương

While Triệu Quang Phục was fighting a guerrilla war from Dạ Trạch marsh, Lý Bí's brother, Lý Thiên Bảo, and a relative named Lý Phật Tử fled to Cửu Chân (Thanh Hóa) with 30,000 men. Chen Baxian followed and defeated them, but Thiên Bảo survived. He gathered the remnants of his army and escaped to the Di Lao region near the border of Ai Lao. There, he found a cave called Dã Năng upstream of the Đào Giang river, set up camp, established a kingdom, and proclaimed himself as Đào Lang Vương (the king of Đào Lang). CM suggests Di Lao is in northern Lao and that Ai Lao is in Yunnan province of China; no one has been able to locate the cave and the river Đào Giang[74,75]

While CM and SKTT record that Lý Thiên Bảo went south to Cửu Chân. I think it is unlikely since, from their last position at Khuất Lão cave in Tam Nông district, it would be more logical for them to escape west to the mountains, headed toward Sơn La, and northern Lao by an overland route or by boats on the Đà river, rather than to go north to Lào Cai (to Ai Lao) or south to Thanh Hóa. The mountain route would make it more difficult for the Liang army to follow. In any event, Chen Baxian must have decided to leave them alone, and the small kingdom of Đào Lang lasted for nearly ten years to 555 when Lý Thiên Bảo died.

Civil war

After Lý Thiên Bảo died, his kinsman, Lý Phật Tử became the new king of Đào Lang, and two years later in 557, Phật Tử led his army east to challenge Triệu Quang Phục at Thái Bình prefecture.[76] By now, the last of Liang troops had long left, and Quang Phục had been the king of the Việt for ten years. They fought each other on five occasions, and ended up in a stalemate. Phật Tử thought Quang Phục had magic so he withdrew, sought reconciliation, and pledged for peace. Quang Phục did not want to fight Lý

Phật Tử to the bitter end because he considered Phật Tử a member of the Lý family. So, he agreed to divide the kingdom whereby he would rule from Long Biên, Vũ Ninh region, east of the Red river, and Phật Tử would reign at Ô Diên, west of the Red river. Ô Diên is now at the commune of Hạ Mỗ, Đan Phượng district, upstream from where the kingdom partition was at the shore of Quân Thần, at the two communes of Thượng Cát, Hà Cát of Từ Liêm district in Hanoi.

Lý Phật Tử then offered his son's hand (Nhã Lang) in marriage to Quang Phục's daughter, Cảo Nương. However, Nhã Lang went on to betray his wife's trust by swapping the magic claw on Quang Phục's helmet with an ordinary claw.[77] With the magic claw in his possession, sometime in 571, Lý Phật Tử broke his pledge and attacked Quang Phục. The latter was easily defeated as he no longer had the magic claw to help him.[78] He and his daughter fled to Đại Nha, at the estuary of the Đáy river, and committed suicide there.[79,80]

11.3 – The Later Lý Nam Đế - facing the wrong way

A PEACEFUL REIGN

With Triệu Quang Phục defeated, Lý Phật Tử proclaimed himself as Lý Nam Đế (Lý, Emperor of the South) in 571. He is known as the Later Lý Nam Đế to distinguish him from his kinsman, Lý Bí, as the Former Lý Nam Đế. Figure 49 shows key locations under the reign of Lý Phật Tử.
It had taken him 30 years since he joined Lý Bí as a young boy in 541 to become the emperor of the realm. It must have been a long struggle for him to get there; half of that time was spent in the highland as the king of Đào Lang and the other half on the plain after he left the mountains in 557.[81]
By all accounts, Phật Tử had a relatively peaceful reign, free from interference from the north for around 30 years.

China was in turmoil at the end of the sixth century from the time Chen Baxian became the emperor of the Chen dynasty in 557, but he ruled for barely two years, and his descendants could not hold the dynasty together after his death. They eventually fell to the Sui dynasty (581-618) in 589, which united China for the first time since the Jin dynasty (266-420).

THE EMPIRE CAME SOUTH

Now that Sui had successfully conquered the northern territories, they began to look south. Giao Châu and Guangzhou had been part of the Chinese realm for so long, and the new dynasty was not about to leave the region outside imperial rule. Even under the short-lived Chen dynasty, the court sent messengers, officials and expeditions to Giao Chỉ to maintain contacts and trades, so both Triệu Quang Phục and Lý Phật Tử had dealings with the northern court during their reigns.[82]

As of 590, Sui annal records Lý Phật Tử as one of ten remaining rebels who must be brought under imperial rule; three of these men claimed "Sons of Heaven" with their courts, and seven claimed "Great Governor-General".[83] But Sui was preoccupied, and Lý Phật Tử maintained a cordial relationship with Ling Huxi, the Sui official responsible for southern China, based in Guizhou of Guangxi province. Lý Phật Tử managed to stay out of the imperial glare for ten years until 601. That year, Ling Huxi forwarded an imperial summons requiring Lý Phật Tử to present himself at the Sui court, a Chinese imperial tradition to ensure loyalty and compliance of vassal states. Lý Phật Tử refused meanwhile, someone in court accused Ling Huxi of taking bribes from Phật Tử – so Huxi was promptly arrested and died en route north.[84]

The die was cast for the invasion of Giao Chỉ, Lý Phật Tử knew war was coming, and he prepared for it by moving his main forces into the ancient citadel of Cổ Loa, north of Hanoi, leaving his top general Lý Phổ Đỉnh to guard his capital at Ô Diên (Hạ Mỗ) in the prefecture of Phong Châu and his nephew Lý Đại Quyền to defend Long Biên.[85,86] Judging from this disposition, it would appear Phật Tử was expecting the invasion to come from the north-east via the traditional route of Lạng Sơn and/or from the south-east by the Red river.

COMING FROM THE REAR

Events did not turn out as Phật Tử expected; in 602, the Sui army under the command of Liu Fang marched south on a completely different route via Yunnan province and entered Giao Chỉ in the north-west direction while Phật Tử was looking the other way. After Liu Fang set out from the Sui capital of Chang'an (modern Xi'an), he took the western route via Sichuan, which he may have been familiar. He once served there as the *cishi* of Guazhou in Gansu province, north of Sichuan. His army counted 27 battalions, a force of 100,000 in total, but by the time they arrived at Chuxiong in Yunnan, some 1,600 kilometres south, many of his troops had died from illness and fatigue.[87,88] They may have been on the march for over four months.[89] The senior civil official fell ill and could not proceed, but Liu Fang, anxious to reach Giao Chỉ before Phật Tử learned of his campaign, left the bulk of his army behind and took with him his best troops.

They crossed the border into north Vietnam sometime in 603. They quickly overwhelmed a frontier fort of Phật Tử forces of 2,000 men at Đỗ Long Mountain, which Maspero located at Dulongzhen, of Maguan prefecture in Yunnan province near Hà Giang on the Lô river.[90,91] They most likely continued down the river, came out at Bạch Hạc, and arrived at Phật Tử's first stronghold at Hạ Mỗ. Liu Fang paused and offered Lý Phật Tử a chance to surrender. Unprepared to face an assault from an unexpected quarter, Lý Phật Tử accepted and was taken back to Xi'an where he died.[92]

His advisors and generals were not so fortunate; they were considered *"deceitful and cruel"* and were all beheaded.[93]

Around two years later, in 605, Liu Fang led an expedition against Linyi and destroyed its capital; this event is described in Chapter 6.

THE LEGACY

One would never know why Lý Phật Tử gave up so easily why nearly 60 years earlier, back in 545, his kinsman held out against Liang forces for over a year. The surrender was also difficult to fathom, particularly when, despite the surprise element, Liu Fang did not arrive with all his battalions. I could only speculate that Liu Fang may have made a good offer to Lý Phật Tử, possibly including a safe passage for him and his family. By 603, Phật Tử was likely an older man, having ruled for 32 years and perhaps no longer wanted to fight. Later Vietnamese historians were scathing of Lý Phật Tử: *"The king was cowardly, but among contemporary civil ministers and military generals, no one ever said a word, as if there were no people in the country"*.[94]

Other recent Vietnamese historians were more sympathetic, portrayed several fierce battles between Liu Fang and Lý Phật Tử forces around Cổ Loa citadel until the latter was overwhelmed by a more superior Sui army.[95]

In a touch of irony, the local people at the estuary of the Đáy river built a temple for Lý Phật Tử at Tiểu Nha, opposite the temple for Triệu Quang Phục, his nemesis, at Đại Nha (Nghĩa Hưng district) where he died.[96]

Lý Bí, Triệu Quang Phục and Lý Phật Tử between themselves ruled ancient Vietnam for nearly 60 years and occupied a special place among the

Vietnamese with many temples dedicated to them.⁹⁷ Their rule lasted as long as the Nguyễn kings (1802-1858) before the French arrived and nearly twice as long as Chen Baxian's dynasty but sadly, there is not much information about their time other than what recorded in Chinese, and much later, in Vietnamese works. It would be another three centuries before the Vietnamese eventually came out of the imperial orbit, which is the period which I will turn to next.

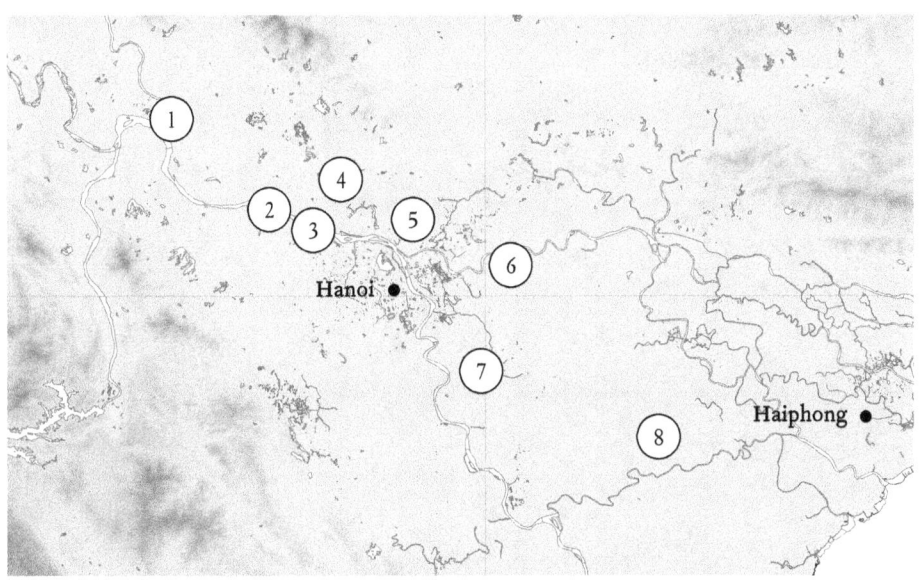

Figure 49 — Key locations under the reign of Lý Phật Tử, not including 2, 4, and 8.
1. Bạch Hạc, 2. Hát Môn, 3. Hạ Mỗ, 4. Hai Bà Trưng Shrine, 5. Cổ Loa citadel, 6. Luy Lâu, 7. Dạ Trạch, 8. Cúc Bồ.

CHAPTER 12

THE BLACK EMPEROR - THE GREAT FATHER AND MOTHER KING OR BỐ CÁI ĐẠI VƯƠNG

SEVENTH AND EIGHTH CENTURIES
GIAO CHÂU IV

STORY TIMELINE: Seventh to eighth centuries.
STORY LOCATION: Northern Vietnam.
KEY CHARACTERS: *Mai Thúc Loan:* the Black Emperor from Nghệ An province, *Yang Si Xu:* a general of the Tang dynasty who defeated the Black Emperor, *The Phùng brothers, Phùng Hưng and Phùng Hải:* led a successful rebellion, *Gao Zheng-ping:* the governor of An Nam who died when under siege by the Phùng brothers, *Zhao Zhang:* protectorate general of An Nam who returned the rule of Tang.
LOCATIONS OF INTEREST: Mai Thúc Loan temple, Nghệ An province. Phùng Hưng temple, Đường Lâm, Sơn Tây, Hanoi. Phùng Hưng tomb, Hanoi.

Chapter summary

The man who defeated Lý Bí went on to found the brief Chen dynasty of 557-589. It was overtaken by the Sui dynasty, which turned out just as short-lived: 581-618. Sui was replaced by a new dynasty, Tang (618-906).

Barring two short interregnums, the Northern Rule period by the Tang dynasty lasted nearly 300 years, leaving a lasting impact on Vietnamese history and culture. During these centuries, north of Ngang pass, Vietnam was deeply embedded in imperial Tang administration as one of the six major protectorates at the periphery of the empire.

Under Tang, Vietnam was part of the Protectorate of Annan (Pacified South, Vietnamese An Nam); the other major protectorates are Andong (Pacified East) on the Korean border; Anxi (Pacified West) on the Tibetan region, Anbei (Pacified North) in Mongolia, Chanyu, west of contemporary Beijing and Beiting in Xinjiang province.

Annan Protectorate territory covers a larger region than Giao Châu under previous dynasties; it includes north and central Vietnam and parts of Guangxi province.[1] There were many changes to Annan Protectorate over the centuries, but effectively, the Tang dynasty only ruled the land north of Ngang pass.

What are these two short interregnums? One was caused by an uprising in the middle of the eighth century. It was led by a man history known as the Black Emperor on account of his dark skin. What is interesting about him is that he somehow managed to form an alliance with Zhenla, Linyi, and Chin-lin – a kingdom in the Malay Peninsula – in his rebellion against Tang, given that the event happened around Nghệ An province, a long way north from any of these kingdoms. Tragically, the uprising did not end well; it happened when the Tang dynasty was at its peak (713-741) – considered one of the golden ages of Chinese history – and the man sent to suppress the rebellion had established himself as one of the most brutal and effective commanders of the empire.

Tang sent a force of 100,000 and caught the Black Emperor unprepared; he was killed with his followers, their bodies piled up to form a huge mound. A massacre was so terrible that the local people have remembered it to this day, centuries later, when they hold the annual ceremony in remembrance of the dead.

One can come to this ceremony, visit the quiet tomb and temple of the Black Emperor (Figure 50). His name, Mai Thúc Loan or Mai Hắc Đế, has been etched into the collective memory of the Vietnamese, with many streets named after him in cities and towns across the whole country.

The second half of the eighth century marked the slow decline of the Tang dynasty; the empire was in turmoil, and An Nam was under repeated raids by pirates from Java. During this time of unrest, two brothers from the north-west of Hanoi formed an army and began to provide protection for the local people. The brothers, the Phùng, were very strong, reputedly able to wrestle a water buffalo and lift six tons of rocks. They were the Vietnamese Atlas and remained so until this day.

They gained control of An Nam by besieging the provincial capital until the Tang commander died from an acute anxiety attack. The older brother ruled for seven years, but his son, who succeeded him, was persuaded to surrender by the next Tang protectorate general. The Vietnamese remember Phùng Hưng as The Great Father and Mother King or *Bố Cái Đại Vương*.

12.1 – The Black Emperor - Mai Thúc Loan and the Hoan Châu Uprising

EARLY LIFE

After Lý Phật Tử's surrender and the arrival of Tang troops at the beginning of the seventh century, no significant event in An Nam was recorded until 687, when a rebellion broke out. It was led by Lý Tự Tiên, the head of the Lý people, over the doubling of taxation by the *dudu*, Liu Yanyou. I do not know if these Lý's were related to Lý Bí or Lý Phật Tử, but in any event, Liu Yanyou killed Lý Tự Tiên. Đinh Kiến, a compatriot of Lý Tự Tiên, then led the rest of the Lý to besiege and ransack the small Tử Thành at Hanoi and put Liu Yanyou to death. However, the rebellion did not last and was suppressed soon after by a Tang major from Guizhou.[2]

Over the next 30 years, Tang rule continued with its oppressive and exploitative policies until a massive rebellion led, this time, by a man of humble origin from the southern frontier of the empire by the name of Mai Thúc Loan in 713 (or 722 by other sources). Mai Thúc Loan grew up in a small coastal village of Mai Phụ, Lộc Hà district, just north of Hà Tĩnh city close to the estuary of the Hạ Vang river. The people in the village traditionally made salt, and most have dark skin from continually being exposed to the sun.[3]

According to local folklore, his mother was unmarried when he was born. Treated as a social pariah, she fled the village and finally settled at Nam Thái commune, Nam Đàn district of Nghệ An province, a remote inland place some 75 kilometres north-west of Mai Phụ.

His mother died when he was ten years old; he survived by working as a labourer, gathering firewood and oxen grazing. However, according to another source, he was looked after by his father's friend and became a son-in-law; his family became wealthy, and a focal point for the gathering of the local elites. Chinese sources referred to him as a tribal leader and a local chieftain.[4] I am inclined to believe he was someone with a significant social standing, judging from the scale of the rebellion and the alliance he formed with foreign kingdoms. An achievement that would have been very difficult if he were just a labourer, albeit a physically strong one – apparently, he had a tiger head, dragon eyes, gibbon arms – and was a fearless, multi-talented person.[5]

THE ALLIANCE

Sometime between 713 and 722, Mai Thúc Loan gathered a force of 400,000 from 32 prefectures in Giao Châu, including contingents from the kingdoms of Linyi, Zhenla and Chin-lin (literally mean "Frontier of Gold"), which may be placed in either Lower Burma or the Malay Peninsula. I would suggest the Malay Peninsula in relation to the history of Funan (Chapter 9).[6] Zhenla is likely Land Zhenla. I had made this assessment based on an event, some four centuries later, in 1150, when Zhenla invaded Nghệ An. SKTT records the expedition was abandoned as most soldiers died from breathing poisonous vapour when they arrived at Mount Vụ Thấp (Vũ Quang of Hà Tĩnh province), and the weather was hot and humid. The route they took was likely along what is now AH15 across the Laos-Vietnam border at the Nam Phao International Checkpoint. The army of Land Zhenla may have taken the same route to join the Black Emperor.

In any case, his army promptly overwhelmed Tang local forces at the southern prefectures of Hoan Châu (which included the place of his birth Hà Tĩnh and the place of his adulthood, Nghệ An), threatened the protectorate capital at Tống Bình (Hanoi) and forced the *duhu*, Guang Chu-Ke to flee north.

The rebellion came to be known by the Vietnamese as the Hoan Châu uprising. Mai Thúc Loan then declared himself as Mai Hắc Đế (Mai, the Black Emperor), returned to his hometown in the valley along Cả (or Lam) river in Nghệ An province, and established his capital at Vạn An (meaning ten thousand safety). Today, there are few remains of this citadel but one can visit his tomb and temple at Vân Diên commune, Nam Đàn district, Nghệ An province (Figure 50). His mother's tomb is around 4 kilometres northwest at Tóc Nhung, Nam Thái commune.

Figure 50 – The temple and tomb of the Black Emperor Mai Hắc Đế.[7]

12.2 – *The Imperial Consort, the lychees and other historical revisions*

THE LYCHEES

For many years, the common explanation for the uprising was that Mai Thúc Loan incited his fellow labourers, lychee carriers doing corvée, to revolt. These lychees were to be taken back to the imperial capital at Chang'an, some 2,500 kilometres north, to satisfy the appetite of the Imperial Consort, Yang Guifei.

This explanation was debunked by historians who noted that Yang Guifei was barely three years old when the uprising was suppressed. Furthermore, lychees would lose their colour and taste after four to five days and thus not edible when they reached the imperial capital months later.

SIZE OF THE REBELLION

Historians also have doubts about the 32 prefectures that joined Mai Thúc Loan when there were only 12 in the whole of An Nam. Similarly, 400,000 rebels under his banner is a vast number; he could not possibly gather that many. They suggest Tang generals deliberately exaggerated these numbers in their report to the emperor to inflate their accomplishments and receive a higher reward.[8] Other sources quote a lesser number, but still a considerable figure, of 300,000.[9]

I agree that these numbers are too high; my study so far has indicated that typical numbers for military forces at the time and place are around ten or twenty thousand. With the additional troops from three foreign countries, Mai Thúc Loan could raise an army of thirty to fifty thousand but not 400,000. Besides, such a large army could not be vanquished so quickly as the event unfolded. I further note that the total number of enlisted troops in the entire Tang armies in 742 is estimated at 500,000.[10] Perhaps it was a mistake, and the figure should read only 40,000.

DURATION

In recent years, Vietnamese historians have also argued that the year of the rebellion should be 713, not 722 as traditionally recorded, and thus the uprising lasted 10 years, not one. They point out that it is only four to five months from July or August when the rebellion broke out until it was suppressed at the end of 722. This would be too short for the news of the rebellion to reach the imperial capital and for the empire to mobilise troops to send south.[11] They also note that VDUL mentions 10 years as the period that the Black Emperor ruled.[12]

My study has indicated that previous campaigns by northern rulers to suppress uprisings in Vietnam would take a lot longer simply due to the distance involved. However, the rebellion occurred during the reign of Emperor Xuanzong (712-756), considered the height of the Tang dynasty, so it is possible Tang could mobilise forces quickly during that time. It should be noted that the *duhu*, Guang Chu-ke, who fled north after the rebellion, returned with imperial troops. While he may have waited for 10 years to return; it would seem unlikely that a person who wanted revenge would have the patience to wait that long, so I support a shorter time frame for the Black Emperor's uprisings.

12.3 – A mound of dead bodies

Whatever the case, the empire mobilised a force 100,000 strong under the command of Yang Si Xu, an imperial official, a eunuch, and the former *duhu*, Guang Chu-Ke. The army embarked on the route that Ma Yuan took in 42 and caught Mai Thúc Loan unprepared. He was killed, and together with his followers, their dead bodies were piled up to form a huge mound. Today, every year, in the middle of the seventh lunar month the shopkeepers and market stall holders at Sa Nam market in Nghệ An province hold a ceremony in their memory. The offered food and fruits are then given to the poor and beggars.[13,14]

The uprising itself is described in Jiu Tang shu as follows:

> *"At the beginning of the Kāiyuán reign (713-741), the leader of Annan, Mei Xuancheng [Mai Thúc Loan], rebelled and called himself "The Black Emperor" and conspired with Linyi, Zhenla countries, threatened Annan capital. Si Xu was sent to quell him. Arriving at Lĩnh Nam [the region south of the Wuling mountains].[15] He recruited more than 100,000 soldiers and horses and took Fubo's [Ma Yuan] old path to advance and surprised [the Black Emperor]. Xuancheng heard the arrival of [Si xu] soldiers and became apprehensive, unable to devise any [defensive] tactics. [Tang] Troops captured or killed all their party at the battlefield, piled up the dead bodies and withdrew".*[16,17]

The biography of Yang Si Xu painted a ruthless and bloodthirsty man, not only in the battle against the Black Emperor but also in the suppression of other uprisings in the southern region of the empire in the years that followed. In 724, he beheaded 30,000 rebels in one uprising. He went on to cut the head off another 3,000 Lao tribesmen and buried 60,000 Man (barbarians) alive. His biography records he ordered the facial skin of prisoners peeled off to reveal the skull and showed the skin to others. His generals and soldiers were so scared, dared not look, and thus, he achieved results.[18,19]

12.4 – The Great Father and Mother King or Bố Cái Đại Vương

VDUL describes Phùng Hưng as:

> *"Metropolitan Lord Phùng was an extraordinary man, of course, he would encounter extraordinary circumstances, but the extraordinary circumstances were there just to treat the extraordinary man. Watch his ability to catch tigers when wanted, he could swallow the star of Ngâu, everyone in the prefecture admired him; if he did not have talents beyond people of the time, how could he be like that?"* [20,21]

The Black Emperor's uprising occurred during the Tang dynasty's golden years under Emperor Xuanzong (712-756). At the end of Xuanzong's reign, the empire was in upheaval due to the An Lushan Rebellion (December 755-February 763), which marked the beginning of the imperial decline.

It is indicated by the high turnover of emperors; over the second half of the eighth century, the Tang dynasty had four emperors compared with one, Xuanzong himself, in the previous 41 years.

ĐƯỜNG LÂM COMMUNE

The slow decline of Tang also affected An Nam as it was roiled from raids by the Kun Lun and She Po pirates (believed to come from Java) in 767 and local rebellions in 782.[22] Against this backdrop, Phùng Hưng and Phùng Hải, two brothers from a wealthy family at Đường Lâm commune, gained control of their surrounding villages, assembled a strong force, surrounded La Thành and ruled An Nam.

Đường Lâm is some 45 kilometres north-west of Hanoi on the southern bank of the Red river. It is the region the legendary Hùng kings governed from the seventh to the second century BCE, where the Trưng sisters first raised their banners against the Han in the early years of the first century and to where Lý Bí retreated in the sixth century.

VIETNAMESE ATLAS

According to SKTT, Phùng Hưng came from a wealthy and prestigious family; his family had held the hereditary title of *Quan Lang* or local chieftain/administrator of the village for generations. Phùng Hưng was very strong, able to wrestle a water buffalo and catch a tiger. His brother Phùng Hải was just as strong: he could carry nearly 6,000 kilograms of rocks over 5 kilometres.[23] The local tribespeople of Di and Lạo were in awe of the brothers. Their father, Phùng Hạp Khanh, apparently joined the Black Emperor in the uprising of 713.[24]

The reign of Emperor Daizong in the Dali era (766-779) was at a time of unrest. Famed for their strength, the Phùng brothers and their band of followers gained widespread support from the neighbouring villages. Phùng Hưng, "ambition satisfied", changed his name to "Great Venerable" and his brother also changed his name to "Great Strength". They claimed themselves as "Metropolitan Lord" and "Metropolitan Guardian" respectively.[25] On the advice of Đỗ Anh Luân (Hàn), a fellow villager, the two brothers and their militia began to patrol not only Đường Lâm and nearby villages but also expanded to the prefectures of Phong, and Trường – covering the western and southern regions of north Vietnam.[26] All people there readily followed them, and their reputation rose.

DEATH FROM ACUTE ANXIETY

The failed rebellion in 782 may have spurred them on, particularly when one of the leaders of that rebellion was the *cishi* of Phong Châu, where the brothers' village is located. Following that event, the brothers let it be known that they wanted to capture the protectorate capital of La Thành.[27] Their cause was also helped by the heavy taxation regime of the *jiedushi*, Gao Zheng-ping. As a military official who helped Zhang Bo-yi fight off the pirates in 767, Gao Zheng-ping certainly had experience in warfare. He was ready for war. The two adversaries fought back and forth without a clear outcome until Đỗ Anh Luân advised the brothers to encircle La Thành completely. They entered it without much bloodshed after Gao Zheng-ping – suffering from acute anxiety because of the blockade – died.

A SEVEN-YEAR REIGN

Phùng Hưng ruled for seven years; upon his death, the people wanted his brother Phùng Hải to succeed him, but the assistant, Bồ Phá Cần, was dead against it. Phá Cần was very brave and incredibly strong, reputedly could move mountains; he wanted Phùng Hưng's son, Phùng An, to be the next king and rallied forces against Phùng Hải. Hải did not want the confrontation, so he left to a cave in the mountain and disappeared.

Phùng An honoured his father with the title *Bố Cái Đại Vương* or The Great Father and Mother King. His reign his reign lasted for barely two years, when the emperor sent a new *jiedushi*, Zhao Zhang in 791 who persuaded Phùng An to surrender peacefully.[28]

A PEACEFUL TRANSFER OF POWER

The Phùng brothers, despite their legendary physical strength, appeared to have gained and lost power peacefully; there was no mound of dead bodies like the Black Emperor nor prolonged fighting like Lý Bí. There was no claim of the emperor's title, merely honoured as the father and mother of the people. Coming down from the hill during the time of unrest to protect the people, perhaps they were not caught in the imperial ambitions of others, and against an overwhelming Tang army (as suggested by other historians) decided to surrender.[29]

Figure 51 – The temple of Phùng Hưng.[34]

Today, one can visit the tomb of Phùng Hưng at Ngõ 2, Giảng Võ Hanoi and a temple dedicated to him at Đường Lâm village (Figure 51), his home village, some 45 kilometres away.[30,31] The tomb is in the middle of a residential area next to a busy street of Hanoi. It appears out of place, but while there, one can light an incense stick and contemplate what it would have been like for Phùng Hưng, over 1,200 years ago, to be buried so far from home.

Today, Vietnamese people remember the brothers who rose against Tang rulers from the ancient land of the Hùng kings and hold them high in their pantheon of heroes.

What became of Zhao Zhang? He stayed in An Nam for 10 years, but after he left, the country was plunged into rebellion and he was recalled. On his second return in 804, everyone was pleased, and the unrest ceased.[32] Zhao Zhang compiled a book called Records of Giao Province (Giao Châu Ký or Jiaozhou Ji), now lost – although some stories were reproduced in VDUL, including that of the Phùng brothers.[33]

CHAPTER 13

SURROUNDED BY RIVERS - A CITY OF LAKES: HANOI, A NATION CAPITAL

GIAO CHÂU V

STORY TIMELINE: Sixth to ninth centuries.
STORY LOCATION: Northern Vietnam.
KEY CHARACTERS: *Lý Bí or the Former Lý Nam Đế:* the emperor who may have first established a base around Hanoi. Subsequent governors, listed below, from the Tang dynasty, built various citadels, which eventually became present-day Hanoi, *Qiu He, Zhang Bo-yi, Zhang Zhou, Wang Shi, Gao Pian.*
LOCATIONS OF INTEREST: The "mountains" of Hanoi. The dykes built by Gao Pian. The archaeological site at 18 Hoàng Diệu St., Hanoi.

Chapter summary

Before the Han army arrived in 111 BCE, the autonomous kingdom of Âu Lạc was ruled from the Cổ Loa citadel. Once Âu Lạc was absorbed into the Han empire, the administration of the region was from Luy Lâu (O), as discussed earlier (Chapter 2).[1] In 142-143, the *cishi* of Giao Chỉ, Zhou Zhang, moved it to Long Biên (or Luy Lâu).

From that time until the middle of the sixth century, for around 400 years, Long Biên remained a major political, religious, and economic capital of northern Vietnam. The brief period of Vietnamese independence in the second half of the sixth century (Chapter 11) saw the capital moved elsewhere, and when the northern rulers returned in the early seventh century during the Sui dynasty, they occupied it briefly and move the capital to Tống Bình, around Hanoi.

Historically, rulers have selected the location of their capitals for many different reasons, among them are easy access to transport and food supplies, easy defence, consideration for the adequacy of existing infrastructure, and last but not least, feng shui or geomancy factors.

I have been unable to find any explanation in historical texts for why the provincial capital was finally moved from Bắc Ninh province to Hanoi, even if the latter was susceptible to flooding. The most likely explanation is that Hanoi – near the Red and Đuống rivers intersection – is a better location for transportation and trades than Long Biên. Whatever the reasons, from the seventh century until the present time, Hanoi has been a relatively continuous power centre of Vietnam with some interruptions in between.[2]

During my research, I have come across the names which often appear in historical records: Tống Bình, Tử Thành, La Thành or An Nam La Thành, and Đại La. I have had many difficulties identifying them, so I will try to decipher these names in this chapter. Tống Bình appears to be a generic name for a location, but the others are specific names of citadels built at different times from the seventh to the ninth centuries. These citadels were close to the Hanoi Flag Tower, built in the 19th century. At the beginning of the 11th century, when Vietnam was ruled by the Vietnamese, Đại La became Thăng Long, but that story will be told in the next volume, so I will not discuss it here.

Today, a traveller can take a leisurely motorbike ride in the early morning around the route that has been once the ramparts of the ancient citadels (Figure 54); climb one of the "Hanoi" mountains (Figure 56), and view the excavation at the heart of these citadels at 18 Hoàng Diệu Street.

I begin this chapter with two maps: one drawn in the 15th century (Figure 52) and the other in the 19th century (Figure 55); by studying these maps, I could identify the approximate locations of Tử Thành, La Thành, and Đại La.

13.1 – Đông Kinh - a 15th-century capital

Over the centuries, the landscape around Hanoi has changed significantly, rivers and lakes were filled in and diverted, and city walls were demolished, but many city features have survived the test of time. I need to study old maps to understand the citadels built from the sixth to the ninth centuries.

TÔ LỊCH RIVER

To my knowledge, the oldest map of the Hanoi area is the map of Đông Kinh, drawn in the 15th century, as shown in Figure 52. It was the capital of the Lê dynasty. On this map, we can see places that have remained unchanged to the present time, such as West Lake (Hồ Tây, 5), the Red river (Nhị Hà, 2), Hoàn Kiếm lake (14), and the Temple of Literature (Quốc Tử Giám, 21). We can also notice where the Đuống river (Thiên Đức Giang, 3) is connected to the Red river at the upper right corner of the map and the entrance to the Tô Lịch river (8) from the Red river by Bạch Mã temple (9, around Chợ Gạo, Nguyễn Siêu Street).[3] From there, the map also shows the Tô Lịch river following the northern side of the city wall to the east at around Bưởi market (not marked on the map) before joining with the Thiên Phù river (28, now filled-in) and turning south outside the west wall of the citadel. It continues to the south (shown in the lower-left corner) and goes off the map. The figures in brackets are those marked in Figure 52.

KIM NGƯU RIVER

The map shows another river, called Kim Ngưu, which forms an arc extended from the eastern corner of the wall by Cửa (gate) Bảo Khánh (22), passes Đàn Nam Giao (Esplanade of Sacrifice to the Heaven and Earth) (17) to the lower right corner of the map. It is connected to a lake, likely Hai Bà Trưng lake (not shown on the map). The river then turns sharp right at around the intersection between Kim Ngưu and Trần Khắc Chân (Ô Đống Mác) streets, flowing southward. It is not clear if the river then flows to the Red river, but

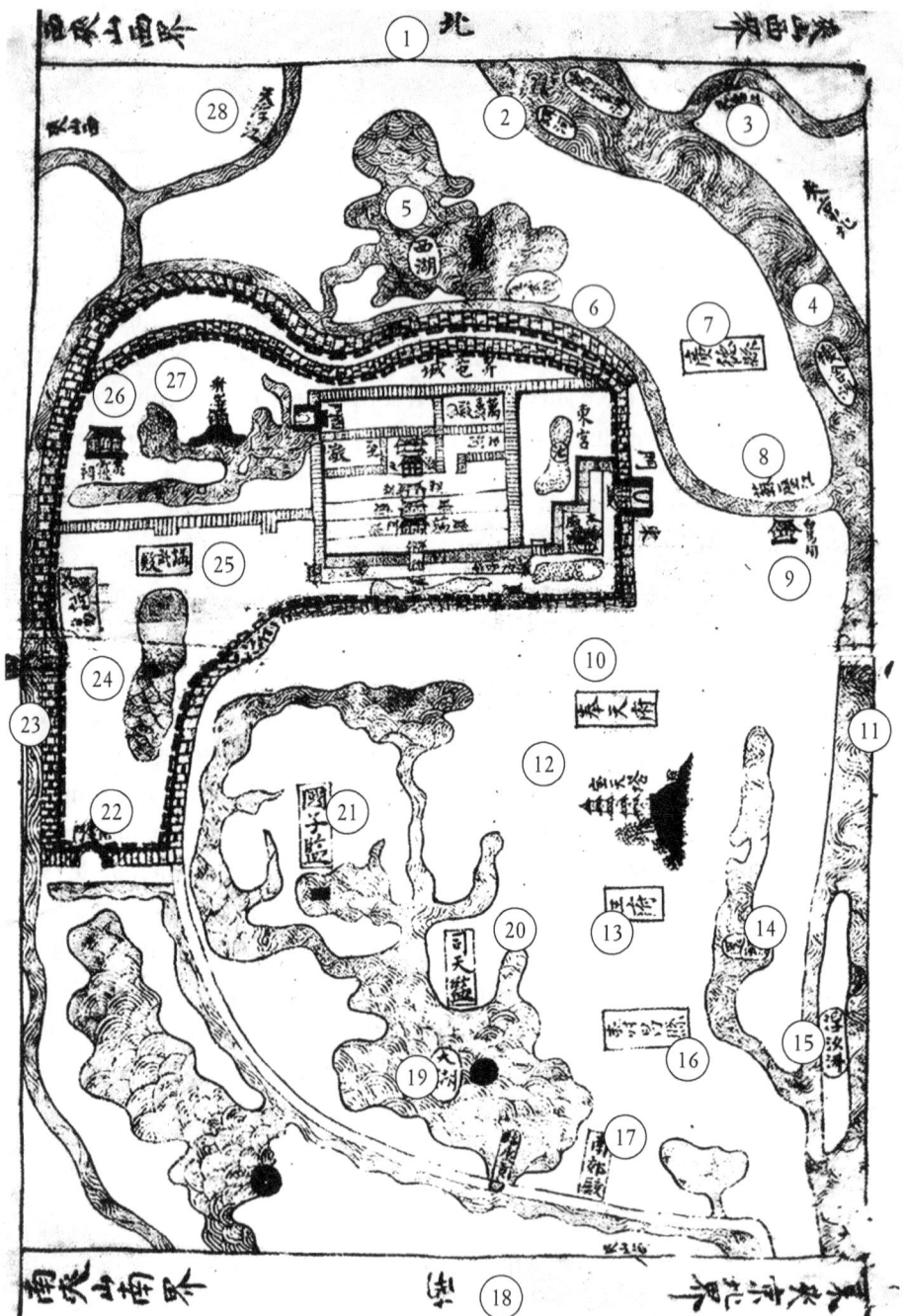

Figure 52 – The map of Đông Kinh

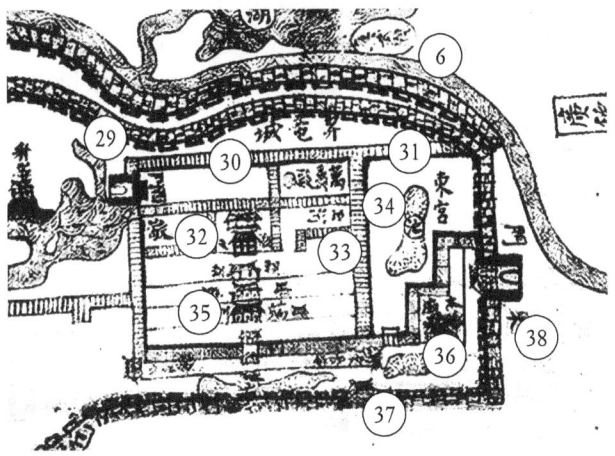

Figure 53 – Details

on the present-day map, there is a canal running along Kim Ngưu street and connecting to lake Yên Sở, linked with the Red river by a canal.

The map shows this river is not connected to the Tô Lịch river but collects its water from Đại Hồ (great lake) (19) and another large lake on the lower-left corner. These lakes are expected to be, from west to east: Thành Công, Đống Đa, Xã Đàn, Ba Mẫu, and Bảy Mẫu respectively. Đàn Nam Giao is now the site of Vincom at 191 Bà Triệu St., east of Bảy Mẫu lake.

Left top: Figure 52 – The map of Đông Kinh (or Trung Đô - the Middle Capital) - 1490.[4]

Keys: 1. *Bắc* = north, 2. *Nhị Hà* = Red river, 3. *Thiên Đức Giang* = Đuống river, 4. *Cơ Xá* = possibly an islet, 5. *Hồ Tây* = West Lake, 6. *Trấn Vũ Quán* = Quán Thánh temple, 7. *Huyện Quảng Đức* = Quảng Đức district, 8. *Sông Tô Lịch* = Tô Lịch river, 9. *Đền Bạch Mã* = Bạch Mã Temple, 10. *Phủ Phụng Thiên* = Phụng Thiên mansion, 11. *Đông* = east, 12. *Tháp Báo Thiên* = Báo Thiên Tower, 13. *Vương Phủ* = Vương's mansion (mansion of a lord), 14. *Hồ Hoàn Kiếm* = Hoàn Kiếm lake, 15. *Bãi Phúc Xá* = another islet, 16. *Huyện Thọ Xương* = Thọ Xương district, 17. *Đàn Nam Giao* = Esplanade of Sacrifice to the Heaven and Earth, 18. *Nam* = south, 19. *Đại Hồ* = great lake, 20. *Khâm Thiên* = Khâm Thiên, 21. *Quốc Tử Giám* = Temple of Literature, 22. *Cửa Bảo Khánh* = Bảo Khánh gate, 23. *Tây* = west, 24. *Hội Thi Đường (or Trường)* = Examination hall (for martial arts and army training), 25. *Điện Giảng Võ* = Giảng Võ palace, 26. *Đền Linh Lang* = Voi Phục temple, 27. *Đền Khán Sơn* = Khán Sơn temple, 28. *Thiên Phù* = Thiên Phù river.

Left bottom: Figure 53 – Details of the Đông Kinh map showing the Inner Wall.

Keys: 6. *Trấn Vũ Quán* = Quán Thánh temple, 29. *Cửa Tây* = west gate, 30. *Cung Vạn Thọ* = Vạn Thọ hall, 31. *Đông Cung* = East Hall, 32. *Kính Thiên* = Kính Thiên palace, 33. *Thần Triều* = Thần Triều, 34. Tri/Hồ Lớn, 35. *Cửa Đoan Môn* = Đoan Môn gate, 36. *Thái Miếu* = Thái Miếu shrine, 37. *Cửa Nam* = south gate, 38. *Cửa Đông* = east gate.

The map also shows what appears to be a road or a dyke following the arc contour of this river. Unfortunately, most of the arc section of Kim Ngưu river has been filled in. This arc is believed to follow La Thành, Xã Đàn, Đại Cồ Việt and Trần Khắc Chân streets.

A CITY OF LAKES

This map also shows many lakes. The builders of Đông Kinh built the walls of the citadel between them and followed the contours of the rivers where they could. The rivers effectively form a moat and the walls provide flood protection; both features also keep the enemies at bay in the time of war.

I have reproduced this 15th-century map in Google Maps, as shown in Figure 54. I aim to fix some of the key locations and dimensions so that the information would help to locate the citadels built between the sixth to the ninth centuries. My study has indicated that all these places were built within the area set out by this map, on the southern bank of Tô Lịch river between Bưởi market on the west and Bạch Mã temple on the east. They were built along a corridor approximately 5 kilometres long in the east-west and 1.5 kilometres wide in the north-south directions, except for a short period when it was north of Tô Lịch river.

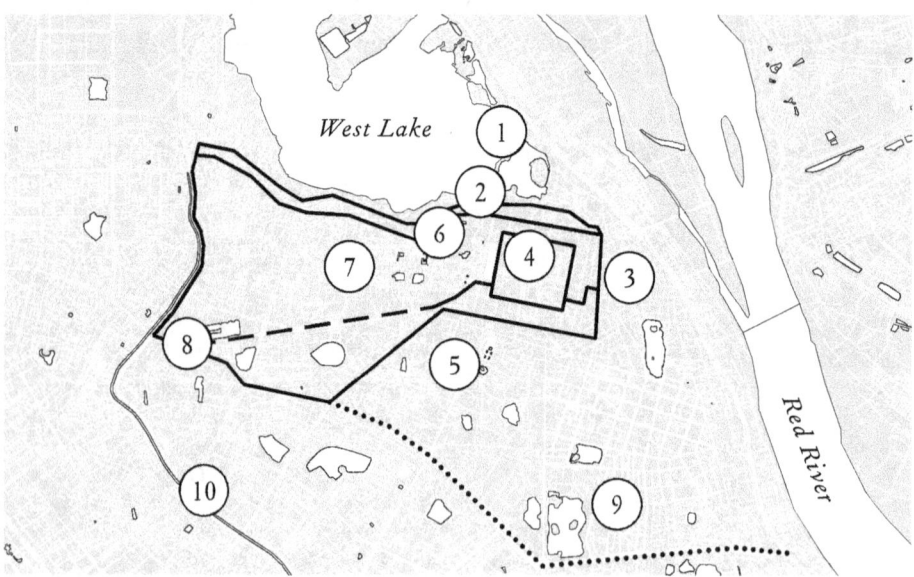

Figure 54 – Outline of the Đông Kinh map.

Left: Figure 54 – Outline of the Đông Kinh map imposed on the map of contemporary Hanoi. The solid line represents the walls, the hyphenated line represents the Dividing Wall, and the dotted line represents a road or a dyke. Keys: 1. Trấn Quốc pagoda, 2. Quán Thánh temple, 3. Bạch Mã temple, 4. Kính Thiên palace, 5. Temple of Literature (Quốc Tử Giám), 6. Núi Sưa, 7. Bát Tháp pagoda, 8. Voi Phục temple. 9. Đàn Nam Giao = Esplanade of Sacrifice to the Heaven and Earth (191 Bà Triệu St.). 10. Tô Lịch river.

13.2 – Hanoi citadel - a 19th-century Vauban-designed fortress

The following map, drawn over three and a half centuries later in 1873, is shown in Figure 55. We could pick out the unchanged natural features such as West Lake (Lac), the Red river (Bô Dê Fl.), and the southern lakes (Etang-Reservoir), which had contracted from the Great Lake (Đại Hồ) over the years. We could also note that Hoàn Kiếm lake (Etang) is near the river bank, but no longer connected to the Red river. The location of the Temple of Literature (Giám Pagode) has not changed, but most of the walls of the citadel under the Lê dynasty citadel has disappeared except for the ruins of the citadel under the Lê dynasty (Ruines de la Citadelle des Lê) in the south-western corner of West Lake.

The map also shows two sections of the ramparts of Hanoi commune (Remparts de la commune de Hanoi); one runs at an approximately forty-five-degree angle which follows the outer wall of Đông Kinh of contemporary Phố Giảng Võ, the other section; shown in the Đông Kinh map as what looks like a dyke, and approximates the routes of La Thành, Xã Đàn, Đại Cồ Việt, Trần Khắc Chân streets to the Red river.

Of interest is the Vauban-designed fortress built by the Nguyễn kings in the 19th century, called the Hanoi citadel, shown in the corner between the West Lake and the Red river where the inner walls of Đông Kinh were. Tragically, the citadel was demolished by the French colonial government in 1894-1897; most of the thick walls were levelled, and the moats were filled in, leaving only the northern gate (Cửa Bắc), Đoan Môn gate, Hanoi Flag Tower and the base of Kính Thiên palace we can still see.[5]

Inside the bastions is a square divided into grids; the square is approximately 4 kilometres in perimeter, with 1 kilometre per side. The north wall is where the north gate currently is; the west, south and east walls follow Hùng Vương, Trần Phú and Lý Nam Đế streets, respectively.[6]

Using these maps as a basis, I can now study the ancient citadels built some 900 years earlier. Before proceeding, I will take a brief detour to discuss citadel terminology in Chinese as they would directly apply to the period.

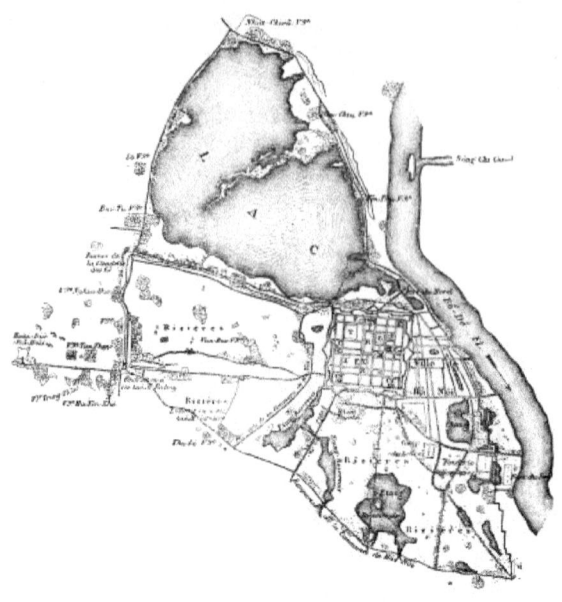

Figure 55 – The map of Hanoi circa 1873.[7] Keys: *Riʒières*: rice fields, *Vge*: village, *Lac*: lake, note *the Ruines de la citadel des Lê*: the ruin of the citadel of the Lê (dynasty), on west side of the *Lac*.

13.3 – Of Thành and Zheng

Thành is a Vietnamese translation of the Chinese term, *ʒheng* which denotes a defensive or fortified wall. For example, *Zi* means a child, so a small wall is *Zi ʒheng*, literally a child wall. It is translated into Vietnamese as Tử Thành, which also means an inner-city.[8] Similarly, *Zijin ʒheng* means Purple Forbidden City: *Zi* means purple and *Jin* forbidden. A wall surrounding an outer city is called *Luo ʒheng* (Vietnamese La Thành); a large *Luo ʒheng* is *Daluo ʒheng* (Vietnamese Đại La Thành).[9,10]

Some Vietnamese historians divide the citadel walls into three categories: the outermost walls are Đại La, the middle walls are Hoàng Thành (Imperial Citadel), and the inner walls, Cấm Thành (Forbidden City).[11,12] While it is tempted to compare Cấm Thành with Tử Thành and Hoàng Thành with La Thành, they are not the same. To avoid confusion, I will not use the terms Hoàng Thành and Cấm Thành in this book. However, Tử Thành and La Thành, while descriptive in meaning, have been used as specific names for citadels in historical records, and I will treat them accordingly.[13]

13.4 – Tử Thành citadel

The relocation of the provincial capital from Long Biên to the Hanoi vicinity may have something to do with Lý Bí. His effort to establish a settlement around the Tô Lịch river mouth in 544 may have attracted the attention of Sui officials on the importance of the area. After he was defeated, Vạn Xuân was abandoned as his successors chose to base their capitals elsewhere, Triệu Quang Phục was believed to stay at Long Biên, and Lý Phật Tử started a new capital at Ô Diên (at Hà Mỗ). However, when the Chinese returned under the Sui dynasty, they made sweeping changes to the administration of Giao Châu; from 604, one single Giao Province, including three prefectures of Giao Chỉ, Cửu Chân, and Nhật Nam, was established. In 618, *taishou* Qiu He built a small citadel of 900 *bu* (1,350 m) in perimeter, near the site where Vạn Xuân capital was. The citadel was called Tử Thành.[14]

Like Vạn Xuân, the exact location of this Tử Thành is still unknown. However, in 2002, during the preparation for the construction of the new National Assembly Hall at 18 Hoàng Diệu St., Hanoi, many archaeological remains were discovered in the excavation of the site. Among those found at the lowest layer of 4 metres below the present ground level were tube-shaped roof tiles with a lotus motif and human faces at the end, bricks with swimming crocodiles, bricks with Chinese characters reading "Jiangxi army", foundations, wood pillars, seven wells, and 15 drainage canals. All were dated back to the Sui-Tang period (seventh-ninth centuries).[15,16,17] Jiangxi is a Chinese province north of Guangdong and the Jiangxi army is likely the same unit that fought against the Man tribes during the Nanzhao-An Nam war in the ninth century, as described in Chapter 14.

The excavation site is within the complex of the Imperial Citadel of Thăng Long, a UNESCO World Heritage Site where one can easily spend the whole day viewing the artefacts over 1,000 years of the site's history from the seventh to the 20th centuries. The complex is south of the now filled northern section of the Tô Lịch river along Phan Đình Phùng street. It is located over 1 kilometre from Bạch Mã temple, which confirms the description of its relative location to the Tô Lịch and Red rivers in historical texts, particularly in the Nanzhao-An Nam war.

13.5 – The "mountains" or Núi of Hanoi

Other than archaeological evidence, I am also looking for high ground in the area on the south bank of the now filled Tô Lịch river as possible sites for citadels. I reason those citadel builders would likely select high ground sites to protect themselves against floods and potential attackers.

Figure 56 – Núi Sưa in Hanoi Botanic Garden.[18]

NÚI SƯA

It is not easy to imagine now since Hanoi is on flat terrain, but at one time, it had several mounds, which were eventually flattened over the centuries. However, one of the surviving mounds, called *Núi Sưa* (hill of Sưa, a type of precious wood) gives us some ideas of what these mounds look like. *Núi Sưa* is inside the Hanoi Botanic Garden, 1 kilometre west of the archaeological site (Figure 56).

The temple of Núi Sưa (circa 19th century) is on the far right of the photograph (only the roof is visible), and the signs on the trees show the red Sưa tree on the left and the white Sưa tree on the right.

NÚI NÙNG

The most significant mound is *Núi Nùng* or Núi Long Đỗ or Long Độ, which means the dragon navel, so named because of the presence of a ventilation hole at the top of the mound.[19,20] It was on this high ground that successive Vietnamese dynasties from the 11th to the 15th centuries built a palace and made it the centre of the forbidden city where the king conducted all his important business. Tragically, in 1886, the palace was demolished by the French colonial government to make way for an artillery command.[21,22] Today, one can only see the remains of the steps with two stone dragons built in the 15th century. This Kính Thiên palace was also called Càn Nguyên and Thiên An at different times.[23,24]

Kính Thiên palace is around 180 metres east of the archaeological site at 18 Hoàng Diệu St., which further confirms that Vạn Xuân and Tử Thành citadels were built around here.

NÚI VẠN BẢO, NÚI CUNG, NÚI THÁI HÒA, NÚI VOI, NÚI KHÁN SƠN

Apart from *Núi Sưa* and *Núi Nùng*, there is a group of historical sites 2 kilometres west of the archaeological site at 18 Hoàng Diệu St.[25] These include the 19th-century Bát Tháp (eight towers) pagoda[26] built on *Núi Vạn Bảo;* the eleventh-century Vĩnh Khánh pagoda next to Vĩnh Phúc temple [27] and *Núi Cung* (so named because a palace was built there, also known as *Núi Thái Hòa)*[28] where many artefacts, dated back to the 11th century, were found.[29] Around 300 metres north of *Núi Cung* was another mound named *Núi Voi*, but it is no longer there as it was flattened during the French colonial period to build a beer factory.[30]

Besides Linh Lang temple, the Đông Kinh map also shows another temple called Khán Sơn which was built on *Núi Khán Sơn*; unfortunately, the exact location of this mound is not precise. Some historians suggest it is between the Presidential Palace and the Office of the Central Committee of the Communist Party in the corner of Hùng Vương, Phan Đình Phùng streets and that the Lê kings used to watch the military practices at Giảng Võ from this mound.[31,32,33] However, Giảng Võ palace is believed to be around lake Ngọc Khánh, some 3 kilometres south-west so it would be quite a distance for the king to see anything clearly from there.

13.6 – La Thành citadel

In any event, Tử Thành was ransacked three times, in 687 by a local rebel, Đinh Kiến, again in 722 by the Black Emperor, and the third time in 767 by the Kun Lun and She Po pirates (from Java). [34] Following this last episode, the *jinglueshi*, Zhang Bo-yi (Trương Bá Nghi) decided to abandon Tử Thành and build a larger citadel at a distance of 200 steps (Chinese *bu* or 300 metres) near Tô Lịch river called La Thành.[35]

However, Zhang Bo-yi did not complete it, and La Thành citadel, larger than Tử Thành, was surrounded by a levee of a few *chis* (less than one metre), but after the rebellion by Phùng Hưng in 791, the new *duhu*, Zhao Zhang (Triệu Xương) strengthened the ramparts and in 803, presumably to create more space, some canals inside the citadel were filled in by another *duhu*, Pei Tai (Bùi Thái).[36]

13.7 – Đại La Thành - a citadel with 6.5-metre-tall walls

Pei Tai was driven out of La Thành by a local rebellion that was quickly suppressed. In 808, the new *duhu*, Zhang Zhou (Trương Chu) invested a massive amount of labour and materials in enlarging it to house weaponry plus fast attacking boats. Zhang Zhou was preparing for war against the southern kingdom of Huanwang – the successor to Linyi – and protecting the empire against future rebellions.

This citadel came to be known as Đại La; the perimeter was increased to 2000 *bu* (2,900 metres) or more than twice that of Tử Thành. Two-hundred-and-fifty thousand workers were employed to build it.[37,38]

Zhang Zhou constructed the citadel on the same site as those who went before him, to Zhang Bo-yi unfinished works 41 years earlier. It was abandoned for a brief period after Zhang Zhou until Gao Pian rebuilt it with an even larger perimeter in 866. The same site became the capital of independent Vietnam in the 11th century and was renamed Thăng Long (rising dragon) under the Lý dynasty. Historical works show a continuity of locations from Zhang Bo-yi, Zhang Zhou, and Gao Pian to Lý, Trần, Lê, and Nguyễn dynasties, as evidenced by the archaeological site at 18 Hoàng Diệu St.[39] One could argue the continuity reached as far back as the time of Lý Bí when he built a wooden fort at the mouth of Tô Lịch river in 544.

13.8 – A headquarters north of the river

Around 17 years later, in 825, the *duhu*, Li Yuan-xi, having seen water flowing in the opposite direction outside the citadel's gate, feared that it was a bad omen for rebellion and sought permission from the Tang court to move the protectorate headquarters to the northern bank of the river.[40,41] However, while his new small citadel was constructed, a geomancer told him:

"Your strength is inadequate to build a large citadel, but in 50 years, there will be a person with the surname Gao who will establish a capital and build palaces at that location." [42]

As explained in Appendix 7, this river is the Tô Lịch river. In 1290, SKTT recorded the same phenomenon in the same river during heavy rains.[43]

13.9 – Gao Pian's La Thành - back to where it all started

In 866, the *jiedushi*, Gao Pian, began the reconstruction of La Thành with a perimeter of 3000 *bu* (or 4,500 m), but other references quoted 3,941 *bu*.[44] Gao Pian may have fulfilled the prophecy made by the soothsayer in 825 as his citadel was massive; the height of the wall was nearly 7.8 metres, taller than what Zhang Zhou built.[45] The base of the wall was also 7.8 metres; on top of the wall – on all four sides – he also built a parapet at the edge of the wall at 1.65 metres tall.[46]

AN ANCIENT DYKE

Gao Pian also built a dyke around and outside the citadel of 4,251.6 *bu* (or 6,377 m) at the height of three *bu* (4.5 m) tall and a base of four *bu* (6 m) wide.[47] Where would this dyke be?

By definition, dykes are built along the riverbank on the side of the land that they are built to protect. At the time of Gao Pian, the rivers are likely the Tô Lịch in the north and west, the Red in the east, and the Kim Ngưu in the south as shown on the map of Đông Kinh (Figure 52). This map shows an outer wall that runs approximately from the intersection of Quán Thánh and Hòe Nhai streets to Bưởi market in the north. It then turns south to Cầu Giấy market along the Tô Lịch river in the west, a total distance of around 6.5 kilometres. It also shows what appears to be a dyke along the Kim Ngưu river, which measures approximately 7.5 kilometres from Cầu Giấy market to the end of Trần Khát Chân street. The total length is 14 kilometres or around 9,333 *bu*, more than twice as long as Gao Pian built. There is no dyke along the Red river shown in Figure 52.

Based on distance and location along the river bank, I would suggest Gao Pian's dyke was built along the Tô Lịch river, where the outer walls of Đông Kinh were as marked in Figure 52. It would be unlikely that Gao Pian built the dykes along the Kim Ngưu and Red rivers, as archaeological evidence indicated that these were built at a much later date by Vietnamese kings.[48]

The detailed discussion of these citadels is shown in Appendix 7 and summarised in Table 5 as follows:

YEARS	CITADELS	BUILT BY	PERIMETER[i]	DISTANCE[ii]
544		Lý Bí	Not known	
618	Tử Thành	Qiu He	900 (600)	225
767	La Thành[iii]	Zhang Boyi	Not known	
808	Đại La[iv]	Zhang Zhou	2,000 (3000)	500
858	La Thành	Wang Shi	3,600 (5,400)	900
866	La Thành	Gao Pian	3,000 or 3,961 (4,500 or 5,941)	750 or 990.25
866	Dykes	Gao Pian	4,251.6 (6,377)	
1490	Đông Kinh (square of the inner walls)		2,240 (3,360)	560
1490	Đông Kinh (outer walls)		8,800 (13,200)	
1803–1805	Hanoi (square)		2,666 (4,000)	666.50

Table 5 – Comparisons between citadels in the vicinity of Hanoi from the sixth to the 19th centuries.

i. Perimeter in *bu* (metres)
ii. Equivalent square, distance of each side in *bu*
iii. The name La Thành is first mentioned in ANCL when Zhang Bo-yi built La Thành at An Nam; it is also known as An Nam La Thành.[49]
iv. Other sources also refer to the citadel built by Zhang Bo-yi and Gao Pian as La Thành.[50,51] But ANCL also refers to La Thành as Đại La.[52] SKTT specifically mentions Đại La as the name of the citadel built by Zhang Zhou; as for other builders, SKTT cited La Thành.[53] For my purposes, to be consistent with other historians' views, I have used La Thành, An Nam La Thành and Đại La interchangeably.[54]

CHAPTER 14

THE NANZHAO-AN NAM WAR

GIAO CHÂU VI

STORY TIMELINE: Ninth century.
STORY LOCATION: South-western China and Northern Vietnam.
KEY CHARACTERS: *Fan Chuo:* Secretary of Cai Xi, An Nam Military Governor (862-863) and author of Man shu; provided an eyewitness account of the Nanzhao-An Nam war, *Li Zhuo:* Governor of An Nam, blamed for causing the war, *Đỗ Tồn Thành:* a local chief killed by Li Zhuo, *Zhu Daogu:* Commander of Nanzhao forces, *Gao Pian:* Prince General of Tang, victor of the war.
LOCATIONS OF INTEREST: Dali by Erhai Lake, Yunnan, China. "Thanh Mai" bell at the National History Museum in Hanoi. Vũ Én, upstream of Phú Thọ city.

Chapter summary

The Phùng brothers were the last to revolt against the Tang until over a century later, when the Khúc family became the first native-born *jiedushi* of An Nam. In the intervening years, An Nam went through a major war with Nanzhao, a kingdom in the contemporary Yunnan province of China.

The Nanzhao-An Nam war does not feature highly in Vietnamese history books, so in this chapter, I will try to piece together the story of a twelve-year war which involved armies of thirty to fifty thousand on both sides. The war resulted in 150,000 Tang troops captured or killed, 30,000 Nanzhao and their allies beheaded, with thousands more on both sides drowning in the Red river. La Thành (Hanoi) was ransacked twice – in 860 and 863 – the first event was relatively short, and Nanzhao forces were driven off within a year. However, for the second time, the occupation lasted for nearly three years, and the invaders left behind a devastated landscape of the surrounding region. Most of the fighting of this war took place at Phong Châu (Phú Thọ), and around La Thành.

The war started in 854 and ended in 866, but its lingering effect was that within 20 years, by 880, the Tang rule of An Nam effectively came to an end, and the dynasty itself collapsed in 907. A brief summary of the timeline of the war is shown in Table 6.

Year	Event
854	Alliance of the northwest mountain chiefs, local Annamese officials and Nanzhao generals.
857	Attacks on frontiers by mountain tribes.
858	Attempts on La Thành by Nanzhao fizzled out.
860	La Thành ransacked by Nanzhao.
861	La Thành retaken by Tang.
862	Attacks by Nanzhao and its allies on La Thành.
863	La Thành fell to Nanzhao. An Nam was under Nanzhao control.
866	La Thành retaken by Gao Pian of Tang. Nanzhao never seriously threatened An Nam again.

Table 6 – A timeline of the Nanzhao-An Nam war.

14.1 – Nanzhao – "a country of cunning and dangerous people"

Figure 57 shows a group of Yi women of Yunnan, China, in their traditional costumes. Back in the seventh to the ninth centuries, their ancestors, the Wu and the Bai ruled a kingdom called Nanzhao (or Southern Zhao), which occupied present-day Yunnan, parts of northern Laos, Myanmar, and northwest of northern Vietnam (Figures 58 and 61).[1,2] Their capital was at Taihe village, just south of Dali on the shore of Erhai Lake in Yunnan.[3] The kingdom had a total of 13 rulers started with Xi-nu-lo (649-674), and ended with Shun-hua-zhen (897-902) over two and half centuries later. Around two-thirds of the time through their reigns, by the early ninth century, Nanzhao began to expand their territory in all directions from the north to Tang China, Tibet, from the south to Myanmar, northern Laos, and northern Vietnam.[4]

At the height of their power, the Nanzhao kingdom occupied La Thành twice, in 860 and 863, during the reign of its king (Meng) Shi-long.

Their power was such that some historians traced the origin of the collapse of the Tang dynasty to the rebellion of the soldiers sent to fight against them.[5] While the history of Nanzhao is fascinating, it is outside the scope of this book to discuss it in detail other than stories related to its invasion of An Nam.

Figure 57 – A photo of the Yi minority in Shilin (Kunming, Yunnan, China).[6]

Fan Chuo, a Tang official, based in La Thành (Hanoi), was aware of the threat of Nanzhao as he reported to Emperor Yizong (Xiantong period, 860-873) in the Book of the Southern Barbarians (Man shu):[7]

"I humbly beg Your Majesty to send down an official notification ordering a detailed survey. Because the Southern Man [Nanzhao] are cunning and treacherous, and (the idea of) attacking and plundering is ever present in their minds, whenever they have some leisure from (cultivating their) fields and mulberry fields, they practice fighting the enemy. If, then, we do not invade and attack them from all four sides, they are violent and bad persons, and difficult to reform. That is why I recorded their cities and garrison-towns, their river valley and plains – mere dust defiling the audience-screen of the Imperial apartments. Perhaps one might hope to wipe out their host of ant-swarms, and purge forever (these) Qiang barbarian rebels."

14.2 – Prelude to a war - A greedy and violent duhu

A RIVER ROUTE TO THE NORTH-WEST

At the time the secretary of the *duhu* of An Nam, by the name of Fan Chuo, lived in La Thành. Fan Chuo knew about Nanzhao and warned the emperor about the coming hostility. When Nanzhao and their allies ransacked La Thành in 863, he barely escaped with his life, but miraculously, and thankfully, he survived the massacre to write a book about the event and the kingdom. Today, we owe much of our knowledge about Nanzhao to him.

In the book Man shu or Book of the Southern Barbarians, Fan Chuo describes the land, the people, their customs, history and products of the kingdom. In one section, he lays out the route from the provincial capital of An Nam (La Thành) to Chü-mieh (the seat of the Man (Nanzhao) king). It includes travelling upstream on the Red river for 25 days to a place called Ku-Yung-Pu (or Manhao in Yunnan, Figure 58), and from there by land for 27 days to Chü-mieh (present-day Dali), a total of 52 days.[8,9,10]

On Google Maps, the distance between these two ancient locations, Dali to Hanoi, is around 1,000 kilometres by road. One could travel this distance by the river route, as indicated by Google Maps. From south of Dali, one could take the West river, follow the Xida/Juli rivers, then continue with the Lishe river at about Xiaojianfang and Bajiao Diregion.[11] From there, the Lishe continues as the Red river to Hanoi, and to the Gulf of Tonkin. Around 846, when Nanzhao raided An Nam, they could have taken this river route or used the land route as described by Fan Chuo or both.[12]

ONE SPECK OF SALT FOR ONE HORSE

According to Fan Chuo, all the places from La Thành to Ku-Yung-Pu along the Red river were dependent on and attached to the administration of An Nam, but the *duhu* may depute the native chiefs to manage them. This convenient alliance was shattered when a new *duhu*, Li Zhuo, arrived in An Nam in 853; he was *"cruel and oppressive"*, *"caused living beings to suffer pain"* and greedy.[13] In 854, he ordered his men to offer only one speck of salt for one horse, or one head of cattle, to the mountain tribe known as Chong-mo Man – who bred cattle and horses, and traded them for salt.[14] The trades normally took place at a place called Lin-Xi-Yuan within the An Nam administration which I believe is by the bank of the Red river, near Vũ Én, upstream of Phú Thọ city, in Tang's Phong prefecture.[15] This new practice caused widespread resentment among the tribes; consequently, the frontier chiefs were *"seduced by the Man* [Nanzhao] *rebels"*, and these places *"fell into rebel hands"*.[16]

THE PEACH-FLOWER PEOPLE

Lin-Xi-Yuan is also a place where the local Dao Hua (Peach-Flower) people did business; their great chieftain, Li you-du, Lord of the Seven *Wan* and Ravines, administered and controlled them on behalf of Tang. They also served as frontier guards on the border, paid the annual land tax, and did other duties to An Nam.[17]

However, on a report from the magistrate of Phong prefecture, Li Zhuo dismissed the winter garrison, 6,000 men in all, who guarded the north-west frontier of Wei, Chen (or Zeng) and Teng (or Deng) Zhou apparently to save cost.[18] These were Tang men stationed there presumably to protect the frontier against Nanzhao. The loss of the winter garrison was too much for Li you-du, who entered into correspondence with the *jiedushi* of Nanzhao, Zhe Dong. The latter saw an opportunity and immediately sent his sister's daughter to marry Li you-du's younger son and got him a job as a Ya-ya (local military commander) in Zhe Dong – later named Shanchan then Kunming – the Nanzhao eastern capital.[19] In due course, it became a staging area for Nanzhao raids on Guangxi and An Nam.[20]

From this time onwards, the Seven *Wan* and Ravines no longer reported to Tang but were administered by Nanzhao. The seven tribes joined a Nanzhao general named Đoàn Tù Thiên (possibly Zhu Daogu) and began to raid Tang outposts and La Thành itself; they called themselves *"The life-*

risking (one-life or suicide) army in white coats".[21] Later historians blame Li Zhuo's actions as the cause of the Nanzhao-An Nam war.[22]

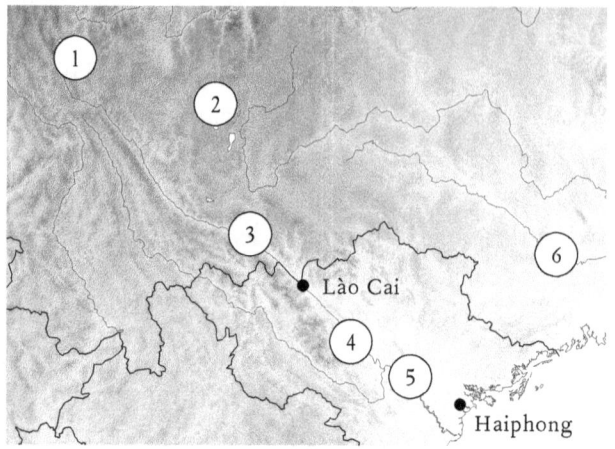

Figure 58 – Key locations related to Nanzhao.
1. Dali (and Taihe), 2. Kunming, 3. Manhao. 4. Vũ Ến, 5. Hanoi (La Thành), 6. Nanning.

14.3 – The killing Đỗ Tồn Thành.[23]

Đỗ Tồn Thành is mentioned briefly in SKTT as a tribal chief, but in other works, he was the prefect of Ái prefecture and a military commander. In 854, he was a major figure, reputedly from a long line of the Đỗ family who fought against the Linyi kings in the fifth century (Chapter 5). Đỗ Tồn Thành could also be a relative of Đỗ Anh Hàn, the adviser to the Phùng brothers in their rebellion over 50 years earlier (Chapter 12). Đỗ Tồn Thành aligned with the mountain chiefs in Phong and rose against Li Zhuo, who succeeded in having him killed, which intensified the war.[24]

Historical events seem to indicate that there was a connection between the people of Phong prefecture in the north-west (Phú Thọ province), and Ái, Hoan, Diễn prefectures (Thanh Hóa, Nghệ An provinces) in the southern part of north Vietnam.[25] Geographically speaking, these regions are the foot of the western mountain range which runs almost parallel to the Red river. The mountain range is at the extreme border of the Tang empire, but the regions are accessible by the Đáy river, which may explain such a connection.

14.4 – Wang Shi and the thorny bamboos

Li Zhuo left in 855, but his actions during the two years in An Nam created an alliance of the mountain chiefs, local An Nam people and Nanzhao generals, united against the Tang administration in the country. For the next two years, fighting continued, and Tang sent two *Duhus* in succession, Sung Ya (857) and Li Hongfu (857-858); neither managed to win a decisive battle against Nanzhao and its allies.

In 858, Tang sent one of its most effective officials, Wang Shi, to take up the post of *duhu*. Wang Shi immediately strengthened La Thành, including moats and thorny bamboo, as discussed in Chapter 13. In the same year, Man troops, including Nanzhao and its allies, got to a half day march to La Thành, but the additional defences must have intimidated them as they did not attack. Wang Shi sent an interpreter to negotiate with the raiders, and overnight, they left, sending their apologies: *"we only came to arrest the Lạo barbarian traitors and not to rob."*[26]

Prior to his arrival, Giao Châu (An Nam) had been in constant unrest and hunger. For six years, it was not able to pay any taxes; there was no bonus or reward for the troops; Wang Shi changed all that by ensuring that taxes and offerings were sent to the Tang court, and troops were rewarded. The situation in An Nam was stabilised, and the kingdoms of Champa and Zhenla sent their envoys to La Thành again and released the people they had captured in their previous raids.[27]

14.5 – The first sacking of La Thành (Hanoi) in 860.

Having stabilised An Nam, in early 860, Wang Shi was recalled by the Tang court to fight off another rebellion in the empire. However, the situation he left behind in An Nam was about to change for the worse because of events in Nanzhao. A year earlier, the king of Nanzhao died and was replaced by his son, king Meng Shi-long (859-877), who declared himself an emperor and continued the aggressive policy of his father. As a result of a diplomatic breakdown between Nanzhao and Tang, Shi-long sent an army into Tang territory to attack Po-chou (Zunyi in Guizhou province, north-east of Kunming).[28]

LI HU - AN AMBITIOUS DUHU

Wang Shi's replacement, an ambitious man by name of Li Hu, decided to recapture Po-chou even though it was outside his jurisdiction, and the campaign was successful. [29] While he was away, the Đỗ family assembled a large force, 30,000 in all, including Nanzhao soldiers to attack La Thành and capture it in the winter of 860.[30] The attack was to revenge the death of Đỗ Thủ Trừng, the son of Đỗ Tồn Thành mentioned earlier.

Li Hu returned to An Nam and drove Nanzhao invaders out of La Thành in the middle of 861, but he was punished by the Tang emperor for the abandonment of the city and was demoted. Meanwhile, Nanzhao forces pulled out of An Nam, circled northeast of the country, and captured Yongzhou (Nanning in Guangxi province). They held it for 20 days and thoroughly plundered it, a sign of things to come when they finally occupied La Thành for a second time in 863.[31,32]

14.6 – The second sacking of La Thành - the war of 862-863

WANG KUANG - APPEASEMENT TO BUY TIME

Li Hu was replaced by Wang Kuang.[33] Recognising that the Đỗ family was still strong, the emperor decided on an appeasement policy: he posthumously granted a title to Đỗ Tồn Thành with an apology for the death of him and his son. The Tang court also punished Li Hu for exceeding his authority by banishing him to Hainan Island.[34]

However, Wang Kuang, with his appeasement policy, was not able to stem the continuing raids by Nanzhao and its allies. He kept asking for more reinforcements, and in 862, the emperor replaced him with *dudu* Cai Xi, who came with an army of 30,000 from eight different provinces in the empire. Their arrival changed the balance of the war, and the Nanzhao offensive stalled.[35] Unfortunately, the stable situation did not last due to the jealousy and ambition of one Tang official, Cai Jing, who was the Tang regional commander based in Yongzhou, a province occupied by Nanzhao earlier. Cai Jing convinced the emperor to order the withdrawal of these troops despite repeated attempts by Cai Xi to keep them in An Nam at a reduced number of 5,000.

THE ATTACK

Once these troops returned north, Cai Xi was left with a small company, including soldiers from the Guangxi army plus possibly a contingent recruited from the local people. The Guangxi army left behind some bricks imprinted with their name that were discovered in 2002, as mentioned in Chapter 13. As Fan Chuo already warned the emperor, Nanzhao and its allies were watching for the weakness in Tang defence, and ready to pounce; the withdrawal of the northern troops provided such an opportunity.

In 862, Nanzhao and its allies, including a number of different mountain tribes coming from Nanzhao, An Nam, totalling 50,000, attacked.[36] The battle intensified around January 863 and reached its final bloody climax a month later when Nanzhao eventually captured La Thành on 28 February 863. They occupied it for three years until they were finally driven out in 866.

THE ELITE FORCES - LUOJUZI

The elite forces of Nanzhao are described by Fan Chuo as follows:

"Luojuzi: These are all recruited after tests from among the local village troops.[37] Therefore, they are called the Juzi (the flower) of the Four Armies. They wear bright helmets on their heads. They wear rhinoceros hide on their backs. They have bronze greaves [armour for the shin]. *They go barefoot through dangerous places as if they were flying."* [38]

Nanzhao, at its height, had a powerful army with well-trained, well-armed soldiers with spears, swords, cutlasses and bows. The elites among them were the Luojuzi, who resembled those bare-footed soldiers shown in Figure 59 from a painting in the 12th century of a procession in the Dali Kingdom (937-1094), which followed Nanzhao. The soldiers depicted in the painting are bare-footed, wear leg-protection, helmets and protective clothing over their arms. They carry spears; one holds a shield and another a cutlass. The Luojuzi were expected to be among the invasion force; as was Nanzhao military practice that every 100 men would have one Luojuzi assistant to control them.[39]

Secretary Fan Chuo was in the thick of the fighting, and he recorded the events vividly in Man shu. The passages, written around 862-864, and translated by scholar Gordon H. Luce, provided a lively account of what happened, so I have decided to quote key passages of his story in full in chronological order instead of a summary so that the reader can hear from Fan Chuo directly as given in Appendix 13.

Figure 59 – A painting of the bare-footed soldiers - possibly the Luojuzi. Cropped from a section of Zhang Shenwen's Kingdom of Dali Buddhist Volume of Paintings.[40]

14.7 – The empire struck back - The arrival of Gao Pian, a prince general

According to SKTT, over the two times Nanzhao occupied La Thành, they captured and killed nearly 150,000 men, which to me seem high given the size of the armies involved in the war of no more than 50,000 on each side. However, if civilians are included, then the number may be reasonable.[41] In any case, while the first occupation in 860 was relatively short, the second sacking of the city in 863 lasted for nearly three years. Nanzhao left behind an occupation force of 20,000, which was more than enough troops to start methodical plunder of homes in the surrounding area and drove the local population to live in caves and ravines.[42] It was a miserable time for the An Nam people.

GOVERNMENT IN EXILE

By July 863, Tang, having abandoned An Nam, installed a government in exile at Hai-men (Beihai in Guangxi province), and began to build up an expedition force with plans to retake their former territory. A year later, Tang had built up an army of 25,000, and the emperor ordered the *jiedushi* of the Lingnan circuit, Zhang Yin, to move south. Zhang Yin was not so sure, hesitated and was soon replaced by one of the best generals of Tang, Gao Pian.

Gao Pian – also a poet and a prince – is a remarkable man of his time.[43] He came from a military family and made his name fighting rebellions in the north. He went on to drive the Nanzhao army out of An Nam in 866. He then strengthened La Thành citadel, fought Nanzhao again at Chengdu in Sichuan province and built similar protective walls there in 875.[44] But towards the end of his life, he and his family were killed while locked up in prison in 887, their bodies were thrown into a single pit. To make it worse for his legacy, later historians blame him for his role in hastening the end of the Tang dynasty.[45,46]

Gao Pian cast a long shadow in Vietnamese history, for his construction of La Thành, his apparent use of witchcraft, and his belief in the spiritual world. LNCQ cites a particularly horrific practice of killing young women to cast spells over spiritual places, as attributed to him.[47]

In September 2001, while dredging the Tô Lịch river near An Phú, workers found eight skeletons; teeth of elephant, horse and water buffalo; potteries, iron utilities, plates, ceramics, knives and coins.[48] Of particular interest were seven wooden poles arranged in a specific way. This caused quite a stir among the local people as it was later reported that some of these workers met with accidents, a few fell ill and several died. Some historians at the time explained that the wooden poles were arranged in the motif of *Bagua* (Eight Trigrams of the I Ching) by Gao Pian, together with other offerings, as a charm to cast a spell on the spirit of the river to stop the bank from collapsing while he was building La Thành.[49]

THE FIRST VICTORY

But for our story, in 864, upon taking over the command of the expedition force, Gao Pian did not know what fate had in store for him over 20 years later, and he was not ready. It took him another year before he was able to take with him 5,000 troops to embark on his campaign to retake An Nam. The plan was for Gao Pian to lead the advance party with the rest of the army, under the command of a eunuch, Li Weizhou, to follow. But Li had other plans; he disliked Gao Pian intensely, and chose to stay behind in Hai-men, hoping that Nanzhao and their Man rebels would wipe out Gao Pian with his small contingent.

As events turned out, Gao Pian and his men arrived at Phong prefecture in October (ninth lunar month) 865, caught the Man rebels out in the open in the middle of the harvest in Nam Định, destroyed them and secured the rice for his troops.[50,51]

REINFORCEMENTS AND THE REVERSE OF ROLES

The fighting then continued without any decisive victory on either side; in the summer of 866, the Nanzhao court promoted Zhu Daogu to the *jiedushi* of Kunming, and other officials were also promoted. In the same year, reinforcements for Gao Pian finally arrived with another 7,000 troops led by Wei Zhongcai. With the additional troops, Gao Pian pushed Nanzhao back, killing and capturing many. Nanzhao's command then withdrew into La Thành. Almost three years after Nanzhao first besieged the citadel, the roles were now reversed with the Tang army on the outside and Man soldiers holed up behind citadel walls.

Gao Pian sent the news of the victory back to Hai-men but Li Weizhou, full of jealousy, decided not to send it on to the Tang court at Chang'an; instead, he reported to the emperor that Gao Pian had halted simply to watch the enemy and refused to attack. By November of 866, La Thành was surrounded for 10 days and was about to fall, but in the middle of the fighting, Gao Pian received an order from the imperial court to hand over the command to general Wang Yanquan and return to Chang'an. The court made this decision on the false information provided by Li Weizhou. As an obedient general, Gao Pian handed the reign to Wei Zhongcai and left for Hai-men with 100 men.

Fortunately, in previous weeks, Gao Pian and Wei Zhongcai sent two trusted officials with the news of victory separately from the official courier to Chang'an. On the way back to Hai-men, these officials saw the ships carrying Li Weizhou and Wang Yanquan; they hid behind one of the islands en route until the flotilla sailed past and in due course, found their way to Chang'an with the message from Gao Pian. The emperor was delighted, reinstated Gao Pian with a new promotion and ordered him to return to An Nam; thus, as soon as he got to Hai-men and received the new directive, Gao Pian turned around and hurried back.

AN ESCAPE AND THE FINAL VICTORY

Meanwhile, Wang Yanquan and Li Weihou arrived at La Thành; Wang was reportedly a coward and relied on Li, who was greedy and cruel. Their staff refused to cooperate and let half of the besieged Man escape from the citadel in protest. Gao Pian returned, exhorted the troops for a final push and entered the citadel sometime in December 866.[52] They killed Nanzhao *jiedushi* Zhu Daogu and beheaded over 30,000 of his men, and over 10,000 local Man rebels surrendered.[53]

14.8 – The aftermath - a dying empire

A PEACEFUL SEA MILITARY DISTRICT

The twelve-year war was over but the Tang court was careful not to antagonise Nanzhao further; the emperor ordered the commanders in An Nam, Yongzhou and Sichuan – three theatres of the Nanzhao-Tang war – to protect their borders and to halt any further fighting against Nanzhao.[54] The emperor changed An Nam from a protectorate into a "Peaceful Sea Military District" (Jinghai-Jun), and appointed Gao Pian as its *jiedushi*. Gao Pian stayed in An Nam for nine years until 874, when he was recalled to go to Sichuan to fight off another Nanzhao invasion in 875. His grandson Gao Xun took over, and in 877, the aide-de-camp that Gao Pian sent on a mission to Chang'an in 866, Zeng Gun, became the new *jiedushi* of An Nam.

ANOTHER INVASION

In 877, Nanzhao king, (Meng) Shi-long, who started the war against An Nam died. His son, Long-shun (877-897) was not giving up his father's ambition and invaded An Nam again. There is not much information on this invasion except that Zeng Gun fled to Yongzhou, and the army he left behind fell apart. As he wanted a negotiated settlement with Nanzhao, Zeng Gun reported to the emperor:

> "*From the end of Xiantong Era (860-873), the Man military betrayed, invaded four zhous: An Nam, Yong, Guang, and Ju* [north Vietnam, Guangxi, Guangdong and Guizhou provinces], *the world has been in turmoil for 15 years; half of the tax collection was not paid to Chang'an* [the imperial capital], *the*

treasury [of the zhous] was empty, the soldiers died from poisonous air, their bones burned, and ash sent back homes; men did not think about their families, risking their lives to rob. It is very painful, not to mention the An Namese military posts are few, and the robbery in the winter is very worrying. Now we can send a messenger to offer peace, although they have not proclaimed a god [king or emperor], we can persuade them to submit, then the country will be calmed." [55]

The emperor agreed, but by then, rebellions against Tang had been suppressed, so he did not take up this recommendation.

History does not record if the Nanzhao invasion of An Nam in 877-878 came to anything, but by then, the focus of the Nanzhao-An Nam war was shifted to Sichuan. As for Zeng Gun, he would have been just a minor footnote, but for the book he is recorded to have compiled, entitled Jiaozhou Ji (*Giao Châu Ký*). The book is now lost, but parts of it were reproduced in a 14th-century book, VDUL, that brought us the remarkable story of the Mountain and Water Spirits (Sơn Tinh and Thủy Tinh), a local folklore that Zeng Gun may have collected during his time in An Nam.[56]

THE BURNING OF THE IMPERIAL CAPITAL OF CHANG'AN

The Tang dynasty was in its death throes by the end of the ninth century. Within three years of Zeng Gun's report, in 883, Chang'an was burned by retreating rebels: between 60 and 70 per cent of its palaces, office buildings, dwellings in its markets, and wards went up in flames. The reconstruction was short-lived and totally demolished by pillaging soldiers again in 888. Fifteen years later, in 904, a powerful warlord, Zhu Wen, sealed the fate of Chang'an, reduced it to a wasteland, beheaded as many as 700 seniors, strangled more than 200 young eunuchs, and drove its inhabitants out of the city to his new capital at Luoyang, some 385 kilometres to the east. By 1 June 907, the last Tang sovereign abdicated, and the Tang dynasty was no more.[57]

THE KINGDOM OF DACHANNGHE

Nanzhao kingdom faced a similar fate. By 897, Long-shun was murdered by one of his ministers; within five years, in 902, another minister murdered the royal family, and usurped the throne, renaming it Dachannghe (902-928).[58] History does not record any interactions between the new kingdom and successive polities in Vietnam. By 1253, the Mongols conquered Yunnan, finally ending the region's independence.

14.9 – A historical footnote on the Đỗ

The name Đỗ appeared a few times in this period of Vietnamese history, but the information on them is scant. We know about Đỗ Viện and his sons, who successfully resisted the Linyi invasion in the fourth and fifth centuries, as discussed in Chapter 5. Đỗ Anh Luân (Hàn) helped the Phùng brothers in the eighth century; Đỗ Tồn Thành and his son were killed in the ninth century.

On 1 April 2011, during an excavation to lay the water pipes at Từ Liêm district, Hanoi, workers found two ancient tombs. On 22 August of the same year, workers found another grave within 100 metres of these two. There are Chinese scripts on the bricks, and one is translated as Đỗ; archaeologists date them to between fourth and the sixth centuries and believe these could be related to the family of Đỗ Viện.[59],[60]

Figure 60 – The Thanh Mai bronze bell.[64]

In early April 1986, a brick maker found a bronze bell when he was digging up the soil to make bricks at the village of Mỹ Dương near Hanoi.[61] The bell is the oldest found in Vietnam, dating back to the 30th of the third lunar month of 798. There are 1530 Chinese characters on the bell, including the names of 234 people contributing to the cost of its casting. Sixty-two of these names have a Đỗ surname, including Đỗ Anh Hàn, adviser to the Phùng brothers cited earlier. At the time of the casting of the bell, there was an assistant *duhu*, Đỗ Anh Sách; also an assistant commissioner for summoning and punishing, and his name is not on the bell. Today, one can view both the bronze bell and the tomb artefacts at the National History Museum in Hanoi.[62,63]

The locations of these artefacts are on the eastern side of the Red river at some 20 to 30 kilometres distance from each other, so it is difficult to form any conclusion if they are linked.

CHAPTER 15

PRELUDE TO INDEPENDENCE

GIAO CHÂU VII

STORY TIMELINE: 10th century.
STORY LOCATION: Northern Vietnam.
KEY CHARACTERS: *Khúc Thừa Dụ:* first Vietnamese-born Military Governor of An Nam, *Khúc Hạo:* son of Khúc Thừa Dụ, *Khúc Thừa Mỹ:* grandson of Khúc Thừa Dụ, *Dương Đình Nghệ:* general in the army of Khúc Hạo, *Liu Yan:* Emperor of the Southern Han dynasty, *Li Jin:* Southern Han governor of An Nam.
LOCATIONS OF INTEREST: Khúc Thừa Dụ temple, Hải Dương province. Dương Đình Nghệ temple, Thanh Hóa province.

Chapter summary

After three centuries, by 907, the Tang dynasty finally collapsed. Its magnificent capital, Chang'an, where over 300 years, emissaries from every corner of the empire, including An Nam, came to pay tributes to the emperors with precious and rare gifts, was turned into a wasteland. China was once again broken up into a period known as the Five Dynasties and Ten Kingdoms period (907-960).[1]

For our story, I only focus on the kingdom of Southern Han (917-971, Figure 61) as events that happened there affected Vietnam. I note with interest that these kingdoms were separated by the borders established by the mountain ranges in Qin and Han times; over 1,000 years earlier. For example, Min was Minyue (Fujian), and Southern Han was Nan-yue (Guangxi and Guangdong provinces).[2] While this may mean that natural features are logical choices for borders between states, it could also mean that the tribal nature of people who live within these borders would tend to reassert itself once the empire disintegrates.

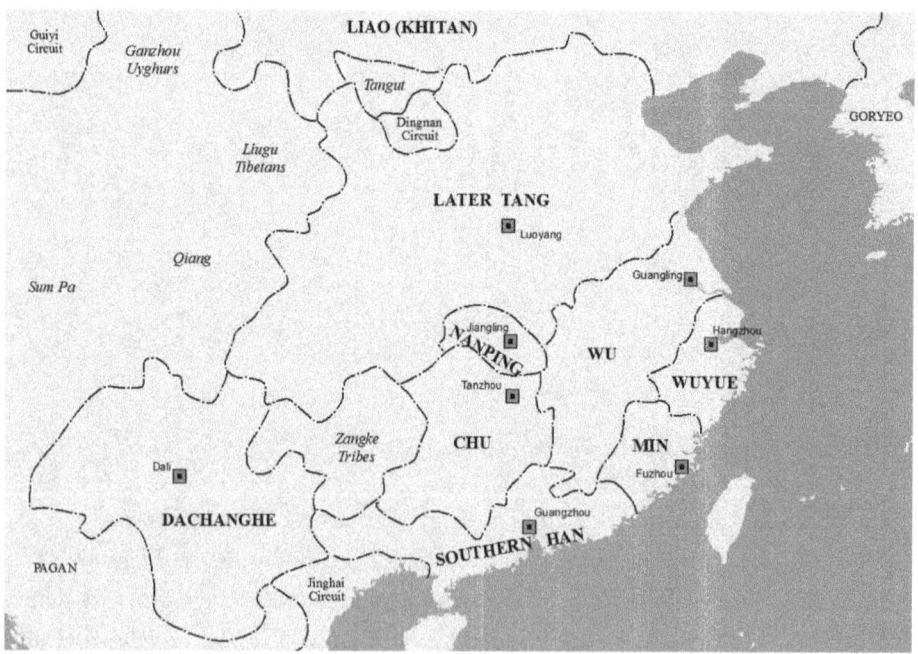

Figure 61 – A map of China around 926, Dachanghe is the successor of the Nanzhao kingdom, Jinghai Circuit is An Nam. The dynasty of Later Tang (923-937) follows that of Later Liang (907-923)(not shown), Jinghai circuit is Giao Châu/ An Nam.[3]

During this time of upheaval in China, the Khúc family, who came from the heart of the Red River Delta, stepped in to take charge of An Nam; thus, began a series of events that eventually led to Vietnamese independence.

Some historians see the Khúc as opportunists; others see them as revolutionists or simply caretakers for the empire. I believe the family was a mixture of all three, the founder was certainly an opportunist, and his son, like a revolutionist, implemented a number of significant changes to the administration of An Nam, but his grandson was timid and loyal to the dying empire. It was no surprise that the reign of the family ended with the grandson who died in exile.

The Northern Rule returned briefly but was driven out by a general from contemporary Thanh Hóa province who served with the Khúc family by the name of Dương Đình Nghệ. He went on to defeat an expedition force from the Southern Han in 931. Despite the victory, Dương Đình Nghệ did not proclaim himself king or emperor; none of the Khúc did either. It must have been difficult for them to do so and to shake free from the Tang dynasty as An Nam was part of the empire for three centuries. But in 938, all that was changed forever, as discussed in the next chapter.

15.1 – The Khúc family (906-930) - the first native jiedushi

KHÚC THỪA DỤ - THE FOUNDER

After Zeng Gun fled An Nam in 880, there were a number of *jiedushi* appointed by Tang in the intervening 25 years from 880 to 905 but most did not stay long; some were in name only and may not have set foot in the country; the last was a Dugu Sun who barely stayed for a few months.[4] During that period, Tang was engulfed in the Huang Chao rebellion (874-884) and never recovered. Taking advantage of the political instability in the north and the power vacuum in An Nam, a man named Khúc Thừa Dụ stepped in.[5] He may not have been aware of it but he was the first Vietnamese ever to hold this position over the three centuries of Tang rule; with the exception of a Japan-born, Abe no Nakamaro (also known as Zhao Heng) who was the *duhu* from 761 to 767, the others were all Chinese.[6] A list of the governors (*cishi*), protectorate generals (*duhu*) and military commissioners (*jiedushi*) from 111 BCE to 937 is shown in Appendix 6.

THE FAMILY VILLAGE

The most fertile land in the Red River Delta is a region of almost a parallelogram in shape with the rivers on four sides: the Đuống in the north, the Luộc in the south, the Red in the west and the Thái Bình in the east. The region captures Hưng Yên, most of Hải Dương, and parts of Hanoi and Bắc Ninh provinces. It includes historical locations such as Chu Diên and Nam Định, which I have already referred to in this book.

Along the northern bank of the Luộc river, some 80 kilometres southeast of Hanoi, we find Ninh Giang district, and that is where the Khúc family came from. Today, there is a temple for the family, "Khúc Thừa Dụ temple", at Cúc Bồ hamlet, Kiến Quốc commune (Figure 49, Chapter 11).[7]

There is not much information recorded in historical works about the family, but they must have been a very influential clan in An Nam. The family of Khúc Thừa Dụ is described in CM as:[8]

> "*The Khúc family was a long-standing family name in Hồng Châu. Thừa Dụ was generous, kind, loving towards others and revered by the people. In turbulent times, as the chief of a prefecture, Thừa Dụ proclaimed himself to be a Military Commissioner (jiedushi) and requested the authorisation from the Tang emperor, who, in that situation, granted it.*"

The transfer of power from a court-appointed, China-based official to a native-born person as the head of An Nam apparently was peaceful, but other sources suggested Khúc Thừa Dụ led an army to occupy Đại La and took over from the last *jiedushi*, Dugu Sun. I am inclined to support the peaceful rise of Khúc Thừa Dụ since Chinese annals did not record any rebellion in An Nam at that time. Whatever the case, his timing was perfect as the Tang dynasty was about to extinguish.[9]

KHÚC HẠO – THE REFORMER

Khúc Thừa Dụ did not rule very long, he died in 907 and his son, Khúc Hạo, became the next *jiedushi*. Khúc Hạo made a number of significant changes to the administration and tax regimes based on the principles of tolerance and simplicity; it was reported that the people enjoyed happy and peaceful lives under ten years of his rule.[10]

In 917, Liu Yin, a Tang-appointed *jiedushi* in Pinyin (Guangzhou), died; his brother, Liu Yan, seized the opportunity, took over from Liu Yin and declared a new kingdom called "Great Việt" (Đại Việt) but he later changed it to Southern Han.[11] Khúc Hạo, sufficiently astute in the politics of the day, decided to send his son Khúc Thừa Mỹ to pay tributes at Pinyin as a friendly gesture between the two polities, even though he was still looking to the dynasty that succeeded Tang as the rightful authority.

KHÚC THỪA MỸ - DIED IN EXILE

Khúc Hạo died in the same year, and Khúc Thừa Mỹ became the new *jiedushi*. Like his father before him, Khúc Thừa Mỹ sent an envoy to Luoyang, the new capital that Zhu Wen established as the seat of his Later Liang dynasty (907-923) to seek two items: a feather flagpole and a large hammer, or "*Tiết Việt*", that represent the emperor's authorisation of his position.[12]

Upon hearing this news, Liu Yan became very angry; presumably, in his mind, Khúc Thừa Mỹ should have sought the authorisation from him, not from Later Liang. Besides, Liu Yan must have wanted to absorb An Nam into his kingdom. He dispatched his generals, Li Shoujuan and Liang Kezhen, to Đại La, captured Khúc Thừa Mỹ, and took him back to Pinyin sometime in 930, where Thừa Mỹ died.[13] Liang Kezhen went on to raid Champa and brought back many treasures, then tasked to hold Đại La.[14]

The Khúc family reigned for a relatively short 30 years before An Nam became governed by the northerners once again, but this time, the ruler barely began before he was forced out.

15.2 – Dương Đình Nghệ - A general from Ái.[15]

With Khúc Thừa Mỹ captured, Liu Yan appointed Li Jin as the new *cishi* of Giao Châu, Li Jin was supported by Liang Kezhen and stationed at Đại La. While Khúc Thừa Mỹ may have been a pushover when he came up against the army of Southern Han, his father's men were not so compliant. One of these men, a junior general from the prefecture of Ái (Thanh Hóa) by the name of Dương Đình Nghệ, marched north from Ái and defeated Liang Kezhen, who fled back to Pinyin.

At Pinyin, Liu Yan decided to change tactics; he offered Dương Đình Nghệ official titles and told his court officials, "*The people of Giao Châu like to revolt; we could only "cơ mi" them* [to keep them loosely controlled]."[16] However, Dương Đình Nghệ had a different plan, he was busily training 3,000 special troops, reported to be his "adopted" sons; Li Jin, in Đại La, was aware of this but acted ignorantly as he was bribed by Dương Đình Nghệ.[17]

VICTORY IN 931

In 931, Dương Đình Nghệ was ready; he and his crack troops marched north and surrounded Đại La. Li Jin urgently sent for help from Pinyin, but before additional troops arrived, Đại La fell. Fortunately for Li Jin, he managed to escape (given his record of accepting bribery, he may have paid his way out of Đại La), but unfortunately for him, his master Liu Yan did not forgive failure easily, not to mention the charge of bribery, put him to death.

The army of Southern Han arrived soon after under Cheng Bao, and the two adversaries squared off outside Đại La in the same year, with the battle ended when Cheng Bao was killed.[18] Dương Đình Nghệ emerged triumphant, declared himself as the new *jiedushi* and ruled for seven years until he was murdered by one of his "adopted "sons – a special force general named Kiều Công Tiễn.[19,20]

THE PATTERN WAS BROKEN

Dương Đình Nghệ and his victory in 931 against the Southern Han army represented a major turning point in Vietnamese history. Before him, those who revolted against the northern dynasties, such as the Trưng sisters, Lý Bí, Mai Thúc Loan, and the Phùng brothers, achieved initial victories only to be suppressed as the empire struck back with troops from the north. This time, however, the pattern was broken as Dương Đình Nghệ fought successfully against a northern reinforcement. The event must have been a boost of confidence to his followers; they now knew they could defeat a northern army. As events turned out, they were to repeat this feat seven years later in 938 when Southern Han sent another expedition force.

TEMPLES

Today there is a temple dedicated to Dương Đình Nghệ at the village of Giàng at Thiệu Dương commune of Thanh Hóa province, where he is believed to have lived and died.[21] The temple is near where two rivers, Mã (or Nam Mã) and Chu meet before flowing out to the sea at Lạch Hới estuary. One could imagine boats on both rivers would meet here for trades before heading out to sea. Those coming in from the coast could sail off to the hinterland on two different routes. Thus, it is no surprise that during Han times, they set up the administrative centre of Cửu Chân commandery here, in the ancient city of Tư Phố. In 42, the forces that joined the Trưng rebellion withdrew to Thanh Hóa; Ma Yuan followed and captured them at Tư Phố. However, a number of his soldiers decided to stay behind, and Tư Phố was near where they settled, as discussed in Appendix 11.

Around 18 kilometres (or 5 kilometres as the crow flies) north of Dương Đình Nghệ temple is the temple of Lady Triệu, who rose against the Eastern Wu in 248, as told in Chapter 3. Historically, Cửu Chân or Ái or Thanh Hóa and the provinces further south had never been entirely under northern controls. The people of these southernmost regions of the northern dynasties, through years of raids from the Linyi kingdom, must have been tough and independent-minded; the Black Emperor raised his army here, and Đỗ Tôn Thành and his men also travelled from here to fight against the Tang with their Nanzhao allies. This may explain why Dương Đình Nghệ was able to raise his crack troops from the same area to defeat the Southern Han.

CHAPTER 16

THE DAWN OF INDEPENDENCE

GIAO CHÂU VIII

STORY TIMELINE: 10th century.
STORY LOCATION: Northern Vietnam.
KEY CHARACTERS: *Kiều Công Tiễn:* the general who betrayed and killed Dương Đình Nghệ, a usurper, *Ngô Quyền:* son-in-law of Dương Đình Nghệ who killed Kiều Công Tiễn, *Liu Yan:* Emperor of the Southern Han dynasty, *Liu Hong-cao:* Prince, son of Liu Yan, who led the invasion of An Nam, lost heavily to Ngô Quyền and was killed.
LOCATIONS OF INTEREST: Ngô Quyền temple, Đường Lâm, Sơn Tây, Hanoi. Relics of Victory on Bạch Đằng river, Hải Phòng.

Chapter summary

Prior to the expedition to Giao (An Nam) in 938, Liu Yan, the ruler of Southern Han, asked Xiao Yi (Tiêu Ích), the envoy from Chongwen for advice. Xiao Yi said:[1,2]

> *"At present, heavy rains have been for several weeks; the sea route is difficult and far; Ngô Quyền is very good and should not be underestimated. The army has to be careful, employ many people to scout the way first, and then advance."* [3]

The advice was ignored, and Liu Yan went ahead with the invasion. In this chapter, I will discuss the events which led to the battle of the Bạch Đằng river in 938, when an armada of ships from Southern Han was lured into the river and sunk by Ngô Quyền's forces. Ngô Quyền is the son-in-law of Dương Đình Nghệ mentioned in the previous chapter. The battle is a major turning point for Vietnam as the Vietnamese have maintained their autonomy from that time to the present day, barring a few intervals under foreign occupations. One could say that was when Vietnam was born.

In many ways, this battle is more significant than the battle of Điện Biên Phủ in 1954, which ended nearly 80 years of French rule. However, it is only described in a short paragraph in a Chinese text, Historical Records of the Five Dynasties (or Wudai Shiji, published in 1073) as follows:

> *"Yang Tingi* [Dương Đình Nghệ] *of Aizhou* [Ái Châu] *defected during the fourth year (931), attacking Jiaozhou* [Giao Châu]*; prefect Li Jin absconded to return the* [Southern] *Han. Yan dispatched Cheng Bao, his recipient for edicts, to retaliate against Yanyi, Bao dying in battle.*
>
> *In the 10th year* [937], *a military attaché to the governor at Jiaozhou, Jiao Gongxian* [Kiều Công Tiễn], *killed Yang Tingi to install himself. Retaliating against Jiaozhou was Wu Quan* [Ngô Quyền], *a one-time commander under Tingyi. Gongxian now approached the Han for military assistance. Yan dispatched troops to the Baiteng river for a drive on Jiaozhou and invested his own son, Hong-cao, as Prince of Jiao [and relief commander]. Yan personally lodged armies at Hai-men. Quan had murdered Gongxian by now and engaged the enemy at the ocean port, planting iron rods in the water. Quan's troops advanced by riding a rising tide, Hong-cao in pursuit. Yet the boats recoiled once tides receded, the iron rods now sticking into the wheel-ruts and overturning all the affected ships. Hong-cao died in battle and Yan regrouped his remaining men to return."* [4]

The Baiteng river is at the estuary of the Xi river, near Jinwan district south of Guangzhou. Wheel-ruts in this context could refer to the grooves between the planks along the bottom of the ship.

In this chapter, I will try to recreate the battle so that it would help me and other travellers to understand this monumental event better while visiting the site of the clash near Hải Phòng.

16.1 – *The betrayal*

As mentioned earlier, Dương Đình Nghệ was murdered by one of his "adopted "sons, a special force general named Kiều Công Tiễn who came from Phong prefecture and served as a junior general under him. Phong was a base for Nanzhao and its allies during the Nanzhao-An Nam war nearly 70 years before. As I have already noted, historical events seem to indicate that there was a connection between the people of Phong and Ái prefectures. It would explain why he served under Dương Đình Nghệ, who came from Ái, even if the two prefectures are over 250 kilometres apart.

Kiều Công Tiễn may have fought against Southern Han in 931 as a loyal officer, but by the spring of 937 in April, his ambition led him to betray, and murder his commander, Dương Đình Nghệ, to claim the title of *jiedushi*.

16.2 – *The revenge*

Kiều Công Tiễn may have overplayed his hand and underestimated the forces lined up against him. The leader of the opposition was another special force general, Ngô Quyền, who happened to be the son-in-law of Dương Đình Nghệ, and at that time, was the prefect of Ái.

In 937, Ngô Quyền was 39 years old, born in 898 at the village of Đường Lâm, of Sơn Tây, Hanoi, where the Phùng brothers grew up over a century earlier.[5] However, historian Trần Trọng Dương made a convincing case that Đường Lâm is not at Sơn Tây in the north-west but is at Hà Tĩnh, just north of Ngang pass.[6] I am inclined to agree with Trần for the simple reason that during the anarchy period (966-967), Ngô Quyền's grandsons both established their bases in the south and not at Đường Lâm. However, this view is yet to be adopted widely, and for travelling purposes, one can still visit his restful tomb at Đường Lâm in Sơn Tây.

Ngô Quyền was destined to do great things. Apparently, when he was born, a strange light flooded his home, his appearance was unusual, and he had three moles on his back. The physiognomist predicted that he would grow up to become the lord of a region, and thus his father named him Quyền, which means power, authority or right. He joined Dương Đình Nghệ's forces and must have been so trusted that he ended up marrying Dương Đình Nghệ's daughter and was appointed as prefect of Ái while Dương Đình Nghệ became the *jiedushi* in Đại La.[7]

Ngô Quyền may have known Kiều Công Tiễn as both would have served under Dương Đình Nghệ during the war against the Southern Han seven years earlier in 931. It must have been a shock to him to learn about the murder of his father-in-law, and he was not about to sit idly; revenge was called for. Like his father-in-law before him over a year earlier, Ngô Quyền assembled his army and in the autumn of 938, in October marched to Đại La.[8] History records he won easily and Kiều Công Tiễn was killed, but before that Kiều Công Tiễn made the ultimate betrayal by sending for help from the Southern Han.

16.3 – Battle of the Bạch Đằng river

Liu Yan, the emperor of Southern Han for nearly 20 years since 917, was pleased to get the request for help from Kiều Công Tiễn. Now, he had a valid reason to invade Giao (An Nam) again after the failure in 931. As quoted above, he sought advice from an envoy who gave it, but the advice was ignored. He immediately appointed one of his many sons, Liu Hong-cao, as the *jiedushi* of Giao as well as the Prince of Giao to lead the expedition. These titles reflected Liu Yan's confidence that Giao would soon be part of Southern Han, and his son would be the new *jiedushi*. However, Liu Yan was sufficiently wary about the southern expedition, so he made himself a general and commanded a force based in the port of Hai-men (Beihai in Guangxi province), ready to reinforce his son if needed.[9]

Liu Hong-cao, his officers, their soldiers, and ships left Hai-men sometime towards the end of 938. They were ready for war. Little did Li Hong-cao and his army know; they were sailing into a trap. Deaths, mostly by drowning, were waiting for them at the Bạch Đằng river by the city of Hải Phòng.

THE TIDES

As already forewarned by Xiao Yi, Ngô Quyền was very shrewd (or very tricky, depending on which sources); he knew the route that the Southern Han flotilla was likely to take. It was the same route that previous northern generals took to invade north Vietnam. They would sail from the southern port of Hai-men, follow the coastline to Hạ Long Bay, from there, enter the Bạch Đằng estuary, sail upstream of the river, take a left turn to the King Thầy river, enter the Đuống river and come out to the Red River, just north of Hanoi; their final destination. The alternative is to get to Hanoi from the south by the Red River, but the entry point is further south. The second route would be more straightforward since the invaders would simply stay on the same river without the twists and turns involved in the first route.

Ngô Quyền also knew about the tides. The river courses and the coastline would have changed over the thousand years from 938, but the tides are not likely to vary much. The tidal regime in the Gulf of Tonkin is diurnal, where there is one high and one low tide every lunar day or roughly 24 hours and 50 minutes.[10] On 27 February 2021, the difference between the highest and lowest tidal marks at Hải Phòng near the Bạch Đằng river was 2.77 metres giving a rate of around 20 centimetres per hour.[11]

THE TRAP

There is a reason this stretch of the river is called Bạch Đằng; it means white swells or waves in strong winds. The river also flows through a forest and is also known as Sông Rừng or the Forest River.[12] Beside one of the river's bends; there is a limestone mountain called Tràng Kênh with many caves, ideal for small boats to hide. Ngô Quyền guessed that Southern Han ships would have to come through here on their way to Đại La and that was where he decided to lay his trap.[13]

Upon hearing that Liu Hong-cao was coming, Ngô Quyền told his general staff:

> "*Hong-cao is a foolish child who brought troops from afar; his soldiers will be tired, and having heard that Kiều Công Tiễn had been killed; thus a loss of an internal* [fifth column] *support, he must be racked with doubts. Our fresh troops, fighting against a tired enemy, would surely defeat them. But they have advantages with their battleships, and if we do not take precautions, then win or lose* [the outcome of the battle] *is not certain. If we order the men to plant tall stakes,*

with pointed irons under the water line at the river mouth, their boats following the high tides to the row of stakes [would be caught at low tides], *then it would be easy for us to overpower and leave them with no escape.*"[14]

The plan was duly implemented with many iron-tips stakes firmly driven to the riverbed and well-hidden in high tides. Upstream from and facing these stakes, hidden by the river banks, Ngô Quyền and the bulk of his men waited for the arrival of the Southern Han fleet.

THE BATTLE

It was sometime in the winter of 938 that the ships of Southern Han arrived just off the coast of the Bạch Đằng river; presumably they would not want to enter the river estuary in the dark nor when the tides were low. So, it would be reasonable to assume that they would wait for high tides and set sail, most likely in the morning.

But their timing was controlled by Ngô Quyền, who also watched the tides. The scenario is likely to play out like this: the ships of Southern Han would come into the estuary as the tide is on the rise, or at least high. Ngô Quyền would send his small boats to engage the flotilla but immediately break off. Eager for a quick victory, Li Hong-cao would order his ships to pursue further into the estuary.

As soon as the flotilla sails into the area where the stakes are hidden, Ngô Quyền's boats would turn around, and his other boats, henceforth hidden along the river banks or the tributaries, would engage. Now the timing is everything. The attack must be just before the tide changes and reveals the stakes. In any case, what happened was that these iron-tipped stakes easily punctured the wooden hulls of Li Hong-cao's ships. Now, Ngô Quyền commanded his army of small boats to close in on the hapless Southern Han ships, water was pouring in, and the ships were on fire; most capsized, and the troops drowned. Liu Hong-cao was captured and killed. The remnants of the Southern Han battle fleet, most likely those outside the killing zone and possibly still at sea waiting for their turn to enter, escaped and returned to Hai-men. On hearing the news of the disaster, Liu Yan broke down and cried. The battle was over, most likely within a day before the tides changed again. An illustration of the battle is shown in Figure 62.

THE DAWN OF INDEPENDENCE

Figure 62 – Battle of the Bạch Đằng river, National Museum of Vietnamese History, Hanoi.[15]

THE PAINTING

One would never know how realistic the above painting is, but it would appear that the artist has tried his best to depict the scene as historically accurate as possible. Firstly, it shows the white swells that give the name to the river; secondly, we know that Ngô Quyền's army was using small, manoeuvrable boats, whereas Southern Han would have sailed south in seagoing battleships, represented here. Back in 808, Zhang Zhou was building 32 fast attacking boats which could each carry 48 men as told in Chapter 13 in Đại La. In 1043, king Lý Thái Tông built hundreds of boats in Thăng Long (Hanoi), so it would be reasonable to assume that Ngô Quyền's men in 938 had the know-how to build war boats.

The painting shows soldiers of Ngô Quyền carrying bows, crossbows, lances, possibly swords, daggers and hooks to board enemy ships; these weapons would be typical at the time.[16] There were no cannons or guns as these did not appear until much later.

As for Southern Han battleships, the nearest comparison would be those built by the Yuan dynasty (1271–1368) adopted from the Song dynasty (960-1127), which followed the demise of Southern Han. River Inspector G.R.G Worcester estimated that some of these ships were 11 metres in beam, 30 metres long and could hold 20 to 70 men.[17]

If there were 50 to 100 boats on each side of the antagonists, which would have been quite a few, then the number of men involved in the battle would be around three to seven thousand for each side. The order of magnitude would be consistent with those engaged in major battles at that time.

The painting appears to show that the Southern Han fleet was heading towards the sun. It would not be correct as they were sailing upstream of the river, which would be in the northern direction; the sun would then be behind the ships, not in front.

The mountain range in the background, if it were Tràng Kênh, then it would mean that the battle took place south of it by the river intersection of Chanh, which could be possible.

THE ARCHAEOLOGICAL EVIDENCE

North of the city of Hải Phòng, by the junction of the Thái and Bạch Đằng rivers, there is a museum aptly named Relics of Victory on Bạch Đằng river (*Di Tích Bạch Đằng Giang*) is dedicated to the three Vietnamese heroes Ngô Quyền, Lê Hoàn and Trần Hưng Đạo who defeated the northern armies of Southern Han, Song and Yuan (Mongols) in 938, 981 and 1288 respectively at the same river.[18]

Downstream of the Bạch Đằng river from the museum is another river junction of the Giá on the west and the Chanh on the east. There, at Yên Giang, by the Chanh river, in 1953, a number of wooden stakes were found (Figure 63); more stakes were found nearby at Đồng Vạn Muối in 2005 and Đồng Má Ngựa in 2010, but these were related to the 1288 battle.[19,20]

North of the museum, in 2019 and 2020, more stakes were found at Cao Quỳ and Đầm Thượng, respectively; however, information to date has indicated that these were also relics of the 1288 battle.[21]

So, unfortunately, my research has not turned up any archaeological evidence of the battle in 938. However, a rough guess could be made based on the estimated position of the coastline in 938 – which was further inland than it is now – the tidal rate and the average travelling speed of the ships to determine where the battle was likely to have taken place. For example, based on a slow sailing speed of, say, four knots or 7.4 kilometres per hour, Southern Han ships would take approximately two to three hours to get from the coast, say at Nam Đình Vũ port, to the museum location. Using modern-day tidal data, the tides would have been retreating, and the water level would have dropped between four to six hundred centimetres by then, which would be low enough to reveal the pointed tips of the stakes. So, somewhere around the museum location could be where the battle was, just south of Tràng Kênh mountain, as seemingly depicted in the painting.

It should be pointed out that Southern Han ships could have sailed up the Chanh river, along the northern side of Hà Nam Island, as this may have been known as Bạch Đằng river in 938, but the outcome would have been the same.[22]

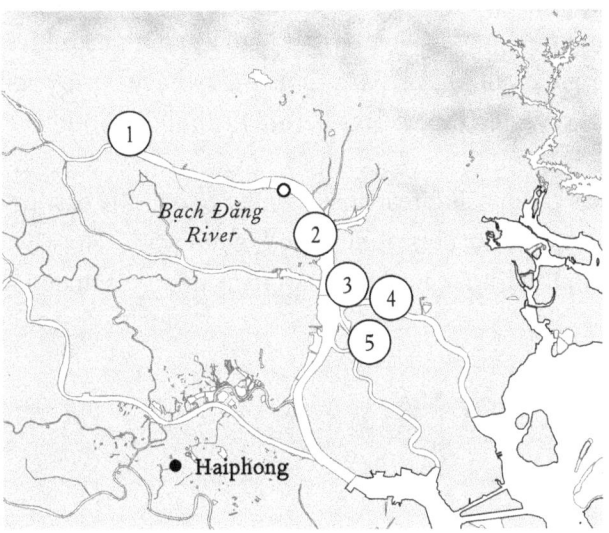

Figure 63 – Locations where stakes were found at the Bạch Đằng river.
1. Bãi Cọc (the stakes zone) Cao Quỳ, 2. Relic of Victory on Bạch Đằng River, 3. Bãi cọc (the stakes zone) Yên Giang-Bạch Đằng 1288, 4. Đồng Cốc, 5. Đình Hải Yến.

AN AMAZING FEAT

Historical works record the battle in a relatively short paragraph, but one could imagine the complexity of the event involved. Firstly, Ngô Quyền must have reliable intelligence to know when the Southern Han ships left Hai-men, and which river estuaries on the east coast of Vietnam they would most likely enter. Secondly, he must have support, and access to local manpower to cut down the trees, cut the stakes, and plant them in the river. Thirdly, he, or one of his men, must make the necessary calculations to know where to place these stakes, how deep, how much below the water level, and how far apart they should be planted, not to mention how to drive them into the river bed.

In preparation for the battle, Ngô Quyền may have moved his command post from Đại La – some 120 kilometres to the east – to Tràng Kênh. To coordinate the logistics of assembling the men, the boats, the weapons, and stakes planting require careful planning and must be done in secret to prevent the information from getting back to Hai-men.

Things could have quickly gone wrong for Ngô Quyền: they may have selected the wrong site to plant the stakes, Southern Han ships may have arrived too early or too late; they may have sent scouts in advance and discovered the stakes, spies may have reported Ngô Quyền's activities back to Li Hong-cao. Worse of all, the attack's timing may have been wrong, and the tides may have revealed themselves before the bulk of Southern Han ships were caught.

In all, it was an amazing feat and possibly one of the best traps in naval warfare of the age. Xiao Yi is right; Ngô Quyền was a shrewd adversary; Liu Yan and his son, Li Hong-cao should not have underestimated him.

16.4 – Aftermath of the battle

DECLARATION AS KING

Ngô Quyền and his men mopped up the remnants of the Southern Han fleet, and returned to Đại La in time to celebrate the Lunar New Year in 939, the year of the Pig. Unlike others before him, this time, he did not see any need to seek northern authorisation to become another *jiedushi*. He declared himself as king, crowned his wife, Dương thị, the daughter of Dương Đình Nghệ, as queen, and established his court at Cổ Loa, the ancient citadel built in the third century BCE.

938 is a major turning point in Vietnamese history; from that time on, the country never came under Northern Rule again except for a short period in the 15th century when the Ming dynasty invaded and stayed for nearly 30 years.

Khúc Thừa Dụ started the independence process in 906, at the end of the Tang dynasty. He was followed by Dương Đình Nghệ in 931, who demonstrated that his local troops could face and defeat a northern army. In 938, Ngô Quyền validated this native military strength with a decisive battle at the Bạch Đằng river.

Lê Văn Hưu, a Vietnamese historian of the 13th century, wrote the following passage about Ngô Quyền:

> "*King Ngô the former was able to take the newly assembled army of our country to defeat the hundreds of thousands of Li Hong-cao's troops, established a kingdom, proclaimed king, and made the northern people dare not come again.*²³ *It is possible to say that getting angry once but creating peace for the people,* [King Ngô] *was not only a good strategist but also good at fighting. Although only proclaimed king, not ascended to become an emperor nor changed the era, but the orthodoxy* [the tradition] *of our country, has been restored* [by these actions]."²⁴

The reference of hundreds of thousands is a little overstated when compared with the typical size of armies at the time in the ten to fifty thousand. Besides, Southern Han was unlikely to have enough ships to transport such a large number of troops. Allowing 50 to 100 troops per ship, they would need one to two thousand ships, which could be too many. Ma Yuan did not have enough ships to transport only 20,000 troops, and the number of boats in contemporary events was only in the hundreds.

Ngô Quyền reigned for six years to 944. After his death at the age of 46, the Giao Châu was plunged into political instability for 60 years and not until 1010 was the situation stabilised under the Lý dynasty (1010-1225).

THE KILLING OF BROTHERS

As for Liu Yan, the defeat at the Bạch Đằng river must have been a shock to him as it happened so quickly, likely within a day, and thoroughly; over half of his soldiers, including his son, were killed. He never invaded An Nam again.

History records Liu Yan as an intelligent but very harsh and cruel man. He was also a sadist who delighted in watching people killed.²⁵ The horrible punishments he handed out included cutting off noses, tongues, dismemberment, slitting pregnant women, tying people to heated iron poles, and boiling people.²⁶ Two years before the death of Ngô Quyền, in the summer of 942 Liu Yan died at the age of 50. The terrible legacy of his cruelty was passed on to his fourth son, Liu Hon-xing.

Within a year of his father's death, Liu Hon-xing began methodically putting to death his brothers, starting with his eldest; in 947, he killed eight; the remaining seven were killed during his reign.²⁷ One could speculate if Liu Hong-cao did not die at the battle at the Bạch Đằng river, he may have suffered the terrible fates of the other brothers. Four years earlier, in 943, Liu Hon-xing became the emperor of Southern Han.²⁸ However, this did not last long and by 971, the Song dynasty finally forced Southern Han to submit to its rule.

CHAPTER 17

CONCLUSIONS

It has been an exciting journey for a traveller to discover so many places I could visit across the whole length of Vietnam related to this period of 1,000 years. Unfortunately, because of the pandemic, my journey to date has involved chiefly poring over ancient texts in Vietnamese, Chinese, English, and French, as well as Google Maps and old charts, but it has been fascinating. There are many stories in Vietnamese history I have discovered representing the diverse and rich environment that is Vietnam.

Hence my first conclusion in this chapter is related to travelling. My second conclusion is about the inscriptions, and my third is to address the question of Vietnamese independence in 938.

17.1 – The river trips

This volume offers many historical sites that a traveller can work out an itinerary to suit; however, the river trips are particularly interesting to me. I summarise them briefly below so that someday I, or someone else, may be able to take them.

IN THE NORTH

1. Take a boat trip downstream of the Red River from Lào Cai in the north-west to Hanoi, then continuing to Hưng Yên, Nam Định, and the National Park at Xuân Thủy at the coast, tracing the route of Lý Bí, Chen Baxian, the Nanzhao warriors, possibly the Indian monks and other foreign merchants.

2. Take a boat trip upstream of the Bạch Đằng river from Hải Phòng to the Kinh Thầy and Đuống rivers and come out at the Red River, checking out the locations of the Bạch Đằng battle in 938.

3. Trace Ma Yuan and other southern expeditions by taking a boat trip downstream of the Đáy river from Đan Phượng commune to Phủ Lý, Ninh Bình to the coast and enter the estuary of the Nam Mã river to Thanh Hóa city.

IN THE NORTH-CENTRAL

1. Take a boat trip upstream of the Gianh river to get an appreciation of the raids from Linyi.

2. Take a boat trip upstream of the Nhật Lệ river to the source to get an understanding of the various battles fought along here during the fourth and fifth centuries.

3. Enter Cửa Việt and travel along the Thạch Hãn river and find a connection to the Ô Lâu river to get to Tam Giang lagoon, from there continue to Cầu Hai and exit to Chân Mây Bay at Cửa Tư Hiền, retracing the water routes taken by the generals of Linyi and northern dynasties. This trip can be taken in reverse.

4. Take a boat trip along the Thu Bồn river in the hinterland to the rock inscriptions of C.105 and C. 135 (Chapter 7).

IN THE MEKONG DELTA

Take a boat trip upstream of the Hậu river (Sông Hậu or Bassac river) from Cần Thơ to Long Xuyên, to Châu Đốc, passing Angkor Borei and finish at Phnom Penh, to visit places related to Funan and Zhenla.

17.2 – The inscriptions and monuments

My second conclusion concerns the inscriptions and monuments left behind by the people of Linyi, Funan, and Zhenla. These people once occupied territory of around 60 per cent of the present-day area of Vietnam; until I wrote this book, I knew little about them, and I suspect most Vietnamese are also just as vague about these kingdoms.[1] There are complex reasons for this lack of knowledge, but the simplest of all is that Vietnamese historians down the centuries have not considered these kingdoms as part of their history. However, in my view, king Bhavavarman of Mỹ Sơn and the Four-armed Buddha at Long Xuyên are as much the segments of the history of Vietnam as Lý Bí and the Thanh Mai bronze bell. I wish I had learned about them in my history lessons at school.

In this book, I have discussed some of the inscriptions and monuments, but the stories of Bahavarman and Rudravarman and others should start with the inscriptions of Võ Cạnh (C.40), Mỹ Sơn A1 (C.72), Gò Tháp (K.5), and continue until the last inscriptions of the 19th century. Such stories should be lifted out from these artefacts, separately from the accounts in the Chinese and Vietnamese annals. The inscriptions will mention Champa and Kamboja but not Linyi, Funan, or Zhenla because these names never appear on the inscriptions. This does not mean the records of these kingdoms in the Chinese and Vietnamese annals are invalid, but these records should be used as supporting evidence and not as drivers of the narratives.

However, I have not done that but may do so at sometime in the future. This is because to embark on such a project requires a scholarly study suitable for a postgraduate degree, for now beyond the scope of this book.

17.3 – The independence question

Finally, it would be remiss of me not to address how Vietnam came out of 1,000 years of Northern Rule as an independent nation. Today, a traveller in Vietnam sooner or later would come across the narrative that *"foreign domination resulted in rebellions leading to independence"*. While this narrative is accurate, it does not reflect the twists and turns of how the country has evolved. Be that the case, the narrative is so central to understanding Vietnamese history that we need to step back a little to review the answers, which, by nature, involve a high degree of generalisation.

CORRUPTED OFFICIALS

At the time of Shi Xie, in 184, the soldiers at Giao Chỉ commandery revolted, killed *cishi* Chu Ngung and sent a representative to the Later Han court to report Chu Ngung's crime. The emperor sent a new *cishi*, Jia Zong, south to take up the post. Upon arrival, Jia Zong asked the people why they rebelled; they replied:

> *"The previous order to pay taxes was very strict, the people were destitute, the road to the capital was far away, and we didn't know who to turn to. The people could not live, so they gathered to resist such policy, not really to rebel"*.[2]

Most of the *cishis* were:

> *"Those who come to work as a cishi, find that the land of Giao Chỉ has many pearls, halcyon's wings, elephant tusks, rhinoceros horns, tortoise-shells, exotic incense, and precious woods. They could not maintain their integrity, fill up their trunks and then move to somewhere else.*[3]

Jia Zong adopted a policy of gathering the homeless, forgiving the taxes, executing the corrupted officials, replacing them with honest ones, and reassuring the people in the commanderies. The policy worked, and the people were able to live in peace. They sang on the roads:

> *"Our father, with the last name of Jia, arrived late, which is why we rebelled previously. Now at peace, who dares to betray again?"*[4]

Jia Zong stayed for three years and was replaced by a native of Giao Châu, Lý Tiến, in 187, and as the Later Han dynasty disintegrated, Shi Xie and his brothers took over the southern land.

HISTORIANS' VIEWS

The enlightened policy of Jia Zong was not applied consistently in the following centuries. The pattern of corrupted, greedy officials followed by a revolt, suppression, and the appointment of an honest official, to reassure the local people repeated many times during the Northern Rule.[5] The implication of such a pattern is that if the northern rulers would only appoint "good" officials, then there would be no rebellion, and the people of Giao Châu or An Nam would be acquiescent to their rule.

However, the answer is not that simple; Chinese historians record that the people of Giao Châu as rebellious in nature.

"However, the newly formed prefectures always rebelled and killed the ruling officials" (around 91 BCE); *"The people [of Giao Châu] are prone to rebellion"* (231); *"The people of Giao Châu like to revolt"* (around 923).[6,7,8]

Vietnamese historians have attributed the Vietnamese people's strong desire for autonomy as the main reason the country rose up against northern rulers. From the poem cited in the 11th century:

The Southern country's mountain[s] and river[s] the Southern Emperor inhabits,
The separation is natural and allotted in Heaven's Book,
If the bandits come to trespass it,
You shall, in doing that, see yourselves to be handed with failure and shame![9]

to the quote by Lê Văn Hưu in the 13th century cited in Chapter 2:

"..the men of our land bowed their heads, folded their arms, and served the northerners; how shameful this is, in comparison with the two Trưng sisters.."

And the view of historian Phan Huy Lê in the 20th century:

"The history of anti-foreign aggression is a prominent feature of Vietnam and plays a decisive role in determining the nation's survival against the risk of foreign invasion and domination."[10]

The message is the same. The land of Vietnam belongs to the Vietnamese and is ruled by them, not by any foreigners. The corollary of this message is that the shame of subjugation would be unbearable, unacceptable so that all foreign rulers must be driven out, no matter the cost or sacrifice.

Phan explained further:

> "*It is this struggle for survival that has forged many noble dignities and developed to a high degree the intelligence and creativity of the nation.*"[11]

Others have attributed the desire for independence to the strength of the traditional villages:

> "*But miraculously,* [while] *our forefathers lost the country, but not the villages. It is the traditional villages of the Vietnamese people that have kept the strength of Vietnamese culture, where the people unite and care for each other to create a binding strength against the yoke of domination and assimilation through struggles to forge bravery and national character.*"[12]

The French historian Henri Maspero asked a similar question but came up with a different answer. In his view:

> "*If An Nam, after being liberated* [by Ma Yuan], *could for centuries to resist the power of China, while all other neighbouring states, Yelang, Dian, Nanzhao* [Yunnan and Guizhou provinces], *have gradually succumbed, it is because only it had been for centuries subjected to the regular Chinese administration and that this one, breaking the particular institutions, local groups, introducing ideas and forms Chinese social networks, gave it cohesion and a form that was always lacking in his neighbours. This advantage is due to Ma Yuan ... this strong Chinese frame allowed it* [An Nam] *to play, since the 10th century, the first role in the history of oriental Indochina*".[13]

Maspero is a highly respected French historian who made significant contributions to the understanding of Vietnamese history. He published the above paragraph in 1918 when Vietnam was a protectorate and a colony of France. Perhaps, he may see things differently if they were not. Leaving that aside, it would seem that Maspero did not pursue the matter further as to why the Vietnamese were not content to be part of imperial China if their native institutions were replaced by the Chinese.

One of the reasons for this, according to Vietnamese historians, continued from the quote above, is that:

> *"The villages themselves are not only places to preserve traditional cultural values but also to selectively absorb advanced exogenous cultural elements, including the fine and authentic culture of the Chinese people. The villages formed fortresses against the malicious assimilation scheme of the enemy."* [14]

A CONTEMPORARY HISTORIAN

Contemporary historian Keith Taylor provides a more succinct conclusion to the same subject, which can be summarised as follows:[15]

a. During the first millennium, the impact of Chinese civilisation on Vietnam was enormous,

b. The impact was most strongly felt at the highest level of government and society; among the middle-and upper-class Vietnamese,

c. As the centuries passed, ruling Vietnam became a luxury that China could not afford,

d. Vietnamese society rested firmly on a foundation of wet-rice agriculture with a robust pre-historic tradition,

e. The Vietnamese retained their language and with it, memories of pre-Chinese civilisation,

f. Their contact with the Chams and Khmers with their non-Chinese culture in the south reinforced their separate culture.

In short, as Taylor put it:

> *"Why did China's impact on Vietnam fall short of turning the Vietnamese into Chinese? The Vietnamese clearly did not want to become Chinese, and this surely lies at the root of their continuing existence as a separate nation."* [16]

A CONTRIBUTION

It would be outside the scope of this book to dwell on the finer points of this subject but having done the research, I will make a contribution as outlined below. Since the independence event of Vietnam happened in 938, I am only considering historical factors that happened *before* that year; those that occurred *after* 938 – may help me to understand the independent question – are not relevant.

Vietnamese culture

One reason the Vietnamese did not want to be Chinese, even after 1,000 years of Northern Rule, is that they already had their own culture. There is a glimpse of it through the bronze drums produced in northern Vietnam, indigenous legends, and myths passing down the generations centuries before the arrival of the Han army, as discussed in Volume One of this series. These stories were recorded in VDUL in the 14th century, and LNCQ in the 15th century, and those collected by the *cishsi* during their time in An Nam in the eighth and ninth centuries. As pointed out by other historians, these stories and annual observances have lived on in the villages and helped maintain a unique local identity.

Limitation of language and movements of people

Chinese scripts are not easy to learn.[17] Until the 19th century, when the French colonial government promoted the Latin-alphabet national script, the number of people who could read and write Chinese, *Hán*, or its Vietnamese derivative, *Nôm*, was limited to a very small number. Prior to the widespread application of the national script, I believe that most Vietnamese could not read or write. Travelling was primarily on foot, carts, horses or by small boats along rivers, and as a result, most people would rarely venture beyond their villages. They communicated in their language; their loyalty was likely to the village and its chiefs and not to some emperors in remote capitals in the north.

Over 1,000 years, most of the 200 recorded *cishis* and *taishous* of Giao Châu were from China. A few stayed for decades, but most stayed for a few years and went back, driven out or killed. A number were banished there as a punishment.[18] It is unlikely that many of them would consider themselves Vietnamese, put down any roots and gain the loyalty of the local people.

Limitation of geography

The other limitation is geography. During the first millennium, the authority of the northern dynasties rarely extended beyond Ngang pass. After the third century, the provinces immediately south of Ngang pass, recorded as part of the empire, were on paper only. Even north of Ngang pass, the control of the northern dynasties around the southern prefectures of contemporary Thanh Hóa, Nghệ An, and the north-western prefectures of contemporary Vĩnh Phúc, was tenuous at best. As events turned out, the people from these regions finally led the charge that gained independence.

It was no coincidence that many Đồng Sơn bronze drums were found in Thanh Hóa, similarly, the legendary Hùng kings came from the region around Phú Thọ where the indigenous culture was deeply embedded.

Land outside the imperial rule

After the third century, the kingdoms south of Ngang pass, like Linyi, Funan, and their successors, developed a distinct Indianised culture, utterly unrelated to those north of the pass. While they had paid tributes, they owed no loyalty to the northern emperors.

Ability to fight

Finally, and arguably the most important factor is that by the ninth century, the Vietnamese knew how to fight: how to build up an army, train their men, organise the logistics, build the ships and weapons. They already knew how to make bronze arrows and crossbows to fight against the Han in the second century BCE, so the knowledge of warfare lived on. No doubt, the battles with Linyi, and the Nanzhao-An Nam war had created a class of warriors and provided the expertise needed to win battles. As repeated events in the second millennium illustrated, if they did not know how to fight and win, they would have easily fallen back into the Northern Rule circuit under the Song, the Yuan, the Ming, and the Qing dynasties.

The second volume of my book series, *"A Traveller's Story of Vietnam's Past"* ends here, and I look forward to sharing my stories with readers in Volume Three to see how an independent Vietnam managed to survive from the 10th to the 16th centuries.

— TAN PHAM (PHẠM LƯƠNG TẤN), Long Bay, June 2022.

APPENDIX I

SOURCES OF VIETNAMESE HISTORY IN THE CHINESE LANGUAGE

Until Vietnam became independent in the 10th century, all writings about its history are Chinese sourced, so to study the characters and events covered by this book, I have to look up these works. There are also Sanskrit and Chamic inscriptions on rocks and stone steles, very useful for the study of Funan and Linyi. A number of these inscriptions have been translated into French, English and Vietnamese.[1] And of course, there are archaeological artefacts and associated papers which I can refer to.

Each dynasty in imperial China compiled its historical texts, called Book or *shu*. In general, each *shu* would cover Annals of the Emperors, Biographies of important characters, Treaties and Records to discuss such items as Astronomy, Geography, Music, Rites and Officials. Many of the stories about Vietnam in the first millennium can be found among the Annals, Geography and Biographies.

A number of these historical works have been translated into English and Vietnamese. Chinese versions one can download from the Chinese Text Project (HTTPS://CTEXT.ORG/) or Chinese Notes (HTTP://CHINESENOTES.COM/) websites.[2]

Below is the list of the relevant works referred to in this book in chronological order, based on the year the work was compiled or published:

1. Han shu or "*Book of Han*" or "*History of the Former Han*" covers the Former Han dynasty from the first emperor in 206 BCE to the fall of Wang Mang in 23. [3,4] The work was composed by Ban Gu (32-92), a Later Han court official. For stories related to Vietnam for this book, the relevant volumes are 28 and 95.[5]

2. Dongguan Hanji or "*Han Records of the Eastern Pavilion*" is a history of the Later Han period (25-220). The name is derived from the palace hall where the historiographic bureau was located.[6] It started out as an official biography for Emperor Guangwu (25-57), founder of the Later Han dynasty, and was compiled by a team of historiographers under the guidance of Ban Gu who also compiled Han shu. Dongguan Hanji is a predecessor of Hou Han shu. For stories related to Vietnam for this book, the relevant volume is the biography of Ma Yuan.[7]

3. Hou Han shu or "*Book of Later Han*", covers the history of the Eastern or Later Han dynasty from 6 to 189.[8] The book was compiled by Fan Ye and others in the fifth century. For stories related to Vietnam, the relevant volumes are 22, 24, 76, 86 and 113.[9]

4. Sanguo zhi or "*Records of the Three Kingdoms*" covers the history of the Later Han dynasty (c. 184–220) and the Three Kingdoms period (220–280). It was written by Chen Shou in the third century.[10] For stories related to Vietnam, the relevant volumes are the Book of Wu, Volumes 49 and 60.[11]

5. Shui Jing Zhu Shu (Thủy kinh chú sớ, TKCS) is a 19th additional explanation of the Shui Jing Zhu (*Commentary on the Water Classic*) compiled by Li Daoyuan during the Northern Wei dynasty (386-534 CE).[12] Shui Jing Zhu is a work on the ancient geography of China, describing its waterways and ancient canals and is expanded from the source text, the older (and now lost) Shui Jing (Water Classic) written during the Three Kingdoms period (220-280 CE). I use the Vietnamese translation of the 19th-century work, published in 1955.[13] It is a thick book (nearly 1000 pages) and the relevant volumes are 36 and 37.

6. Nan Qi shu or *"Book of Southern Qi (Nan Qi shu) or the Book of Qi (Qi shu)"* covers the period from 479 to 502 of the Southern Qi dynasty.[14] It was written by Xiao Zixian (489-537). For stories related to Vietnam, the relevant volume is Volume 58.[15]

7. Song shu or *"Book of Song"* is a historical text of the Liu Song dynasty from 420 to 479. It was written in 492–493 by Shen Yue (441-513).[16] For stories related to Vietnam, the relevant volumes are 38, 76, 92 and 97.[17]

8. Liang shu or *"Book of Liang"* was compiled under Yao Silian and completed in 635. It covers the Liang (or Southern Liang) dynasty (502–557).[18] For stories related to Vietnam, the relevant volumes are 3 and 58.[19]

9. Chen shu or *"Book of Chen"* is the official history of the Chen dynasty. It was compiled by Yao Silian, a historian of the Tang dynasty and completed in 636.[20] For stories related to Vietnam, the relevant volume is 1.[21]

10. Sui shu or *"Book of Sui"* is the official history of the Sui dynasty. It was written by Yan Shigu, Kong Yingda, and Zhangsun Wuji, with Wei Zheng as the lead author. The Book of Sui was completed in 636, the same year as the Book of Chen was completed.[22] For stories related to Vietnam, the relevant volumes are 2, 31, 53, 56 and 82.[23]

11. Jin shu or *"Book of Jin"* is an official Chinese historical text covering the history of the Jin dynasty from 266 to 420. It was compiled in 648 by a number of officials commissioned by the imperial court of the Tang dynasty, with chancellor Fang Xuanling as the lead editor.[24] For stories related to Vietnam, the relevant volumes are 7, 15, 57, 97.[25]

12. Bei shi or *"History of the Northern Dynasties"*, the book was started by Li Dashi and, following his death, completed by his son, Li Yanshou, between 643 and 659. For stories related to Vietnam, the relevant volume is 95.[26]

13. Man shu or *"The Book of the Man barbarians"* also known as Yunnan zhi *"Local gazetteer of Yunnan"*, Nanyi zhi, *"Treatise on the Southern barbarians"*, and other names, is a geographical description of China's remote south-west during the Tang period (618-907). The book was compiled by Fan Chuo (late ninth century). Modern editions are based on Fang Guoyu's (1903-1983) edition.[27]

14. Jiu Tang shu or *"Old Book of Tang"*, or simply the *Book of Tang*, is a historical work about the Tang dynasty. The credited editor was chief minister Liu Xu (888-947), but the bulk (if not all) of the editing work was actually completed by his predecessor Zhao Ying.[28] For stories related to Vietnam, the relevant volumes are 35, 41, 59 and 197.[29]

15. Tongdian means *"Comprehensive Institutions"* is a Chinese institutional history and encyclopaedia text covering antiquity to 756. The book was written by Du You from 766 to 801.[30] For stories related to Vietnam, the relevant volume is 188 (Border defence).

16. Tang Huiyao, "Institutional history of the Tang dynasty", compiled by Wang Pu and presented to Emperor Taizu of Song in 961. For stories related to Vietnam, the relevant volume is 98.[31]

17. Xin Tang shu or *"New Book of Tang"* is an official history covering the Tang dynasty. The work was compiled by a team of scholars of the Song dynasty, led by Ouyang Xiu and Song Qi, and completed in 1060.[32] For stories related to Vietnam, the relevant volumes are 9, 167, 170, 201, 207, 222c, 224.[33]

18. Wudai Shiji or *"Historical Records of the Five Dynasties"* is a history book of the Five Dynasties period (907–960), written by Ouyang Xiu, an official of the Song dynasty. It was not published until 1073, a year after his death. Frequently referred to as *"The New History of the Five Dynasties (Xin Wudai Shi)"*. An abridged English translation by Richard L. Davis was published in 2004.[34] For stories related to Vietnam, the relevant volumes are 65 and 74.[35]

19. Zizhi Tongjian literally means *"Comprehensive Mirror in Aid of Governance"* (or government) is a reference work in Chinese historiography, published in 1084 in the form of a chronicle. It took historian Sima Guang (1019–1086) and other scholars nineteen years to complete this universal history of China. The *Zizhi Tongjian* records Chinese history from 403 BCE to 959, covering 16 dynasties and spanning almost 1,400 years.[36]

APPENDIX 2

SOURCES OF VIETNAMESE HISTORY BY VIETNAMESE AUTHORS WRITTEN PRE-19TH CENTURY.

Vietnamese historical works first appeared in the 12th century. The writers most likely referred to the Chinese sources for the earlier periods of Vietnamese history, so whenever applicable and possible, I have used the original Chinese references in the dynastic annals.

However, the compilers of Vietnamese works also included records from local temples, and pagodas not included in Chinese sources, offered explanations, made notes and expressed their views. I have found these helpful in collecting materials for this book. The lists below are key documents in chronological order with a short description; a more detailed account of these works can be found in Volume One of my book series.

1. *An Nam Chí Lược* (ANCL, Abridged Annals of An Nam).[1]

There are 20 introductions to this book, with the one dated in 1307 as the earliest and the one dated in 1884 as the latest. The author, Lê Tắc, also wrote his introduction in 1333. So, it appears that Lê Tắc wrote his book soon after he escaped from Đại Việt (Vietnam was called Đại Việt at the time) and settled in China in 1292. His book covers the period from Zhao Tuo of Nan-Yue to the time when he fled Đại Việt at the end of the 13th century.

2. *Việt Điện U Linh* (VDUL, Compilation of the Departed Spirits in the Realm of Viet).[2]

VDUL was written by Lý Tế Xuyên, an official (possibly a librarian) under the reign of King Trần Hiến Tông (1329-1341). The preface of the book as written by him was dated 1329.[3] Lý Tế Xuyên made a number of references to two books[4] now lost, *Giao Châu Ký*[5] *(Records of Jiaozhou)* written by Zhao Zhang (Triệu Vương or Triệu Xương)[6] and *Giao Chỉ Ký (Records of Jiaozhi)*[7] written by Zeng Gun (Tăng Công or Tăng Cồn).[8] It is a little confusing as SKTT refers to the book written by Zeng Gun as *Giao Châu Ký* but makes no reference to any book written by Zhao Chang.[9] Zhao Chang was the *duhu* of An Nam twice, in 791-802 and 804-806, Zeng Gun was the *jiedushi* of An Nam in 878-880 under the Tang dynasty.

The title of *Giao Châu Ký* also appears under different authors, Diêu Văn Thức of the Later Han (25-220), Đặng Trung Phẫu, Lưu Hân Kỳ of the Jin (265-420), Lưu Trường Chi of the Liu Song (420-479) and Zeng Gun of Tang (618-906). All were lost except for a few pages by Lưu Hân Kỳ that was found.[10] VDUL does not mention other authors except Zeng Gun for *Giao Chỉ Ký*.

These two books are also known as as *Triệu Công Giao Châu Ký* or *Triệu Vương Giao Châu Ký* and *Tăng Công Giao Châu Ký*.[11]

3. *Việt Sử Lược* (An Abridged History of Viet or Veritable records of Việt, VSL) with the word Đại (or Great) removed.[12]

VSL covers the period from the Hùng kings to the final king of the Lý dynasty in 1225, with a list of kings of the Trần dynasty until 1377. The author of this book is cited as Sử Hy Nhan, but the version that I use does not have this name.[13]

4. *Lĩnh Nam Chích Quái* (LNCQ, A Collection of Strange Stories from Lingnan).[14]

Vũ Quỳnh (1452-1516), a scholar-official during the Lê dynasty and Kiều Phú, restored and edited LNCQ, attributed to Trần Thế Pháp. This book is of a similar genre to VDUL. Vũ Quỳnh suggests the original authors lived under the Lý (1009-1225) and Trần dynasties (1225-1400).[15]

However, in terms of Vietnamese history books, the most important work is:

5. *Đại Việt Sử Ký Toàn Thư* (SKTT, Complete Book of the Historical Records of Great Viet).[16]

It was compiled by Ngô Sĩ Liên in 1479. The oldest version of the book was found by Professor Phan Huy Lê (1934-2018), a Vietnamese historian, at the library of the Société Asiatique in Paris, France. This version, termed Chính Hòa, was printed from woodcuts in 1697.[17]

SKTT covers the history of Vietnam from the time of Hùng kings to 1675. One can find an online version at HTTP://WWW.NOMFOUNDATION.ORG/NOM-PROJECT/HISTORY-OF-GREATER-VIETNAM/FULLTEXT/100-TUC-BIEN-TU?UILANG=VN.

6. *Khâm Định Việt Sử Thông Giám Cương Mục* (CM, The Imperially Ordered Annotated Text Completely Reflecting the History of Viet).[18]

CM is a Vietnamese historical work edited by Phan Thanh Giản, first printed by the Bureau of History of the Nguyễn Dynasty (*Quốc Sử Quán Triều Nguyễn*) in 1884, covering the period from the Hùng kings to the last king of the Lê dynasty in 1789.

APPENDIX 3

NAMES IN VIETNAMESE, PINYIN CHINESE AND ENGLISH

Imperial China adopted a hierarchical system of administration centred around the emperor at the top. The empire was divided into many provinces, which were further split up into prefectures or counties. Below the prefecture level, were further subdivisions into smaller administration units.
There were changes over the centuries, but the hierarchical principle had remained the same with the three tiers structure. However, during Sui-Tang times, the line between *zhou* (province) and *jun* (commandery) became blurred, and *jun* was eventually phased out.

During Former Han times, the head of each *jun* was called *taishou* (Governor). He was to report to a *cishi* (Regional Inspector) who reported back to the court.[1] At the time of Emperor Cheng (8 BCE) of the Former Han, another title *zhou mu* (Governor) appeared with a salary more than six times that of *cishi*. Barely three years later, in 5 BCE, it reverted back to *cishi*, only to be changed back to *zhou mu* in 1 BCE. For all intent and purposes, both *zhou mu* and *cishi* are the same.[2] In later times, *cishi* became the head of *zhou*, and *taishou* disappeared under Sui (581-618).

Under Tang, *zhou* became smaller, for example, Giao châu (a *zhou*) until Sui times includes Giao Chỉ, Cửu Chân and Nhật Nam commanderies, but under Tang, it only covers roughly Giao Chỉ commandery. The head of a *zhou* or several *zhous* is no longer a *cishi* but a *dudu* (Governor-General) or a *duhu* (Protectorate General), and later on, when the *zhou* was changed to a *jinghai*, it became the or *jiedushi* (Military Governor) or *jing lue shi* (Imperial Commissioner).[3] In this book, to avoid confusion, I have generally used the Chinese titles and not their English translation as there are several of such translations.

VIETNAMESE	PINYIN CHINESE	ENGLISH
\multicolumn{3}{c}{I. ADMINISTRATIVE UNITS}		
\multicolumn{3}{c}{*Qin/Former Han Dynasty*}		
Bộ[4]	Zhōu (州)	Circuit (also translated as Province).[5] e.g. *Giao Chỉ circuit*
Quận	Jùn (郡)	Commandery. e.g. *Nhật Nam commandery.*
Huyện	Hien (縣) Xian	Prefecture (also translated as District and County).[6] e.g. *Chu Ngô prefecture.*
\multicolumn{3}{c}{*Later Han/Six Dynasties*}		
Châu	Zhōu (州)	Province (also translated as Circuit).[7] e.g. *Giao Châu province.*
Quận	Jùn (郡)	Commandery e.g. *Nhật Nam commandery.*
Huyện	Hien (縣) Xian	Prefecture (also translated as District and County). e.g *Chu Ngô prefecture.*
\multicolumn{3}{c}{*Sui-Tang Dynasties*}		
Đạo	Dào (道)	Circuit, e.g. *Lingnan circuit.*
Châu	Zhōu (州)	Province (also translated as Department, Prefecture).[8] e.g. *Giao province.* Note that Giao Châu in Sui-Tang times is not the same as Giao Châu in Later Han times. The latter is much larger, more equivalent to a circuit.
Quận	Jùn (郡)	Commandery
Huyện	Hien (縣) Xian	Prefecture (also translated as Sub-prefecture, Arrondissement, District and County).[9] e.g *Tống Bình prefecture.*
Phủ	Fu (府)	Superior prefecture
Đô Đốc Phủ	Dūdū fǔ (都督府)	Office of the Governor General.
Đô Hộ Phủ	Dūhu fǔ (都护府)	Protectorate
	Fānzhèn (藩鎮)	Military district or buffer town
Tĩnh Hải Quận	Jinghai-Jun (靜海軍)	Peaceful Sea Military District

APPENDIX 3

VIETNAMESE	PINYIN CHINESE	ENGLISH

2. DYNASTIES-KINGDOMS

VIETNAMESE	PINYIN CHINESE	ENGLISH
Ân	Shang or Yin	
Chu	Zhou	
Đông Hán		Eastern (or Later) Han
Đường	Tang	
Hạ	Xia	
Lỗ	Lu	
Lương	Liang	
Lưỡng Tấn		Western Jin and Eastern Jin
Lưu Tống	Liu Song	
Minh	Ming	
Ngô	Wu	
Nguyên	Yuan	
Ngụy	Wei	
Sở	Chu	
Tam Quốc (Tào Ngụy, Thục Hán, Đông Ngô)	Cao Wei, Shu Han, Dong Wu	Three Kingdoms (Cao Wei, Shu Han, Eastern Wu)
Tần	Qin	
Tấn	Jin	
Tây Hán		Western (or Former) Han
Tề (Nam Tề)	Qi (Nan Qi)	
Thanh	Qing	
Thương	Shang or Yin	
Tống	Song	
Triệu	Zhao	
Tùy	Sui	
Yên	Yan	

3. HISTORICAL WORKS/DESCRIPTION

VIETNAMESE	ENGLISH
Chí	Annals
Chính Biên	Principal
Cương	Sketch, general, summary.[10]

VIETNAMESE	PINYIN CHINESE	ENGLISH
Cựu Đường Thư	Jiu Tang shu	Old Book of Tang
Ký	Ji	Records
Hán Thư	Han shu	Book of Han
Hậu Hán Thư	Hou Han shu	Book of Later Han
Hoài Nam Tử	Huainanzi	
Lã Thị Xuân Thu	Lüshi Chunqiu	
Lược		Summary, abridged, annotated
Lục		Records, copies
Lục Độ Tập Kinh	Liudu ji jing	Six Perfection Sutras
Lương Thư	Liang shu	Book of Liang
Lý Hoặc Luận	Lihou lun	Treatise on Alleviating Doubt
Man Thư	Man shu	Book of the Southern Man barbarians
Mục		Details expanded from "Cương"
Nam Tề Thư	Nan Qi shu	Book of Southern Qi
Sử Ký	Shiji	
Tả truyện / Tả thị Xuân Thu	Zuo Zhuan	The Commentary of Zuo
Tam Quốc Chí – Ngô Thư	Sanguo zhi – Wu Shu	The Records of the Three Kingdoms – Book of Wu
Tân Đường Thư	Xin Tang shu	New Book of Tang
Tân Ngũ Đại Sử	Xin Wudai Shi	New History of the Five Dynasties
Tấn Thư	Jin shu	Book of Jin
Thiền Uyển Tập Anh	Zhan Yuan Jiying	Collection of Outstanding Figures of the Zen Garden
Thông		Complete
Thông Điển	Tongdian	Comprehensive Institutions
Thực (Thật) lục		Veritable records
Thủy Kinh Chú Sớ	Shuijing zhu shi	
Tiền Biên		Prequel
Tống Thư	Song shu	Book of Song
Trần Thư	Chen shu	Book of Chen
Tự Trị Thông Giám	Zizhi Tongjian	Comprehensive Mirror in Aid of Government (Governance)

VIETNAMESE	PINYIN CHINESE	ENGLISH
Tục Biên		Sequel
Tùy Thư	Sui shu	Book of Sui
Xuân Thu	Chunqiu	

4. LOCATIONS

VIETNAMESE	PINYIN CHINESE
Ba Thục	Ba Shu
Châu Nhai	Zhuya
Chiết Giang	Zhejiang
Chu Giang	Zhujiang
Chu Ngô	Zhuwu
Côn Minh	Kunming
Cửu Chân	Jiuzhen
Cửu Nghi (Mạnh Chử Lĩnh)	Mengzhuling
Đam Nhĩ	Dan'er
Dạ Lang	Yelang
Đại Dũ	Dayuling
Dự Chương	Yuzhang
Dương Sơn	Yang-san
Dư Can	Yugan
Giang Tây	Jiangxi
Giao Châu	Jiaozhou
Giao Chỉ	Jiaozhi
Giang Tô	Jiangsu
Hà Nam	Henan
Hồ Bắc	Hubei
Hồ Nam	Hunan
Hợp Phố	Hepu
Khu Túc	Qusu
Kinh Châu	Jingzhou
Lạc Dương	Luoyang, capital of Later Han
Lâm Lư	Lung-lu
Lĩnh Nam	Lingnan

VIETNAMESE	PINYIN CHINESE	ENGLISH
Linh Lăng	Lingling	
Lô Dung	Lurong	
Lục Lương	Luliang	
Luy Lâu	Leilou	
Nam Hải	Nan-hai	
Nam Kinh	Nanjing or Jianye	
Nam Ninh	Nanning	
Nam Việt	Nan-yue	
Ngô Châu	Wuzhou	
Ngũ Lĩnh	Wuling	
Nhật Nam	Rinan	
Phiên Ngung	Panyu	
Phủ Châu	Fuzhou	
Phúc Kiến	Fujian	
Phong Khê	Fengxi	
Quảng Châu	Guangzhou	
Quảng Đông	Guangdong	
Quảng Tây	Guangxi	
Quảng Tín	Guangxin	
Quế Dương	Guiyang	
Quế Lâm (under Qin) and Uất Lâm (under Han)[11]	Guilin	
Quý Châu	Guizhou	
Tây An	Xi'an	
Tây Quyển	Xijuan	
Tây Vu	Xi Yu	
Thạc Môn	Shih-men	
Thành Đô	Chengdu	
Thương Ngô	Cangwu	
Thiệu Hưng	Shaoxing	
Thượng Hải	Shanghai	
Tín Giang	Xinjiang	

VIETNAMESE	PINYIN CHINESE	ENGLISH
Tống Bình	Songping	
Trùng Khánh	Chongqing	
Trường An	Chang'an, capital of Former Han	
Trường Sa	Changsa	
Tư Phố	Xupu	
Tứ Xuyên	Sichuan	
Tượng Lâm	Xianglin	
Tỷ Ảnh	Bijing	
Vân Nam	Yunnan	
Vọng Hải	Wanghai	
Vũ Hán	Wuhan	
Xa Cừ	Chequ	
Yết Dương	Jiejang	

5. MEASUREMENTS

bộ	bu	pace
cân	jin	
đấu	dou	
hộc	ge	
lí, dặm	li	mile
lượng, lạng	liang/ tael	
phân	fen	
thăng	shen	
thốn, tấc	cun	inch
trượng	zhang	
xích/ thước	chi	foot

6. OFFICIAL TITLES

Châu Mục	Zhou mu (州牧)	Governor
Công Tào	Gongcao 功曹	Officer of Merit, Labour Section Serviceman
Đại Tướng Quân	Da Jiangjun	Commander-in-Chief
Đô Úy	Duwei (都尉)	Commandant

VIETNAMESE	PINYIN CHINESE	ENGLISH
Đô Đốc	Dūdū (都督)	Governor General
Đô Hộ	Dūhu (都护)	Protectorate General
Đốc Bưu	Duyou (督郵)	Investigator/Local Inspector
Hầu	Hou	Marquis
Hiếu Liêm	Xiaolian	Candidate of Probity and Piety
Huyện Lệnh	Xianling (縣令)	County Magistrate
Kinh Lược Sứ	Jing Lue Shi (经略使)	Imperial Commissioner
Lâu Thuyền Tướng Quân	Lou Chuan Jiangjun	General of Tower Ships
Mậu Tài	Maocai	Candidate of Accomplished Talent
Phục Ba Tướng Quân	Fubo Jiangjun	Wave-Calming General
Tam Công	Sangong	Three Ducal Ministers or Three Dukes
Thái Thú	Taishou (太守)	Governor (also translated as Grand Administrator or Administrator)
Thị Ngự Sử	Shi Yushi (侍御史)	Imperial Clerk, Attendant Censor
Thứ Sử	Cishi (刺史)	Regional Inspector (also as Inspector) in Han times. Prefect (Head of local prefecture) in Sui-Tang times.
Thượng Thư Lang	Shangshu lang	Gentleman of Writing
Tiết Độ Sứ	Jiedushi (节度使)	Military Governor/Commissioner
Tổng Quản		Administrator (overall management)
Tư Mã	Sima (司馬)	Major (or Commander) in charge of horses
Tư Đồ	Situ 司徒	Minister of the Masses

7. PEOPLE

Chất Đa Tư Na	She-to-ssu-na	Citrasena (Sanskrit)
Chi Cương Lương		Kalasivi (Sanskrit)
Đàm Thiên	Tan Tian	
Đổng Trác	Dong Zhuo	
Già La Đồ Lê		Kalacarya (Sanskrit)
Già Xương	Jia Zhang	

APPENDIX 3

VIETNAMESE	PINYIN CHINESE	ENGLISH
Hồ	Hu	
Khâu Đà La		Ksudra (Sanskrit)
Khu Liên	Qu Lian	
Khương Tăng Hội	Kang Shenghui	
Lộ Bá Đức	Lu Bode	
Lưu Biểu	Liu Biao	
Lý Cố	Li Gu	
Ma-la-kỳ-vực		Mahajivaka (Sanskrit)
Mã Viện	Ma Yuan	
Mâu Tử	Mouzi	
Nhâm Diên	Ren Yan	
Ô Hử	Wuhu	
Sái Lợi	Cha li	Kṣatriya (Sanskrit)
Sĩ Huy	Shi Hui	
Sĩ Khuông	Shi Kuang	
Sĩ Nhất	Shi Yi	
Sĩ Nhiếp	Shi Xie	
Sĩ Tứ	Shi Ci	
Sĩ Vĩ	Shi Wei	
Sĩ Vũ	Shi Wu	
Sĩ Ngẩm	Shi Xin	
Tích Quang	Xi Guang	
Trần Bá Tiên	Chen Baxian	
Triệu Ẩu (Bà Triệu)		Lady Triệu
Tỳ Ni Đa Lưu Chi	Vinitaruci	
Tô Định	Su Ding	
Tôn Quyền	Sun Quan	
Người Tráng (Choang)	Zhuangzu	
Triệu Đà	Zhao Tuo	
Trưng Trắc	Zheng Ce	
Trưng Nhị	Zheng Er	
Vương Mãng	Wang Mang	

VIETNAMESE	PINYIN CHINESE	ENGLISH
Y Xa Na Tiên		Īśānasena (Sanskrit)

8. RIVERS, MOUNTAINS, LAKES

VIETNAMESE	PINYIN CHINESE	ENGLISH
Bá Dương (hồ)	Poyang lake	
Cô Tô (núi)	Mount Gusu	
Cối Khê (núi)	Mount Kuaiji	
Đại Dữu (or Đại Dũ, núi)	Mount Dayu	
Đỗ Bang (núi)	Mount Dupang	
Động Đình (hồ)	Dongting lake	
Dương Tử (sông)	Yangtze or Yangzi (river)	
Hoàng Hà (sông)	Huang He (river)	Yellow river
Hữu Giang (sông)	Youjiang (river)	
Kỵ Điền (núi)	Mount Qitian	
Minh (or Manh) Chử or Cửu Nghi, núi)	Mount Mengzhu	
Ngũ Lĩnh (núi)	Wuling or Nanling mountains	
Tả Giang (sông)	Zuojiang (river)	
Tín Giang (or Dư Can or Dư Hãn, sông)	Xinjiang (river) – Yugan is a county	
Việt Thành (or Đàm Thành)[12] (núi)	Mount Yuechengling	
Vũ Di (núi)	Mount Wuyi	

9. STATES, KINGDOMS

VIETNAMESE	PINYIN CHINESE	ENGLISH
An Nam	An nan	Annam (French)
Chân Lạp	Zhenla	
Chiêm Thành		Champa
Dạ Lang	Yelang	
Đông Âu	Dong-ou	
Đông Ngô	Eastern Wu	
Đường Minh	Tangming	
Hoàn Vương	Huanwang	
Lâm Ấp	Linyi	

APPENDIX 3

VIETNAMESE	PINYIN CHINESE	ENGLISH
Mân Việt	Min-yue	
Nam Giao	Nanzhao	
Nam Việt	Nan-yue	
Phù Nam	Funan	
Tam Quốc		Three Kingdoms
Tào Ngụy	Cao Wei	
Thục Hán	Shu Han	
Việt	Yue	

APPENDIX 4

POLITIES UNDER THE NORTHERN RULE PERIOD

APPENDIX 4

TIMELINES	CHINESE DYNASTIES	POLITIES	COMMANDERIES & PROVINCES[i]
111 – 1 BCE	Former Han	Giao Chỉ (circuit)	Three commanderies of: Giao Chỉ (10)[1] - Cửu Chân (7)[2] - Nhật Nam (5)[3]
1-199 CE	Former/Later Han	Funan Giao Chỉ (circuit)	Same as above
200-299 CE	Later Han/ Six Dynasties	Funan Linyi Giao Chỉ / Giao Châu (from 203)	Three commanderies of: Giao Chỉ (12)[4] - Cửu Chân (5) - Nhật Nam (5)
300-399 CE	Six Dynasties	Funan Linyi Giao Châu	Six commanderies of:[5] Giao Chỉ (14) - Tân Xương (6) - Vũ Bình (7) - Cửu Chân (7) - Cửu Đức (8) - Nhật Nam (5)
500-699 CE	Liang/Cheng/Sui	Funan Linyi Giao Châu, Vạn Xuân, An Nam Duhufu (679)	Six commanderies of:[6] Giao Chỉ (9) - Cửu Chân (6) - Nhật Nam (8) - Tỷ Ảnh - Hải Âm - Tượng Lâm.
700-799 CE	Tang	Zhenla, Water Zhenla and Land Zhenla Linyi An Nam Duhufu, Trấn Nam Duhufu (757), An Nam (766)	Ten provinces:[7] Giao (8) -Phong (5) - Trường-Ái (6) - Diễn Hoan (4) - Phúc Lộc-Lục (3)[8] – Lâm - Ảnh
800-899 CE	Tang	Zhenla, Water Zhenla and Land Zhenla Huanwang (757-859) An Nam Duhufu, Jinghai Qu (866)	
900-999 CE	Tang/Five Dynasties	Khmer Empire Champa Jinghai Qu/ Giao Châu	

Table 7 – Polities in three regions of Vietnam from the first to the 10th centuries.

i. Related to Vietnam only. Number of prefectures in brackets.

APPENDIX 5

GIAO CHỈ, GIAO CHÂU, LUY LÂU AND LONG BIÊN

Much of my time has been spent locating sites of historical interest mentioned in historical works. For the stories associated with north and central Vietnam, the names of Giao Chỉ (Jiaozhi), Giao Châu (Jiaozhou), Luy Lâu (Leilou), and Long Biên (Longbian) appear frequently. They get very confusing, so in the Appendix, I will attempt to clarify their locations and put forward my suggestions on where these might be.

A5.1 – Giao Chỉ and Giao Châu - Circuit and Province - A confusion of names

GIAO CHỈ CIRCUIT

Five years after defeating Nan-yue, in 106 BCE, the Former Han dynasty placed seven commanderies under the Giao Chỉ circuit, including 55 prefectures covering the land that once Nan-yue.[1] The head of the circuit is called a *cishi* (Regional Inspector).

During the reign of Emperor Shun of Han (126-144), around 136, the *taishou* (Governor) of Giao Chỉ commandery, Zhou Zhang, sought permission to change Giao Chỉ to a *zhou*, Giao Châu, at a level higher than a commandery and on a par with other *zhous* in the empire. Presumably, he wanted more benefits and power, but the emperor turned him down. Since *zhou* in Pinyin Chinese is *Châu* in Vietnamese, translated as a province in English, Giao Châu *or Jiaozhou* is Giao province. However, as Giao Châu or Jiaozhou is a more commonly used term, I will use Giao Châu and not Giao province or Giao Châu province.

GIAO CHÂU

In 203, the *cishi* of the Giao Chỉ circuit, Zhang Jin, and the *taishou* of Giao Chỉ, commandery, Shi Xie, tried again and made a joint submission to the Later Han court. This time the last Emperor of Later Han, Xiaoxian, agreed. Giao Chỉ circuit became Giao Châu, Zhang Jin became its governor, *zhou mu* (Châu Mục), but Giao Chỉ as a commandery remained the same with Shi Xie as its head.[2] The name Giao Châu started from then, the year 203.

Other than rewards and power, I suspect that Shi Xie played a long game. He wanted to become a *zhou mu*, and as events turned out, not only was he tasked to be in charge of all seven commanderies, but his three brothers also became *taishou* of three.

Over 20 years later, at the death of Shi Xie in 226, Giao Châu was divided into two: Giao Châu and Guangzhou, where Giao Châu includes three commanderies of Giao Chỉ, Cửu Chân, Nhật Nam whereas Guangzhou incorporates the remaining four commanderies under Giao Chỉ circuit, Hepu, Nan-hai (contemporary Guangzhou), Yulin (contemporary Guilin) and Cangwu (near contemporary Wuzhou). The administrative centre of Giao Châu was moved to Long Biên, but that of Guangzhou stayed in Pinyin.

The split did not last long; in the same year, Eastern Wu decided to remove Guangzhou and restore Giao Châu, but nearly 40 years later, in 264, Giao Châu was divided once again into Giao Châu and Guangzhou, but this time Hepu stayed with Giao Châu.

The official record shows Giao Châu includes seven commanderies: Giao Chỉ, Cửu Chân, Nhật Nam, Hepu, Jiude, Xinchang, and Wuping, with the administrative centre Long Biên. The first three are in central and northern Vietnam, and the others are in contemporary Guangxi province, but this time, it includes Hepu.[3,4] The administrative centres stay at Long Biên and Pinyin, respectively. Guangzhou province includes 10 commanderies: Nan-hai, Linhe, Shi'an, Shi xing, Cangwu, Yulin, Guilin, Gaoliang, Gaoxing, and Ningpu, with the administrative centre Panyu, in Guangzhou. These are in the south and east of China in Guangdong province.

LOSS OF HEPU

In 471 CE, the Liu Song dynasty split Hepu from Giao Châu and with parts of Guangzhou, formed Việt Châu (Yuezhou), which includes the southern third of Guangxi, the south-western third of Guangdong and is administered from Hepu. Việt Châu is the area that consists the Leizhou Peninsula, Nanning, possibly Guilin, and Wuzhou.

A SUMMARY

From 111 BCE to 203 or nearly 300 years, the Giao Chỉ circuit occupies roughly the same land coverage as Nan-yue, contemporary north and north-central Vietnam and four provinces of southern China. From 203, the circuit became Giao Châu, and in 226, it was split and became smaller, but in the same year, it was restored. In 264, it was divided again and included only the land that is contemporary central and north Vietnam plus Hepu in the southern Guangxi province of China. In 471, Hepu split from Giao Châu.[5] From then until the beginning of the seventh century under the Sui dynasty,

A5.2 – Luy Lâu and Long Biên - The long-lost capitals

ADMINISTRATIVE CENTRES (OR SEATS)

Under the Former Han and subsequent dynasties, each commandery or circuit has an administrative centre where the *cishi* or *taishou*, his team of officials, together with their families, live and govern. The first prefecture listed in the official record usually is where the administrative centre of a particular commandery or *zhou* is located. In the case of the Giao Chỉ commandery, its first administrative centre was at Mê Linh, a military camp that also doubled up as an administrative centre in the early years of the Former Han rule in 111 BCE.[6,7]

By 106 BCE, when the Giao Chỉ circuit is established, the administrative centre was at a place named Luy Lâu (or Liên Lâu, Liên Thụ), near Hanoi, which first appeared in Han shu.[8,9,10] For my purposes, I refer to it as Luy Lâu (O), O is for original. Some historians believe it is the same place that existed from the time of Nan-yue; the Former Han simply continued to use it as the administrative centre of Giao Chỉ commandery when they took over in 111 BCE.[11,12]

The administrative centre of the circuit was then moved from Luy Lâu (O) to Guangxin (Wuzhou) in Cangwu county of Guangxi province, China. It stayed there for around a century until 210; by then, the Giao Chỉ circuit had become Giao Châu, and the administrative centre was then relocated to Panyu in Guangzhou province.[13] By 226, the Han court decided to reduce Giao Châu from seven commanderies to three, and created another province, Guangzhou, to include the other four. Panyu remains the administrative centre of Guangzhou, but that of Giao Châu was moved to Long Biên.[14]

In the same year, Guangzhou became Giao Châu again, but in 264, when it was broken up once more, the administrative centres of the two provinces still stayed at Panyu and Long Biên.

LONG BIÊN

Long Biên first appears in Hou Han shu as the leading prefecture of Giao Chỉ commandery. In 137, there was a major rebellion in the southernmost commandery of the empire, Nhật Nam, the Khu Liên revolt, as discussed in Chapter 4. The rebellion must have shaken the confidence of the local Han officials, and the new *taishou* of Giao Chỉ, Zhou Zhang, moved the administrative centre of Giao Chỉ commandery from Luy Lâu (O) to Long Biên in 142-143 and strengthened in 144.[15,16] The decision was made apparently because its location is easier to defend.[17] This is the same Zhou Zhang who made the submission to change the Giao Chỉ circuit to Giao Châu as cited earlier.

From that time until the middle of the sixth century, for around 400 years, Long Biên remained a major political, religious, and economic capital of northern Vietnam. The brief period of Vietnamese independence in the second half of the sixth century (as discussed in Chapter 11) saw the capital move elsewhere. When the northern rulers returned in the early seventh century during the Sui dynasty, they occupied it briefly and moved the capital to Tống Bình, now around Hanoi. From the seventh to the ninth centuries, the administrative centre at Tống Bình was called by different names: Tử Thành, La Thành, and Đại La discussed in Chapter 13.

Long Biên faded from history, and for centuries no one knows for certain where it is. Recent archaeological evidence points to a location known as the Ancient Capital of Luy Lâu (*Thành cổ Luy Lâu*), around 25 kilometres east of Hanoi in the Thuận Thành district of Bắc Ninh province. However, there is no definite consensus among historians if this place is indeed the famed capital of Long Biên. Having visited the site and reviewed the papers by researchers, including an excellent summary by researcher Phạm Lê Huy, I conclude that the Ancient Capital of Luy Lâu, as discussed in Chapter 2 is indeed Long Biên.[18] My conclusion is based on:

- Archaeological evidence from the work of archaeologist Nishimura Masanari and others.[19]

- The title of Shi Xie is the "Marquis of Long Biên".[20] His residence and tomb are at Luy Lâu.

- Today, there is a place called Đồng Biền close to Luy Lâu that Wintrebert first suggests as the deformation of Long Biên.[21]

- The area is surrounded by ancient pagodas and tombs, proving it as a major settlement.[22,23]

- Luy Lâu is positioned at a strategic location by the bank of the Đuống river and can be easily accessed by the river route from the coast by Bạch Đằng or Thái Bình rivers. It can also be accessed by the land route by what is known as the ancient invaders' route connected with Hạ Long by the coast by national highways QL 17 and QL 18. In fact, many historical sites from Han times, from the first to the third centuries, were found along this route from Phả Lại, Đông Triều, Tràng Bạch, Uông Bí, Yên Lập to Vạn Yên.[24,25]

- An article in the Vietnam National Museum of History states that Luy Lâu and Long Biên are the same.[26]

- However, according to some historians, this Luy Lâu citadel, which a Vietnamese 19th-century geographical text refers to as the Lũng Khê citadel, is not the same as Long Biên (Lũng Khê itself is the village close to the citadel). They refer to a fifth-century Chinese work, *Shu jing zhu* (reproduced as TKCS), in which Luy Lâu and Long Biên are cited as two separate locations.[27] The same reference points out that Long Biên is also not Thăng Long.[28]

THE TWO LUY LÂUS

Luy Lâu east of Hanoi

I now have two contradictory propositions, and both are correct if I consider that there are two separate Luy Lâus cited in historical texts, the first one is Luy Lâu (O), west of Hanoi, and the second one is Luy Lâu, east of Hanoi; an idea first noted by Phạm.[29]

The Luy Lâu, which I call Luy Lâu (O) is mentioned in *Yuanhe junxian zhi* as:

> "the old *Leilou* [Luy Lâu] *Citadel is located 75 li* [around 34 kilometres] *in the west of Songping* [Tống Bình] *County—formerly a county under the Han, a part of the Jiaozhi* [Giao Chỉ] *commandery. In the Later Han, the Jiaozhi's cishi located the headquarters here, but it was later moved to Longbian* [Long Biên]".[30]

There are other historical texts which support the proposition that Luy Lâu (O) is west of Hanoi as summarised by Phạm.[31] On the other hand, the present-day ancient capital named Luy Lâu is east of Hanoi.

Madrolle suggests there is an error in *Yuanhe junxian zhi*'s passage, and west should read east.[32] The present-day Luy Lâu is around 25 kilometres east of Hanoi (measured to Hanoi Flag Tower), so it is comparable with the description if the passage does not refer to Luy Lâu but to Luy Lâu (O).

I would suggest Zhou Zhang, in the middle of the second century, who moved the capital from Luy Lâu (O) to Luy Lâu or Long Biên. It is also at Luy Lâu (O) that the Trưng sisters captured Su Ding in their rebellion and not Luy Lâu since the latter was not settled until the second century, according to archaeological records.

Luy Lâu west of Hanoi

If that is the case, where is Luy Lâu (O)? Maspero, based on the passage in *Yuanhe junxian zhi* quoted above where he cites 65 *li*, (or around 29 kilometres) of distance, not 75 as mentioned, deduces Luy Lâu (O) is south of the city of Hà Đông by the Nhuệ river. This location is around 10 kilometres south-west of Hanoi, closer than the estimated distance, but I cannot to locate any significant ancient landmarks in the vicinity.

Pham hypothesises the 10th century of Quèn citadel in Cổ Hiền hamlet, Tuyết Nghĩa commune, and Quốc Oai district could be Luy Lâu (O) where several artefacts were found which have many Han features.[33,34] While the distance from there to Hanoi, around 42 kilometres, seems close to the estimated distance, Cổ Hiền hamlet is nowhere near a major river such as the Red river. It is upstream of Tích Giang, a small tributary that flows into the Đáy river. I do not believe this is Luy Lâu (O) as I expect a major citadel like it would be by the bank of a larger river.

One place that may fit such a description is Ô Diên in Hạ Mỗ hamlet, Đan Phượng district, where Lý Phật Tử established his capital in the sixth century, as discussed in Chapter 11. It is by the bank of the Red river, northwest of Hanoi, and at a distance of around 30 kilometres which matches the distance described in *Yuanhe junxian zhi*. I have no archaeological evidence of any kind to support this proposition, but compared with Hà Đông and Quèn, Ô Diên appears a better candidate for Luy Lâu (O).

A5.3 – A summary

TIMELINES	LOCATIONS	ADMINISTRATIVE CENTRES
111 – 106 BCE	Giao Chỉ commandery	Luy Lâu (O), west of Hanoi.
106 BCE – 142 CE	Giao Chỉ commandery	Luy Lâu (O), west of Hanoi.
	Giao Chỉ circuit	Wuzhou, Guangxi.
142-203	Giao Chỉ commandery	Luy Lâu or Long Biên, east of Hanoi.
	Giao Chỉ circuit	Wuzhou, Guangxi.
203-210	Giao Chỉ commandery	Luy Lâu or Long Biên, east of Hanoi.
	Giao Châu	Wuzhou, Guangxi.
210-226	Giao Chỉ commandery	Luy Lâu or Long Biên, east of Hanoi.
	Giao Châu	Panyin, Guangzhou.
226-264	Giao Chỉ commandery	Luy Lâu or Long Biên, east of Hanoi.
	Giao Châu	Luy Lâu or Long Biên, east of Hanoi.
	Guangzhou	Panyin, Guangzhou.
264 – middle of the sixth century	Giao Châu	Luy Lâu or Long Biên, east of Hanoi.
From the beginning of the seventh century		Provincial capital moved from Long Biên to Tống Bình (Hanoi).

Table 8 – A summary of Giao Chỉ, Giao Châu, Luy Lâu, and Long Biên.

APPENDIX 6

LIST OF GOVERNORS, PREFECTS, PROTECTORATE GENERALS, GOVERNOR GENERALS AND MILITARY COMMISSIONERS DURING THE NORTHERN RULE PERIOD

The list of names below is taken from ANCL, the years are approximated and when a range is given, it indicates the reign of the emperor under which the person is appointed. ANCL has listed the names under three periods: Three Kingdoms, Six Dynasties and Tang.[1] I have copied the names as they appear in ANCL, which generally are in chronological order. Most of these people came from China; the names of those who are natives of Vietnam are in italics. The names in bold are mentioned in this book.

For completeness, I have also included names cited in SKTT and CM but not in ANCL. However, as pointed out in CM, before 203, the head of the Giao Chỉ circuit was a *quan mục* (or *zhou mu, châu mục*) or a *cishi*. There is no such title as *cishi* of Giao Châu before this year as Giao Châu was named from 203 as a replacement for the Giao Chỉ circuit.[2] However, to be truthful to ANCL, I have copied these titles as per ANCL.

I have also included the list of names under the Tang dynasty by researcher Lư Vĩ An.[3] These are underlined.

VIETNAMESE	PINYIN CHINESE	YEARS	TITLES	LOCATIONS
\multicolumn{5}{c}{III BCE TO FIRST CENTURY CE}				
		Former Han Dynasty[4]		
Thạch Đái[5]	Shi Dai ?	110 BCE	cishi	Giao Chỉ
Chu Chương[6]		87-74 BCE	cishi	Giao Chỉ
		FIRST TO EARLY THIRD CENTURIES		
		Later Han Dynasty		
Đặng Huân			zhou mu (châu mục)	Giao Châu
Ích Cư Xương		57-54 BCE[7]	cishi	Giao Châu
Đặng Nhượng		23	quan mục[8]	Giao Chỉ
Tích Quang	Xi Guang	1-6	taishou	Giao Chỉ
Nhâm Diên	Ren Yan	25	taishou	Cửu Chân
Tô Định	Su Ding	34	taishou	Giao Chỉ
Lý Thiện			taishou	Nhật Nam
Trương Khôi			taishou	Giao Chỉ
Hồ Cống			duwei	Giao Chỉ
Phan Diễn	Fan Ye	137	cishi	Giao Chỉ
Trương Kiều	Zhang Qiao	138	cishi	Giao Châu
Chúc Lương	Zhu Liang	136-141	taishou	Cửu Chân
Châu (Chu?) Xưởng[9]	Zhou Zhang	141	taishou	Giao Chỉ
Hạ Phương	Xia Fang	144	cishi	Giao Châu
Lưu Tháo[10]		147-167	cishi	Giao Chỉ
Sĩ Tứ[11]	Shi Ci	147-167	taishou	Nhật Nam
Dương Phò			cishi	Giao Châu
Nghê Thức	Ni Shih ?		taishou	Cửu Chân
Nguy Lãng	Wei Lang	157	duwei	Cửu Chân
Chúc Điềm		159	cishi	Giao Châu
Cát Kỳ		163		

VIETNAMESE	PINYIN CHINESE	YEARS	TITLES	LOCATIONS
Đinh Cung	Ting Kung	147-167	cishi	Giao Châu
Trương Bàn		158-166	cishi	Giao Châu
Ngu Thiều			taishou	Nhật Nam
Châu (Chu) Tuấn	Zhu Zhuan	181	cishi	Giao Châu
Chu Ngung[12]		181	cishi	Giao Châu
Giả Mạnh Kiên (Giả Tông)	Jia Zong	184	cishi	Giao Châu
Lý Tiến (Tiến)[13]		184-189	cishi	Giao Châu
Chu Thặng		184	cishi	Giao Châu
Kiến Lang			taishou	Giao Chỉ
Lại Tiên			taishou	Giao Chỉ
Hoàng Cái			taishou	Nhật Nam
Đam Manh			taishou	Cửu Chân
Chu Phù	Zhu Fu		cishi	Giao Chỉ
Trương Tân	Zhang Jin	201	cishi	Giao Châu
Lại Cung			cishi	Giao Châu
Ky Vô Hạp			cishi	Giao Châu
Chu Trị		202	taishou	Cửu Chân
Sĩ Nhiếp	Shi Xie	190?	taishou	Giao Chỉ
Sĩ Vỹ	Shi Yi		taishou	Cửu Chân

Table 9 – Cishis and taishous of Giao Châu under the Han dynasty.

VIETNAMESE	PINYIN CHINESE	YEARS	TITLES	LOCATIONS
THIRD CENTURY				
Eastern Wu Dynasty				
Bộ Chất	Bu Zhi	210	cishi	Giao Châu
Sĩ Huy	Shi Hui	226	taishou	Giao Chỉ
Trần Thời	Zhen Shi	226	taishou	Giao Chỉ
Đái Lương[14]	Dai Liang	226	cishi	Giao Châu
Lữ (Lã) Đại	Lu Dai	226	cishi	Giao Châu
Tiết Tông			taishou	Giao Chỉ and Hepu
Lục Duệ (or Lục Doãn)	Lu Yin	248-258	cishi	Giao Châu
Tôn Sư (or Tôn Tư)	Sun Xu	258-264	taishou	Giao Chỉ
Trần Tập		264	quan mục	Giao Châu
Ngu Phiếm		269	cishi	Giao Châu
Cốc Lãng			taishou	Cửu Chân
Ky Vô Hậu			cishi	Giao Châu
Tu Tắc			dudu	Giao Châu
Lưu Tuấn			cishi	Giao Châu
Eastern Wu/Shu Han				
Hấn Tông[15]			cishi	Giao Châu
Mao Quýnh			taishou	Giao Chỉ

Table 10 – Cishis and taishous of Giao Châu under the Eastern Wu and Shu Han kingdoms.

VIETNAMESE	PINYIN CHINESE	YEARS	TITLES	LOCATIONS
\multicolumn{5}{c}{THIRD TO FIFTH CENTURIES}				
	Jin Dynasty			
Đồng Nguyên		265-316	taishou	Cửu Chân
Soán Cốc			taishou	Giao Chỉ
Mã Dung			taishou	Giao Chỉ
Dương Tắc			taishou	Giao Chỉ
Mạnh Cán	Meng Kan		taishou	Nhật Nam
Đào Hoàng[16]	Tao Huang	280	cishi	Giao Châu
Ngô Ngạn (Nghiệm)	Wu Yen		cishi	Giao Châu
Cố Bí	Gu Pi (Mi)		cishi	Giao Châu
Cố Sâm	Gu Zan		cishi	Giao Châu
Cố Thọ[17]	Gu Shou			
Đào Oai (or Đào Uy)	Tao Wei (son of Tao Huang)		cishi	Giao Châu
Đào Thục[18]	Tao Shu (brother of Tai Wei)		cishi	Giao Châu
Vương Đôn[19]	Wang Chi		cishi	Giao Châu
Vương Cơ			cishi	Giao Châu
Lương Thạc	Liang Shih?		cishi	Giao Châu
Vương Lượng	Wang Liang		taishou	Giao Chỉ
Đào Khản	Tao Kan	318	cishi	Giao Châu
Biện Triển[20]			cishi	Giao Châu
Chử Đào			taishou	Cửu Chân
Trương Liễn		328	cishi	Giao Chỉ
Nguyên (Nguyễn) Phóng	Ruan Fu	328	cishi	Giao Châu
Hạ Hầu Lãm	Xi Houlan	345-356	taishou	Nhật Nam
Chu Phiên	Zhu Fan	347	cishi	Giao Châu
Dương Bình	Yang Ping	351	cishi	Giao Châu
Nguyễn Phu	Yuan Fu	353	cishi	Giao Châu
Ôn Phóng Chi	Wen Fangzhi	357-361	cishi	Giao Châu

VIETNAMESE	PINYIN CHINESE	YEARS	TITLES	LOCATIONS
Đỗ Bửu			taishou	Giao Chỉ
Đặng Hàm	Teng Ham	361	cishi	Giao Châu
Cát Hồng[21]			magistrate	Câu Lậu
Khương Tráng			cishi	Giao Châu
Lý (Nguyễn) Tốn			taishou	Cửu Chân
Đỗ Viện[22]	Du Yuan	Appointed at the end of Eastern Jin 317-419	taishou	Nhật Nam and Giao Châu, also *cishi* of Giao Châu
Đỗ Tuệ Độ	Du Hui-du	411	cishi	Giao Châu
Đỗ Tuệ Hựu	Du Hungzhi		taishou	Giao Châu
Phó Vĩnh			taishou	Giao Châu
Đặng Tốn			cishi	Giao Châu
Đỗ Hoàng Văn	Du Hungwen	427-453	cishi	Giao Châu

Table 11 – Cishis and taishous of Giao Châu under the Jin dynasty.

VIETNAMESE	PINYIN CHINESE	YEARS	TITLES	LOCATIONS
\multicolumn{5}{c}{FIFTH TO SIXTH CENTURIES}				
\multicolumn{5}{c}{*Liu Song Dynasty*}				
Vương Huy		427	cishi	Giao Châu
Lưu Nghĩa Khang[23]		424-453	dudu	
Nguyễn Di Chi	Yuan Mizhi	424-453	cishi	Giao Châu
Nguyễn Nghiên			cishi	Giao Châu
Trương Mục Chi				
Đàn Hòa Chi	Tan Hezhi	453	cishi	Giao Châu
Hoàn Hoằng	Huan Hung	454-464	cishi	Giao Châu
Lưu Mục				
Lưu Bột	Liu Po		cishi	Giao Châu
Nguyễn (Lý) Trường Nhân)		465-472	cishi	Giao Châu
Thẩm Hoán		479-482	cishi	Giao Châu
Nguyễn (Lý) Thúc Hiến[24]		479	taishou cishi	Vũ Bình, Tân Xương Giao Châu
\multicolumn{5}{c}{*Nan Qi Dynasty*}				
Phòng Pháp Thừa[25]	Fang Fa Zheng	483-493 (or 494-498)	cishi	Giao Châu
Lưu Khải		479-482	cishi	Giao Châu
\multicolumn{5}{c}{*Nan Qi/Liang Dynasty*}				
Lý Khải		505	cishi	Giao Châu
\multicolumn{5}{c}{*Liang Dynasty*}				
Lý Tắc			cishi	Giao Châu
Tiêu Tư	Xiao Zu	535	cishi	Giao Châu
Dương Phiêu	Yang Piao		cishi	Giao Châu
Trần Bá Tiên	Chen Baxian		dudu/cishi	Giao Châu
\multicolumn{5}{c}{*Tang Dynasty*}				
Vương Nhiếp[26]			cishi	Giao Châu

APPENDIX 6

VIETNAMESE	PINYIN CHINESE	YEARS	TITLES	LOCATIONS
Chen Dynasty				
Âu Dương Hột[27]		569	dudu	Giao Châu and Guangzhou
Dương Tần			dudu	Giao Châu and Ái Châu
Dương Hựu Phổ[28]	Yang Xiu-pu		dudu	Giao Châu
SEVENTH CENTURY				
Sui Dynasty				
Lý (? Name unknown)		601-604	cishi	Giao Châu
Sui/Tang Dynasty				
Khâu Hòa[29]	Qui He	622	taishou/Grand Administrator	**Giao Châu Đại Tổng Quản Phủ** (Grand Administrative Province of Giao, 622-624)[30]

Table 12 – Cishis and taishous of Giao Châu under the Southern Dynasties.

VIETNAMESE	PINYIN CHINESE	YEARS	TITLES	LOCATIONS
\multicolumn{5}{c}{SEVENTH TO EIGHTH CENTURIES}				
\multicolumn{5}{c}{*Tang Dynasty*}				
Vương Chí Viễn		624	dudu	**Giao Châu Đại Đô Đốc Phủ** (Dudu fu, Grand Office of the Governor General of Giao Châu Province, 624-679)
Lý Đại Lượng		627	dudu	Giao Châu
Lý Thọ	Li Shou	628	dudu	Giao Châu
Lư Tổ Thượng[31]	Lu Zu-shang	628	zhoumu (châu mục)	Giao Châu
Phổ Tán			dudu	Giao Châu
Lý Đạo Hưng	Li Dao-xing	635-638	dudu	Giao Châu
Lý Đạo Ngạn		627-649	cishi	Giao Châu
Lý Giám			cishi	Giao Châu
Liễu Sở Hiền		627-649	dudu	Giao Châu and Guizhou
Lý Hoằng Sức		640	dudu	Giao Châu
Đỗ Chánh Luân	Du Zheng-lun	643	dudu	Giao Châu
Lý Tổ Lập			duhu	Giao Châu
Khương Giản			duhu	Giao Châu
Đậu Đức Minh			taishou	Ái Châu
Ninh Đạt		685-705	taishou	Ái Châu
Chử Toại Lương	Zhu Sui-liang	649	taishou	Ái Châu
Sài Triết Uy		650-661	dudu	Giao Châu
Lý Càn Hựu			dudu	Giao Châu
Lang Dư Khánh	Lang She-qing	674	cishi	Giao Châu
Lương Nạn Địch			dudu	Giao Châu
Lưu Diên Hựu	Liu Yan-you	687	duhu	**Annam (Peaceful South) Duhu fu** (679-757)
Dương Mẫn			duhu	An Nam
Thôi Huyền Tín			duhu	An Nam
Đặng Hựu			duhu	An Nam

VIETNAMESE	PINYIN CHINESE	YEARS	TITLES	LOCATIONS
Khúc Lãm[32]		705-710	duhu	An Nam
Lưu Hựu	Liu You		duhu	An Nam
Nguyên (Quang) Sở Khách	Guang Chu-ke	713	duhu	An Nam
Tân Tử Ngôn			duhu	An Nam
Tống Chi Đễ		713-741	tổng quản	An Nam
Đỗ Minh Cử	Du Ming-zhu		duhu	An Nam
Hà Lý Quang	He Li-guang	749-751	duhu	An Nam
Vương Tri Tiến		751	duhu	An Nam
Khang Khiêm			duhu	An Nam

Table 13 – List A of cishis, taishous of Giao Châu under the Tang dynasty.

VIETNAMESE	PINYIN CHINESE	YEARS	TITLES	LOCATIONS
		EIGHTH TO NINTH CENTURIES		
		Tang Dynasty		
Đậu Mông			duhu	Trấn Nam (Zhennan, Guarded South) Duhufu (757-766)
Trương Thuận[33]		756-763	duhu	Trấn Nam
Triều Hoàng	Zhao Heng (Abe no Nakamaro)	761-766	duhu	Trấn Nam
Trương Bá Nghi	Zhang Bo-yi	767	jing lue shi	Annam Duhufu (766-863)
Ô Sùng Phúc			duhu	An Nam
Phụ Lương Giao	Fu Liang-jiao	782	duhu	An Nam
Cao Chính Bình	Gao Zeng-ping	763-779	jing lue shi	An Nam
Trương Ứng	Zhang Ying		jing lue shi	An Nam
Bàng Phục		789	duhu	
Triệu Xương[34]	Zhao Zhou	791-802	duhu/jing lue shi	An Nam
Bùi Thái	Pei Tai	802-903	duhu	An Nam
Triệu Xương	Zhao Zhou	804-806	duhu	An Nam
Trương Châu (Chu)	Zhang Zhou	808	duhu	An Nam
Mã Tổng (Ấn)	Ma Zong	806-810	duhu	An Nam
Trương Miễn		813	duhu	
Bùi Thành Lập	Pei Xing-li	813-817	duhu	
Lý Tượng Cổ	Li Xiang-gu	818-819	duhu	An Nam
Quế Trọng Vũ	Gui Zong-wu	819-820	duhu	An Nam
Bùi Thành Lập	Pei Xing-li	820	jing lue shi	An Nam
Vương Thừa Biện (Thừa Nghiệp)		822	duhu	
Lý Nguyên Thiện (Hỷ)	Li Yuan-xi	822-826	duhu	An Nam
Hàn Ước	Han Yue	828	duhu	An Nam
Trịnh Xước		831	duhu	An Nam
Lưu Mân		833	duhu	An Nam

VIETNAMESE	PINYIN CHINESE	YEARS	TITLES	LOCATIONS
Hàn Uy		834	duhu	An Nam
Điền Tảo	Tian Zao	826-830	duhu	An Nam
Mã Thực	Ma Zhi	836-840	duhu	An Nam
Vũ Hồn	Wu Hun	841-843	jing lue shi	An Nam
Bùi Nguyên Dụ		846-847	jing lue shi	An Nam
Điền Tại Hựu		849-850	duhu	An Nam
Thôi Cảnh		852	duhu	An Nam
Lý Trác	Li Zhuo	853-855	duhu	An Nam
Tống Nhai		857	duhu	An Nam
Lý Hoằng Phủ		857-858	duhu	An Nam

Table 14 – List B of cishis, taishous of Giao Châu under the Tang dynasty.

VIETNAMESE	PINYIN CHINESE	YEARS	TITLES	LOCATIONS
Ninth to 10th Centuries				
Tang Dynasty				
Vương Thức	Wang Shi	847-859	jing lue shi	An Nam
Lý Vu (Lý Hộ)	Li Hu	860-861	duhu	An Nam
Vương Khoan	Wang Guan	861-862	jing lue shi/kinh lược chiêu thảo sứ	An Nam
Thái (Sái) Tập	Cai Xi	862-863	jing lue shi	An Nam
Tống Nhung	Song Rong	863	jing lue shi	Hành Giao Châu[35]
Trương Nhân		864	jing lue shi	Hành Giao Châu
Cao Biền		864-866	jing lue shi	Hành Giao Châu
Vương Án Quyền		866	jing lue shi	Hành Giao Châu
Cao Biền	Gao Pian	866-868	jiedushi	Jinghai-jun (866-905)
Cao Tầm	Gao Xun	868-873	jiedushi	Jinghai-jun
Tăng Cổn	Zeng Gun	880	jiedushi	Annam/Jinhhai-jun
Cao Mậu Khanh		882	jiedushi	Jinghai-jun
Tạ Triệu		884	jiedushi	Jinghai-jun
An Hữu Quyền		897-900	jiedushi	Jinghai-jun
Tôn Đức Chiêu		901	jiedushi	Jinghai-jun
Kinh Ngạn Tông			cishi	Ái Châu
Thôi Lập Tín[36]			duhu	Annam/Jinhhai-jun
Chu Toàn Dục[37]	Zhu Quan-yu	905	jiedushi	Jinghai-jun
Độc Cô Tổn[38]	Dugu Sun	905	jiedushi	Jinghai-jun
Southern Han Dynasty				
Khúc Thừa Dụ	Qu Cheng-yu	906	jiedushi	Giao Châu[39]
Khúc Hạo	Qu Hao	907-917	jiedushi	Giao Châu
Khúc Thừa Mỹ	Qu Cheng-mei	918-923/30	jiedushi	Giao Châu
Dương Đình Nghệ	Yang Ting-yi	931	jiedushi	Giao Châu
Kiều Công Tiễn	Jiao Gong-xian	937	jiedushi	Giao Châu

Table 15 – Cishis and taishous of Giao Châu under the Tang dynasty and Southern Han.

APPENDIX 7

IN SEARCH OF ANCIENT HANOI

A7.1 – Đông Kinh - a 15th-century capital

INNER WALLS AND THE MAGIC SQUARE

Figure 52 in Chapter 13 shows the Đông Kinh map with the Outer Wall (the darkened brick walls in an inverted L-shape including gates 22, 37 and 38) and the Inner Walls (the lighter walls with vertical or horizontal stripes). The Inner Walls can be described in three parts, from left to right: a "Dividing Wall", a "Square" and an "Enclosure". The Dividing Wall connects the Outer Wall with the Square in the centre, which shares a common wall with the Enclosure on the eastern side. The Enclosure encloses a lake and the Đông Cung (eastern palace) with a zig-zag section at the south-eastern corner.

According to historians, this Square had changed little from what was built under the Lý (11th, 12th), the Trần (13th, 14th), and the Lê dynasties in the 15th century when the Đông Kinh map was drawn. Most of the changes over those four centuries were in the Enclosure, the Dividing Wall and the Outer Wall.[1,2]

I am focusing on the Square since it is a common design layout in ancient Chinese and Vietnamese citadels based on the Magic Square as a mandala of Buddhism. Like a Sudoku, it is a 9x9 grid and is widely applied as a layout for royal cities. It reached its most sophisticated form during the Sui-Tang periods (581-618, 618-907) when the first citadel in Hanoi was built.[3] If I can locate this Square on the present-day map, I could retrace the outline of the original citadels built during the Lý, Trần dynasties. From there, I can go back in time and assess the likely position of the citadels built in Hanoi under Sui and Tang dynasties in the seventh and eighth centuries, as this is the period which this book covers. I assume that the Square of the citadels built under the Sui and Tang dynasties is in the same position as that built under the successive Vietnamese kings, as it is a Magic Square design feature.

FORBIDDEN CITY AND THE SQUARE

I should note that in the study of the ancient citadels at Hanoi, Vietnamese historians divide the citadel walls into three categories: the outermost wall is called Đại La, the middle wall is called Hoàng Thành (Imperial Citadel), and the inner wall, Cấm Thành (Forbidden City).[4,5] Thus on Figure 52, the inner wall including the Square is the Forbidden City, and the outer wall is Imperial Citadel, but the western wall is called Đại La.[6]

They also make a distinction between this Đại La and the Đại La citadel under Sui-Tang times, so to avoid confusion, for my purposes. I will not use these names but refer to these walls simply as Inner and Outer Walls.[7]

To locate the Square, I have relied on the locations of two monuments in Figure 53, unchanged over the centuries to the present-day: Kính Thiên palace and Đoan Môn gate. Sadly, the former was demolished, and only the steps are left. The latter survived but has been rebuilt and modified from the one shown on the Đông Kinh map.

I have also relied on archaeological finds at 18 Hoàng Diệu street, where artefacts dated back to the Sui-Tang period (seventh-ninth centuries) were found. Similarly, artefacts dated back to the Lê dynasty were found at the base of the North Gate (Cửa Bắc).[8] Based on this fact, I can now set the northern wall of the Square there and the centre of the Square at Kính Thiên palace, as generally agreed to by most historians, and construct the sides of the Square accordingly. As measured by Google Maps, the distance between the North Gate and Kính Thiên palace is around 420 metres.

Measured in a line parallel to Phan Đình Phùng street, 420 metres from Kính Thiên palace to the east is around Tôn Thất Thiệp street, and in the opposite (western) direction, it is slightly beyond Độc Lập street. At 420 metres south of Kính Thiên palace is just north of the Hanoi Flag pole.

I can now join a "Square" of 840 metres per side with the eastern side along Tôn Thất Thiệp street; the southern side along Lê Hồng Phong/ Nguyễn Tri Phương streets; the northern side through the North Gate; and the western side along in parallel to Độc Lập street but at 35 metres west of it. The total perimeter of this Square is 3,360 metres or 2240 *bu*, with each side measured at 840 metres or 573 *bu*. I had decided to use *bu* as the unit of measurement as it was used at the time when these citadels were built. The advantage of using *bu* instead of the metric equivalent is that the original measurements have tended to be rounded, e.g. 900, 2000 *bu* etc., so it would help to improve the accuracy of the estimates.[9]

On this basis, a side of 573 *bu* seems odd, it should be, say, 500 or 600 *bu*, but it is clear that the archaeological site at 18 Hoàng Diệu street, towards the north-west corner, is well within it. I have not been able to obtain sufficient evidence to verify the exact position of this Square, but I am reasonably confident that this is the area where the Sui and Tang governors and possibly Lý Bí built their capitals. So for my purposes, despite the slightly uneven *bu* measurements, I am using these dimensions. Other historians suggest the Forbidden City (my "Square" equivalent) of Thăng Long citadel under the Lý dynasty is a square shape of 700-metre length on each side (or 466 *bu*), giving a perimeter of 2,800 metres or 1867 *bu* with the southern wall ran near Hanoi Flag pole, the western wall near the east of One Pillar pagoda (Chùa Một Cột), the north wall just south of Phan Đình Phùng street with Kính Thiên palace at the centre.[10]

Finally, my reasoning for using modern roads or streets as a guide for the location of ancient walls is based on the assumption that the base of the walls would have been compacted during the construction and gradually settled under the weight of the wall itself and thus would form a good base for a road. Similarly, a moat or canal, when filled in, could be used to build a road as the route would not interfere with other land use.

THE OUTER WALLS

Historians have suggested the northeastern corner of the Outer Wall is somewhere near the intersection of Phan Đình Phùng, Hàng Cót streets.[11] Starting from there and moving anti-clockwise, the Outer Wall continues westward following two paths, one follows Hoàng Hoa Thám, Thụy Khuê, Đồng Cổ to Bưởi market. The other path follows Quán Thánh and Thụy

Khuê streets to Bười market. From there, two walls become one and head south along Đường Bưởi to Cầu Giấy (Giấy bridge). The wall continues east along La Thành and turns in the north-east direction along Phố Giảng Võ to join the southern boundary around Kim Mã bus station.

From Kim Mã bus station, the wall follows Trần Phú street until it reaches Hàng Da. The intersection of Trần Phú and Tôn Tháp Thiệp streets is the location of the south-western gate in the 1890 map, which could be at the location of the South Gate (Cửa Nam) on the Đông Kinh map. In the present-day map, south of this area has a South Gate (Cửa Nam) street and Southern Gate market, which could mean that the South Gate is in proximity.[12]

The eastern wall of the Outer Wall has an Eastern Gate (Cửa Đông) and Phan estimates the position of this gate at around 38B Hàng Đường, 8 Hàng Cân and 8 Lãn Ông.[13] Phan also suggests the eastern wall of the Outer Wall runs somewhere along Thuốc Bắc street. It is a little confusing as today's Thuốc Bắc street does not run continuously to join the northern and southern sections of the Outer Wall. On the other hand, Hàng Da/Hàng Gà/Hàng Cót streets do connect with Phan Đình Phùng street. So, I suggest the eastern side of the Outer Wall would run along these Hàng streets instead.

ENCLOSURE

As for the eastern "Enclosure", I have to guess based on the estimated position of the eastern wall at Hàng Gà street. The zig-zag wall then follows the east-west section of Tôn Thất Thiệp street to Phùng Hưng street, turns east at Hàng Vải street, just above East Gate street (Phố Cửa Đông) before joining Hàng Gà street. I cannot to locate the lake inside the Enclosure or other features shown on the Đông Kinh map.

DIVIDING WALL

On the Đông Kinh map, the Dividing Wall starts south of Voi Phục temple, runs north of Giảng Võ palace and joins the western wall of the Square. On today's map, this would be Kim Mã street. The Đông Kinh map also shows the gate of Bảo Khánh, which could be near the intersection to Láng Hạ and Giảng Võ street where a gate to the Bảo Khánh village was found.[14]

A7.2 – Hanoi "mountains" or Núi

Other than the mounds of *Núi Sưa* and *Núi Nùng*, there is a group of historical sites 2 kilometres west of the archaeological site at 18 Hoàng Diệu.[15] The existence of these sites led some historians such as Trần, Quốc Vượng to suggest the citadel built during the 11th century would be in this area centred around Liễu Giai district and shifted west during the Nguyễn dynasty in the 19th century.[16] This could imply that the early Sui-Tang era citadels may have been built there too as suggested by Papin.

Papin believes Núi Cung was at the centre of Tử Thành and An Nam La Thành (commonly known as La Thành) citadel, built nearly 200 years later in 806.[17] However, the discovery of the 18 Hoàng Diệu have quelled these suggestions, Phan makes it clear that there is no west to east shift but the Lý, Lê, Trần and Nguyễn dynasties all built their citadels on the same area of Núi Nùng or Kính Thiên palace.[18] I am inclined to support Phan, as other than the archaeological evidence, Đông Kinh map (Figure 52) shows a large lake west of the "square" towards Linh Lang temple (Đền Voi Phục). The lake has shrunk in size to the lake of Thủ Lệ by Hanoi Zoo, but the size of the lake on the old map indicates the region is low-lying. Thus, it would be difficult to imagine any citadel of significant size built there.

A7.3 – La Thành citadel

Maspero suggests La Thành was built north of Tô Lịch river. To locate this citadel, I drew a line at 300 metres (200 steps or *bu* as recorded in historical text) north of where Tô Lịch river (now filled-in) was. On a present-day map, this line would run approximately parallel to Phan Đình Phùng, Hoàng Hoa Thám streets to Bưởi market. The line shows clearly that there are only two places La Thành could have been situated; one is on the south-western side of the West Lake and the other is on the south-eastern side of West Lake between the lake and Red river, anywhere in between would be in the lake itself.[19,20]

The south-eastern site would seem a more likely candidate as it is closer to the archaeological sites and Núi Nùng. While my estimated position would be similar to the one suggested by Papin, I do not believe where Zhang Bo-yi built his La Thành as this is not supported by archaeological evidence. I would suggest it was built south of the river where Đông Kinh was.[21]

A7.4 – Đại La Thành - a citadel with 6.5 metre walls

In 808, the new *duhu*, Zhang Zhou (Trương Chu) built Đại La. The citadel's perimeter was increased to 2000 *bu* (3,000 metres) or more than twice that of Tử Thành and employed 250,000 workers to build it. The walls are two *zhang* and two *chi* high (or 22 *chi*), equivalent to 6.6 metres, or around the same height as the walls of the 19th-century Imperial City in Huế. The citadel had gates on the east, west and south walls. Both gates on the east and west walls had three entrances, but the south gate had five. There is no gate on the north wall. The gates had higher storeys; on the gates were drums and horns (presumably to be used as warning devices).

Ten buildings (or palaces) stood inside the citadel, each on the left and right. Previously, in the army, there were only 3,000 weaponry items, now increased to 30,000, housed in 30 new arsenals. Zhang Zhou also built thirty-two "*đồng mông*" type boats (long narrow boats designed for fast speed during attacks) to replace previously slower and fewer boats. Each of these boats carries 25 sailors, 23 rowers and two devices that can shoot arrows like crossbows. It is reported that the boats could go forwards and backwards as fast as the wind.[22]

The location is definitely on the south side of the Tô Lịch river, not north of it, as there would not be sufficient space. Papin suggests Zhang Zhou built a new citadel, and not complete what Zhang Bo-yi started as recorded in ANCL, which he calls An Nam La Thành centred around Núi Cung as mentioned earlier.[23] I have doubts about this proposition as the citadel that Zhang Zhou built was substantial and should have left behind some archaeological evidence but to date, little, if any, of such evidence was found around the area of Núi Cung.

A7.5 – An headquarter north of the river

Figure 52 (Đông Kinh map) of Chapter 13 shows West Lake is connected to the Tô Lịch river. Today, segments of the Tô Lịch river can be seen along Đồng Cổ street, and there is a community house in the village of Hồ Khẩu around 200 metres west of West Lake. Hồ means lake and Khẩu means mouth and that is probably where the ancient Tô Lịch river joined to the lake.[24] The same map also shows the Tô Lịch river is connected to the Red river, which archaeologists believe at Chợ Gạo.[25] These connections are now filled in so we could not easily locate them. However, in Tang times, water from West Lake would normally flow out to the Tô Lịch river and from there to the Red river, from Hồ Khẩu to Chợ Gạo. However, during heavy rainy seasons, water collected from the surrounding area may flow in reverse, into West Lake, to the lake by Hồ Khẩu.[26] In 825, when *duhu* Li Yuan-xi saw the river water outside the citadel's gate flowing in the opposite direction to its normal course, this is likely what happened. From the map, I am convinced that the river in question is the Tô Lịch river.

The new headquarters that Li Yuan-xi moved to is likely in the southeast corner of the West Lake, between the Tô Lịch and the Red rivers. However, shortly after, he moved it back to Đại La; given that Đại La was a substantial fortress and offered significant protection, this would seem a logical choice.[27]

A7.6 – Đại La continuity

As mentioned previously, in the early ninth century, Zhang Zhou built Đại La citadel in the face of threats from the southern kingdom of Huanwang, which he eventually eliminated. In the middle of the century, a new threat came from Nanzhao; Đại La was repaired and strengthened by successive *duhus* and *jiedushis*. Around 843, *jing lue shi* Wu Hun strengthened the citadel, but his effort led to a rebellion whereby the buildings on the walls were burned, and the protectorate storehouse was robbed. Wu Hun escaped to Guangzhou.[28,29] In 858, a talented Tang official named Wang Shi, impatient with the slow and expensive method of using timber to build walls by his predecessors, decided to plant trees instead. He used the tax money for one year to plant *"táo gai"*, a type of Crataegus (hawthorn) which can grow to 15 metres with thorny branches, to a perimeter of 12 *li* or 3600 *bu* (5.4 kilometres), long enough to surround Đại La's perimeter of 2,000 *bu*. He also dug a moat and planted thorny bamboo, so raiders could not easily penetrate.[30]

While these measures helped Wang Shi to hold back the Nanzhao raiders, barely two years later, after he left, in the winter of 860, Nanzhao forces overwhelmed the defence and ransacked La Thành. Presumably, the hawthorn trees he planted had not grown sufficiently high to form a strong barrier against the invaders. A year later, La Thành was retaken by the Tang but fell in 863 after 24 days of siege; it took one of Tang's best generals, Gao Pian, to finally force out the Nanzhao army in 866.

A7.7 – Gao Pian's La Thành

Gao Pian began the reconstruction of La Thành with a perimeter of 3000 *bu* (or 4,500 m), but other references quoted 3000 *bu*. Interestingly, both of these dimensions are within the perimeter of the trees Wang Shi planted eight years earlier at 3,600 *bu*; perhaps Gao Pian was following the course that Wang Shi set out.

There were 55 watch towers[31], five tower gates[32], six sheltered gates[33], three moats or canals[34] and 34 stairways.[35]

A wall of this size at the base was most likely rammed earth sandwiched between brick walls. Today, there is no information on where these watch towers were located but assuming that they were spread around on top of the walls, they would be spaced at around 70 *bu* or 100 metres distance.

There were five tower gates which would seem reasonable compared with three that Zhang Zhou built in 808. The six sheltered gates would increase the number of entrance gates to the citadel to 11 unless five of these were outside the tower gates; in that case, there would only be a total of six gates. I am inclined to believe the latter as more gates would make the citadel more vulnerable. Gao Pian was not a man who took unnecessary risks with his formidable fortress judging from the number of watchtowers, the thickness of the wall, and the three moats. Three moats or canals would make sense if the north wall were backed against the Tô Lịch river, so there was no need for a ditch on that side.

As for the stairways, it is difficult to visualise what they were; one source indicated that these were roads.[36] However, one could only imagine that there must have been stairways or steps to allow troops access to the battlement at the top of the wall; such access is called Ma Dao in Chinese (Horse route).[37] Since there were 55 towers, it would seem to make sense to build 34 stairways to get access to them from within the citadel, one for roughly two towers.

APPENDIX 8

MA YUAN'S EXPEDITIONS (41-44)

A8.1 – Ma Yuan's expedition to Giao Chỉ

THE ROUTE

In January 41, Ma Yuan was appointed as the Wave-Calming General (Fubo Jiangjun) with Liu Long as his deputy, supported by the General of Tower Ships (Lou Chuan Jiangjun), Duan Zhi.[1,2,3,4] He took 8,000 regular troops from the commanderies of Changsha, Guiyang, Lingling, Cangwu, and 12,000 local militias from Guangdong, totalling 20,000.[5] They were to assemble at a port in Hepu, and board 2,000 ships to Giao Chỉ, but the ships were insufficient; to make the matter worse, Duan Zhi fell ill and died.

Ma Yuan decided to take the land route and ordered his ships to sail along the coast to Giao Chỉ. Historical text reports he cut a path through the mountains and forests for 1,000 *li* (or around 450 kilometres). From Hepu, this route would involve marching through the territory of Ô hứa (or Ô Hử) and through Đông Triều mountains, where the distance from Hepu, as estimated by Google Maps, seems to match 1000 li (450 m) as recorded.[6,7,8]

On the sea route, his ships could have entered Bái Tử Long bay, sailed up Bạch Đằng river and followed Đuống river to Mê Linh on the bank of the Red river. Figure 64 shows the possible expedition routes, key locations of the revolt and the subsequent suppression.

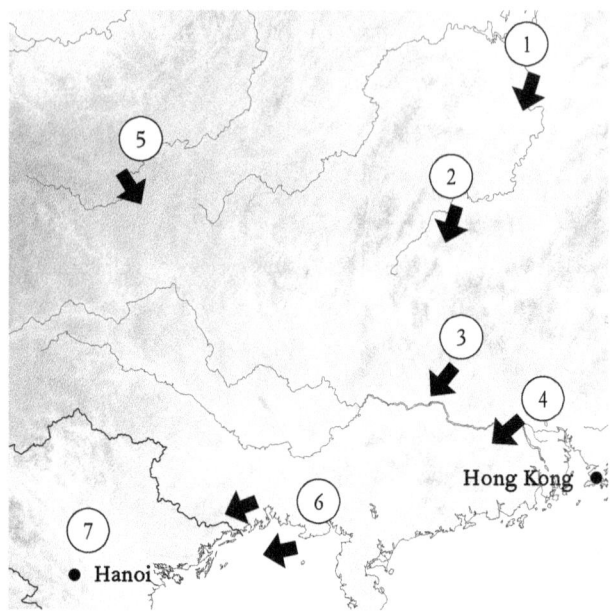

Figure 64 – Mobilisation of the Later Han armies under Ma Yuan to Hepu (from locations 1 to 5) and the sea routes to Mê Linh (from 6 to 7). Keys: 1. Changsa, 2. Lingling District, 3. Cangwu County, 4. Guangzhou, 5. Guiyang, 6. Hepu County, 7. Mê Linh.

LÃNG BẠC

Ma Yuan's biography in Hou Han shu does not mention Luy Lâu but only cites Lãng Bạc (Lang Po), Tây Vu and Cẩm Khê as places where his army camped. At Lãng Bạc, Tây Vu, they fought and won a decisive battle. They also won the final battle at Cẩm Khê.[9] Historians agreed that Lãng Bạc was Mount Tiên Du.[10,11] This mountain is Mount Lạn Kha where Phật Tích pagoda now is.[12,13] This position would be consistent with a passage in TKCS that refers to the high ground at Lãng Bạc as the reason for Ma Yuan to camp there.[14] The reference to Lãng Bạc as today's West Lake (Hồ Tây) in Hanoi has been rejected by historians.[15,16]

TÂY VU

But before the battle at Lãng Bạc, Ma Yuan may have marched straight to Mê Linh but was beaten back and decided to take a defensive position at the high ground at Mt Tiên Du. Tây Vu was one of ten counties under the Han, north of the Đuống river and Vietnamese historians believe battle took place at the ancient citadel of Cổ Loa, a major fort of Tây Vu.[17] Looking at the map, the following battle plan seems feasible: Ma Yuan and his combined forces arrived and proceeded by land and river to Mê Linh but Cổ Loa was in their path, the Trưng sisters beat them back there and they retreated to Mt Tiên Du. His biography does not mention this battle.

In any case, history recorded that he had a moment of doubt while waiting at Lãng Bạc from his biography:

> "*My cousin* [my brother in the text of Dongguan hanji] *Shaoyou constantly laments my efforts and my ambition, saying: "The man in this life only needs clothes and food. He rides in a low chariot with short axles; he rides a small, slow horse; he is just a small civil servant in the commandery, but he keeps the tombs (of his ancestors), and the neighbours call him a good man. To seek the superfluous is to make one's own misfortune."* When I was in between the Lãng Bạc and Tây Vu camps and the rebels were not yet subdued, the rain was falling; there were rising vapours; there were pestilential fumes, and the heat was scorching; I even saw a flying hawk falling into the water (struck down by these emanations). Lying down, I was thinking about Shaoyou's discourse on life and quietly (asking myself) how we could achieve them."[18]

CẨM KHÊ

Maspero also suggests that the Trưng sisters' forces, emboldened perhaps by the first success, attacked Ma Yuan forces at Lãng Bạc and were decisively defeated with losses of several thousand before retreating to the mountains, chased by Han troops. Ma Yuan's biography records beheading 1,000 and capturing 10,000 of the sisters' followers. Vietnamese military historians thought the battle of Lãng Bạc was a major blunder by the sisters against an experienced general with seasoned regular troops. They suggest the sisters should have adopted a guerrilla warfare strategy instead.[19]

SKTT reports the battle differently, whereby the sisters saw that the enemy was strong, their troops were undisciplined, and would not be able to resist, so they decided to withdraw to Cẩm Khê (or Kim Khê). The troops believed that the queens, being women, would not be able to fight, and also scattered, so the nation was lost.[20]

One of the chiefs, Đô Dương (Du Yang), with his supporters escaped to Cửu Chân, probably by the Đáy river. The sisters remained in Mê Linh and were pursued by Ma Yuan's deputy, Liu Long, to Cẩm Khê when Trưng Nhị was taken and put to death with 1,000 of their followers.[21] The rest surrendered, and the population of the highland to the number of more than 20,000 men submitted, and the heads of the two sisters were sent to Luoyang.[22] Vietnamese historians, on the other hand, record that the sisters committed suicide by drowning at Hát Giang river, a section of the Red river.[23]

There are different opinions on where the location of Cẩm Khê is; Đinh places it at the eastern foot of Ba Vì mountain, whereas CM identifies it at Vĩnh Tường in Vĩnh Phúc province.[24,25,26] I tend to support CM (and Maspero) locations since it would be difficult to support a camp of any size in the mountainous region with difficult access, for any length of time as compared with a site near the junction of three main rivers.[27]

A8.2 – Ma Yuan's expedition to Cửu Chân

In November 43, Ma Yuan reported to his emperor that he took 12,000 crack troops from Giao Chỉ together other regular troops to form an army of 20,000 with 2,000 ships of different sizes to Cửu Chân (modern-day Thanh Hóa province).[28] Unlike the expedition to Giao Chỉ where the main battle was fought and lost at Lãng Bạc, in Cửu Chân the followers of the Trưng sisters appeared to put up fierce resistance. TKCS described at least four battles as being fought at Vô Công, Dư Phát, Vô Biên and finally, Cư Phong.[29]

THE FIRST BATTLE AT VÔ CÔNG

According to Maspero, Ma Yuan forces sailed down the Red river, as far south as Hưng Yên, and connected with the Đáy river at (Châu Cầu) Phủ Lý, by the Châu Giang river.[30] When he arrived at Vô Công (also Vô Thiết), the chief of the rebellion surrendered, and he advanced to Dư Phát. Đào placed Vô Công at Gia Viễn Nho Quan, Gia Viễn district, by Bôi river, just north-west of the 11th-century capital of Hoa Lư. Vô Công was a strategic location as it guarded one of the main roads to Cửu Chân along the Nho Quan Phố Cát route (QL12B and QL45); the Han had a military garrison there (similar to Mê Linh).[31] Having overcome the resistance at Vô Công,

Ma Yuan turned to the coast, possibly along Vân and Vạc rivers to Cửa (sea gate) Thần Phù, and headed to Dư Phát. To avoid having to go around the dangerous headland at Thần Phù, Ma Yuan ordered his troops to dig a channel through the mountain and created a rock dyke for his army to pass.[32]

THE SECOND BATTLE AT DƯ PHÁT

Once he came through Thần Phù, Ma Yuan arrived at the fort of Dư Phát; according to Đào, Dư Phát was located between Hậu Lộc and Nga Sơn districts near Cửa Lạch Trường at the Trường Giang river mouth.[33,34] Đào forms this conclusion on many artefacts dated back to the Later Han times found there. But according to Maspero, Dư Phát was at the junction of the Mã and Lèn rivers called Ngã Ba Bông further to the west, presumably because it is on the river route leading to the main river of Mã.[35] In any case, Chu Bá, the rebel leader at Dư Phát escaped to the deep forest where there were many rhinoceros, thousands of buffaloes and elephants.[36] Đào suggests Ma Yuan went upstream of Mã river, captured Cửu Chân's administrative centre of Tư Phố (now believed to be at Thiệu Khánh, Thiệu Dương communes) where the Chu and Mã rivers meet at Ngã Ba Đầu, before flowing to the sea.[37] Over the years, the local people have found many bronze weapons, pottery, and graves from the Han era near Vồm pagoda at Thiệu Khánh.

THE THIRD BATTLE AT VÔ BIÊN

After Tư Phố, Đào believes Ma Yuan continued further upstream of the Mã river, and took the Vô Biên fort located at Vĩnh Lộc district near the 15th-century citadel of Hồ. Maspero proposed a different route whereby Ma Yuan, from Dư Phát at Ngã Ba Bông, went south on the Mã river to the junction at Ngã Ba Đầu. From there, he split his forces in two, one went up the Chu river to as far as Thọ Xuân and Cầu Bái Thượng to the west, near the historic place of Lam Kinh, to chase the remnants of Chu Bá troops. There, at Cư Phong district, the rebels refused to surrender and gave battle; Han troops killed and captured over 5,000, which put an end to the rebellion. The second column of his force sailed down the Mã river and captured Vô Biên in the vicinity of Thanh Hóa city. The difference between Đào and Maspero interpretation is in the locations of Dư Phát and Vô Biên, but they generally agree on the places of Vô Công and Cư Phong.[38] These locations are shown in Figure 65.

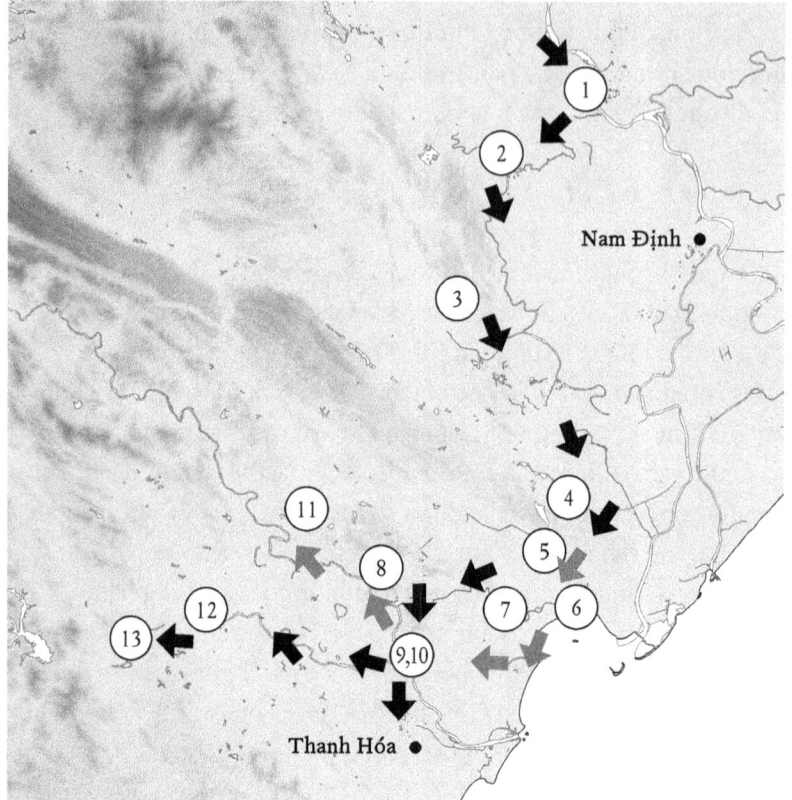

Figure 65 – Possible routes of Ma Yuan expedition into Cửu Chân (43-44). Route of dark arrows is based on Mapsero, that of light arrows is based on Đào.

1. Hưng Yên, 2. Phủ Lý, 3. Gia Viên District, 4. Cửa Thần Phù, 5. Nga Sơn District, 6. Cửa Lạch Trường, 7. Hậu Lộc, 8. Ngã Ba Bông, 9. Ngã Ba Đầu, 10. Thọ Xuân District, 11. Vĩnh Lộc, 12. Thọ Xuân District, 13. Cầu Bái Thượng.

APPENDIX 9

THE KINGS OF LINYI

Right: Table 16 – The kings of Linyi from the second to the fifth centuries.

i. After Majumdar[1]
ii. Volume
iii. Years tributes received at Chinese imperial court
iv. Fan Yi died in 337
v. Fan Zhunong died en route at sea in 498

APPENDIX 9

PINYIN CHINESE	VIETNAMESE	REIGN[i]	CHINESE ANNALS[ii]	TRIBUTES[iii]
		Eastern Wu Dynasty		
Qu Lian	Khu Liên (Đạt)[2]	2nd century	Jin shu (97) Liang shu (54) Sui shu (82)	
		Jin Dynasty		
Fan Xiong	Phạm Hùng	c. 270-280	Jin shu (97) Liang shu (54) Sui shu (82)	
Fan Yi[iv]	Phạm Dật	c. 280-336	Jin shu (97) Liang shu (54) Sui shu (82)	
Fan Wen	Phạm Văn	336-349	Jin shu (97) Nan Qi shu (58) Liang shu (54) Sui shu (82)	
Fan Fo (or Fu)	Phạm Phật	349-380	Jin shu (97) Liang shu (54) Sui shu (82)	
Fan Huda	Phạm Hồ (or Tu) Đạt	380-413	Jin shu (97) Liang shu (54)	
Di Zhen	Dịch Chân	413-c. 415	Liang shu (54)	
		Liu Song Dynasty		
Wen Di	Văn Địch		Liang shu (54)	
Fan Yangmai I	Phạm Dương Mại I	420-c. 425?	Song shu (97) Liang shu (54)	421
Fan Yangmai II	Phạm Dương Mại II	c. 425 - 446	Song shu (97) Nan Qi shu (58) Liang shu (54)	
Fan Shencheng	Phạm Thần Thành	c.454-c.480	Song shu (97) Liang shu (54)	455, 458, 472 (in Song shu). Several times during 454 – 464 (in Liang shu).
		Nan Qi Dynasty		
Fan Danggenchun	Phạm Đương (or Đáng) Căn Thuần	c.480-c.491	Nan Qi shu (58)	491
Fan Zhunong[v]	Phạm Chư Nông	491-498	Nan Qi shu (58)	

PINYIN CHINESE	VIETNAMESE	REIGN[i]	CHINESE ANNALS[ii]	TRIBUTES[iii]
Liang Dynasty				
Fan Wenzan (Wenkouan)	Phạm Văn Tán (or Khoản)	c.500-c.508	Liang shu (54)	Several times during 483-493
Fan Tiankai[iv]	Phạm Thiên Khải	c.508-c.520	Liang shu (54)	510, 511, 514
Bicuibamo	Bật Nhuế (or Tuyệt) Bạt Ma	c.520-c.529 for Vijayavarman	Liang shu (54)	
Gaoshi Shengkai	Cao Thức Thắng Khải		Liang shu (54)	526, 527
Gaoshi Lutu-oluobamo	Cao Thức Luật Đà La Bạt Ma		Liang shu (54)	530, 534
Sui/Tang Dynasties				
Fan Fanzhi	Phạm (Phạn) Chí		Sui shu (82) Jiu Tang shu (197) Xin Tang shu (222c)	623, 625
Tang Dynasty				
Fan Touli	Phạm Đầu Lê		Jiu Tang shu (197) Xin Tang shu (222c)	630, 631
Fan Zhenlong[v]	Phạm Trấn Long		Jiu Tang shu (197) Xin Tang shu (222c)	
Fan Zhenlong's son-in-law			Xin Tang shu (222c)	From 650 to 756 sent tributes three times
Daughter of Fan Touli			Xin Tang shu (222c)	
Zhugedi	Chư Cát Địa		Xin Tang shu (222c)	
	Kien-to-ta-mo		Tang Hui yao (98)	713, 731

Table 17 – The kings of Linyi from the sixth to the eighth centuries.

i. After Majumdar[3]
ii. Volume
iii. Years tributes received at Chinese imperial court
iv. Fan Tiankai died soon after 514
v. Killed in 645 by Ma Ha Mạn Đa Già Độc

APPENDIX 9

KINGS	INSCRIPTIONS	REIGN[i]	REIGN[ii]
	Jin/Liu Song/Nan Qi Dynasties		
Śrīmāra	C.40		
Bhadravarman	C.72 C.73A C.41 C.81		
Gaṅgārāja Gaṅgeśvara	C.96 C.81		
	Nan Qi/Liang Dynasties		
Manorathavarman	C.96		
Rudravarman	C.96 – Reigned from 400 Śaka to...	c. 529-c. 565	539-541
	Siu/Tang Dynasties		
Śambhuvarman	C.73A C.74 C.96 C.99	c. 565-629	595-629
	Tang Dynasty		
Kandarpadharma	C.73A C.96 C.111 – Only mentioned "...varma (or dharma)"	629-c.640	630-631
Prabhasadharma	C.96 C.81	c.640-645	640-645
Daughter of Kandarpadharma	C.96	645-653	
Satyakauśikasvāmi	C.96	645-653	
Bhadreśvaravarman	C.96	653-655	
Jagaddharma	C.96	653-655	

KINGS	INSCRIPTIONS	REIGN[i]	REIGN[ii]
Prakāśadharma (or Prakāśadharma - Vikrāntavarman I) Vikrāntavarman II	C.73 A C.73 B C.74 C.79 C.81 C.87 – A date of 687 is given when king Prakāśadharma donated a kosa. Same donations were given by king Vikrāntavarman. C.96 – Stele erected 658 C.127 C.135 C.136 C.137 C.173	c.655-c.690	657-679
Naravāhanavarman	C.74 – 653 Śaka or 741 CE is recorded.	c.690-c.710	
Vikrantavarman II	C.74 C.81 – the year of 63x Śaka is recorded. C.77 C.80 C.97 C.99	c.710-730?	713-731
Rudravarman II		c. 730?-757	

Table 18 – The kings, based on inscriptions from the fourth to the eighth centuries.

i. After Majumdar[4]
ii. After BFEO[5]

APPENDIX 9

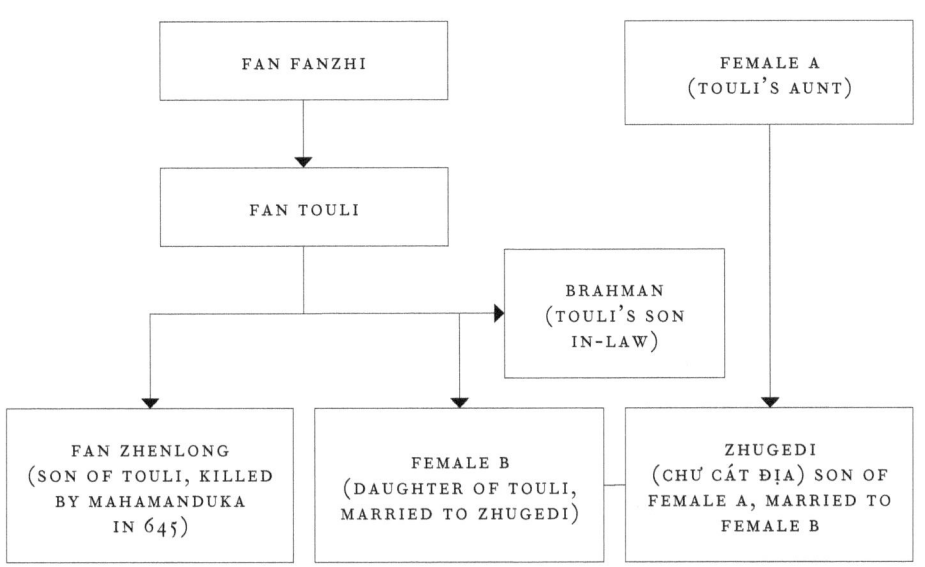

Figure 66 – Family tree of the kings of Linyi from the middle of the sixth century to the middle of the seventh based on Chinese annals.

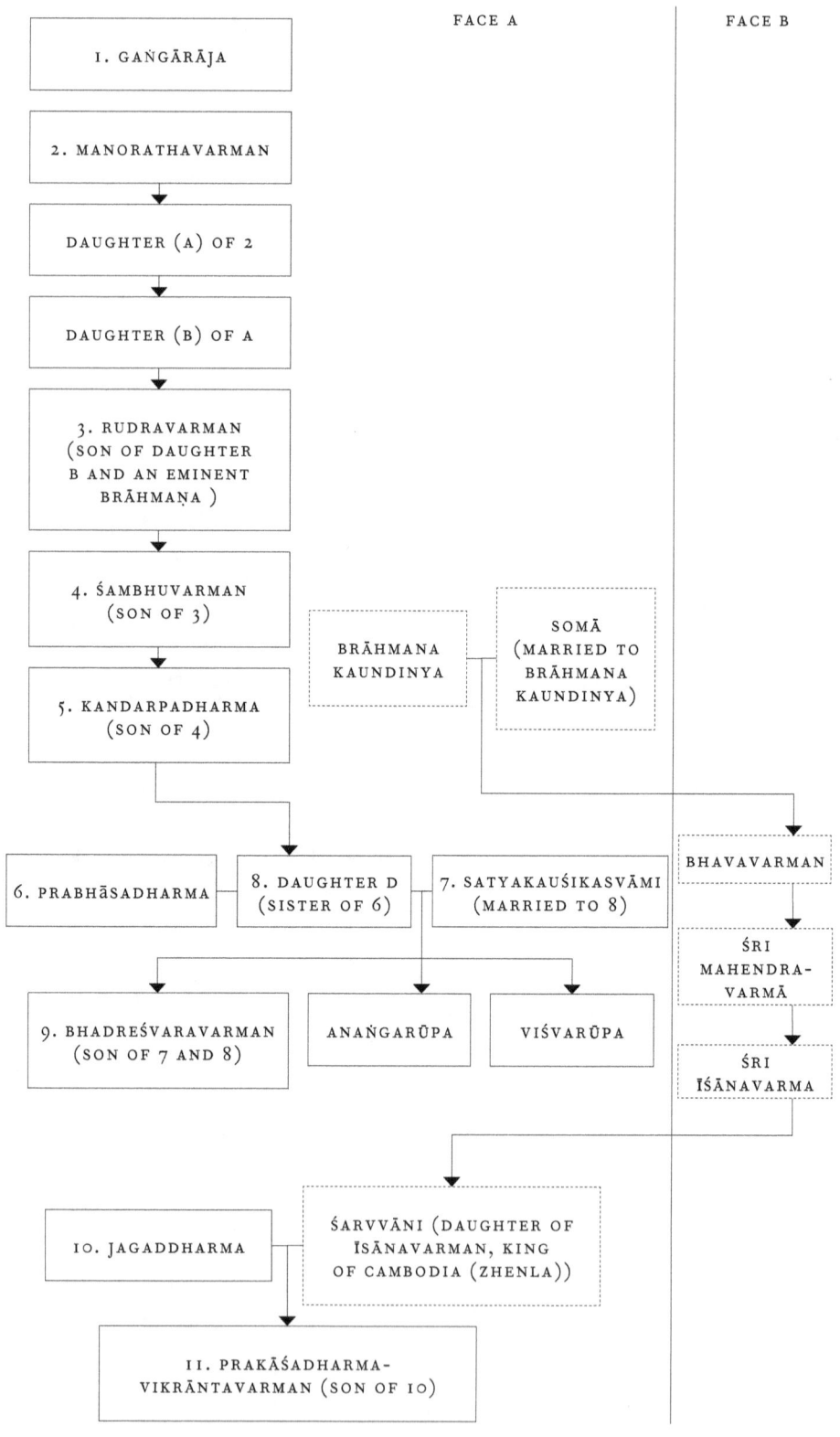

Left: Figure 67 – Family tree of the kings of Linyi, based on Inscription C.96 (Mỹ Sơn E6), erected by king no. 11 in 657 [6] The solid line is Champa, dotted line is Zhenla.

There are several different interpretations of the family tree, particularly in relation to Jagaddharma. In my interpretation, which aligns with Majumdar, Jagaddharma is the great-grandson of Kandarpadharma but in the dynastic list published in the *Bulletin de l'Ecole française d'Extrême-Orient*, Jagaddharma is not mentioned at all; the list shows Prakasadharma as the great-grandson of Kanharpadharma.[7] On the other hand, Maspero's chart displays Jagaddharma as the grandson of Rudravarman and thus a cousin of Kanharpadharma.[8] Lương Ninh is uncertain about the status of Jagaddharma as to whether he was a son, or grandson of Prabhasadharma. If he were a son then he would be a grandson of Kanharpadharma.[9]

As for the connection with the Fans, while most historians identify Śambhuvarman with Fan Fanzhi, however, Southworth identifies Kandarpadharma with Fan Fanzhi, and Jagaddharma as Zhugedi.[10] It can get confusing, so I am inclined to keep the information separate and leave the attempts to link them with the professional historians. However, I have some observations:

- The information from the inscriptions, produced locally, is likely more accurate than what is written down by the annal compilers years later, at some offices situated thousands of kilometres away.

- However, the annal compilers are generally accurate on years when the kings of vassal kingdoms sent their tributes, it is their job.

- Imperial envoys and field commanders are expected to submit their reports to the court. Information from such a report is likely to find its way to the annals so there is a certain degree of reliability on major events such as wars.

APPENDIX 10

THE KINGS OF FUNAN AND ZHENLA

APPENDIX 10

PINYIN CHINESE	VIETNAMESE	YEAR[1]	CHINESE ANNALS[i]	TRIBUTES[ii]
Later Han Dynasty				
Ye-liu (ot Liu-ye)	Diệp Liễu (or Liễu Diệp)	First/second century?	Nan Qi shu (58) Jin shu (97) Song shu (58) Liang shu (54)	
Hun-houei (or Hun-tian)	Hỗn Hội (or Hỗn Điền)	First/second century?	Nan Qi shu (58) Jin shu (97) Song shu (58) Liang shu (54)	
Hun Pan-huang	Hỗn Bàn Huống	Second century	Nan Qi shu (58) Liang shu (54)	
Pan-pan	Bàn Bàn	Late second century	Liang shu (54)	
Eastern Wu Dynasty				
Fan Shiman	Phạm Sư Man/ Phạm Man	Early third century	Nan Qi shu (58) Liang shu (54)	
Fan Jinsheng (or Kin-cheng)	Phạm Kim Sinh		Nan Qi shu (58) Liang shu (54)	
Fan Zhan	Phạm Chiên	c. 230 – c. 243	Nan Qi shu (58) Liang shu (54)	
Fan Chang	Phạm Trường		Nan Qi shu (58) Liang shu (54)	
Fan Xun	Phạm Tầm	245/50-287	Jin shu (58) Liang shu (54)	266/267, 280
Jin Dynasty				
Chu Zhantan (or Tianzhu Zhantan)	Trúc Chiên Đàn (Thiên Trúc Chiên Đàn)	c. 357	Jin shu (58)	357/368
Jin/Liu Song Dynasties				
Qiaochenru	Kiều Trần Như (Kauṇḍinya in Sanskrit)	c. 420	Liang shu (54)	
Liu Song Dynasty				
Chilituobamo	Trì Lê Đà Bạt Ma	c. 430-c. 440	Song shu (58)	434, 435, 438

PINYIN CHINESE	VIETNAMESE	YEAR	CHINESE ANNALS[i]	TRIBUTES[ii]
Nan Qi Dynasty				
Qiaochenru Sheseibamo	Kiều Trần Như Xà Da Bạt Ma	484-514	Nan Qi shu (58) Liang shu (54)	484, 503, 511, 514
Liang Dynasty				
Liutuobamo	Lưu Đà Bạt Ma	514-c. 545	Liang shu (54)	517, 519, 520, 530, 535, 539
Tang Dynasty				
No name is given			Xin Tang shu (222c)	618-626, 626-649

Table 19 – The kings of Funan based on Chinese records.

i. Volume
ii. Years tributes received at imperial court

APPENDIX 10

PINYIN CHINESE	VIETNAMESE		YEAR[2]	CHINESE ANNALS[i]	TRIBUTES[ii]
		Liang/Sui Dynasties			
		Bhavavarman I	Second half of the sixth century to c. 598		
		Sui Dynasty			
Chali She-to-ssu-na	Sái Lợi Chất Đa Tư Na	Kṣatriya Citrasena or Mahendravarman	Around 600-616 CE	Sui shu (82)	
		Tang Dynasty			
Y-che-na-sien-tai or Yishenaxiandai	Y Xa Na Tiên	Īśānavarman	616-635	Sui shu (82)	623, 628 Jiu Tang shu (222c)
		Bhavavarman II	Before 639-before 657		During 649-683. Jiu Tang shu (222c)
		Jayavarman I	Around 657-after 690		During 649-683. Jiu Tang shu (222c)
		Two Zhenlas (705-707)		Jiu Tang shu (222c)	
		Queen Jayadevi	713		During 690-705. Jiu Tang shu (222c)
		Pushka or Pushkarākṣa	716		During 712-756. Jiu Tang shu (222c)
		Rājendravarman I			
		Mahipativarman	to 802		

Table 20 – The kings, based on pre-Angkor inscriptions.

i. Volume
ii. Years tributes received at imperial court

The genealogy from Bhavavarman I to Queen Jayadevi is generally clear from the inscriptions but after that the information becomes a little confused. Apparently, there is a line from kings Bālādiya to Nṛipāditya to Pushkarāksha, for Water Zhenla.³ And there is another line from Pushkarāksha to Rājendravarman I and Mahipativarman. A king by the name of Sambhuvarman (eighth century) is also cited in some sources.

The break-up of the two Zhenlas may happen during the time of Queen Jayadevi or at the beginning of Pushkarāksha.

APPENDIX II

THE LAND THAT WAS LINYI

Historians generally agree that Linyi occupied the land that is north-central Vietnam between Quảng Bình province south of Ngang pass and Quảng Nam province south of Hải Vân pass. This land, under the Han, was the commandery of Nhật Nam. However, historical documents have provided a conflicting picture of the locations of the citadels, the prefectures, and the battlefields. The kings of Linyi and the generals from Eastern Wu, Jin, Song, Sui, and finally Tang dynasties fought many battles between the third and the seventh centuries, but these battlefields are not easily identifiable on the map.

In this Appendix, I will try to recreate the map of Linyi by reviewing works by historians, astronomical measurements recorded in Chinese annals, and Google Maps to better understand where these places are during the travel through this land.

I am approaching from two directions: one is by geography, based around the rivers, mountains, and two is by tracing back historical events. My first assumption is that battles are likely fought near the rivers where settlements and army camps or forts are located. My second assumption is that prefecture borders are likely rivers, and they remain relatively unchanged under the

Han, other northern dynasties, Linyi, and Champa so geography is where I will begin.

A11.1 – *The land and its rivers - Of water and sand*

The land between Ngang and Hải Vân passes stretches over 300 kilometres and is effectively divided into two flat terrains with Mũi Lay (Cape Lay) roughly in the centre. Mũi Lay is where the Trường Sơn mountain range branches off to the sea, and there is a lighthouse there. Geographically, Mũi Lay forms a natural border, reflected in the separation of the province of Quảng Bình, located north of Mũi Lay to Ngang pass, and the two provinces south of Mũi Lay extended to Hải Vân pass, of Quảng Trị and Thừa Thiên-Huế.

Seven main rivers flow to the sea between these two passes, as shown in Figure 68 and Table 21. The latter also lists the rivers immediately north of Ngang and south of Hải Vân passes.

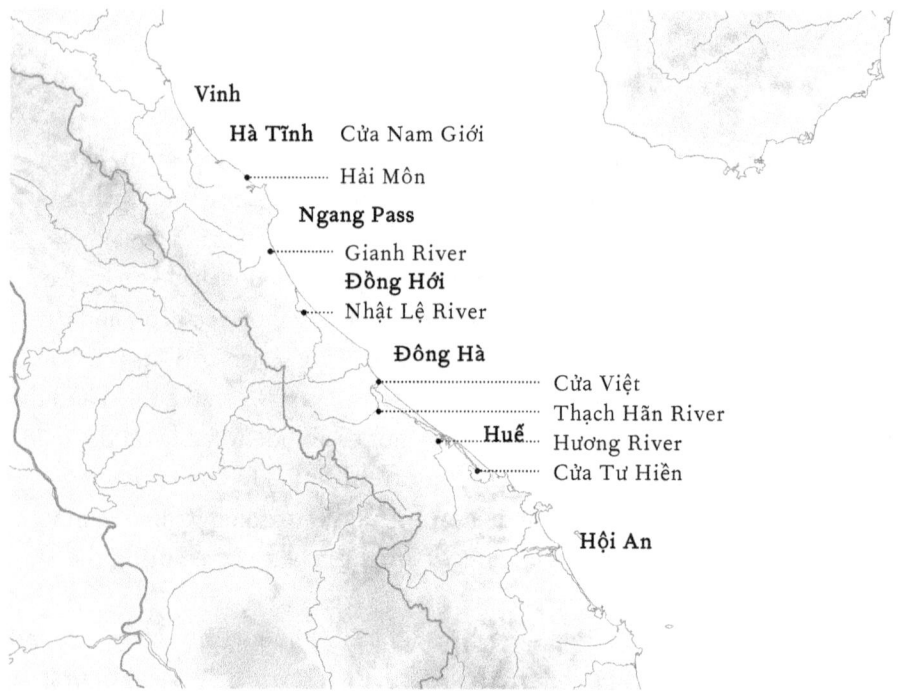

Figure 68 – The map of some of the main rivers in north-central Vietnam. Mũi Lay (not shown) is the point just north of Đông Hà.

RIVERS[i]	ESTUARIES	OTHER NAMES	SETTLEMENTS[ii]	DISTANCE[iii]	DISTANCE[iv]
Mã (or Nam Mã)			Thanh Hóa	Thanh Hóa – Vinh: 140 km	283 km
Cả	Cửa Hội, Cửa Lò		Vinh	Vinh – Hà Tĩnh: 49 km	137 km
Hạ Vàng		Nam Giới	Hà Tĩnh	Hà Tĩnh – Ba Đồn: 113 km	87 km
Ngang pass					0
Ròn					13 km
Gianh	Gianh		Ba Đồn	Ba Đồn – Đồng Hới: 42 km	28 km
Nhật Lệ [1]	Nhật Lệ		Đồng Hới	Đồng Hới – Đông Hà: 99 km	67 km
			Mũi Lay		144 km
Bến Hải	Cửa Tùng	Cửa Minh Linh	Xuân Mỹ	Đồng Hới – Xuân Mỹ: 81 km	146 km
Thạch Hãn [2]	Cửa Việt		Đông Hà, Quảng Trị	Đông Hà – Quảng Trị: 15 km	164 km
Ô Lâu					200 km
Hương	Cửa Thuận An		Huế	Đông Hà – Huế: 72 km	232 km
	Cửa Tư Hiền	Cửa Tư Dung, Tư Minh, Tư Khách, Ô Long			283 km
Hải Vân pass					314 km
Hàn			Đà Nẵng	Huế – Đà Nẵng: 92 km	330 km
Thu Bồn	Cửa Đại		Hội An	Đà Nẵng – Hội An: 30 km	360 km

Table 21 – The list of the main rivers in north-central Vietnam.

i. From north to south
ii. Major settlements close to the rivers
iii. Distance between major settlements
iv. Approximate distance from Ngang pass

Between the Nhật Lệ river and Mũi Lay, there is a very long stretch of sand called the Great Length of Sand (*Đại Trường Sa*); south of Mũi Lay to Cửa Thuận An there is also another stretch of sand called Small Length of Sand (*Tiểu Trường Sa*).[3,4]

The map indicates there is no river or canal route to connect the Ròn, Gianh, and Nhật Lệ rivers north of Mũi Lay. However, south of it, Google Maps shows one can travel from the Bến Hải to Thạch Hãn to Ô Lâu and Hương rivers by boat without having to sail along a more exposed coastline.[5] A map drawn in the 15th century (Figure 69) also shows a river route that connects the entrance to the Thạch Hãn river at Cửa Việt to the entrance of the Ô Lâu and Hương rivers at Cửa Tư Dung (or Tư Hiền).[6] In other words, Cửa Việt and Cửa Tư Hiền are major entrance/exit points of river transport up and down this stretch of the coast. This may explain why major naval battles were fought there during Linyi and Champa times, as explained elsewhere.

The significance of this observation is that Linyi troops can move relatively easily from their base in Huế by ships to the south of Mũi Lay, a distance of just over 100 kilometres in two or three days as compared with eight or nine days on foot.[7] There is no historical text to support this observation but for a kingdom that lived by raids and plunder of northern towns in imperial territory, the area around Cửa Việt – the settlement of contemporary Đông Hà, would have been very strategically important to Linyi as a staging area for such raids. There is also another factor which also makes Đông Hà a vital post to the Linyi economy is that it is on the trade route connecting Laos, west of Trường Sơn mountain range to the coast, via the border town of Lao Bảo as noted by historian Li Tana.[8] Furthermore, around 20 kilometres north of Đông Hà is the ancient and rich rice production terraces of Gio Linh as first identified by archaeologist Madeleine Colani.[9]

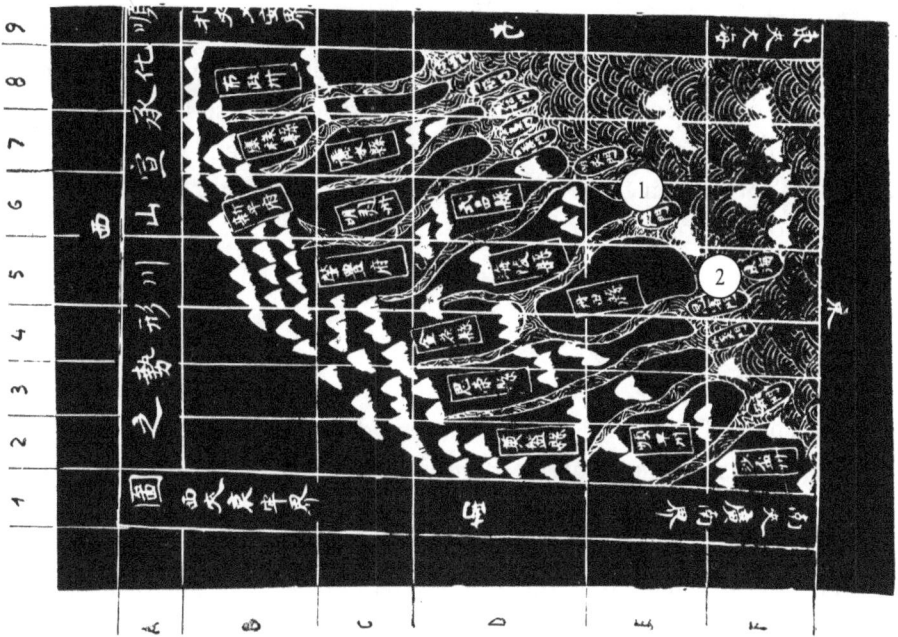

Figure 69 – A 15th-century map of Thuận Hóa (contemporary Thừa Thiên-Huế and Quảng Trị provinces).[10,11] 1. Cửa Việt, 2. Cửa Tư Dung (or Tư Hiền).

A11.2 – Land of the Chams

Once the imperial ruler was forced out, north Vietnam, north of Ngang pass, became an independent kingdom of Đại Việt (from the 10th to 19th centuries). Linyi, by that time, had become Champa (from the ninth to 19th centuries)[12]. Champa left many ruins, including towers, steles, vestiges, and citadels. North of Hải Vân pass, the largest number of Champa ruins are in Quảng Trị (29 ruins) as compared with its nearby provinces of Quảng Bình (13 ruins) and Thừa Thiên-Huế (25 ruins).[13] The favourable conditions for rice farming in Quảng Trị as discussed in Chapter 4 may have explained the difference. While not all these ruins were left behind by the Linyi people, it is likely that the Chams settled or built on former Linyi sites, so knowing what and where these ruins sites are would help us understand the land of Linyi.

Some of the ruins in Quảng Trị province are shown on a map in Tana's paper, where 27 ruins were listed, including five wells and a cluster of 14 wells spread between its southern and northern borders.[14] Local newspapers listed a few more sites including citadels and defensive walls.[15] Among these, one site at 10 kilometres east of Đông Hà is dated between the seventh and eighth centuries, the other site, at the rice terraces of Gio Linh, is older, between the second and sixth century, both were built during Linyi times.[16,17] There may be others of this time, but most were at Linyi and Champa times (seventh to 13th century); covering the districts of Gio Linh, Vĩnh Linh, and Cam Lộ around Đông Hà.

EXCHANGE LAND FOR FREEDOM

History records in 1069, Champa king, Chế Củ was captured by the Đại Việt king, Lý Thánh Tông (1054-1072). He surrendered three northern counties of Champa to exchange for his freedom.[18] These three counties from north to south were:

- Bố Chính, which includes the northern half of Quảng Bình province (the districts of Bố Trạch, Minh Hóa, Tuyên Hóa, Quảng Trạch and Ba Đồn town) from the Ròn to Nhật Lệ rivers.

- Địa Lý, which covers the southern half of the same province, between Nhật Lệ and Mũi Lay (the districts of Quảng Ninh and Lệ Thủy).

- Ma Linh, which includes the northern part of Quảng Trị province around Mũi Lay, Bến Hải and Thạch Hãn rivers (the districts of Gio Linh, Vĩnh Linh and Cam Lộ around Đông Hà).[19]

EXCHANGE LAND FOR A WIFE

Around 250 years later, in 1306, Đại Việt king, Trần Anh Tông, married his daughter, Princess Huyền Trân, to the Champa king, Chế Mân. The latter who offered two prefectures: Châu Ô and Châu Lý (or Rí) as a dowry but the names were changed to Thuận Châu and Hóa Châu a year later.[20] The former occupied a region overlapping southern Quảng Trị and northern Thừa Thiên-Huế provinces, covering roughly the land between the Thạch Hãn and Hương rivers.[21] Hóa Châu includes the districts south of the Hương river to the north of Thu Bồn rivers.[22]

The region between Ngang and Hải Vân passes became a contested area between Đại Việt and Champa over many years, but that is another story to be told in a separate volume. For now, I can summarise the northern prefectures or counties under Champa in the 11th and 14th centuries and compare them with those under the Han dynasty in the first and second centuries, shown in Table 22:

CHAMPA PREFECTURES[i]	LOCATION[ii]	ANCIENT CITADELS[iii]	LOCATION[iv]
Bố Chính	Between Ngang pass and the Nhật Lệ river	Cao Lao Hạ	Tây Quyển
Địa Lý	Between the Nhật Lệ river and the Kiến Giang river/Mũi Lay	Thành Nhà Ngo (Ninh Viễn)	Ti Ảnh
Ma Linh/Minh Linh	Between the Kiến Giang river/Mũi Lay and the Thạch Hãn river	Thành Cổ Lũy	Chu Ngô
Châu Ô (Thuận Châu)	Between the Thạch Hãn and Ô Lâu rivers	Thuận Châu	Lô Dung
Châu Lý (Hóa Châu)	Between the Ô Lâu and Thu Bồn rivers	Hóa Châu, Thành Lồi, Trà Kiệu	Tượng Lâm

Table 22 – Northern Champa prefectures.

i. From north to south
ii. Approximate
iii. Ancient citadels found at the locations
iv. Approximate locations of prefectures under the Han and Jin dynasties

RUINS OF CHAMPA CITADELS

In Table 22, I have also included the ruins of Champa citadels: Cao Lao Hạ, just south of Ba Đồn town, Thành Nhà Ngo (or Ninh Viễn), by the bank of the Kiên Giang river that flows into the Nhật Lệ river[23], Thành Cổ Lũy[24] by the Bến Hải river, Thuận Châu[25] by the Thạch Hãn river and Hóa Châu citadel near the Bồ river (Figure 70).[26]

When the first Nguyễn lord and entourage went south in 1588 to establish his new domain, he chose to camp at Ái Tử (1558-1570). Ái Tử is on the bank of Thạch Hãn river, south of Đông Hà. They chose this site as they sailed up the river from the estuary of Cửa Việt.[27] Over the next 70 years, his camp (or capital) moved to two other sites at Dinh Trà Bát (1570-1600) and Dinh Cát (1600-1626). All three are within 3 kilometres radius of the Champa citadel at

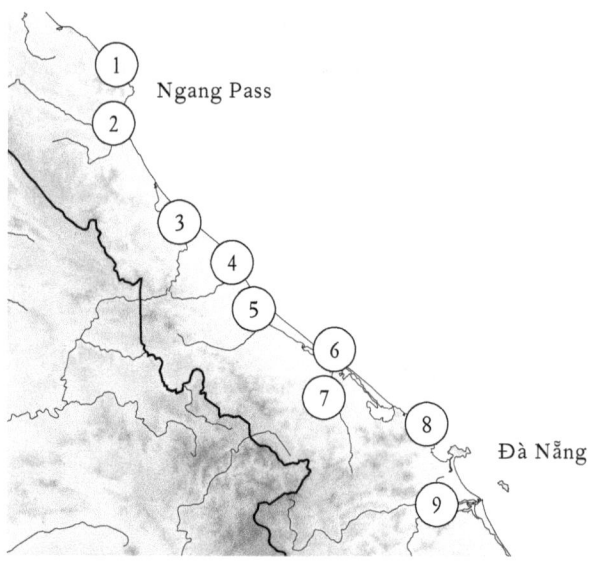

Figure 70 – Locations of Linyi and Champa citadels. 1. Ngang pass, 2. Cao Lao Hạ, 3. Thành Nhà Ngo, 4. Thành Cổ Lũy, 5. Thuận Châu, 6. Hóa Châu, 7. Thành Lồi, 8. Hải Vân pass, 9. Trà Kiệu.

Thuận Châu on the eastern side of the Thạch Hãn river.[28,29] Cửa Việt went on to become a major trading port for the Nguyễn lords which confirms the strategic importance of the region around Đông Hà as explained earlier.

A Vietnamese 19th-century geographical work entitled "A Unification Record of Đại Nam" or Đại Nam Nhất Thống Chí mentions a number of Champa citadels:

a. Thành Lồi at Nguyệt Biều commune, Hương Thủy district,

b. Thành Trung commune, Quảng Điền district,

c. Đan Duệ commune, Minh Linh district, Quảng Trị, where a citadel foundation can be found.

d. Hóa Châu citadel at Đan Điền district, Triệu Phong, location unknown.

e. Thuận Châu citadel at Hải Lăng, location unknown.[30]

Today, a) Thành Lồi is where it is now (Chapter 4), b) is Hóa Châu, c) could be Thành Cổ Lũy, as Đan Duệ is Đơn Duệ commune at Vĩnh Hòa district near Vĩnh Giang, d) could be the same as Thuận Châu. I have not been able to locate e) near Hải Lăng.

A11.3 – Gnomon measurements - Shadow of the sun

Another important source of information is the gnomon measurements taken by imperial expedition armies against Linyi. The measurements would be taken at noon on the summer solstice, the longest daylight of the year, using a "stick" of a standard height of 8 *chi* (*chi* is the Chinese foot).
A paragraph in ANCL records this practice as follows:[31]

> *"In the Yuanjia era of the reign of Emperor Wen (424-453), the Song dynasty went south to fight Linyi country. On a day in May, [they] planted a stick [a gnomon] and watched the sun's shadow. If the sun is north of the stick, [the shadow] is 9 cun 1 fen [273 mm], then the shadow at Giao Châu, south of the stick, is 2 cun 3 fen [69 mm]. Giao Châu, along the land and water routes, away from Luoyang, is more than 7,000 li [3,150 km]. Because of the winding mountains and rivers, the road becomes longer. [If we] take the sticks and stretch a string straight between them, the number [distance] is 1,000 li [450 km].*
>
> *In the 12th year of Kaiyuan (724), the Tang dynasty, again, took the measurement of Giao Châu: during the summer solstice, the sun's shadow in the south of the stick is 3 cun 2 fen [96 mm], compared to the measurement taken during the Yuanjia era of the Song Dynasty, is similar.*
>
> *The book Lunheng of* [astronomer and philosopher] *Wang Chong [27-97] says Nhật Nam prefecture is 10,000 li [4,500 km] from Luo-yang, which is why it is called Nhật Nam.* [A Taoist under the Tang dynasty] *Li Yun said that Annan fu [fu is a large prefecture] is 7,250 li [3,262 km] from Chang'an; Mạnh Quân said: the Annan Circuit is at the bottom of China. Now from La Thành to Kinh Sư* [Beijing?]*, there are approximately 115 stations added up to more than 7,700 li [3,465 km]."*

To determine where the gnomon's readings were taken, I have worked out a relationship between the location, latitude, and the gnomon readings.

The latitude of the Tropic of Cancer is ø. If a person stands at a spot along the Tropic of Cancer latitude on the summer solstice day, his sun shadow would be where his feet are. At a place away from the Tropic of Cancer, this person would see a shadow. For our purposes, the latitude of the gnomon planted there is angle α.

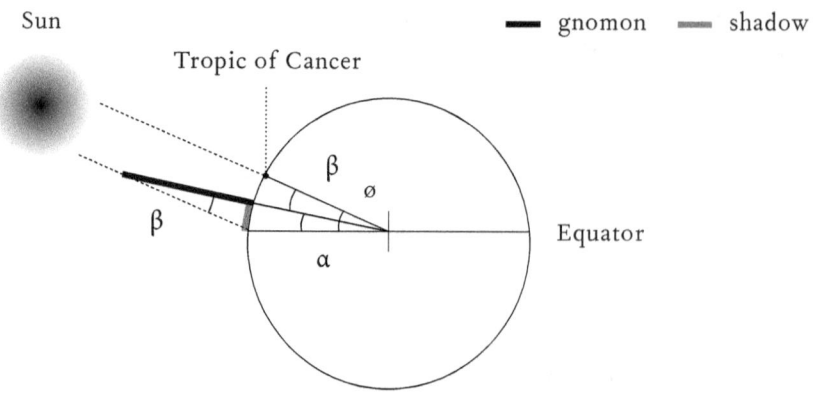

Figure 71 – An illustration of the gnomon latitude during the summer solstice.

From the diagram in Figure 71, α = ø – β, (if the gnomon is north of the Tropic of Cancer, then α = ø + β), where tan (β) = shadow/height of gnomon.[32]

In 2021, ø was 23°26"11.3" (or 23.436472°) north of the Equator.[33] Using this relationship, I can calculate the latitudes from the gnomon measurements reported in ANCL and TKCS, shown in decreasing degrees:

HEIGHT[i]	SHADOW[ii]	LATITUDE[iii]	LATITUDE[iv]	DATA	LOCATION[v]	YEAR[vi]
8	2.3	21.789676	21° 47' 23"	ANCL[35]	Giao Châu	446[36]
8	3.2	21.145867	21° 08' 45"	ANCL[37]	Giao Châu	724
8	8	17.725892	17° 43' 33"	TKCS[38,39]	Khu Túc citadel	351
8	9.1	16.946986	16° 56' 49"	TKCS[40] Tongdian[41] Old Book of Tang[42]	Linyi (during Tan Hezhi expedition)	446

Table 23 – Gnomon measurements.[34]

i. Gnomon height, *chi*
ii. Gnomon shadow, *cun*
iii. Latitude in decimal degrees
iv. Latitude in degrees, minutes
v. Where measurements were taken
vi. Year measurements were taken

I have matched up these locations with modern places of similar latitudes, as in Table 24 below. The result indicates that measurement no. 1 appears odd, and only the last three measurements are meaningful. The three respective locations are Luy Lâu, Ba Đồn, and Cửa Việt, the entrance to the Nhật Lệ river.

LOCATION[i]	LATITUDE[ii]	NOTES
1a. Yên Trạch, near Lạng Sơn. **1b. Citadel of Lạng Sơn.**	1a. 21°47'06.0"N 106°45'31.3"E 21.784999, 106.758698 1b. 21°50'29.9"N 106°45'19.0"E 21.841630, 106.755264	Lạng Sơn is a Vietnamese town near the border with southern China. It has been on the main land route to Hanoi from China for centuries. It would be unusual to have a gnomon measurement taken here by an expedition force as its location is already known. The other place in southern China of a similar latitude is near Beihai port, where Chinese southern expedition ships normally sailed from (Shiwan Post branch bureau, Hepu county, 21°45'58.3"N). On the same rationale, there is no reason for a gnomon measurement to be taken here either.
2a. Bái Uyên market, Bắc Ninh. **2b. Thành Cổ Luy Lâu, Bắc Ninh.**	2a. 21°08'36.8"N 106°02'21.4"E 21.143550, 106.039275 2b. 21°02'20.5"N 106°02'24.2"E 21.039014, 106.040047	Luy Lâu was the administrative centre of Giao Châu during Han times; the measurement was likely to be taken here for Giao Châu.
3a. Quảng Long district, north of Ba Đồn. **3b. Ba Đồn (172-178 Chu Văn An).**	3a. 17°46'26.0"N 106°25'25.3"E 17.773899, 106.42370 3b. 17°45'12.6"N 106°25'25.7"E 17.753511, 106.423817	Ba Đồn is located on the bank of the Gianh river and is believed to be the location of a significant frontier defensive fort for Linyi.
4a. An Mỹ pagoda. **4b. Thạch Hãn river inlet (Port of Cửa Việt.)**	4a. 16°57'09.9"N 107°06'49.6"E 16.952749, 107.113771 4b. 16°54'20.6"N 107°11'30.5"E 16.905709, 107.191791	An Mỹ pagoda is at Gio Linh around 20 kilometres north of Đông Hà.

Table 24 – Latitudes of places in Vietnam checked against historical gnomon measurements.

i. North to south
ii. Latitudes close to gnomon measurements

The distance between locations 1a and 4a is around 600 kilometres as the crow flies – a little higher than the estimate of 1000 *li* or 450 kilometres. Similarly, the road distance between Luoyang and Cửa Việt is around 2,500 kilometres by Google Maps – which is less than the estimates of over 3,000 kilometres.

A11.4 – Five prefectures of Nhật Nam commandery - A very confusing picture

Based on Vietnamese historical records, local information and archaeological digs, I now have a fairly good idea of how the land between Ngang and Hải Vân passes was historically occupied from the 11th century. However, to understand the same region in Linyi times, I need to go to Chinese works and subsequent research by historians.

In 111 BCE, after the Former Han dynasty conquered Nan-yue, they created three commanderies in the north and north-central Vietnam. From north to south, these are Giao Chỉ, Cửu Chân and Nhật Nam. Historians agree that Cửu Chân is in Thanh Hóa, Nghệ An, Hà Tĩnh with the southern border set at Hoành Sơn mountain range where Ngang pass is. They also agree that this is also the northern border of Nhật Nam.

Nhật Nam was then divided into five prefectures; historians agree that the southernmost county is Tượng Lâm and that is where Linyi was first established. However, there is a disagreement about the order of the prefectures from north to south, as summarised in Table 25, and where the southern border of Nhật Nam was. Aurousseau and Đào believe the southern border was as far as Cả pass, between Phú Yên and Khánh Hòa provinces; others disagree and place it at Hải Vân pass. Having reviewed Champa prefectures as illustrated above, I believe Tượng Lâm would likely be Châu Lý (Hóa Châu) and reach as far south as the Thu Bồn river. In fact, in later centuries, this river was the border between Đại Việt and Champa for nearly 100 years.[43]

While the order of the locations from north to south, as shown in Table 25, varies between sources, one common factor is that each prefecture is generally separated from the others by a river, as demonstrated in TKCS.[50]

History also records that most battles during this period took place in the rivers, at the estuaries, and the forts along the river bank. It would make sense as both antagonists rely on ships to transport their soldiers, and in particular, Linyi uses ships to raid many coastal towns of the empire north of their capital.

HAN SHU[45]	HOU HAN SHU[46]	JIN SHU[47]	SHUIJING ZHU SHU	ĐÀO[48]	AUROUSSEAU[49]
Chu Ngô (Zhuwu)	Tây Quyển	Tượng Lâm	Tây Quyển	Tây Quyển	Lô Dung
Tỷ Ảnh (Bijing)	Chu Ngô	Lô Dung	Lô Dung	Tỷ Ảnh	Tỷ Ảnh
Lô Dung (Lurong)	Lô Dung	Chu Ngô	Tỷ Ảnh	Chu Ngô	Chu Ngô
Tây Quyển (Xijuan)	Tượng Lâm	Tây Quyển	Chu Ngô	Lô Dung	Tây Quyển
Tượng Lâm (Xianglin)	Tỷ Ảnh	Tỷ Ảnh	Tượng Lâm	Tượng Lâm	Tượng Lâm

Table 25 – The distribution of five prefectures in Nhật Nam from different sources (from north to south). Information from the first four columns is also shown in Southworth.[44]

TÂY QUYỂN

TKCS states that Tây Quyển is the administrative centre of Nhật Nam and that Chu Ngô is 200 *li* (90 kilometres) from Tây Quyển. It is also deduced that Tây Quyển is also 400 *li* (180 kilometres) from Linyi.[51,52] We know that Linyi is south of Nhật Nam, so the order of these locations would be Tây Quyển – Chu Ngô - Linyi from north to south. At these distances, on Google Maps, Linyi is around Huế, Tây Quyển is south of the Gianh river, and north of Đồng Hới.

Aurousseau, on the other hand, believes Tây Quyển is just north of Tượng Lâm as the king of Linyi, Fan Wen, in his northern campaign, would logically occupy it as his next stage.[53] He did occupy Tây Quyển but razed it to the ground and returned to Linyi. Historical records also tell us Fan Wen demanded that the northern border be set at Ngang pass, which meant that his troops must have reached the Gianh and Ròn rivers, just south of Ngang pass. Based on the geography discussed earlier, Wen's forces, once they started from Huế, could easily go north using the river route. They got to Chu Ngô within a week by ships and continued from there along the coast from Cửa Việt or Cửa Tùng.

North of Ngang pass was Jin territory, and it makes sense where Tây Quyển is immediately south of it. This is because it was razed to the ground by Fan Wen; he did this presumably to create a no-man land buffer zone south of Ngang pass before returning to his base, possibly south of Mũi Lay. There is another possible reason, for revenge, as Wen was a slave at Tây Quyển in his youth.

On the subject of Tây Quyển, Đào suggests Chinese annals typically list the name of the prefecture, where the seat of the administration of the commandery, first thus under Han shu, it is Chu Ngô, and under Hou Han shu it is Tây Quyển.[54] He further explains the administrative centre was moved north from Chu Ngô to Tây Quyển during the time of Wang Mang rebellion (9-23). This is to provide additional protection due to the unrest caused by rebellions at the southern border of Nhật Nam.[55] His reasoning supports the position of Tây Quyển as north of Chu Ngô.

CHU NGÔ

Earlier, I recounted that Tan Hezhi arrived at Chu Ngô in 446 and had a gnomon reading taken; this establishes the position of Chu Ngô by Thạch Hãn river in Quảng Trị province (Figure 68). This is also the position taken by Đào and Pelliot and confirms the strategic importance of Đông Hà. The area was heavily settled by the Chams in later years, which became the prefecture of Ma Linh.[56]

I have now established Tượng Lâm in the south, Chu Ngô in the centre and Tây Quyển in the north, in the geographical order of south to north, but where would Tỷ Ảnh (or Tỉ Cảnh) and Lô Dung be?

LÔ DUNG

Aurousseau quotes the Jin shu Di Dao Ki (the geographical section of Jin Shu), which locates Chu Ngô at 200 *li* (90 kilometres) from Tây Quyển and Lô Dung at 300 *li* (135 kilometres) from the same prefecture. This means Lô Dung is 100 *li* (45 kilometres) from Chu Ngô. On the current map, it is placed just north of Huế, around Phong Điền/Quảng Điền districts.[57] Similarly, Jin shu and Hou Han shu both put Lô Dung and Tượng Lâm next to each other – consistent with this description.

TỶ ẢNH

On the other hand, TKCS mentions to get to Chu Ngô, one catches a boat to Lô Dung, then from there to Vô Biến (also known as Vô Lao, a sub-prefecture of Tỷ Ảnh), Phong Hỏa, and Tỷ Ảnh, from there, take another boat to Chu Ngô.⁵⁸,⁵⁹,⁶⁰ This passage confirms Tỷ Ảnh is north of Chu Ngô, but the reference to Lô Dung as north of Chu Ngô is incorrect.⁶¹ Since in another paragraph, TKCS mentions Lô Dung prefecture is 200 *li* (90 kilometres) from the estuary of the Lô Dung river, and also the old seat of Tượng Lâm. It also notes this river entrance is probably more than 200 *li* (90 kilometres) from Linyi.⁶²,⁶³ Comparing this with the earlier paragraph would indicate that this prefecture should read Tây Quyển, not Lô Dung. A footnote in TKCS explains that Lô Dung prefecture is Thừa Thiên-Huế.⁶⁴

A SUMMARY

Having studied TKCS, and the narratives of the various campaigns against Linyi, I support the order of the five prefectures of Nhật Nam commandery from north to south as: Tây Quyển - Tỷ Ảnh (Ti Cảnh) - Chu Ngô - Lô Dung - Tượng Lâm, and believe they generally align with locations of the Champa prefectures 500 years later as shown in Table 22. This order is the same as identified in a nineteenth-century Vietnamese geography work.⁶⁵

A11.5 – Đại Việt campaign against Champa in 1044 and 1069

Another source of information that has helped my understanding of the Linyi locations is the two campaigns of Đại Việt against Champa in 1044 and 1069. These campaigns were recorded with some details and shed light on the previous expeditions by the Jin, the Liu Song and Sui armies against Linyi in the fourth, fifth and seventh centuries.⁶⁶ Both campaigns were by ships that departed from Thăng Long (Hanoi), followed the Đáy river to the coast. They then sailed south from the river estuary of Đại An (previously Đại Ác) near Thanh Hóa.⁶⁷ Over 1,000 years earlier, Ma Yuan also took the Đáy river route as it was the most direct river route from Hanoi to the coast when travelling south. Cửa Đại An is not very far from where Ma Yuan led his ships up the Mã river in Thanh Hóa to attack the remnants of the Trưng sisters' rebellion (Appendix 8).

YEAR 1044

In the 1044 campaign, Đại Việt's fleet arrived at Cửa Tư Minh (Cửa Tư Hiền), landed and won a decisive battle against Champa forces where the Champa king was killed. ⁶⁸,⁶⁹ By this time, the Champa capital had shifted to Vijaya. This was where king Lý Thái Tông and his ships arrived in July of 1044. They entered Vijaya and captured many of the wives and concubines of the dead Champa king.[70] In August, Lý Thái Tông returned to Đại Việt with his booty and arrived at Thăng Long in September of 1044. Vijaya is believed to be Quy Nhơn.

YEAR 1069

Twenty-five years later, on 8 March 1069, his son, king Lý Thánh Tông, commanded another Đại Việt forces. They were led by a general, admiral, and eunuch by the name of Lý Thường Kiệt and set out from the capital of Thăng Long to invade Champa again. While history record does not mention where the armada sailed from but I have assumed that the expedition would follow the same river route that was to sail down the Đáy river and took the coastal route from Cửa Đại An.[71]

On 23 March, they entered the Nhật Lệ river and successfully destroyed the Champa defence there. On 3 April, the armada of Đại Việt king arrived at Shilibinai (Thi lị bì nại), or present-day Cửa Thị Nại, Quy Nhơn, won a major battle and captured Chế Củ.

On 19 June, they departed Quy Nhơn, passed Cửa Tư Hiền in Huế and finally arrived at Thăng Long on 17 July 1069 with Chế Củ paraded as a prisoner. Chế Củ eventually surrendered three northern prefectures in the present-day Quảng Bình, Quảng Trị provinces to Đại Việt to exchange for his freedom, as mentioned earlier.

The two campaigns note the battles of Cửa Tư Hiền and Nhật Lệ on the ways south, but there is no mention of the Champa defence at the Gianh nor Thạch Hãn rivers. On the other hand, gnomon measurements taken by the Jin in the fifth century indicate battles at these rivers. I could only speculate that the forts were destroyed in previous battles, and Champa may have decided to establish their defensive lines further south.

Table 26 provides estimated data on the average speed of Đại Việt troops' movements by the sea route measured in land distance equivalent. It is between 40 and 50 kilometres per day by ship. This data is helpful to estimate the locations of the battles during Linyi times. It is interesting to note that my approximation matches Pelliot's estimates of six days to travel from Đồng Hới to Quảng Nam (a road distance of around 300 kilometres).[72]

LOCATION	DISTANCE[i]	TIME[ii]	SPEED[iii]	NOTES
Thăng Long (Hanoi) – Vinh (Cửa Nghệ An) via Nghĩa Hưng (Cửa Đại Ác)	341	7	48.7	8 to 15 March 1069
Vinh – Hà Tĩnh (Cửa Nam Giới)	49	3	16.3	15 to 18 March 1069. It took three days to cover 49 kilometres which indicate the expedition must have stopped at Hà Tĩnh, just north of Ngang pass, for provisions since beyond Ngang pass; they would come into Champa territory or at least to a no-man land.
Hà Tĩnh – Đồng Hới (Cửa Nhật Lệ)	152	5	30.4	18 to 23 March 1069
Đồng Hới – Cửa Tư Hiền (Tư Dung)	219	5	43.8	23 to 28 March 1069
Cửa Tư Hiền (Tư Dung) – Quy Nhơn (Cửa Thị Nại)	373	6	62.2	28 March to 3 April 1069
Total	1,134	26		
Return trip: Quy Nhơn – Hanoi	1,134	28	40.5	19 June to 17 July 1069

Table 26 – Routes taken in the 1069 campaign by Đại Việt against Champa.[73]

i. Land distance, *km*
ii. Time taken by ships, *days*
iii. Speed, *km per day*

A11.6 – The trip of Jia Dan

Another record of sailing duration and distances was provided by a scholar-official, geographer Jia Dan in the eighth century under the Tang dynasty. It is shown in Table 27 and Figure 72. In Figure 72, I have mapped out the distances between the destinations recorded by Jia Dan as straight lines using Google Maps. The distances between them are proportioned based on the duration; that is a 4-day sailing distance would be twice as long as a 2-day trip and so on. While sailing duration depends on the wind speed and the earth is round, not flat, this method does provide a reasonable estimate of locations.

The estimation is assisted by a number of destinations which could be identified with a high degree of accuracy as per Pelliot's paper.[74] These are Guangzhou, Cù Lao Chàm island, Côn Đảo (Côn Sơn or Poulo Condore), and the strait of Malacca. The results show an average sailing speed of over 100 km of road distance per day (for example: from Cam Ranh to Phan Rang-Tháp Chàm is 52 km by road and 0.5 day sailing by Jia Dan's record). This is faster than the 50 km/day estimated above, which likely reflects that a trader on a sailing ship is expected to travel faster than a flotilla of a naval expedition force.

APPENDIX II

Positions from the north to south are shown in Table 27:[75,76]

	ORIGINAL NAMES	CONTEMPORARY LOCATIONS	SAILING DURATION
1.	Canton	Guangzhou	0
2.	Mount Tun-men	Near Lantau island, Hong Kong.	South-eastern direction, not recorded
3.	Jiu zhou Shi (Nine Islands)	Qi or Taya islands, north-east point of Hainan.	Western direction, two days from Mount Tun-men.
4.	Xiang Shi (Tu-chu-shen, or Tchan-pou-lao or Elephant Rock)	Tinhosa (Dazhou Island) of Hainan.	Southern direction, two days from Nine islands.
5.	Mount Zhan-bu-lau (Tchan-pou-lao)	Cù Lao Chàm, off the coast of Hội An.	South-western direction, three days from Elephant Rock.
6.	Mount Ling	North of Quy Nhơn, around con Trâu islet, off Đầm Nước Ngọt (Freshwater bay) – the outlet of the La Tinh river. Pelliot suggests Cape Sa-hoi, Cape Batangan (Ba Làng An or Ba Tân Gân). Sa-hoi is just south of Sa Hùynh commune.[77] Batangan is north of Quảng Ngãi city. However, both are further north in Quảng Ngãi province and too close to Cù Lao Chàm for a 3 days sailing.	South direction, two days from Mount Zhan-bu-lau.
7.	Kingdom of Mendu (Men-tou)	Just north of Cả pass, the kingdom of Mentu	Southern direction, one day from Mount Ling.
8.	Kingdom of Guda (Kou-tan)	Between Nha Trang city and Cam Ranh bay, Ku-ta is the kingdom of Kauṭhāra.	Southern direction, one day from Mendu.
9.	Pen-tuo-lang (Pen-t'o-lang)	Phan Rang (kingdom of Pāṇḍuraṅga)	Southern direction, 0.5 day from Guda.
10.	Zhun-tu-nong (Kiun-t'ou-nong) island	Côn Đảo island (Poulo Condore)	Southern direction, two days from Pen-tuo-lang
11.	Strait	Malacca strait perhaps by Singapore	Southern direction, five days from Zhun-tu-nong.

Table 27 – Details of Jia Dan's trip in the eighth century.

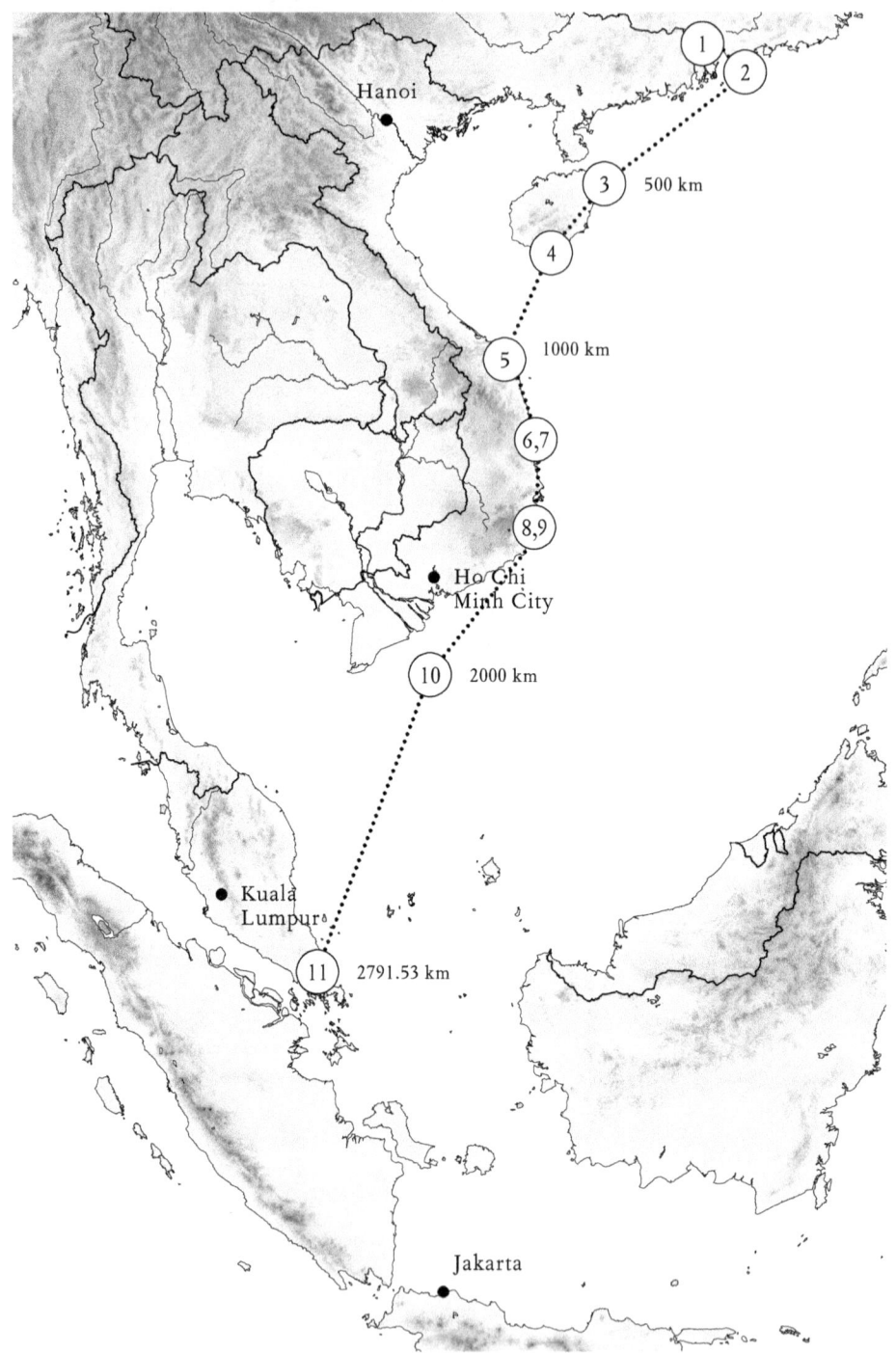

Figure 72 – Estimated positions of Jia Dan's trip. See Table 27 for the explanation of the numbers.

A11.7 – Ma Yuan's bronze pillars

BRONZE PILLARS AT THANH HÓA

TKCS, quotes the book "*Tiên*", written by a certain Du Đinh Kỳ, an official of the Eastern Wu (220-280) dynasty, as below. He wrote it after an inspection tour of Nhật Nam.[78] It is the oldest passage related to the Mã Lưu people, and subsequent corresponding paragraphs in the Book of Liang (635) and Xin Tang shu (1060) are likely its copy.

Du Đinh Kỳ wrote:

> "*Mã Văn Uyên (Ma Wenyuan or Ma Yuan) erected two bronze pillars on the [river bank] north of Linyi. There were 10 families of soldiers who were left behind and did not return [to China], on the south bank of the Thọ Linh [river], facing the bronze columns. All of them took the last name Ma, married between themselves, now there are 200* [300 in the next paragraph of TKCS] *households. The Giao Châu people consider them exiles, so they call them Mã Lưu* [the Mã exiles or the remaining men of Mã]. *Their language and eating habits are still similar to the Chinese. The mountains and rivers have changed, the bronze pillars are now in the sea, but thanks to these people, we know the ancient location of the bronze pillars.*"[79]

I have established that Thọ Linh is the Gianh river; based on this passage, Ma Yuan's bronze pillars are at the Gianh river.

However, the pillars may be at Thanh Hóa. In 1953, archaeologist Olov Janse found 29 Han graves at Lạch Trường harbour of Thanh Hóa province. Some historians suggest these belong to those Han soldiers who accompanied Ma Yuan in his expedition against the Trưng sisters in 41-44.[80]

The only difficulty of matching the archaeological finds with the historical text is that Lạch Trường harbour is at the Nam Mã river mouth, whereas the Thọ Linh river (the present-day Gianh river) is some 300 kilometres south. However, if Du Đinh Kỳ is wrong in identifying the name of the river, then the archaeological artefacts would be consistent with his description. Ma Yuan and his troops fought the last battle in the 41-43 campaign in Thanh Hóa, so it makes sense that where he left them, not at some place further south.

As discussed earlier, Linyi and Eastern Wu were at war in 248, so when Du Đinh Kỳ visited, the region around Ngang pass may still be the war zone; hence he may not have gone further than the pass when he wrote his report. This would support the explanation that the bronze pillars are at Thanh Hóa.

BRONZE PILLARS AT HUẾ

TCKS then quotes the book Records of Linyi (Linyi ji) that Ma Yuan erected two bronze pillars south of Tượng Lâm prefecture, the border between the Han territory and the kingdom of Xitu. The local people explained that the inhabitants were called *Mã Lưu*, who, for generations, had claimed to be descendants of the Han.[81] In the same paragraph, TKCS mentions the pillars must be south of Quảng Hòa (present-day Quảng Trị) province.

The biography of Liu Fang describes Ma Yuan's bronze pillars as a marker for his campaign against Linyi in 605. My analysis of this campaign has indicated that these pillars are likely at Huế or Hải Vân pass. In Liang shu (635), Linyi is described as follows:

> "*The country of Linyi, originally the prefecture of Tượng Lâm of Nhật Nam commandery under the Han dynasty, is the frontier of the land of Việt Thường in antiquity. Fubo Jiangjun Ma Yuan of the Han dynasty expanded the realm in the south for the Han, and established this prefecture. The land is 600 li (270 km) long, the administrative centre is 120 li (54 km) from the coast, away from the boundary of Nhật Nam by 400 li (180 km); the north is the border with Cửu Đức prefecture. The southern border is more than 200 li (90 km) by water or land routes. There is a Di (barbarian) country in the west that also claims the title of king. That is where Ma Yuan erected two bronze pillars to mark the border of the Han*".[82]

Xin Tang shu (1060) describes Huangwang, following Linyi, as:

> "*At the great harbour in the south of that country, there are five bronze pillars, the mountain there looks like an inclined canopy. There are many peaks in the west, the sea borders the cliffs on the east. These are the bronze pillars which Ma Yuan built during the Han dynasty. There were also Xitu barbarians; when Ma Yuan returned home, he left them there. There were* [originally] *only 10 households but by the end of the Sui dynasty, the descendants had multiplied to 300 households.*[83] *They all took the Ma family name; the local custom treated them as exiles so they referred to them as "Mã Lưu Nhân" (the people left behind by Ma Yuan). They shared the southern part of the land with Linyi*".[84]

Let us study these passages in a little more detail:

a. Cửu Đức prefecture is contemporary Hà Tĩnh province, so the northern border of Linyi would be at Ngang pass.

b. The length of Linyi at 270 km is surprisingly close to the distance between Ngang, and Hải Vân passes measured by Google Maps (314 km by road or 260 km by the crow flies) or to Hội An (358 km and 304 km respectively).

c. The administrative centre, 54 km from the coast, is too far inland; it would be at the Trường Sơn mountain range. None of the present settlements is that far from the coast.

d. The administrative centre is 180 km south of Ngang pass, which could be around the Champa citadel of Thuận Châu, south of Đông Hà in Quảng Trị province.

e. Both passages indicate that the bronze pillars are at the southern border of Linyi, which would be in the vicinity of Hải Vân pass by this time.

f. The description of the inclined canopy mountains appears to match the pass as viewed from the north, and the great wharf seems to fit Chân Mây bay, immediately north of the pass. Similarly, the same description could match the mountains around Ngang pass and Vũng Áng bay north of the same pass.

To my knowledge, there are no archaeological finds of Han artefacts around either bays or passes. So, to reconcile with Janse's findings above, it would seem to me that the Mã Lưu Nhân left behind by Ma Yuan had to be at Thanh Hóa.

However, at the time of Ma Yuan, the southern border of the Han empire was further south and possibly at Hải Vân pass, so Ma Yuan was likely to order the bronze pillars erected there. To illustrate the southern extent of the empire, Hou Han shu recorded that in 102, the family of the Later Han Empress Yin, including her grandmother, Deng Zhu, her brothers and household staff, were exiled to Tỷ Ảnh, in Đồng Hới by the Nhật Lệ river.[85] One could imagine the shock of the natives to see the large entourage of this ex-royal family arrive at the entrance of the Nhật Lệ river!. Fortunately for the empress' family, in 110, they were allowed to return to China, regained their confiscated wealth and received a payment of 500 taels of silver in compensation.

Based on the description in Xin Tang shu, I would suggest Ma Yuan bronze pillars were likely erected at Chân Mây bay, possibly by the Bu Lu river estuary. However, the Mã Lưu Nhân probably settled around the Nam Mã river.

A11.8 – The kingdom of Xitu

XITU DI – BARBARIANS "TU" IN THE WEST

In Chapter 5, Ma Duanlin describes Linyi as:

> *"This country has mountains which contain gold mines, of which the ore is red. The gold generated in these mines produces, during the night, fires that resemble those of glowworms."*

Ma Duanlin may have copied it from Liang shu (635). However, in the original text of Liang shu, while the description is under Linyi heading, it specifically refers to a region 200 *li* south of Linyi (around 90 km): *"there is a Di (barbarian) country in the west also claim the title of king"*.[86] In Xin Tang shu (1060), a similar passage under Huanwang mentions a place:

> *"where mountains that appear to [reach] the inclining canopy. In the west are continuous cliffs, and the east is the shoreline. Also to its east are the Tu barbarians"*.[87]

However, in the earlier Nan Qi shu (537), there is no mention of the Tu barbarians but just a direct statement that *"Linyi has a golden mountain, and golden water flows to the shore of the river."*[88]

I have established that the description of gold mines fits contemporary Quảng Nam province. The inclined canopy mountain appears to match Hải Vân pass viewed from the north. Based on these passages and other documents, historians have concluded that the kingdom in the Thu Bồn river valley of Quảng Nam province is Xitu (Xi means west), and this kingdom existed in the fifth century, ruled by king Bhadravarman, independent of Linyi to the north.[89,90]

In this narrative, the territory of Linyi to the north of the Hải Vân pass followed Fan Yang Mai's line, south of the pass, Xitu took up the lineage of Di Zhen/ Gaṅgārāja (Chapter 6) in the Thu Bồn river valley until it absorbed Linyi in the early sixth century as Rudravarman went north to attack Lý Bôn.[91] Following the same narrative, from the fifth century on, apparently, the Chinese texts differentiate between Linyi north of Hải Vân pass and Xitu, south of the pass.[92] Other historians argue Linyi could have absorbed Xitu at an earlier date.[93]

BOLIAO AND QUDUQUIAN

Other than Xitu, Chinese annals also mention two other kingdoms: Boliao (Ba Liêu), 100 *li* (around 45 kilometres) south of Xitu and Quduqian (Khuất Đồ Kiền) at some 3,000 *li* by boat south of Boliao.[94] Forty-five kilometres south of Xitu, taken from the Thu Bồn river estuary, is around Tam Kỳ, but 3,000 li (or 1,350 kilometres) south of it would be well outside Vietnamese territory. Perhaps it should read 300 *li*, which would be around the estuary of the Trà Khúc river in Quảng Ngãi province.[95]

KINGDOMS OR TRIBES?

I am not so convinced about the significance of the above kingdoms in Vietnamese history, as indicated by the above narratives when compared with Linyi and Funan. To my knowledge, they are not recorded in Chinese annals as sending any tributes to the imperial court. Some historians suggest the Chinese writers got Xitu and Linyi mixed up.[96] However, I would propose that these kingdoms could well be similar to the small states Fan Wen conquered when he first became king (Chapter 4).

TKCS says that during Han times, the people of Chu Ngô could not cope with the heavy taxation from the local magistrate, so they fled to Khuất Đồ Kiền to establish a kingdom. TKCS also notes the translation of "kingdom" may be incorrect, and the text might refer to Khuất Đồ Kiền robbers. It records Khuất Đồ is the people of Di (or barbarian), but Khuất Đồ Kiền (Quduqian) is the same as one of the states Fan Wen conquered, as cited earlier.[97] TKCS also mentions 2,000 households of Chu Ngô people living there including the rebels.[98] I have established that Chu Ngô is located near contemporary northern Quảng Trị overlapping southern Quảng Bình provinces and that is where Quduqian is likely to be.

The other alternative explanation is that the people of Chu Ngô fled their hometown to escape the heavy taxation, but it would be difficult to believe they would flee as far south as the Trà Khúc river south of Hải Vân pass. In all likelihood, they would escape west to the mountains nearby as it would be a lot closer and more difficult for the pursuers to follow.

A location 3,000 *li* north of Chu Ngô would be somewhere in Guangdong province, which would not make sense for the location of the Boliao kingdom. However, if the distance is only 300 *li*, then Xitu, at 400 li (180 kilometres) north of Chu Ngô, would be around Ngang pass – a possibility as it would be within the Linyi domain.

However, Xitu is mentioned in relation to Ma Yuan bronze pillars, and as discussed earlier, these pillars are likely to be at Chân Mây bay in Huế. In that case, Xitu would be in Quảng Nam and according to Xin Tang shu, the Xitu people are the barbarians Ma Yuan left behind, even if TKCS refers to them as soldiers who came with Ma Yuan. However, archaeological findings indicate that these people were in Thanh Hóa!.

These contradictions, and the reference to the Tu barbarians in the west in the text have given me doubt as to whether Xitu would be of such a significant size to absorb Linyi

APPENDIX 12

CITADELS OF BLOOD AND GOLD - KHU TÚC (QUSU), ĐIỂN XUNG (DIAN CHONG), AND OTHER BATTLEFIELDS

Historical records of the expedition of Tan Hezhi of the Liu Song dynasty against Linyi in 446 mention two major citadels: KHU TÚC, where Tan Hezhi troops beheaded everyone over 15 years old, and ĐIỂN XUNG, where they melted down the golden statues and took away tons of gold.

Historians have long tried to locate these citadels, and in this Appendix, I will add my contribution based on the analysis in Appendix 11 and the description in TKCS. Similarly, I will attempt to identify the locations of the battles between the kings of Linyi and the generals of the northern dynasties in the fourth and fifth centuries, as it is not easy to relate them to modern settings.

A12.1 – Ancient locations

A CONFUSION OF RIVERS

TKCS is based on the work by Li Daoyuan (470-527) in the sixth century about rivers in the Chinese empire. With respect to the rivers in Linyi, historians generally agree that there are mistakes and discrepancies in his work. One of the main reasons is that Li did not visit the region of Linyi but relied on other sources, chief among them is the Records of Linyi (or Linyi Ji), now lost.

Uất Thủy river

However, in the absence of other sources, the description in TKCS is extremely valuable for reconstructing the geography of Linyi, keeping in mind these discrepancies. Since the book is about rivers, I will follow its narration of the Uất Thủy river, a common thread in the TKCS story of Linyi. In TKCS, this river flows from Guilin (Quế Lâm or Uất Lâm) commandery to the sea at Tứ Hội (Sihui) river mouth, with Tứ Hội means where four rivers meet.[1,2,3] It also flows to the west of Nan-hai, or Guangdong province, and based on this description, this estuary is likely in Guangzhou with the four rivers as Yingu, Xi, Bei, and Dong respectively.[4] As for the Uất Thủy river, it resembles the Xunjiang and Xi rivers in southern China. In other words, these natural features have little to do with Linyi in north-central Vietnam.

As that is the case, the Tứ Hội estuary mentioned in TKCS, related to the event of 431, is not the same as the Tứ Hội estuary of the Uất Thủy river since there is no way that Linyi king, Fan Yangmai, and his ships would sail that far north to Guangzhou.

However, for my purposes, I will continue with the Uất Thủy river in TKCS, accepting that the name is incorrect for Linyi. It flows south past the Tứ Hội Phố river and connects upstream to a place called Cổ Lang Cửu Phố, west of Lô Dung prefecture; it then passes the estuary of Nội Tào Khẩu where Ma Yuan transported his supplies by sea.[5] In Ma Yuan's expedition of 41, they left Hepu and most likely entered Bái Tử Long bay to the Bạch Đằng river by Hải Phòng, a long way north of Linyi so the description here is also likely related to southern China.

Lô Dung river

The Uất Thủy river then flows into lake Lang which receives its water from the ravine or spring of Kim Sơn Lang Cứu, where Kim Sơn means golden mountain.[6] This spring flows north, connecting with two rivers: Lô Dung (Lurong), and Thọ Linh (Shouling) rivers.[7] The Lô Dung river collects water from a high mountain south of Khu Túc citadel and flows in the southwest direction. This mountain is connected to a chain of mountains in the west like a natural curtain. The Lô Dung river then accumulates water at Ẩn Sơn mountain, flows around the west, circles to the north, and then to the east on the northern side of Khu Túc citadel. It then continues to the east and joins with the Thọ Linh river on the right, which flows from the border of Thọ Linh prefecture.[8] The joined river flows east to Lang Cửu gully, which stores water in a lake called the mouth of the Lang Hồ (Lake Lang) Phố Khẩu.

The Uất Thủy river flows south from the Thọ Linh (Shouling) prefecture to the sea. There are places named Shouling in southern China in the vicinity of Uất Thủy (Yu, Xunjiang, and Xi) rivers, but these are not the same as Thọ Linh prefecture split from Tây Quyển in Jin times.[9,10,11]

Based on this description, I have produced a sketch of the rivers and Khu Túc citadel, as shown in Figure 73.

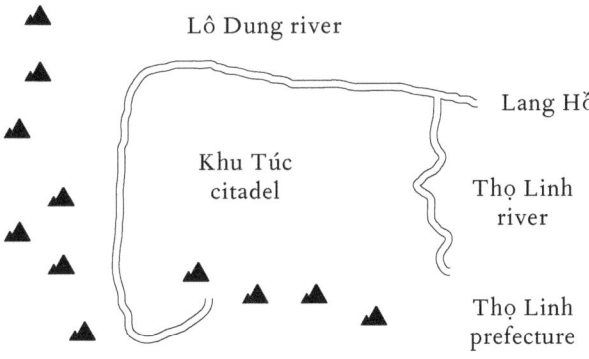

Figure 73 – The Lô Dung river as described in TKCS. The jagged black shapes denote mountains.

Lô Dung river mouth

It would not be unreasonable to assume that the Lô Dung river is in Lô Dung prefecture as naming a location after the main river was a common practice at the time. As discussed earlier, Lô Dung prefecture is Thừa Thiên-Huế province, so the Lô Dung river is likely the Hương river. The Lô Dung river mouth (or Cửa Lô Dung) is then likely the present-day Cửa Tư Hiền.

However, this may not be the only explanation, and the Lô Dung river mouth could be elsewhere. TKCS, citing "Records of Funan" (Funan Ji) by Kang Tai (Chapter 9), that Cửa Lô Dung is more than 200 *li* (90 kilometres) from Linyi and travelling to Funan would leave from this river mouth.[12]

From north to south, there are four possible locations Kang Tai may refer to as Linyi. In the first location, it could be immediately south of Ngang pass, but at the time of Kang Tai in the middle of the third century, Fan Wen was yet to be born, and the area was still under contention between Linyi and Eastern Wu. Kang Tai is unlikely to refer to it as Linyi. The second location is south of Mũi Lay at around Cửa Việt, which could be possible, given that Linyi had fought their way north during Kang Tai's time; in that case, more than 90 kilometres north of it would be at around the Giang river inlet. So depending on where Linyi is, we can locate Cửa Lô Dung.

The third location is at Huế, 90 kilometres north of it would be around Cửa Việt, which could also be a major port to leave. The fourth location is Quảng Nam then 90 kilometres north of it would be around Cửa Tư Hiền. When Kang Tai mentioned Linyi, presumably, he referred to the capital of the kingdom where he was heading. In the middle of the third century, around 50 years after the Khu Liên rebellion and the founding of Linyi, its capital probably was at Quảng Nam. So in the absence of other evidence, I believe the entrance of the Lô Dung river is still Cửa Tư Hiền.

THÀNH LỒI IN HUẾ AS KHU TÚC CITADEL

TKCS describes the Khu Túc citadel as where the Linyi army kept all their weapons and other war materials. The citadel is surrounded by

> *"high rocky mountains and rugged land"* and it is *"located between two rivers, three sides close to the mountains, the north and south sides both looked out to rivers, there are small streams at the base of the citadel walls in the east and west, the western wall follows a winding path with 10 corners"* .[13, 14]

Based on this description, Figure 73, and the map of the Hương river, it would seem that the ancient Champa citadel of Thành Lồi in Huế best matches Khu Túc. Thành Lồi is located at the river bend of the Hương river flowing around it in a clockwise direction from the south to the west and then to the north. The curve is shaped like a horizontal U (or a horseshoe), appearing as if the citadel were between two rivers. The citadel is also surrounded by mountains on the south and west. The western mountain is part of the Trường Sơn mountain range.

The Hương river flows to the large body of brackish water of Tam Giang lagoon in the north-west and Cầu Hai lagoon in the south-east; the former is connected to the sea at Thuận An, and the latter at Cửa Tư Hiền. Downstream of Thành Lồi, the Hương river branches off to the right and becomes the An Cựu (formerly Phú Cam) river which also flows to the Cầu Hai lagoon. By the TKCS description, the An Cựu river would be the Thọ Linh river, and the Cầu Hai lagoon would be Lake Lang. Aurousseau reaches the same conclusion.[15]

Tao Huang, in his 280 accounts of the threat from Linyi, refers to its kings hidden in dangerous, deep remote places, which tend to confirm the location of Thành Lồi. It is not an easy place to get to in the third century. As discussed earlier, the Gianh and Nhật Lệ rivers are not connected; there are no tributaries to join the Nhật Lệ and Thạch Hãn rivers so any attack by ships on Linyi strongholds south of Mũi Lay has to enter Cửa Việt or Cửa Tư Hiền. To get there, ships of a military expedition from the north of Ngang pass would have to sail along the coast, enter the river inlet at Cửa Việt, then follow Thạch Hãn, Ô Lâu rivers to Tam Giang lagoon. Alternatively, they could enter Cửa Tư Hiền to Cầu Hai lagoon further south and reach the Hương river from there.[16]

RUINS OF CHAMPA CITADELS

There are four Champa citadel ruins between Hải Vân pass and Mũi Lay, including Thành Lồi, so Khu Túc could be one of them. The northernmost ruin is Thành Cổ Lũy by the Bến Hải river, but this location is north of where Tan Hezhi landed in 446. Since he was heading south to attack Linyi, Khu Túc has to be south of where he landed, so it cannot be Thành Cổ Lũy.

The next ruin is Thuận Châu, but while this is south of where Tan Hezhi landed, it is too close to Hezhi's initial position before the attack began, and we know that it took time for Tan Hezhi's forces to get to Khu Túc, so it does not make sense for it to be there. That leaves Hóa Châu or Thành Lồi as a possible location for Khu Túc, but archaeologists agree that Hóa Châu was built at a much later date, so Thành Lồi is the most likely candidate.

It should be noted that other than Thành Lồi, the other Champa citadel ruins are generally on flat terrain, close to the river entrances, which could be easily overwhelmed by enemies coming from the sea. A battle-hardened, cunning, and successful commander like Fan Wen would be more likely to keep all his war materials in a place like Thành Lồi than in an area near the northern border like Ba Đồn or Thuận Châu on the Thạch Hãn river.

KHU TÚC CITADEL NEAR BA ĐỒN

However, there are two issues with the above conclusion; one is that a gnomon reading a Khu Túc citadel indicated its location is near Ba Đồn and not at Huế at some 200 kilometres south. However, I believe the location where the gnomon reading was taken refers to another Linyi citadel but not Khu Túc at Thành Lồi. This is because Ba Đồn and the Champa citadel of Cao Lao Hạ, north of Đông Hà, are on relatively flat ground, not surrounded by high and rocky mountains.

The second issue is that Thọ Linh prefecture is supposed to be on the east or south-east of Khu Túc according to TKCS, but Thọ Linh was split from Tây Quyển, so they were neighbouring prefectures. As Tây Quyển is believed to be at the Ròn and Gianh rivers near Ba Đồn, not at Huế, this account would make sense if applied to the Khu Túc citadel near Ba Đồn.

One other possible conclusion is that TKCS keeps referring to different Linyi citadels as Khu Túc; in that case, there are at least two. One is at Ba Đồn, and one is at Huế.

To firm up these conclusions, I will review the campaigns against Linyi in the fourth and fifth centuries as recorded in Chinese annals, which help to identify Khu Túc and the locations where the battles were fought.

A12.2 – Campaigns against Fan Wen

In 349, the Jin emperor sent a combined force of soldiers from Giao Châu, Guangzhou under Deng Zhun to crush Fan Wen, and the battle took place at the entrance to the Lô Dung river (or Cửa Lô Dung). Wen defeated them, and Deng Zhun withdrew to Cửu Chân, but that year, Fan Wen died from wounds suffered during the battle; his son Fan Fo became the next king of Linyi and remained in Nhật Nam.[17]

Historians have different views on where this battle took place; according to Aurousseau, Cửa Lô Dung is Cửa Tư Hiền; Đào also notes the same from another historian, Đặng Xuân Bảng.[18]

Southworth suggests the battle was fought near Hà Tĩnh north of Ngang pass; this would imply that Fan Wen's navy intercepted the Chinese armada on its way south as Hà Tĩnh (or Cửu Đức) was still in Jin territory.[19] While this is possible, it means Wen knew in advance when and where Deng Zhun launched his campaign, which would seem unlikely.

Taylor puts Cửa Lô Dung as the river mouth of the Gianh river just south of Ngang pass.[20] There was a major naval battle near there in 248 between Linyi and imperial troops, so it is possible Fan Wen fought them at the same place.

Another possibility is that the battle was fought at the Nhật Lệ river mouth. We know that Wen's soldiers had already ravaged Cửu Đức, Cửu Chân north of Ngang pass, and he had already razed Tây Quyển prefecture, south of Ngang pass, to the ground. So, it would be reasonable to assume that he set up his northern front line somewhere south of Tây Quyển, or south of the Gianh river, using Tây Quyển as a "no-man land" buffer zone. The estuary of the Nhật Lệ river, as the next major river south, would seem a sensible choice; it was there that Đại Việt forces defeated the Chams in 1044 as described later.

However, on balance, based on the historical text and geographical analysis, I would support the proposition that the battle in 349 was at Cửa Tư Hiền.

A12.3 – Campaigns against Fan Fo

DENG ZHUN/GUAN CUI IN 351

Three slightly different versions of this event could happen at three different places on three different rivers. From north to south, the rivers are Giang, Nhật Lệ and Thạch Hãn.

Gianh river

TKCS explains the name Ti Cảnh also reads Ti Ảnh. The term means at noon on the summer solstice, a person's body and its shadow match; he would be standing over his own shadow.[21] This is incorrect as this phenomenon only happens at the Tropic of Cancer – a long way north of Ti Ảnh.

TKCS also notes Guan Cui defeated Linyi forces at Bắc Cảnh prefecture of Cảnh Châu and also explains Tỉ Cảnh is the same as Bắc Cảnh. At Khu Túc citadel, they took a gnomon reading on one day of the fifth lunar month. As a matter of interest, the summer solstice in the northern hemisphere is 20 June. According to TKCS, the shadow of the sun is on the south side of the gnomon, which is why the name of the commandery was called Nhật Nam (or south of the sun).[22]

TCKS also notes a gnomon reading of eight *cun* over 8 *chi* in another paragraph as described earlier.[23] I have not been able to connect this reading to the 351 event, but if it were then the location would be near Ba Đồn by the Gianh river as analysed previously. This would be consistent with the story that, instead of being attacked, Fan Fo besieged Guan Cui in the capital of Cửu Chân north of Ngang pass but was driven back by a relief column by Yang Ping and Deng Zhu, who then defeated him south of the pass (Versions 1 and 2, Chapter 5).

The presence of the ramparts Fan Wen reportedly built north of the Gianh river would tend to support the proposition that the 351 battle was fought just south of Ngang pass.

Nhật Lệ river

In version 3, the forces of Deng Zhun and Guan Cui forces arrived at the Thọ Linh river, camped at lake Lang and fought Fan Fo at the former administrative centre of Nhật Nam, Chu Ngô.[24]

I have identified the Thọ Linh river as the Gianh river, so the battlefield would match the location as per Versions 1 and 2. However, the reference to lake Lang is confusing as I have already suggested this lake is the contemporary Cầu Hai lagoon – a long way south of this river. However, there is a lake called Bầu Tró near the entrance to the Nhật Lệ river, that could be what TKCS refers to as lake Lang, and in this setting, Thọ Linh could be the Nhật Lệ river.[25]

Nhật Lệ river would be consistent with the TKCS reference to Tỷ Ảnh as where this prefecture is expected to be, south of the Nhật Lệ river. There is a ruin of a Champa citadel at Thành Nhà Ngo (Ninh Viễn) on the Kiên Giang river that flows into the Nhật Lệ river, and that battle could have taken place there.

Thạch Hãn river

TKCS' reference to Chu Ngô complicates the search for the battlefield as this would indicate that the battle took place near the Thạch Hãn river and not at the Nhật Lệ river. TKCS also noted that Fan Fo was defeated, and chased to Linyi, which would confirm the location of the Thạch Hãn river as a possible location since if it were at Nhật Lệ river, he would not be able to escape south by the river route as there is no river interconnection between Nhật Lệ and Thạch Hãn. However, that did not mean he was not able to escape on foot from the Nhật Lệ river via its tributary Kiên Giang to Bến Hải rivers, a distance of around 20 kilometres.

The ramparts or defensive stonewalls

A 17th-century map covering today's Quảng Bình, Quảng Trị provinces shows extensive ramparts of a military defence between the area around Ngang pass and the Nhật Lệ river extending to Mũi Lay.[26] Given the date when the maps were drawn, the ramparts were likely built by the southern Nguyễn lords in their war against the Trịnh lords of the north and not earlier. There is no evidence that these were built on the original Linyi or Champa's foundation, but they indicate the strategic importance of these locations.[27]

In conclusion, based on gnomon measurements, the existence of the ancient ramparts, and the lack of consistency in TKCS records, I believe the area around the Gianh river is the most likely battlefield of the 351 battles.

YUAN FU IN 353

The destruction of the ramparts related to the battle against Yuan Fu would indicate that it likely occurred not very far from the Gianh river, possibly near the Nhật Lệ river.

WEN FANGZHI IN 359

In TKCS, there is no mention of ramparts or encampment destruction in this expedition which would indicate that Wen Fangzhi had gone further south than his predecessors since these structures are located close to the northern border between Linyi and the imperial territory north of Ngang pass. However, TKCS notes Ôn Công river branch, Ôn Công walls as named after Wen Fangzhi since he took this route and built these walls during his campaign against Fan Fo in the fourth century.[28] Here, TKCS gets a little muddled; and unfortunately, I am unable to decipher these locations.

Ôn Công would be next to Thọ Linh and thus north of Hải Vân pass, but TKCS also mentions Ôn Công walls are south of the citadel of Linyi (in this case, Điển Xung, at around 5 *li*, or 2.25 kilometres), south of the same pass.[29,30]

I do not believe Wen Fangzhi got as far as Điển Xung in his campaign because over 70 years later, Yuan Jianjin, another imperial general, never did. According to TKCS, he took the same river route as Wen Fanzhi to attack Linyi. Similarly, it seems doubtful that, even if he did, Wen Fangzhi would build the walls to strike Điển Xung from the south, and a northern invader would attack it from the north, as Tan Hezhi did.

In 359, Fan Fo lost heavily as he retreated south, and references to the Ôn Công river in the campaigns against his successors in 431, as discussed below, would indicate that the battle took place in northern Quảng Trị. Today, there is a ruin of a Champa citadel at Thuận Châu at Triệu Long commune, Triệu Phong district by Thạch Hãn river; this could be the citadel that Fan Fo decided to take a stand, and surrendered to Wen Fangzhi.

A12.4 – Yuan Jianjin's campaign in 431

THE RAID

Chinese annals tell us Fan Yangmai raided Cửu Đức prefecture, north of Ngang pass, located in contemporary Hà Tĩnh and Nghệ An. Linyi troops got as far as the river estuaries of Tứ Hội but were driven back, so Tứ Hội (Sihui) would be somewhere north of Ngang pass, but this Tứ Hội is not the same as Tứ Hội at Guangzhou as discussed earlier. I believe it is at Cửa Nam Giới by Hà Tĩnh where the 1069 expedition of Đại Việt stopped on the way south, presumably to stock up, which would mean that the settlement there was of a reasonable size to attract Linyi's piracy intention. Cửa Nam Giới is also identified in TKCS as Cửa Sót at Hà Tĩnh, and is in Cửu Đức prefecture, just north of Ngang pass.[31,32,33]

APPENDIX 12

THE COUNTERATTACK

In the counterattack, Liu Song's general Yuan Jianji's forces left the river estuary of Tứ Hội and spent three days and three nights non-stop sailing along the coast to get to Khu Túc. Assuming there is no major change in local boat building technique from the fifth to the 11th centuries, based on the analysis of the Đại Việt campaign discussed previously, a non-stop six days sailing would cover a distance of 300 kilometres of land equivalent that far south of Hà Tĩnh would bring us to slightly north-west of Huế, around where the Ô Lâu river joins Tam Giang lagoon. However, if they were a bit slower, they could get to Đông Hà, where Tan Hezhi arrived 15 years later. Based on the time taken, it is unlikely that Yuan Jianji ever got to Cửa Tư Hiền because that would be too far south. In either case, Khu Túc would be south of Đông Hà and north of Hải Vân pass.

THE RIVER BATTLES

Liu Song and Linyi forces clashed at a naval battle in a narrow river branch of Thọ Linh to a draw; Yuan Jianji, having lost many ships at sea during a storm, decided to withdraw and returned to Thọ Linh and reached the river branch of Ôn Công (or Wen Kong). This account would indicate the following order in the north-south direction: Thọ Linh prefecture, the river branch of Ôn Công, and the river branch of Thọ Linh; the latter joined with the Vô Lao Cứu stream. Vô Lao itself is the name of a lake that the river branch Chu Ngô at the border of Chu Ngô prefecture flows into.[34]

Since the location of Chu Ngô is known with some certainty from the gnomon measurement, it is reasonable to assume that the river of Chu Ngô is today's Thạch Hãn river. The river branch Chu Ngô would be a tributary of the Thạch Hãn river that flows into lake Vô Lao, which would most likely be the Tam Giang lagoon.[35] Yuan Jianji ships would have to come south this way from Cửa Việt to get to Khu Túc, and the battle most likely took place in one of the river branches which connects Thạch Hãn and Ô Lâu rivers. So, in this campaign, the river branch of Thọ Linh is the Ô Lâu river and not the Thạch Hãn river. Since Yuan Jianji did not have many ships left, it would make good tactical sense that he fought in a river branch against superior Linyi forces (of 300 ships) in the dark and directed at the command ship of Fan Yangmai. Out in the open water of the lagoon, Yuan Jianji would have been quickly overwhelmed.

From the above description, I believe the battles against Yuan Jianji in 431 occurred at the Ô Lâu river, north of Huế.

A12.5 – Tan Hezhi expedition in 446

ARRIVED AT CỬA VIỆT AND RANSACKED KHU TÚC

Based on the gnomon measurement of 446, I am reasonably sure that Tan Hezhi expedition entered Cửa Việt near Đông Hà. The mention of Chu Ngô as a location where he started from, also confirms the location of this prefecture in this area, north of Quảng Trị province, as concluded in Appendix 11. From there, his troops attacked Khu Túc and Điển Xung in that order, so Khu Túc would be south of Đông Hà, and Điển Xung must be south of Khu Túc.

After he entered Cửa Việt, Tan Hezhi set up camps and sent his delegation to negotiate with Fan Yangmai. As mentioned earlier in Chapter 5, negotiations failed, and Hezhi decided to attack. His forces took the river branch of Tứ Hội Phố to lake Lang and carried out the assault of Khu Túc, burning, looting and killing everyone over 15 years old inside the citadel.[36] We know from current and old maps that it is possible to travel south from Đông Hà to the lagoons in Huế using the river route, and I believe that was what Tan Hezhi took. On Google Maps, from Cửa Việt, Hezhi ships could have sailed up the Thạch Hãn river, followed small river branches to the Ô Lâu river to Tam Giang and Cầu Hai lagoons, arrived at Khu Túc/ Thành Lồi by the Hương river itself or other river branches that flow from it.

Having ransacked Khu Túc, Tan Hezhi forces pressed on to Điển Xung. So which route did they take? Noting that their ships were still moored in the rivers or at the lagoons.

HEADED TO ĐIỂN XUNG

Today, to reach the sea by the river route from Đông Hà, one has to exit at Cửa Thuận An or Cửa Tư Hiền. Before the 15th century, Thuận An was silted up, and the only connection between the fresh water network between Đông Hà and the sea was by the estuary of Tư Hiền.[37] The location of Tư Hiền had moved several times over the centuries as the sand and silt closed it and reopened it somewhere else during that time. However, Cửa Tư Hiền occupies a critical position as one of two entry points from the coast to the interior between Mũi Lay and Hải Vân pass. I believe this is where Tan

Hezhi forces must have exited on their way to Điển Xung.

From the north, to get from Khu Túc to Điển Xung, TKCS tells us Tan Hezhi's forces travelled through the river branch of Ôn Công Phố, Tân La Loan bay, Yên Hạ, and Bành Long Loan bay, their flags almost covered the sea as their ships came to the last bay.[38] There are no river routes connecting the two citadels, so Tan Hezhi's ships had to sail in the open sea along the coast thus explaining the story about flags covering up the ocean.

From the south, TKCS also notes the capital of Linyi is south of the Hoài river. Travelling north from this capital, one crosses this river over a bridge, then continues to Bành Long; from there, if one keeps going northward, one would arrive at Khu Túc. The distance between Khu Túc and Linyi capital is given in TKCS at around 400 *li* (or 183 kilometres).[39] TKCS also records Fan Yangmai fell off his elephant during the battle against Tan Hezhi at this bridge across the Hoài river on his route to Bành Long.

Most historians agree that Điển Xung is at the Champa ruin of Trà Kiệu, and that the Hoài river is the present-day Thu Bồn river.[40,41] Its location would fit the above description in TKCS whereby Bành Long Loan bay would be the bay of Đà Nẵng, and Tân La Loan bay would be Chân Mây bay. North of Chân Mây bay is Lăng Cô bay, but it is more of a lagoon than a bay. Once his ships were in Đà Nẵng bay, they would sail up the Hàn river or march south on foot over some 20 kilometres to get to the north bank of the Thu Bồn river to face Linyi troops, where Fan Yangmai fell off his elephants as Zong Que used his mocked lions to defeat the Linyi army.

A12.6 – Liu Fang expedition in 605

In this expedition, Liu Fang forces headed to Tỉ Ảnh by ships, arrived at the sea gate in 605, fought off Linyi troops and reached the Đồ Lê river. His forces crossed the river, fought a major battle at 30 li (13.5 kilometres) against Linyi elephants and overcame Khu Túc, passed Lục Lí and came to the Đại Duyên river, where they fought another battle. Eight days beyond the Ma Yuan bronze pillars, they arrived at the capital of Linyi.

So where are these places?

I have established the location of Tỉ Ảnh prefecture with some degree of confidence. The other is the Đại Duyên river; it was called Đại Duyên (great winding river) but apparently was changed to Nhật Lệ (a sad, tearful day) in 1069 after the campaign of Đại Việt's king Lý Thánh Tông (Appendix 11).[42]

Unfortunately, I have not been able to locate the original reference of this name change.

Based on these two locations, let us explore a possible campaign route:

THE CAMPAIGN ROUTE

In his biography, the Sui shu, Volume 53, Liu Fang's forces were transported by ships and arrived at a sea gate. They could have taken the route that Ma Yuan took in 43 from Hanoi down the Đáy river to the coast, the same route that Đại Việt's kings took in 1044 and 1069. Once there, they would sail along the coastline and land, in this case at a sea gate. North of Ngang pass is the bay of Vũng Áng, where two rivers, Vịnh and Quyền flow into. The river estuary there was named Hải Khẩu Môn (seaport gate) on a fifteenth-century map, present-day Cửa Khẩu. Under this scenario, this was where Liu Fang forces landed, based on the reference to a sea gate.[43] Presumably, that was where Liu Fang met up with the rest of the Sui troops who came down by the land route.

As mentioned earlier, Linyi built a number of stone ramparts on the southern side of Ngang pass. These were probably those that his biography referred to as "dangerous places", but Liu Fang forces overcame them and pushed south. They got to the Đồ Lê river, crossed it and fought a battle nearly 14 kilometres south of the river, put Linyi troops to rout and overcame Khu Túc. Khu Túc, in this context, as discussed previously, is near Ba Đồn or within the vicinity of the Gianh river. It is around 15 kilometres south of the Ròn river in a straight line, so Đồ Lê is the Ròn river, close to the description in the text. It should be noted that Southworth, quoting Maspero, identifies Đồ Lê as the Nhật Lệ river.[44]

They passed Lục Lí, which could be the Gianh river and reached the Đại Duyên river, Nhật Lệ river. The geography so far matches his biography reasonably well. However, the biography recorded that he passed Ma Yuan bronze pillars and took eight days to get to the capital of Linyi.

If I base the soldier's marching speed on an average of 30 li (13.5 kilometres) per day (Chapter 4), eight days of march would be around 100 kilometres. If the pillars were at the Nhật Lệ river then 100 kilometres south of it would take us to about Đông Hà, but Đông Hà is too far north as the capital of Linyi.

Since Liu Fang intended to rob and pillage, it would be reasonable to assume that he wanted to get to Điển Xung where Tan Hezhi found the treasures in 446. Điển Xung or Trà Kiệu is in Quảng Nam province, and 80 km north of this location is around Chân Mây bay, just before Hải Vân pass. It should be noted that the bulk of Liu Fang's army was on foot. Back in 605, the land route over Hải Vân pass was likely a goat track if it existed at all, so at a marching speed of 13.5 kilometres per day, they could march the distance of 80 kilometres within eight days as recorded.

The only issue with this route is that Liu Fang's biography recorded that their ships were heading to Tỷ Ảnh, south of Ngang pass, but on this route, he landed at Cửa Khẩu, north of it. One possible explanation is that the text indicates Tỷ Ảnh as a final destination or a general direction but not the place where he landed.

It should be noted that in 446, Tan Hezhi landed at Cửa Việt in Chu Ngô prefecture, south of Tỷ Ảnh and that the bulk of his forces was travelling by ships. They arrived at Điển Xung from Huế by sailing around the headland of Hải Vân pass.

So, I believe Chân Mây bay is the likely location of Ma Yuan bronze pillars.

APPENDIX 13

AN EYEWITNESS ACCOUNT OF THE NANZHAO-AN NAM WAR

Fan Chuo, secretary of the Protectorate General (*duhu*) of An Nam, was living in La Thành in the middle of the ninth century as war broke out; he barely escaped with his life, and recorded the battle as summarised below. All the translations were translated by Luce.[1]

Fan Chuo started by recording his effort to negotiate with the leaders of Nanzhao invasion forces in April 862, who were mostly Wu Man (black barbarians) – the ancestors of those shown in Figure 57 – with a common surname of Yang. Their commander was called Yang Si-jin.

APPENDIX 13

6 APRIL 862: "*On the fourth day of the third month, Spring, of the third year of Xiantong (April sixth, 862 CE), I, your humble servant, received from my superior officer, the Shang-Shu (Board President) Cai Xi, handwritten instructions secretly deputing me, your humble servant, to ride alone, with not more than 20 sturdy foot soldiers, and deeply penetrate the camp and stockade of the rebel commander, Zhu Dao-guo.² On the eighth day of the third month (April 10) we entered the double enclosure of the rebels* [around Phú Thọ].³

The Man rebel leaders, Yang Bing, Zhung Da-qiang, Yang A-ch'u and Yang qiu-sheng, were all WU MAN.⁴ *The rebels received me in a body. Their words were cunning and deceitful. Your humble servant broke off (negotiations) and returned. Point by point I explained everything to the Du-hu Wang Kuang.⁵ Wang Kuang was conceited and stupid, quite incapable of making farsighted plans. He received your humble servant's written report, but entirely failed to issue any directions. Without authority he allowed the army to return, and had the impertinence to ask for commendations from the court.⁶ All this resulted in your humble servant's superior officer, Cai Xi, being uselessly wounded with arrows and stones and in the fall and loss of the moated city. If one asks the cause of all this it can be no other than Wang Kuang.*" (Man shu, p. 35).

In another passage of Man shu,

10 APRIL 862: "*... Your humble servant took the opportunity to call on the Man Pan-guan (Judge) of Zhe Dong* [Kunming], *Yang Zhong-yi. Behind his back he had at his command eight Man holding bows and spears. Your humble servant took the opportunity to ask the rebel commander, Zhu Daogu about their source and origin. He explained that they were* DAO HUA MEN. *Now also they are called Dao hua Man. Originally, they lived on each side of the Seven Wan and Ravines (Tung) of Lin-xi-yuan of An Nam. The people wear sheep-skins. Some wear felt. They comb their hair into a knot in front* [note the black knobs on the helmets in Figure 59]. *Although adhering to the Man, their hearts are all inclined towards Tang civilisation.*" (Man shu p. 45).

Fan Chuo also mentioned the meeting in another chapter of the book where he tried to gather more information about the origin of the Man rebels.

"*I took the opportunity to enter the camp-stockade of the rebel, Zhu Daogu. All day long I talked with the Man rebel generals, Da-Qiang ("the great Qiang"), Yang A-ch'u, Yang Jiu-sheng, and the Pan-guan (Judge) of Zhe Dong, Yang Zhong-yi. I got their clan-names and personal names, and (learned) their reasons*

> *for having set up a frontier city and made themselves into a kingdom of their own. Their ancestors were descendants of Pan-gu.*[7] *The Man rebel, Yang Qiang, and others said: Zhan* [or Qiang] *was a descendant of Pan-gu."* (Man shu, p. 99).

However, negotiation failed, and shortly after, Nanzhao and its allies began their siege of La Thành.

> 23 APRIL 862: *"On the 21st day of the third month of the third year of Xiantong (April 23rd 862 CE) there were barely five or six thousand of their men* [Dao hua] *encamped below the west corner of An Nam city* [La Thành]. *The Man rebel, Yang Si-jin deputed the magistrate of Fu-xie-xian of Luo-fu-zhou, Ma Guang-gao, to command them".* (Man shu, p. 46).

Nine months later, more tribes arrived, and 30,000 troops who came with Cai Xi had returned north, leaving the defenders exposed to the aggressive tribesmen and Nanzhao crack troops. At Cai Xi's urgent request, in the winter of 862 (November), the emperor sent 2,000 troops from Jingnan (around Hubei, Hunan provinces) plus 3,000 volunteers to assemble at Nanning to come to the rescue. In January 863, Cai Xi requested more troops, and the emperor sent 1,000 archers armed with crossbows from Shannan East Circuit (Dong dao, around Hubei) by then La Thành was surrounded, and the relief columns could not enter.[8]

> 14 JANUARY 863: *"On the 21st day of the 12th month of the third year of Xiantong (Jan. 14th, 863 CE), there were also these* MANG MAN *mustered on the Su-li* [Tô Lịch] *riverbank of An Nam - a regiment of two or three thousand men".*[9] (Man shu, p. 44).

> "LUO-XING MAN *(Naked Man). (They have their nests and holes 300 li west of Xun-chuan city.*[10] *They are called the* YEH MAN *(Wild Man). These Man are not warlike by habit, but are naturally friendly and submissive).... they too were formed into a regiment, in the front line of the battle-array. If any of them did not advance or charge, the Man directing the battle front would at once cut them down from behind."* (Man shu, p. 40)

And over a week later, the pressure on the besieged city dramatically increased:

20 JANUARY 863: *"In the third year of Xiantong, 12th month, 27th day (Jan 20, 863 CE), the Man rebels closely besieged the moated city of Jiaozhou* [La Thành]. *The* HO MAN *set up their camp in the old city of Su-li* [Tô Lịch].[11] *When stations were assigned to the rebel hosts on the wooden rafts and bamboo rafts, there were hardly more than two thousand men."* (Man shu, p. 38).

On the same day, Cai Xi managed to capture and killed 100 Man rebels, and it appeared that the defenders were starving, and forced into cannibalism:

"Your humble servant's superior officer, Cai Xi, on the 27th day of the 12th month of the third year of Xiantong (Jan. 20th, 863 CE), got over one hundred of (these) men with small spears and pointed weapons. When your servant's superior officer, Cai Xi, asked Liang Ke[12] *(about them), as soon as he saw that they had bamboo to cage their heads and pig-skin to tie their waists, he at once said they were* XUN-CHUAN MAN[13], *and told us all about them. The troops of the Jiangxi General took the flesh of these Man and broiled it."*[14] (Man shu, p.40).

But Nanzhao did not let up the pressure despite desperate attempts from Tang command, holed up in La Thành, including shooting a copy of the loyalty oath into Nanzhao camp, but it made no difference to the war:

"In the first month of the fourth year of Xiantong (Jan. 23rd-Feb. 21st, 863 CE) I, your humble servant, received an order from my superior officer, the Shang-shu (Board President) Cai Xi, signifying his wish. I ordered a scribe (Shu-li) to write out several copies of the oath sworn by the Man king, Yi-mou-xun[15]. *All these documents were fastened on to a mechanical crossbow and shot flying into the rebel's camp. Your humble servant perused the whole text of Yi-mou-xun's oath. The drawing-up of the covenant was extremely apposite. At present the descendants of the Southern Man have disregarded and turned their backs on their former oath. I humbly suppose that the Way of Heaven is bound to punish them."* (Man shu p. 28)

The fighting was savage, and Fan Chuo found out that they had a spy, Liang Ke, in their midst:

25 JANUARY 863: *"Your humble servant's superior officer, Cai Xi, on the third day of the first month of the fourth year of Xian Tong (Jan. 25th, 863 CE), on the battle front, captured alive some Pu-zi Man.*[16] *When examined under*

flogging, none of them said a word. When their wrists were severed, they also made no sound.

Liang Ke, a yu-hou (attendant) of An-nan-ẓi city [La Thành] *is said to be a Pu-ẓi Man. Liang Ke is now to be seen among the rebels, arrogating to himself the title of magistrate (ling) of Chu-yuan-xian"* [Chu Diên prefecture]*"* (Man shu p. 39).

And even a strange monk appeared among the rebel camps:

28 JANUARY 863: *"In the fourth year Xiantong, 1st month, sixth day (Jan 28th, 863 CE) between 3 and 5 a. m, there was a Hu (? Central Asian) Buddhist monk, naked, holding a staff bound with white silk, who strutted forwards and backward making passes. This was on the south of the perimeter of An Nam city. At this moment your servant's superior officer, Cai Xi, took a bow and shot an arrow, and hit in the breast of this scheming Hu monk. Lots of the Man helped in carrying him back to the camp. Within the city there were none among the officers or men who did not make a din with the drums."*, (Man shu p. 91).

Fighting continued into the first month of the Lunar New Year in February:

14 FEBRUARY 863: *"On the 23rd day of the first month of the fourth year of Xiantong (Feb. 14th, 863 CE), Cai Xi on the city wall, with a mechanical crossbow (? ballista), shot down two hundred men of the* WANG-JU-ZI[17] *and over thirty horses."* (Man shu p. 41).

A fortnight later, La Thành fell but not without a last-ditch and suicide attempt to break out by the defenders. Fan Chuo managed to escape with the seal of the office by swimming across the river, likely the Red river. His commander, Cai Xi, together with his followers, perished.

28 FEBRUARY 863: *On the seventh day of the second month (Feb. 28th, 863) the city fell. And your humble servant's superior officer, Cai Xi, was hit by an arrow in the left shoulder. His principal followers(?) were already dead. Your humble servant was hit by an arrow in the right wrist. I took off the seal, swam, and crossed the river* [Red river].[18] *The officers and able-bodied men of Jingnan*[19], *Jiangxi, Eyue, and Xiang-ẓhou*[20], *numbering around four hundred men or more, holding mo (?) cutlasses and riding on horseback, rushed out to the water edge east of the city. The Du-yu-hou (Head Attendant?) of Jingnan, Yuan*

Wei-de, the Guan-du-tou (General Manager?) Tan Ke Yan and the Jun-pan-guan (Army-Judge) of Jiangxi, Chuan Men, addressed the officers and men saying: "Now, my lads, we've all reached the river, but there are no boats. If we enter the river, we are sure to die. But if we form a band of brothers, and each of us manages to kill two Man rebels, we too shall gain something".

Thereupon they went in a body and entered the eastern perimeter of the city, and crowded inside the gate. On one side they drew up the 'long cutlasses', on the other side the 'Long (?) Horses', to charge the Man rebels. (The Man), having gone outside the city wall and reached the water, now rode their horses (back) to the gate, taking no precautions whatsoever against a (possible) enemy. Your humble servant saw a Buddhist monk, Chi Ai, who told me, saying:

"On this day, before noon, they went on to kill rebels, together with their horses: nearly two or three thousand rebels, and over three hundred horses. The Man rebel, Yang Si-jin was inside the inner city. It was only in the first watch of the night that he knew (about it), and went out to the rescue. At dawn the following day, they distributed horse-flesh to 12 camps of rebel hosts."

In another passage, with a seemingly contradictory date, Fan Chou recounted the event:

"My superior officer, Cai Xi, last year, on the 14th day of the first month (Feb. 5th, 863 CE) in the fourth division? four times? was hit by an arrow at Shi-jia-kou (? river mouth).[21]*. Together with his principal followers, over seventy men, they all perished at the place of the rebels. Your humble servant's eldest son, Tao, and servants and maid-servants, fourteen persons, all were trapped in this far corner of the Man. Your humble servant, morning and night, mourns and remembers my superior officer, Cai Xi. Whether I walk or sit, my heart aches insistently when I think of the Man rebels still in occupation of An Nam."*

After the loss of La Thành, Tang officials retreated to Hai-men (Beihai in Guangxi province). The above passage seems to indicate that Fan Chou and his family were still in An Nam, but it would seem more likely that they had withdrawn to Hai-men. Meanwhile, other enclaves of Tang rule in An Nam were left to defend themselves against Nanzhao.

"At present Jiang-yuan and likewise the various zhou (divisions [prefecture]) each guard itself firmly. The native chieftains (shou-ling) and military and civil officers (jiang-li), last year, both in spring and summer, unceasingly appealed for troops to rescue them. From that time Hai-men (Sea Gate) refused

to dispatch (troops). [22] *At the same time, it failed to supply spears, armour, bows, crossbows, thus causing the Man rebels to invade and plunder the troops of the divisions (chou). Your humble servant is of the opinion that from old up to the present day, whenever the Southern Man capture or raid various places, the common people fall under the control of the barbarians, I (or) Liao.* [23] *Then (everyone) from the chieftains of Gui and Jiang-yuan downwards, knows this business of dual (or transferred?) control.* [24] *Assuredly one feels sorry for the Fu-qing (assistant minister). (We) must certainly combine forces and be of one mind, and all together, resist the injuries and violence of the Man barbarians."* (Man shu p. 98).

25 JUNE 863: *"In the fourth year of Xiantong, sixth month, sixth day (June 25th, 863 CE), over four thousand of the Man rebels, (with) 2000 men under the petty rebel Zhu-Daogu, together rowing several hundred small boats, took Jun ẓhou* [a prefecture in Guangxi].[25] *They captured the general Ya-Ya of An Nam, Zhang Qing-ẓong and Du Cun-ling* [Đỗ Tồn Lăng]. *The prefect of Wu-an ẓhou* [Quảng Ninh province], *Qian Xing-yu, took ten large sailing junks (hang-bo) and war boats, and rammed and damaged the boats of the Man: over thirty were sunk."* [26] (Man shu, p. 93).

Fan Chuo received the news nearly five months later that most of the Man rebels drowned:

5 NOVEMBER 863: *"On the 21st day of the ninth month (Nov. fifth, 863 CE), your humble servant saw at Deng-ẓhou the Yu-hou (attendant of An Nam, Shih Xiao-min, and also got a letter from the Bing-ma-shi (army officer?) Xu Chong-ya (both averred that) the Man rebels were unable to swim, so every one of them drowned."* [27] (Man shu, p. 94).

APPENDIX 14

THE POPULATION QUESTION

Han shu records the total number of "mouths" for Giao Chỉ, Cửu Chân, Nhật Nam, and Hepu commanderies in year 2 CE as over one million (1,060,715 to be exact, Table 28). When I first came across this information, I was puzzled as to whether this is a reasonable number, for 700 years later, during the Tang dynasty, the equivalent figures for similar provinces are much lower. To answer that question, I have decided to take a little detour in this Appendix to review the issue more closely, even if it is of more interest to a historian than a traveller.

Of "mouth" and "đinh"

One item that was surrendered to the commander of the Former Han army in 111 BCE was the household records. TKCS describes the event as follows: when Lu Bode arrived at Hepu, the king of Yue sent envoys with 100 cows, 1000 jars of rice wine, and the household records (returns of the population) of the two prefectures: Giao Chỉ and Cửu Chân as an offering to Lu Bode.

Lu Bode appointed the two envoys (or legates) as *taishou* of these commanderies. However, the Lạc Tướng still governed the people.[1,2] SKTT tells the story slightly differently:

> "Our country sent three envoys with 300 water buffaloes ... and the household records of three districts Giao Chỉ, Cửu Chân, and Nhật Nam to surrender to Lu Bode. He appointed all three to be the governors of these districts."[3]

So how many people were listed in the household records in 111 BCE? According to Han shu, it was 400,000 *"mouths"* from Âu Lạc, which I believe to include Giao Chỉ, Cửu Chân, Nhật Nam, and Hepu commanderies.[4,5]

Imperial administrators need such records to collect taxes. Subsequent northern dynasties also continued the practice, which went on well into the 19th century by the Nguyễn kings. Court historians record them, and we can now access the information from the various *"shus"* down the centuries.

As mentioned earlier, in year 2 CE, Han officials recorded in Han shu a total of 159,041 households and 1,060,715 mouths or 6.67 mouths per household.[6] The "mouth" compounding growth rate over this period, from 111 BCE to 2 CE, works out as 0.87% per annum. In year 140, similar data were also collected; however, the annual growth rate from 2 CE to 140 CE is much slower at 0.07% for Hepu and 0.17% for Cửu Chân.

In the 19th century, the officials of the Nguyễn dynasty recorded the number of taxpayers, or *"đinh"*, by different provinces, *"đinh"* included men from 18 to 59 years of age but not women, children, and men older than 59.[7] Therefore, the record of *"đinh"* is not the same as that of the population. In 1819, the total number of *"đinh"* of Thanh Hóa, Nghệ An, and Hà Tĩnh provinces combined was 111,330; in 1870, it increased to 148,737 or an annual increase of 0.57% (Table 30).

"đinh" and "mouth", while recording for tax collection, are not the same. If they were, then the data would not make sense. The number of *"đinh"* recorded in the above three provinces, roughly the size of the ancient Cửu Chân commandery, at 111,330, would be smaller than that recorded in 2 CE at 166,013 over 1,800 years earlier. It would make more sense to compare *"đinh"* with the number of households, which for Cửu Chân were 35,743, and 46,153 in years 2 and 140, respectively. The average annual growth rate of the household for Cửu Chân from 35,743 in 2 CE to 111,330 in 1819 then works out as 0.06%; by comparison, the world population growth rate is 0.04% from 10,000 BCE to 1700.[8,9]

	FORMER HAN (2 CE)	LATER HAN (140)	TANG (CIRCA 700)	TANG (740)	TANG (742)
Hepu	78,980	86,617			
Giao Chỉ	746,237				
Cửu Chân	166,013	209,894			
Nhật Nam	69,485	100,676			
Giao			88,788	99,660	99,652
Phong			6,435	5,119	
Ái			36,519	135,030	
Hoan			16,689	53,818	50,818
Lục				2,710	2,674
Trường				3,040	
Total	1,060,715	397,187	148,431	299,377	153,144

Table 28 – The number of mouths (or heads) in the commanderies (and zhou).[10]

	FORMER HAN (2 CE)	LATER HAN (140)	JIN (275-420)	SONG (420-479)	SUI (581-681)
Hepu	15,398	23,121	2,000		
Giao Chỉ	92,440		12,000	4,233	30,516
Tân Xương			3,000		
Vũ Bình			5,000	1,490	
Cửu Chân	35,743	46,153	3,000	2,328	16,135
Cửu Đức				809	9,915
Nhật Nam	15,460	18,263	600	402	
Total	159,041	87,537	25,600	9,262	56,566
	TANG (CIRCA 700)	TANG (726)	TANG (740)	TANG (742)	TANG (807)
Giao	17,523	25,690	24,730	24,230	27,135
Phong	5,444	3561	1,920	1,920	1,483
Ái	9,080	14,056	40,700	14,700	5,379
Hoan	6,579	6,694	9,629	9,619	3,843
Lục		1934	490	494	231
Trường			630		648
Diễn			Included in Hoan		1,450
Phúc Lộc					317
Total	38,626	51,935	78,099	50,963	40,486

Table 29 – The number of households (or hearths) in the commanderies (and zhou)

The anomalies

By 700, the Tang census shows 148,431 "mouths" for the "zhous" of Giao, Phong, Ái, and Hoan, and by 742, the figure for the "zhous" of Giao, Hoan, and Lục is 153,144 (Table 28). These are much lower than the one million number cited earlier, albeit without the records for Hepu commanderies. Historian Keith Taylor offers a number of explanations in his book, but the one I think is most likely is that the ascendance of great landowning families turned independent farmers into tenants and thus no longer required to register as taxpayers.[11]

There are two other possible causes: one is that later dynasties had lost control of a large region of the territories when compared to the Han; two, it is not in the interest of the officials in later dynasties to record a high number of taxpayers, for doing so would put them at risk of getting punished when they were not able to collect the taxes. Furthermore, a low recorded number of taxpayers would enable them to pocket the collection from the "off the book" taxpayers for themselves.

The loss of control is obvious when one reviews the data for Nhật Nam; from the Jin dynasty (265–420) onwards, the numbers were minimal as wars against Linyi had made the region ungovernable.

Conclusions

While a complete study of how the population of Vietnam has developed over the past 2,000 years is beyond the scope of this book, a brief analysis of the data has provided us with some interesting observations. I summarise them as follows:

1. The figure of one million population, as recorded by Han shu, for Giao Chỉ, Cửu Chân, Nhật Nam, and Hepu commanderies (contemporary upper central, northern Vietnam, and southern Guangxi) seems high. However, on balance, in the absence of evidence to indicate otherwise, I would accept this number at face value without further comments.

2. Of the three commanderies, Giao Chỉ is the most populated, followed by Cửu Chân and Nhật Nam. The pattern has remained the same for over 2,000 years, from years 2 CE to 2019.

3. Nhật Nam commandery, the equivalent provinces of Quảng Bình and Quảng Trị, immediately south of Ngang pass, consistently have the smallest population when compared with other provinces immediately north of Ngang pass, such as Nghệ An and Thanh Hóa over the same period (Table 30). This would indicate that the land has never been sufficiently fertile to support a large population and may explain why the Linyi kings had to resort to raids across Ngang pass to support themselves.

	"ĐINH" 1819	POPULATION 1936	POPULATION 2019
1. Thanh Hóa	33,230	844,000	3,645,800
2. Nghệ An	65,400	746,000	3,337,200
3. Hà Tĩnh	12,700	400,000	1,290,300
4. Quảng Bình	13,500	223,000	896,600
5. Quảng Trị		172,000	633,400
6. Phủ Thừa Thiên incl. Quảng Trị	50,300	302,000	1,129,500
7. Quảng Nam + Đà Nẵng	36,900	792,000	2,638,600
Total 1 to 3	111,330	1,990,000	8,273,300
Total 4 to 6	63,800	697,000	2,659,500
Total 4 to 7	100,700	1,489,000	5,298,100

Table 30 – The number of registered taxpayers and population of some of the provinces in Central Vietnam.[12]

APPENDIX 15

OF LI, BU, CHI, LIANG, AND JIN — CHINESE UNITS OF MEASUREMENTS[1]

DYNASTIES	CHI[i]	BU	MILE[ii]
Qin/Former Han	23.1 cm	6 chi = 1.386 m	300 bu = 415.8 m
Later Han	23.75 - 24.2 cm	6 chi = 1.425-1.452 m	300 bu = 427.5-436.6 m
Southern & Northern Dynasties / Sui	24.5 - 29.6 cm	6 chi = 1.47-1.776 m	300 bu = 441-532.8 m
Tang	30 cm (short)	5 chi = 1.50 m	300 bu = 450 m
Tang	36 cm (long)[2]	5 chi = 1.80 m	300 bu = 540 m
Song/Yuan	31.2 cm	5 chi = 1.56 m	300 bu = 468.00 m

Table 31 – The Chinese unit of measurements (length).

Notes: *chi* is Chinese foot, *cun* is Chinese inch and 1 *cun* equals 10 *fen*. To simplify the estimates in this book, I have used 1 *li* = 450 metres and hence 1 *bu* = 1/300 li = 1.5 m

i. 1 *zhang* = 10 *chi*, 1 *chi* = 10 cun
ii. customary 1 *li* = 500 m

DYNASTIES	DOU[i]	JIN	LIANG
Qin	2 litres		
Former Han	2 litres	248 g	15.5 g = 1/16 jin
Later Han	2 litres	220 g	13.8 g = 1/16 jin
Southern & Northern Dynasties	2-3 litres	regionally different	
Sui	6 litres (large)	661 g (large)	41.3 g (large)
	2 litres (small)	220 g (small)	13.8 g (small)
Tang	6 litres (large)	661 g	1 qian = 4.13 g = 1/10 liang
	2 litres (small)		
Song	6.7 litres		
Ming/Qing	10 litres	590 g	1 qian = 3.69 g = 1/10 liang

Table 32 – The Chinese unit of measurements (weight).

i. 1 *dou* = 10 *sheng*, 1 *sheng* = 10 *ge*

APPENDIX 16

MUSEUMS IN SOUTHERN VIETNAM WITH EXHIBITS OF THE ÓC EO CIVILISATION

PROVINCE	MUSEUM	ADDRESS[i]	SITES[ii]
An Giang	An Giang Museum	11 Tôn Đức Thắng St., Mỹ Bình ward, Long Xuyên city.	Óc Eo, Gò Cây Thị, 10°13'45.8"N 105°09'33.7"E (10.229384, 105.159361)
Bạc Liêu	Bạc Liêu Museum	25 Hai Bà Trưng, Phường 3, Bạc Liêu.	Vĩnh Hưng ancient tower, Vĩnh Hưng A, Vĩnh Lợi, 9°23'33.5"N 105°34'41.5"E, (9.392629, 105.578189)
Bến Tre	Bến Tre Provincial Museum	146 Hùng Vương, Ward 3, Bến Tre city	Giồng Nổi, Bình Phú ?
Cà Mau[iii]	Cà Mau Provincial Museum	Phường 1, Tân Xuyên, Ca Mau, Vietnam.	
Cần Thơ	Cần Thơ Museum	1 Đại Lộ Hoà Bình, Tân An, Ninh Kiều, Cần Thơ.	Nhơn Thành hamlet, Nhơn Nghĩa commune, Phong Điền district, Cần Thơ.
Đồng Tháp	Đồng Tháp Provincial Museum	162, Nguyễn Thái Học St., Ward 4, Cao Lãnh. https://baotang.dongthap.gov.vn/	Gò Tháp, Hamlet 1, Tân Kiều commune, Tháp Mười district, Đồng Tháp province also 10°36'04.0"N 105°49'38.2"E (10.601103, 105.827280)
Hậu Giang[iv]	Hậu Giang Provincial Museum	8 Hồ Sen (Hồ Xuân Hương), Ward 1, Vị Thanh, Hậu Giang.	
Kiên Giang	Kiên Giang Museum	27 Nguyễn Văn Trỗi St., Thanh Vân ward, Rạch Giá city.	Cạnh Đền, Vĩnh Phong, Vĩnh Thuận, Kiên Giang.
Long An	Long An Museum	No. 400, Highway 1, Ward 4, Tân An city.	Bình Tả, the archaeological sites are in the vicinity of 10°49'45.4"N 106°28'12.3"E, (10.829268, 106.470091)
Sóc Trăng	Sóc Trăng Provincial Museum	Hùng Vương, Ward 6, Sóc Trăng.	

APPENDIX 16

PROVINCE	MUSEUM	ADDRESS	SITES[i]
Tiền Giang	Tiền Giang Museum	2A Trương Vĩnh Ký, Ward 7, Mỹ Tho City.	Gò Thành, Tân Thành hamlet, Tân Thuận Bình commune, Chợ Gạo district. 10°23'26.8"N 106°27'33.2"E (10.390766, 106.459224)
Trà Vinh	Museum of Ethnic Khmer Culture	Nguyễn Du, Phường 8, Trà Vinh. This museum may not have Óc Eo artefacts which were found at Lò Gạch Pagoda in 2014.	Bờ Lũy - Lò Gạch (Kompong Thmo) pagoda. Lương Hòa, Châu Thành District, Trà Vinh Province. 9°55'02.5"N 106°17'44.2"E, (9.917363, 106.295600)
Vĩnh Long	Vĩnh Long Museum	1 Phan Bội Châu, Phường 1, Vĩnh Long.	Thành Mới, spread across the hamlets of Ruột Ngựa, Bình Phụng of Trung Hiệp commune and Bình Thành hamlet of Trung Hiếu commune, Vũng Liêm district, Vĩnh Long. I do not have information about the precise location.

Table 33 – Museums in 13 provinces in the Mekong Delta.

i. Websites only listed if available
ii. Nearby archaeological sites
iii. This museum does not appear to have any Óc Eo exhibits
iv. I do not have a lot of information about this museum

PROVINCE	MUSEUM	ADDRESS[i]	SITES[ii]
Bà Rịa - Vũng Tàu	Bà Rịa - Vũng Tàu Provincial Museum	4 Trần Phú, Ward 1, Vũng Tàu City, Bà Rịa - Vũng Tàu.	Giồng Lớn, hamlet 3, Rạch Già commune, Long Sơn island, Vũng Tàu.[1]
Bình Dương[iii]	Bình Dương Provincial Museum	565 Bình Dương Highway, Hiệp Thành, Thủ Dầu Một, Bình Dương.	
Bình Phước[iii]	Bình Phước Provincial Museum	Hồ Xuân Hương St., Tân Phú, Đồng Xoài, Bình Phước. http://baotang.tayninh.gov.vn/	
Đồng Nai[iii]	Đồng Nai Provincial Museum	1 Nguyễn Ái Quốc, Tân Tiến, Biên Hòa City. http://baotang.tayninh.gov.vn/	
Tây Ninh	Tây Ninh Museum	4A Hoàng Lê Kha, KP3, Ward 3, Tây Ninh City. http://baotang.tayninh.gov.vn/	Tower of Bình Thạnh at Bình Phú hamlet, Bình Thạnh commune, Trảng Bàng district, Tây Ninh. Later period of Óc Eo (VIII-IX centuries). (11°01'08.6"N 106°13'09.2"E, 11.019050, 106.219232) The tower of Chóp Mạt (Tháp Chóp Mạt), ấp Xóm Mới, Tân Phong, Tân Biên, Tây Ninh, Vietnam. (11°27'50.2"N 106°00'36.7"E 11.463948, 106.010197)
Thành phố Hồ Chí Minh	History Museum	2 Nguyễn Bình Khiêm Street, Bến Nghé Ward, District 1. http://www.baotanglichsutphcm.com.vn/	

Table 34 – Museums in five provinces around Ho Chi Minh City.

i. Websites only listed if available
ii. Nearby archaeological sites
iii. This museum does not appear to have any Óc Eo exhibits

ENDNOTES

PREFACE

1. Pham, T. (2021). *The Bronze Drums and The Earrings* (Vol. 1). 315Kio Publishing.

2. There are three different names in this period of independence, Đại Cồ Việt (Great Viet, 968 to 1054), Đại Việt (Great Viet, 1054-1400) and Đại Ngu (Happy and Peaceful Viet, 1400-1407). Between 1407-1414 and 1414-1427, the country was under the rule of the Ming dynasty from China and its name was reverted to Giao Chỉ, its title under the Former Han dynasty 500 years earlier. Once the Ming was forced out, the name returned to Đại Việt (Great Viet, 1428-1804). I have adopted Đại Việt for this period as it was used for the most extended period of time

3. N Rama, & Lakshmanan, M. (2010). An Algorithm Based on Empirical Methods, for Text-to-Tuneful-Speech Synthesis of Sanskrit Verse. *International Journal of Computer Science and Network Security*, *10*, 281-288.

4. While the Linyi rebellion started at the end of the second century, the Jin dynasty (following the Later Han) did not move the border north of Ngang pass until around the third century. Đào, D. A. (2006). *Lịch sử Việt Nam - Từ nguồn gốc đến thế kỷ XIX*. NXB Văn Hóa Thông Tin. (1957), p. 116, p. 123.

5. Taylor, K. W. (1983). *The Birth of Vietnam*. Berkeley: University of California Press., p. 118. See also Đào, D. A. (2005). *Đất nước Việt Nam qua các đời - Nghiên cứu địa lý học lịch sử Việt Nam*. NXB Văn Hóa Thông Tin., p. 106.

CHAPTER I

1. I am using the Lạc and the Sa Huỳnh people in a generic sense; in reality there were many different groups of people who lived in these regions.

2. The total area of the Vietnamese provinces south of Ngang pass is 192,261 km2. It is 58 per cent of the country's area of 331,170 km2.

3. Phan, H. L. (2018). *Lịch sử và văn hóa Việt Nam tiếp cận bộ phận* (P. T. Phan, Ed. 4th ed.). NXB Đại Học Quốc Gia Hà Nội., p. 12.

4. Map edited by the author based on a map created by Sadalmelik - Public domain. (2007). *Topographic map of Vietnam. Created with GMT from publicly released GLOBE data*. https://commons.wikimedia.org/wiki/File:Vietnam_Topography.png

5. Taylor, K. W. (1983). *The Birth of Vietnam*. Berkeley: University of California Press., p. 188, p. 228. See also Bộ Quốc Phòng - Viện Lịch Sử Quân Sự Việt Nam, Trần, Q. V., & Lê, Đ. S. (2001). *Lịch Sử Quân Sự Việt Nam - Tập 2 - Đấu tranh giành độc lập tự chủ (từ năm 179 TCN đến năm 938)*. NXB Chính Trị Quốc Gia., p. 9.

6. A detailed description of the Dương Thanh revolt can be found in Phạm, L. H. Khảo cứu lại khởi nghĩa Dương Thanh (819-820). *Tạp chí Nghiên cứu Lịch sử, 12.2012*.

7. SKTT, Vol. 1, p. 186. "*Nam-Bắc mạnh yếu điều có từng lúc. Đương khi phương Bắc yếu thì ta mạnh, phương Bắc mạnh thì ta cũng thành yếu. Thế lớn trong thiên hạ là như vậy.*"

8. Although I began the "*Northern Rule*" in 111 BCE, it could be argued that this period began approximately 60 years earlier, in 179 BCE when Zhao Tuo, a Qin general defeated An Dương Vương. An Dương Vương's kingdom Âu Lạc became part of the latter's kingdom of Nan-yue, which the Former Han in turn conquered in the winter of 111 BCE. Most historians use the 111 BCE date. See Pham, T. (2021). *The Bronze Drums and The Earrings* (Vol. 1). 315Kio Publishing., p. 115.

9. The chronology of dynasties is provided by Cynthia L. Chennault, K. N. K., Alan J. Berkowitz, and Albert E. Dien. (2015). *Early Medieval Chinese Texts: A Bibliographical Guide* (Vol. 71).

10. Three Kingdoms: Cao Wei (220-265), Shu Han (221-263), and Dong (Eastern) Wu (220-280). *Jin* (265–420): Western Jin (265-317) and Eastern Jin (318-420). Northern Dynasties and Southern Dynasties: *Liu Song* (420–479), *Southern Qi* (479–502), *Liang* (502–557), *Chen* (557–589), Northern Wei (386-534), Eastern Wei (534-550), Northern Qi (550-577), Western Wei (535-557), Northern Zhou (557-581). The term Six Dynasties refers to Eastern Wu, Eastern Jin, Liu Song, Southern Qi, Liang and Chen.

11. Five dynasties in the 10th century are Later Liang, Later Tang, Later Jin, Later Han, and Later Zhou. Ten states are Wu, Wu/yue, Min, Southern Han, Chu, Later Han, Former Shu, Later Shu, and Southern Tang.

12. Trần, T. K. (1999). *Việt Nam Sử Lược*. Văn Hóa Thông Tin. (1921), p. 606.

13. Map edited by the author from a map created by and used with permission from Ebrey, P. B. *A Visual Sourcebook of Chinese Civilization, China proper*. https://depts.washington.edu/chinaciv/geo/proper.htm, refer to the email dated 20 April 2020.

14. The five mountains are Yuecheng (or Yuechengling, Hunan-Guangxi border), Dupang (Hunan-Guangxi border), Mengzhu (Hunan-Guangxi border), Qitian (near Hunan-Guangzhou border), and Dayu (Jiangxi-Guangdong) south of Ganzhou. Approximate coordinates from Google Maps are Yuechengling (25°52'38.1"N 110°25'16.9"E, 25.877252, 110.421369), Dupang (25°19'09.6"N 111°09'06.2"E, 25.319320, 111.151709), Mengzhu Ling (24°52'59.6"N 111°41'59.3"E, 24.883225, 111.699802), Qitian mountain (24°52'59.6"N 111°41'59.3"E, 24.883225, 111.699802), Dayu Ling (25°20'01.0"N 114°27'59.8"E, 25.333610, 114.466610), Mount Wuyi (Wuyishan, 25°20'01.0"N 114°27'59.8"E, 25.333610, 114.466610).

15. Peak Advisor. *Nanling Mountains*. https://peakvisor.com/range/nanling-mountains.html.

CHAPTER 2

1. Historians divide the Han dynasty into two periods: Former (or Western) Han (202 BCE-9 CE) and Later (or Eastern) Han (25-220). In the period this book covers, I am dealing with both. I have used the terms "Former" and "Later" rather than "Western" and "Eastern" to avoid any confusion that may arise from the perception that the two dynasties may exist at the same time if a geographical term of east or west is used.

2. Pham, T. (2021). *The Bronze Drums and The Earrings* (Vol. 1). 315Kio Publishing., p. 136.

3. The southernmost border of the empire is as far south as Cả pass, according to one historian, and to Hải Vân pass, according to another (thus the dotted line).

4. After Loewe. *The Cambridge History of China: Volume 1: The Ch'in and Han Empires, 221 BC–AD 220*. (1986). (D. Twitchett & M. Loewe, Eds. Vol. 1). Cambridge University Press. https://doi.org/DOI: 10.1017/CHOL9780521243278, Map 8. Zhuya and Dan'er not shown.

5. The envoys brought "*100 cows, 1000 jars of rice wine and household records*", CM, Vol. 1, p. 106.

6. TKCS, Vol. 37, p. 423.

7. Taylor notes Luy Lâu was established by Zhao Tuo, the founder of Nan-yue many years earlier, but I have not been able to locate the original reference. Taylor, K. W. (1983). *The Birth of Vietnam*. Berkeley: University of California Press., p. 73.

8. TKCS, Vol. 37, p. 423.

9. English translation from Vietnamese by, Châu, H. Đ. (2018). *An Nam Truyện - Ghi chép về Việt Nam trong chính sử Trung Quốc xưa*. Hội Nhà Văn., p. 188. See also Hou Han shu, Volume 86,Fan Ye. (5th century). *Hou Han shu - Book of the Later Han*. https://ctext.org/hou-han-shu, https://ctext.org/hou-han-shu/nan-man-xi-nan-yi-lie-zhuan, paragraph 14 of Volume 86 "Treatise on the Nanman, Southwestern Barbarians".

10. A figure of 12,000 is quoted in another work, see Đào, D. A. (2006). *Lịch sử Việt Nam - Từ nguồn gốc đến thế kỷ XIX*. NXB Văn Hóa Thông Tin. (1957), p. 95.

11. VDUL, p. 56.

12. LNCQ, p. 82.

13. CM, Vol. 1, p. 116.

14. Trần, T. K. (1999). *Việt Nam Sử Lược*. Văn Hóa Thông Tin. (1921), p. 50. See also Đào, D. A. (2006). *Lịch sử Việt Nam - Từ nguồn gốc đến thế kỷ XIX*. NXB Văn Hóa Thông Tin. (1957), p. 96.

15. Trần, T. K. (1999). *Việt Nam Sử Lược*. Văn Hóa Thông Tin. (1921), p. 50.

16. "*Đền Hát Môn*", Hát Môn village, Phúc Thọ district, Sơn Tây province.

17. Copied from the 2002 Đông Hồ calendar. Đông Hồ paintings are traditionally produced by the people of Đông Hồ village, Song Hồ commune, Thuận Thành district, Bắc Ninh province, near Luy Lâu.

18. Lý, T. X. (2012). *Việt điện u linh* (Đ. R. Trịnh & G. K. Đinh, Trans.). NXB Hồng Bàng. (1329), p. 57. The expression "the face of a flower, eyebrows like a willow" or "*mặt phù dung, mày dương liễu*" in VDUL is based on a line in a famous poem by Bai Juyi (772-846) during the Tang dynasty "Song of Everlasting Sorrow" about Yang Guifei (719-756), the consort of Emperor Xuanzong and is one of the most beautiful women of ancient China. The flower in question, *phù dung* is a Hibiscus mutabilis or Confederate Rose. The author, Lý, an educated person in his time, must have been familiar with this poem. He uses the expression to express the beauty of the sisters. See also Chapter 12 about Yang Guifei.

19. O'Harrow, S. (1979). From Co-loa to the Trung Sisters' revolt: Viet-Nam as the Chinese found it. *Asian perspectives.*, 22(2), 140-164., p. 151., p. 175.

20. Nguyễn, Q. N. (2012). *Chinese domination and the resistance against it: remains of the material culture - Bắc thuộc và chống Bắc thuộc: Những dấu tích văn hóa vật chất*. Perspectives on the archaeology of Vietnam international colloquium, Hanoi 29th February - 2nd March 2012 = Toàn cảnh khảo cổ học Việt Nam, Hanoi, Vietnam., p. 175.

21. Chinese Text Project. (2006-2020). *Shiji-Historical Records- [Western Han] 109 BC-91 BC Sima Qian*. https://ctext.org/shiji, https://ctext.org/shiji/ping-zhun-shu, Chapter 30, Level (stabilisation) book, Paragraph 46. Translated from Sima Qian, & translated by Phan Ngọc. (2018). *Sử ký Tư Mã Thiên : (trọn bộ hai tập)* (Vol. 1, 2). Văn học. Vol.1, p. 161.

22. Taylor, K. W. (1983). *The Birth of Vietnam*. Berkeley: University of California Press., p. 36.

23. O'Harrow, S. (1979). From Co-loa to the Trung Sisters' revolt: Viet-Nam as the Chinese found it. *Asian perspectives.*, 22(2), 140-164., p. 159.

24. Holmgren, J. (1980). *Chinese colonisation of northern Vietnam: administrative geography and political development in the Tongking Delta, first to sixth centuries A.D*. Australian National University., p. 5.

25. Xi Guang appeared during the time of one of the last of the Former Han emperors, Emperor Ping of Han (1-5), and continued to the beginning of the Emperor Guangwu of the Later Han (25-57). He could have stayed until at least 30 CE, ibid. p. 4.

26. SKTT, Vol. 1, p. 155.

27. Fan Ye. (5th century). *Hou Han shu - Book of the Later Han.* https://ctext.org/hou-han-shu, Biography 84, https://ctext.org/hou-han-shu/nan-man-xi-nan-yi-lie-zhuan, paragraph 13 or Volume 86, *Treatise on the Nanman, Southwestern Barbarians.*

28. Ibid., Biography 71, https://ctext.org/hou-han-shu/xun-li-lie-zhuan, paragraphs 10, 11 or Volume 76, *Biographies of Upright Officials.*

29. SKTT, Vol. 1, p. 155.

30. De Crespigny, R. (2007). *A biographical dictionary of Later Han to the Three Kingdoms (23-220 AD).* Brill., p. 721.

31. Fan Ye. (5th century). *Hou Han shu - Book of the Later Han.* https://ctext.org/hou-han-shu, Biography 71, https://ctext.org/hou-han-shu/xun-li-lie-zhuan, paragraph 11 or Volume 76, *Biographies of Upright Officials.*

32. CM, Vol. 1, p. 113.

33. Pham, T. (2021). *The Bronze Drums and The Earrings* (Vol. 1). 315Kio Publishing., p. 53.

34. Holmgren, J. (1980). *Chinese colonisation of northern Vietnam: administrative geography and political development in the Tongking Delta, first to sixth centuries A.D.* Australian National University., p. 4, puts this year as 37; 34 is based on CM, p. 114.

35. ANCL, p. 162.

36. SKTT, Vol. 1, p. 156.

37. Trần, B. Đ., Mạc, Đ., Tô, B. G., Phan, V. H., Lê, V. N., Nguyễn, N., & Tôn, N. Q. T. (2005). *Lịch Sử Việt Nam (Từ Đầu Đến Năm 938) - Tập 2* (V. G. Trần, B. Đ. Trần, & Đ. Mạc, Eds.). NXB Trẻ., p. 133. Also *Biography of Ma Yuan.* (2020?). https://ctext.org/dong-guan-han-ji/ma-yuan. Biography 7, paragraph 27.

38. TKCS, Vol. 37, p. 425.

39. SKTT, Vol. 1, p. 156.

40. Đào, D. A. (2006). *Lịch sử Việt Nam - Từ nguồn gốc đến thế kỷ XIX.* NXB Văn Hóa Thông Tin. (1957), p. 92.

41. Maspero, H. (1918). Études d'histoire d'Annam. *Bulletin de l'Ecole française d'Extrême-Orient*, 1-36. https://www.persee.fr/doc/befeo_0336-1519_1918_num_18_1_588., p. 13.

42. Trần, B. Đ., Mạc, Đ., Tô, B. G., Phan, V. H., Lê, V. N., Nguyễn, N., & Tôn, N. Q. T. (2005). *Lịch Sử Việt Nam (Từ Đầu Đến Năm 938) - Tập 2* (V. G. Trần, B. Đ. Trần, & Đ. Mạc, Eds.). NXB Trẻ., p. 135.

43. SKTT, Vol. 1, p. 156 also includes the commandery of Nan-hai, but this is likely incorrect as Nan-hai is a long way northeast from other commanderies, and Hou Han shu never mentions it.

44. The ten counties are Mê Linh (Miling), Tây Vu (Xiyu), Long Biên (Longbian), Bắc Đái (Beidai), Kê Từ (Jixu), Khúc Dương (Quyang), Liên Lâu or Luy Lâu (Leilou), An Định (Anding), Câu Lậu (Goulou), Chu Diên (Zhugou) located in a clockwise direction with Liên Lâu roughly in the centre. Vietnamese names are taken from Đào, D. A. (2005). *Đất nước Việt Nam qua các đời - Nghiên cứu địa lý học lịch sử Việt Nam.* NXB Văn Hóa Thông Tin., p. 36. Pinyin names are taken from Brindley, E. (2018). *Ancient China and the Yue : perceptions and identities on the southern frontier, c.400 BCE - 50 CE.*, p. 235.

45. Đinh, V. N. (1980). Đất Mê Linh - Trung tâm chính trị, quân sự và kinh tế của huyện Mê Linh thời Hai Bà Trưng. *Nghiên Cứu Lịch Sử - Viện Sử Học*, *1*, 35-53., p. 37.

46. SKTT, Vol.1, p. 156.

47. Maspero, H. (1918). Études d'histoire d'Annam. *Bulletin de l'Ecole française d'Extrême-Orient*, 1-36. https://www.persee.fr/doc/befeo_0336-1519_1918_num_18_1_588., p. 13.

48. It is where the shrine is now at Hà Lôi hamlet, but Đinh believed that this location was incorrect and it should be on the eastern side of Ba Vì mountain, see Đinh, V. N. (1980). Đất Mê Linh - Trung tâm chính trị, quân sự và kinh tế của huyện Mê Linh thời Hai Bà Trưng. *Nghiên Cứu Lịch Sử - Viện Sử Học*, 1, 35-53., p. 51.

49. Giao Chỉ has ten prefectures, Cửu Chân seven, Nhật Nam five, and Hepu five, totalling 27. See Gu, B. (111). *Han shu - Book of Han*. https://ctext.org/han-shu/zh, https://ctext.org/han-shu/di-li-zhi-xia, paragraphs 33 to 39, Volume 28, Treatise of Geography.

50. Ibid., https://ctext.org/han-shu/di-li-zhi-xia, paragraphs 33 to 39, Volume 28, Treatise of Geography.

51. "*Hai Ba Trung Shrine*" at Hạ Lôi hamlet, Mê Linh commune, Mê Linh district, Hanoi.

52. Kim Khánh. Di tích lịch sử Đền Hai Bà Trưng. https://sites.google.com/site/cauchuyenvanhocnghethuat/vhnt-93

53. Phan, H. L. (2018). *Di sản văn hóa Việt Nam dưới góc nhìn lịch sử*. NXB Đại Học Quốc Gia Hà Nội., p. 943.

54. SKTT, Vol. 1, p. 157.

55. Photo by author, 4 December 2019.

56. Đinh, V. N. (1980). Đất Mê Linh - Trung tâm chính trị, quân sự và kinh tế của huyện Mê Linh thời Hai Bà Trưng. *Nghiên Cứu Lịch Sử - Viện Sử Học*, 1, 35-53. p. 37.

57. Đào, D. A. (2005). *Đất nước Việt Nam qua các đời - Nghiên cứu địa lý học lịch sử Việt Nam*. NXB Văn Hóa Thông Tin., p. 70.

58. Taylor, K. W. (1983). *The Birth of Vietnam*. Berkeley: University of California Press., p. 46 and Fan Ye. (5th century). *Hou Han shu - Book of the Later Han*. https://ctext.org/hou-han-shu, https://ctext.org/hou-han-shu/ma-yuan-lie-zhuan, Biography 14, paragraph 17 or Volume 24, Biography of Ma Yuan.

59. Maspero, H. (1918). Études d'histoire d'Annam. *Bulletin de l'Ecole française d'Extrême-Orient*, 1-36. https://www.persee.fr/doc/befeo_0336-1519_1918_num_18_1_588., p. 24.

60. *The boundary stone of Han Dynasty in Suma Bay*. (18 May 2018). http://www.chinadaily.com.cn/regional/2015-05/18/content_20750795.htm

61. https://www.zdic.net/hans/金馬門

62. Maspero, H. (1918). Études d'histoire d'Annam. *Bulletin de l'Ecole française d'Extrême-Orient*, 1-36. https://www.persee.fr/doc/befeo_0336-1519_1918_num_18_1_588., p. 27 and Fan Ye. (5th century). *Hou Han shu - Book of the Later Han*. https://ctext.org/hou-han-shu, https://ctext.org/hou-han-shu/ma-yuan-lie-zhuan, Biography 14, paragraph 19 or Volume 24, Biography of Ma Yuan.

63. ANCL, p. 194.

64. ANCL, p. 197.

65. One request was made in 1272, CM Vol. 1, p. 500, and one in 1345, CM Vol. 1, p. 619.

66. CM, Vol. 1, p. 117. Also Chính Đạo. (2017). *Trụ đồng Mã Viện : Sự đàn hồi của biên giới đế quốc Trung Hoa*. Van Hoa Publishing Co. https://nghiencuulichsu.com/2017/07/19/tru-dong-ma-vien-su-dan-hoi-cua-bien-gioi-de-quoc-trung-hoa/

67. Edmondson, J. A. (1994). Change and Variation in Zhuang. *University of Texas at Arlington*. http://sealang.net/sala/archives/pdf8/edmondson1994change.pd., p. 149.

68. CM, Vol. 1, p. 114.

69. Châu, H. Đ. (2018). *An Nam Truyện - Ghi chép về Việt Nam trong chính sử Trung Quốc xưa*. Hội Nhà Văn., p. 192. See also Hou Han shu, Volume 86.

70. CM, Vol. 1, p. 156. The remnants of the ex-*cishi* of Guangzhou, Lư Tuấn and ex-*taishou* of Cửu Chân, Lý Thoát, joined with the Lý, Lạo to attack Long Biên, they got to the river south of it. I am unable to locate this river; the nearest river is the Đuống river, but it is north of Luy Lâu (Long Biên).

71. Pham, T. (2021). *The Bronze Drums and The Earrings* (Vol. 1). 315Kio Publishing., pp. 97-105.

72. Madrolle, C. (1937). I. Le Tonkin ancien. Lei-leou et les districts chinois de l'époque des Han. La population. Yue-chang. *Bulletin de l'Ecole française d'Extrême-Orient*, 263-332. https://www.persee.fr/doc/befeo_0336-1519_1937_num_37_1_535., p. 267, p. 274.

73. Ibid., pp. 270-271.

74. Ibid., p. 269.

75. Ibid., p. 268.

76. Ibid., p. 270.

77. Pham, T. (2021). *The Bronze Drums and The Earrings* (Vol. 1). 315Kio Publishing., p. 76.

78. Thanh Khương commune, Thuận Thành district, Bắc Ninh province.

79. Phan, H. L. (2018). *Di sản văn hóa Việt Nam dưới góc nhìn lịch sử*. NXB Đại Học Quốc Gia Hà Nội. p. 951. See the paper of Noriko, N. (2017). An Introduction to Dr. Nishimura Masanari's Research on the Lung Khe Citadel. *Asian Review of World Histories*, 5(2), 11-27. https://doi.org/https://doi.org/10.1163/22879811-12340003 . Page 12 of this paper shows 680, 520, 320, and 328 metres, respectively.

80. Madrolle, C. (1937). I. Le Tonkin ancien. Lei-leou et les districts chinois de l'époque des Han. La population. Yue-chang. *Bulletin de l'Ecole française d'Extrême-Orient*, 263-332. https://www.persee.fr/doc/befeo_0336-1519_1937_num_37_1_535., p. 269.

81. Phan, H. L. (2018). *Di sản văn hóa Việt Nam dưới góc nhìn lịch sử*. NXB Đại Học Quốc Gia Hà Nội., p. 951. The communes of Đình Tổ, Trà Lâm, Tư Thế, Trí Quả, Công Hà and Hà Mãn are believed to be on its route. See V. Thanh. (6 June 2014). *Về sông Dâu*. http://www.dongky.bacninh.com/xem-tin-tuc/68721/ve-song-dau.html

82. Photo by author, 4 December 2019.

83. Photo by author, 4 December 2019.

84. Noriko, N. (2017). An Introduction to Dr. Nishimura Masanari's Research on the Lung Khe Citadel. *Asian Review of World Histories*, 5(2), 11-27. https://doi.org/https://doi.org/10.1163/22879811-1234000., p. 11.

85. Phan, H. L. (2018). *Di sản văn hóa Việt Nam dưới góc nhìn lịch sử*. NXB Đại Học Quốc Gia Hà Nội., pp. 954-955.

86. Vu, H. L., & Sharrock, P. D. (2014). *Descending dragon, rising tiger: a history of Vietnam.*, p. 34.

87. Noriko, N. (2017). An Introduction to Dr. Nishimura Masanari's Research on the Lung Khe Citadel. *Asian Review of World Histories*, 5(2), 11-27. https://doi.org/https://doi.org/10.1163/22879811-1234000., p. 13.

CHAPTER 3

1. The original text cited Giao Châu, but at the time of Wang Mang, it did not exist, only the Giao Chỉ circuit (Appendix 5).

2. Châu, H. Đ. (2018). *An Nam Truyện - Ghi chép về Việt Nam trong chính sử Trung Quốc xưa*. Hội Nhà Văn., pp. 197-200. See also Sanguo zhi, Book of Wu, Volume 4.

3. *Shangshu* means "presenting writings", and *lang* means gentlemen. *Shangshu* also translates as "Office of the Masters of Writing". See De Crespigny, R., Ban, G., Australian National, U., & Centre of Oriental, S. (1967). *Official titles of the Former Han dynasty*. Centre of Oriental Studies in association with Australian National University Press., p. 19.

4. CM, Vol. 1, p. 129. Xiaolian (Candidate of Probity and Piety) and Maocai (Candidate of Accomplished Talent) – translation taken from O'Harrow, S. (1986). Men of Hu, Men of Han, Men of the hundred man. *Bulletin de l'Ecole française d'Extrême-Orient*, 249-266. https://www.persee.fr/doc/befeo_0336-1519_1986_num_75_1_170., p. 259.

5. Wikipedia. (-r). *Shi Xie*. https://en.wikipedia.org/wiki/Shi_Xie, in O'Harrow, S. (1986). Men of Hu, Men of Han, Men of the hundred man. *Bulletin de l'Ecole française d'Extrême-Orient*, 249-266. https://www.persee.fr/doc/befeo_0336-1519_1986_num_75_1_170., p. 259. Wu prefecture is located in present-day Sichuan province, west of Chongqing.

6. SKTT, Vol. 1, p. 164.

7. The Five Classics are the Odes (Shi), the Documents (Shu), the Three Rites Canons, the Changes (Yi), and the Spring and Autumn Annals (Chunqiu).

8. O'Harrow, S. (1986). Men of Hu, Men of Han, Men of the hundred man. *Bulletin de l'Ecole française d'Extrême-Orient*, 249-266. https://www.persee.fr/doc/befeo_0336-1519_1986_num_75_1_170., p. 251.

9. Hà, V. T. (2018). *The making of Việt Nam*. Thế Giới., p. 85.

10. Ibid., p. 86.

11. Taylor, K. W. (1983). *The Birth of Vietnam*. Berkeley: University of California Press., p. 218.

12. Gia Đông, Thuận Thành, Bắc Ninh, 21°01'59.3"N 106°03'52.4"E, 21.033127, 106.064562. Photo by author, 5 December 2019.

13. Thich, N. H. (1998). *The Three Doors of Liberation - The Heart of the Buddha's Teachings*. http://www.mpcmontreal.org/sites/pleineconscience.org/files/The%20Three%20Doors%20of%20Liberation-%20Emptiness.pdf

14. O'Harrow, S. (1986). Men of Hu, Men of Han, Men of the hundred man. *Bulletin de l'Ecole française d'Extrême-Orient*, 249-266. https://www.persee.fr/doc/befeo_0336-1519_1986_num_75_1_170., p. 260.

15. The timing is a little strange as Ting Kung was the *cishi* of Giao Châu during the reign of Emperor Huan of the Later Han (146-168), and at the same time, Shi Xie's father was the *taishou* of Nhật Nam reporting to Ting Kung. Shi Xie may have pulled a few strings to have his son, Shi Yi, appointed as an Investigator with Ting Kung. When Tung King left Giao Châu to come to the capital, Luoyang, to take up the offer from the emperor, which happened sometime after 168, it is reasonable to assume that Shi Yi would follow soon after. However, if Shi Yi returned home in 189, it was 21 years later. This appears inconsistent with the record indicating he fled shortly after arriving at Luoyang.

16. Map by SY CC BY-SA 4.0 <https://creativecommons.org/licenses/by-sa/4.0> via Wikimedia Commons. (7 July 2017). *Warlords in the End of the Han Dynasty*. https://commons.wikimedia.org/wiki/File:End_of_Han_Dynasty_Warlords.png

17. ANCL, p. 133.

18. O'Harrow, S. (1986). Men of Hu, Men of Han, Men of the hundred man. *Bulletin de l'Ecole française d'Extrême-Orient*, 249-266. https://www.persee.fr/doc/befeo_0336-1519_1986_num_75_1_170., p. 261.

19. In the ancient Chinese military, the General on the Left is inferior to the General on the Right.

20. O'Harrow, S. (1986). Men of Hu, Men of Han, Men of the hundred man. *Bulletin de l'Ecole française d'Extrême-Orient*, 249-266. https://www.persee.fr/doc/befeo_0336-1519_1986_num_75_1_170., p. 263.

21. Hsu, E. H.-l. (2017). In *History of Liuli Glazed Ceramics* (pp. 38-69). Brill. https://doi.org/https://doi.org/10.1163/9789004335868_00., p. 39.

22. Wang, Y., Sastra, L., & Boonsom, Y. (2018). Pearl Raising in Guangxi Province and Its Importance to the Local Economy. *International Journal of East Asia Studies, 22(1)*, 20-41.

23. Châu, H. Đ. (2018). *An Nam Truyện - Ghi chép về Việt Nam trong chính sử Trung Quốc xưa*. Hội Nhà Văn., p. 205. See also report by Tao Huang in Jin shu, Volume 57: Fang Xuanling. (648). *Book of Jin (Jin shu)*. http://chinesenotes.com/jinshu.html, Book of Jin, Volume 57 Biographies 27, http://chinesenotes.com/jinshu/jinshu057.html

24. Yuan Fang. (May 2017). *The favorite animal: the horse as mingqi in Han tombs* Cornell University]. https://ecommons.cornell.edu/bitstream/handle/1813/51570/Fang_cornell_0058O_10102.pdf?sequence=1&isAllowed=y</author></authors></contributors><titles><title>The favorite animal: the horse as mingqi in Han tombs</title><secondary-title>Faculty of the Graduate School</secondary-title></titles><volume>Master of Arts</volume><dates><year>May 2017</year></dates><publisher>Cornell University</publisher><urls><related-urls><url>https://ecommons.cornell.edu/bitstream/handle/1813/51570/Fang_cornell_0058O_10102.pdf?sequence=1&isAllowed=y</url></related-urls></urls></record></Cite></EndNote>

25. Translated from Vietnamese in Châu, H. Đ. (2018). *An Nam Truyện - Ghi chép về Việt Nam trong chính sử Trung Quốc xưa*. Hội Nhà Văn., p. 198. See also Sanguo zhi, Book of Wu, Volume 4.

26. O'Harrow, S. (1986). Men of Hu, Men of Han, Men of the hundred man. *Bulletin de l'Ecole française d'Extrême-Orient*, 249-266. https://www.persee.fr/doc/befeo_0336-1519_1986_num_75_1_170., p. 261.

27. Châu, H. Đ. (2018). *An Nam Truyện - Ghi chép về Việt Nam trong chính sử Trung Quốc xưa*. Hội Nhà Văn., pp. 197-200. See also Sanguo zhi, Book of Wu, Volume 4 and O'Harrow, S. (1986). Men of Hu, Men of Han, Men of the hundred man. *Bulletin de l'Ecole française d'Extrême-Orient*, 249-266. https://www.persee.fr/doc/befeo_0336-1519_1986_num_75_1_170., pp. 259-265.

28. Cheng Shou. (3rd century CE). *Record of the Three Kingdoms, Sanguo zhi*. https://ctext.org/sanguozhi/zh, Book of Wu, Volume 15, Biographies of He, Quan, Lü, Zhou, and Zhongli, https://ctext.org/sanguozhi/60/zh

29. Ibid., Book of Wu, Volume 15, Biographies of He, Quan, Lü, Zhou, and Zhongli, https://ctext.org/sanguozhi/60/zh

30. O'Harrow, S. (1986). Men of Hu, Men of Han, Men of the hundred man. *Bulletin de l'Ecole française d'Extrême-Orient*, 249-266. https://www.persee.fr/doc/befeo_0336-1519_1986_num_75_1_170., p. 265.

31. Trần, V. G. (1932). X Le bouddhisme en Annam, des origines au XIIIe siècle. Ibid., 191-268. https://www.persee.fr/doc/befeo_0336-1519_1932_num_32_1_455., p. 206.

32. Ibid., p. 220.

33. Dinh, M. C., Ly, K. H., Ha, T. M., Ha, V. T., Hoang Thi, T., & Nguyen, T. T. (2008). *The History of Buddhism in Vietnam*. The Council for Research in Values and Philosophy., p. 28.

34. LNCQ describes the tree as *cây phù dung* (Hibiscus mutabilis) but it is more likely a Dâu wood. The rose tree mentioned would be too small to have a large hollow for a baby, see also below.

35. LNCQ, pp. 84-86. In another reference, the tree is a banyan tree, not a confederate rose as per LNCQ. See Dinh, M. C., Ly, K. H., Ha, T. M., Ha, V. T., Hoang Thi, T., & Nguyen, T. T. (2008). *The History of Buddhism in Vietnam*. The Council for Research in Values and Philosophy., p. 28. Another explanation for this tree is a Dâu wood tree, common in the area (Baccaurea sapida, Allospondias tonkinensis).

36. Ibid., p. 27.

37. *Tứ Pháp.* (2020). https://vi.wikipedia.org/wiki/T%E1%BB%A9_ph%C3%A1p

38. In Vietnamese; *"Nhất nước, nhì phân, tam cần, tứ giống"*

39. Dinh, M. C., Ly, K. H., Ha, T. M., Ha, V. T., Hoang Thi, T., & Nguyen, T. T. (2008). *The History of Buddhism in Vietnam.* The Council for Research in Values and Philosophy., pp. 27-28.

40. Photo by Thế Tử Đại Lý. (2018). *Goddess of (Lightning) Flash statue.* Located in Trí Quả Buddhist Temple, Thuan Thanh, Bac Ninh, Viet Nam. Taken without usual decorative clothes. Public domain via Wikimedia Commons. https://upload.wikimedia.org/wikipedia/commons/0/0c/T%C6%B0%E1%BB%A3ng_Ph%C3%A1p_%C4%90i%E1%BB%87n_khi_ch%C6%B0a_phong_y_%C3%A1o.jpg

41. Photo by author, 5 December 2019.

42. An Bình. (2012). *Phòng VH&TT huyện Thuận Thành trả lời đơn xin lại tượng Pháp Vũ của nhân dân thôn Đông Cốc.* https://phatgiao.org.vn/phong-vhtt-huyen-thuan-thanh-tra-loi-don-xin-lai-tuong-phap-vu-cua-nhan-dan-thon-dong-coc-d10319.html

43. Dinh, M. C., Ly, K. H., Ha, T. M., Ha, V. T., Hoang Thi, T., & Nguyen, T. T. (2008). *The History of Buddhism in Vietnam.* The Council for Research in Values and Philosophy., p. 28.

44. Trần, V. G. (1932). X Le bouddhisme en Annam, des origines au XIIIe siècle. *Bulletin de l'Ecole française d'Extrême-Orient,* 191-268. https://www.persee.fr/doc/befeo_0336-1519_1932_num_32_1_455., p. 219.

45. Ibid., p. 212.

46. Dinh, M. C., Ly, K. H., Ha, T. M., Ha, V. T., Hoang Thi, T., & Nguyen, T. T. (2008). *The History of Buddhism in Vietnam.* The Council for Research in Values and Philosophy., p. 11.

47. Trần, V. G. (1932). X Le bouddhisme en Annam, des origines au XIIIe siècle. *Bulletin de l'Ecole française d'Extrême-Orient,* 191-268. https://www.persee.fr/doc/befeo_0336-1519_1932_num_32_1_455., p. 212.

48. Pham, T. (2021). *The Bronze Drums and The Earrings* (Vol. 1). 315Kio Publishing., pp. 68-70.

49. Dinh, M. C., Ly, K. H., Ha, T. M., Ha, V. T., Hoang Thi, T., & Nguyen, T. T. (2008). *The History of Buddhism in Vietnam.* The Council for Research in Values and Philosophy.

50. Three Baskets are the Sutra Piṭaka, the Vinaya Piṭaka, and the Abhidhamma Piṭaka. In Vietnamese, these are: *Tam Tăng Kinh Điển.*

51. Trần, V. G. (1932). X Le bouddhisme en Annam, des origines au XIIIe siècle. *Bulletin de l'Ecole française d'Extrême-Orient,* 191-268. https://www.persee.fr/doc/befeo_0336-1519_1932_num_32_1_455., p. 213. The text quotes the translation of the original source as *"he had extensively examined the six classic books"*. I am unable to identify these classic books but a Vietnamese translation refers to them as *Lục Thư* (six letters), It means six different ways to construct the Chinese characters. See also Trần, V. G., & Tuệ Sỹ. (1968). *Phật Giáo Việt Nam từ khởi nguyên đến thế kỷ XIII - Le Bouddhisme en Annam* (T. Sỹ, Trans.). Ban Tu Thư Viện Đại Học Vạn Hạnh 1968. .

52. Huynh, T. (2018). *The early Sinification of the Buddha's relics and the case in which Kang Senghui prayed for those sacred relics by Dr. Trung Huynh* 7th International Conference Buddhism & Australia, http://www.buddhismandaustralia.com/ba/index.php?title=Presentations_2018

53. Huynh, T. (2016). *The Early Development of Buddhism in the Red River Delta Basin, Jiaozhi, and Southern China: The Case of a Sogdian-Jiaozhi Buddhist Monk Kang Senghui* 康僧會 University of the West]. https://web.archive.org/web/20160911172427/http://thichhangdat.com/wp-content/uploads/2016/07/Kang-senghui-PhD.pdf, p. 38.

54. *Jing'an Temple predates city's birth*. (1 November 2004). http://www.chinadaily.com.cn/english/doc/2004-11/01/content_387373.htm

55. Dinh, M. C., Ly, K. H., Ha, T. M., Ha, V. T., Hoang Thi, T., & Nguyen, T. T. (2008). *The History of Buddhism in Vietnam*. The Council for Research in Values and Philosophy., p. 37.

56. Duong, V. C. (2016). Buddhism from India to Vietnam: A Study of Early Introduction. *Imperial Journal of Interdisciplinary Research (IJIR)*, *2*(9), 1171-1175. http://www.onlinejournal.in/IJIRV2I9/184.pd., p. 1173.

57. Trần, V. G. (1932). X Le bouddhisme en Annam, des origines au XIIIe siècle. *Bulletin de l'Ecole française d'Extrême-Orient*, 191-268. https://www.persee.fr/doc/befeo_0336-1519_1932_num_32_1_455., p. 213.

58. Ibid., p. 214.

59. Ibid., p. 214.

60. Nguyễn, L. (1973). *Việt Nam Phật Giáo Sử Luận*. Lá Bối., p. 42.

61. Dinh, M. C., Ly, K. H., Ha, T. M., Ha, V. T., Hoang Thi, T., & Nguyen, T. T. (2008). *The History of Buddhism in Vietnam*. The Council for Research in Values and Philosophy., p. 32.

62. Nguyễn, L. (1973). *Việt Nam Phật Giáo Sử Luận*. Lá Bối., p. 43.

63. Ibid. p. 43.

64. Mouzi is likely to have taken the traditional route from Luy Lâu (or La Thành at a later date) to the imperial capital at Chang'an (or Xi'an). This route would go through contemporary Bắc Ninh, Bắc Giang, Lạng Sơn, cross the border into China, continues north via Chongzuo, Nanning, Guilin (Guangxi province) then to Youngzhou, Hengyang, Changsha, passes the eastern shore of Dongting lake (Hunan province), to Wuhan, Xiangyang and arrives at Xi'ian. See also map in Lư, V. A. (2014). *Bộ máy An Nam Đô Hộ Phủ của Trung Quốc thời Đường (679 – 905)* Đại Học Quốc Gia Thành Phố Hồ Chí Minh - Trường Đại Học Khoa Học Xã Hội và Nhân Văn]. Ho Chi Minh City., p. 28.

65. Nguyễn, L. (1973). *Việt Nam Phật Giáo Sử Luận*. Lá Bối., p. 43.

66. Lê, M. T. (2001). *Tổng Tập Văn Học Phật Giáo Việt Nam - Tập I* (Vol. 1). Nhà Xuất Bản Thành Phố Hồ Chí Minh., p. 94.

67. Keenan, J. P., & Mou, t. (1994). *How Master Mou Removes Our Doubts: A Reader-response Study and Translation of the Mou-tzu Li-huo Lun (SUNY Series in Buddhist Studies)*. State University of New York Press.

68. *Selections from Mouzi's Disposing of Error (Lihou Lun)*. http://afe.easia.columbia.edu/ps/cup/mouzi_disposing_error.pdf

69. Dinh, M. C., Ly, K. H., Ha, T. M., Ha, V. T., Hoang Thi, T., & Nguyen, T. T. (2008). *The History of Buddhism in Vietnam*. The Council for Research in Values and Philosophy., p. 31.

70. Lê, M. T. (2001). *Tổng Tập Văn Học Phật Giáo Việt Nam - Tập I* (Vol. 1). Nhà Xuất Bản Thành Phố Hồ Chí Minh., p. 30.

71. Ibid., p. 175.

72. Dinh, M. C., Ly, K. H., Ha, T. M., Ha, V. T., Hoang Thi, T., & Nguyen, T. T. (2008). *The History of Buddhism in Vietnam*. The Council for Research in Values and Philosophy., p. 33.

73. Ibid., p. 34, p. 35.

74. Nguyễn, L. (1973). *Việt Nam Phật Giáo Sử Luận*. Lá Bối., p. 78.

75. Kim Sơn - Thiền phái Trúc Lâm. (1337). *Thiền Uyển Tập Anh* (Lê Mạnh Thát (Dựa trên bản in năm 1715), Trans.). Đại Học Vạn Hạnh - Saigon. http://www.thuvienhaiphu.com.vn/datafile1/BE015404.pdf

76. Ibid., p. 50.

77. Photo by author, 5 December 2019.

78. CM, Vol.1, p. 143.

79. VDUL, p. 142.

80. *Giao Chỉ Chí* is believed to be the same as *Giao Chỉ Ký* written by Zeng Gun in the ninth century (now lost).

81. SKTT, Vol. 1, p. 167.

82. Bộ Quốc Phòng - Viện Lịch Sử Quân Sự Việt Nam, Trần, Q. V., & Lê, Đ. S. (2001). *Lịch Sử Quân Sự Việt Nam - Tập 2 - Đấu tranh giành độc lập tự chủ (từ năm 179 TCN đến năm 938)*. NXB Chính Trị Quốc Gia., p. 121 and Minh Thư. (2007). *Tuyển chọn ca dao hay nhất*. NXB Văn hóa dân tộ., p. 37:

    Ru con con ngủ cho lành
    Để mẹ gánh nước rửa bành cho voi
    Muốn coi lên núi mà coi
    Coi Bà Triệu tướng cưỡi voi đánh cồng
    Túi gấm cho lẫn túi hồng
    Têm trầu cánh phượng cho chồng ra quân.

83. Cheng Shou. (3rd century CE). *Record of the Three Kingdoms, Sanguo zhi*. https://ctext.org/sanguozhi/zh, Volume 61: Book of Wu 16-Biographies of Pan Jun and Lu Kai, http://chinesenotes.com/sanguozhi/sanguozhi061.html.

84. SKTT, Vol. 1, p. 167, quotes 30,000 households, which is incorrect. Sanguo zhi (Vol. 61) cites only 3,000 families.

85. Bộ Quốc Phòng - Viện Lịch Sử Quân Sự Việt Nam, Trần, Q. V., & Lê, Đ. S. (2001). *Lịch Sử Quân Sự Việt Nam - Tập 2 - Đấu tranh giành độc lập tự chủ (từ năm 179 TCN đến năm 938)*. NXB Chính Trị Quốc Gia., pp. 122-123.

86. VDUL, p. 142.

87. Photo by author, 12 December 2019.

88. Photo by author, 12 December 2019.

89. VDUL, p. 136, p. 137. The original Vietnamese version is:

    "Em chỉ muốn cưỡi gió đạp sóng, chém cá kình lớn ở biển đông, quét sạch bờ cõi, cứu dân ra khỏi cảnh chìm đắm há lại bắt chước người đời cúi đầu khom lưng làm tì thiếp kẻ khác, cam tâm phục dịch ở trong nhà ư?"

CHAPTER 4

1. Taylor, K. W. (1983). *The Birth of Vietnam*. Berkeley: University of California Press., p. 60.

2. Schweyer, A.-V. (2019). *The Birth of Champa*., p. 1 and Ngô, V. D. (2002). *Văn hóa cổ Champa*. NXB Văn Hóa Dân Tộc., p. 51.

3. SKTT, Vol. 1, p. 158. Also Fan Ye. (5th century). *Hou Han shu - Book of the Later Han.* https://ctext.org/hou-han-shu, https://ctext.org/hou-han-shu/nan-man-xi-nan-yi-lie-zhuan, paragraph 16 or Volume 86, *Treatise on the Nanman, Southwestern barbarians.*

4. CM, Vol. 1, p. 122.

5. The advice makes interesting reading, but one should note that the Later Han (and Chinese armies at different periods) also travelled by ships (refer to the attack on Nan-yue and Ma Yuan's expedition), so the time taken is likely shorter.

6. ANCL, p. 131.

7. Fan Ye. (5th century). *Hou Han shu - Book of the Later Han.* https://ctext.org/hou-han-shu, https://ctext.org/hou-han-shu/nan-man-xi-nan-yi-lie-zhuan, paragraph 16 or Volume 86, *Treatise on the Nanman, Southwestern barbarians.*

8. Lĩnh region refers to the Nanling mountains (see Figure 3). In 179 BCE, an army sent by Han Empress Lu Zhi to invade Nan-yue had to turn back at these mountains due to illness, see Phạm, T. (2021). *The Bronze Drums and The Earrings* (Vol. 1). 315Kio Publishing., p. 128.

9. This appears slow but is probably a reasonable estimate if supply trains are included in the march. A standard loaded Roman army march would be 29.62 kilometres over six hours. Wikipedia. (2015). *Loaded march.* https://en.wikipedia.org/wiki/Loaded_march

10. The original text is "*hộc*" or ge = 10 sheng. An army of 40,000 soldiers would consume 60,000,000 sheng of rice over a 300-day expedition or 60,000 dan with one dan equals 100 sheng. Five sheng of rice per day seems realistic based on the typical rice ration of Japanese soldiers in WWII.

11. 3,038 kilometres equals 2,248 kilometres from Jinan to Pingxiang, on the Chinese border, plus 790 kilometres from Lạng Sơn, on the Vietnamese border, to Huế.

12. Army, U., Service, M. I., & War Department. (1942). *Intelligence Bulletin.* (Vol. I, No. 1, September 1942). GPO.

13. SKTT, p. 159.

14. A region to the west of Thanh Hóa city covering Nhồi mountain, Triệu Sơn, Quảng Xương the southern side of the Nhà Lê river (Bồn Giang). See Đào, D. A. (2005). *Đất nước Việt Nam qua các đời - Nghiên cứu địa lý học lịch sử Việt Nam.* NXB Văn Hóa Thông Tin., p. 56.

15. Located in the upland, south of the Mã river, see Appendix 8.

16. Taylor, K. W. (1983). *The Birth of Vietnam.* Berkeley: University of California Press., p. 65. Also Fan Ye. (5th century). *Hou Han shu - Book of the Later Han.* https://ctext.org/hou-han-shu, https://ctext.org/hou-han-shu/nan-man-xi-nan-yi-lie-zhuan, paragraph 17 or Volume 86, *Treatise on the Nanman, Southwestern barbarians*, and ANCL, p. 165.

17. Bộ Quốc Phòng - Viện Lịch Sử Quân Sự Việt Nam, Trần, Q. V., & Lê, Đ. S. (2001). *Lịch Sử Quân Sự Việt Nam - Tập 2 - Đấu tranh giành độc lập tự chủ (từ năm 179 TCN đến năm 938).* NXB Chính Trị Quốc Gia., pp. 105-106.

18. There are different explanations for the official position of Gongcao or Vietnamese "Công Tào". Under the Tang dynasty, it is an official responsible for construction and repairs (public works), see Lư, V. A. (2014). *Bộ máy An Nam Đô Hộ Phủ của Trung Quốc thời Đường (679 – 905)* Đại Học Quốc Gia Thành Phố Hồ Chí Minh - Trường Đại Học Khoa Học Xã Hội và Nhân Văn]. Ho Chi Minh City., pp. 62-63. In another source, it is an official responsible for staff and other activities in the prefecture besides the prefect, a "chief of staff" position, see TKCS, Vol. 36, p. 377. In Trần, B. Đ., Mạc, Đ., Tô, B. G., Phan, V. H., Lê, V. N., Nguyễn, N., & Tôn, N. Q. T. (2005). *Lịch Sử Việt Nam (Từ Đầu Đến Năm 938) - Tập 2* (V. G. Trần, B. Đ. Trần, & Đ. Mạc, Eds.). NXB Trẻ., p. 132. "*Công Tào Tòng sự*" is one of seven assistants to the *zhou mu* (or *cishi*) responsible for staff appointment and citizen affairs.

19. Châu, H. Đ. (2018). *An Nam Truyện - Ghi chép về Việt Nam trong chính sử Trung Quốc xưa*. Hội Nhà Văn., p. 247. See also Jin shu, Volume 97: Fang Xuanling. (648). *Book of Jin (Jin shu)*. http://chinesenotes.com/jinshu.html. https://ctext.org/wiki.pl?if=gb&chapter=282778, paragraph 43 of Volume 97, *Four Barbarian Tribes*.

20. Southworth, W. A. (2001). *The origins of Campa in Central Vietnam: a preliminary review* /z-wcorg/. http://catalog.hathitrust.org/api/volumes/oclc/57480138.html, p. 285.

21. Phan, H. L. (2018). *Lịch sử và văn hóa Việt Nam tiếp cận bộ phận* (P. T. Phan, Ed. 4th ed.). NXB Đại Học Quốc Gia Hà Nội., p. 162.

22. Đổng, T. D. (2018). *Đặt lại vấn đề thời điểm ra đời của nhà nước Lâm Ấp*. http://nghiencuuquocte.org/2018/05/27/dat-lai-van-de-thoi-diem-ra-doi-cua-nha-nuoc-lam-ap/

23. Đào, D. A. (2006). *Lịch sử Việt Nam - Từ nguồn gốc đến thế kỷ XIX*. NXB Văn Hóa Thông Tin. (1957), p. 112.

24. Lương Ninh. (2013). Lại bàn về nước Lâm Ấp-Champa. *Nghiên Cứu Lịch Sử - Viện Sử Học, 5*.

25. Cheng Shou. (3rd century CE). *Record of the Three Kingdoms, Sanguo zhi*. https://ctext.org/sanguozhi/zh, https://ctext.org/sanguozhi/60/zh, paragraph 5. Volume 60 (Book of Wu No. 15), Biographies of He, Quan, Lü, Zhou, and Zhongli.

26. Pelliot, P. (1903). Le Fou-nan. *Bulletin de l'Ecole française d'Extrême-Orient*, 248-303. https://www.persee.fr/doc/befeo_0336-1519_1903_num_3_1_121., p. 251.

27. Gungwu, W. (1958). The Nanhai Trade: A Study of the Early History of Chinese Trade in the South China Sea. *Journal of the Malayan Branch of the Royal Asiatic Society, 31*(2 (182)), 1-135. http://www.jstor.org/stable/41503138, p.31.

28. Schweyer, A.-V. (2019). *The Birth of Champa*., p. 2.

29. For a discussion of this subject, see Pham, T. (2021). *The Bronze Drums and The Earrings* (Vol. 1). 315Kio Publishing., p. 143.

30. The five prefectures are, from north to south, Tây Quyền (Xijuan) by the Gianh river, Tỷ Ảnh (Bijing) by Nhật Lệ river, both are in Quảng Bình provinces south of Ngang pass; Chu Ngô (Zhuwu) by the Thạch Hãn river in Quảng Trị province, Lô Dung (Lurong) by the Hương and Bồ rivers in Thừa Thiên-Huế province and Tượng Lâm (Xianglin) by the Chợ Cùi (Thu Bồn) river according to Đào, D. A. (2005). *Đất nước Việt Nam qua các đời - Nghiên cứu địa lý học lịch sử Việt Nam*. NXB Văn Hóa Thông Tin., p. 61. See also Gu, B. (111). *Han shu - Book of Han*. https://ctext.org/han-shu/zh, https://ctext.org/han-shu/di-li-zhi, paragraph 39 or Volume 28, Part 2, *Treatise on Geography*.

31. According to Đào, Tượng Lâm also includes Quảng Ngãi, Bình Định and Phú Yên provinces to Cả pass. See Đào, D. A. (2005). *Đất nước Việt Nam qua các đời - Nghiên cứu địa lý học lịch sử Việt Nam*. NXB Văn Hóa Thông Tin., p. 62.

32. Tượng Lâm (Xianglin) means elephant and forest. It has been confused with Tượng Quận (Xiang), the name of a commandery under Qin times, see TKCS, Vol. 36, p. 366, but Tượng Quận did not include today's Vietnam See also Pham, T. (2021). *The Bronze Drums and The Earrings* (Vol. 1). 315Kio Publishing., p. 144.

33. Maspero, H. (1918). Études d'histoire d'Annam. *Bulletin de l'Ecole française d'Extrême-Orient*, 1-36. https://www.persee.fr/doc/befeo_0336-1519_1918_num_18_1_588., p. 23.

34. Bảo tàng Nhân học. (2010). *Lâm Ấp qua những tài liệu khảo cổ học – 1. Về vị trí của Lâm Ấp*. http://baotanglichsu.vn/vi/Articles/3127/6629/lam-ap-qua-nhung-tai-lieu-khao-co-hoc-1-ve-vi-tri-cua-lam-ap.html

35. Đào, D. A. (2005). *Đất nước Việt Nam qua các đời - Nghiên cứu địa lý học lịch sử Việt Nam*. NXB Văn Hóa Thông Tin., p. 60.

36. Aurousseau, L. (1914). Georges Maspero: Le Royaume de Champa. *Bulletin de l'Ecole française d'Extrême-Orient*, 8-43. https://www.persee.fr/doc/befeo_0336-1519_1914_num_14_1_285., p. 33.

37. Translated from Vietnamese from Châu, H. Đ. (2018). *An Nam Truyện - Ghi chép về Việt Nam trong chính sử Trung Quốc xưa*. Hội Nhà Văn., pp. 256-257. See also Xiao Zixian (537). *Book of Southern Qi - Volume 58, Biographies 39: Other Peoples from the Southeast*. http://chinesenotes.com/nanqishu/nanqishu058.html.

38. Southworth, W. A. (2001). *The origins of Campa in Central Vietnam: a preliminary review* /z-wcorg/. http://catalog.hathitrust.org/api/volumes/oclc/57480138.html, p. 198, p. 374.

39. *Varman* in Sanskrit means "shield" but could also be derived from the Tamil word *Varamban* as in the royal title "*Vaava Varamban*", Wikipedia. *Varman (surname)*. https://en.wikipedia.org/wiki/Varman_(surname).

40. Aspell, W. (2013). Southeast Asia in the Suishu: A Translation of Memoir 47 with Notes and Commentary. *Asia Research Institute - Working Paper Series No. 208*. https://ari.nus.edu.sg/wp-content/uploads/2018/10/wps13_208.pdf, footnote 18.

41. Châu, H. Đ. (2018). *An Nam Truyện - Ghi chép về Việt Nam trong chính sử Trung Quốc xưa*. Hội Nhà Văn., p. 282. See also Xin Tang shu, Volume 222c:Xiu, O., Qi, S., & Fan, Z. (1060). *New Book of Tang (Xin Tang shu) - Volume 222c Biographies 147c: Southern Man 3*. http://chinesenotes.com/xintangshu/xintangshu222c.html

42. Of 206 full or partial inscriptions discovered and catalogued, only 81 have been translated, see Lapont, P. B., Poklaun, H., & Council for the Social-Cultural Development of, C. (2011). *Vương quốc Champa-Địa dư, Dân cư và Lịch sử.*, p. 132. I do not have an updated figure for 2022.

43. Ibid., p. 134.

44. Southworth, W. A. (2001). *The origins of Campa in Central Vietnam: a preliminary review* /z-wcorg/. http://catalog.hathitrust.org/api/volumes/oclc/57480138.html, pp. 241-242.

45. Schweyer, A.-V. (2019). *The Birth of Champa.*, p. 2.

46. Bellwood as quoted in Pham, T. (2021). *The Bronze Drums and The Earrings* (Vol. 1). 315Kio Publishing., p. 156.

47. Vickery, M. (2005). Champa revised., p. 17, p. 24.

48. Klamer, M. (2019). The dispersal of Austronesian languages in Island South East Asia: Current findings and debates. *Language and Linguistics Compass*, *13*(4), e12325. https://doi.org/10.1111/lnc3.12325

49. Edmondson, J. A., & Gregerson, K. J. (2007). The Languages of Vietnam: Mosaics and Expansions. Ibid., *1*(6), 727-749. https://doi.org/10.1111/j.1749-818X.2007.00033.x

50. Châu, H. Đ. (2018). *An Nam Truyện - Ghi chép về Việt Nam trong chính sử Trung Quốc xưa*. Hội Nhà Văn., p. 248.

51. Fang Xuanling. (648). *Book of Jin (Jin shu)*. http://chinesenotes.com/jinshu.html. Volume 97 Biographies 67: Four Barbarian Tribes. http://chinesenotes.com/jinshu/jinshu097.html.

52. Schweyer, A.-V. (2019). *The Birth of Champa.*, p. 4.

53. Gianh and Nhật Lệ rivers are in Quảng Bình province; Thạch Hãn and Bến Hải rivers are in Quảng Trị province; Hương and Ô Lâu rivers are in Thừa Thiên-Huế province.

54. Fang Xuanling. (648). *Book of Jin (Jin shu)*. http://chinesenotes.com/jinshu.html. Volume 3 Annals 3: Emperor Wu. http://chinesenotes.com/jinshu/jinshu003.html.

55. Several thousand *li*, say, 3000 *li* is around 1350 kilometres, but the distance between Hanoi (near Luy Lâu) and Hội An (near Trà Kiệu) is only around 900 kilometres, so this may be a little overestimation. In CM, this distance is quoted as 700 *li* or 315 kilometres, which is more reasonable when compared with the distance between Ngang pass to Hội An at 350 kilometres. CM, Vol. 1, p. 149.

56. ANCL, p. 134.

57. Fang Xuanling. (648). *Book of Jin (Jin shu)*. http://chinesenotes.com/jinshu.html. Volume 57 Biographies 27: Luo Xian; Teng Xiu; Ma Long; Hu Fen; Tao Huang; Wu Yan; Zhang Guang; Zhao You. http://chinesenotes.com/jinshu/jinshu057.html.

58. TKCS, Vol. 36, pp. 359-360.

59. Li Daoyuan. (466). *Shui Jing Zhu*. https://ctext.org/shui-jing-zhu. Volume 36, https://ctext.org/wei-jin-and-north-south?searchu=%E6%9E%97%E9%82%91, paragraph 11.

60. Đào, D. A. (2005). *Đất nước Việt Nam qua các đời - Nghiên cứu địa lý học lịch sử Việt Nam*. NXB Văn Hóa Thông Tin., p. 62.

61. Ibid., p. 68.

62. Châu, H. Đ. (2018). *An Nam Truyện - Ghi chép về Việt Nam trong chính sử Trung Quốc xưa*. Hội Nhà Văn., p. 248.

63. Fang Xuanling. (648). *Book of Jin (Jin shu)*. http://chinesenotes.com/jinshu.html. Volume 97.

64. TKCS, Vol. 36, p. 380.

65. Gungwu, W. (1958). The Nanhai Trade: A Study of the Early History of Chinese Trade in the South China Sea. *Journal of the Malayan Branch of the Royal Asiatic Society*, *31*(2 (182)), 1-135. http://www.jstor.org/stable/4150313., p. 40.

66. TKCS, Vol. 36, p. 379., p. 248. See also Jin shu, Volume 97.

67. Châu, H. Đ. (2018). *An Nam Truyện - Ghi chép về Việt Nam trong chính sử Trung Quốc xưa*. Hội Nhà Văn., p. 248. See also Jin shu, Volume 97.

68. I am unable to decipher or locate these states, but they are: Đại Kỳ Giới, Tiểu Kỳ Giới, Thức Bộc (Che Pou), Từ Lang (Siu Lang), Khuất Đô (Khiu Tou), Kiền (Càn) Lỗ (Kan Lou), Phù Đơn (Đan, Fou Tan) based on TKCS, Vol. 36, p. 380 and Jin shu, Volume 97 Biographies 67: Four Barbarian Tribes.

69. Southworth, W. A. (2001). *The origins of Campa in Central Vietnam: a preliminary review* /z-wcorg/. http://catalog.hathitrust.org/api/volumes/oclc/57480138.html, p. 298.

70. TKCS, Vol. 36, p. 381.

71. Châu, H. Đ. (2018). *An Nam Truyện - Ghi chép về Việt Nam trong chính sử Trung Quốc xưa*. Hội Nhà Văn., p. 248. See also Jin shu, Volume 97.

72. Fang Xuanling. (648). *Book of Jin (Jin shu)*. http://chinesenotes.com/jinshu.html. Volume 7 Annals 7: Emperor Cheng; Emperor Kang. http://chinesenotes.com/jinshu/jinshu007.html.

73. Southworth, W. A. (2001). *The origins of Campa in Central Vietnam: a preliminary review* /z-wcorg/. http://catalog.hathitrust.org/api/volumes/oclc/57480138.html, p. 298.

74. Châu, H. Đ. (2018). *An Nam Truyện - Ghi chép về Việt Nam trong chính sử Trung Quốc xưa*. Hội Nhà Văn., p. 248. See also Jin shu, Volume 97.

75. Under the Jin dynasty, Cửu Chân prefecture was made smaller and a new prefecture Cửu Đức was added. See Đào, D. A. (2005). *Đất nước Việt Nam qua các đời - Nghiên cứu địa lý học lịch sử Việt Nam*. NXB Văn Hóa Thông Tin., pp. 73-74.

76. Gungwu, W. (1958). The Nanhai Trade: A Study of the Early History of Chinese Trade in the South China Sea. *Journal of the Malayan Branch of the Royal Asiatic Society*, 31(2 (182)), 1-135. http://www.jstor.org/stable/4150313., p. 40.

77. TKCS, Vol. 36, p. 369.

78. TKCS, Vol. 36, p. 382.

79. ANCL, p. 181.

80. Liu Xiong's title in Vietnamese is Đốc Hộ but I am unable to find the English translation. Taylor refers to him as a Governor-General. See Taylor, K. W. (1983). *The Birth of Vietnam*. Berkeley: University of California Press., p. 108. It would appear that this military position is alongside, or just below, the civilian position of governor of a circuit. In the case of Giao Châu, Liu Xiong would have been Zhu Fans right-hand man, and headed the military, see Bộ Quốc Phòng - Viện Lịch Sử Quân Sự Việt Nam, Trần, Q. V., & Lê, Đ. S. (2001). *Lịch Sử Quân Sự Việt Nam - Tập 2 - Đấu tranh giành độc lập tự chủ (từ năm 179 TCN đến năm 938)*. NXB Chính Trị Quốc Gia., p. 130. Ngô translates it as *Đô Đốc*, which means Admiral, see Ngô, V. D. (2002). *Văn hóa cổ Champa*. NXB Văn Hóa Dân Tộc., p. 55.

81. TKCS, Vol. 36, p. 366.

82. Taylor, K. W. (1983). *The Birth of Vietnam*. Berkeley: University of California Press., p. 108.

83. Châu, H. Đ. (2018). *An Nam Truyện - Ghi chép về Việt Nam trong chính sử Trung Quốc xưa*. Hội Nhà Văn., p. 264. See also Liang shu, Volume 54: Yao Silian. (635). *Book of Liang (Liang shu) - Volume 54 - The Various Barbarians* http://chinesenotes.com/liangshu/liangshu054.html.

84. Yao Silian. (635). *Book of Liang (Liang shu) - Volume 54 - The Various Barbarians* http://chinesenotes.com/liangshu/liangshu054.html.

85. Quốc Sử Quán Triều Nguyễn, Viện Khoa Học Xã Hội Việt Nam, & Viện Sử Học. (2006). *Đại Nam Nhất Thống Chí* (T. Đ. Phạm & D. A. Đào, Trans.). NXB Thuận Hóa., Volume II, Quyển 3. Tỉnh Quảng Bình, p. 53.

86. CM, Vol.1, p. 153.

87. Trần, T. K. (1999). *Việt Nam Sử Lược*. Văn Hóa Thông Tin. (1921), pp 57-59.

88. Quốc Sử Quán Triều Nguyễn, Viện Khoa Học Xã Hội Việt Nam, & Viện Sử Học. (2006). *Đại Nam Nhất Thống Chí* (T. Đ. Phạm & D. A. Đào, Trans.). NXB Thuận Hóa., p. 53.

89. TKCS, Vol. 36, p. 362.

90. Khu Túc, as noted in TKCS, measures 650 *bu* (975 m, 1 *bu* = 1.50 m, 1 *li* = 300 bu = 450 m, see Appendix 15) in the east-west direction, and the perimeter of this rectangular citadel is given at 6 *li* 170 *bu* or 1970 *bu* which would produce a width in the north-south direction of 335 *bu* or 502.5 metres for a rectangle. The walls are measured at 2 *zhang* or 20 *chi*, *1 chi* = 0.25 m. See TKCS, Vol. 36, p. 362. Khu Túc, at 975x502 m, is a lot larger than Cao Lao Hạ at 250 by 180 m.

91. Near Thôn (hamlet) 1, Hạ Trạch commune, Bố Trạch district, Quảng Bình province.

92. Lê, Đ. P. (2018). *Khảo cổ học Champa : khai quật và phát hiện = Champa archeology : excavations and discoveries*. NXB Khoa Học Xã Hội., pp. 434-435.

93. Taken from ibid., pp. 430-431 with the ramparts having a dimension of North: 8.6 m base width, 3.8 m top width, 0.8-1.2 m height, South: 8.2 m base width, 3.6 m top width, 1.5-2.0 m height, East: 12.5 m base width, 5.0 m top width, West: 10-12 m base width, 3.5-4.0 m top width, 1.5-2.0 m height.

94. Measured from Google Maps as 243 m N, 187 m W, 252 m S, 186 m E.

95. Ngô, V. D. (2002). *Văn hóa cổ Champa*. NXB Văn Hóa Dân Tộc., p. 222.

96. TKCS, Vol. 36, p. 363.

97. The same information is given in Nan Qi shu, Volume 58, see Châu, H. Đ. (2018). *An Nam Truyện - Ghi chép về Việt Nam trong chính sử Trung Quốc xưa*. Hội Nhà Văn., p. 257.

98. Southworth, W. A. (2001). *The origins of Campa in Central Vietnam: a preliminary review* /z-wcorg/. http://catalog.hathitrust.org/api/volumes/oclc/57480138.html, p. 301, footnote 6, and p. 255.

99. It is a reasonable approximation given the method employed over 1,600 years ago to make the measurements. The actual latitude of Ba Đồn Town People's Committee building provided by Google Maps is 17°45'11.4"N 106°25'26.1"E. The 17°40' 00"N location is around 10 kilometres south of this building in a straight line. The centre of Cao Lao Hạ is located at 17°42'45.2"N 106°25'11.0"E, or around 4.6 kilometres south of the same building in a straight line.

100. TKCS, Vol. 1, p. 361.

101. Aurousseau, L. (1914). Georges Maspero: Le Royaume de Champa. *Bulletin de l'Ecole française d'Extrême-Orient*, 8-43. https://www.persee.fr/doc/befeo_0336-1519_1914_num_14_1_285., p. 31.

102. Tana, L. (2019). The changing landscape of the former Linyi in the provinces of Quảng Trị and Thừa Thiên -Huế. In *Yusof Ishak Institute Nalanda-Sriwijaya Centre working paper series* (pp. 1-16). Yusof Ishak Institute Nalanda-Sriwijaya Centre., p. 7. Tana suggests Khu Túc (Qu Su) is romanised erroneously, it should have read Oli of the original Ulik, and that Oli could be by the Ô Lâu river where a cluster of Cham citadels and Nguyễn lords' capitals were found.

103. Quốc Sử Quán Triều Nguyễn, Viện Khoa Học Xã Hội Việt Nam, & Viện Sử Học. (2006). *Đại Nam Nhất Thống Chí* (T. Đ. Phạm & D. A. Đào, Trans.). NXB Thuận Hóa., Volume 1, p. 85, p. 194.

104. Lâm, T. M. D. (2018). *Sa Huỳnh - Lâm Ấp - Chămpa: Thế kỷ 5 trước công nguyên đến thế kỷ 5 sau công nguyên (một số vấn đề khảo cổ học) = Sa Huynh - Linyi - Champa: 5th century BC - 5th century AD: some archaeological issues*. NXB Thế Giới., p. 212.

105. Lê, Đ. P. (2018). *Khảo cổ học Champa : khai quật và phát hiện = Champa archeology : excavations and discoveries*. NXB Khoa Học Xã Hội., p. 450.

106. 26mx21m on the east wall, 25mx15m on the south wall, and 37mx36m on the southeast corner.

107. Nguyễn, V. Q. (2016). Nhận thức mới về Thành Lồi (Thừa Thiên- Huế) qua kết quả điều tra khảo cổ học. *Tạp chí Nghiên cứu và Phát triển*, *4 (130)*, 57-69., p. 63.

108. Lê, Đ. P. (2018). *Khảo cổ học Champa : khai quật và phát hiện = Champa archeology : excavations and discoveries*. NXB Khoa Học Xã Hội., p. 446-449.

109. Following the tracing shown in Figure 22, the west rampart measures 560 m, the east rampart 600 m, including the dog leg, and the north rampart 850 metres, to produce a perimeter of around 2.5 kilometres.

110. The slab dimensions are 60x23x22 cm, 70x20x22 cm, 56x52x22 cm (LxWxD) as per Nguyễn, V. Q. (2016). Nhận thức mới về Thành Lồi (Thừa Thiên- Huế) qua kết quả điều tra khảo cổ học. *Tạp chí Nghiên cứu và Phát triển*, *4 (130)*, 57-69.

111. Lâm, T. M. D. (2018). *Sa Huỳnh - Lâm Ấp - Chămpa: Thế kỷ 5 trước công nguyên đến thế kỷ 5 sau công nguyên (một số vấn đề khảo cổ học) = Sa Huynh - Linyi - Champa: 5th century BC - 5th century AD: some archaeological issues*. NXB Thế Giới., p. 308.

112. Ibid., p. 207.

113. Photo by Nguyễn, Phạm Phúc Nhân on 8 August 2021 at 16°26'46.0"N 107°33'25.6"E (16.446122, 107.557118).

114. Photo by Nguyễn, Phạm Phúc Nhân on 8 August 2021 at 16°26'57.6"N 107°33'02.4"E (16.449333, 107.550659).

CHAPTER 5

1. Taylor, K. W. (1983). *The Birth of Vietnam*. Berkeley: University of California Press., p. 108. I am unable to locate the original reference for this version.

2. TKCS Vol. 36, p. 367.

3. Châu, H. Đ. (2018). *An Nam Truyện - Ghi chép về Việt Nam trong chính sử Trung Quốc xưa*. Hội Nhà Văn., p. 264. See also Liang shu, Volume 54. In TKCS, a slightly different story is told, whereby it was Yang Ping, the governor of Giao Châu and not Guan Cui (Quán Thúy), who commanded the attack. No citadel was mentioned, but Jin forces faced a stone wall of 50 *li* (22.5 kilometres) long and defeated Phật with soldiers *"as many as ants"*, see TKCS Vol. 36, p. 367.

4. TKCS Vol. 36, p. 367.

5. TKCS Vol. 36, p. 367, see also ANCL, p. 182. Other works cite 50 stone walls (SKTT, Vol.1, p. 172; CM, Vol.1, p. 153).

6. TKCS, pp. 383-384. See also Taylor, K. W. (1983). *The Birth of Vietnam*. Berkeley: University of California Press., p. 108.

7. TKCS, Vol. 36, p. 375.

8. Southworth, W. A. (2001). *The origins of Campa in Central Vietnam: a preliminary review* /z-wcorg/. http://catalog.hathitrust.org/api/volumes/oclc/57480138.html, p. 299.

9. Châu, H. Đ. (2018). *An Nam Truyện - Ghi chép về Việt Nam trong chính sử Trung Quốc xưa*. Hội Nhà Văn., p. 265. See also Liang shu, Volume 54.

10. Around modern Hải Dương province, see Đào, D. A. (2005). *Đất nước Việt Nam qua các đời - Nghiên cứu địa lý học lịch sử Việt Nam*. NXB Văn Hóa Thông Tin., p. 87.

11. Châu, H. Đ. (2018). *An Nam Truyện - Ghi chép về Việt Nam trong chính sử Trung Quốc xưa*. Hội Nhà Văn., p. 207. See also Song shu, Volume 92: Yue, S. (492-493). *Book of Song (Song shu)-Volume 92 Biographies 52: Liang Li* http://chinesenotes.com/songshu/songshu092.html

12. Đào, D. A. (2005). *Đất nước Việt Nam qua các đời - Nghiên cứu địa lý học lịch sử Việt Nam*. NXB Văn Hóa Thông Tin., pp. 73-74.

13. Châu, H. Đ. (2018). *An Nam Truyện - Ghi chép về Việt Nam trong chính sử Trung Quốc xưa*. Hội Nhà Văn., p. 265. See also the Liang shu, Volume 54.

14. Ibid., p. 208. See also Song shu, Volume 92.

15. Kapok is a tree cultivated for its fibre and used for blanket or pillow filling. In this context, Kapok is the fibre filling, not the tree.

16. Châu, H. Đ. (2018). *An Nam Truyện - Ghi chép về Việt Nam trong chính sử Trung Quốc xưa*. Hội Nhà Văn., p. 265. See also Liang shu, Volume 54.

17. Southworth, W. A. (2001). *The origins of Campa in Central Vietnam: a preliminary review* /z-wcorg/. http://catalog.hathitrust.org/api/volumes/oclc/57480138.html, p. 300.

18. TKCS, Vol. 36, p. 385.

19. In TKCS, p. 385, it appears Dương Mại II became king at the death of Dương Mại I after the destruction of the Linyi capital in 446 but in the Nan Qi shu, Vol. 58, Biography 39, Dương Mại I died much earlier, and it was Dương Mại II that fought against Tan Hezhi. See Châu, H. Đ. (2018). *An Nam Truyện - Ghi chép về Việt Nam trong chính sử Trung Quốc xưa*. Hội Nhà Văn., p. 255. See also the Book of Southern Qi, Volume 58: Xiao Zixian. (537). *Book of Southern Qi - Qi Shu*. http://chinesenotes.com/nanqishu.html, Volume 58 Biographies 39: Other Peoples from the Southeast, http://chinesenotes.com/nanqishu/nanqishu058.html.

20. 430, 433, 435, 438, 441 CE see Châu, H. Đ. (2018). *An Nam Truyện - Ghi chép về Việt Nam trong chính sử Trung Quốc xưa*. Hội Nhà Văn., p. 251 and Yue, S. (492-493). *Book of Song (Song shu)*. http://chinesenotes.com/songshu.html, Volume 97 Biographies 57: Yi Man, http://chinesenotes.com/songshu/songshu097.html

21. Đỗ Hoàng Văn was a former governor of Cửu Chân, also a Marquis of Long Biên, with oversight of over 1,000 households, a title that his father held before his death.

22. Châu, H. Đ. (2018). *An Nam Truyện - Ghi chép về Việt Nam trong chính sử Trung Quốc xưa*. Hội Nhà Văn., p. 209. See also Song shu, Volume 92 and CM, Vol.1, p.158.

23. TKCS, Vol. 36, p. 375 and ibid., p. 251. See also Song shu, Volume 97: Yue, S. (492-493). *Book of Song (Song shu)*. http://chinesenotes.com/songshu.html, Volume 97 Biographies 57: Yi Man, http://chinesenotes.com/songshu/songshu097.html.

24. As per Appendix 12, the raid was at Cửu Đức, in today's Hà Tĩnh, Nghệ An, so this river inlet is likely the Hạ Vang river. In CM, Vol. 1, p. 159, the raid took place at Cửu Chân, which at this time, is by Thanh Hóa province further north. Since Cửu Đức is recorded in earlier texts, I have used Cửu Đức.

25. TKCS, Vol. 36, p. 375.

26. TKCS, Vol. 36, p. 371.

27. Châu, H. Đ. (2018). *An Nam Truyện - Ghi chép về Việt Nam trong chính sử Trung Quốc xưa*. Hội Nhà Văn., p. 251. See also Song shu, Volume 97.

28. Yanzhou is in present-day Shandong province.

29. Hồ (or Hu), in this context, refers to the people of Linyi and not southern or central Asia such as Sogdians and Indians (Chapter 3).

30. CM, Vol. 1, p. 161.

31. The Liu Song dynasty (420-479) did not last very long, barely 60 years and Emperor Wen's reign, at thirty years (424-453), is the longest and the most prosperous.

32. Yue, S. (492-493). *Book of Song (Song shu) - Volume 76 Biographies 36: Zhu Xiuzhi, Zong Que, Wang Xuanmo*. http://chinesenotes.com/songshu/songshu076.html

33. In Vietnamese *"Chấn Võ (Vũ) Tướng Quân"*

34. In CM, Vol. 1, p. 160, Zong Que led the front-line troops.

35. Châu, H. Đ. (2018). *An Nam Truyện - Ghi chép về Việt Nam trong chính sử Trung Quốc xưa*. Hội Nhà Văn., p. 255. See also the Nan Qi shu, Volume 58. In this reference, Duong Mai II also offered to return the territories of Nhật Nam that Linyi had occupied.

36. See (8 June 2022) https://www.monex.com/gold-prices/

37. *Gold Reserves*. https://tradingeconomics.com/country-list/gold-reserves

38. The delegation included Khương Trọng Cơ (Governor), Kiều Hoàng Dân, Tất Nguyện, Cao Tinh Nô. Kiều Hoàng Dân was released, the others were retained, and what became of them was not recorded.

39. TKCS, Vol. 36, p. 362. The wall was 2 *zhang* tall, 1 *zhang* = 2.5 m (Appendix 15).

40. TKCS, Vol. 36, p. 365.

41. A reference to a Hindu temple or shrine. See Southworth, W. A. (2001). *The origins of Campa in Central Vietnam: a preliminary review* /z-wcorg/. http://catalog.hathitrust.org/api/volumes/oclc/57480138.html, p. 302.

42. TKCS, Vol. 36, p. 376.

43. *"mấy chục vạn"* means several *vạn* (1 vạn = 10,000)

44. CM, Vol. 1, p. 161. Also TKCS, Vol. 36, p. 385.

45. TKCS, Vol. 36, p. 383.

46. TKCS, Vol. 36, p. 384.

47. Trà Kiệu means a place where the Champa people used to live but is now occupied by new settlers (Trà comes from Chùm Chà or Champa people), and Kiệu comes from Kiều, referring to "overseas" people, in this case, newcomers from the north who settled there in 1628. See *Đức Mẹ Trà Kiệu*. (2019). https://vi.wikipedia.org/wiki/%C4%90%E1%BB%A9c_M%E1%BA%B9_Tr%C3%A0_Ki%E1%BB%87u

48. The current building of the shrine was built in 1971.

49. Based on a map in, Giang, Đ., Tomomi, S., Văn Quảng, N., & Mariko, Y. (2020). Champa Citadels: An Archaeological and Historical Study., p. 72.

50. Ibid., p. 71.

51. Ibid., p. 72.

52. From https://www.britannica.com/ *Apsara, Indian religion and mythology*. https://www.britannica.com/topic/apsara, *In Indian religion and mythology, one of the celestial singers and dancers who, together with the gandharvas, or celestial musicians, inhabit the heaven of the god Indra, the lord of the heavens. Originally water nymphs, the apsaras provide sensual pleasure for both gods and men. They have been beautifully depicted in sculpture and painting in India and throughout areas of South and Southeast Asia influenced by Hinduism and Buddhism.*

53. Photo by Jean-Pierre Dalbéra from Paris France / CC BY (https://creativecommons.org/licenses/by/2.0). (31 January 2010). *Les Apsaras Style de Tra Kieu Xè siècle Grès*. https://upload.wikimedia.org/wikipedia/commons/2/2b/Apsaras_%28mus%C3%A9e_Cham%2C_Da_Nang%29_%284394717693%29.jpg.

54. Cropped photo from one taken by Daderot / CC0. (7 August 2014). *Dancer, Tra Kieu, Quang Nam, 10th century AD, sandstone - Museum of Vietnamese History - Ho Chi Minh City*. https://commons.wikimedia.org/wiki/File:Dancer,_Tra_Kieu,_Quang_Nam,_10th_century_AD,_sandstone_-_Museum_of_Vietnamese_History_-_Ho_Chi_Minh_City_-_DSC06144.JPG.

55. Lâm, T. M. D. (2018). *Sa Huỳnh - Lâm Ấp - Chămpa: Thế kỷ 5 trước công nguyên đến thế kỷ 5 sau công nguyên (một số vấn đề khảo cổ học) = Sa Huynh - Linyi - Champa: 5th century BC - 5th century AD: some archaeological issues*. NXB Thế Giới., p. 258.

56. Giang, Đ., Tomomi, S., Văn Quảng, N., & Mariko, Y. (2020). Champa Citadels: An Archaeological and Historical Study., p. 74.

57. Ibid., p. 79.

58. Ma Duanlin (Ma-Touan-Lin), & Le Marquis d'Hervey de Saint-Senys - de l'Institut de France. (Jan 1883). *Ethnographie des peuples étrangers à la Chine: ouvrage composé au XIIIe siècle de notre ère, Méridionaux, Volume 2*. Geneve, H. Georg. - TH. Muller. https://play.google.com/store/books/details/Duanlin_Ma_Ethnographie_des_peuples_%C3%A9trangers_%C3%A0_la?id=4F0LAAAAIAA., p. 420, p. 422

59. A similar description can be found in TKCS, Vol. 36, p. 364, and Châu, H. Đ. (2018). *An Nam Truyện - Ghi chép về Việt Nam trong chính sử Trung Quốc xưa*. Hội Nhà Văn., p. 247. See also Jin shu, Volume 97.

60. *"Kan-lan"* is a term used in the dwellings built by the ancient indigenous people of southern China, see footnote 22 of Ma Duanlin (Ma-Touan-Lin), & Le Marquis d'Hervey de Saint-Senys - de l'Institut de France. (Jan 1883). *Ethnographie des peuples étrangers à la Chine: ouvrage composé au XIIIe siècle de*

notre ère, Méridionaux, Volume 2. Geneve, H. Georg. - TH. Muller. https://play.google.com/store/books/details/Duanlin_Ma_Ethnographie_des_peuples_%C3%A9trangers_%C3%A0_la?id=-4F0LAAAAIAAJ

61. Du You. (766-801). *Tongdian - Volume 188: Border defence four Southern barbarians*. https://zh.wikisource.org/zh-hant/%E9%80%9A%E5%85%B8/%E5%8D%B7188

62. Bồng Miêu goldmine is at Tam Lãnh commune, Phú Ninh district, Quảng Nam province. Phước Sơn gold mine is at Phước Sơn district, Quảng Nam province.

63. Hà, S. (2019). Tỉnh nào có nhiều vàng nhất nước ta? https://zingnews.vn/tinh-nao-co-nhieu-vang-nhat-nuoc-ta-post965839.html

64. *Active Gold Mines in Vietnam's Jungle*. (2015). https://raregoldnuggets.com/?p=1968.

65. Scientific names are Aquilaria crassna, Pierre ex Lecomte, Thymelaeaceae

66. Vietnamese *Trầm Hương*, see Ma Duanlin (Ma-Touan-Lin), & Le Marquis d'Hervey de Saint-Senys - de l'Institut de France. (Jan 1883). *Ethnographie des peuples étrangers à la Chine: ouvrage composé au XIIIe siècle de notre ère, Méridionaux, Volume 2*. Geneve, H. Georg. - TH. Muller. https://play.google.com/store/books/details/Duanlin_Ma_Ethnographie_des_peuples_%C3%A9trangers_%C3%A0_la?id=4F0LAAAAIAA., p. 421.

67. Quách, T. (2002). *Xứ Trầm Hương*. Hội Văn Học Nghệ Thuật Khánh Hòa., p. 339.

68. Vietnamese *Xứ Trầm Hương*

69. Tana, L. (2019). The changing landscape of the former Linyi in the provinces of Quảng Trị and Thừa Thiên -Huế. In *Yusof Ishak Institute Nalanda-Sriwijaya Centre working paper series* (pp. 1-16). Yusof Ishak Institute Nalanda-Sriwijaya Centre., p. 3.

70. Lapont, P. B., Poklaun, H., & Council for the Social-Cultural Development of, C. (2011). *Vương quốc Champa-Địa dư, Dân cư và Lịch sử*., p. 112.

CHAPTER 6

1. Châu, H. Đ. (2018). *An Nam Truyện - Ghi chép về Việt Nam trong chính sử Trung Quốc xưa*. Hội Nhà Văn., p. 274. See also the Book of Sui, Volume 82: Wei Zheng, Shigu, Y., Yingda, K., & Wuji, Z. (636). *Book of Sui* http://chinesenotes.com/suishu.html, Volume 82 Biographies 47: The Nanman. http://chinesenotes.com/suishu/suishu082.html.

2. Châu, H. Đ. (2018). *An Nam Truyện - Ghi chép về Việt Nam trong chính sử Trung Quốc xưa*. Hội Nhà Văn., p. 216. See also the Book of Sui, Volume 53: Wei Zheng, Shigu, Y., Yingda, K., & Wuji, Z. (636). *Book of Sui* http://chinesenotes.com/suishu.html, Volume 53 Biographies 18: Daxi Zhangru, Helou Zigan, Shi Wansui, Liu Fang, http://chinesenotes.com/suishu/suishu053.html.

3. Châu, H. Đ. (2018). *An Nam Truyện - Ghi chép về Việt Nam trong chính sử Trung Quốc xưa*. Hội Nhà Văn., p. 275. See also the Book of Sui, Volume 82.

4. Southworth, W. A. (2001). *The origins of Campa in Central Vietnam: a preliminary review* /z-wcorg/. http://catalog.hathitrust.org/api/volumes/oclc/57480138.html, p. 312.

5. Majumdar, R. C. (1927). *Ancient Indian colonies in the Far East. Vol. I, Champa / by R.C. Majumdar*. Punjab Sanskrit Book Depot., p. 38.

6. National Organization for Rare Disorders. (2009). *Elephantiasis*. https://rarediseases.org/rare-diseases/elephantiasis/

7. Goguryeo is the name of a Korean kingdom that once occupied the northern and central parts of the Korean Peninsula plus the southern and central parts of Manchuria.

8. Wei Zheng, Shigu, Y., Yingda, K., & Wuji, Z. (636). *Book of Sui* http://chinesenotes.com/suishu.html, Volume 31 Treatises 26: Geography 3. http://chinesenotes.com/suishu/suishu031.html#?highlight=%E6%9E%97%E9%82%91 1

9. Trần, B. Đ., Mạc, Đ., Tô, B. G., Phan, V. H., Lê, V. N., Nguyễn, N., & Tôn, N. Q. T. (2005). *Lịch Sử Việt Nam (Từ Đầu Đến Năm 938) - Tập 2* (V. G. Trần, B. Đ. Trần, & Đ. Mạc, Eds.). NXB Trẻ., p. 252.

10. Đào, D. A. (2005). *Đất nước Việt Nam qua các đời - Nghiên cứu địa lý học lịch sử Việt Nam*. NXB Văn Hóa Thông Tin., p. 90.

11. Châu, H. Đ. (2018). *An Nam Truyện - Ghi chép về Việt Nam trong chính sử Trung Quốc xưa*. Hội Nhà Văn., p. 278. See also Jiu Tang shu, Volume 197: Zhao Ying, Liu Xu, Zhang Zhao, Jia Wei, & Zhao Xi. (941-945). *Old Book of Tang (Jiu Tang shu)*. https://ctext.org/wiki.pl?if=gb&res=456206, Volume 197 Biographies 147: Southern Man, Southwest Man, http://chinesenotes.com/jiutangshu/jiutangshu209.html.

12. Xiu, O., Qi, S., & Fan, Z. (1060). *New Book of Tang (Xin Tang shu) - Volume 222c Biographies 147c: Southern Man 3*. http://chinesenotes.com/xintangshu/xintangshu222c.html

13. Châu, H. Đ. (2018). *An Nam Truyện - Ghi chép về Việt Nam trong chính sử Trung Quốc xưa*. Hội Nhà Văn., p. 279. See also Jiu Tang shu, Volume 197.

14. In Listes dynastiques. (1915). *Bulletin de l'Ecole française d'Extrême-Orient*, 181-184. https://www.persee.fr/doc/befeo_0336-1519_1915_num_15_1_5479, Kandarpadharma's reign is shown to last one year from 630 to 631. However, as his son ascended the throne in 640, I would suggest that 640, as recorded by Majumdar, is more likely.

15. Châu, H. Đ. (2018). *An Nam Truyện - Ghi chép về Việt Nam trong chính sử Trung Quốc xưa*. Hội Nhà Văn., p. 279. See also Jiu Tang shu, Volume 197.

16. Mahamanduka is based on Goble, G. (May 2014). Maritime Southeast Asia: The view from Tang–Song China *Nalanda-Sriwijaya Centre Working Paper No 16*. http://www.iseas.edu.sg/nsc/documents/working_papers/nscwps016.pd., p. 16. However, Majumdar suggests Mahamantradhikrta, see Majumdar, R. C. (1927). *Ancient Indian colonies in the Far East. Vol. I, Champa / by R.C. Majumdar*. Punjab Sanskrit Book Depot., p. 40.

17. Châu, H. Đ. (2018). *An Nam Truyện - Ghi chép về Việt Nam trong chính sử Trung Quốc xưa*. Hội Nhà Văn., p. 279. See also Jiu Tang shu, Volume 197.

18. Xiu, O., Qi, S., & Fan, Z. (1060). *New Book of Tang (Xin Tang shu) - Volume 222c Biographies 147c: Southern Man 3*. http://chinesenotes.com/xintangshu/xintangshu222c.html

19. Goble, G. (May 2014). Maritime Southeast Asia: The view from Tang–Song China *Nalanda-Sriwijaya Centre Working Paper No 16*. http://www.iseas.edu.sg/nsc/documents/working_papers/nscwps016.pd., p. 11.

20. In 657, 669, 670, 686, 691, 695, 699, 702, 703, 706, 707, 709, 711, 712 and 713. Wang Pu. (961). *Tang huiyao, "Institutional history of the Tang dynasty"*. http://www.chinaknowledge.de/Literature/Historiography/tanghuiyao.html.

21. *"Tang Hui Yao" Volume Ninety-eight. Foreign countries: Uyghurs, Xicuan, Mikun, Linyi, Zhenla, Baigou Qiang, Caoguo, Shuna, Bayegu, Xi, Tanguts*. http://guoxue.httpcn.com/html/book/CQAZUYRN/UYPWUYKOUY.shtml.

22. Maspero, G. (1928). *Le royaume de Champa* (G. Vanoest, Ed.). Librairie Nationale d'Art et d'Histoire., pp. 523-525.

23. Châu, H. Đ. (2018). *An Nam Truyện - Ghi chép về Việt Nam trong chính sử Trung Quốc xưa*. Hội Nhà Văn., p. 283. See also Xin Tang shu, Volume 222c: Xiu, O., Qi, S., & Fan, Z. (1060). *New Book of Tang (Xin Tang shu) - Volume 222c Biographies 147c: Southern Man 3*. http://chinesenotes.com/xintangshu/xintangshu222c.html.

24. Quốc Sử Quán Triều Nguyễn, Viện Khoa Học Xã Hội Việt Nam, & Viện Sử Học. (2006). *Đại Nam Nhất Thống Chí* (T. Đ. Phạm & D. A. Đào, Trans.). NXB Thuận Hóa., Vol. 2, Book 7, p. 430.

CHAPTER 7

1. Southworth, W. A. (2001). *The origins of Campa in Central Vietnam: a preliminary review* /z-wcorg/. http://catalog.hathitrust.org/api/volumes/oclc/57480138.html, p. 361.

2. Ibid., pp. 241-242.

3. *Varman* in Sanskrit means "shield" but could also be derived from the Tamil word *Varamban* as in the royal title "*Vaava Varamban*", Wikipedia. *Varman (surname)*. https://en.wikipedia.org/wiki/Varman_(surname).

4. Ngô, A. (2011). *Võ Cạnh - bia sớm nhất của vương quốc Chăm Pa* http://baotanglichsu.vn/vi/Articles/2001/65904/vo-canh-bia-som-nhat-cua-vuong-quoc-cham-pa.html.

5. Filliozat, J. (1969). VI. L'inscription dite "de Vo-çanh". *Bulletin de l'Ecole française d'Extrême-Orient*, 107-116. https://www.persee.fr/doc/befeo_0336-1519_1969_num_55_1_485., p. 116.

6. Ibid., p. 116.

7. Southworth, W. A. (2001). *The origins of Campa in Central Vietnam: a preliminary review* /z-wcorg/. http://catalog.hathitrust.org/api/volumes/oclc/57480138.html, p. 205, p. 420.

8. Around 2.5 m tall, 72 cm wide and 67 cm deep. Hoangkid. (2020). *Vo Canh Stele (the original stele at National Museum of Vietnamese History in Hanoi) - a National Treasure of Vietnam*. https://upload.wikimedia.org/wikipedia/commons/f/f7/Vo_Canh_stele_%28National_Museum_of_Vietnamese_History%29.jpg, photo quotes 320x110x80 (HxWxD in centimetres).

9. Filliozat, J. (1969). VI. L'inscription dite "de Vo-çanh". *Bulletin de l'Ecole française d'Extrême-Orient*, 107-116. https://www.persee.fr/doc/befeo_0336-1519_1969_num_55_1_485., pp. 113-114.

10. Hardy, A. D. C. M. Z. P. (2012). *Champa and the archaeology of My Son (Vietnam)*. NUS Press., p. 3.

11. Kieu, O. L. o. T. https://vietnamcatholictours.vn/destination/our-lady-of-tra-kieu-2/

12. Hardy, A. D. C. M. Z. P. (2012). *Champa and the archaeology of My Son (Vietnam)*. NUS Press., p. 199.

13. Ibid., p. 17.

14. Ibid., p. 198.

15. Ibid., p. 3.

16. Lê, Đ. P. (2019). *Mỹ Sơn - Vùng đất thiêng vương quốc cổ Champa* Nhà Xuất Bản Khoa Học Xã Hội., pp. 63-64.

17. Trần, K. P. (2009). The Architecture of the Temple-Towers of Ancient Champa (Central Vietnam) - Chapter 6. In A. C. M. Z. P. Hardy (Ed.), *Champa and the archaeology of Mỹ Sơn (Vietnam)*. NUS Press., p. 181.

18. Finot, L. (1902). Notes d'épigraphie. *Bulletin de l'Ecole française d'Extrême-Orient*, 185-191. https://www.persee.fr/doc/befeo_0336-1519_1902_num_2_1_111., p. 187.

19. Ngô, V. D. (2004). *Thánh địa Mỹ Sơn* (2 ed.). NXB Trẻ., p. 121.

20. Hardy, A. D. C. M. Z. P. (2012). *Champa and the archaeology of My Son (Vietnam)*. NUS Press., pp. 199-201.

21. Smith, C. R. U. S. M. C. H., & Museums, D. (1988). *U.S. Marines in Vietnam: high mobility and stand down, 1969.*, p. 86, p. 184. There were 10 military operations by the US-South Vietnamese forces in 1969 in Quảng Nam province in Jan/Feb (Linn River), Feb/June (Quảng Nam), March (Cane Field), March/May (Oklahoma Hills), April (Muskogee Meadows), April/May (Bristol Boots), May/November (Pipestone Canyon), June/July (Forsyth Grove), July 12/Aug 15 (Campbell Steamer), July 20/Aug 13 (Durham Peak). Operation Durham Peak was the tenth operation and involved a large number of US Marines as well as the ARVN Rangers. This was likely the operation when Mỹ Sơn was bombed because of its size and location. See *List of allied military operations of the Vietnam War (1969)*. https://en.wikipedia.org/wiki/List_of_allied_military_operations_of_the_Vietnam_War_(1969).

22. Coedès, G., Cowing, S. B., Vella, W. F., & Press, A. N. U. (1968). The Indianized States of Southeast Asia. http://hdl.handle.net/1885/11518., p. 19.

23. *The Trimurti*. https://iskconeducationalservices.org/HoH/practice/worship/the-trimurti/.

24. *Nature of God and existence in Hinduism*. (2022). https://www.bbc.co.uk/bitesize/guides/z44bcj6/revision/3#:~:text=Three%20of%20the%20most%20significant,and%20Shiva%20is%20the%20destroyer.

25. Majumdar, R. C. (1927). *Ancient Indian colonies in the Far East. Vol. I, Champa / by R.C. Majumdar*. Punjab Sanskrit Book Depot., Book I, p. 180.

26. Thakur, U. (1986). *Some aspects of Asian history and culture*. Abhinav publications., p. 86.

27. Majumdar, R. C. (1927). *Ancient Indian colonies in the Far East. Vol. I, Champa / by R.C. Majumdar*. Punjab Sanskrit Book Depot., Book III, pp. 6-8.

28. *Quang Nam Province*. https://en-us.topographic-map.com/maps/9dda/Quang-Nam-Province/

29. Finot, L. (1904). Notes d'épigraphie : XI. Les inscriptions de Mi-Sơn. *Bulletin de l'Ecole française d'Extrême-Orient*, 897-977. https://www.persee.fr/doc/befeo_0336-1519_1904_num_4_1_140., pp. 918-925.

30. Majumdar, R. C. (1927). *Ancient Indian colonies in the Far East. Vol. I, Champa / by R.C. Majumdar*. Punjab Sanskrit Book Depot., Book III, pp. 16-26.

31. C.72 (Mỹ Sơn A1), C. 73A (Mỹ Sơn A1), C. 81 (Mỹ Sơn B1) and C.137 (Trà Kiệu).

32. Photo courtesy of Timothy M. Ciccone, www.orientalarchitecture.com.

33. Majumdar, R. C. (1927). *Ancient Indian colonies in the Far East. Vol. I, Champa / by R.C. Majumdar*. Punjab Sanskrit Book Depot., Book I, p36.

34. Ibid., Book III, The Inscription of Champa, p. 22 (or p. 412 of pdf).

35. Southworth, W. A. (2001). *The origins of Campa in Central Vietnam: a preliminary review* /z-wcorg/. http://catalog.hathitrust.org/api/volumes/oclc/57480138.html, Table 5, p. 422 also p. 314.

36. Phúc Kiến is Vietnamese for Fukien or Fujian, a province north of Guangdong.

37. Translated from French translation by Huber, E. (1911). Études indochinoises. *Bulletin de l'Ecole française d'Extrême-Orient*, 259-311. https://www.persee.fr/doc/befeo_0336-1519_1911_num_11_1_269., p. 260.

38. Cadiere explains the blocks served as a step to an Annamese pagoda, see Cadière, L. (1905). Monuments et souvenirs chams du Quảng-tri et du Thừa-thiên. Ibid., 185-195. https://www.persee.fr/doc/befeo_0336-1519_1905_num_5_1_263., p. 193.

39. Southworth, W. A. (2001). *The origins of Campa in Central Vietnam: a preliminary review* /z-wcorg/. http://catalog.hathitrust.org/api/volumes/oclc/57480138.html, Table 5, p. 422, p. 425.

40. This figure was originally published in the Bulletin de l'École française d'Extrême-Orient, Tome 11, 1911, p. 259. Reproduced with permission from BEFEO. See Huber, E. (1911). Études indochinoises. *Bulletin de l'Ecole française d'Extrême-Orient*, 259-311. https://www.persee.fr/doc/befeo_0336-1519_1911_num_11_1_2693 .

41. The UNESCO World Heritage sites in Vietnam are Complex of Huế Monuments, Ha Long Bay, Hoi An Ancient Town, My Son Sanctuary, Phong Nha-Ke Bang National Park, Central Sector of Imperial Citadel of Thang Long – Hanoi, Citadel of the Ho Dynasty, Trang An Landscape Complex. See *World Heritage List*. https://whc.unesco.org/en/list/&order=country#alphaM.

42. Majumdar, R. C. (1927). *Ancient Indian colonies in the Far East. Vol. I, Champa / by R.C. Majumdar*. Punjab Sanskrit Book Depot., Book I, p. 27.

43. Ngô, V. D. (2004). *Thánh địa Mỹ Sơn* (2 ed.). NXB Trẻ., p. 43.

44. Southworth, W. A. (2004). The coastal states of Champa. In B. P. IGlover I (Ed.), *Southeast Asia: from prehistory to history*. (pp. 209-233). Routledge Curzon., p. 222.

45. Schweyer, A.-V. (2019). *The Birth of Champa*., p. 9.

46. Finot, L. (1902). Notes d'épigraphie. *Bulletin de l'Ecole française d'Extrême-Orient*, 185-191. https://www.persee.fr/doc/befeo_0336-1519_1902_num_2_1_111., p. 186.

47. Chợ Dinh (or Dinh market) is by the Đà Rằng river, east of Champa's Nhạn tower (Tháp Nhạn) and the intersection of Dinh and Đà Rằng rivers, Tuy Hoà, Phú Yên, see Nguyễn, Đ. C. (2005). *Cầu Sông Dinh – chợ Dinh*. http://www.baophuyen.com.vn/120/729/cau-song-dinh-%E2%80%93-cho-dinh.html.

48. Majumdar, R. C. (1927). *Ancient Indian colonies in the Far East. Vol. I, Champa / by R.C. Majumdar*. Punjab Sanskrit Book Depot., Book III, The Inscription of Champa, p. 4 (or p. 394 of pdf).

49. Finot, L. (1902). Notes d'épigraphie. *Bulletin de l'Ecole française d'Extrême-Orient*, 185-191. https://www.persee.fr/doc/befeo_0336-1519_1902_num_2_1_111., pp. 185-186.

50. Basak, B. (2012). *Understanding the Champa polity from archaeological and epigraphic evidence - a critical stocktaking* European Association of Southeast Asian archaeology, 14 (EurASEAA 14), Dublin, Ireland., p. 72.

51. TKCS, Vol. 36, p. 383.

52. Finot, L. (1902). Notes d'épigraphie. *Bulletin de l'Ecole française d'Extrême-Orient*, 185-191. https://www.persee.fr/doc/befeo_0336-1519_1902_num_2_1_111., pp. 186-187. Finot locates it at the village of Chimson, Duy Xuyên district, Quảng Nam province, around 28 kilometres S-S-W of Đà Nẵng. Today, there is a Chiêm Sơn village at Duy Trinh commune, Duy Xuyên district but the exact location of Hòn Cục is not known, see Antontruongthang's Blog. (2015). *Văn Khắc Champa: Hòn... Cup, Chiêm Sơn*. https://antontruongthang.wordpress.com/a-da-nang-may-2015/van-khac-champa-honcup-chiem-son/

53. Translated from French by Finot, L. (1902). Notes d'épigraphie. *Bulletin de l'Ecole française d'Extrême-Orient*, 185-191. https://www.persee.fr/doc/befeo_0336-1519_1902_num_2_1_111., p. 187.

54. Majumdar, R. C. (1927). *Ancient Indian colonies in the Far East. Vol. I, Champa / by R.C. Majumdar*. Punjab Sanskrit Book Depot., Book III, p. 21.

55. Southworth, W. A. (2001). *The origins of Campa in Central Vietnam: a preliminary review* /z-wcorg/. http://catalog.hathitrust.org/api/volumes/oclc/57480138.html, p. 304.

56. Majumdar, R. C. (1927). *Ancient Indian colonies in the Far East. Vol. I, Champa / by R.C. Majumdar*. Punjab Sanskrit Book Depot., Book I, p. 42.

57. Maspero, G. (1928). *Le royaume de Champa* (G. Vanoest, Ed.). Librairie Nationale d'Art et d'Histoire., p. 90.

58. Schweyer, A.-V. (2019). *The Birth of Champa.*, p. 12.

59. Vickery, M. (2000). Coedès' Histories of Cambodia. *Silpakorn University International Journal (Bangkok), 1, Number 1*(January-June 2000), 61-108., p. 11.

60. Southworth, W. A. (2001). *The origins of Campa in Central Vietnam: a preliminary review* /z-wcorg/. http://catalog.hathitrust.org/api/volumes/oclc/57480138.html, p. 308.

61. Pelliot refers to him as Lieou-t'o-pa-mo in BEFEO Chinese or Liu-tuo-ba-mo in Pinyin Chinese, see Pelliot, P. (1903). Le Fou-nan. *Bulletin de l'Ecole française d'Extrême-Orient*, 248-303. https://www.persee.fr/doc/befeo_0336-1519_1903_num_3_1_121., p. 270. Golzio also uses the same, see Golzio, K.-H. Kauṇḍinya in Southeast Asia, How a historical figure was transformed into a mythical Hero. https://www.academia.edu/6874876/Kau%E1%B9%87%E1%B8%8Dinya_in_Southeast_Asia_How_a_historical_figure_was_transformed_into_a_mythical_Hero_., p. 7 (page number not listed).

62. Southworth, W. A. (2001). *The origins of Campa in Central Vietnam: a preliminary review* /z-wcorg/. http://catalog.hathitrust.org/api/volumes/oclc/57480138.html, diagram 4, p. 331.

63. Vickery, M. (2005). Champa revised., p. 26.

64. Translation by Majumdar, R. C. (1927). *Ancient Indian colonies in the Far East. Vol. I, Champa / by R.C. Majumdar*. Punjab Sanskrit Book Depot., Book III, The Inscription of Champa, p. 21 (or p. 411 of pdf).

65. Finot, L. (1904). Notes d'épigraphie : XI. Les inscriptions de Mi-Sơn. *Bulletin de l'Ecole française d'Extrême-Orient*, 897-977. https://www.persee.fr/doc/befeo_0336-1519_1904_num_4_1_140., p. 918.

66. Translation by Majumdar, R. C. (1927). *Ancient Indian colonies in the Far East. Vol. I, Champa / by R.C. Majumdar*. Punjab Sanskrit Book Depot., Book III, The Inscription of Champa, p. 15 (or p. 405 of pdf).

67. Southworth, W. A. (2001). *The origins of Campa in Central Vietnam: a preliminary review* /z-wcorg/. http://catalog.hathitrust.org/api/volumes/oclc/57480138.html, p. 242.

68. Huber, E. (1911). Études indochinoises. *Bulletin de l'Ecole française d'Extrême-Orient*, 259-311. https://www.persee.fr/doc/befeo_0336-1519_1911_num_11_1_269., p. 261.

69. Lê, T. (2021). *Bia Chăm trên Hòn Kẽm - Đá Dừng*. https://baodanang.vn/channel/6058/201606/bia-cham-tren-hon-kem-da-dung-2490464/.

70. Goble, G. (May 2014). Maritime Southeast Asia: The view from Tang–Song China *Nalanda-Sriwijaya Centre Working Paper No 16*. http://www.iseas.edu.sg/nsc/documents/working_papers/nscwps016.pd., p. 9.

71. Daši, T., Weiyi, H., Qiyan, Z., Xuan, O., Haowen, L., Yi, W., & Zongduan, Y. (1346). *History of Song (Song Shi)*. http://chinesenotes.com/songshi.html, Volume 489 Biographies 248: Foreign States 5 - Champa, Siem Reap, Bagan, Miaoli, Srivijaya, Sheponanpi, Brunei, Chola, Nakhon Si Thammarat.

CHAPTER 8

1. Coedès, G., Cowing, S. B., Vella, W. F., & Press, A. N. U. (1968). The Indianized States of Southeast Asia. http://hdl.handle.net/1885/11518., p. 28. There are also other land routes not included here, as cited by Coedès.

2. Rivers, P. J. (2004). Monsoon rhythms and trade patterns: ancient times east of Suez. *Journal of the Malaysian Branch of the Royal Asiatic Society*, 77(2 (287)), 59-93. http://www.jstor.org/stable/4149352., p. 63, p. 68, p. 77.

3. Gungwu, W. (1958). The Nanhai Trade: A Study of the Early History of Chinese Trade in the South China Sea. *Journal of the Malayan Branch of the Royal Asiatic Society*, 31(2 (182)), 1-135. http://www.jstor.org/stable/41503138, p.6.

4. Coedès, G., Cowing, S. B., Vella, W. F., & Press, A. N. U. (1968). The Indianized States of Southeast Asia. http://hdl.handle.net/1885/11518., p. 19.

5. Jia (Chia in Wades-Giles or Kia in EFEO), Dan (Tan in Wade-Giles).

6. Pelliot, P. (1904). Deux itinéraires de Chine en Inde à la fin du VIIIe siècle. *Bulletin de l'Ecole française d'Extrême-Orient*, 131-413. https://www.persee.fr/doc/befeo_0336-1519_1904_num_4_1_129., p. 217.

7. Filliozat, J. (1971). Louis Malleret (1901-1970) [note biographique]. Ibid., 58, 1971, 4-15. https://www.persee.fr/doc/befeo_0336-1519_1971_num_58_1_5073, also Tingley, N., with essays by Andreas Reinecke, Pierre-Yves Manguin, Kerry Nguyen-Long, & Nguyen Dinh Chien. (2009). *Arts of Ancient Viet Nam: From River Plain to Open Sea*. Asia Society; The Museum of Fine Arts; Yale University Press [distr.]., pp. 105-106. Malleret was not a trained archaeologist.

8. Cropped photo of an original taken by Bùi Thụy Đào Nguyên CC BY-SA 3.0. (29 November 2013). *Trên đường Gò Cây Thị nhìn về núi Ba Thê thuộc Thoại Sơn, An Giang, Việt Nam*. https://commons.wikimedia.org/wiki/File:N%C3%BAi_Ba_Th%C3%AA_%E1%BB%9F_Tho%E1%BA%A1i_S%C6%A1n.jpg

9. Malleret, L. (1951). IV. Les fouilles d'Oc-èo (1944). Rapport préliminaire. *Bulletin de l'Ecole française d'Extrême-Orient*, 75-88. https://www.persee.fr/doc/befeo_0336-1519_1951_num_45_1_551., pp. 75-76.

10. Ibid., pp. 86-87.

11. Ibid., p. 77.

12. Filliozat, J. (1971). Louis Malleret (1901-1970) [note biographique]. Ibid., 58, 1971, 4-15. https://www.persee.fr/doc/befeo_0336-1519_1971_num_58_1_507., p. 3.

13. Malleret, L. (1959). *L'archéologie du Delta du Mékong* (Vol. 1. L'exploration archéologique et les fouilles d'Oc-Eo). Publications de l'École française d'Extrême-Orient, v. 43 (XLIII)., pp. 451-454.

14. Demandt, M., xc, & Le H, S. (2015). Early Gold Ornaments of Southeast Asia: Production, Trade, and Consumption. *Asian Perspectives*, 54(2), 305-330. http://www.jstor.org/stable/2635768., p. 308.

15. Located at Phan Thanh Giản St., Oc Eo, Thoại Sơn, An Giang, Vietnam

16. Tingley, N., with essays by Andreas Reinecke, Pierre-Yves Manguin, Kerry Nguyen-Long, & Nguyen Dinh Chien. (2009). *Arts of Ancient Viet Nam: From River Plain to Open Sea*. Asia Society; The Museum of Fine Arts; Yale University Press [distr.]., p. 144.

17. Vallerin, M., & Manguin, P.-Y. (1997). Viêt Nam. La mission « Archéologie du delta du Mékong ». *Bulletin de l'Ecole française d'Extrême-Orient*, 408-414. https://www.persee.fr/doc/befeo_0336-1519_1997_num_84_1_249., p. 409.

18. Nguyễn, T. S. T. (2015). *Đời sống văn hóa của cư dân Óc Eo ở Tây Nam Bộ (Qua tư liệu khảo cổ học)*. Bộ Văn Hóa, Thể Thao và Du Lịch Bộ Giáo Dục và Đào Tạo, Trường Đại Học Văn Hóa Hà Nội]. Hanoi., p. 32, p. 35.

19. Tingley, N., with essays by Andreas Reinecke, Pierre-Yves Manguin, Kerry Nguyen-Long, & Nguyen Dinh Chien. (2009). *Arts of Ancient Viet Nam: From River Plain to Open Sea*. Asia Society; The Museum of Fine Arts; Yale University Press [distr.]., p. 162.

20. Lê, T. L. (2006). *Nghệ thuật Phật giáo và Hindu giáo ở đồng bằng sông Cửu Long trước thế kỷ X*. Nhà xuất bản Thế Giới., pp. 220-221.

21. Ibid., p. 42.

22. Ibid., p. 208.

23. Baotanglichsutphcm. (2018). *PHẬT*. http://www.baotanglichsutphcm.com.vn/phat-3

24. Other wooden statues were carved from *gỗ Mù u* (Calophyllum inophyllum, Lợi Mỹ - Đồng Tháp, BTLS 1617) and *gỗ Bằng Lăng* (Lagerstroemia calyculata, Bình Hòa - Long An, BTLS 1618).

25. Việt Nữ. (2018). *Những con đường rợp bóng cây cổ thụ ở Sài Gòn*. https://tuoitre.vn/nhung-con-duong-rop-bong-cay-co-thu-o-sai-gon-20180120200829412.htm

26. *Abhanga, Ābhaṅga, Abhaṅga, Abhamga: 7 definitions*. (2021). https://www.wisdomlib.org/definition/abhanga.

27. Cropped photo of original taken Gary Todd from Xinzheng China CC0 via Wikimedia Commons. (27 September 2013). *Vietnam History Museum, Ho Chi Minh City (Saigon), 2013. Complete indexed photo collection at WorldHistoryPics.com., A photograph taken in the Museum of Vietnamese History in Hồ Chí Minh City (HCMC / TPHCM) by Professor Gary Lee Todd*. https://commons.wikimedia.org/wiki/File:Oc-Eo_Culture_(9980674965).jpg.

28. The Metropolitan Museum of Art. *Buddha in Meditation, 8th–9th century, Southern Vietnam*. https://www.metmuseum.org/art/collection/search/77598

29. Guy, J. B. P., & Metropolitan Museum of Art. (2014). *Lost kingdoms: Hindu-Buddhist sculpture of early Southeast Asia*. The Metropolitan Museum of Art., p. 99.

30. Kang, H. (2013). The Spread of Sarnath-Style Buddha Images in Southeast Asia and Shandong, China, by the Sea Route., p. 44.

31. Lê, T. L. (2006). *Nghệ thuật Phật giáo và Hindu giáo ở đồng bằng sông Cửu Long trước thế kỷ X*. Nhà xuất bản Thế Giới., p. 209.

32. Photo from VNA. (9 February 2021). *Ethnic cultures, national treasures on display at An Giang Museum*. https://en.qdnd.vn/culture-sports/culture/ethnic-cultures-national-treasures-on-display-at-an-giang-museum-526838. Giồng Xoài site is located at Mỹ Hiệp Sơn commune, Hòn Đất district, An Giang province.

33. Photo by Gary Todd - CC0 - via Wikimedia Commons. (28 November 2012). *Oc Eo Culture Gallery*. https://commons.wikimedia.org/wiki/File:Oc_Eo_Culture_Vishnu_Statue_2.jpg

34. Tingley, N., with essays by Andreas Reinecke, Pierre-Yves Manguin, Kerry Nguyen-Long, & Nguyen Dinh Chien. (2009). *Arts of Ancient Viet Nam: From River Plain to Open Sea*. Asia Society; The Museum of Fine Arts; Yale University Press [distr.]., p. 172.

CHAPTER 9

1. Vickery, M. (2003). Funan Reviewed: Deconstructing the Ancients. *Bulletin de l'Ecole française d'Extrême-Orient*, 101-143. https://www.persee.fr/doc/befeo_0336-1519_2003_num_90_1_360., p. 101.

2. Gungwu, W. (1958). The Nanhai Trade: A Study of the Early History of Chinese Trade in the South China Sea. *Journal of the Malayan Branch of the Royal Asiatic Society*, *31*(2 (182)), 1-135. http://www.jstor.org/stable/4150313., p. 33.

3. Lustig, E. J. (2009). *Power and pragmatism in the political economy of Angkor* Sydney eScholarship. http://hdl.handle.net/2123/5356, Appendixes, p. 44.

4. Dates are taken from Briggs, L. P. (1947). A Sketch of Cambodian History. *The Far Eastern Quarterly*, 6(4), 354-363. https://www.jstor.org/stable/2049431?seq=1 ( ) <style face="italic"> 6</style>(4, p. 345.

5. Vickery states Funan existed from the first to the seventh centuries. I had used Briggs's middle of the sixth century by as it fits with the timing of the last recorded king of Funan and the date when Zhenla sent tributes to the northern court. See Vickery, M. (2003). Funan Reviewed: Deconstructing the Ancients. *Bulletin de l'Ecole française d'Extrême-Orient*, 101-143. https://www.persee.fr/doc/befeo_0336-1519_2003_num_90_1_360., p. 101.

6. Fang Xuanling. (648). *Book of Jin (Jin shu) - Volume 97 Biographies 67: Four Barbarian Tribes.* http://chinesenotes.com/jinshu/jinshu097.html, translated from a French translation by Paul Pelliot, Pelliot, P. (1903). Le Fou-nan. *Bulletin de l'Ecole française d'Extrême-Orient*, 248-303. https://www.persee.fr/doc/befeo_0336-1519_1903_num_3_1_121., p. 254. Pelliot noted that the Hou (or Hu) people are the people of Central Asia with alphabets roughly similar to the Indian script. See also Châu, H. Đ. (2018). *An Nam Truyện - Ghi chép về Việt Nam trong chính sử Trung Quốc xưa*. Hội Nhà Văn., p. 249.

7. Pelliot, P. (1903). Le Fou-nan. *Bulletin de l'Ecole française d'Extrême-Orient*, 248-303. https://www.persee.fr/doc/befeo_0336-1519_1903_num_3_1_121., p. 303.

8. Xiao Zixian. (489-537). *Book of Southern Qi*. http://chinesenotes.com/nanqishu.html, Volume 58 Biographies 39: Other Peoples from the Southeast, http://chinesenotes.com/nanqishu/nanqishu058.html. Yue, S. (492-493). *Book of Song (Song shu)*. http://chinesenotes.com/songshu.html, Volume 97 Biographies 57: Yi Man, http://chinesenotes.com/songshu/songshu097.html. Yao Silian (635). *Book of Liang (Liang shu)*. http://chinesenotes.com/liangshu/liangshu054.html, Volume 54: Various Barbarians.

9. Wei Zheng, Yan Shigu, Kong Yingda, & Zhangsun Wuji. (636). *Book of Sui* http://chinesenotes.com/suishu.html, Volume 82 Biographies 47: The Nanman, http://chinesenotes.com/suishu/suishu082.html. Zhao Ying, Liu Xu, Zhang Zhao, Jia Wei, & Zhao Xi. (941-945). *Old Book of Tang (Jiu Tang shu)*. https://ctext.org/wiki.pl?if=gb&res=456206, Volume 197 Biographies 147: Southern Man, Southwestern Man, http://chinesenotes.com/jiutangshu/jiutangshu209.html. Xiu, O., Qi, S., & Fan, Z. (1060). *New Book of Tang (Xin Tang shu) - Volume 222c Biographies 147c: Southern Man 3.* http://chinesenotes.com/xintangshu/xintangshu222c.html.

10. Vickery, M. (2003). Funan Reviewed: Deconstructing the Ancients. *Bulletin de l'Ecole française d'Extrême-Orient*, 101-143. https://www.persee.fr/doc/befeo_0336-1519_2003_num_90_1_360., p. 106.

11. Translated from the French translation by Paul Pelliot, Pelliot, P. (1903). Le Fou-nan. Ibid., 248-303. https://www.persee.fr/doc/befeo_0336-1519_1903_num_3_1_121., p. 254.

12. Coedès, G., Cowing, S. B., Vella, W. F., & Press, A. N. U. (1968). The Indianized States of Southeast Asia. http://hdl.handle.net/1885/11518., p. 37.

13. Vickery, M. (2003). Funan Reviewed: Deconstructing the Ancients. *Bulletin de l'Ecole française d'Extrême-Orient*, 101-143. https://www.persee.fr/doc/befeo_0336-1519_2003_num_90_1_360., p. 106.

14. Ibid., p. 109.

15. Coedès, G., Cowing, S. B., Vella, W. F., & Press, A. N. U. (1968). The Indianized States of Southeast Asia. http://hdl.handle.net/1885/11518., p. 38.

16. Vickery, M. (2003). Funan Reviewed: Deconstructing the Ancients. *Bulletin de l'Ecole française d'Extrême-Orient*, 101-143. https://www.persee.fr/doc/befeo_0336-1519_2003_num_90_1_360., p. 107.

17. Golzio, K.-H. Kauṇḍinya in Southeast Asia, How a historical figure was transformed into a mythical Hero. https://www.academia.edu/6874876/Kau%E1%B9%87%E1%B8%8Dinya_in_Southeast_Asia_How_a_historical_figure_was_transformed_into_a_mythical_Hero_1

18. Vickery, M. (2003). Funan Reviewed: Deconstructing the Ancients. *Bulletin de l'Ecole française d'Extrême-Orient*, 101-143. https://www.persee.fr/doc/befeo_0336-1519_2003_num_90_1_360., p. 105.

19. Pelliot, P. (1903). Le Fou-nan. Ibid., 248-303. https://www.persee.fr/doc/befeo_0336-1519_1903_num_3_1_121., p. 291.

20. In Wade-Giles Chinese, these are Ch'ü-tu-k'un, Chiu-chih, Tien-sun. See Coedès, G., Cowing, S. B., Vella, W. F., & Press, A. N. U. (1968). The Indianized States of Southeast Asia. http://hdl.handle.net/1885/11518., p. 38.

21. Yao Silian (635). *Book of Liang (Liang shu)*. http://chinesenotes.com/liangshu/liangshu054.html, Volume 54: Various Barbarians.

22. Vickery, M. (2003). Funan Reviewed: Deconstructing the Ancients. *Bulletin de l'Ecole française d'Extrême-Orient*, 101-143. https://www.persee.fr/doc/befeo_0336-1519_2003_num_90_1_360., p. 119, also Coedès, G., Cowing, S. B., Vella, W. F., & Press, A. N. U. (1968). The Indianized States of Southeast Asia. http://hdl.handle.net/1885/11518., p. 39 and Wheatley, P. (1956). Tun-Sun (頓 遜). *Journal of the Royal Asiatic Society of Great Britain and Ireland*(1/2), 17-30. http://www.jstor.org/stable/2522278., p. 25.

23. Pelliot, P. (1903). Le Fou-nan. *Bulletin de l'Ecole française d'Extrême-Orient*, 248-303. https://www.persee.fr/doc/befeo_0336-1519_1903_num_3_1_121., p. 292.

24. Ye Myint Swe, Cho Cho Aye, & Khin Zaw. (2017). Chapter 25 Gold deposits of Myanmar. *Geological Society, London, Memoirs*, *48*(1), 557-572. https://doi.org/10.1144/m48.25, Figure 25.1.

25. Monument Mining. Factsheet. https://www.monumentmining.com/site/assets/files/4223/mmy_factsheet_march_19_2021.pdf .

26. Vickery, M. (2003). Funan Reviewed: Deconstructing the Ancients. *Bulletin de l'Ecole française d'Extrême-Orient*, 101-143. https://www.persee.fr/doc/befeo_0336-1519_2003_num_90_1_360., p. 111. See also Manguin, P.-Y. (1980). The Southeast Asian Ship: An Historical Approach. *Journal of Southeast Asian Studies*, *11*(2), 266-276. http://www.jstor.org/stable/20070359 .

27. Gungwu, W. (1958). The Nanhai Trade: A Study of the Early History of Chinese Trade in the South China Sea. *Journal of the Malayan Branch of the Royal Asiatic Society*, *31*(2 (182)), 1-135. http://www.jstor.org/stable/41503138, p.38.

28. Châu, H. Đ. (2018). *An Nam Truyện - Ghi chép về Việt Nam trong chính sử Trung Quốc xưa*. Hội Nhà Văn., p. 270. See also Liang shu, Volume 54.

29. Pelliot, P. (1903). Le Fou-nan. *Bulletin de l'Ecole française d'Extrême-Orient*, 248-303. https://www.persee.fr/doc/befeo_0336-1519_1903_num_3_1_121., p. 292.

30. Ibid., p. 292.

31. Coedès, G., Cowing, S. B., Vella, W. F., & Press, A. N. U. (1968). The Indianized States of Southeast Asia. http://hdl.handle.net/1885/11518., p. 28.

32. Pelliot, P. (1903). Le Fou-nan. *Bulletin de l'Ecole française d'Extrême-Orient*, 248-303. https://www.persee.fr/doc/befeo_0336-1519_1903_num_3_1_121., p. 292.

33. Majumdar, R. C. (1943). *Kambujadesa*. https://www.vifindia.org/sites/default/files/145799028-Kambujadesa-1943.pdf quotes MS Levi, who suggested Pataliputra.

34. Sou-wou and Chen-song are most likely the Chinese transcription of local names. In another page, Pelliot explains the horses are Indo-Scythe and are presents from the Indian king to Fan Chan, see Pelliot, P. (1903). Le Fou-nan. *Bulletin de l'Ecole française d'Extrême-Orient*, 248-303. https://www.persee.fr/doc/befeo_0336-1519_1903_num_3_1_121., p. 292.

35. Ibid., p. 271. *zhong-lang* (中郎],a person responsible for the security of the palace).

36. Châu, H. Đ. (2018). *An Nam Truyện - Ghi chép về Việt Nam trong chính sử Trung Quốc xưa*. Hội Nhà Văn., p. 258, p.270. See also Liang shu, Volume 54.

37. Pelliot, P. (1903). Le Fou-nan. *Bulletin de l'Ecole française d'Extrême-Orient*, 248-303. https://www.persee.fr/doc/befeo_0336-1519_1903_num_3_1_121., p. 292.

38. Châu, H. Đ. (2018). *An Nam Truyện - Ghi chép về Việt Nam trong chính sử Trung Quốc xưa*. Hội Nhà Văn., p. 271. See also Liang shu, Volume 54.

39. Pelliot refers to him as Lieou-t'o-pa-mo in BEFEO Chinese or Liu-tuo-ba-mo in Pinyin Chinese, see Pelliot, P. (1903). Le Fou-nan. *Bulletin de l'Ecole française d'Extrême-Orient*, 248-303. https://www.persee.fr/doc/befeo_0336-1519_1903_num_3_1_121., p. 270. Southworth and Golzio refer to him as Lutuoluobamo, see Southworth, W. A. (2001). *The origins of Campa in Central Vietnam: a preliminary review* /z-wcorg/. http://catalog.hathitrust.org/api/volumes/oclc/57480138.html, p. 308 and Golzio, K.-H. Kauṇḍinya in Southeast Asia, How a historical figure was transformed into a mythical Hero. https://www.academia.edu/6874876/Kau%E1%B9%87%E1%B8%8Dinya_in_Southeast_Asia_How_a_historical_figure_was_transformed_into_a_mythical_Hero_1 . I use Pelliot's version.

40. Pelliot refers to him Chō-sie-pa-mo in BEFEO Chinese or She-sie-ba-mo in Pinyin Chinese, see Pelliot, P. (1903). Le Fou-nan. *Bulletin de l'Ecole française d'Extrême-Orient*, 248-303. https://www.persee.fr/doc/befeo_0336-1519_1903_num_3_1_121., p. 269.

41. In 434, 435, 438, 484, 503, 511, 514, 517, 519, 520, 530, 535, and 539, Châu, H. Đ. (2018). *An Nam Truyện - Ghi chép về Việt Nam trong chính sử Trung Quốc xưa*. Hội Nhà Văn., p. 254, p. 271. See also Liang shu, Volume 54.

42. Pelliot, P. (1903). Le Fou-nan. *Bulletin de l'Ecole française d'Extrême-Orient*, 248-303. https://www.persee.fr/doc/befeo_0336-1519_1903_num_3_1_121., p. 294.

43. Briggs, L. P. (1951). *The ancient Khmer Empire*. American Philosophical Society., p. 48.

44. Châu, H. Đ. (2018). *An Nam Truyện - Ghi chép về Việt Nam trong chính sử Trung Quốc xưa*. Hội Nhà Văn., p. 283. See also Xin Tang shu, Volume 222c.

45. Ibid., p. 280. See also Jiu Tang shu, Volume 197.

46. See also Vickery, M. (2003). Funan Reviewed: Deconstructing the Ancients. *Bulletin de l'Ecole française d'Extrême-Orient*, 101-143. https://www.persee.fr/doc/befeo_0336-1519_2003_num_90_1_360., p. 122.

47. See also ibid., p. 136.

48. Ibid., p. 131.

49. Stark, M. (2006). From Funan to Angkor Collapse and Regeneration in Ancient Cambodia. In (pp. 144-167)., p. 151.

50. Pelliot, P. (1903). Le Fou-nan. *Bulletin de l'Ecole française d'Extrême-Orient*, 248-303. https://www.persee.fr/doc/befeo_0336-1519_1903_num_3_1_121., p. 261, p. 264, p. 268, p. 269 and Châu, H. Đ.

(2018). *An Nam Truyện - Ghi chép về Việt Nam trong chính sử Trung Quốc xưa*. Hội Nhà Văn., pp. 260-261 (Book of Southern Qi, Volume 58), pp. 268-272 (Book of Liang, Volume 54).

51. Vickery, M. (2003). Funan Reviewed: Deconstructing the Ancients. *Bulletin de l'Ecole française d'Extrême-Orient*, 101-143. https://www.persee.fr/doc/befeo_0336-1519_2003_num_90_1_360., p. 125.

52. Lương, N. (2010). Nước Phù Nam và Hậu Phù Nam. *Tạp chí Nghiên cứu Lịch sử*, 1.2010, 3-17.

53. Châu, H. Đ. (2018). *An Nam Truyện - Ghi chép về Việt Nam trong chính sử Trung Quốc xưa*. Hội Nhà Văn., p. 265. See also Liang shu, Volume 54.

54. Ibid., p. 251. See also Song shu, Volume 97.

55. Ibid., p. 261. See also the Book of Southern Qi, Volume 58.

56. Ibid., p. 259. See also the Book of Southern Qi, Volume 58.

57. Pelliot is not sure what a *po-lo* unit is. He suggests it should read *bhāra*, an ancient Indian unit of weight measurement, which equates to 2,000 *pala* where one pala is 64 *māsa* which varies between 15 to 17 Troy grains. One Troy grain is 0.062 g, so one *bhāra* varies between 2000×64×15×0.062=119 kg or 134.9 kg. In Pelliot's estimation, five *bhāra* would be between 600 and 700 kg. In another reference, one *bhāra* is 96 kg (refer https://www.wisdomlib.org/definition/bhara). In ibid., p. 259, the author suggests *po-lo* should read *Bà lan* where one *Bà lan* is *300 jin* or 179 kg, so five *p'o-lo* would be nearly 900 kg. In today's value (8 June 2022), the estimated value of five *po lo* of gold, say 900 kg, would be around USD 53.5 million.

58. Southworth, W. A. (2001). *The origins of Campa in Central Vietnam: a preliminary review* /z-wcorg/. http://catalog.hathitrust.org/api/volumes/oclc/57480138.html, p. 306, also Châu, H. Đ. (2018). *An Nam Truyện - Ghi chép về Việt Nam trong chính sử Trung Quốc xưa*. Hội Nhà Văn., p. 256. See also the Book of Southern Qi, Volume 58.

59. Wei Zheng, Yan Shigu, Kong Yingda, & Zhangsun Wuji. (636). *Book of Sui* http://chinesenotes.com/suishu.html, Volume 82 Biographies 47: The Nanman, http://chinesenotes.com/suishu/suishu082.html. Zhao Ying, Liu Xu, Zhang Zhao, Jia Wei, & Zhao Xi. (941-945). *Old Book of Tang (Jiu Tang shu)*. https://ctext.org/wiki.pl?if=gb&res=456206, Volume 197 Biographies 147: Southern Man, Southwestern Man, http://chinesenotes.com/jiutangshu/jiutangshu209.html. Xiu, O., Qi, S., & Fan, Z. (1060). *New Book of Tang (Xin Tang shu) - Volume 222c Biographies 147c: Southern Man 3.* http://chinesenotes.com/xintangshu/xintangshu222c.html. Daši, T., Weiyi, H., Qiyan, Z., Xuan, O., Haowen, L., Yi, W., & Zongduan, Y. (1346). *History of Song (Song Shi)*. http://chinesenotes.com/songshi.html, Volume 489 Biographies 248: Foreign States 5, http://chinesenotes.com/songshi/songshi489.html. Li Yanshou. (643-659). *Beishi: History of the Northern Dynasties*. http://chinesenotes.com/songshi/songshi489.html, Volume 95 Biographies 83: Man, Lao, Linyi, Chi Tu, Zhenla, Poli. http://chinesenotes.com/beishi/beishi095.html.

60. Châu, H. Đ. (2018). *An Nam Truyện - Ghi chép về Việt Nam trong chính sử Trung Quốc xưa*. Hội Nhà Văn., p. 275. See also Sui shu, Volume 82.

61. Pelliot, P. (1903). Le Fou-nan. *Bulletin de l'Ecole française d'Extrême-Orient*, 248-303. https://www.persee.fr/doc/befeo_0336-1519_1903_num_3_1_121., p. 272 translates ancestors not grandfather.

62. SLK. (5 February 2009). *The history of Cambodia from 1st century to 20th century [5] Why did Chinese call Cambodia "Chenla"?* https://sokheounnews.files.wordpress.com/2010/05/5-why-did-chinese-call-cambodia-chenla.pdf, p. 1.

63. Vickery, M. (1994). What and Where was Chenla? *Recherches nouvelles sur le Cambodge*, 197-212. (Publiées sous la direction de F. Bizot. École française d'Extrême-Orient, Paris), p.1.

64. Heng, P., & Lavy, P. (2018). *Pre-Angkorian cities: Ishanapura and Mahendraparvata*. https://angkordatabase.asia/publications/pre-angkorian-cities-ishanapura-and-mahendraparvata, p. 138.

65. Hendrickson, M., Leroy, S., Hua, Q., Phon, K., & Voeun, V. (2017). Smelting in the Shadow of the Iron Mountain: Preliminary Field Investigation of the Industrial Landscape around Phnom Dek, Cambodia (Ninth to Twentieth Centuries A.D.). *Asian Perspectives*, 56(1), 55-91. http://www.jstor.org/stable/26357707

66. Vickery, M. (1994). What and Where was Chenla? *Recherches nouvelles sur le Cambodge*, 197-212. (Publiées sous la direction de F. Bizot. École française d'Extrême-Orient, Paris., p. 8.

67. Vickery, M. (2003). Funan Reviewed: Deconstructing the Ancients. *Bulletin de l'Ecole française d'Extrême-Orient*, 101-143. https://www.persee.fr/doc/befeo_0336-1519_2003_num_90_1_360., p. 134.

68. Châu, H. Đ. (2018). *An Nam Truyện - Ghi chép về Việt Nam trong chính sử Trung Quốc xưa*. Hội Nhà Văn., p. 283. See also Jiu Tang shu, Volume 197 and Coedès, G., Cowing, S. B., Vella, W. F., & Press, A. N. U. (1968). The Indianized States of Southeast Asia. http://hdl.handle.net/1885/11518., p. 65.

69. Coedès, G., Cowing, S. B., Vella, W. F., & Press, A. N. U. (1968). The Indianized States of Southeast Asia. http://hdl.handle.net/1885/11518., p. 68.

70. Châu, H. Đ. (2018). *An Nam Truyện - Ghi chép về Việt Nam trong chính sử Trung Quốc xưa*. Hội Nhà Văn., p. 280. See also Jiu Tang shu, Volume 197.

71. Ibid., p. 284.

72. Vickery, M. (1994). What and Where was Chenla? *Recherches nouvelles sur le Cambodge*, 197-212. (Publiées sous la direction de F. Bizot. École française d'Extrême-Orient, Paris., p. 16.

73. SLK. (5 February 2009). *The history of Cambodia from 1st century to 20th century [5] Why did Chinese call Cambodia "Chenla"?* https://sokheounnews.files.wordpress.com/2010/05/5-why-did-chinese-call-cambodia-chenla.pdf, p. 17.

CHAPTER 10

1. Soutif, D., & Chollet, C. (2017). *Inventaire CIK des inscriptions Khmères (Corpus of Khmer Inscriptions)*. Siem Reap EFEO Center https://cik.efeo.fr/wp-content/uploads/2017/04/Inventaire-CIK-09042017.pdf

2. As of 2021, the number of Khmer inscriptions has increased to 1562, see Chollet, C. (2021). *About the recent activities of the CIK (Corpus of Khmer Inscriptions)*. https://dharma.hypotheses.org/3659

3. Coedès, G., Cowing, S. B., Vella, W. F., & Press, A. N. U. (1968). The Indianized States of Southeast Asia. http://hdl.handle.net/1885/11518., p. 65.

4. Kambuja appears on the following inscriptions listed in the format of (Inscription K. number and name - Cœdès IC: Inscriptions du Cambodge, Volume, page number - year)

   K. 61 (Preah Vihear Kuk ou Vat Chakret) – IC. VII, p. 22 - 834 or 912 CE,
   K. 86 (Yah Hom) - IC. V, p. 283 - tenth century Śaka,
   K. 177 (Preah Theat Khvav) - IC. VII, p. 39 – 13th to 14th centuries Śaka,
   K. 258 (Samrong) - IC. IV, p.189 - after 1029 Śaka,
   K. 522 (Prasat Sla Ket) - IC. V, p. 123 - ninth century Śaka,
   K. 675 (Prasat Andon) - IC. I, p.66 - ninth century Śaka,
   K. 713 (Preah Ko) - IC. I, p.24 - 801 or 879 CE,
   K. 806 (Pre rup) - IC. I, p.110 - 883 or 961 CE, (inscription also describes a genealogy of kings),
   K. 842 (Banteay Srei) - IC. I, p.154 - 889 or 967 CE,
   K. 853 (Phnom Bayan) - IC. I, p. 258 - ninth century Śaka,

K. 923 (Bakong) - IC. IV, p. 42 - ninth century Śaka,
K. 216 (Phnom Preah Netr Preah) - IC. III, p.42 - 927 or 1005 CE,
K. 958 (Prasat Kuk Chak) - IC. VII, p.144 – 869 or 947 CE.

5. Professor George Cœdès was born in Paris on 10 August 1886. It appears he showed his talent for languages early. At the age of 18, he published in the BEFEO (Bulletin de l'École française d'Extrême-Orient) his first article on an inscription from Cambodia in Khmer and Sanskrit. At 19, he gained a teaching license in German. At 25, in 1911, he sailed to Cambodia, married an aristocratic Khmer, and became the curator of the National Library of Siam (Thailand). There he stayed until he moved to Hanoi in 1930 to take up the position as the Director of EFEO (l'École française d'Extrême-Orient). He stayed there until he retired in 1947 and became the curator of Musée d'Ennery in Paris. See EFEO. *George Cœdès*. https://www.efeo.fr/biographies/notices/codes.htm. Among his numerous articles and books, the monumental eight volumes: *Inscriptions du Cambodge* (commonly abbreviated as IC), Hanoi/Paris, EFEO (Textes et documents sur l'Indochine, 3), (1937, 1942, 1951, 1952, 1953, 1954, 1964, 1966) stand out. In the words of historian Milton Osborne : "*The translations and annotations contained in the eight volumes of Les Inscriptions du Cambodge represent the most important single corpus of epigraphic research to be prepared by an individual scholar of Southeast Asia in the present century.*" See Osborne, M. Professor George Coedes, 1866-1969: A Memoir. https://www.cambridge.org/core/services/aop-cambridge-core/content/view/433EC6CA2E601BB57A87D96D-8616A30C/S0022463400000035a.pdf/professor-george-coedes-1866-1969-a-memoir.pdf.

6. Beckwith, J. A. (2002). *Pre-Angkor Cambodia: The Transition from Prehistory to History* University of Otago]. Dunedin., pp. 24-25.

7. Ibid., pp. 121-123. One inscription, K. 124 is dated 803 but I have not included it as it is not pre-Angkor.

8. Jenner, P. N. (1980). Chrestomathy of Pre-Angkorian Khmer I, Dated Inscriptions from the Seventh and Eighth Centuries. *Center for Southeast Asian Studies. School of Hawaiian, Asian, and Pacific Studies. University of Hawaii at Manoa.* listed 34 inscriptions in 1980.

9. Beckwith, J. A. (2002). *Pre-Angkor Cambodia: The Transition from Prehistory to History* University of Otago]. Dunedin., pp. 31-34.

10. Soutif, D., & Chollet, C. (2017). *Inventaire CIK des inscriptions Khmères (Corpus of Khmer Inscriptions)*. Siem Reap EFEO Center https://cik.efeo.fr/wp-content/uploads/2017/04/Inventaire-CIK-09042017.pdf

11. Tonlé Sap has a minimum surface area of 2,700 km2, almost four times as large as the land area of Singapore (at 728.6 km2) and a maximum of 16,000 km2.

12. Soutif, D., & Chollet, C. (2017). *Inventaire CIK des inscriptions Khmères (Corpus of Khmer Inscriptions)*. Siem Reap EFEO Center https://cik.efeo.fr/wp-content/uploads/2017/04/Inventaire-CIK-09042017.pdf. The full list is Battambang, Siem Reap, Preah Vihear, Stung Treng provinces in Cambodia; Ayutthaya, Lopburi, Prachin-Buri, Nakhon-Ratchasima, Chaiyaphum, Buri Ram, Surin, Khon Kaen, Phitsanulok provinces in Thailand; and Muang Champasak in Laos.

13. The full list includes Kampot, Takeo, Kandal, Kompong Speu, Prey Veng, Kompong Chhnang, Svay Rieng, Kompong Cham provinces, and further to the east at Kratié. Across the border to Vietnam includes An Giang and Đồng Tháp.

14. Soutif, D., & Chollet, C. (2017). *Inventaire CIK des inscriptions Khmères (Corpus of Khmer Inscriptions)*. Siem Reap EFEO Center https://cik.efeo.fr/wp-content/uploads/2017/04/Inventaire-CIK-09042017.pdf

15. Cœdès, G. (1908). Inventaire des inscriptions du Champa et du Cambodge. *Bulletin de l'Ecole française d'Extrême-Orient*, 37-92. https://www.persee.fr/doc/befeo_0336-1519_1908_num_8_1_418., p. 50, p. 52.

16. Soutif, D., & Chollet, C. (2017). *Inventaire CIK des inscriptions Khmères (Corpus of Khmer Inscriptions)*. Siem Reap EFEO Center https://cik.efeo.fr/wp-content/uploads/2017/04/Inventaire-CIK-09042017.pdf

17. Cœdès, G. (1931). Etudes cambodgiennes. XXV, Deux inscriptions sanskrites du Fou-nan. XXVI, La date de Kôh Ker. XXVII, La date du Bàphûon. *Bulletin de l'Ecole française d'Extrême-Orient*, 1-23. https://www.persee.fr/doc/befeo_0336-1519_1931_num_31_1_441., p. 4.

18. Trần, B. Đ., Mạc, Đ., Tô, B. G., Phan, V. H., Lê, V. N., Nguyễn, N., & Tôn, N. Q. T. (2005). *Lịch Sử Việt Nam (Từ Đầu Đến Năm 938) - Tập 2* (V. G. Trần, B. Đ. Trần, & Đ. Mạc, Eds.). NXB Trẻ., p. 287.

19. Majumdar, R. C. (1953). Inscriptions of Kambuja. *The Asiatic Society Monograph Series, VIII*, 1-635., p. 3.

20. Ibid., p. 5.

21. Cœdès, G. (1931). Etudes cambodgiennes. XXV, Deux inscriptions sanskrites du Fou-nan. XXVI, La date de Kôh Ker. XXVII, La date du Bàphûon. *Bulletin de l'Ecole française d'Extrême-Orient*, 1-23. https://www.persee.fr/doc/befeo_0336-1519_1931_num_31_1_441., pp. 7. Cœdès notes "*Vikramin "walker" is a nickname for Visnu conquering the world in three steps (Trivikrama). But vikramin also has the meaning of "valiant" and "lion".*"

22. Translated from French by ibid., pp. 11.

23. Vickery, M. (2003). Funan Reviewed: Deconstructing the Ancients. Ibid., 101-143. https://www.persee.fr/doc/befeo_0336-1519_2003_num_90_1_360., p. 122.

24. *Proposed inscriptions for the permanent exhibition*. https://www.efeo.fr/CIK/Documents/InscriptionsMNPP/SelectionExpoPermanente5.htm

25. Soutif, D., & Chollet, C. (2017). *Inventaire CIK des inscriptions Khmères (Corpus of Khmer Inscriptions)*. Siem Reap EFEO Center https://cik.efeo.fr/wp-content/uploads/2017/04/Inventaire-CIK-09042017.pdf

26. Coedès, G. (1937). A New Inscription from Fu-Nan. *The Journal of The Greater India Society, IV, No. 1*, 117-121., p. 117.

27. I am unable to locate this temple.

28. Barth, A. M.-E. (1885). *Inscriptions sanscrites du Cambodge. Extrait des notices et extraits des manuscrits de la Bibliothèque Nationale tome XXVII, 1st partie.* Paris Imprimerie Nationale., p. 65. See also Majumdar, R. C. (1953). Inscriptions of Kambuja. *The Asiatic Society Monograph Series, VIII*, 1-635., p. 39.

29. Coedès, G., Cowing, S. B., Vella, W. F., & Press, A. N. U. (1968). The Indianized States of Southeast Asia. http://hdl.handle.net/1885/11518., p. 68. See also Barth, A. M.-E. (1885). *Inscriptions sanscrites du Cambodge. Extrait des notices et extraits des manuscrits de la Bibliothèque Nationale tome XXVII, 1st partie.* Paris Imprimerie Nationale., p. 71.

30. Coedès, G., Cowing, S. B., Vella, W. F., & Press, A. N. U. (1968). The Indianized States of Southeast Asia. http://hdl.handle.net/1885/11518., p. 68.

31. Higham, C. (1999). *The archaeology of mainland Southeast Asia : from 10,000 B.C. to the fall of Angkor.* Cambridge University Press., p. 267. See also Heng, P., & Lavy, P. (2018). *Pre-Angkorian cities: Ishanapura and Mahendraparvata*. https://angkordatabase.asia/publications/pre-angkorian-cities-ishanapura-and-mahendraparvata, p. 146 and Schweyer, A.-V. (2019). *The Birth of Champa.*, p. 12.

32. Barth, A. M.-E. (1903). Inscription sanscrite du Phou Lokhon (Laos). *Bulletin de l'Ecole française d'Extrême-Orient*, 442-446. https://www.persee.fr/doc/befeo_0336-1519_1903_num_3_1_123., p. 442.

33. Soutif, D., & Chollet, C. (2017). *Inventaire CIK des inscriptions Khmères (Corpus of Khmer Inscriptions)*. Siem Reap EFEO Center https://cik.efeo.fr/wp-content/uploads/2017/04/Inventaire-CIK-09042017.pdf

34. Seidenfaden, E. (1922). Complément à l'Inventaire descriptif des monuments du Cambodge pour les quatre provinces du Siam Oriental. *Bulletin de l'Ecole française d'Extrême-Orient*, 55-99. https://www.persee.fr/doc/befeo_0336-1519_1922_num_22_1_2912

35. Ibid., p. 58. See also Majumdar, R. C. (1953). Inscriptions of Kambuja. *The Asiatic Society Monograph Series, VIII*, 1-635., p. 20.

36. Coedès, G., Cowing, S. B., Vella, W. F., & Press, A. N. U. (1968). The Indianized States of Southeast Asia. http://hdl.handle.net/1885/11518., p. 68 and p. 288.

37. Other inscriptions are K.151, K. 439, and K. 1250. See Heng, P., & Lavy, P. (2018). *Pre-Angkorian cities: Ishanapura and Mahendraparvata*. https://angkordatabase.asia/publications/pre-angkorian-cities-ishanapura-and-mahendraparvata, p. 142. K. 61 (Preah Vihear Kuk ou Vat Chakret) records the date of Īśānavarman's reign at 548 Śaka or 627 CE.

38. Translated from French translation by archaeologist Louis Finot (1864-1935), see Finot, L. (1928). Nouvelles inscriptions du Cambodge. *Bulletin de l'Ecole française d'Extrême-Orient*, 43-80. https://www.persee.fr/doc/befeo_0336-1519_1928_num_28_1_311., p. 45.

39. Heng, P., & Lavy, P. (2018). *Pre-Angkorian cities: Ishanapura and Mahendraparvata*. https://angkordatabase.asia/publications/pre-angkorian-cities-ishanapura-and-mahendraparvata, p. 140.

40. The inscriptions are K. 1, K. 3 at An Giang; K. 5, K. 6, K. 7, K. 8, and K. 9 at Đồng Tháp (Prasat Pram Loveng). See Soutif, D., & Chollet, C. (2017). *Inventaire CIK des inscriptions Khmères (Corpus of Khmer Inscriptions)*. Siem Reap EFEO Center https://cik.efeo.fr/wp-content/uploads/2017/04/Inventaire-CIK-09042017.pdf K. 1 (Vat ThLen, Thling) was found.

41. Using the coordinates supplied by Siddham, 10°30'13"N 104°59'6"E, this pagoda is Chùa Phật Lớn (Big Buddha Temple), see Siddham the Asia inscriptions database. (2020). *Vat Thlen stele with an inscription (K.1) in Old Khmer*. https://siddham.network/object/objectk1/. At around 500 metres west of this pagoda, there is another pagoda named Chùa Vạn Linh, which sounds close to Vat ThLen. However, my research has not shown any mention of ancient inscriptions in either pagoda. Soutif, D., & Chollet, C. (2017). *Inventaire CIK des inscriptions Khmères (Corpus of Khmer Inscriptions)*. Siem Reap EFEO Center https://cik.efeo.fr/wp-content/uploads/2017/04/Inventaire-CIK-09042017.pdf describes the K. 1 inscription as *"in situ; in the masonry of the altar of the pagoda in the village of Lê Hoat, Châu Đốc"*. I am unable to locate this village. The village of Tenot Chum is mentioned in Majumdar, R. C. (1953). Inscriptions of Kambuja. *The Asiatic Society Monograph Series, VIII*, 1-635., p. 51 for K. 1 inscription but I have not been able to locate its whereabouts in Châu Đốc.

42. Majumdar, R. C. (1953). Inscriptions of Kambuja. *The Asiatic Society Monograph Series, VIII*, 1-635., pp. 51-52.

43. Majumdar suggests the god is Śiva and not Vishnu, even if a Vishnu statue was found nearby, see ibid., p. 27.

44. Photos cropped from those taken by Bùi Thụy Đào Nguyên CC BY-SA 3.0. (2007). *Tượng Phật bốn tay và tấm bia đá cổ có từ thời vương quốc Phù Nam, hiện ở trong chùa Linh Sơn (Ba Thê); tọa lạc tại thị trấn Óc Eo, huyện Thoại Sơn, tỉnh An Giang, Việt Nam*. https://upload.wikimedia.org/wikipedia/commons/1/1d/T%C6%B0%E1%BB%A3ng_Ph%E1%BA%ADt_b%E1%BB%91n_tay.jpg and Thuydaonguyen CC BY-SA 3.0. Bàn thờ chính trong chùa Linh Sơn, núi Ba Thê, huyện Thoại Sơn, An Giang, Việt Nam. https://upload.wikimedia.org/wikipedia/commons/6/6d/B%C3%A0n_th%E1%BB%9D_ch%C3%ADnh_trong_ch%C3%B9a_Linh_S%C6%A1n.jpg .

45. See https://vi.wikipedia.org/wiki/Ch%C3%B9a_Linh_S%C6%A1n_(Ba_Th%C3%AA) and https://web.archive.org/web/20131021190011/http://www.dch.gov.vn/pages/news/preview.aspx?n=539&c=25.

46. The History Museum in Ho Chi Minh City has a Champa bronze statue of Avalakitesvara (a Buddhist Bodhisattva), dated the 9th century found in Hoài Nhơn, Bình Định, museum registered number

BTLS. 1290. The statue has four arms. The two right hands hold a prayer bead (aksamala) and a lotus (padma). The two left arms hold an oblong water pot (kamandalu) and a book (pustaka). Refer to https://www.facebook.com/baotanglichsu/posts/pfbid0SP8MeiburaQPqnfhAsRdyCnmycechjn-V2a42hixUnjTxpJJNnEBz2a9cfdbeihBPl.

47. Majumdar, R. C. (1953). Inscriptions of Kambuja. *The Asiatic Society Monograph Series, VIII*, 1-635., No. 21, p. 26.

48. Coedès, G. (1942). *Inscriptions du Cambodge/editées et traduites par G. Cœdès.* (Vol. II). École française d'Extrême-Orient., p. 79.

49. Beckwith, J. A. (2002). *Pre-Angkor Cambodia: The Transition from Prehistory to History* University of Otago]. Dunedin., pp. 124-125.

50. Soutif, D., & Chollet, C. (2017). *Inventaire CIK des inscriptions Khmères (Corpus of Khmer Inscriptions)*. Siem Reap EFEO Center https://cik.efeo.fr/wp-content/uploads/2017/04/Inventaire-CIK-09042017.pdf

51. Beckwith, J. A. (2002). *Pre-Angkor Cambodia: The Transition from Prehistory to History* University of Otago]. Dunedin., pp. 126-127.

52. Soutif, D., & Chollet, C. (2017). *Inventaire CIK des inscriptions Khmères (Corpus of Khmer Inscriptions)*. Siem Reap EFEO Center https://cik.efeo.fr/wp-content/uploads/2017/04/Inventaire-CIK-09042017.pdf

53. Chronique. (1909). *Bulletin de l'Ecole française d'Extrême-Orient*, 613-630. https://www.persee.fr/doc/befeo_0336-1519_1909_num_9_1_196., p. 619.

54. Coordinates 12°23'57.6"N 104°48'39"E.

55. Parmentier, H. (1909b). Relevé archéologique de la province de Tây-Ninh (Cochinchine). *Bulletin de l'Ecole française d'Extrême-Orient*, 739-756. https://www.persee.fr/doc/befeo_0336-1519_1909_num_9_1_197., p. 754.

56. Located at Xóm Mới hamlet, Tân Phong, Tân Biên, Tây Ninh, Vietnam, coordinates 11°27'50.2"N 106°00'36.8"E. Photo by Ola Xuân Xuân (Cô Tết, 22 March 2020), used with permission by Ola Xuân Xuân, 9 May 2022.

57. *Hiện vật khai quật tại tháp Bình Thạnh*. https://baotang.tayninh.gov.vn/bo-suu-tap-hien-vat/hien-vat-khai-quat-tai-thap-binh-thanh/603.html. However, the stele at the site shows the date to be between the eighth and the ninth century. I am inclined to adopt the museum's dates.

58. Lunet de Lajonquière, E. (1911). *Inventaire descriptif des monuments du Cambodge, Tome Troisième.* (Vol. 3). Imprimerie Nationale., p. 469. Figure 122 of this reference shows a site at Phước Mỹ, around 10 kilometres of Bình Thạnh tower. However, de Lajonquière did not mention any tower, he only described a debris of bricks and a stone lintel found there. In Parmentier's paper, he identifies a tower named Teai-ho which de Lajonquière locates it at the junction of two rivers: Prek Kampong Spean and Vàm Cỏ Đông. I am unable to locate such a tower but the plan of the tower, which Parmentier drew, resembles Bình Thạnh so I thought that Parmentier may have mistaken it for the Teai-ho tower but the lintel he drew is not Bình Thạnh's, it looks like that of Chóp Mạt. See Parmentier, H. (1909b). Relevé archéologique de la province de Tây-Ninh (Cochinchine). *Bulletin de l'Ecole française d'Extrême-Orient*, 739-756. https://www.persee.fr/doc/befeo_0336-1519_1909_num_9_1_197., p. 742, p. 744 and p. 745.

59. Photo by Śisp Thiên (April 2021), used with permission by Sakaisp Thiên, 10 May 2022. The tower is located at Bình Hòa, Trảng Bàng, Tây Ninh, Vietnam, coordinates 11°01'07.8"N 106°13'09.4"E.

60. Soutif, D., & Chollet, C. (2017). *Inventaire CIK des inscriptions Khmères (Corpus of Khmer Inscriptions)*. Siem Reap EFEO Center https://cik.efeo.fr/wp-content/uploads/2017/04/Inventaire-CIK-09042017.pdf and Coedès, G. (1942). *Inscriptions du Cambodge/editées et traduites par*

G. Cœdès. (Vol. II). École française d'Extrême-Orient., p. 80, also Chronique. (1917). *Bulletin de l'Ecole française d'Extrême-Orient*, 35-57. https://www.persee.fr/doc/befeo_0336-1519_1917_num_17_1_534., p. 48.

61. Cropped photo of original taken by Nguyễn Hoàng Nhật Thiên Nam - CC BY-SA 4.0 via Wikimedia Commons. (2021). *Tháp cổ Vĩnh Hưng thuộc ấp Trung Hưng IB, xã Vĩnh Hưng A, Vĩnh Lợi, Bạc Liêu*. https://upload.wikimedia.org/wikipedia/commons/1/1b/Vinh_Hung_tower%2C_Vinh_Loi%2C_Bac_Lieu.jpg. The tower is located at Vĩnh Hưng A, Vĩnh Lợi, Bạc Liêu, Vietnam, coordinates 9°23'33.0"N 105°34'41.4"E.

62. Eade, C. (2011). Vatt Samrong Ek: the Inscription, the Buddha Pedestal, and the Numbers. *Aséanie, Sciences humaines en Asie du Sud-Est*, 101-104. https://www.persee.fr/doc/asean_0859-9009_2011_num_27_1_2172, located at QL53, Phường 8, Trà Vinh, Vietnam, coordinates 9°54'56.7"N 106°18'38.5"E.

CHAPTER 11

1. SKTT, Vol. 1, p. 182.

2. Shi Ci (Xie's father, *taishou* of Nhật Nam), Shi Xie (137-226, *taishou* of Giao Chỉ), Shi Yi (Xie's brother, *taishou* of Hepu), Shi Hui (Xie's brother, *taishou* of Cửu Chân), Shi Wu (Xie's brother, *taishou* of Nan-hai), Shi Xin (Xie's son, *taishou* of Giao Chỉ).

3. Tao Huang (270-290 CE, *cishi* of Giao Châu), Tao Wei (Huang's son, *cishi* of Giao Châu), Tao Shu (Đào Thục, Huang's son, *cishi* of Giao Châu)

4. Đỗ Viện (327-410, *cishi* of Giao Châu), Đỗ Tuệ Độ (Viện's son, *cishi* of Giao Châu), Đỗ Tuệ Kỳ (Viện's son, *taishou* of Cửu Chân), Đỗ Hoàng Văn (*cishi* of Giao Châu).

5. Taylor, K. W. (1983). *The Birth of Vietnam*. Berkeley: University of California Press., p. 73.

6. Ibid., p. 127.

7. Bộ Quốc Phòng - Viện Lịch Sử Quân Sự Việt Nam, Trần, Q. V., & Lê, Đ. S. (2001). *Lịch Sử Quân Sự Việt Nam - Tập 2 - Đấu tranh giành độc lập tự chủ (từ năm 179 TCN đến năm 938)*. NXB Chính Trị Quốc Gia., p. 137.

8. The Wang Mang rebellion (9-13), the civil war during the Three Kingdoms period (220-280), and the transition to Sui-Tang dynasties in the sixth-seventh century produced many refugees. As for the exiles, see ANCL, pp. 211-218.

9. See Tao Huang biography, Châu, H. Đ. (2018). *An Nam Truyện - Ghi chép về Việt Nam trong chính sử Trung Quốc xưa*. Hội Nhà Văn., p. 205. See also Jin shu, Volume 57.

10. Other sources cite eleventh-generation, which fits the five hundred years or so timeline from Wang Mang to the fifth century better, see Nguyễn, D. H. (2019). *Văn Minh Đại Việt*. NXB Hồng Đức., p. 163.

11. CM, Vol. 1, p. 167.

12. Nguyễn, D. H. (2019). *Văn Minh Đại Việt*. NXB Hồng Đức., p. 161, other sources cite 503.

13. Hồng Anh. (10 October 2012). *Một số vấn đề về vương triều Tiền Lý và quê hương của vua Lý Nam Đế*. http://baotanglichsu.vn/vi/Articles/3091/12680/mot-so-van-dje-ve-vuong-trieu-tien-ly-va-que-huong-cua-vua-ly-nam-dje.html

14. Taylor, K. W. (1983). *The Birth of Vietnam*. Berkeley: University of California Press., p. 136. See also Yao Silian. (636). *Book of Chen (Chen Shu), Volume 1: Emperor Wu 1*. http://chinesenotes.com/chenshu/chenshu001.html, Vol. 1.

15. SKTT, Vol. 1, p. 179.

16. In SKTT, Vol. 1, p. 179, this position is recorded as *Thượng Thư Bộ Lại* (Minister of the Ministry of Personnel)

17. Taylor, K. W. (1983). *The Birth of Vietnam*. Berkeley: University of California Press., p. 135.

18. Taylor puts this date at 523, ibid., p. 135, other, Bộ Quốc Phòng - Viện Lịch Sử Quân Sự Việt Nam, Trần, Q. V., & Lê, Đ. S. (2001). *Lịch Sử Quân Sự Việt Nam - Tập 2 - Đấu tranh giành độc lập tự chủ (từ năm 179 TCN đến năm 938)*. NXB Chính Trị Quốc Gia., p. 140 dates this event as before 521. The rebellion was not in full swing until 541, nearly 20 years after their return. If both Lý Bí, and Tinh Thiều began the revolt together soon after they returned from China, then it would seem a very long time for them to achieve victory. A possible explanation is that they already had a network of like-minded individuals and seized the opportunity to move against the Liang, not in 523, but at a much later date when the timing was right. If Lý Bí returned in 521 or 523, he must have been in his twenties which would seem reasonable if he was born in 499 or 503.

19. According to SKTT, Vol. 1, p. 179 but in Taylor, they travelled back to Giao Châu together. See Taylor, K. W. (1983). *The Birth of Vietnam*. Berkeley: University of California Press., p. 135.

20. The husband of Trưng Trắc, Thi Sách, came from a county of the same name, but Chu Diên, during Lý Bí's time, had shifted eastward from the region between Đáy and Hồng rivers in Han times to the land between the Red and Thái Bình rivers. SKTT, Vol. 1, p. 179, notes it was part of Hải Hưng, which was divided into Hưng Yên and Hải Dương provinces.

21. Taylor, K. W. (1983). *The Birth of Vietnam*. Berkeley: University of California Press., p. 136.

22. Silian, Y. (635). *Book of Liang (Liang shu) - Volume 3: Emperor Wu 3*. http://chinesenotes.com/liang-shu/liangshu003.html#?highlight=%E6%9D%8E%E8%B3%81 also Bộ Quốc Phòng - Viện Lịch Sử Quân Sự Việt Nam, Trần, Q. V., & Lê, Đ. S. (2001). *Lịch Sử Quân Sự Việt Nam - Tập 2 - Đấu tranh giành độc lập tự chủ (từ năm 179 TCN đến năm 938)*. NXB Chính Trị Quốc Gia., p. 144. This event was not mentioned in Chens Shu (the Book of Chen).

23. Since Lý Bí may have begun his rebellion from Cửu Đức (Hà Tĩnh) south of Ái Châu (Thanh Hóa), presumably he would have vanquished any Liang resistance on his way north to Long Biên. While it is possible, it would appear unconvincing that surviving Liang forces at Ái Châu were called upon to march against him later.

24. Bộ Quốc Phòng - Viện Lịch Sử Quân Sự Việt Nam, Trần, Q. V., & Lê, Đ. S. (2001). *Lịch Sử Quân Sự Việt Nam - Tập 2 - Đấu tranh giành độc lập tự chủ (từ năm 179 TCN đến năm 938)*. NXB Chính Trị Quốc Gia., p. 144.

25. SKTT, Vol.1, p. 179 cites *"unhealthy air rising in spring and asked for a delay to autumn"*

26. A similar epidemic struck down the invasion forces of the Han army in the second century BCE during their invasion of Nan-yue. See Pham, T. (2021). *The Bronze Drums and The Earrings* (Vol. 1). 315Kio Publishing. .

27. Durand, M. (1951). La dynastie des Lý antérieurs d'après le Viêt diên u linh tâp. *Bulletin de l'Ecole française d'Extrême-Orient*, 437-452. https://www.persee.fr/doc/befeo_0336-1519_1951_num_44_2_517., p. 440.

28. Bộ Quốc Phòng - Viện Lịch Sử Quân Sự Việt Nam, Trần, Q. V., & Lê, Đ. S. (2001). *Lịch Sử Quân Sự Việt Nam - Tập 2 - Đấu tranh giành độc lập tự chủ (từ năm 179 TCN đến năm 938)*. NXB Chính Trị Quốc Gia., p. 145. Note that SKTT, Vol. 1, p. 179 does not mention any ambush; besides, it would have been a major undertaking for Lý Bí to take the fight to the Liang at Hepu. To get there, he would have to follow the routes Ma Yuan took in reverse, involving a distance of some 500 kilometres on foot and possibly a week of sailing on many ships. This may have been possible for an established state, but it would likely be too far for a rebellious force that wanted to consolidate its gain and establish a nation.

29. SKTT, Vol. 1, p. 179.

30. Bộ Quốc Phòng - Viện Lịch Sử Quân Sự Việt Nam, Trần, Q. V., & Lê, Đ. S. (2001). *Lịch Sử Quân Sự Việt Nam - Tập 2 - Đấu tranh giành độc lập tự chủ (từ năm 179 TCN đến năm 938)*. NXB Chính Trị Quốc Gia., p. 151.

31. Taylor, K. W. (1983). *The Birth of Vietnam*. Berkeley: University of California Press., p. 138.

32. Silian, Y. (635). *Book of Liang (Liang shu) - Volume 3: Emperor Wu 3*. http://chinesenotes.com/liangshu/liangshu003.html#?highlight=%E6%9D%8E%E8%B3%81

33. SKTT, Vol. 1, p. 179.

34. Taylor, K. W. (1983). *The Birth of Vietnam*. Berkeley: University of California Press., p. 138.

35. Pham, T. (2021). *The Bronze Drums and The Earrings* (Vol. 1). 315Kio Publishing., p. 145.

36. Taylor, K. W. (1983). *The Birth of Vietnam*. Berkeley: University of California Press., p. 138.

37. SKTT, Vol. 1, p. 179.

38. Trần, Q. V., & Vũ, T. S. (2004). *Hà Nội Nghìn Xưa*. NXB Quân Đội Nhân Dân., p. 120-121. In Phan's paper, Van Xuân citadel was built in the centre of Hanoi, see Phan, H. L. (2012). *Power centres in North Vietnam during the period of Chinese occupation - Những trung tâm quyền lực ở miền bắc Việt Nam thời kỳ Trung Hoa đô hộ*. Perspectives on the archaeology of Vietnam international colloquium, Hanoi 29th February - 2nd March 2012 = Toàn cảnh khảo cổ học Việt Nam, Hanoi, Vietnam., p. 196.

39. Others suggest that the capital could be near lake "Vạn Xuân" in Vạn Phúc commune, Thanh Trì district, south of Hanoi, see CM, Vol. 1, p. 169. However, there are only two small ponds near Tiên Linh pagoda (20°54'46.7"N 105°53'31.0"E), not a lake in the vicinity. A study by Tran in *Hà Nội Nghìn Xưa* suggests lake "Vạn Xuân" or "Vạn Xoan" is between the communes of Thanh Trì and Vĩnh Tuy. Today, the whole area is shallow, with many lakes and ponds so that it could be there. The largest lake is called Thanh Trì, next to the office of the People's Committee of Thanh Trì ward (20°59'41.9"N 105°53'10.3"E), and that could be lake Vạn Xuân. However, from historical records, we know that Lý Bí made a strong stand at the mouth of the Tô Lịch river, around 7 kilometres north of the lake. His attackers were coming from the south and would reach the lake first; thus it would not make sense if he abandoned his capital at lake Thanh Trì to take a defensive position at a relatively short distance north of it. It would be more understandable if his capital was not at lake Thanh Trì but further away from the mouth of the Tô Lịch river, upstream of the river to the east. It would explain why he defended the capital at the river mouth to prevent his attackers from getting to the capital. Taylor suggests his capital was at Gia Ninh, further to the east on the north bank of the Red River, possibly opposite Sơn Tây city, see Taylor, K. W. (1983). *The Birth of Vietnam*. Berkeley: University of California Press., p. 140. It is possible, but for the position of the Khai Quốc pagoda, which Lý Bí built, would be some 45 kilometres west of the capital, this would likely be too far. One could imagine that the king wanted to pray at a pagoda close to his capital.

40. Bửu, C., Đỗ, V. A., Pham, H. T., & Trương, B. L. (1962). *Hồng Đức Bản Đồ*. Tủ Sách Viện Khảo Cổ-Publications of the Institute of Historical Research - Publications de l'institut de Recherches Historiques - Số III., p.9.

41. Quốc Sử Quán Triều Nguyễn, Viện Khoa Học Xã Hội Việt Nam, & Viện Sử Học. (2006). *Đại Nam Nhất Thống Chí* (T. Đ. Phạm & D. A. Đào, Trans.). NXB Thuận Hóa., Vol. 3, p. 215.

42. unknown. (19th century). *King Lý Nam Đế and his Queen*. https://www.vnfam.vn/en/artifact/5af2af3d4e501e0026539520. 112 x 182 cm

43. Stefan Fussan / CC BY-SA (https://creativecommons.org/licenses/by-sa/3.0). (20 December 2011). Trấn Quốc Pagoda, Hanoi, Vietnam. https://upload.wikimedia.org/wikipedia/commons/3/3d/Hanoi_-_Tran-Quoc-Pagode_0002.JPG

44. See Team Wanderlust. (10 February 2017). *10 incredibly beautiful pagodas from around the world.* https://www.wanderlust.co.uk/content/10-incredible-pagodas-from-around-the-world/.

45. Xiao Bo's father was a cousin of the emperor (See Taylor, K. W. (1983). *The Birth of Vietnam*. Berkeley: University of California Press., p. 141), he may have been a relative of the other Xiao Zi, and Xiao Yong mentioned elsewhere.

46. Yao Silian. (636). *Book of Chen (Chen Shu), Volume 1: Emperor Wu 1*. http://chinesenotes.com/chenshu/chenshu001.html, Vol. 1: Emperor Wu 1, http://chinesenotes.com/chenshu/chenshu001.html.

47. Ma Yuan left from the port of Beihai in Hepu, south of Panyu; the Liang army could have sailed from there instead.

48. Unknown, translated by Trần Quốc Vượng (1959), & compared and corrected by Đinh Khắc Thuân. (2005). *Việt Sử Lược*. Thuận Hóa. (1377), p. 31. This event is not mentioned in the Book of Chen, Vol.1 or Liang shu, Vol. 3.

49. Maspero, H. (1916). Études d'histoire d'Annam. *Bulletin de l'Ecole française d'Extrême-Orient*, 1-55. https://www.persee.fr/doc/befeo_0336-1519_1916_num_16_1_527., p. 20. I am unable to find the primary reference for this description, according to other historians, based on Liang shu, Volume 3: Emperor Wu 3, http://chinesenotes.com/liangshu/liangshu003.html, Lý Bí built a wooden fort at the mouth of Tô Lịch river and that seems to be the basis to reach the conclusion that where his capital was. See Trần, Q. V., & Vũ, T. S. (2004). *Hà Nội Nghìn Xưa*. NXB Quân Đội Nhân Dân., pp. 120-121. Again, I am unable to locate the relevant passage in the primary reference.

50. Gia Ninh is the name of a county under Phong prefecture during the Tang dynasty; according to Maspero, it included Việt Trì, Vĩnh Yên, and Sơn Tây and extended from Ba Vì mountain in the west to the Cà Lồ river in the east. See Maspero, H. (1910). Le Protectorat général d'Annam sous les T'ang : essai de géographie historique, II. *Bulletin de l'Ecole française d'Extrême-Orient*, 665-682. https://www.persee.fr/doc/befeo_0336-1519_1910_num_10_1_206., pp. 666-667. There is little information on the location of the Gia Ninh fort, but since rivers were the main transport routes at that time, I would suggest that it was near the intersection between the Cà Lồ and Red rivers, somewhere in the Yên Lạc district, Vĩnh Phúc province. The location at the Cà Lồ river would allow Lý Bí to receive support from his birthplace in Tiên Phong district, Thái Nguyên province. Đào indicates Gia Ninh at Yên Lãng, Phúc Yên (one of the two cities that was combined into Vĩnh Yên, the other was Vĩnh Yên) which should read Yên Lạc as Yên Lãng is in Phú Thọ province on the west bank of Đà river. See Đào, D. A. (2006). *Lịch sử Việt Nam - Từ nguồn gốc đến thế kỷ XIX*. NXB Văn Hóa Thông Tin. (1957), p. 125.

51. Bộ Quốc Phòng - Viện Lịch Sử Quân Sự Việt Nam, Trần, Q. V., & Lê, Đ. S. (2001). *Lịch Sử Quân Sự Việt Nam - Tập 2 - Đấu tranh giành độc lập tự chủ (từ năm 179 TCN đến năm 938)*. NXB Chính Trị Quốc Gia., p. 153. According to VDUL, the person who fought against Champa is Lý Phục Man (Lý, the conqueror of the barbarians), the barbarians in his title refers to those tribes who lived at Đường Lâm near Sơn Tây, north-west of Hanoi where he died, see VDUL, p. 87. There is a temple for him at the Yên Sở, Đắc Sở communes, Hoài Đức district, Hanoi. Historians have different opinions as to whether Phạm Tu and Lý Phục Man are the same person, ibid., p. 141.

52. There are three hills on the west side of the Thao river, also known as the Red River, which the locals refer to as Cổ Bồng, Tam Khu or Khu Lăng surrounded by a marsh, and where Khuất Lão is believed to be, see ibid., p. 159. Cổ Bồng hillock is some 500 metres from the riverbank with a shape like a three-branch lotus, and next to two places I have not been able to identify on Google Maps: Liên Giang lagoon and Đính Trại.

53. Yao Silian. (636). *Book of Chen (Chen Shu), Volume 1: Emperor Wu 1*. http://chinesenotes.com/chenshu/chenshu001.html, Vol. 1: Emperor Wu 1 and SKTT, Vol. 1, p. 180.

54. Bộ Quốc Phòng - Viện Lịch Sử Quân Sự Việt Nam, Trần, Q. V., & Lê, Đ. S. (2001). *Lịch Sử Quân Sự Việt Nam - Tập 2 - Đấu tranh giành độc lập tự chủ (từ năm 179 TCN đến năm 938)*. NXB Chính Trị Quốc Gia., p. 159.

55. Yao Silian. (636). *Book of Chen (Chen Shu), Volume 1: Emperor Wu 1*. http://chinesenotes.com/chenshu/chenshu001.html, Vol. 1: Emperor Wu 1 and Silian, Y. (635). *Book of Liang (Liang shu)-Volume 3: Emperor Wu 3*. http://chinesenotes.com/liangshu/liangshu003.html#?highlight=%E6%9D%8E%E8%B3%81 Vol. 3: Emperor Wu 3.

56. CM, Vol.1, p. 173.

57. Bộ Quốc Phòng - Viện Lịch Sử Quân Sự Việt Nam, Trần, Q. V., & Lê, Đ. S. (2001). *Lịch Sử Quân Sự Việt Nam - Tập 2 - Đấu tranh giành độc lập tự chủ (từ năm 179 TCN đến năm 938)*. NXB Chính Trị Quốc Gia., p. 158.

58. Taylor, K. W. (1983). *The Birth of Vietnam*. Berkeley: University of California Press., p. 143.

59. Lý Bí Temple, Văn Lương, Tam Nông, Phú Thọ, coordinates: 21.306603 N, 105.251137 E.

60. Lý, T. X. (2012). *Việt điện u linh* (Đ. R. Trịnh & G. K. Đinh, Trans.). NXB Hồng Bàng. (1329), p. 49.

61. At Khoái Châu district, Hưng Yên province.

62. For a reference to the Chử Đồng Tử legend, see Pham, T. (2021). *The Bronze Drums and The Earrings* (Vol. 1). 315Kio Publishing., p. 68.

63. LNCQ, p. 54.

64. SKTT, Vol.1, p. 183

65. SKTT, Vol.1, p. 182 records Triệu Quang Phục moved from Long Biên to Vũ Ninh shortly after. It notes that Vũ Ninh is in Quế Võ district, just around 15 kilometres east of Bắc Ninh. This is where Mt Châu Sơn (or Trâu Sơn) is (also known as Mt Vũ Ninh), see Pham, T. (2021). *The Bronze Drums and The Earrings* (Vol. 1). 315Kio Publishing., p. 115.

66. At the end of the nineteenth century, a revolt against the French colonial government held out for several years at Bãi Sậy swamp, in the same area at Dạ Trạch. See http://baotanglichsu.vn/vi/Articles/3097/15111/9-1885-bung-no-cuoc-khoi-nghia-bai-say.html.

67. SKTT, Vol. 1, p. 181.

68. Pham, T. (2021). *The Bronze Drums and The Earrings* (Vol. 1). 315Kio Publishing., p. 68.

69. The text describes it as *"mũ đâu mâu"*, a helmet made from bronze or iron with a short, pointed shape in the centre of the top of the helmet.

70. LNCQ, p. 54.

71. Photo by author, 20 January 2020.

72. "Đền Hóa Dạ Trạch", Photo by author, 20 January 2020.

73. SKTT, Vol. 1, p. 184.

74. Di Lao could be the ancient kingdoms of Luang Prabang (Nam Chưởng) and Muang Phuan (Xiang Khouang, Trấn Man).

75. CM, Vol. 1, p. 176.

76. Thái Bình county during Tang dynasty is on the eastern bank of the Red River generally around the Cà Lồ river whereas Ô Diên county is on the opposite river bank. It is not present-day Thái Bình province. See Maspero, H. (1910). Le Protectorat général d'Annam sous les T'ang : essai de géographie historique, I. *Bulletin de l'Ecole française d'Extrême-Orient*, 539-584. https://www.persee.fr/doc/befeo_0336-1519_1910_num_10_1_204., p. 680a. Lý Bí family came from Thái Bình prefecture and perhaps that is why Lý Phật Tử returned there to contest power with Triệu Quang Phục.

77. This story is very similar to the story of the magic crossbow nearly seven hundred years earlier, see Pham, T. (2021). *The Bronze Drums and The Earrings* (Vol. 1). 315Kio Publishing. which leads some

historians to doubt the story of Triệu Quang Phục as historical. See Maspero, H. (1916). Études d'histoire d'Annam. *Bulletin de l'Ecole française d'Extrême-Orient*, 1-55. https://www.persee.fr/doc/befeo_0336-1519_1916_num_16_1_527., p. 10. who points out that ANCL never mentions him (ibid. p. 12). This is of no surprise as ANCL relied on Chinese sources.

78. The timing seems a little odd, Lý Phật Tử moved out of the mountain to challenge Triệu Quang Phục in 557, and his son married Quang Phục's daughter at about the same time. However, not until 570, or thirteen years later, that his son stole the golden claw, which led to the defeat of Quang Phục. One would have thought duplicity like this would have happened within the first year or two of the marriage.

79. Đại Nha is also known as Đại Ác and Đại An, at Nghĩa Hưng district, Nam Định province.

80. SKTT, Vol.1, pp. 183-185.

81. While historical text does not record this, it would not be unreasonable to assume that he had been with Lý Bí from the beginning of 541 as he escaped with Lý Bí's brother to the mountains after the battle of lake Điển Triệt in 546.

82. Taylor, K. W. (1983). *The Birth of Vietnam*. Berkeley: University of California Press., pp. 148-149.

83. Zheng, W., Shigu, Y., Yingda, K., & Wuji, Z. (636). *Book of Sui - Volume 2 Annals 2: Gaozu 2*. http://chinesenotes.com/suishu/suishu002.html. In Taylor, K. W. (1983). *The Birth of Vietnam*. Berkeley: University of California Press., p. 159. Lý Phật Tử was recorded as Lý Xuân (Li Chun) from Giao Chỉ. Some of the others were in Guangxi (such as Wuzhou), the coast of Fujian, Zhejiang, and Jiangsu provinces (such as Quanzhou, Yuhang, Yongjia, and Suzhou).

84. Taylor, K. W. (1983). *The Birth of Vietnam*. Berkeley: University of California Press., p. 161, also Wei Zheng, Yan Shigu, Kong Yingda, & Zhangsun Wuji. (636). *Book of Sui - Volume 56 Biographies 21: Lu Kai, Ling Huxi, Xue Zhou, Yu Wenbi, Zhang Heng, Yang Wang* http://chinesenotes.com/suishu/suishu056.html.

85. For a detailed discussion of the Cổ Loa citadel, see Pham, T. (2021). *The Bronze Drums and The Earrings* (Vol. 1). 315Kio Publishing., p. pp. 97-102.

86. SKTT, Vol. 1, p. 185.

87. Bộ Quốc Phòng - Viện Lịch Sử Quân Sự Việt Nam, Trần, Q. V., & Lê, Đ. S. (2001). *Lịch Sử Quân Sự Việt Nam - Tập 2 - Đấu tranh giành độc lập tự chủ (từ năm 179 TCN đến năm 938)*. NXB Chính Trị Quốc Gia., p. 174.

88. Maspero, H. (1916). Études d'histoire d'Annam. *Bulletin de l'Ecole française d'Extrême-Orient*, 1-55. https://www.persee.fr/doc/befeo_0336-1519_1916_num_16_1_527., p. 25.

89. Based on a marching speed of 12.45 kilometres per day, see Chapter 4.

90. Maspero points out that the location (called Tụ Long) is in the region of a dispute between colonial France and the Qing dynasty in 1887; France ceded this region to China, see *"Convention relative à la délimitation de la frontière entre la Chine et le Tonkin"* signed in 1887.

91. Also known as Clear river, Maspero, H. (1916). Études d'histoire d'Annam. *Bulletin de l'Ecole française d'Extrême-Orient*, 1-55. https://www.persee.fr/doc/befeo_0336-1519_1916_num_16_1_527., p. 25. On the other hand, Đào locates Đỗ Long somewhere in Nanning, Guangxi province, which would be in the wrong direction from Yunnan. Without any additional information, I would use Maspero's reference even if it would be a strange choice for Lý Phật Tử to have 2,000 men stationed in such a remote area, even if it is near the Chinese border.

92. SKTT, Vol. 1, pp. 186-187.

93. Ibid., p. 187.

94. Ibid., p. 186.

95. Bộ Quốc Phòng - Viện Lịch Sử Quân Sự Việt Nam, Trần, Q. V., & Lê, Đ. S. (2001). *Lịch Sử Quân Sự Việt Nam - Tập 2 - Đấu tranh giành độc lập tự chủ (từ năm 179 TCN đến năm 938)*. NXB Chính Trị Quốc Gia., p. 175.

96. I am unable to locate these temples. There is a large temple for Triệu Quang Phục at Giáp Ba temple, Nam Giang, Nam Trực district, Nam Định province (20°20'16.1"N 106°10'54.8"E). As for Lý Phật Tử, there are not many temples dedicated to him, but in Hanoi, he is worshipped at the village communal house of Mai Dịch, Cầu Giấy, located at 16 Hồ Tùng Mậu (21°02'13.6"N 105°46'44.9"E).

97. According to a reference quoted in Kiều, T. H. (2016). *Góp phần nghiên cứu lịch sử văn hóa Việt Nam - Thời kỳ thiên niên kỷ đầu công nguyên*. NXB Thế Giới., p. 564, across north Vietnam, Lý Bí are worshipped at 20 different villages; 26 for Triệu Quang Phục; 16 for Lý Phật Tử, 15 of which are at Phúc Yên province; ten for his son, Nhã Lang; 19 for Lý Phục Man, and a surprisingly high number of 143 villages for two of Triệu Quang Phục's generals: Trương Hống, Trương Hát.

CHAPTER 12

1. Annan Protectorate, at one time (660-663), is part of the Lingnan circuit that includes Guangdong province; at another time (745), it is part of the Lingnan Jiedushi, and at a later time, it is part of 49 military districts or *fanzhen*.

2. Unknown, translated by Trần Quốc Vượng (1959), & compared and corrected by Đinh Khắc Thuân. (2005). *Việt Sử Lược*. Thuận Hóa. (1377), p. 43.

3. Bộ Quốc Phòng - Viện Lịch Sử Quân Sự Việt Nam, Trần, Q. V., & Lê, Đ. S. (2001). *Lịch Sử Quân Sự Việt Nam - Tập 2 - Đấu tranh giành độc lập tự chủ (từ năm 179 TCN đến năm 938)*. NXB Chính Trị Quốc Gia., p. 227.

4. Phan, H. L. (2009). Khởi nghĩa Mai Thúc Loan - Những vấn đề cần xác minh. *Nghiên Cứu Lịch Sử - Viện Sử Học, Vol. 2.2009.*, p. 7.

5. Lý, T. X. (2012). *Việt điện u linh* (Đ. R. Trịnh & G. K. Đinh, Trans.). NXB Hồng Bàng. (1329), p. 146.

6. This has been identified with Suvarnabhumi, "Land of Gold" or Suvarnakudya, "Wall of Gold", Hall, D. G. E. (1999). *A history of South-East Asia*. MacMillan., p. 27.

7. Located at 18°41'49.6"N 105°28'36.3"E. by the foot of Đụn (Hùng Sơn) mountain. Photo used with permission from https://www.facebook.com/lamhmk/photos/2874975272515336, 5 January 2021.

8. CM, Vol.1, p. 188.

9. ANCL, p. 118.

10. Benn, C. D. (2004). *China's golden age: everyday life in the Tang dynasty*. Oxford University Press.

11. Phan, H. L. (2009). Khởi nghĩa Mai Thúc Loan - Những vấn đề cần xác minh. *Nghiên Cứu Lịch Sử - Viện Sử Học, Vol. 2.2009.*, p. 13.

12. Lý, T. X. (2012). *Việt điện u linh* (Đ. R. Trịnh & G. K. Đinh, Trans.). NXB Hồng Bàng. (1329), p. 150.

13. On Sa Nam Street, near the intersection of Sa Nam and Mai Hắc Đế streets, Nam Đàn district, Nghệ An province.

14. Hồ, H. (5 February 2012). *Thực hư chuyện kinh đô Vạn An trên đất Nghệ An: Những bí mật chờ giải mã*. https://giadinh.net.vn/xa-hoi/thuc-hu-chuyen-kinh-do-van-an-tren-dat-nghe-an-nhung-bi-mat-cho-giai-ma-20120202104119991.htm

15. Including Guangxi and Guangdong provinces, see Pham, T. (2021). *The Bronze Drums and The Earrings* (Vol. 1). 315Kio Publishing., p. 145.

16. Zhao Ying, Liu Xu, Zhang Zhao, Jia Wei, & Zhao Xi. (941-945). *Old Book of Tang (Jiu Tang shu)*. https://ctext.org/wiki.pl?if=gb&res=456206, Volume 184 Biographies 134: Imperial Officials, http://chinesenotes.com/jiutangshu/jiutangshu188.html. Xin Tang shu, Volume 207 has a similar passage but includes Chin-lin.

17. Phan, H. L. (2009). Khởi nghĩa Mai Thúc Loan - Những vấn đề cần xác minh. *Nghiên Cứu Lịch Sử - Viện Sử Học, Vol. 2.2009.*, p. 12.

18. Châu, H. Đ. (2018). *An Nam Truyện - Ghi chép về Việt Nam trong chính sử Trung Quốc xưa*. Hội Nhà Văn., pp. 220-221. See also Xin Tang Shu, Volume 207.

19. Taylor, K. W. (1983). *The Birth of Vietnam*. Berkeley: University of California Press., p. 193.

20. The star of Ngâu is a reference to the Vietnamese version of *"Ngưu Lang Chức Nữ"*, a Chinese folktale called *"Cowherd and the Weaver Girl"*, a forbidden love story between a cattle grazier (*Ngưu Lang*) and the weaver (*Chức Nữ*), symbolizing the stars of Vega and Altair on the opposite sides of the heavenly river (the Milky Way). Its citation is related to Phùng Hưng's ability to wrestle a water buffalo or an ox.

21. Lý Tế, X., & Lê Hữu, M. (1961). *Việt điện u-linh tập*. Khai-Trí. //catalog.hathitrust.org/Record/001356016 http://hdl.handle.net/2027/mdp.39015023991485, ibid., p. 28.

22. In 782, the military commander of Diễn prefecture (north of present-day Nghệ An province), Lý Mạnh Thu, and the prefect of Phong (present-day Phú Thọ province), Lý Bì Ngạn rebelled but were captured and beheaded. See ANCL, p. 195.

23. Lý, T. X. (2012). *Việt điện u linh* (Đ. R. Trịnh & G. K. Đinh, Trans.). NXB Hồng Bàng. (1329), p. 45. The reference cites "ten thousand *cân* of rock … over ten *dặm*". One *cân*, or one *jin* (Chinese pound), is 16 *lang* (Chinese ounce) or 661 g in Tang times. Ten thousand *jin* (or 6,610 kg) is a massive weight for a mortal to carry. As a matter of comparison, the heaviest weight ever lifted by a human being in a back lift is 2,840 kg, according to the Guinness Book of Worlds Record (1985 edition). Perhaps the number should read 1,000 *cân* or 595 kg !!. Ten *dặm* or *li* (Chinese mile) is 4.5 kilometres.

24. This is based on information from a stele erected in 1841. See Phan, H. L. (2009). Khởi nghĩa Mai Thúc Loan - Những vấn đề cần xác minh. *Nghiên Cứu Lịch Sử - Viện Sử Học, Vol. 2.2009.*, p. 16.

25. "Great Venerable", Vietnamese Cự Lão, "Great Strength", Vietnamese Cự Lực, see Taylor, K. W. (1983). *The Birth of Vietnam*. Berkeley: University of California Press., p. 202 and Lý, T. X. (2012). *Việt điện u linh* (Đ. R. Trịnh & G. K. Đinh, Trans.). NXB Hồng Bàng. (1329), p. 45 and CM, Vol. 1, p. 191, also SKTT, Vol. 1, p. 191.

26. or Đỗ Anh Hàn in other sources

27. History is not clear on the timing, in Lý, T. X. (2012). *Việt điện u linh* (Đ. R. Trịnh & G. K. Đinh, Trans.). NXB Hồng Bàng. (1329) p. 46, Phùng Hưng died after seven years of rule, and his son Phùng An ascended the throne for another two years to 791, which means the brothers entered La Thành in 782. However, the *duhu* of 782 was Fu Liang-jiao, not Gao Zheng-ping. It is possible, of course, that Gao Zheng-ping, the next *duhu* after Fu Liang-jiao, replaced him in the same year, see ANCL, p. 195. Another source, CM, Vol. 1, p. 191, indicates Phùng Hưng died soon after he captured La Thành, which means this event happened closer to 791, say 788 or 789, to allow for the two years of his son's rule. 791 was the year when Phùng An surrendered to Zhao Zhang, the new protectorate general sent by Tang. Since Gao Zheng Ping already appeared in history in 767 as a *Jing Lue Shi*, it seems a long time, over 20 years, from then until he became a *duhu*. I would suggest that the year 782 or sometime after seems to make sense as it was soon after the *taishou* of Phong was beheaded, thus providing a strong motivation for the brothers, who came from Phong, to take revenge and attack La Thành.

28. ANCL, p. 195 records another Protectorate General, Zhang Zing, who died on the job between Gao Zheng Ping, and Zhao Zhang and that the rebellion was led by Đỗ Anh Hàn (Luân), a tribal chief. ANCL does not mention the Phùng brothers.

29. Đào, D. A. (2006). *Lịch sử Việt Nam - Từ nguồn gốc đến thế kỷ XIX*. NXB Văn Hóa Thông Tin. (1957), p. 142.

30. Kim Mã, Ba Đình at 21°01'52.8"N 105°49'44.4"E.

31. Located at 21°08'54.5"N 105°27'47.5"E.

32. ANCL, p. 196.

33. Taylor, K. W. (1983). *The Birth of Vietnam*. Berkeley: University of California Press., p. 223.

34. Photo by Ngokhong from Vietnamese Wikipedia, C. B.-S. (2010). *Shrines of Phung Hung in Son Tay town, Hanoi*. https://upload.wikimedia.org/wikipedia/commons/c/c8/DenPhungHung1.jpg.

CHAPTER 13

1. Ma Yuan built a citadel named Kiển Giang at Phong Khê county in 43 CE (see SKTT, Vol. 1, p. 157). The citadel is in a round shape like a cocoon (*ổ kén*) that is why it is named "Kiển". This citadel could be the same as Cổ Loa, see Đào, D. A. (2005). *Đất nước Việt Nam qua các đời - Nghiên cứu địa lý học lịch sử Việt Nam*. NXB Văn Hóa Thông Tin., p. 44, but there is no evidence that it was used as the commandery capital.

2. The other places which became the capitals of Vietnam are Hoa Lư (968-1010), Tây Đô (1400-1407), Huế (1802-1945), and Saigon (1955-1975) for the Republic of South Vietnam.

3. Phan, H. L. (2018). *Lịch sử và văn hóa Việt Nam tiếp cận bộ phận* (P. T. Phan, Ed. 4th ed.). NXB Đại Học Quốc Gia Hà Nội., p. 752.

4. The map is taken from Bửu, C., Đỗ, V. A., Pham, H. T., & Trương, B. L. (1962). *Hồng Đức Bản Đồ*. Tủ Sách Viện Khảo Cổ-Publications of the Institute of Historical Research - Publications de l'institut de Recherches Historiques - Số III., p. 9. The translation of location names is taken from Lê Thánh Tông (1442 - 1497) Public domain, v. W. C. (2016). *Bản đồ kinh thành Thăng Long (kèm chú thích) theo Hồng Đức bản đồ sách (洪德版圖冊), ban hành vào đời vua Lê Thánh Tông, năm Hồng Đức thứ 21 (tức năm 1490)*. https://upload.wikimedia.org/wikipedia/commons/6/62/B%E1%BA%A3n_%C4%91%E1%BB%93_kinh_th%C3%A0nh_Th%C4%83ng_Long_%28k%C3%A8m_ch%C3%BA_th%C3%AD-ch%29%2C_theo_H%E1%BB%93ng_%C4%90%E1%BB%A9c_b%E1%BA%A3n_%C4%91%E1%BB%93_s%C3%A1ch_%E6%B4%AA%E5%BE%B7%E7%89%88%E5%9C%96%E5%86%8A_%281490%29.jpg. The original map shows *Vương Phủ* (王府) which means a place for a lord appointed by the king but the lord may not be Lord Trịnh. The name of the map is *Trung Đô* (middle capital). Under the Lý dynasty, it was called *Thăng Long* but changed to *Đông Đô* in 1397 by the Trần dynasty and became *Đông Kinh* under the Lê dynasty. I use Đông Kinh for our discussion. See Phan, H. L. (2012). *Thăng Long-Hà Nội vị thế lịch sử và di sản văn hóa*. 8.2012., p. 5.

5. Phan, H. L. (2018). *Lịch sử và văn hóa Việt Nam tiếp cận bộ phận* (P. T. Phan, Ed. 4th ed.). NXB Đại Học Quốc Gia Hà Nội., p.785.

6. Ibid., p. 780.

7. Downloaded from Frederic Romanet du Caillaud, Public domain via Wikimedia Commons, & Vinhtantran. (1873 4 June 2009). *Map of Hanoi c. 1873 - Source La conquete du delta du Tong-King by Frederic Romanet du Caillaud, published in 1877*. https://upload.wikimedia.org/wikipedia/commons/7/70/Map_of_Hanoi.png.

8. *Chinese fortification: an overview of parts and terminology — Part 1: The wall.* (2019). https://greatmingmilitary.blogspot.com/2019/06/chinese-fortification-p1.html.

9. The Chinese script for Cheng is 城 and for Guo is 郭 which means outer wall. However, in other sources, the term used is Luo 羅 which means net or silk. But La 欏 can also mean a wooden fence. There is an interpretation of La as dyke or stopbank, but the Chinese script for that is 堤防 or Difang, entirely unrelated to La.

10. Nguyen, P. L. (1975). Les nouvelles recherches archéologiques au Việtnam (Complément au Việtnam de Louis Bezacier). *Arts Asiatiques*, 3-151. https://www.persee.fr/doc/arasi_0004-3958_1975_num_31_1_109., p. 24-25.

11. Phan, H. L. (2018). *Lịch sử và văn hóa Việt Nam tiếp cận bộ phận* (P. T. Phan, Ed. 4th ed.). NXB Đại Học Quốc Gia Hà Nội., p. 751.

12. Ibid., p. 753. Also known as *Cung Thành*.

13. See Taylor, K. W. (1983). *The Birth of Vietnam.* Berkeley: University of California Press., p. 250, footnote 2.

14. Ibid., p. 174. Taylor suggests Tử Thành was built where Lý Bí built the fortification to resist Chen Baxian in 545. On the archaeological evidence that Han graves were found at Chèm, brick graves from the Tang dynasty and wells at Nhật Tảo, Đông Ngạc commune (the Ciputra tombs mentioned in the footnotes of Chapter 14), Phan believes the Sui built a capital which he terms Tống Bình somewhere there, to the west of West lake by the bank of the Thiên Phù river which has now disappeared. See Phan, H. L. (2012). *Power centres in North Vietnam during the period of Chinese occupation - Những trung tâm quyền lực ở miền bắc Việt Nam thời kỳ Trung Hoa đô hộ*. Perspectives on the archaeology of Vietnam international colloquium, Hanoi 29th February - 2nd March 2012 = Toàn cảnh khảo cổ học Việt Nam, Hanoi, Vietnam., p. 195. Both locations are on the southern bank of the Red River, by the Thăng Long bridge.

15. Nguyễn, Q. N. (ibid.). *Chinese domination and the resistance against it: remains of the material culture - Bắc thuộc và chống Bắc thuộc: Những dấu tích văn hóa vật chất.*, p. 353.

16. Jiangxi is a large province in China, south of the Yangtze River and sandwiched between Hunan and Fujian provinces.

17. Nguyễn, Q. N. (2012). *Chinese domination and the resistance against it: remains of the material culture - Bắc thuộc và chống Bắc thuộc: Những dấu tích văn hóa vật chất.* Perspectives on the archaeology of Vietnam international colloquium, Hanoi 29th February - 2nd March 2012 = Toàn cảnh khảo cổ học Việt Nam, Hanoi, Vietnam., p. 186 also Phan, H. L. (ibid.). *Power centres in North Vietnam during the period of Chinese occupation - Những trung tâm quyền lực ở miền bắc Việt Nam thời kỳ Trung Hoa đô hộ.*, p. 205.

18. Photo by Daderot - CC0. (3 August 2014). *Daderot, CC0, via Wikimedia Commons*. https://upload.wikimedia.org/wikipedia/commons/e/e6/Steps_-_Hanoi_Botanical_Garden_-_Hanoi%2C_Vietnam_-_DSC03633.JPG.

19. "*Núi*" in Vietnamese means mountain, but I would not refer to these natural features as mountains; they are more like small hills.

20. Trần, Q. V., & Vũ, T. S. (2004). *Hà Nội Nghìn Xưa*. NXB Quân Đội Nhân Dân., p. 25.

21. Tống, T. T. (2012). *A general outline on the history of archeology in Vietnam - Vài nét về lịch sử khảo cổ học Việt Nam.* Perspectives on the archaeology of Vietnam International Colloquium, Hanoi 29th February - 2nd March 2012 = Toàn cảnh khảo cổ học Việt Nam, Hanoi, Vietnam., p. 315.

22. Phan, H. L. (2018). *Lịch sử và văn hóa Việt Nam tiếp cận bộ phận* (P. T. Phan, Ed. 4th ed.). NXB Đại Học Quốc Gia Hà Nội., p. 776.

23. Co-ordinates (21°02'12.6"N 105°50'25.3"E).

24. Phan, H. L. (2018). *Lịch sử và văn hóa Việt Nam tiếp cận bộ phận* (P. T. Phan, Ed. 4th ed.). NXB Đại Học Quốc Gia Hà Nội., p. 763.

25. Tống, T. T. (2012). *A general outline on the history of archeology in Vietnam - Vài nét về lịch sử khảo cổ học Việt Nam*. Perspectives on the archaeology of Vietnam International Colloquium, Hanoi 29th February - 2nd March 2012 = Toàn cảnh khảo cổ học Việt Nam, Hanoi, Vietnam., p. 316.

26. At 209 phố Đội Cấn, Ba Đình, Hà Nội, built on Núi Vạn Bảo.

27. At 267 ngõ Hoàng Hoa Thám, Ba Đình, Hà Nội.

28. Somewhere near 63 Ngõ 279 Đội Cấn, Ba Đình, Hà Nội.

29. Phan, H. L. (2018). *Lịch sử và văn hóa Việt Nam tiếp cận bộ phận* (P. T. Phan, Ed. 4th ed.). NXB Đại Học Quốc Gia Hà Nội., p. 761.

30. Now at HABECO, Hanoi Beer Company, 183 Hoàng Hoa Thám, Ba Đình, Hanoi. Nguyễn, Q. N. (1998). Vị trí của chùa Chân Giáo và một hướng tìm di tích thành Thăng Long thời kỳ mới định đô Kỷ yếu hội thảo quốc tế Việt Nam học lần thứ nhất (1998) Hanoi., p. 141.

31. Previously Lycée Albert-Saraut.

32. Phan, H. L. (2018). *Lịch sử và văn hóa Việt Nam tiếp cận bộ phận* (P. T. Phan, Ed. 4th ed.). NXB Đại Học Quốc Gia Hà Nội., p. 765, Papin, P. (2001). *Histoire de Hanoi*. Fayard., p. 48.

33. Phan, H. L. (2018). *Lịch sử và văn hóa Việt Nam tiếp cận bộ phận* (P. T. Phan, Ed. 4th ed.). NXB Đại Học Quốc Gia Hà Nội., p. 771.

34. Taylor, K. W. (1983). *The Birth of Vietnam*. Berkeley: University of California Press., p. 188.

35. Maspero uses the French terms *pas* and *pied* in his paper for the measurements where he explains one *pas* equals six *pieds* and one pied is slightly less than 0.3 metres. These terms are translated into English as step and foot, and the original Chinese would be *bu* and *chi*. Under the Tang dynasty, one chi is either 0.30 or 0.36 metres (Appendix 15) and one *bu* is five *chi* or 1.5 or 1.8 metres. See Maspero, H. (1910). Le Protectorat général d'Annam sous les T'ang : essai de géographie historique, I. *Bulletin de l'Ecole française d'Extrême-Orient*, 539-584. https://www.persee.fr/doc/befeo_0336-1519_1910_num_10_1_204., p. 557.

36. SKTT, Vol. 1, p. 192.

37. Taylor, K. W. (1983). *The Birth of Vietnam*. Berkeley: University of California Press., p. 226. SKTT, Vol. 1, p.192. In ANCL, p. 53, Zhang Bo-yi built La Thành, but on p. 196, he built Đại La, so it would appear that ANCL treats both terms synonymously. Phan adopts the same approach (Phan, H. L. (2012). *Power centres in North Vietnam during the period of Chinese occupation - Những trung tâm quyền lực ở miền bắc Việt Nam thời kỳ Trung Hoa đô hộ*. Perspectives on the archaeology of Vietnam international colloquium, Hanoi 29th February - 2nd March 2012 = Toàn cảnh khảo cổ học Việt Nam, Hanoi, Vietnam., p. 202). In the same page, ANCL notes Zhang Zhou built Đại La. For my purposes, I treat La Thành as a citadel built by Zhang Bo-yi and Đại La as a citadel built by Zhang Zhou, and Gao Pian. But as explained previously, Đại La is a larger version of La Thành.

38. ANCL, p. 53.

39. ANCL, p. 56.

40. SKTT, Vol. 1, p. 193 dated this event at 824, ANCL, p. 198 put it at 825.

41. ANCL, p. 198. The term used in ANCL, "*phủ lị*", describe an administrative centre of the protectorate that Li Yuan-xi sought permission to shift, not a fortified wall "*thành*". However, later historians refer to this event as the construction of a new citadel, see SKTT Vol. 1, p. 193. I prefer ANCL's explanation as it is older than SKTT.

42. VSL, p. 33.

43. SKTT, Vol. 2, p. 67.

44. Unknown, translated by Trần Quốc Vượng (1959), & compared and corrected by Đinh Khắc Thuân. (2005). *Việt Sử Lược*. Thuận Hóa. (1377), p. 36, cites 1980 *zhang* and five *chi* (or 19805 *chi* or 3961 *bu* or 5,941 m, the equivalent square is 990.25 *bu* or 1,485 m for each side). Other references quote 3,000 *bu*, see Maspero, H. (1910). Le Protectorat général d'Annam sous les T'ang : essai de géographie historique, I. *Bulletin de l'Ecole française d'Extrême-Orient*, 539-584. https://www.persee.fr/doc/befeo_0336-1519_1910_num_10_1_204., p. 557.

45. 2 *zhang* 6 *chi* or 5.2 *bu* or 7.8 m

46. Vietnamese "Nữ Tường" (Chinese Nu Qiang) or "Woman's wall" at 5 *chi* and 5 *cun* or 1.65 m tall.

47. CM, Vol. 1, p.214. 2,125 *zhang* and 8 *chi* or 4251.6 *bu*, 1 *zhang* 5 *chi* or 3 *bu*.

48. Nguyễn, D. V. (2020). Nhận Diện La Thành Thăng Long Qua Tư Liệu Thư Tịch và Khảo Cổ Học. *Văn Hóa Truyền Thống và Phát Triển, Volume 9, Issue 1.*, p. 100.

49. ANCL, p. 53.

50. Unknown, translated by Trần Quốc Vượng (1959), & compared and corrected by Đinh Khắc Thuân. (2005). *Việt Sử Lược*. Thuận Hóa. (1377), p. 33, p. 36.

51. Đào, D. A. (2005). *Đất nước Việt Nam qua các đời - Nghiên cứu địa lý học lịch sử Việt Nam*. NXB Văn Hóa Thông Tin., p. 94, p. 96.

52. ANCL, p. 56, p. 194, p. 196

53. SKTT, Vol. 1, p. 192.

54. Phan, H. L. (2012). *Power centres in North Vietnam during the period of Chinese occupation - Những trung tâm quyền lực ở miền bắc Việt Nam thời kỳ Trung Hoa đô hộ*. Perspectives on the archaeology of Vietnam international colloquium, Hanoi 29th February - 2nd March 2012 = Toàn cảnh khảo cổ học Việt Nam, Hanoi, Vietnam., p. 202.

CHAPTER 14

1. The predecessors of the Yi people are the Wu Man or black barbarians. The other dominant ethnic group in Yunnan is the Bai people or Bai Man or white barbarians. There is an ongoing debate as to whether the Bai, the Yi or the Tai ethnic people are the original rulers of Nanzhao. According to researcher Yuqing Yang, the current view is that Nanzhao was populated by the people who are the ancestors of the Bai and the Yi nationality.

2. Lempert, D. (2018). Nan Zhao Invasions and Buddha idols of Northern Thailand and Laos in the 7th to 9th Centuries, Lao Studies, Volume 6, No. 1, pages 26 - 55, 2018. http://www.laostudies.org/system/files/subscription/Lempert.pdf. 6., p. 30.

3. There is a Taihe City Ruins of Nanzhao Kingdom near the village of Taihe near Dali, Taihecheng Relic Site, near Taihe, coordinates 25°37'51.3"N 100°12'23.7"E.

4. Lempert, D. (2018). Nan Zhao Invasions and Buddha idols of Northern Thailand and Laos in the 7th to 9th Centuries, Lao Studies, Volume 6, No. 1, pages 26 - 55, 2018. http://www.laostudies.org/system/files/subscription/Lempert.pdf. 6., p. 30.

5. Yuqing Yang. (June 2008). *The role of Nanzhao history in the formation of Bai identity* University of Oregon]., p. 65.

6. Cropped photo of original taken by Brücke Osteuropa. (2009). *Representatives of the Yi Minority in Shilin (Kunming/Yunnan)*. https://commons.wikimedia.org/wiki/File:Yi-Minority.JPG.

7. Man shu, p. 8. Fan Chuo was the Secretary of Cai Xi, An Nam Military Governor (862-863).

8. This place could be Manhao (23°01'10.7"N 103°20'53.4"E, 23.019636, 103.348152). During the French colonial period in the late nineteenth century, goods transported on the Red River from Hanoi or Haiphong were offloaded here and taken by pack animals to Mengzi at Honghe Hani and Yi Autonomous Prefecture. See Wikipedia. (-n). *Mengzi City*. https://en.wikipedia.org/wiki/Mengzi_City

9. Man shu records Chü-mieh or Yang-chü-mieh as the main palace of Nanzhao. It also mentions two other places: Ta-ho city, 15 *li* or 6.885 kilometres to the north, and Ta-li city, 40 *li* or 18.36 kilometres to the south of Yang-chü-mieh.

10. Man shu, p. 4.

11. Coordinates 25°03'53.0"N 100°32'49.1"E, 25.064730, 100.546977

12. SKTT, Vol. 1, p. 193.

13. Man shu, p. 87.

14. "Man" is a generic Chinese term for barbarians. Another source quotes one *dou*, a Chinese measurement of volume. One *dou* is 10 *sheng* or 6 litres (Appendix 15). See Backus, C. (1981). *The Nan-chao kingdom and T'ang China's southwestern frontier*. Cambridge University Press., p. 132.

15. Fan Chuo records Li-Xi-Yuan is of Zhen Deng Zhou (Man shu, p. 59), and Deng Zhou is two days from Feng Zhou, identified on the map as the area around Bạch Hạc where three rivers: Red, Đà, and Lô meet (Man shu, p. 117). Feng Zhou, (Phong Châu), is recorded at a distance of two days from La Thành (Man shu, p. 4) so a rough estimate would indicate that Lin-Xi-Yuan is upstream of Phú Thọ, somewhere near Vũ Én railway station.

16. Man shu p. 4.

17. Man shu, p. 45.

18. Man shu, p. 45. Other than Deng zhou (see the previous footnote), I am unable to locate the other places on the map.

19. Man shu, p 45.

20. Backus, C. (1981). *The Nan-chao kingdom and T'ang China's southwestern frontier*. Cambridge University Press., p. 132.

21. CM, Vol. 1, p. 202, Vietnamese equivalent "*Bạch Y Một Mệnh Quân (quân áo trắng liều mạng or quân cảm tử áo trắng*" (ANCL, p. 199). CM also quotes Xiu, O., Qi, S., & Fan, Z. (1060). *New Book of Tang (Xin Tang shu) - Volume 222c Biographies 147c: Southern Man 3*. http://chinesenotes.com/xintangshu/xintangshu222c.html. CM refers to Đỗ Tôn Thành as a tribal chief and not a governor of Ái, this information comes from Taylor, K. W. (1983). *The Birth of Vietnam*. Berkeley: University of California Press., p. 240.

22. ANCL, p. 199.

23. The killing of Đỗ Tôn Thành is not mentioned in Man shu, which does not record Đoàn Tù Thiên either.

24. Taylor, K. W. (1983). *The Birth of Vietnam*. Berkeley: University of California Press., p. 240.

25. The father of the Phùng brothers (in Phong prefecture) fought with the Black Emperor (in Hoan prefecture) in the 713 uprisings, and the governors of Phong and Diễn rebelled in 782. Phùng brothers' military adviser is a Đỗ person.

26. ANCL, p. 199 and SKTT, Vol. 1, p. 194. ANCL refers to the barbarians as *Mán* (Vietnamese for Man), but SKTT cites *Lạo*. At the time of Nanzhao, there was a Lao tribe who lived north of modern Hà Giang in Vietnam. See the map in Man shu.

27. CM, Vol. 1, p. 203.

28. Backus, C. (1981). *The Nan-chao kingdom and T'ang China's southwestern frontier*. Cambridge University Press., p. 135.

29. Zunyi is over 1,000 kilometres north of La Thành (Hanoi), so it is difficult to believe Li Hu would march all that way over mountainous terrains to fight Nanzhao without an expressed order from the Tang emperor. In any case, he was away from Annam when Nanzhao struck La Thành. But in CM, see below, he fled La Thành during the attack, so he must have been there.

30. Taylor, K. W. (1983). *The Birth of Vietnam*. Berkeley: University of California Press., p. 243. Note that CM, Vol. 1, p. 204 only mentions the killing of Đỗ Thủ Trừng, and that Li Hu fled La Thành when Nanzhao attacked but nothing about his campaign to recapture Po-chou.

31. Nanning is about 800 kilometres east of Kunming, the eastern capital during Nanzhao time, quite a distance. However, Nanzhao troops could have reached Nanning by the rivers, and the long distance illustrates the power of the Nanzhao army that it could move troops at such a long distance.

32. Backus, C. (1981). *The Nan-chao kingdom and T'ang China's southwestern frontier*. Cambridge University Press., p. 136.

33. According to ANCL, p. 200, the loss of the winter garrison occurred during Wang Kuang time (861-862,) even if Li Zhuo made the request in 854-855. Given how events unfolded after Li Zhuo's departure in 855, by the time Wang Kuang arrived, most of the north-west frontier between An Nam and Nanzhao would have been in rebels' hands, and the winter garrison would have long gone.

34. CM Vol.1, p. 204 and Taylor, K. W. (1983). *The Birth of Vietnam*. Berkeley: University of California Press., p. 243.

35. CM Vol.1, p. 205: "*Hứa, Hoạt, Từ, Biện, Kinh, Tường, Đàm, Ngạc*". I have not been able to locate these locations in China, but since Cai Xi is an official from Hunan province, these troops could have come from there.

36. The Wu Man was in charge, supported by the Man of Mang, Luo-xing (apparently used as cannon fodder), Ho, Xun-chuan, Pu-zi and Wang-ju-zi (employed as vanguard troops). These tribes came from the regions on the east and west of Dali. The Dao-hua Man, a tribe that lived around modern Phú Thọ, also joined Nan-zhao.

37. Tests included climbing to the top of Dian Cang (Tien-ts'ang, Cangshan?) mountain west of Dali City in Yunnan province, jumping over a pit of 1 *zhang* 3 *chi* (3.9 m) wide, swimming upstream (or staying afloat) of a fast-flowing river for 2000 Chinese feet (600 m), excelling in sword playing and carrying one picul and five pecks (60 kg ?) for 40 *li* (18 kilometres).

38. Man shu p. 82.

39. Man shu p. 82.

40. Cropped photo of an original provided by Yprpyqp. (27 February 2018). *A shieldbearer in the Dali Kingdom of Yunnan*. https://commons.wikimedia.org/wiki/File:Dali_Shield.jpg. The original painting was completed in 1180 by Zhang Shengwen entitled "Kingdom of Dali Buddhist Volume of Paintings". It is 30.4 cm tall by 16.655 m long and is held at the National Palace Museum, Taipei, Taiwan. This section is located at the far-right end of the painting.

41. SKTT, Vol. 1, p. 193.

42. Taylor, K. W. (1983). *The Birth of Vietnam*. Berkeley: University of California Press., p. 247.

43. Gao Pian is the Prince of Bohai. Bohai Sea is east of Beijing and Hubei province, north of the Shandong peninsula. Another source refers to Bohai as a kingdom north of modern North Korea, around Heilongjiang, China.

44. Backus, C. (1981). *The Nan-chao kingdom and T'ang China's southwestern frontier*. Cambridge University Press., p. 152.

45. Guang, S., Shu, L., Ban, L., & Zuyu, F. (1084). *Zizhi Tongjian - Comprehensive Mirror in Aid of Governance* http://www.guoxue.com/shibu/zztj/zztjml.htm.

46. Verellen, F. (2015). *Prince Gao's occupation of Annan and the rise of regional autonomy under the late Tang*. Hong Kong University Press.

47. LNCQ, p. 93.

48. The location is near the intersection of Hoàng Quốc Việt and Bưởi streets, Nghĩa Đô district, Hanoi.

49. Phan, L. H. (2015). Phép thuật Cao Biền tại An Nam-Từ ảo tượng đến chân tướng. *Tạp Chí Nghiên Cứu Tôn Giáo, 17, no. 3(141), March 2015*, 105-132.

50. SKTT, Vol. 1, p. 198 cites 50,000 Man troops were rice harvesting and got routed by Gao Pian; the number seems excessively high given that Nanzhao only left 20,000 troops after they took La Thành. Other sources, Backus, C. (1981). *The Nan-chao kingdom and T'ang China's southwestern frontier*. Cambridge University Press. (p. 141) mentions only the resistance of the local people, who were doing the rice harvesting, not Nanzhao troops.

51. Under Tang, Nam Định is one of eight counties within Giao prefecture that covers the area south of the Đuống river in present-day Hải Dương province. However, it is not the same as the contemporary city of Nam Định. The location is at the heart of the rice-growing region of the Red River Delta, and thus, it is possible Gao Pian caught Nanzhao soldiers out in the open doing the rice harvesting there on his way to La Thành. He presumably took the sea route from Hai-men, entering An Nam by the Bạch Đằng river. See Đào, D. A. (2005). *Đất nước Việt Nam qua các đời - Nghiên cứu địa lý học lịch sử Việt Nam*. NXB Văn Hóa Thông Tin., p. 96 and Maspero, H. (1910). Le Protectorat général d'Annam sous les T'ang : essai de géographie historique, I. *Bulletin de l'Ecole française d'Extrême-Orient*, 539-584. https://www.persee.fr/doc/befeo_0336-1519_1910_num_10_1_204., p. 551, p. 568. The mention of Phong prefecture in ANCL, p. 201, reads as if Gao Pian got to Phong first, but this would not be the case as Phong is further inland from the coast than Nam Định. By geography, Gao Pian would retake La Thành first before he attacked the main camp of the Man rebels at Phong.

52. The event of Gao Pian's officials travelling to Chang'an – some 2,000 kilometres north of La Thành – the transmission of the new directive from the emperor at Chang'an to Gao Pian at Hai-men; plus Gao Pian's travelling back to La Thành, apparently took place within a month or so from November to December 866. It seems a very short time for these events to occur such a long distance.

53. SKTT, Vol. 1, pp. 198-199.

54. Backus, C. (1981). *The Nan-chao kingdom and T'ang China's southwestern frontier*. Cambridge University Press., p. 143.

55. ANCL, p. 205.

56. Lý, T. X. (2012). *Việt điện u linh* (Đ. R. Trịnh & G. K. Đinh, Trans.). NXB Hồng Bàng. (1329), p. 107. See also Pham, T. (2021). *The Bronze Drums and The Earrings* (Vol. 1). 315Kio Publishing.

57. Benn, C. D. (2004). *China's golden age: everyday life in the Tang dynasty*. Oxford University Press., pp. 291-292.

58. Backus, C. (1981). *The Nan-chao kingdom and T'ang China's southwestern frontier*. Cambridge University Press., p. 161.

59. These tombs are known as the Ciputra tombs in reference to where they were found, at Nhật Tảo hamlet, Đông Ngạc commune, Từ Liêm district (nearby coordinates 21°5'1"N 105°47'18"E). Anoth-

er tomb found at Tân Hòa commune, Hoài Đức district, east of Hanoi, is also believed to be related to the Đỗ family. See Nguyễn, V. (2011). *Chủ nhân mộ cổ Ciputra là người Việt?* http://baotanglichsu.vn/vi/Articles/2001/62685/chu-nhan-mo-co-ciputra-la-nguoi-viet.html and Nguyễn, L. C. (2011). *Bí ẩn của hai ngôi mộ cổ ở Ciputra.* http://nguoihanoi.com.vn/bi-an-vu-hai-ngoi-mo-co-o-ciputra_217062.html.

60. Phạm, L. H. (2012). Một vài suy nghĩ nhân sự kiện phát lộ các ngôi mộ cổ tại Đông Ngạc (Từ Liêm, Hà Nội). *Thông Báo Hán Nôm Học Năm 2010-2011 - Viện Khoa Học Xã Hội Viện Nam - Viện Nghiên Cứu Hán Nôm*, 704-712.

61. Bãi Rồng area, Phú An neighbourhood, My Dương hamlet, Thanh Mai commune, Thanh Oai district, Hà Nội. See Hương, T. (2020). *Độc đáo chuông Thanh Mai.* https://nhipsonghanoi.hanoimoi.com.vn/tin-tuc/van-hoa/823443/doc-dao-chuong-thanh-mai

62. Phạm, L. H. *Một số thủ lĩnh An Nam thời thuộc Đường.* *VNH3.TB1.543.*, p. 21. Also see Phạm, L. H. (2009). *Về một số thủ lĩnh An Nam thời thuộc Đường.* *Tạp chí Nghiên cứu Lịch sử*, No. 9, 2009, 46-58.

63. Man shu, p. 86.

64. 60 cm in height x 36.5 cm in diameter, 35.5 kg weight. Photo by Daderot CC0 via Wikimedia Commons. (2014). Bell for ritual use (replica). https://upload.wikimedia.org/wikipedia/commons/5/5a/Bell_for_ritual_use_%28replica%29%2C_Thanh_Mai_pagoda%2C_Ha_Tay_province%2C_cast_in_798_AD%2C_bronze_-_National_Museum_of_Vietnamese_History_-_Hanoi%2C_Vietnam_-_DSC05548.JPG .

CHAPTER 15

1. The five dynasties are Later Liang, Later Tang, Later Jin, Later Han, and Later Zhou (basically occupied the same region in central China centred around the former Tang capital at Chang'an but with different names at different times). The Ten Kingdoms are Yang Wu, Wuyue, Min, Ma Chu, Southern Han, Former Shu, Later Shu, Jingnan, Southern Tang and Northern Han.

2. Pham, T. (2021). *The Bronze Drums and The Earrings* (Vol. 1). 315Kio Publishing., p. 104.

3. SS. (3 July 2017). *Map of Later Tang, one of Five Dynasties SS, CC BY-SA 4.0* <https://creativecommons.org/licenses/by-sa/4.0>, *via Wikimedia Commons*. https://commons.wikimedia.org/wiki/File:Later_Tang.png.

4. Bộ Quốc Phòng - Viện Lịch Sử Quân Sự Việt Nam, Trần, Q. V., & Lê, Đ. S. (2001). *Lịch Sử Quân Sự Việt Nam - Tập 2 - Đấu tranh giành độc lập tự chủ (từ năm 179 TCN đến năm 938)*. NXB Chính Trị Quốc Gia., p. 249. Also CM, Vol. 1, p. 218.

5. Khúc Thừa Dụ is not mentioned in ANCL nor SKTT, these works only record his son, Khúc Hạo, but CM makes a reference to Khúc Thừa Dụ.

6. There was a brief period when a local leader, Dương Thanh, held power for a short time during an uprising in the early years of the ninth century (819-820).

7. Co-ordinates: 20°42'41.3"N 106°19'49.1"E (20.711460, 106.330311), also known as Dương Xá.

8. CM, Vol. 1, p. 218.

9. Bộ Quốc Phòng - Viện Lịch Sử Quân Sự Việt Nam, Trần, Q. V., & Lê, Đ. S. (2001). *Lịch Sử Quân Sự Việt Nam - Tập 2 - Đấu tranh giành độc lập tự chủ (từ năm 179 TCN đến năm 938)*. NXB Chính Trị Quốc Gia., p. 251.

10. CM, Vol. 1, p. 218.

11. Liu Yan has several names, including Liu Zhi and Liu Gong.

12. Khúc Thừa Mỹ sent an envoy to Luoyang to seek a *"Tiết Việt"*, one of two items a Chinese emperor grants to the head of a vassal state as a symbol of his authorization. One is a flag pole with feathers hung at the end of it (*Tiết Mao* or *Mao Tiết* (Mao Jie), and the other (*Việt*) is a large hammer with a long handle). See CM, Vol. 1, p. 219.

13. Xiu, O., & Davis, R. L. (2004). *Historical Records of the Five Dynasties*. Columbia University Press., Chapter 65: Heredity House of Southern Han. SKTT, Vol.1, p.202 notes a different general, Lý Khắc Chính, and the year was August 923.

14. Guang, S., Shu, L., Ban, L., & Zuyu, F. (1084). *Zizhi Tongjian - Comprehensive Mirror in Aid of Governance* http://www.guoxue.com/shibu/zztj/zztjml.htm, Volume 277: Later Tang.

15. Also known as Dương Diên Nghệ, see CM, Vol. 1, p. 220.

16. CM, Vol. 1, p. 220. During Tang times, the empire controlled the remote regions by allowing the local chiefs to rule with Tang-appointed titles such as governor or prefect; these positions were passed on from father to son. These regions were called CO MI (Cơ Mi or Ky Mi). Literally, CO MI means a contraption of straps attached around the head of a horse and an ox respectively to control them. See CM, Vol. 1, p. 199,

17. In SKTT, Vol. 1, p. 202, once Li Yin learned of Dương Đình Nghệ's activity, he sent an urgent message back to Liu Yan for reinforcements; there was no mention of the bribery. In ANCL, p. 225, the story is different in that Liu Yan granted Dương Đình Nghệ a title at the same time as he appointed Li Yin and Lý Khắc Chính but Dương Đình Nghệ turned against Li Yin a year later, and defeated Lý Khắc Chính (or Liang Kezhen). The more likely story would be that after Khúc Thừa Mỹ was captured, Southern Han may have left the southern provinces of Ái, and Hoan to be ruled by people appointed under the Khúc family, thus explaining the reference to COMI by Liu Yan to his officials. As for the southern raid, Liang Kezhen was likely to take the coastal route to Champa's capital (around modern Quảng Nam), bypassing Ái and Hoan. Meanwhile, Dương Đình Nghệ was biding his time; the fact that he was training 3,000 men indicates he was a patient commander and not rushed to battle until he was ready. Using the same strategy, he may have bribed or paid Li Yin to downplay his threat to Đại La until he was prepared to attack. Once the attack commenced, Li Yin was so alarmed that he sent for reinforcements, but after Liang Kezhen was beaten, there was no one to prevent Dương Đình Nghệ from entering Đại La to begin his reign.

18. Guang, S., Shu, L., Ban, L., & Zuyu, F. (1084). *Zizhi Tongjian - Comprehensive Mirror in Aid of Governance* http://www.guoxue.com/shibu/zztj/zztjml.htm, Volume 277: Later Tang.

19. In CM, Vol. 1, p. 220, 3,000 crack troops were called *"nha binh"* or "special forces" and Kiều Công Tiễn was a *"nha tướng"* or a special force general.

20. SKTT, Vol. 1, p. 202, also Xiu, O., & Davis, R. L. (2004). *Historical Records of the Five Dynasties*. Columbia University Press., Vol. 65: Heredity House of Southern Han.

21. Coordinates 19°52'27.0"N 105°45'54.5"E, 19.874156, 105.765149, next to Phúc Hưng pagoda.

CHAPTER 16

1. There is a district named Chongwen near Beijing, but I am not certain if this is the same place where the envoy Xiao Yi came from.

2. CM, Vol. 1, p. 222 also Guang, S., Shu, L., Ban, L., & Zuyu, F. (1084). *Zizhi Tongjian - Comprehensive Mirror in Aid of Governance* http://www.guoxue.com/shibu/zztj/zztjml.htm, Vol. 281 – Later Jin.

3. In SKTT, Vol.1, p. 203. Ngô Quyền is referred to as a devious person (*kiệt hiệt*). In Zizhi Tongjian, Vol. 281, the paragraph reads: "Wu Quan (Ngô Quyền) is not to be taken lightly.."

4. Xiu, O., & Davis, R. L. (2004). *Historical Records of the Five Dynasties*. Columbia University Press., p. 540.

5. In fact, according to local legends, Phùng Hưng helped Ngô Quyền to defeat the Southern Han army at the battle of Bạch Đằng river, see VDUL, p. 47.

6. Trần, T. D. (2019). *Việt Nam Thế Kỷ X: Những Mảnh Vỡ Lịch Sử*. Nhà Xuất Bản Đại Học Sư Phạm., pp. 51-88.

7. SKTT, Vol. 1. p. 203.

8. This date is given in CM, Vol.1, p. 221 but in SKTT, Vol. 1, p. 203, the date is shown three months later in the winter, December/January 938. One would never know why Ngô Quyền waited for over for over a year before marching. It could be that he was not ready, or maybe he just waited to see how Kiều Công Tiễn fared, or it could be that the dates are incorrect.

9. SKTT, Vol. 1, p. 203.

10. Nguyen, M., Marchesiello, P., Florent, L., Ouillon, S., Cambon, G., Allain, D., & Van Uu, D. (2014). Tidal characteristics of the gulf of Tonkin. *Continental Shelf Research*, 91, 37-56. https://doi.org/10.1016/j.csr.2014.08.00., p. 4.

11. *Haiphong tide times and tide charts - 27-28 Feb. 2021*. (2021). https://www.tideschart.com/Vietnam/Hai-Phong/Haiphong/, on 27 February 2021, the highest tide of 3.21 m was at 4.21 am local time, the lowest tide of 0.44 m was at 6.31 pm, a difference of 2.77 m, the tides were retreating almost on a sloping straight-line at a rate of approximately 20 cm per hour.

12. Today, a the ferry terminals on this river is called Forest ferry (*phà rừng*).

13. Trần, B. Đ., Mạc, Đ., Tô, B. G., Phan, V. H., Lê, V. N., Nguyễn, N., & Tôn, N. Q. T. (2005). *Lịch Sử Việt Nam (Từ Đầu Đến Năm 938) - Tập 2* (V. G. Trần, B. Đ. Trần, & Đ. Mạc, Eds.). NXB Trẻ., p. 239.

14. SKTT, Vol. 1, p. 203.

15. Photo was taken by Daderot CC0 via Wikimedia Commons. (6 August 2014). *Model of Battle in Bach Dang River in 938 AD*. https://commons.wikimedia.org/wiki/File:Model_of_Battle_in_Bach_Dang_River_in_938_AD_-_DSC05544.JPG.

16. Bộ Quốc Phòng - Viện Lịch Sử Quân Sự Việt Nam, Trần, Q. V., & Lê, Đ. S. (2001). *Lịch Sử Quân Sự Việt Nam - Tập 2 - Đấu tranh giành độc lập tự chủ (từ năm 179 TCN đến năm 938)*. NXB Chính Trị Quốc Gia., p. 280.

17. Worcester, G. R. (2020). *Junks and Sampans of the Yangtze*. NAVAL INSTITUTE PRESS.

18. Relic of Victory on Bạch Đằng river (*Di Tích Bạch Đằng Giang*) at Minh Đức, Thủy Nguyên, Hải Phòng city.

19. Both sites are on Hà Nam Island, the first site is east of Đồng Cốc and the second is north of Hải Yến.

20. Lê, T. L., Pham, C., Staniforth, M., Delgado, J., Kimura, J., & Sasaki, R. (2011). Understanding the Bach Dang Battlefield from recent research results.

21. The sites are at Liên Khê and Lại Xuân communes of Thủy Nguyên district respectively.

22. Đào, D. A. (2005). *Đất nước Việt Nam qua các đời - Nghiên cứu địa lý học lịch sử Việt Nam*. NXB Văn Hóa Thông Tin., p. 258.

23. This is likely to be an overestimate, see the earlier discussion.

24. SKTT, Vol. 1, p. 204. The original Vietnamese version is:

Tiền Ngô Vương có thể lấy quân mới họp của nước Việt ta mà đánh tan được trăm vạn quân của Lưu Hoằng Tháo, mở nước xưng vương, làm cho người phương Bắc không dám lại sang nữa. Có thể nói là một lần nổi giận mà yên được dân, mưu giỏi mà đánh cũng giỏi vậy. Tuy chỉ xưng vương, chưa lên ngôi đế, đổi niên hiệu, nhưng chính thống của nước Việt ta, ngõ hầu đã nối lại được.

25. Châu, H. Đ. (2018). *An Nam Truyện - Ghi chép về Việt Nam trong chính sử Trung Quốc xưa*. Hội Nhà Văn., p. 233 and Xiu, O., & Davis, R. L. (2004). *Historical Records of the Five Dynasties*. Columbia University Press., Chapter 65: Heredity House of Southern Han.

26. Guang, S., Shu, L., Ban, L., & Zuyu, F. (1084). *Zizhi Tongjian - Comprehensive Mirror in Aid of Governance* http://www.guoxue.com/shibu/zztj/zztjml.htm, Vol. 283 – Later Jin

27. Xiu, O., & Davis, R. L. (2004). *Historical Records of the Five Dynasties*. Columbia University Press., Chapter 65: Heredity House of Southern Han. The two oldest sons of Liu Yan died young.

28. Guang, S., Shu, L., Ban, L., & Zuyu, F. (1084). *Zizhi Tongjian - Comprehensive Mirror in Aid of Governance* http://www.guoxue.com/shibu/zztj/zztjml.htm, Vol. 285, 287, 291, 292.

CHAPTER 17

1. In present-day Vietnam, there are 63 provinces, 27 north of Ngang pass and 36 south of it. The areas are 138,909 and 192,261 km2, respectively. See Tổng Cục Thống Kê - General Statistics Office. (2020). *Kết quả toàn bộ tổng điều tra dân số và nhà ở - Completed results of the 2019 Vietnam population and housing census*. Nhà xuất bản Thống Kê 2020. Statistical Publishing House 2020.

2. CM, Vol. 1, p. 127.

3. CM, Vol. 1, p. 127.

4. CM, Vol. 1, p. 127, ANCL, p. 167, and Taylor, K. W. (1983). *The Birth of Vietnam*. Berkeley: University of California Press., p. 68.

5. In 231, the *taishou* of Hepu noted several "bad" officials in his submission to convince the emperor of Eastern Wu, Sun Quan, to keep Lu Dai, as a "good" official, in Giao Châu as its *cishi*: ".. but there (in Giao Châu), the land is large with many people, dangerous forest, poisoned water, and the people are prone to rebellion". He mentioned the *taishou* of Nhật Nam, Hoàng Cái, was driven out of the commandery for killing the key organizer of his reception committee upon his arrival; the *taishou* of Cửu Chân, Đam Mạnh, died when the rebels attacked the administration centre because he beat up the local Công Tào during a party of his father-in-law; the *cishi* Zhu Fu was chased to the coast and disappeared because he appointed a number of his friends from his village to key positions at the prefectures and commanderies. These were corrupted and forced heavy taxation on the local people. See CM, Vol. 1, p. 140.

6. Chinese Text Project. (2006-2020). *Shiji-Historical Records- [Western Han] 109 BC-91 BC Sima Qian*. https://ctext.org/shiji, Chapter 30, Level (stabilization) book, Paragraph 46. Translated from Sima Qian, & translated by Phan Ngọc. (2018). *Sử ký Tư Mã Thiên : (trọn bộ hai tập)* (Vol. 1, 2). Văn học., Vol.1, p. 161.

7. CM, Vol. 1, p. 140.

8. CM, Vol. 1, p. 220.

9. Translated by Vuving, A. L. (2001). The References of Vietnamese States and the Mechanisms of World Formation. *ASIEN (Journal of the German Association for Asian Studies), no. 79 (April 2001)*, 62-86., p. 65 from the original Hán-Nôm in Lý, T. X. (2012). *Việt điện u linh* (Đ. R. Trịnh & G. K.

Đinh, Trans.). NXB Hồng Bàng. (1329), p. 83.

Nam quốc sơn hà, nam đế cư
Tiệt nhiên phận định tại thiên thư.
Như hà nghịch lỗ lai xâm phạm,
Nhữ đẳng hành khan thủ bại hư.

Historian Trần Trọng Kim is believed to have translated the poem to Vietnamese as:

Sông núi nước Nam vua Nam ở
Rành rành định phận ở sách trời.
Cớ sao lũ giặc sang xâm phạm,
Chúng bây sẽ bị đánh tơi bời!

See https://plo.vn/nhung-ban-dich-bai-tho-nam-quoc-son-ha-post362458.html.

10. Phan, H. L. (2018). *Lịch sử và văn hóa Việt Nam tiếp cận bộ phận* (P. T. Phan, Ed. 4th ed.). NXB Đại Học Quốc Gia Hà Nội., p. 17.

11. Ibid., p. 17.

12. Bộ Quốc Phòng - Viện Lịch Sử Quân Sự Việt Nam, Trần, Q. V., & Lê, Đ. S. (2001). *Lịch Sử Quân Sự Việt Nam - Tập 2 - Đấu tranh giành độc lập tự chủ (từ năm 179 TCN đến năm 938)*. NXB Chính Trị Quốc Gia., p. 11.

13. Maspero, H. (1918). Études d'histoire d'Annam. *Bulletin de l'Ecole française d'Extrême-Orient*, 1-36. https://www.persee.fr/doc/befeo_0336-1519_1918_num_18_1_588., p. 27.

14. Bộ Quốc Phòng - Viện Lịch Sử Quân Sự Việt Nam, Trần, Q. V., & Lê, Đ. S. (2001). *Lịch Sử Quân Sự Việt Nam - Tập 2 - Đấu tranh giành độc lập tự chủ (từ năm 179 TCN đến năm 938)*. NXB Chính Trị Quốc Gia., p. 11.

15. Taylor, K. W. (1983). *The Birth of Vietnam*. Berkeley: University of California Press. pp. 296-301.

16. Ibid, p.299.

17. Chinese is one of the five most difficult languages to learn. An educated Chinese person would know about 8,000 characters out of 20,000 listed in the dictionary, but one would only need about 2-3,000 to be able to read a newspaper, see *Real Chinese - Mini-guides - Chinese characters*. (2014). https://www.bbc.co.uk/languages/chinese/real_chinese/mini_guides/characters/characters_howmany.shtml#:~:text=How%20many%20characters%20are%20there,able%20to%20read%20a%20newspaper. This would be equivalent to an HSK (Hanyu Shuiping Kaoshi), or the Chinese Proficiency Test, of Level 6 which would take a year and a half full-time study to reach. See Billman, S. (2021). *How Long Does It Take To Learn Chinese?* https://www.china-admissions.com/blog/how-long-does-it-take-to-learn-chinese/.

18. Lu Zu-shang was appointed as a *cishi* but did not want to go, explaining that *"Lingnan is full of poisonous gas, go there will not return"*; he was beheaded for disobedience (ANCL, p. 191). Lang She-qing made a mistake and was demoted as a *cishi* of Giao Chau (ANCL, p. 193).

APPENDIX I

1. For example, Thái, V. C. (2009). *Nghiên cứu chữ viết cổ trên bia ký ở Đông Dương*. NXB Khoa Học Xã Hội. .

2. For example, Oey, G. P., & Luce, G. H. (1961). *The Man shu*. Department of Far Eastern Studies Cornell University. and Châu, H. Đ. (2018). *An Nam Truyện - Ghi chép về Việt Nam trong chính sử Trung Quốc xưa*. Hội Nhà Văn. . One can find a useful bibliography in Cynthia L. Chennault, K. N. K., Alan J. Berkowitz, and Albert E. Dien. (2015). *Early Medieval Chinese Texts: A Bibliographical Guide* (Vol. 71).

3. Gu, B. (111). *Han shu - Book of Han*. https://ctext.org/han-shu/zh .

4. Wikipedia *Book of Han*. https://en.wikipedia.org/wiki/Book_of_Han.

5. Volume 28: Treatise of Geography (part II); Volume 95: Traditions of the Yi of the southeast, the two Yues, and Chosun (Korea) – Nanyue and Min Yue.

6. *Dongguan hanji*. (2020?). http://www.chinaknowledge.de/Literature/Historiography/dongguan-hanji.html

7. https://ctext.org/dong-guan-han-ji/ma-yuan.

8. Wikipedia. (-k). *Book of the Later Han*. https://en.wikipedia.org/wiki/Book_of_the_Later_Han.

9. Volume 22: Biographies of Zhu, Jing, Wang, Du, Ma, Liu, Fu, Jian, Ma; Volume 24 (or 14 if number 1 biography is counted as 1): Ma Yuan Biography; Volume 76: Biographies of Upright Officials; Volume 86: Treatise on the Nanman, Southwestern Barbarians; Volume 113: Record 23: Commanderies and States Part Five.

10. Wikipedia. (-q). *Records of the Three Kingdoms*. https://en.wikipedia.org/wiki/Records_of_the_Three_Kingdoms.

11. Book of Wu - Volume 49 (or 4): Biographies of Liu Yao, Taishi Ci, and Shi Xie; Volume 60 (or 15): Biographies of He, Quan, Lü, Zhou, and Zhongli.

12. Wikipedia. (-l). *Commentary on the Water Classic*. https://en.wikipedia.org/wiki/Commentary_on_the_Water_Classic. Also https://ctext.org/shui-jing-zhu

13. Lịch Đạo Nguyên, (Li Daoyuan), Dương Thủ Kính, (Yang, Shoujing), Hùng Hội Trinh, (Xiong, Huizhen), Đoàn Huy Trọng, (Duan, Xizhong), Trần Kiều Dịch, (Chen, Qiaoyi), & Nguyễn Bá Mão. (2005). *Thủy Kinh Chú Sớ* (Nguyễn Bá Mão, Trans.). NXB Thuận Hóa ; Trung tâm văn hóa ngôn ngữ Đông Tây. (Giang Tô, China 1999), p.5.

14. Wikipedia. (-j). *Book of Qi*. https://en.wikipedia.org/wiki/Book_of_Qi.

15. Nan Qi Shu, Volume 58, Biographies 39: Other Peoples from the Southeast.

16. Wikipedia. (-g). *Book of Song*. https://en.wikipedia.org/wiki/Book_of_Song.

17. Volume 38: Treatises 28: Administrative District 4; Volume 76: Biographies 36: Zhu Xiuzhi, Zong Que, Wang Xuanmo; Volume 92: Biographies 52: Liang Li; Volume 97: Biographies 57: Yi Man.

18. Wikipedia. (-f). *Book of Liang (Liang shu)*. https://en.wikipedia.org/wiki/Book_of_Liang.

19. Volume 3: Emperor Wu; Volume 54: The various barbarians.

20. Wikipedia. (-e). *Book of Chen (Chen shu)*. https://en.wikipedia.org/wiki/Book_of_Chen.

21. Volume 1: Emperor Wu 1.

22. Wikipedia. (-h). *Book of Sui*. https://en.wikipedia.org/wiki/Book_of_Sui.

23. Volume 2: Gaozu; Volume 31: Treatise 26, Geography; Volume 53: Biography 18: Daxi Zhangru; Shi Wansui; Liu Fang; Volume 56: Biography 21: Lu Kai, Ling Huxi, Xue Zhou, Yu Wenbi, Zhang Heng, Yang Wang; Volume 82: Biography 47, The Nanman.

24. Wikipedia. (-i). *Book of Jin (Jin shu)*. https://en.wikipedia.org/wiki/Book_of_Jin.

25. Volume 7: Emperor Cheng, Emperor Kang; Volume 15: Treatise 5, Geography Part Two; Volume 57:Biography 27: Luo Xian; Teng Xiu; Ma Long; Hu Fen; Tao Huang; Wu Yan; Zhang Guang; Zhao You; Volume 97: Four barbarian tribes.

26. Volume 95 Biographies 83: Man, Lao, Linyi, Chi Tu, Zhenla, Poli. See http://chinesenotes.com/beishi/beishi095.html.

27. Theobald, U. (12 July 2010). *Manshu*. http://www.chinaknowledge.de/Literature/Historiography/manshu.html.

28. Wikipedia. (-p). *Old Book of Tang (Jiu Tang shu)*. https://en.wikipedia.org/wiki/Old_Book_of_Tang.

29. Volume 35: Treatise 15, Astronomy; Volume 41: Treatise 21, Geography 4; Volume 59: Biography 9, Qu Tutong, Ren Gui, Qiu He, Xu Shao, Li Xizhi, Jian Mo. Volume 197: Biography 147: Southern Man, Southwestern Man.

30. Wikipedia. *Tongdian*. https://en.wikipedia.org/wiki/Tongdian.

31. *"Tang Hui Yao" Volume Ninety-eight. Foreign countries: Uyghurs, Xicuan, Mikun, Linyi, Zhenla, Baigou Qiang, Caoguo, Shuna, Bayegu, Xi, Tanguts.* http://guoxue.httpcn.com/html/book/CQAZUYRN/UYPWUYKOUY.shtml.

32. Wikipedia. (-o). *New Book of Tang (Xin Tang shu)*. https://en.wikipedia.org/wiki/New_Book_of_Tang.

33. Volume 9: Annal 9; Emperor Yizong, Emperor Xizong; Volume 167: Biography 92: Bai Pei, Cui Wei, Li Huangfu, Wang; Volume 170: Biography 95; Volume 201: Biography 126, Literature and Arts; Volume 207: Biography 132, Imperial Officials 1; Volume 222b: Biography 147b: Southern Man; Volume 224b Biography 149b: Treasonous Ministers 2.

34. Wikipedia. *Historical Records of the Five Dynasties*. https://en.wikipedia.org/wiki/Historical_Records_of_the_Five_Dynasties.

35. Volume 65: Heredity House of the Southern Han; Volume 74: Appendix on the Four Barbarians.

36. Wikipedia. *Zizhi Tongjian*. https://en.wikipedia.org/wiki/Zizhi_Tongjian.

APPENDIX 2

1. Lê, T. (2002). *An Nam Chí Lược* (Ủy ban phiên dịch sử liệu Việt Nam của Viện Đại Học Huế (1961), Trans.). Thuận Hóa. (1285).

2. Taylor, K. W. (1983). *The Birth of Vietnam*. Berkeley: University of California Press., p. 152.

3. Lý, T. X. (2012). *Việt điện u linh* (Đ. R. Trịnh & G. K. Đinh, Trans.). NXB Hồng Bàng. (1329).

4. Taylor, K. W. (1983). *The Birth of Vietnam*. Berkeley: University of California Press., pp. 353-354.

5. Lý, T. X. (2012). *Việt điện u linh* (Đ. R. Trịnh & G. K. Đinh, Trans.). NXB Hồng Bàng. (1329), p. 45.

6. Lê, T. (2002). *An Nam Chí Lược* (Ủy ban phiên dịch sử liệu Việt Nam của Viện Đại Học Huế (1961), Trans.). Thuận Hóa. (1285).

7. Lý, T. X. (2012). *Việt điện u linh* (Đ. R. Trịnh & G. K. Đinh, Trans.). NXB Hồng Bàng. (1329), p. 107.

8. Appointed in 877 as the Protector General of Annam (previously Giao Chỉ) under the Tang dynasty. Lê, T. (2002). *An Nam Chí Lược* (Ủy ban phiên dịch sử liệu Việt Nam của Viện Đại Học Huế (1961), Trans.). Thuận Hóa. (1285), p. 205.

9. SKTT, Vol. 1, p. 201.

10. Trần, V. G. (1966). Sách "Vĩnh-Lạc đại điển bản Giao-Châu ký" mới bị phát hiện là một nguy thư (sách giả tạo). *Tạp chí Nghiên cứu Lịch sử, Số 84 (Tháng 3)*, 26-28. (Viện Khoa học Xã hội Việt Nam., p. 28.

11. Phạm, L. H. Một số thủ lĩnh An Nam thời thuộc Đường. *VNH3.TB1.543*.

12. Unknown, translated by Trần Quốc Vượng (1959), & compared and corrected by Đinh Khắc Thuân. (2005). *Việt Sử Lược*. Thuận Hóa. (1377).

13. Trần, T. D. (2019). *Việt Nam Thế Kỷ X: Những Mảnh Vỡ Lịch Sử*. Nhà Xuất Bản Đại Học Sư Phạm., p. 96.

14. Trần, T. P. (2011). *Lĩnh nam chích quái* (restored and edited by Vũ Quỳnh and Kiều Phú, Đinh Gia Khánh, Nguyễn Ngọc San, Trans.). NXB Trẻ; Hồng Bàng. (1492).

15. LNCQ, p. 29, p. 30.

16. Ngô Sĩ Liên. (1998). *Đại Việt Sử Ký Toàn Thư* Khoa Học Xã Hội (Social Science) (1998). (Chính Hòa version (1697).) For the electronic copy, see Văn phòng Nôm Na (Hà Nội). (1993). *Phiên bản Alpha, Đại Việt Sử Ký Toàn Thư, Bản in Nội các quan bản, Mộc bản khắc năm Chính Hoà thứ 18 (1697)*. http://www.nomfoundation.org/nom-project/history-of-greater-vietnam/Preface?uiLang=vn.

17. Chính Hòa is the *niên hiệu* (era) of King Lê Hy Tông (1680-1705)

18. Quốc Sử Quán Triều Nguyễn, & Viện Sử Học. (1998). *Khâm Định Việt Sử Thông Giám Cương Mục* (Hoa Bằng, Phạm Trọng Điềm, & Trần Văn Giáp (1957), Trans.). Giáo dục.

APPENDIX 3

1. Đào, D. A. (2006). *Lịch sử Việt Nam - Từ nguồn gốc đến thế kỷ XIX*. NXB Văn Hóa Thông Tin. (1957), p. 86.

2. CM, Vol. 1, p. 120.

3. ANCL, p. 175, p. 190.

4. Đào, D. A. (2005). *Đất nước Việt Nam qua các đời - Nghiên cứu địa lý học lịch sử Việt Nam*. NXB Văn Hóa Thông Tin., p. 36.

5. Taylor, K. W. (1983). *The Birth of Vietnam*. Berkeley: University of California Press., p. 363. Also Holmgren, J. (1980). *Chinese colonisation of northern Vietnam: administrative geography and political development in the Tongking Delta, first to sixth centuries A.D.* Australian National University., p. 4.

6. Holmgren, J. (1980). *Chinese colonisation of northern Vietnam: administrative geography and political development in the Tongking Delta, first to sixth centuries A.D.* Australian National University., p. 26.

7. During the Later Han, *circuit* and *province* were essentially interchangeable, see ibid., p. 55.

8. Maspero, H. (1910). Le Protectorat général d'Annam sous les T'ang : essai de géographie historique, I. *Bulletin de l'Ecole française d'Extrême-Orient*, 539-584. https://www.persee.fr/doc/befeo_0336-1519_1910_num_10_1_204., p. 549, to avoid confusion, I have not used Maspero's translation.

9. Ibid., p. 549.

10. Quốc Sử Quán Triều Nguyễn, Viện Khoa Học Xã Hội Việt Nam, & Viện Sử Học. (2006). *Đại Nam Nhất Thống Chí* (T. Đ. Phạm & D. A. Đào, Trans.). NXB Thuận Hóa., p. 12.

11. SKTT, Vol. 1, p. 153.

12. Đàm Thành is also known as Việt Thành, Cửu Nghi is also known as Mạnh Chử, see Kiều, T. H. (2016). *Góp phần nghiên cứu lịch sử văn hóa Việt Nam - Thời kỳ thiên niên kỷ đầu công nguyên*. NXB Thế Giới., p. 36.

APPENDIX 4

1. Đào, D. A. (2005). *Đất nước Việt Nam qua các đời - Nghiên cứu địa lý học lịch sử Việt Nam*. NXB Văn Hóa Thông Tin., p. 36.

2. Ibid., p. 48.

3. Ibid., p. 57.

4. Ibid., p. 70.

5. Ibid., pp. 73-74.

6. Ibid., pp. 85-86.

7. Maspero, H. (1910). Le Protectorat général d'Annam sous les T'ang : essai de géographie historique, I. *Bulletin de l'Ecole française d'Extrême-Orient*, 539-584. https://www.persee.fr/doc/befeo_0336-1519_1910_num_10_1_204., p. 550.

8. Đào, D. A. (2005). *Đất nước Việt Nam qua các đời - Nghiên cứu địa lý học lịch sử Việt Nam*. NXB Văn Hóa Thông Tin., pp. 90-103.

APPENDIX 5

1. CM, Vol.1, p.108.

2. CM, Vol. 1, p. 121, p. 132.

3. CM, Vol. 1, p. 138, p. 144.

4. See Fang Xuanling. (648). *Book of Jin (Jin shu)*, *Volume 15 Treatise 5: Geography Part Two*. http://chinesenotes.com/jinshu/jinshu015.html#?highlight=%E6%AF%94%E6%99%AF.

5. Anderson, J., & Whitmore, J. K. (2015). *China's encounters on the South and Southwest: reforging the fiery frontier over two millennia*., p. 59.

6. Trần, Q. V. (2001). Vị thế Luy Lâu. *Nghiên Cứu Lịch Sử - Viện Sử Học*, 315, 3-7. https://repository.vnu.edu.vn/handle/VNU_123/7109., p. 3.

7. TKCS, Vol. 37, p. 423.

8. Phạm, L. H. (2017). A Reconsideration of the Leilou – Longbian Debate: A Continuation of Research by Nishimura Masanari. *Asian Review of World Histories*, 5(2), 28-52. https://doi.org/https://doi.org/10.1163/22879811-1234000., p. 35.

9. CM, Vol. 1, p. 111.

10. In Han shu, Luy Lâu is listed first out of ten prefectures in Giao Chỉ commandery, indicating that where the administrative centre is located. See Gu, B. (111). *Han shu - Book of Han*. https://ctext.org/han-shu/zh, https://ctext.org/han-shu/di-li-zhi, paragraph 37, Volume 28, Treatise of Geography and Đào, D. A. (2005). *Đất nước Việt Nam qua các đời - Nghiên cứu địa lý học lịch sử Việt Nam*. NXB Văn Hóa Thông Tin., p. 36.

11. Taylor notes Luy Lâu was established by Zhao Tuo, the founder of Nan-yue many years earlier, but I have not been able to locate the original reference. Taylor, K. W. (1983). *The Birth of Vietnam*. Berkeley: University of California Press., p. 73.

12. Madrolle, C. (1937). I. Le Tonkin ancien. Lei-leou et les districts chinois de l'époque des Han. La population. Yue-chang. *Bulletin de l'Ecole française d'Extrême-Orient*, 263-332. https://www.persee.fr/doc/befeo_0336-1519_1937_num_37_1_535., p. 280.

13. CM, Vol. 1, p. 111.

14. Hou Han shu, Long Biên is listed first out of ten prefectures in Giao Chỉ commandery, indicating where the administrative centre is located. See Fan Ye. (5th century). *Hou Han shu - Book of the Later Han*. https://ctext.org/hou-han-shu, Volume 113: 23: Commanderies and States Part Five. https://ctext.org/hou-han-shu/jun-guo-wu, paragraphs 521-535. See also Đào, D. A. (2005). *Đất nước Việt Nam qua các đời - Nghiên cứu địa lý học lịch sử Việt Nam*. NXB Văn Hóa Thông Tin., p. 73.

15. Maspero, H. (1910). Le Protectorat général d'Annam sous les T'ang : essai de géographie historique, I. *Bulletin de l'Ecole française d'Extrême-Orient*, 539-584. https://www.persee.fr/doc/befeo_0336-1519_1910_num_10_1_204., p. 569. According to TKCS, Vol. 37, p. 429, the name Long Biên, changed from its old name of Long Uyên, occurred in 218. Maspero dates the change at 142-143, p. 575. However, Madrolle wrote that the name was not officially consecrated until the Liu Song dynasty (420-479). See Madrolle, C. (1937). I. Le Tonkin ancien. Lei-leou et les districts chinois de l'époque des Han. La population. Yue-chang. Ibid., 263-332. https://www.persee.fr/doc/befeo_0336-1519_1937_num_37_1_535., p. 297.

16. Madrolle, C. (1937). I. Le Tonkin ancien. Lei-leou et les districts chinois de l'époque des Han. La population. Yue-chang. *Bulletin de l'Ecole française d'Extrême-Orient*, 263-332. https://www.persee.fr/doc/befeo_0336-1519_1937_num_37_1_535., p. 296.

17. Taylor, K. W. (1983). *The Birth of Vietnam*. Berkeley: University of California Press., p. 63. Luy Lâu is by the Đuống river, and Bắc Ninh is by the Cầu river, but attackers from the south would reach Luy Lâu first as the Cầu river is further north.

18. Phạm, L. H. (2017). A Reconsideration of the Leilou – Longbian Debate: A Continuation of Research by Nishimura Masanari. *Asian Review of World Histories*, 5(2), 28-52. https://doi.org/https://doi.org/10.1163/22879811-12340004

19. Noriko, N. Ibid.An Introduction to Dr. Nishimura Masanari's Research on the Lung Khe Citadel. 11-27. https://doi.org/https://doi.org/10.1163/22879811-12340003 .

20. CM, Vol. 1, p. 136.

21. Madrolle, C. (1937). I. Le Tonkin ancien. Lei-leou et les districts chinois de l'époque des Han. La population. Yue-chang. *Bulletin de l'Ecole française d'Extrême-Orient*, 263-332. https://www.persee.fr/doc/befeo_0336-1519_1937_num_37_1_535., p. 268.

22. Lê, T. L. (2017). Lung Khe and the Cultural Relationship between Northern and Southern Vietnam. *Asian Review of World Histories*, 5(2), 53-69. https://doi.org/https://doi.org/10.1163/22879811-12340005

23. Masanari, N. (2005). Settlement patterns on the Red River plain from the late prehistoric period to the 10th century AD. https://journals.lib.washington.edu/index.php/BIPPA/article/download/11920/10546

24. Madrolle, C. (1937). I. Le Tonkin ancien. Lei-leou et les districts chinois de l'époque des Han. La population. Yue-chang. *Bulletin de l'Ecole française d'Extrême-Orient*, 263-332. https://www.persee.fr/doc/befeo_0336-1519_1937_num_37_1_535., p. 277.

25. Masanari, N. (2005). Settlement patterns on the Red River plain from the late prehistoric period to the 10th century AD. https://journals.lib.washington.edu/index.php/BIPPA/article/download/11920/1054., p. 105, Figure 5.

26. Tourism, M. o. C.-S. a., & BẢO TÀNG LỊCH SỬ QUỐC GIA VIETNAM NATIONAL MUSEUM OF HISTORY. (8 July 2010). *Từ Luy Lâu - Long Biên đến Thăng Long - Hà Nội (I)*. http://baotanglichsuquocgia.vn/vi/Articles/2001/65224/tu-luy-lau-long-bien-djen-thang-long-ha-noi-i.html

27. Trần, Q. V. (2001). Vị thế Luy Lâu. *Nghiên Cứu Lịch Sử - Viện Sử Học, 315*, 3-7. https://repository.vnu.edu.vn/handle/VNU_123/7109., p. 5.

28. Trần, Q. V., & Vũ, T. S. (2004). *Hà Nội Nghìn Xưa*. NXB Quân Đội Nhân Dân., p. 118.

29. Phạm, L. H. (2017). A Reconsideration of the Leilou – Longbian Debate: A Continuation of Research by Nishimura Masanari. *Asian Review of World Histories, 5*(2), 28-52. https://doi.org/https://doi.org/10.1163/22879811-1234000., p. 52.

30. Li Jifu. (813). *Yuanhe junxian zhi - Treatise on all districts from the Yuanhe reign-period (806-820).*, Volume 38, Circuit of Lingnan - https://ctext.org/wiki.pl?if=gb&chapter=80194&remap=gb, paragraph 112. Translation copied from Phạm, L. H. (2017). A Reconsideration of the Leilou – Longbian Debate: A Continuation of Research by Nishimura Masanari. *Asian Review of World Histories, 5*(2), 28-52. https://doi.org/https://doi.org/10.1163/22879811-1234000., p. 36. See also Maspero, H. (1918). Études d'histoire d'Annam. *Bulletin de l'Ecole française d'Extrême-Orient*, 1-36. https://www.persee.fr/doc/befeo_0336-1519_1918_num_18_1_5888, note 3, p. 11.

31. Phạm, L. H. (2017). A Reconsideration of the Leilou – Longbian Debate: A Continuation of Research by Nishimura Masanari. *Asian Review of World Histories, 5*(2), 28-52. https://doi.org/https://doi.org/10.1163/22879811-1234000., p. 33.

32. Madrolle, C. (1937). I. Le Tonkin ancien. Lei-leou et les districts chinois de l'époque des Han. La population. Yue-chang. *Bulletin de l'Ecole française d'Extrême-Orient*, 263-332. https://www.persee.fr/doc/befeo_0336-1519_1937_num_37_1_535., p. 267.

33. Đỗ, V. N. (1970). Thành Quèn, căn cứ của Đỗ Cảnh Thạc, một trong mười hai sứ quân hồi thế kỷ X. *Nghiên Cứu Lịch Sử - Viện Sử Học, 132*, 91-97. https://repository.vnu.edu.vn/handle/VNU_123/69074

34. Phạm, L. H. (2017). A Reconsideration of the Leilou – Longbian Debate: A Continuation of Research by Nishimura Masanari. *Asian Review of World Histories, 5*(2), 28-52. https://doi.org/https://doi.org/10.1163/22879811-1234000., p. 52.

APPENDIX 6

1. ANCL, pp. 161-201, Volumes 7, 8, and 9.

2. CM, Vol. 1, p. 121.

3. Lư, V. A. (2014). *Bộ máy An Nam Đô Hộ Phủ của Trung Quốc thời Đường (679 – 905)* Đại Học Quốc Gia Thành Phố Hồ Chí Minh - Trường Đại Học Khoa Học Xã Hội và Nhân Văn]. Ho Chi Minh City., pp. 116-119.

4. ANCL does not appear to list any name under the Former Han period.

5. CM, Vol. 1, p. 110. Thạch Đái was the head of the Giao Chỉ circuit, but the footnote in CM states the position of *cishi* was not established until 106 BCE, so he could not have been a *cishi*. SKTT, Vol. 1, p. 155, lists him as a *taishou*.

6. SKTT, Vol. 1, p. 155.

7. The translator of ANCL pointed out that there may be a mistake in the date (see ANCL p. 174).

8. I am unable to find what this tile is; it could be the same as Châu Mục, the Head of a *Zhou* (a governor).

9. SKTT, Vol. 1, p. 158 mentions a Chu Xưởng, a *taishou* of Giao Châu in 136. He is probably the same as Châu Xưởng cited in ANCL (p. 164), a *taishou* of Giao Chỉ in 141.

10. Unknown, translated by Trần Quốc Vượng (1959), & compared and corrected by Đinh Khắc Thuân. (2005). *Việt Sử Lược*. Thuận Hóa. (1377), p. 25.

11. Sĩ Tú is not separately listed in ANCL but is mentioned in relation to Shi Xie (ANCL, p. 169)

12. Unknown, translated by Trần Quốc Vượng (1959), & compared and corrected by Đinh Khắc Thuân. (2005). *Việt Sử Lược*. Thuận Hóa. (1377), p. 25.

13. SKTT, Voll. 1, p. 160 Lý Tiến or Nguyễn Tiến ibid., p. 26.

14. Trần Thời was appointed to replace Shi Xie but both he and Đái Lương were opposed by Sĩ Huy.

15. ANCL notes Hẳn Tông, Mao Quýnh could have been officials under Shu (Han), but other sources cites Jin.

16. His father, Đào Cơ, was also a *cishi* of Giao Châu but I am unable to find a record of him. See CM, Vol. 1, p. 151.

17. Cố Thọ wanted to become the *cishi* of Giao Châu, but the people did not want him, so he killed Hồ Triệu, the *trường sử* (chief secretary). Both he and his mother were then arrested and poisoned by Lương Thạc, the taishou of Giao Chỉ (ANCL, p. 178).

18. His son, Đào Tuy, was also a *cishi* of Giao Châu, but I am unable to find a record of him. See CM, Vol. 1, p. 151.

19. Vương Đôn was a generalissimo in charge of the military affairs for all six zhous: *Giang, Hoài, Kinh, Tướng, Giao and Quảng*. (ANCL, p. 178).

20. If he were a *taishou* then the location should read Giao Chỉ but if it were indeed Giao Châu, then he should have been a *cishi*.

21. Not sure why he was listed in ANCL (p. 182) as his position was not a *cishi* nor *taishou*.

22. ANCL, pp. 266-267.

23. Military Governor (*Dudu*) of Giang, Giao and Quảng (ANCL, p. 183).

24. Listed as Phòng Pháp Tông in Unknown, translated by Trần Quốc Vượng (1959), & compared and corrected by Đinh Khắc Thuân. (2005). *Việt Sử Lược*. Thuận Hóa. (1377), p. 30 as a Qi appointment.

25. Ibid., p. 30.

26. ANCL lists him as a *cishi* under Tang, which could be an error as Tang's cishis are shown in Volume 9, p. 190, and not in Volume 8. The next *cishi* listed is under Liang.

27. Military Governor (*dudu*) of sixteen zhous, including Giao and Quảng (ANCL, p. 187).

28. ANCL (p. 188) referred to the loss of the Jin dynasty when he was appointed, but it should have read Chen dynasty.

29. He was also appointed as the Tổng Quản (Administrator) of Giao Châu.

30. Taken from Lư, V. A. (2014). *Bộ máy An Nam Đô Hộ Phủ của Trung Quốc thời Đường (679 – 905)* Đại Học Quốc Gia Thành Phố Hồ Chí Minh - Trường Đại Học Khoa Học Xã Hội và Nhân Văn]. Ho Chi Minh City.

31. Lu Zu-shang refused to take up the post at Giao Châu and was beheaded (ANCL, p. 190).

32. Unknown, translated by Trần Quốc Vượng (1959), & compared and corrected by Đinh Khắc Thuân. (2005). *Việt Sử Lược*. Thuận Hóa. (1377), p. 32.

33. Trương Thuận is the father of Trương Bá Nghi. He defeated the raid of Guangzhou and An Nam by the Arabs and the Persians in 757, see Vĩ, A. L. (2016). *Sự kiện người Arab (Đại Thực) tấn công An Nam đô hộ phủ giữa thế kỉ VII (2014)*. https://www.academia.edu/19954557/S%E1%BB%B1_ki%E1%BB%87n_ng%C6%B0%E1%BB%9Di_Arab_%C4%90%E1%BA%A1i_Th%E1%BB%B-1c_t%E1%BA%A5n_c%C3%B4ng_An_Nam_%C4%91%C3%B4_h%E1%BB%99_ph%E1%BB%A7_gi%E1%BB%AFa_th%E1%BA%BF_k%E1%BB%89_VII.

34. ANCL appears to abbreviate "Kinh Lược" (Jing Lue) and not "Kinh Lược Sứ" (Jing Lue Shi). However, I have used Jing Lue Shi.

35. An Nam was under Nanzhao's occupation during 863-866, Tang's administration was in exile; thus, it was named Hành (temporary) Giao Châu.

36. This is the last name cited in ANCL under the Tang dynasty.

37. The name of Chu Toàn Dục is taken from SKTT, Vol. 1, p. 201.

38. Dugu Sun is not mentioned in ANCL or SKTT. It is listed here as taken from Unknown, translated by Trần Quốc Vượng (1959), & compared and corrected by Đinh Khắc Thuân. (2005). *Việt Sử Lược*. Thuận Hóa. (1377), p. 37.

39. Under Southern Han, An Nam is called Jiao or Giao prefecture. See Xiu, O., & Davis, R. L. (2004). *Historical Records of the Five Dynasties*. Columbia University Press., p. 537.

APPENDIX 7

1. Phan, H. L. (2018). *Lịch sử và văn hóa Việt Nam tiếp cận bộ phận* (P. T. Phan, Ed. 4th ed.). NXB Đại Học Quốc Gia Hà Nội., p. 772.

2. Ibid., p. 767.

3. Schinz, A. (1996). *The Magic Square: Cities in Ancient China*. Edition Axel Menges., p. 9.

4. Phan, H. L. (2018). *Lịch sử và văn hóa Việt Nam tiếp cận bộ phận* (P. T. Phan, Ed. 4th ed.). NXB Đại Học Quốc Gia Hà Nội., p. 751.

5. Ibid., p. 753. Also known as *Cung Thành*.

6. Tống, T. T. (2012). *Contributions to the Structure of the Thăng Long Citadel - Đóng góp vào việc nghiên cứu cấu trúc kinh thành Thăng Long* Perspectives on the archaeology of Vietnam international colloquium, Hanoi 29th February - 2nd March 2012 = Toàn cảnh khảo cổ học Việt Nam, Hanoi, Vietnam., p. 325.

7. Phan, H. L. (2018). *Lịch sử và văn hóa Việt Nam tiếp cận bộ phận* (P. T. Phan, Ed. 4th ed.). NXB Đại Học Quốc Gia Hà Nội., p. 751.

8. Ibid., p. 781.

9. For example, a wall estimated at 300 metres long is around 203.6 *bu*, it would be more accurate to estimate it at 200 *bu* (295.5 m) rather than 300 metres.

10. Tống, T. T. (2012). *A general outline on the history of archeology in Vietnam - Vài nét về lịch sử khảo cổ học Việt Nam*. Perspectives on the archaeology of Vietnam International Colloquium, Hanoi 29th February - 2nd March 2012 = Toàn cảnh khảo cổ học Việt Nam, Hanoi, Vietnam., p. 318.

11. Tống, T. T. (2012). *Contributions to the Structure of the Thăng Long Citadel - Đóng góp vào việc nghiên cứu cấu trúc kinh thành Thăng Long* Perspectives on the archaeology of Vietnam international colloquium, Hanoi 29th February - 2nd March 2012 = Toàn cảnh khảo cổ học Việt Nam, Hanoi, Vietnam., p. 318.

12. Phan, H. L. (2018). *Lịch sử và văn hóa Việt Nam tiếp cận bộ phận* (P. T. Phan, Ed. 4th ed.). NXB Đại Học Quốc Gia Hà Nội., p. 783 and Trần, Q. V., & Vũ, T. S. (2004). *Hà Nội Nghìn Xưa*. NXB Quân Đội Nhân Dân., p. 168.

13. Phan, H. L. (2018). *Lịch sử và văn hóa Việt Nam tiếp cận bộ phận* (P. T. Phan, Ed. 4th ed.). NXB Đại Học Quốc Gia Hà Nội., p. 756.

14. Near house no. 55, ngõ 612 Giảng Võ Street. See ibid., p. 769.

15. Tống, T. T. (2012). *A general outline on the history of archeology in Vietnam - Vài nét về lịch sử khảo cổ học Việt Nam*. Perspectives on the archaeology of Vietnam International Colloquium, Hanoi 29th February - 2nd March 2012 = Toàn cảnh khảo cổ học Việt Nam, Hanoi, Vietnam., p. 316.

16. Phan, H. L. (2018). *Lịch sử và văn hóa Việt Nam tiếp cận bộ phận* (P. T. Phan, Ed. 4th ed.). NXB Đại Học Quốc Gia Hà Nội., p. 746.

17. Papin, P. (2001). *Histoire de Hanoi*. Fayard., p. 41.

18. Phan, H. L. (2018). *Lịch sử và văn hóa Việt Nam tiếp cận bộ phận* (P. T. Phan, Ed. 4th ed.). NXB Đại Học Quốc Gia Hà Nội., p. 762, p. 764.

19. Around the office of the People's Committee of Bưởi ward at 10 Võng Thị street.

20. Somewhere in the quadrant formed by Phạm Hồng Thái, Cửa Bắc, Nguyễn Trường Tộ and Hàng Bún streets, on the western side of Yên Phụ flood bank (dyke).

21. Papin, P. (2001). *Histoire de Hanoi*. Fayard., p. 41.

22. ANCL, p. 196 cites 32 boats but SKTT, Vol. 1, p. 192 records a higher number at three hundred boats.

23. ANCL, p. 53.

24. The village community hall can be found at Ngõ 378 Thụy Khuê, Bưởi, Tây Hồ, Hà Nội, coordinates 21°02'49.0"N 105°48'46.0"E.

25. Around the coordinates 21°02'13.0"N 105°51'10.2"E.

26. Phan, H. L. (2012). *Power centres in North Vietnam during the period of Chinese occupation - Những trung tâm quyền lực ở miền bắc Việt Nam thời kỳ Trung Hoa đô hộ*. Perspectives on the archaeology of Vietnam international colloquium, Hanoi 29th February - 2nd March 2012 = Toàn cảnh khảo cổ học Việt Nam, Hanoi, Vietnam., p. 203.

27. Ibid., p. 203.

28. SKTT, Vol. 1, p. 193,

29. Nguyễn, H. T. (2009). Thư tịch cổ viết về Vũ Hồn. *Tạp chí Nghiên cứu Lịch sử*, 4.2009.

30. CM, Vol. 1, p. 200.

31. Vietnamese "dịch lâu or lâu vọng dịch", Chinese "Zhong lou".

32. Vietnamese "môn lâu", Chinese "men lou"

33. Vietnamese "Úng (or ủng) môn", Chinese "Weng cheng" (literally Urn fort), is a fortified wall that encloses the gatehouse, it is typically rectangular or semicircular, similar to a barbican. See *Chinese fortification: an overview of parts and terminology — Part 1: The wall.* (2019). https://greatmingmilitary.blogspot.com/2019/06/chinese-fortification-p1.html.

34. Vietnamese "thủy cừ or kênh/ngòi nước".

35. Unknown, translated by Trần Quốc Vượng (1959), & compared and corrected by Đinh Khắc Thuân. (2005). *Việt Sử Lược*. Thuận Hóa. (1377), p. 36. Also CM, Vol. 1, p. 214 and Phan, H. L. (2012). *Power centres in North Vietnam during the period of Chinese occupation - Những trung tâm quyền lực ở miền bắc Việt Nam thời kỳ Trung Hoa đô hộ*. Perspectives on the archaeology of Vietnam international colloquium, Hanoi 29th February - 2nd March 2012 = Toàn cảnh khảo cổ học Việt Nam, Hanoi, Vietnam., p. 203.

36. CM, Vol. 1, p. 214.

37. *Chinese fortification: an overview of parts and terminology — Part 1: The wall.* (2019). https://greatmingmilitary.blogspot.com/2019/06/chinese-fortification-p1.html.

APPENDIX 8

1. A title that was conferred upon Lu Bode around 150 years earlier during the conquest of Nan-yue.

2. Fan Ye. (5th century). *Hou Han shu - Book of the Later Han.* https://ctext.org/hou-han-shu, https://ctext.org/hou-han-shu/zhu-jing-wang-du-ma-liu, Biography 12, paragraph 29 or Volume 22, "*Biographies of Zhu, Jing, Wang, Du, Ma, Liu, Fu, Jian, Ma*"

3. Ibid. https://ctext.org/hou-han-shu/ma-yuan-lie-zhuan, Biography 14, paragraph 16 or Volume 24, Biography 24. Biography of Ma Yuan.

4. In another part of Hou Han shu, the year of 42 CE is quoted, see Chapter 2, but since this is Ma Yuan's biography, 41 CE is likely the year allowing time for the mobilisation.

5. Maspero, H. (1918). Études d'histoire d'Annam. *Bulletin de l'Ecole française d'Extrême-Orient*, 1-36. https://www.persee.fr/doc/befeo_0336-1519_1918_num_18_1_588., p. 14.

6. The region between Lạng Sơn and Nanning, see ibid., p. 15.

7. Holmgren, J. (1980). *Chinese colonisation of northern Vietnam: administrative geography and political development in the Tongking Delta, first to sixth centuries A.D.* Australian National University., p. 12.

8. Today, one can travel from Beihai in Hepu County to Dongxing (a distance of 202 kilometres). From there, one can travel from Móng Cái, on the Vietnamese side of the China/Vietnam border, to Đông Triều district across the mountains (via QL1B, DT330, QL279, DT326), at a distance of 235 kilometres, total 437 kilometres.

9. Fan Ye. (5th century). *Hou Han shu - Book of the Later Han.* https://ctext.org/hou-han-shu, https://ctext.org/hou-han-shu/ma-yuan-lie-zhuan, Biography 14, paragraph 16 or Volume 24, Biography 24. Biography of Ma Yuan.

10. Maspero, H. (1918). Études d'histoire d'Annam. *Bulletin de l'Ecole française d'Extrême-Orient*, 1-36. https://www.persee.fr/doc/befeo_0336-1519_1918_num_18_1_588., p. 16.

11. Đào, D. A. (2006). *Lịch sử Việt Nam - Từ nguồn gốc đến thế kỷ XIX*. NXB Văn Hóa Thông Tin. (1957), p. 95.

12. Lê, V. S. (2003). *Việt Nam văn minh sử: lược khảo, tập thượng, từ nguồn gốc đến thế kỷ thứ X*. Lao Động., p. 147.

13. Đào, D. A. (2005). *Đất nước Việt Nam qua các đời - Nghiên cứu địa lý học lịch sử Việt Nam*. NXB Văn Hóa Thông Tin., p. 46.

14. Lịch Đạo Nguyên, (Li Daoyuan), Dương Thủ Kính, (Yang, Shoujing), Hùng Hội Trinh, (Xiong, Huizhen), Đoàn Huy Trọng, (Duan, Xizhong), Trần Kiều Dịch, (Chen, Qiaoyi), & Nguyễn Bá Mão. (2005). *Thủy Kinh Chú Sớ* (Nguyễn Bá Mão, Trans.). NXB Thuận Hóa ; Trung tâm văn hóa ngôn ngữ Đông Tây. (Giang Tô, China 1999), p. 429.

15. SKTT, footnote 3, p. 156.

16. Quốc Sử Quán Triều Nguyễn, Viện Khoa Học Xã Hội Việt Nam, & Viện Sử Học. (2006). *Đại Nam Nhất Thống Chí* (T. Đ. Phạm & D. A. Đào, Trans.). NXB Thuận Hóa., p. 115.

17. Bộ Quốc Phòng - Viện Lịch Sử Quân Sự Việt Nam, Trần, Q. V., & Lê, Đ. S. (2001). *Lịch Sử Quân Sự Việt Nam - Tập 2 - Đấu tranh giành độc lập tự chủ (từ năm 179 TCN đến năm 938)*. NXB Chính Trị Quốc Gia., p.65.

18. Maspero, H. (1918). Études d'histoire d'Annam. *Bulletin de l'Ecole française d'Extrême-Orient*, 1-36. https://www.persee.fr/doc/befeo_0336-1519_1918_num_18_1_588., p. 16. Also *Biography of Ma Yuan*. (2020?). https://ctext.org/dong-guan-han-ji/ma-yuan, paragraph 25.

19. Bộ Quốc Phòng - Viện Lịch Sử Quân Sự Việt Nam, Trần, Q. V., & Lê, Đ. S. (2001). *Lịch Sử Quân Sự Việt Nam - Tập 2 - Đấu tranh giành độc lập tự chủ (từ năm 179 TCN đến năm 938)*. NXB Chính Trị Quốc Gia., p. 74-75.

20. SKTT, p. 156.

21. This is according to Liu Long's biography, but in Ma Yuan's biography, it is Ma Yuan who chased and killed both sisters at Cấm Khê.

22. Maspero, H. (1918). Études d'histoire d'Annam. *Bulletin de l'Ecole française d'Extrême-Orient*, 1-36. https://www.persee.fr/doc/befeo_0336-1519_1918_num_18_1_588., p. 18. And Fan Ye. (5th century). *Hou Han shu - Book of the Later Han*. https://ctext.org/hou-han-shu, https://ctext.org/hou-han-shu/zhu-jing-wang-du-ma-liu, Biography 12, paragraph 29 or Volume 22, "*Biographies of Zhu, Jing, Wang, Du, Ma, Liu, Fu, Jian, Ma*"

23. Đinh, V. N. (1980). Đất Mê Linh - Trung tâm chính trị, quân sự và kinh tế của huyện Mê Linh thời Hai Bà Trưng. *Nghiên Cứu Lịch Sử - Viện Sử Học*, *1*, 35-53., p. 38. Other source mentioned Hát Giang is near where Đáy and Red rivers intersect.

24. Ibid., p. 42.

25. At the "golden creek" flowing into today's Tích Giang river between Thạch Thất and Quốc Oai.

26. CM, p. 115. There is a Cấm Khê district in Phú Thọ province, but Maspero chooses to ignore it as the name first appeared in 1841. He thought a location near the Đà (black) river, north-west of Mê Linh, as suggested by CM, was the most likely.

27. The route of the battles described follows these locations: Tây Vu (at Cổ Loa) – Lãng Bạc (at Mount Lạn Kha, north of Đuống river) – Cấm Khê (Vĩnh Tường). In a 2010 paper, historian Nguyễn Quang Ngọc suggests a different route and positions: Lãng Bạc (based on a small mound found somewhere in Gia Lương, Gia Bình, and Lương Tài districts - south of the Đuống River) - Tây Vu (at Cổ Loa) - Cấm Khê (stretched from Ba Vì mountain to Hương pagoda, a distance of some 90 kilometres). I favour the first route as Mount Lạn Kha is a significant landmark, large enough to accommodate the soldiers of Ma Yuan,, but I am unable to locate any site of significant elevation within the area suggested by Nguyễn. See Nguyễn, Q. N. (2010). Cuộc khởi nghĩa Hai Bà Trưng sau 1970 năm nhìn lại *Tạp chí Nghiên cứu Lịch sử*, 3. 2010, 3-15., pp.8-9.

28. These numbers look suspiciously the same as those he employed during his expedition to Giao Chỉ.

29. TKCS, Vol. 37. pp. 434-435.

30. Đào, D. A. (2005). *Đất nước Việt Nam qua các đời - Nghiên cứu địa lý học lịch sử Việt Nam*. NXB Văn Hóa Thông Tin. p. 51.

31. ANCL, p. 59.

32. At the time of Ma Yuan, Cửa Thần Phù (sea gate) is the name of a point at the end of the mountain range forming a natural barrier to Cửu Chân. It reaches the sea and is known as a dangerous place for boats to go around. These days, the silt from the Đáy river has pushed it out to the sea shore to around 10 kilometres.

33. Đào, D. A. (2005). *Đất nước Việt Nam qua các đời - Nghiên cứu địa lý học lịch sử Việt Nam*. NXB Văn Hóa Thông Tin., p. 52.

34. On current map, there are two large areas formed by the Lèn river in north, the Tào/Bút/Trường Giang rivers in the south, and Dư Phát could be located in these areas, at Hậu Lộc and Nga Sơn districts. Lịch Đạo Nguyên, (Li Daoyuan), Dương Thủ Kính, (Yang, Shoujing), Hùng Hội Trinh, (Xiong, Huizhen), Đoàn Huy Trọng, (Duan, Xizhong), Trần Kiều Dịch, (Chen, Qiaoyi), & Nguyễn Bá Mão. (2005). *Thủy Kinh Chú Sở* (Nguyễn Bá Mão, Trans.). NXB Thuận Hóa ; Trung tâm văn hóa ngôn ngữ Đông Tây. (Giang Tô, China 1999).

35. Maspero, H. (1918). Études d'histoire d'Annam. *Bulletin de l'Ecole française d'Extrême-Orient*, 1-36. https://www.persee.fr/doc/befeo_0336-1519_1918_num_18_1_588., p. 24. In Maspero's paper, Lâu is the Lèn river, Lương is the Chu river.

36. TKCS, Vol. 37, p. 435.

37. Phan, H. L. (2012). *Power centres in North Vietnam during the period of Chinese occupation - Những trung tâm quyền lực ở miền bắc Việt Nam thời kỳ Trung Hoa đô hộ*. Perspectives on the archaeology of Vietnam international colloquium, Hanoi 29th February - 2nd March 2012 = Toàn cảnh khảo cổ học Việt Nam, Hanoi, Vietnam., p. 194. Tư Phố is also known as Dương Xá, Kẻ Giàng, (or Kẻ Ràng) and Kẻ Vồm.

38. Cư Phong is a region to the west of Thanh Hóa city covering Nhồi mountain, Triệu Sơn, Quảng Xương located at the southern side of the Nhà Lê river (Bồn Giang). See Đào, D. A. (2005). *Đất nước Việt Nam qua các đời - Nghiên cứu địa lý học lịch sử Việt Nam*. NXB Văn Hóa Thông Tin., p. 56.

APPENDIX 9

1. Taken from Majumdar, R. C. (1927). *Ancient Indian colonies in the Far East. Vol. I, Champa / by R.C. Majumdar*. Punjab Sanskrit Book Depot., pp.33-34.

2. Also known as Khu Đạt in Liang shu, Châu, H. Đ. (2018). *An Nam Truyện - Ghi chép về Việt Nam trong chính sử Trung Quốc xưa*. Hội Nhà Văn., p. 263. See also Liang shu, Volume 54.

3. Taken from Majumdar, R. C. (1927). *Ancient Indian colonies in the Far East. Vol. I, Champa / by R.C. Majumdar*. Punjab Sanskrit Book Depot., pp.33-34.

4. Ibid., Book I, pp. 47-48.

5. Listes dynastiques. (1915). *Bulletin de l'Ecole française d'Extrême-Orient*, 181-184. https://www.persee.fr/doc/befeo_0336-1519_1915_num_15_1_5479

6. Majumdar, R. C. (1927). *Ancient Indian colonies in the Far East. Vol. I, Champa / by R.C. Majumdar*. Punjab Sanskrit Book Depot., p. 43, p. 47, p. 48.

7. Listes dynastiques. (1915). *Bulletin de l'Ecole française d'Extrême-Orient*, 181-184. https://www.persee.fr/doc/befeo_0336-1519_1915_num_15_1_5479

8. Maspero, G. (1910). Le royaume de Champa: Chapitre III. Le Lin-Yi (Suite). *T'oung Pao, 11*(4), 489-526. http://www.jstor.org/stable/452616., p. 526.

9. Lương Ninh. (2013). Lại bàn về nước Lâm Ấp-Champa. *Nghiên Cứu Lịch Sử - Viện Sử Học, 5.*, p. 8.

10. Southworth, W. A. (2001). *The origins of Campa in Central Vietnam: a preliminary review* /z-wcorg/. http://catalog.hathitrust.org/api/volumes/oclc/57480138.html, diagram 4, p. 331.

APPENDIX 10

1. Dates are taken from Wikipedia. (-m). *Funan.* https://en.wikipedia.org/wiki/Funan

2. Dates are taken from Coedès, G., Cowing, S. B., Vella, W. F., & Press, A. N. U. (1968). The Indianized States of Southeast Asia. http://hdl.handle.net/1885/11518., pp. 65-86.

3. Ibid., p. 86. See also Briggs, L. P. (1951). *The ancient Khmer Empire.* American Philosophical Society., p. 63 and also https://www.globalsecurity.org/military/world/cambodia/history-chenla.htm.

APPENDIX 11

1. Kiến Giang and Long Đại rivers flow into the Nhật Lệ river.

2. The Hiếu river flows into the Thạch Hãn river.

3. Lê, Q. Đ., Nam, V. K. H. X. H. V., & Viện Sử Học. (2007). *Phủ Biên Tạp Lục* (M. K. Đỗ, T. H. Nguyễn, N. T. Nguyễn, & D. A. Đào, Trans.). NXB Văn Hóa Thông Tin. (1776), p. 127.

4. Đào, D. A. (2005). *Đất nước Việt Nam qua các đời - Nghiên cứu địa lý học lịch sử Việt Nam.* NXB Văn Hóa Thông Tin., p. 228.

5. Colani made a similar observation, see Schweyer, A.-V. (2019). *The Birth of Champa.*, p.7.

6. Atlas of Hồng Đức - Bửu, C., Đỗ, V. A., Pham, H. T., & Trương, B. L. (1962). *Hồng Đức Bản Đồ.* Tủ Sách Viện Khảo Cổ-Publications of the Institute of Historical Research - Publications de l'institut de Recherches Historiques - Số III., p. 48.

7. Based on 30 to 50 kilometres per day by river transport and 12 to 15 kilometres per day on foot.

8. Tana, L. (2019). The changing landscape of the former Linyi in the provinces of Quảng Trị and Thừa Thiên -Huế. In *Yusof Ishak Institute Nalanda-Sriwijaya Centre working paper series* (pp. 1-16). Yusof Ishak Institute Nalanda-Sriwijaya Centre., p. 2. There is a pass of Aihao en route to Lao Bảo from Đông Hà.

9. Schweyer, A.-V. (2019). *The Birth of Champa.*, p. 6.

10. Hienzquynh / CC BY-SA (https://creativecommons.org/licenses/by-sa/4.0). (23 August 2017). *Bức bản đồ thừa tuyên Thuận Hóa trong tập thứ nhất thuộc Hồng Đức Bản Đồ.* https://commons.wikimedia.org/wiki/File:B%E1%BA%A3n_%C4%91%E1%BB%93_Th%E1%BB%ABa_Tuy%C3%AAn_Thu%E1%BA%ADn_H%C3%B3a_trong_b%E1%BB%99_H%E1%BB%93ng_%C4%90%E1%BB%A9c_B%E1%BA%A3n_%C4%90%E1%BB%93.jpg.

11. *Hồng Đức Bản Đồ Sách* = Book of Hồng Đức (1490 CE) maps, *Thuận Hóa Thừa Tuyên Sơn Xuyên Hình Thế Chi Đồ* = Map (Chart) of mountains, rivers and setting (locality) of Thuận Hóa province, *Bắc*=north, *Tây*=west, *Nam* = south, *Đông*=east, *Bắc giáp Nghệ An giới* = north to Nghệ An, *Tây*

giáp *Ai Lao giới* = west to Ai Lao (modern Laos), *Nam giáp Quảng Nam giới* = south to Quảng Nam, *Đông giáp Đại Hải* = east to Great Sea.

12. Historians such as Maspero put the end date of Champa in the 15th century. Others use a later date of the nineteenth century. I prefer the later date as Champa still existed as a political entity until then.

13. For a list of these ruins, see Parmentier, H. (1909). *Inventaire descriptif des monuments Cams de l'Annam* (Vol. Planches). de l'École française d'Extrême-Orient, Ernest Leroux., Parmentier, H. (1909a). *Inventaire descriptif des monuments. Cams de l'Annam* (Vol. Tome Premier - Description des Monuments). de l'École française d'Extrême-Orient, Ernest Leroux. .

14. Tana, L. (2019). The changing landscape of the former Linyi in the provinces of Quảng Trị and Thừa Thiên -Huế. In *Yusof Ishak Institute Nalanda-Sriwijaya Centre working paper series* (pp. 1-16). Yusof Ishak Institute Nalanda-Sriwijaya Centre., Map 1, p. 5. These are, from north to south: Vĩnh Tú (Vĩnh Linh district), Duy Viên (Vĩnh Lâm district), Vĩnh Sơn (Vĩnh Linh district), An Xá (Trung Sơn district), Gio Mỹ well (Gio Linh district), Gio An 14 wells (Gio Linh district), Hảo Sơn (Gio Linh district), Cam An (Đông Hà district), Triệu Đại (Triệu Phong district), Phường 2 (Đông Hà district), Triệu Thuận (Triệu Phong district), Phường 3 (Đông Hà district), Phường 4 (Đông Hà district), Phương Sơn (Triệu Phong district), Trà Liên Tây (Triệu Phong district), Cam Hiếu (Đông Hà district), Bích La Thượng (Triệu Phong district), Ngô Xá (Chùa Ngô Xá Đông, Triệu Phong district), Hải Thiện (Hải Lăng district), Hải Thành (Hải Lăng district), Hải Trường (Hải Lăng district) and five unidentified sites.

15. *Về các loại hình văn hóa Chămpa ở Quảng Trị*. (11 December 2011). https://gioithieu.quangtri.gov.vn/index.php?language=vi&nv=news&op=Lich-su-Van-hoa/Ve-cac-loai-hinh-van-hoa-Champa-o-Quang-Tri-34.

16. Dương Lệ Đông hamlet, Triệu Thuận commune, Triệu Phong district, see Lâm, T. M. D. (2018). *Sa Huỳnh - Lâm Ấp - Chămpa: Thế kỷ 5 trước công nguyên đến thế kỷ 5 sau công nguyên (một số vấn đề khảo cổ học) = Sa Huynh - Linyi - Champa: 5th century BC - 5th century AD: some archaeological issues*. NXB Thế Giới., p. 307.

17. Cồn Chùa, Gio Mai, Gio Linh. See ibid., p. 307.

18. CM, p. 345.

19. Phan, K. (1967). *Việt Sử: Xứ Đàng Trong 1558-1777 - Cuộc Nam Tiến của Dân Tộc Việt Nam*. Nhà Sách Khai Trí., pp. 52-53.

20. CM, pp. 571-572.

21. Covering the districts of Triệu Phong, Hải Lăng, Phong Điền, Quảng Điền, Hương Trà. See Phan, K. (1967). *Việt Sử: Xứ Đàng Trong 1558-1777 - Cuộc Nam Tiến của Dân Tộc Việt Nam*. Nhà Sách Khai Trí., p. 67.

22. Covering the districts of Phú Vang, Phú Lộc on the north side of Hải Vân pass and Hòa Vang, Đại Lộc, Điện Bàn, and Duy Xuyên, south of Hải Vân pass.

23. Between Uẩn Áo and Quy Hậu hamlets of Liên Thủy commune, Lệ Thủy district, Quảng Bình province. See Ngô, V. D. (2002). *Văn hóa cổ Champa*. NXB Văn Hóa Dân Tộc., p. 223. It is rectangular, measured 600mx300m (east-west x north-south). From a map in a local newspaper, I believe that this citadel is at 17°12'51.2"N 106°47'57.9"E, see https://www.baoquangbinh.vn/dat-va-nguoi-quang-binh/202110/mien-man-chieu-ninh-vien-thanh-2194355/.

24. Located at Cổ Lũy hamlet, Vĩnh Giang commune, Vĩnh Linh district, Quảng Trị province. See *Về các loại hình văn hóa Chămpa ở Quảng Trị*. (11 December 2011). https://gioithieu.quangtri.gov.vn/index.php?language=vi&nv=news&op=Lich-su-Van-hoa/Ve-cac-loai-hinh-van-hoa-Champa-o-Quang-Tri-34.

25. Located at Vệ Nghĩa hamlet, Triệu Long commune, Triệu Phong district, Quảng Trị province.

26. Thành Trung commune, Quảng Điền district, Thừa Thiên-Huế province.

27. The first site is on a sand dune west of Giang Hến hamlet on the west bank of the Thạch Hãn river, near An Mô bridge in Triệu Phong district. See Lê, Đ. T. (20 Feb 2018). *Nguyễn Hoàng - "Người mồ côi" Đàng Trong*. https://laodong.vn/van-hoa/nguyen-hoang-nguoi-mo-coi-dang-trong-591698.ldo

28. The second site is north from Ái Tử, also on the west bank of the Thạch Hãn river, by Trà Liên hamlet, Triệu Giang commune. It is now near Liễu Bông (or Liễu Ba, Miếu Bông) pagoda and close to the cemetery. See Lê, Đ. D. (13 Dec 2008). *Dinh xưa, cảng cũ bây giờ*. https://tuoitre.vn/dinh-xua-cang-cu-bay-gio-292392.htm

29. The third site is south-west of the second site and is on Phước Mỹ hamlet, Triệu Giang commune, Triệu Phong district by the bank of Ái Tử river. See Lê, Đ. T. (20 Feb 2018). *Nguyễn Hoàng - "Người mồ côi" Đàng Trong*. https://laodong.vn/van-hoa/nguyen-hoang-nguoi-mo-coi-dang-trong-591698.ldo

30. Quốc Sử Quán Triều Nguyễn, Viện Khoa Học Xã Hội Việt Nam, & Viện Sử Học. (2006). *Đại Nam Nhất Thống Chí* (T. Đ. Phạm & D. A. Đào, Trans.). NXB Thuận Hóa., Vol. 1, pp. 194-195.

31. ANCL, p. 73.

32. Trương, T. D. (2018). *Khảo chứng tiền sử Việt Nam - Researching of Vietnam prehistory*. NXB Tổng Hợp Thành Phố Hồ Chí Minh., p. 258 also Sabanski, C. *The Sundial Primer*. https://www.mysundial.ca/tsp/gnomon_height.html.

33. *Tropic of Cancer*. (2021). https://en.wikipedia.org/wiki/Tropic_of_Cancer

34. In 1917, it was exactly 23° 27'N, the Tropics of Cancer moved southward at a rate of 0.468 arcseconds or 0.0001300 decimal degrees per year, see ibid. So in 446, when the gnomon measurement was taken, it would be around 12 minutes (0.20475 degrees) further north than where it is now. However, the relative positions of the gnomon and the Tropics of Cancer should stay the same, so for our purposes; I have not adjusted for this southward drift.

35. ANCL, p. 73.

36. Taken when the Song forces attacked Linyi.

37. ANCL, p. 73.

38. TKCS, Vol. 36, p. 363.

39. See also Châu, H. Đ. (2018). *An Nam Truyện - Ghi chép về Việt Nam trong chính sử Trung Quốc xưa*. Hội Nhà Văn., p. 257.

40. TKCS, Vol. 36, p. 363.

41. Du You. (766-801). *Tongdian - Volume 188: Border defence four Southern barbarians*. https://zh.wikisource.org/zh-hant/%E9%80%9A%E5%85%B8/%E5%8D%B7188.

42. Zhao Ying, Liu Xu, Zhang Zhao, Jia Wei, & Zhao Xi. (941-945). *Old Book of Tang, (Jiu Tang shu), Volume 35 Treatises 15: Astronomy 1*. http://chinesenotes.com/jiutangshu/jiutangshu039.html.

43. Hồ, T. T. (2019). *Có 500 năm như thế - Bản sắc Quảng Nam và Đàng Trong từ góc nhìn phân kỳ lịch sử* (6th ed.). NXB Đà Nẵng. http://books.google.com/books?id=KMTCxLyvLco., p. 41.

44. Southworth, W. A. (2001). *The origins of Campa in Central Vietnam: a preliminary review* /z-wcorg/. http://catalog.hathitrust.org/api/volumes/oclc/57480138.html, pp. 282-283.

45. Gu, B. (111). *Han shu - Book of Han*. https://ctext.org/han-shu/zh, https://ctext.org/han-shu/di-li-zhi, Geography II, paragraph 40 or Volume 28 Part II, Treatise on Geography.

46. Fan Ye. (5th century). *Hou Han shu - Book of the Later Han*. https://ctext.org/hou-han-shu, https://ctext.org/hou-han-shu/jun-guo-wu/zhs, paragraph 544, or Records volume 113, 23: Commanderies and States Part Five.

47. Fang Xuanling. (648). *Book of Jin (Jin shu)*, *Volume 15 Treatise 5: Geography Part Two*. http://chinesenotes.com/jinshu/jinshu015.html#?highlight=%E6%AF%94%E6%99%AF.

48. Đào, D. A. (2005). *Đất nước Việt Nam qua các đời - Nghiên cứu địa lý học lịch sử Việt Nam*. NXB Văn Hóa Thông Tin., p. 61.

49. Aurousseau, L. (1914). Georges Maspero: Le Royaume de Champa. *Bulletin de l'Ecole française d'Extrême-Orient*, 8-43. https://www.persee.fr/doc/befeo_0336-1519_1914_num_14_1_285., p. 26.

50. TKCS, Vol. 36, pp. 372-373

51. TKCS, Vol. 36, p. 374.

52. TKCS, Vol. 36, pp. 359-p. 361. See also Quốc Sử Quán Triều Nguyễn, Viện Khoa Học Xã Hội Việt Nam, & Viện Sử Học. (2006). *Đại Nam Nhất Thống Chí* (T. Đ. Phạm & D. A. Đào, Trans.). NXB Thuận Hóa., Volume 1, Book 2. Phủ Thừa Thiên, p. 102.

53. Aurousseau, L. (1914). Georges Maspero: Le Royaume de Champa. *Bulletin de l'Ecole française d'Extrême-Orient*, 8-43. https://www.persee.fr/doc/befeo_0336-1519_1914_num_14_1_285., p. 27.

54. Đào, D. A. (2005). *Đất nước Việt Nam qua các đời - Nghiên cứu địa lý học lịch sử Việt Nam*. NXB Văn Hóa Thông Tin., pp. 57-58. This is consistent with the listing of the counties for Giao Chỉ and Cửu Chân commanderies where Luy Lâu (or Liên Lâu –Lianlou) and Tư Phố (Xupu) are listed first. Both are administrative towns for the commanderies respectively.

55. Ibid., p. 58.

56. Ibid., p. 57.

57. Aurousseau, L. (1914). Georges Maspero: Le Royaume de Champa. *Bulletin de l'Ecole française d'Extrême-Orient*, 8-43. https://www.persee.fr/doc/befeo_0336-1519_1914_num_14_1_285., p. 26, footnote (2). See also Quốc Sử Quán Triều Nguyễn, Viện Khoa Học Xã Hội Việt Nam, & Viện Sử Học. (2006). *Đại Nam Nhất Thống Chí* (T. Đ. Phạm & D. A. Đào, Trans.). NXB Thuận Hóa., Volume 1, Book 2. Phủ Thừa Thiên, p. 102.

58. It is not Vô Biên, a county in Cửu Chân commandery north of Ngang pass during Han times.

59. Đào, D. A. (2005). *Đất nước Việt Nam qua các đời - Nghiên cứu địa lý học lịch sử Việt Nam*. NXB Văn Hóa Thông Tin., p. 62

60. Ibid., p. 74.

61. TKCS, Vol. 36, pp. 371-372.

62. TKCS, Vol. 36, p. 366.

63. TKCS, Vol. 36, p. 367.

64. TKCS, Vol. 36, p. 366.

65. Quốc Sử Quán Triều Nguyễn, Viện Khoa Học Xã Hội Việt Nam, & Viện Sử Học. (2006). *Đại Nam Nhất Thống Chí* (T. Đ. Phạm & D. A. Đào, Trans.). NXB Thuận Hóa., Volume 1, Book 2. Phủ Thừa Thiên, p. 102.

66. Unknown, translated by Trần Quốc Vượng (1959), & compared and corrected by Đinh Khắc Thuân. (2005). *Việt Sử Lược*. Thuận Hóa. (1377), pp 96-98.

67. Located in Nghĩa Hưng district, Nam Định province.

68. Đào suggests these could be Sơn Dương island and Vũng Chùa (Chùa bay) accordingly.

69. Or Ô Long, Tư Khánh, Tư Dung.

70. Thành Đồ Bàn or Chà Bàn.

71. Đào, D. A. (2005). *Đất nước Việt Nam qua các đời - Nghiên cứu địa lý học lịch sử Việt Nam*. NXB Văn Hóa Thông Tin., p. 229.

72. Pelliot, P. (1904). Deux itinéraires de Chine en Inde à la fin du VIIIe siècle. *Bulletin de l'Ecole française d'Extrême-Orient*, 131-413. https://www.persee.fr/doc/befeo_0336-1519_1904_num_4_1_129., p. 198.

73. Dates taken from Unknown, translated by Trần Quốc Vượng (1959), & compared and corrected by Đinh Khắc Thuân. (2005). *Việt Sử Lược*. Thuận Hóa. (1377), pp. 96-97.

74. Pelliot, P. (1904). Deux itinéraires de Chine en Inde à la fin du VIIIe siècle. *Bulletin de l'Ecole française d'Extrême-Orient*, 131-413. https://www.persee.fr/doc/befeo_0336-1519_1904_num_4_1_129., pp. 215-218.

75. Gungwu, W. (1958). The Nanhai Trade: A Study of the Early History of Chinese Trade in the South China Sea. *Journal of the Malayan Branch of the Royal Asiatic Society*, *31*(2 (182)), 1-135. http://www.jstor.org/stable/4150313., pp. 104-105.

76. Phạm, H. Q. (2011). Những ghi chép liên quan đến biển Đông Việt Nam trong chính sử Trung Quốc. *Nghiên cứu Trung Quốc*, *6 (118)*, 22-55., p. 33.

77. United States Office of Geography United States Board on Geographic Names. (1961). *Southern Vietnam and the South China Sea; Official Standard Names Approved by the United States Board on Geographic Names*. U.S. Government Printing Office., p. 183.

78. Trần, B. Đ., Mạc, Đ., Tô, B. G., Phan, V. H., Lê, V. N., Nguyễn, N., & Tôn, N. Q. T. (2005). *Lịch Sử Việt Nam (Từ Đầu Đến Năm 938) - Tập 2* (V. G. Trần, B. Đ. Trần, & Đ. Mạc, Eds.). NXB Trẻ., p. 258.

79. TKCS, Vol. 36, pp. 394-395.

80. Đào, D. A. (2005). *Đất nước Việt Nam qua các đời - Nghiên cứu địa lý học lịch sử Việt Nam*. NXB Văn Hóa Thông Tin., p. 52.

81. TKCS, Vol. 36, p. 395.

82. Châu, H. Đ. (2018). *An Nam Truyện - Ghi chép về Việt Nam trong chính sử Trung Quốc xưa*. Hội Nhà Văn., p. 263. See also Liang shu, Volume 58.

83. This represents an annual growth rate of 0.61% from around years 43 to 605, not too out of scale with those shown in Appendix 14.

84. Châu, H. Đ. (2018). *An Nam Truyện - Ghi chép về Việt Nam trong chính sử Trung Quốc xưa*. Hội Nhà Văn., p. 281. See also Xin Tang shu, Volume 222c.

85. Trần, B. Đ., Mạc, Đ., Tô, B. G., Phan, V. H., Lê, V. N., Nguyễn, N., & Tôn, N. Q. T. (2005). *Lịch Sử Việt Nam (Từ Đầu Đến Năm 938) - Tập 2* (V. G. Trần, B. Đ. Trần, & Đ. Mạc, Eds.). NXB Trẻ., p. 258, the brothers are Âm Dật and Âm Xưởng. See also Fan Ye. (5th century). *Hou Han shu - Book of the Later Han*. https://ctext.org/hou-han-shu, Volume 10 (part 1), Annals of Empresses, Guo Shengtong; Empress Yin Lihua; Empress Ma; Consort Jia; Empress Dou; Empress Yin; Empress Deng Sui. https://ctext.org/hou-han-shu/huang-hou-ji-shang.

86. Châu, H. Đ. (2018). *An Nam Truyện - Ghi chép về Việt Nam trong chính sử Trung Quốc xưa*. Hội Nhà Văn., p. 263. See also Liang shu, Volume 58.

87. Goble, G. (May 2014). Maritime Southeast Asia: The view from Tang–Song China *Nalanda-Sriwijaya Centre Working Paper No 16*. http://www.iseas.edu.sg/nsc/documents/working_papers/nscwps016.pd., p. 10. See also Xin Tang shu, Volume 222c. In the Vietnamese translation of the same passage, Châu translates "the people of Tây Đồ barbarians", see Châu, H. Đ. (2018). *An Nam Truyện - Ghi chép về Việt Nam trong chính sử Trung Quốc xưa*. Hội Nhà Văn., p. 281.

88. Châu, H. Đ. (2018). *An Nam Truyện - Ghi chép về Việt Nam trong chính sử Trung Quốc xưa*. Hội Nhà Văn., p. 255. See also the Book of Southern Qi, Volume 58.

89. Schweyer, A.-V. (2019). *The Birth of Champa.*, p. 9.

90. Southworth, W. A. (2001). *The origins of Campa in Central Vietnam: a preliminary review* /z-wcorg/. http://catalog.hathitrust.org/api/volumes/oclc/57480138.html, pp. 291-293.

91. Ibid., p. 309, p. 335.

92. Schweyer, A.-V. (2019). *The Birth of Champa.*, p. 5.

93. Lê, Q. Đ. (1773). *Vân Đài Loại Ngữ* (V. G. Trần, V. K. Trần, & X. H. Cao, Trans.). NXB Văn Hóa Thông Tin (2006)., p. 140.

94. TKCS, Vol. 36, p. 374.

95. Southworth, W. A. (2001). *The origins of Campa in Central Vietnam: a preliminary review* /z-wcorg/. http://catalog.hathitrust.org/api/volumes/oclc/57480138.html, pp. 293-294.

96. Schweyer, A.-V. (2019). *The Birth of Champa.*, p. 5.

97. TKCS, Vol. 36, p. 374.

98. TKCS, Vol. 36, p. 374.

APPENDIX 12

1. TKCS, Vol. 36, p. 342.

2. TKCS, Vol. 36, p. 346.

3. Southworth, W. A. (2001). *The origins of Campa in Central Vietnam: a preliminary review* /z-wcorg/. http://catalog.hathitrust.org/api/volumes/oclc/57480138.html, p. 301.

4. TKCS, Vol. 36, p. 357.

5. TKCS, Vol. 36, p. 358.

6. TKCS, Vol. 36, p. 358.

7. TKCS, Vol. 36, pp. 361-362.

8. TKCS, Vol. 36, pp. 358-359.

9. TKCS, Vol. 36, p. 394.

10. Yue, S. (492-493). *Book of Song (Song shu)- Volume 38 Treatises 28: Administrative Districts 4.* http://chinesenotes.com/songshu/songshu038.html.

11. Đào, D. A. (2005). *Đất nước Việt Nam qua các đời - Nghiên cứu địa lý học lịch sử Việt Nam*. NXB Văn Hóa Thông Tin., p. 74.

12. TKCS, Vol. 36, p. 367.

13. TKCS, Vol. 36, p. 362.

14. TKCS, Vol. 36, p. 362.

15. Aurousseau, L. (1914). Georges Maspero: Le Royaume de Champa. *Bulletin de l'Ecole française d'Extrême-Orient*, 8-43. https://www.persee.fr/doc/befeo_0336-1519_1914_num_14_1_285., p. 30.

16. The alternative to Cửa Việt is to use the river inlet at the Bến Hải river, around 15 kilometres north, then follow the Cánh Hòm river to the Thạch Hãn river. However, while historical records mention Cửa Việt as an entry point, they do not refer to the estuary at the Bến Hải river as an alternative, presumably because the two rivers are only around 15 kilometres apart, so it would make sense to continue the sea route along the coast from the Bến Hải to Thạch Hãn rivers rather than taking the parallel river route of Cánh Hòm.

17. TKCS, Vol. 36, p. 366.

18. Đào, D. A. (2005). *Đất nước Việt Nam qua các đời - Nghiên cứu địa lý học lịch sử Việt Nam*. NXB Văn Hóa Thông Tin., p. 69.

19. Southworth, W. A. (2001). *The origins of Campa in Central Vietnam: a preliminary review* /z-wcorg/. http://catalog.hathitrust.org/api/volumes/oclc/57480138.html, p. 298.

20. Taylor, K. W. (1983). *The Birth of Vietnam*. Berkeley: University of California Press., p. 108.

21. TKCS, Vol. 36, p. 373.

22. Tỉ Cảnh means at noon on the summer solstice when a person's body and its shadow match or a person would look down on his own shadow.

23. TKCS, Vol. 36, p. 363.

24. TKCS, Vol. 36, p. 367.

25. TKCS, Vol. 36, p. 367.

26. Bửu, C., Đỗ, V. A., Phạm, H. T., & Trương, B. L. (1962). *Hồng Đức Bản Đồ*. Tủ Sách Viện Khảo Cổ-Publications of the Institute of Historical Research - Publications de l'institut de Recherches Historiques - Số III., maps 89, 90 pp.117-118 and map 141, p. 169.

27. Ibid., page XII, p. 9.

28. TKCS, Vol. 36, p. 375.

29. TKCS, Vol. 36, p. 383.

30. TKCS, Vol. 36, p. 384.

31. TKCS, Vol. 36, p. 371.

32. Quốc Sử Quán Triều Nguyễn, Viện Khoa Học Xã Hội Việt Nam, & Viện Sử Học. (2006). *Đại Nam Nhất Thống Chí* (T. Đ. Phạm & D. A. Đào, Trans.). NXB Thuận Hóa., Vol. 2, Book 5, Nghệ An, p. 209.

33. TKCS, Vol. 36, p. 371.

34. TKCS, Vol. 36, p. 374.

35. Đào, D. A. (2005). *Đất nước Việt Nam qua các đời - Nghiên cứu địa lý học lịch sử Việt Nam*. NXB Văn Hóa Thông Tin., p. 69.

36. TKCS, Vol. 36, p. 365.

37. *Cửa Tư Hiền*. https://vi.wikipedia.org/wiki/C%E1%BB%ADa_T%C6%B0_Hi%E1%BB%81n

38. TKCS, Vol. 36, p. 376.

39. TKCS, Vol. 36, p. 388.

40. Aurousseau, L. (1914). Georges Maspero: Le Royaume de Champa. *Bulletin de l'Ecole française d'Extrême-Orient*, 8-43. https://www.persee.fr/doc/befeo_0336-1519_1914_num_14_1_285., p. 33.

41. Lê, T. M., & Zhang, Z. Đô thành Điển Xung của Vương Quốc Lâm Ấp trong sách Thủy Kinh Chú -The Dian Chong capital of Lin Yi kingdom in Shui Jing Zhu book,

42. Trần, B. Đ., Mạc, Đ., Tô, B. G., Phan, V. H., Lê, V. N., Nguyễn, N., & Tôn, N. Q. T. (2005). *Lịch Sử Việt Nam (Từ Đầu Đến Năm 938) - Tập 2* (V. G. Trần, B. Đ. Trần, & Đ. Mạc, Eds.). NXB Trẻ., p. 251.

43. Bửu, C., Đỗ, V. A., Pham, H. T., & Trương, B. L. (1962). *Hồng Đức Bản Đồ*. Tủ Sách Viện Khảo Cổ-Publications of the Institute of Historical Research - Publications de l'institut de Recherches Historiques - Số III., p. 114, map on page 86.

44. Southworth, W. A. (2001). *The origins of Campa in Central Vietnam: a preliminary review* /z-wcorg/. http://catalog.hathitrust.org/api/volumes/oclc/57480138.html, p. 312.

APPENDIX 13

1. Oey, G. P., & Luce, G. H. (1961). *The Man shu*. Department of Far Eastern Studies Cornell University.

2. It could be one of the departments just below the governor.

3. It took Fan Chuo two days of horse riding to get to the rebel camp, at an average speed of six kilometres per hour for eight hours; his horse would get him to the rebel camp at around Phú Thọ, possibly as far as Li Xi Yuan (somewhere near Vũ Ến railway station). This is consistent with his mention of the two days of water travel to get to Phong prefecture (Feng Zhou), around modern Bạch Hạc, from La Thành. Horse riding is expected to be faster than travelling by boat; thus, I expect him to get further than Bạch Hạc.

4. "Wu Man" or back barbarians, a tribe who lived on the eastern side of Yunan, *"they have no cotton cloth nor silk. Men and women all wear the skins of cattle or sheep"*. Man shu, p. 10.

5. A note in the Man shu (p. 35) points out that Wang Kuang had already left at that time, and the person responsible for the troop withdrawal was not him but Cai Jing who was jealous of Cai Xi.

6. Referring to 30,000 troops who came with Cai Xi.

7. This passage cites Pangu or P'an Ku, a cosmological demigod in the Chinese legends of creation. At the beginning of time, the universe had the shape of an egg. When the egg broke, a giant, P'an-Ku, came out of it along with two basic elements: Yin and Yang. Yang formed the sky and Yin condensed to become the Earth. However, Fan Chuo did not mention any of this in the following pages but instead explained another myth of P'an-hu, which means "Plate-Gourd", the name of a dog who mated with a princess and gave birth to 12 children. (Man shu p. 100). There is no connection between these two myths that appear to derive from Southern China. See Birrell, A. (1999). *Chinese mythology: an introduction*. Johns Hopkins University Press., p. 119.

8. SKTT, Vol. 1, p. 196. SKTT records the volunteers came from Quế Quản, I am unable to locate this region but it could be a combination of the Quế (Gui) and the Quản (Guan) provinces: modern Guizhou and Guangxi, Guangdong provinces.

9. Mang Man is another barbarian tribe, *"they live in pile-propped houses. They have no cities with outer or inner walls. Some lacquer their front teeth. All wear trousers of blue cloth, and tangle their waists with canes and strips of bamboo. With red silk cloth they bind their headdress, leaving the spill of it to hang behind as an ornament. Their womenfolk wear so-lo cages 155 (smocks of silk cotton passed over the head) of all five colours. Pea-fowl nest on the trees (near) the people's houses. They have elephants the size of the water buffalo. The native custom is to rear elephants to till the fields. Also, they burn their dung"*. Man shu, p. 43.

10. A region north-west of modern Dali city, Yunnan, modern Jianchuan and Eryuan counties.

11. Ho Man, Ho barbarians who used to live by Erhai Lake at Dali but were driven out and settled at Zhe Dong (modern Kunming). Man shu, p. 37.

12. A local attendant belongs to one of the tribes that came with Nanzhao.

13. Xun-chuan Man is a different barbarian tribe, described by Fan Chuo as *"they go barefoot, and can tread on brambles and thorns. Holding bows in their hands and arrows under their arms, they shoot porcupines and pigs and eat their flesh raw. They take their two (canine) teeth and stick both in the sides of their head-dress as an adornment. Also, they use strips of pig-skin to tie their waist. Whenever they fight in battle, they encage their heads with wicker cages, like metal -caps or helmets in appearance."*, Man shu, p. 40.

14. Fan Chuo may have referred to soldiers from Jiangxi province, China.

15. Yi-mou-xun (I-mou-hsun) is a Nanzhao king who reigned between 778 and 808, the oath was signed in 794.

16. Fan Chuo described Pu-zi Man as a *brave, fierce, nimble, and active people*.

17. A tribe who lived to the west of Lan-cang-jiang (modern Lancang river) near the border of Myanmar and China. According to Fan Chuo, they are warlike, nimble, and good at using the lance and the chan (?) on horseback, and are usually deployed as a vanguard in battles.

18. SKTT, Vol.1. p. 196 refers to the east gate of La Thành next to the river, as discussed in Chapter 13, this would be the Red River.

19. Jingnan and Eyue are in contemporary Hubei and Henan provinces. I am unable to locate Xiangzhou. These are all south of the imperial capital at Chang'an.

20. Jiangxi is a province in China, I am unable to locate the other places mentioned here.

21. This could be the Tô Lịch river mouth which has long been filled in and is now around Chợ Gạo, Hanoi.

22. Fan Chuo may have written this passage in late 863 or early 864. Since La Thành fell in the winter of 863, it makes sense that the call for help from local prefectures would be after that in the spring and summer of the same year.

23. I am unclear if "I or Liao" refers to two different tribes or the name of a location. The other reference in Man shu to I-liao (or the I and the Liao) is in relation to a route that one of Nanzhao envoys took under the reign of Yi-mou-xun (778-808) on the way to pay tribute to the Tang emperor at Chang'an: *"one way going out by I-liao (or the I and the Liao) and (entering) from the An Nam road"*, Man shu, p. 106. In this context, I-liao is likely a location, but I am unable to locate it on the map. Since An Nam road is the route upstream of the Red River to Yunan, I-liao is likely to be around Ku-Yung-pu (modern Manhao). Man shu, p. 60, also mentions Yongchang city (modern Baohan, west of Dali), the old Ai-lao land, but this Ai-lao is not the same as I-liao. There are Lao tribes shown on the map in Man shu, p. 117, who lived north of modern Hà Giang in Vietnam.

24. Gui and Jing-yuan are probably different types of administrative units such as *xian* (county) and *zhou* (prefecture).

25. According to SKTT, Vol. 1, p. 197, note 4, Jun zhou (or *Dung Châu* in Vietnamese) is modern Beiliu county, Yulin, Guangxi, but this location would be deep in Tang territory and has little military or economic value for Nanzhao to attack. Given that the Man rebels captured two Tang generals of An Nam there, Jun zhou is likely to be in An Nam territory.

26. Đào, D. A. (2005). *Đất nước Việt Nam qua các đời - Nghiên cứu địa lý học lịch sử Việt Nam*. NXB Văn Hóa Thông Tin., p. 103 explains Wu-an zhou (Võ An châu) is at Guangxi but CM, Vol. 1, p. 184, quotes Phan Huy Chú cited Vũ An Châu as Quảng Yên or modern Quảng Ninh province on the east coast of north Vietnam.

27. It is strange that Fan Chuo saw the attendant at Teng zhou, north of modern Phú Thọ, well inside Man territory in November 863. This is because, by that time, he should have been at Hai-men in China.

APPENDIX 14

1. Maspero, H. (1918). Études d'histoire d'Annam. *Bulletin de l'Ecole française d'Extrême-Orient*, 1-36. https://www.persee.fr/doc/befeo_0336-1519_1918_num_18_1_588., p. 11.

2. TKCS, Book 37, p. 423.

3. SKTT Vol. 1, p. 153.

4. Gu, B. (111). *Han shu - Book of Han*. https://ctext.org/han-shu/zh, https://ctext.org/han-shu/xi-nan-yi-liang-yue-zhao, Volume 95, Traditions of the Yi of the southeast, the two Yue, and Chosun (Korea) – Nanyue and Min Yue, Paragraph 27.

5. Sima, Q., & Chan, C. M. (2016). *The Grand Scribe's Records, Volume X : Volume X: The Memoirs of Han China, Part III* [Book]. Indiana University Press., Memoir 53 or Chapter 113, p. 19, footnote 120.

6. This number is skewed by the high density in Giao Chỉ (8.07) as compared with the southern commanderies of Cửu Chân (4.64) and Nhật Nam (4.49).

7. Tana, L. (2002). *Nguyễn Cochinchina: Southern Vietnam in the seventeenth and eighteenth centuries* (Second ed.). Southeast Asia Program Publications., p. 170.

8. Tana concludes "*đinh*" is no reliable data to estimate the population. She uses the number of villages instead. On this basis, she estimates the population of north Vietnam in 1417, 1490 and 1539 as 1,861,750, 4,372,500, and 5,625,400 respectively. The annual growth rate works out to be 0.91% from 1417 to 1539 and 1.29% from 1417 to 149, see ibid., p. 171. In recent times, the rate for the whole of Vietnam has steadily declined from 1.11% in 2000 (pop. 79.9 m) to 0.91% in 2020 (pop. 97.3 m), with a peak of 3.07% in 1959 (pop. 31.7 m), see macrotrends. (2021). *Vietnam Population 1950-2021*. https://www.macrotrends.net/countries/VNM/vietnam/population.

9. ourworldindata.org. (2021). *World population from 10,000 BC to today*. https://ourworldindata.org/world-population-growth

10. Taylor, K. W. (1983). *The Birth of Vietnam*. Berkeley: University of California Press., p. 55, p.120, p. 167, and p. 176, taken from Han shu (Vol. 28, part 1, Treatise on Geography), Hou Han shu (Vol. 113, Records 23, Commanderies and States Part Five), Jin shu (Vol. 15, Treatise 5, Geography Part 2), Song shu (Vol. 38, Treatise 28: Administrative Districts 4), Sui shu (Vol. 31, Treatise 26: Geography 3), Jiu Tang shu(Volume 41 Treatises 21: Geography 4), Xin Tang shu (Volume 43a, Treatises 37: Geography 7a).

11. Ibid., p. 180.

12. Data is taken from Quốc Sử Quán Triều Nguyễn, Viện Khoa Học Xã Hội Việt Nam, & Viện Sử Học. (2006). *Đại Nam Nhất Thống Chí* (T. Đ. Phạm & D. A. Đào, Trans.). NXB Thuận Hóa., Vol. 1, p. 140; Vol. 2, p. 18, p. 101, p. 172, p. 286, p. 398; Banens, M. (1999). Vietnam: A Reconstitution of its 20th Century Population History. hal- 00369251 https://hal.archives-ouvertes.fr/hal-0036925., p. 39 and General Statistics Office of Vietnam. (2021). *Area, Population and Population Density by Cities, Provinces, Year, and Items*. https://www.gso.gov.vn/en/px-web/?pxid=E0201&theme=Population%20and%20Employment.

APPENDIX 15

1. Taken from Theobald, U. (2016). *duliangheng* 度量衡, *weights and measures*. http://www.chinaknowledge.de/History/Terms/duliangheng.html.

2. According to Schinz, A. (1996). *The Magic Square: Cities in Ancient China*. Edition Axel Menges., p. 179, under Tang, there were large *li* and smaller *li*, the former is used for all measurements in general, and the latter is permitted only in connection with the emperor. In this book, I use the smaller *li*, *chi*, and *bu*, as they are more in line with measurements at other periods; one *bu* is 1.5 m.

APPENDIX 16

1. I am unable to locate the location, see Trương, Đ. C. (2018). *Các nhóm mộ táng tại di tích Giồng Lớn (Bà Rịa - Vũng Tàu)*. https://baotanglichsu.vn/vi/Articles/3127/68782/cac-nhom-mo-tang-tai-di-tich-giong-lon-ba-ria-vung-tau.html.

BIBLIOGRAPHY

Abhanga, Ābhaṅga, Abhaṅga, Abhamga: 7 definitions. (2021). HTTPS://WWW.WISDOMLIB.ORG/DEFINITION/ABHANGA

Active Gold Mines in Vietnam's Jungle. (2015). HTTPS://RAREGOLDNUGGETS.COM/?P=1968

An Bình. (2012). *Phòng VH&TT huyện Thuận Thành trả lời đơn xin lại tượng Pháp Vũ của nhân dân thôn Đông Cốc.* HTTPS://PHATGIAO.ORG.VN/PHONG-VHTT-HUYEN-THUAN-THANH-TRA-LOI-DON-XIN-LAI-TUONG-PHAP-VU-CUA-NHAN-DAN-THON-DONG-COC-D10319.HTML

Anderson, J., & Whitmore, J. K. (2015). *China's encounters on the South and Southwest: reforging the fiery frontier over two millennia.*

Antontruongthang's Blog. (2015). *Văn Khắc Champa: Hòn...Cụp, Chiêm Sơn.* HTTPS://ANTONTRUONGTHANG.WORDPRESS.COM/A-DA-NANG-MAY-2015/VAN-KHAC-CHAMPA-HONCUP-CHIEM-SON/

Apsara, Indian religion and mythology. HTTPS://WWW.BRITANNICA.COM/TOPIC/APSARA

Army, U., Service, M. I., & War Department. (1942). *Intelligence Bulletin.* (Vol. I, No. 1, September 1942). GPO.

Aspell, W. (2013). Southeast Asia in the Suishu: A Translation of Memoir 47 with Notes and Commentary. *Asia Research Institute - Working Paper Series No. 208.* HTTPS://ARI.NUS.EDU.SG/WP-CONTENT/UPLOADS/2018/10/WPS13_208.PDF

Aurousseau, L. (1914). Georges Maspero: Le Royaume de Champa. *Bulletin de l'Ecole française d'Extrême-Orient*, 8-43. https://www.persee.fr/doc/befeo_0336-1519_1914_num_14_1_2850

Backus, C. (1981). *The Nan-chao kingdom and Tang China's southwestern frontier*. Cambridge University Press.

Banens, M. (1999). Vietnam: A Reconstitution of its 20th Century Population History. *hal- 00369251* https://hal.archives-ouvertes.fr/hal-00369251

Bảo tàng Nhân học. (2010). *Lâm Ấp qua những tài liệu khảo cổ học – 1. Về vị trí của Lâm Ấp*. http://baotanglichsu.vn/vi/articles/3127/6629/lam-ap-qua-nhung-tai-lieu-khao-co-hoc-1-ve-vi-tri-cua-lam-ap.html

Baotanglichsutphcm. (2018). *PHẬT*. http://www.baotanglichsutphcm.com.vn/phat-3

Barth , A. M.-E. (1885). *Inscriptions sanscrites du Cambodge. Extrait des notices et extraits des manuscrits de la Bibliothèque Nationale tome XXVII, 1st partie*. Paris Imprimerie Nationale.

Barth, A. M.-E. (1903). Inscription sanscrite du Phou Lokhon (Laos). *Bulletin de l'Ecole française d'Extrême-Orient*, 442-446. https://www.persee.fr/doc/befeo_0336-1519_1903_num_3_1_1236

Basak, B. (2012). *Understanding the Champa polity from archaeological and epigraphic evidence - a critical stocktaking* European Association of Southeast Asian archaeology, 14 (EurASEAA 14), Dublin, Ireland.

Beckwith, J. A. (2002). *Pre-Angkor Cambodia: The Transition from Prehistory to History* University of Otago]. Dunedin.

Benn, C. D. (2004). *China's golden age: everyday life in the Tang dynasty*. Oxford University Press.

Billman, S. (2021). *How Long Does It Take To Learn Chinese?* https://www.china-admissions.com/blog/how-long-does-it-take-to-learn-chinese/

Biography of Ma Yuan. (2020?). https://ctext.org/dong-guan-han-ji/ma-yuan

Birrell, A. (1999). *Chinese mythology: an introduction*. Johns Hopkins University Press.

Bộ Quốc Phòng - Viện Lịch Sử Quân Sự Việt Nam, Trần, Q. V., & Lê, Đ. S. (2001). *Lịch Sử Quân Sự Việt Nam - Tập 2 - Đấu tranh giành độc lập tự chủ (từ năm 179 TCN đến năm 938)*. NXB Chính Trị Quốc Gia.

The boundary stone of Han Dynasty in Suma Bay. (18 May 2018). http://www.chinadaily.com.cn/regional/2015-05/18/content_20750795.htm

Briggs, L. P. (1947). A Sketch of Cambodian History. *The Far Eastern Quarterly*, 6(4), 354-363. https://www.jstor.org/stable/2049431?seq=1 ( )

Briggs, L. P. (1951). *The ancient Khmer Empire*. American Philosophical Society.

Brindley, E. (2018). *Ancient China and the Yue : perceptions and identities on the southern frontier, c.400 BCE - 50 CE*.

Brücke Osteuropa. (2009). *Representatives of the Yi Minority in Shilin (Kunming/Yunnan)*. https://commons.wikimedia.org/wiki/file:yi-minority.jpg

Bùi Thụy Đào Nguyên CC BY-SA 3.0. (29 November 2013). *Trên đường Gò Cây Thị nhìn về núi Ba Thê thuộc Thoại Sơn, An Giang, Việt Nam*. https://commons.wikimedia.org/wiki/file:n%c3%bai_ba_th%c3%aa_%e1%bb%9f_tho%e1%ba%a1i_s%c6%a1n.jpg

Bùi Thụy Đào Nguyên CC BY-SA 3.0. (2007). *Tượng Phật bốn tay và tấm bia đá cổ có từ thời vương quốc Phù Nam, hiện ở trong chùa Linh Sơn (Ba Thê); tọa lạc tại thị trấn Óc Eo, huyện Thoại Sơn, tỉnh An Giang, Việt Nam.* https://upload.wikimedia.org/wikipedia/commons/1/1d/t%c6%b0%e1%bb%a3ng_ph%e1%ba%adt_b%e1%bb%91n_tay.jpg

Bửu, C., Đỗ, V. A., Pham, H. T., & Trương, B. L. (1962). *Hồng Đức Bản Đồ*. Tủ Sách Viện Khảo Cổ-Publications of the Institute of Historical Research - Publications de l'institut de Recherches Historiques - Số III.

Cadière, L. (1905). Monuments et souvenirs chams du Quảng-tri et du Thừa-thiên. *Bulletin de l'Ecole française d'Extrême-Orient*, 185-195. https://www.persee.fr/doc/befeo_0336-1519_1905_num_5_1_2637

The Cambridge History of China: Volume 1: The Ch'in and Han Empires, 221 BC–AD 220. (1986). (D. Twitchett & M. Loewe, Eds. Vol. 1). Cambridge University Press. https://doi.org/doi:10.1017/CHOL9780521243278

Châu, H. Đ. (2018). *An Nam Truyện - Ghi chép về Việt Nam trong chính sử Trung Quốc xưa.* Hội Nhà Văn.

Cheng Shou. (3rd century CE). *Record of the Three Kingdoms, Sanguo zhi.* https://ctext.org/sanguozhi/zh

Chinese Text Project. (2006-2020). *Shiji-Historical Records- [Western Han] 109 BC-91 BC Sima Qian.* https://ctext.org/shiji

Chinese fortification: an overview of parts and terminology — Part 1: The wall. (2019). https://greatmingmilitary.blogspot.com/2019/06/chinese-fortification-p1.html

Chính Đạo. (2017). *Trụ đồng Mã Viện : Sự đàn hồi của biên giới đế quốc Trung Hoa*. Van Hoa Publishing Co. https://nghiencuulichsu.com/2017/07/19/tru-dong-ma-vien-su-dan-hoi-cua-bien-gioi-de-quoc-trung-hoa/

Chollet, C. (2021). *About the recent activities of the CIK (Corpus of Khmer Inscriptions)*. https://dharma.hypotheses.org/3659

Chronique. (1909). *Bulletin de l'Ecole française d'Extrême-Orient*, 613-630. https://www.persee.fr/doc/befeo_0336-1519_1909_num_9_1_1965

Chronique. (1917). *Bulletin de l'Ecole française d'Extrême-Orient*, 35-57. https://www.persee.fr/doc/befeo_0336-1519_1917_num_17_1_5342

Cœdès, G. (1908). Inventaire des inscriptions du Champa et du Cambodge. *Bulletin de l'Ecole française d'Extrême-Orient*, 37-92. https://www.persee.fr/doc/befeo_0336-1519_1908_num_8_1_4180

Cœdès, G. (1931). Etudes cambodgiennes. XXV, Deux inscriptions sanskrites du Fou-nan. XXVI, La date de Kôh Ker. XXVII, La date du Bàphùon. *Bulletin de l'Ecole française d'Extrême-Orient*, 1-23. https://www.persee.fr/doc/befeo_0336-1519_1931_num_31_1_4415

Coedès, G. (1937). A New Inscription from Fu-Nan. *The Journal of The Greater India Society*, *IV, No. 1*, 117-121.

Coedès, G. (1942). *Inscriptions du Cambodge/editées et traduites par G. Cœdès.* (Vol. II). École française d'Extrême-Orient.

Coedès, G., Cowing, S. B., Vella, W. F., & Press, A. N. U. (1968). *The Indianized States of Southeast Asia*. HTTP://HDL.HANDLE.NET/1885/115188

Cửa Tư Hiền. HTTPS://VI.WIKIPEDIA.ORG/WIKI/C%E1%BB%ADA_T%C6%B0_HI%E1%BB%81N

Cynthia L. Chennault, K. N. K., Alan J. Berkowitz, and Albert E. Dien. (2015). *Early Medieval Chinese Texts: A Bibliographical Guide* (Vol. 71).

Daderot - CC0. (3 August 2014). *Daderot, CC0, via Wikimedia Commons*. HTTPS://UPLOAD.WIKIMEDIA.ORG/WIKIPEDIA/COMMONS/E/E6/STEPS_-_HANOI_BOTANICAL_GARDEN_-_HANOI%2C_VIETNAM_-_DSC03633.JPG

Daderot CC0 via Wikimedia Commons. (2014). Bell for ritual use (replica). HTTPS://UPLOAD.WIKIMEDIA.ORG/WIKIPEDIA/COMMONS/5/5A/BELL_FOR_RITUAL_USE_%28REPLICA%29%2C_THANH_MAI_PAGODA%2C_HA_TAY_PROVINCE%2C_CAST_IN_798_AD%2C_BRONZE_-_NATIONAL_MUSEUM_OF_VIETNAMESE_HISTORY_-_HANOI%2C_VIETNAM_-_DSC05548.JPG

Daderot / CC0. (7 August 2014). *Dancer, Tra Kieu, Quang Nam, 10th century AD, sandstone - Museum of Vietnamese History - Ho Chi Minh City*. HTTPS://COMMONS.WIKIMEDIA.ORG/WIKI/FILE:DANCER,_TRA_KIEU,_QUANG_NAM,_10TH_CENTURY_AD,_SANDSTONE_-_MUSEUM_OF_VIETNAMESE_HISTORY_-_HO_CHI_MINH_CITY_-_DSC06144.JPG

Daderot CC0 via Wikimedia Commons. (6 August 2014). *Model of Battle in Bach Dang River in 938 AD*. HTTPS://COMMONS.WIKIMEDIA.ORG/WIKI/FILE:MODEL_OF_BATTLE_IN_BACH_DANG_RIVER_IN_938_AD_-_DSC05544.JPG

Đào, D. A. (2006). *Lịch sử Việt Nam - Từ nguồn gốc đến thế kỷ XIX*. NXB Văn Hóa Thông Tin. (1957)

Đào, D. A. (2005). *Đất nước Việt Nam qua các đời - Nghiên cứu địa lý học lịch sử Việt Nam*. NXB Văn Hóa Thông Tin.

Daši, T., Weiyi, H., Qiyan, Z., Xuan, O., Haowen, L., Yi, W., & Zongduan, Y. (1346). *History of Song (Song Shi)*. HTTP://CHINESENOTES.COM/SONGSHI.HTML

De Crespigny, R. (2007). *A biographical dictionary of Later Han to the Three Kingdoms (23-220 AD)*. Brill.

De Crespigny, R., Ban, G., Australian National, U., & Centre of Oriental, S. (1967). *Official titles of the Former Han dynasty*. Centre of Oriental Studies in association with Australian National University Press.

Demandt, M., xc, & Le H, S. (2015). Early Gold Ornaments of Southeast Asia: Production, Trade, and Consumption. *Asian Perspectives, 54*(2), 305-330. HTTP://WWW.JSTOR.ORG/STABLE/26357682

Dinh, M. C., Ly, K. H., Ha, T. M., Ha, V. T., Hoang Thi, T., & Nguyen, T. T. (2008). *The History of Buddhism in Vietnam*. The Council for Research in Values and Philosophy.

Đinh, V. N. (1980). Đất Mê Linh - Trung tâm chính trị, quân sự và kinh tế của huyện Mê Linh thời Hai Bà Trưng. *Nghiên Cứu Lịch Sử - Viện Sử Học, 1*, 35-53.

Đỗ, V. N. (1970). Thành Quèn, căn cứ của Đỗ Cảnh Thạc, một trong mười hai sứ quân hồi thế kỷ X. *Nghiên Cứu Lịch Sử - Viện Sử Học, 132*, 91-97. HTTPS://REPOSITORY.VNU.EDU.VN/HANDLE/VNU_123/69074

Đồng, T. D. (2018). *Đặt lại vấn đề thời điểm ra đời của nhà nước Lâm Ấp*. http://nghiencuuquocte.org/2018/05/27/dat-lai-van-de-thoi-diem-ra-doi-cua-nha-nuoc-lam-ap/

Dongguan hanji. (2020?). http://www.chinaknowledge.de/literature/historiography/dongguanhanji.html

Du You. (766-801). *Tongdian - Volume 188: Border defence four Southern barbarians*. https://zh.wikisource.org/zh-hant/%E9%80%9A%E5%85%B8/%E5%8D%B7188

Đức Mẹ Trà Kiệu. (2019). https://vi.wikipedia.org/wiki/%C4%90%E1%BB%A9c_M%E1%BA%B9_Tr%C3%A0_Ki%E1%BB%87u

Duong, V. C. (2016). Buddhism from India to Vietnam: A Study of Early Introduction. *Imperial Journal of Interdisciplinary Research (IJIR)*, 2(9), 1171-1175. http://www.onlinejournal.in/ijirv2i9/184.pdf

Durand, M. (1951). La dynastie des Lý antérieurs d'après le Viêt diên u linh tập. *Bulletin de l'Ecole française d'Extrême-Orient*, 437-452. https://www.persee.fr/doc/befeo_0336-1519_1951_num_44_2_5179

Eade, C. (2011). Vatt Samrong Ek: the Inscription, the Buddha Pedestal, and the Numbers. *Aséanie, Sciences humaines en Asie du Sud-Est*, 101-104. https://www.persee.fr/doc/asean_0859-9009_2011_num_27_1_2172

Ebrey, P. B. *A Visual Sourcebook of Chinese Civilization, China proper*. https://depts.washington.edu/chinaciv/geo/proper.htm

Edmondson, J. A. (1994). Change and Variation in Zhuang. *University of Texas at Arlington*. http://sealang.net/sala/archives/pdf8/edmondson1994change.pdf

Edmondson, J. A., & Gregerson, K. J. (2007). The Languages of Vietnam: Mosaics and Expansions. *Language and Linguistics Compass*, 1(6), 727-749. https://doi.org/10.1111/j.1749-818x.2007.00033.x

EFEO. *George Cœdès*. https://www.efeo.fr/biographies/notices/codes.htm

Fan Ye. (5th century). *Hou Han shu - Book of the Later Han*. https://ctext.org/hou-han-shu

Fang Xuanling. (648). *Book of Jin (Jin shu)*. http://chinesenotes.com/jinshu.html

Fang Xuanling. (648). *Book of Jin (Jin shu), Volume 15 Treatise 5: Geography Part Two*. http://chinesenotes.com/jinshu/jinshu015.html#?highlight=%E6%AF%94%E6%99%AF

Fang Xuanling. (648). *Book of Jin (Jin shu) - Volume 97 Biographies 67: Four Barbarian Tribes*. http://chinesenotes.com/jinshu/jinshu097.html

Filliozat, J. (1969). VI. L'inscription dite "de Vo-çanh". *Bulletin de l'Ecole française d'Extrême-Orient*, 107-116. https://www.persee.fr/doc/befeo_0336-1519_1969_num_55_1_4856

Filliozat, J. (1971). Louis Malleret (1901-1970) [note biographique]. *Bulletin de l'Ecole française d'Extrême-Orient*, 58, 1971, 4-15. https://www.persee.fr/doc/befeo_0336-1519_1971_num_58_1_5073

Finot, L. (1902). Notes d'épigraphie. *Bulletin de l'Ecole française d'Extrême-Orient*, 185-191. https://www.persee.fr/doc/befeo_0336-1519_1902_num_2_1_1119

Finot, L. (1904). Notes d'épigraphie : XI. Les inscriptions de Mi-Sơn. *Bulletin de l'Ecole française d'Extrême-Orient*, 897-977. HTTPS://WWW.PERSEE.FR/DOC/BEFEO_0336-1519_1904_NUM_4_1_1405

Finot, L. (1928). Nouvelles inscriptions du Cambodge. *Bulletin de l'Ecole française d'Extrême-Orient*, 43-80. HTTPS://WWW.PERSEE.FR/DOC/BEFEO_0336-1519_1928_NUM_28_1_3116

Frederic Romanet du Caillaud, Public domain via Wikimedia Commons, & Vinhtantran. (1873 4 June 2009). *Map of Hanoi c. 1873 - Source La conquete du delta du Tong-King by Frederic Romanet du Caillaud, published in 1877.* HTTPS://UPLOAD.WIKIMEDIA.ORG/WIKIPEDIA/COMMONS/7/70/MAP_OF_HANOI.PNG

Gary Todd - CC0 - via Wikimedia Commons. (28 November 2012). *Oc Eo Culture Gallery.* HTTPS://COMMONS.WIKIMEDIA.ORG/WIKI/FILE:OC_EO_CULTURE_VISHNU_STATUE_2.JPG

Gary Todd from Xinzheng China CC0 via Wikimedia Commons. (27 September 2013). *Vietnam History Museum, Ho Chi Minh City (Saigon), 2013. Complete indexed photo collection at WorldHistoryPics.com., A photograph taken in the Museum of Vietnamese History in Hồ Chí Minh City (HCMC / TPHCM) by Professor Gary Lee Todd.* HTTPS://COMMONS.WIKIMEDIA.ORG/WIKI/FILE:OC-EO_CULTURE_(9980674965).JPG

General Statistics Office of Vietnam. (2021). *Area, Population and Population Density by Cities, Provinces, Year, and Items.* HTTPS://WWW.GSO.GOV.VN/EN/PX-WEB/?PXID=E0201&THEME=POPULATION%20AND%20EMPLOYMENT

Giang, Đ., Tomomi, S., Văn Quảng, N., & Mariko, Y. (2020). Champa Citadels: An Archaeological and Historical Study.

Goble, G. (May 2014). Maritime Southeast Asia: The view from Tang–Song China *Nalanda-Sriwijaya Centre Working Paper No 16.* HTTP://WWW.ISEAS.EDU.SG/NSC/DOCUMENTS/WORKING_PAPERS/NSCWPS016.PDF

Gold Reserves. HTTPS://TRADINGECONOMICS.COM/COUNTRY-LIST/GOLD-RESERVES

Golzio, K.-H. Kauṇḍinya in Southeast Asia, How a historical figure was transformed into a mythical Hero. HTTPS://WWW.ACADEMIA.EDU/6874876/KAU%E1%B9%87%E1%B8%8DINYA_IN_SOUTHEAST_ASIA_HOW_A_HISTORICAL_FIGURE_WAS_TRANSFORMED_INTO_A_MYTHICAL_HERO_1

Gu, B. (111). *Han shu - Book of Han.* HTTPS://CTEXT.ORG/HAN-SHU/ZH

Guang, S., Shu, L., Ban, L., & Zuyu, F. (1084). *Zizhi Tongjian - Comprehensive Mirror in Aid of Governance* HTTP://WWW.GUOXUE.COM/SHIBU/ZZTJ/ZZTJML.HTM

Gungwu, W. (1958). The Nanhai Trade: A Study of the Early History of Chinese Trade in the South China Sea. *Journal of the Malayan Branch of the Royal Asiatic Society, 31*(2 (182)), 1-135. HTTP://WWW.JSTOR.ORG/STABLE/41503138

Guy, J. B. P., & Metropolitan Museum of Art. (2014). *Lost kingdoms: Hindu-Buddhist sculpture of early Southeast Asia.* The Metropolitan Museum of Art.

Hà, S. (2019). Tỉnh nào có nhiều vàng nhất nước ta? HTTPS://ZINGNEWS.VN/TINH-NAO-CO-NHIEU-VANG-NHAT-NUOC-TA-POST965839.HTML

Hà, V. T. (2018). *The making of Việt Nam.* Thế Giới.

Haiphong tide times and tide charts - 27-28 Feb. 2021. (2021). https://www.tideschart.com/vietnam/hai-phong/haiphong/

Hall, D. G. E. (1999). *A history of South-East Asia*. MacMillan.

Hardy, A. D. C. M. Z. P. (2012). *Champa and the archaeology of My Son (Vietnam)*. NUS Press.

Hendrickson, M., Leroy, S., Hua, Q., Phon, K., & Voeun, V. (2017). Smelting in the Shadow of the Iron Mountain: Preliminary Field Investigation of the Industrial Landscape around Phnom Dek, Cambodia (Ninth to Twentieth Centuries A.D.). *Asian Perspectives, 56*(1), 55-91. http://www.jstor.org/stable/26357707

Heng, P., & Lavy, P. (2018). *Pre-Angkorian cities: Ishanapura and Mahendraparvata*. https://angkordatabase.asia/publications/pre-angkorian-cities-ishanapura-and-mahendraparvata

Hiện vật khai quật tại tháp Bình Thạnh. https://baotang.tayninh.gov.vn/bo-suu-tap-hien-vat/hien-vat-khai-quat-tai-thap-binh-thanh/603.html

Hienzquynh / CC BY-SA (https://creativecommons.org/licenses/by-sa/4.0). (23 August 2017). *Bức bản đồ thừa tuyên Thuận Hóa trong tập thứ nhất thuộc Hồng Đức Bản Đồ*. https://commons.wikimedia.org/wiki/file:b%e1%ba%a3n_%c4%91%e1%bb%93_th%e1%bb%aba_tuy%c3%aan_thu%e1%ba%adn_h%c3%b3a_trong_b%e1%bb%99_h%e1%bb%93ng_%c4%90%e1%bb%a9c_b%e1%ba%a3n_%c4%90%e1%bb%93.jpg

Higham, C. (1999). *The archaeology of mainland Southeast Asia : from 10,000 B.C. to the fall of Angkor*. Cambridge University Press.

Hồ, H. (5 February 2012). *Thực hư chuyện kinh đô Vạn An trên đất Nghệ An: Những bí mật chờ giải mã*. https://giadinh.net.vn/xa-hoi/thuc-hu-chuyen-kinh-do-van-an-tren-dat-nghe-an-nhung-bi-mat-cho-giai-ma-20120202104119991.htm

Hồ, T. T. (2019). *Có 500 năm như thế- Bản sắc Quảng Nam và Đàng Trong từ góc nhìn phân kỳ lịch sử* (6th ed.). NXB Đà Nẵng. http://books.google.com/books?id=kmtcxlyvlcoc

Hoangkid. (2020). *Vo Canh Stele (the original stele at National Museum of Vietnamese History in Hanoi) - a National Treasure of Vietnam*. https://upload.wikimedia.org/wikipedia/commons/f/f7/vo_canh_stele_%28national_museum_of_vietnamese_history%29.jpg

Holmgren, J. (1980). *Chinese colonisation of northern Vietnam: administrative geography and political development in the Tongking Delta, first to sixth centuries A.D.* Australian National University.

Hồng Anh. (10 October 2012). *Một số vấn đề về vương triều Tiền Lý và quê hương của vua Lý Nam Đế*. http://baotanglichsu.vn/vi/articles/3091/12680/mot-so-van-dje-ve-vuong-trieu-tien-ly-va-que-huong-cua-vua-ly-nam-dje.html

Hsu, E. H.-l. (2017). In *History of Liuli Glazed Ceramics* (pp. 38-69). Brill. https://doi.org/https://doi.org/10.1163/9789004335868_004

Huber, E. (1911). Études indochinoises. *Bulletin de l'Ecole française d'Extrême-Orient*, 259-311. https://www.persee.fr/doc/befeo_0336-1519_1911_num_11_1_2693

Hương, T. (2020). *Độc đáo chuông Thanh Mai*. https://nhipsonghanoi.hanoimoi.com.vn/tin-tuc/van-hoa/823443/doc-dao-chuong-thanh-mai

Huynh, T. (2016). *The Early Development of Buddhism in the Red River Delta Basin, Jiaozhi, and Southern China: The Case of a Sogdian-Jiaozhi Buddhist Monk Kang Senghui* 康僧會 University of the West]. https://web.archive.org/web/20160911172427/http://thichhangdat.com/wp-content/uploads/2016/07/kang-senghui-phd.pdf

Huynh, T. (2018). *The early Sinification of the Buddha's relics and the case in which Kang Senghui prayed for those sacred relics by Dr. Trung Huynh* 7th International Conference Buddhism & Australia, http://www.buddhismandaustralia.com/ba/index.php?title=presentations_2018

Jean-Pierre Dalbéra from Paris France / CC BY (https://creativecommons.org/licenses/by/2.0). (31 January 2010). *Les Apsaras Style de Tra Kieu Xè siècle Grès*. https://upload.wikimedia.org/wikipedia/commons/2/2b/apsaras_%28mus%c3%a9e_cham%2c_da_nang%29_%284394717693%29.jpg

Jenner, P. N. (1980). Chrestomathy of Pre-Angkorian Khmer I, Dated Inscriptions from the Seventh and Eighth Centuries. *Center for Southeast Asian Studies.*

School of Hawaiian, Asian, and Pacific Studies. University of Hawaii at Manoa.

Jing'an Temple predates city's birth. (1 November 2004). http://www.chinadaily.com.cn/english/doc/2004-11/01/content_387373.htm

Kang, H. (2013). The Spread of Sarnath-Style Buddha Images in Southeast Asia and Shandong, China, by the Sea Route.

Keenan, J. P., & Mou, t. (1994). *How Master Mou Removes Our Doubts: A Reader-response Study and Translation of the Mou-tzu Li-huo Lun (SUNY Series in Buddhist Studies)*. State University of New York Press.

Kieu, O. L. o. T. https://vietnamcatholictours.vn/destination/our-lady-of-tra-kieu-2/

Kiều, T. H. (2016). *Góp phần nghiên cứu lịch sử văn hóa Việt Nam - Thời kỳ thiên niên kỷ đầu công nguyên*. NXB Thế Giới.

Kim Khánh. Di tích lịch sử Đền Hai Bà Trưng. https://sites.google.com/site/cauchuyenvan-hocnghethuat/vhnt-93

Kim Sơn - Thiền phái Trúc Lâm. (1337). *Thiền Uyển Tập Anh* (Lê Mạnh Thát (Dựa trên bản in năm 1715), Trans.). Đại Học Vạn Hạnh - Saigon. http://www.thuvienhaiphu.com.vn/datafile1/be015404.pdf

Klamer, M. (2019). The dispersal of Austronesian languages in Island South East Asia: Current findings and debates. *Language and Linguistics Compass, 13*(4), e12325. https://doi.org/10.1111/lnc3.12325

Lâm, T. M. D. (2018). *Sa Huỳnh - Lâm Ấp - Chămpa: Thế kỷ 5 trước công nguyên đến thế kỷ 5 sau công nguyên (một số vấn đề khảo cổ học) = Sa Huynh - Linyi - Champa: 5th century BC - 5th century AD: some archaeological issues*. NXB Thế Giới.

Lapont, P. B., Poklaun, H., & Council for the Social-Cultural Development of, C. (2011). *Vương quốc Champa-Địa dư, Dân cư và Lịch sử*.

Lê, Đ. D. (13 Dec 2008). *Dinh xưa, cảng cũ bây giờ*. https://tuoitre.vn/dinh-xua-cang-cu-bay-gio-292392.htm

Lê, Đ. P. (2019). *Mỹ Sơn - Vùng đất thiêng vương quốc cổ Champa* Nhà Xuất Bản Khoa Học Xã Hội.

Lê, Đ. P. (2018). *Khảo cổ học Champa : khai quật và phát hiện = Champa archeology : excavations and discoveries.* NXB Khoa Học Xã Hội.

Lê, Đ. T. (20 Feb 2018). *Nguyễn Hoàng - "Người mồ côi" Đàng Trong.* https://laodong.vn/van-hoa/nguyen-hoang-nguoi-mo-coi-dang-trong-591698.ldo

Lê, M. T. (2001). *Tổng Tập Văn Học Phật Giáo Việt Nam - Tập I* (Vol. 1). Nhà Xuất Bản Thành Phố Hồ Chí Minh.

Lê, Q. Đ. (1773). *Văn Đài Loại Ngữ* (V. G. Trần, V. K. Trần, & X. H. Cao, Trans.). NXB Văn Hóa Thông Tin (2006).

Lê, Q. Đ., Nam, V. K. H. X. H. V., & Viện Sử Học. (2007). *Phủ Biên Tạp Lục* (M. K. Đỗ, T. H. Nguyễn, N. T. Nguyễn, & D. A. Đào, Trans.). NXB Văn Hóa Thông Tin. (1776)

Lê, T. (2002). *An Nam Chí Lược* (Ủy ban phiên dịch sử liệu Việt Nam của Viện Đại Học Huế (1961), Trans.). Thuận Hóa. (1285)

Lê, T. (2021). *Bia Chăm trên Hòn Kẽm - Đá Dừng.* https://baodanang.vn/channel/6058/201606/bia-cham-tren-hon-kem-da-dung-2490464/

Lê Thánh Tông (1442 - 1497) Public domain, v. W. C. (2016). *Bản đồ kinh thành Thăng Long (kèm chú thích) theo Hồng Đức bản đồ sách (洪德版圖冊), ban hành vào đời vua Lê Thánh Tông, năm Hồng Đức thứ 21 (tức năm 1490).* https://upload.wikimedia.org/wikipedia/commons/6/62/b%e1%ba%a3n_%c4%91%e1%bb%93_kinh_th%c3%a0nh_th%c4%83ng_long_%28k%c3%a8m_ch%c3%ba_th%c3%adch%29%2c_theo_h%e1%bb%93ng_%c4%90%e1%bb%a9c_b%e1%ba%a3n_%c4%91%e1%bb%93_s%c3%a1ch_%e6%b4%aa%e5%be%b7%e7%89%88%e5%9c%96%e5%86%8a_%281490%29.jpg

Lê, T. L. (2006). *Nghệ thuật Phật giáo và Hindu giáo ở đồng bằng sông Cửu Long trước thế kỷ X.* Nhà xuất bản Thế Giới.

Lê, T. L. (2017). Lung Khe and the Cultural Relationship between Northern and Southern Vietnam. *Asian Review of World Histories, 5*(2), 53-69. https://doi.org/https://doi.org/10.1163/22879811-12340005

Lê, T. L., Pham, C., Staniforth, M., Delgado, J., Kimura, J., & Sasaki, R. (2011). Understanding the Bach Dang Battlefield from recent research results.

Lê, T. M., & Zhang, Z. Đô thành Điển Xung của Vương Quốc Lâm Ấp trong sách Thủy Kinh Chú -The Dian Chong capital of Lin Yi kingdom in Shui Jing Zhu book

Lê, V. S. (2003). *Việt Nam văn minh sử: lược khảo, tập thượng, từ nguồn gốc đến thế kỷ thứ X.* Lao Động.

Lempert, D. (2018). Nan Zhao Invasions and Buddha idols of Northern Thailand and Laos in the 7th to 9th Centuries, Lao Studies, Volume 6, No. 1, pages 26 - 55, 2018. http://www.laostudies.org/system/files/subscription/lempert.pdf. 6.

Li Daoyuan. (466). *Shui Jing Zhu.* https://ctext.org/shui-jing-zhu

Li Jifu. (813). *Yuanhe junxian zhi - Treatise on all districts from the Yuanhe reign-period (806-820).*

Li Yanshou. (643-659). *Beishi: History of the Northern Dynasties.* http://chinesenotes.com/songshi/songshi489.html

Lịch Đạo Nguyên, (Li Daoyuan), Dương Thủ Kính, (Yang, Shoujing), Hùng Hội Trinh, (Xiong, Huizhen), Đoàn Huy Trọng, (Duan, Xizhong), Trần Kiều Dịch, (Chen, Qiaoyi), & Nguyễn Bá Mão. (2005). *Thủy Kinh Chú Sớ* (Nguyễn Bá Mão, Trans.). NXB Thuận Hóa ; Trung tâm văn hóa ngôn ngữ Đông Tây. (Giang Tô, China 1999)

List of allied military operations of the Vietnam War (1969). HTTPS://EN.WIKIPEDIA.ORG/WIKI/LIST_OF_ALLIED_MILITARY_OPERATIONS_OF_THE_VIETNAM_WAR_(1969)

Listes dynastiques. (1915). *Bulletin de l›Ecole française d›Extrême-Orient*, 181-184. HTTPS://WWW.PERSEE.FR/DOC/BEFEO_0336-1519_1915_NUM_15_1_5479

Lư, V. A. (2014). *Bộ máy An Nam Đô Hộ Phủ của Trung Quốc thời Đường (679– 905)* Đại Học Quốc Gia Thành Phố Hồ Chí Minh - Trường Đại Học Khoa Học Xã Hội và Nhân Văn]. Ho Chi Minh City.

Lunet de Lajonquière, E. (1911). *Inventaire descriptif des monuments du Cambodge, Tome Troisième.* (Vol. 3). Imprimerie Nationale.

Lương, N. (2010). Nước Phù Nam và Hậu Phù Nam. *Tạp chí Nghiên cứu Lịch sử*, 1.2010, 3-17.

Lương Ninh. (2013). Lại bàn về nước Lâm Ấp-Champa. *Nghiên Cứu Lịch Sử - Viện Sử Học*, 5.

Lustig, E. J. (2009). *Power and pragmatism in the political economy of Angkor* Sydney eScholarship. HTTP://HDL.HANDLE.NET/2123/5356

Lý Tế, X., & Lê Hữu, M. (1961). *Việt điện u-linh tập*. Khai-Trí. //catalog.hathitrust.org/Record/001356016

HTTP://HDL.HANDLE.NET/2027/MDP.39015023991485

Lý, T. X. (2012). *Việt điện u linh* (Đ. R. Trịnh & G. K. Đinh, Trans.). NXB Hồng Bàng. (1329)

Ma Duanlin (Ma-Touan-Lin), & Le Marquis d›Hervey de Saint-Senys - de l›Institut de France. (Jan 1883). *Ethnographie des peuples étrangers à la Chine: ouvrage composé au XIIIe siècle de notre ère, Méridinaux, Volume 2*. Geneve, H. Georg. - TH. Muller. HTTPS://PLAY.GOOGLE.COM/STORE/BOOKS/DETAILS/DUANLIN_MA_ETHNOGRAPHIE_DES_PEUPLES_%C3%A9TRANGERS_%C3%A0_LA?ID=4F0LAAAAIAAJ

macrotrends. (2021). *Vietnam Population 1950-2021*. HTTPS://WWW.MACROTRENDS.NET/COUNTRIES/VNM/VIETNAM/POPULATION

Madrolle, C. (1937). I. Le Tonkin ancien. Lei-leou et les districts chinois de l›époque des Han. La population. Yue-chang. *Bulletin de l›Ecole française d›Extrême-Orient*, 263-332. HTTPS://WWW.PERSEE.FR/DOC/BEFEO_0336-1519_1937_NUM_37_1_5354

Majumdar, R. C. (1927). *Ancient Indian colonies in the Far East. Vol. I, Champa / by R.C. Majumdar*. Punjab Sanskrit Book Depot.

Majumdar, R. C. (1943). *Kambujadesa*. HTTPS://WWW.VIFINDIA.ORG/SITES/DEFAULT/FILES/145799028-KAMBUJADESA-1943.PDF

Majumdar, R. C. (1953). Inscriptions of Kambuja. *The Asiatic Society Monograph Series*, *VIII*, 1-635.

Malleret, L. (1951). IV. Les fouilles d›Oc-èo (1944). Rapport préliminaire. *Bulletin de l›Ecole française d›Extrême-Orient*, 75-88. HTTPS://WWW.PERSEE.FR/DOC/BEFEO_0336-1519_1951_NUM_45_1_5512

Malleret, L. (1959). *L'archéologie du Delta du Mékong* (Vol. 1. L'exploration archéologique et les fouilles d'Oc-Eo). Publications de l'École française d'Extrême-Orient, v. 43 (XLIII).

Manguin, P.-Y. (1980). The Southeast Asian Ship: An Historical Approach. *Journal of Southeast Asian Studies, 11*(2), 266-276. http://www.jstor.org/stable/20070359

Masanari, N. (2005). Settlement patterns on the Red River plain from the late prehistoric period to the 10th century AD. https://journals.lib.washington.edu/index.php/bippa/article/download/11920/10546

Maspero, G. (1910). Le royaume de Champa: Chapitre III. Le Lin-Yi (Suite). *T'oung Pao, 11*(4), 489-526. http://www.jstor.org/stable/4526168

Maspero, G. (1928). *Le royaume de Champa* (G. Vanoest, Ed.). Librairie Nationale d'Art et d'Histoire.

Maspero, H. (1910). Le Protectorat général d'Annam sous les T'ang : essai de géographie historique, I. *Bulletin de l'Ecole française d'Extrême-Orient*, 539-584. https://www.persee.fr/doc/befeo_0336-1519_1910_num_10_1_2046

Maspero , H. (1910). Le Protectorat général d'Annam sous les T'ang : essai de géographie historique, II. *Bulletin de l'Ecole française d'Extrême-Orient*, 665-682. https://www.persee.fr/doc/befeo_0336-1519_1910_num_10_1_2062

Maspero, H. (1916). Études d'histoire d'Annam. *Bulletin de l'Ecole française d'Extrême-Orient*, 1-55. https://www.persee.fr/doc/befeo_0336-1519_1916_num_16_1_5270

Maspero, H. (1918). Études d'histoire d'Annam. *Bulletin de l'Ecole française d'Extrême-Orient*, 1-36. https://www.persee.fr/doc/befeo_0336-1519_1918_num_18_1_5888

Minh Thư. (2007). *Tuyển chọn ca dao hay nhất*. NXB Văn hóa dân tộc

Monument Mining. Factsheet. https://www.monumentmining.com/site/assets/files/4223/mmy_factsheet_march_19_2021.pdf

N Rama, & Lakshmanan, M. (2010). An Algorithm Based on Empirical Methods, for Text-to-Tuneful-Speech Synthesis of Sanskrit Verse. *International Journal of Computer Science and Network Security, 10*, 281-288.

National Organization for Rare Disorders. (2009). *Elephantiasis*. https://rarediseases.org/rare-diseases/elephantiasis/

Nature of God and existence in Hinduism. (2022). https://www.bbc.co.uk/bitesize/guides/z44bcj6/revision/3#:~:text=three%20of%20the%20most%20significant,and%20shiva%20is%20the%20destroyer.

Ngô, A. (2011). *Võ Cạnh - bia sớm nhất của vương quốc Chăm Pa* http://baotanglichsu.vn/vi/articles/2001/65904/vo-canh-bia-som-nhat-cua-vuong-quoc-cham-pa.html

Ngô Sĩ Liên. (1998). *Đại Việt Sử Ký Toàn Thư* Khoa Học Xã Hội (Social Science) (1998). (Chính Hòa version (1697).)

Ngô, V. D. (2002). *Văn hóa cổ Champa*. NXB Văn Hóa Dân Tộc.

Ngô, V. D. (2004). *Thánh địa Mỹ Sơn* (2 ed.). NXB Trẻ.

Ngokhong from Vietnamese Wikipedia, C. B.-S. (2010). *Shrines of Phung Hung in Son Tay town, Hanoi*. https://upload.wikimedia.org/wikipedia/commons/c/c8/denphunghung1.jpg

Nguyễn, Đ. C. (2005). *Cầu Sông Dinh – chợ Dinh*. http://www.baophuyen.com.vn/120/729/cau-song-dinh-%e2%80%93-cho-dinh.html

Nguyễn, D. H. (2019). *Văn Minh Đại Việt*. NXB Hồng Đức.

Nguyễn, D. V. (2020). Nhận Diện La Thành Thăng Long Qua Tư Liệu Thư Tịch và Khảo Cổ Học. *Văn Hóa Truyền Thống và Phát Triển, Volume 9, Issue 1*.

Nguyễn Hoàng Nhật Thiên Nam - CC BY-SA 4.0 via Wikimedia Commons. (2021). *Tháp cổ Vĩnh Hưng thuộc ấp Trung Hưng IB, xã Vĩnh Hưng A, Vĩnh Lợi, Bạc Liêu*. https://upload.wikimedia.org/wikipedia/commons/1/1b/vinh_hung_tower%2c_vinh_loi%2c_bac_lieu.jpg

Nguyễn, H. T. (2009). Thư tịch cổ viết về Vũ Hồn. *Tạp chí Nghiên cứu Lịch sử, 4.2009*.

Nguyễn, L. (1973). *Việt Nam Phật Giáo Sử Luận*. Lá Bối.

Nguyễn, L. C. (2011). *Bí ẩn của hai ngôi mộ cổ ở Ciputra*. http://nguoihanoi.com.vn/bi-an-vu-hai-ngoi-mo-co-o-ciputra_217062.html

Nguyen, M., Marchesiello, P., Florent, L., Ouillon, S., Cambon, G., Allain, D., & Van Uu, D. (2014). Tidal characteristics of the gulf of Tonkin. *Continental Shelf Research, 91*, 37-56. https://doi.org/10.1016/j.csr.2014.08.003

Nguyen, P. L. (1975). Les nouvelles recherches archéologiques au Việtnam (Complément au Việtnam de Louis Bezacier). *Arts Asiatiques*, 3-151. https://www.persee.fr/doc/arasi_0004-3958_1975_num_31_1_1092

Nguyễn, Q. N. (1998). Vị trí của chùa Chân Giáo và một hướng tìm di tích thành Thăng Long thời kỳ mới định đô Kỷ yếu hội thảo quốc tế Việt Nam học lần thứ nhất (1998) Hanoi.

Nguyễn, Q. N. (2010). Cuộc khởi nghĩa Hai Bà Trưng sau 1970 năm nhìn lại *Tạp chí Nghiên cứu Lịch sử, 3. 2010*, 3-15.

Nguyễn, Q. N. (2012). *Chinese domination and the resistance against it: remains of the material culture - Bắc thuộc và chống Bắc thuộc: Những dấu tích văn hóa vật chất*. Perspectives on the archaeology of Vietnam international colloquium, Hanoi 29th February - 2nd March 2012 = Toàn cảnh khảo cổ học Việt Nam, Hanoi, Vietnam.

Nguyễn, T. S. T. (2015). *Đời sống văn hóa của cư dân Óc Eo ở Tây Nam Bộ (Qua tư liệu khảo cổ học)*. Bộ Văn Hóa, Thể Thao và Du Lịch Bộ Giáo Dục và Đào Tạo, Trường Đại Học Văn Hóa Hà Nội]. Hanoi.

Nguyễn, V. (2011). *Chủ nhân mộ cổ Ciputra là người Việt?* http://baotanglichsu.vn/vi/articles/2001/62685/chu-nhan-mo-co-ciputra-la-nguoi-viet.html

Nguyễn, V. Q. (2016). Nhận thức mới về Thành Lồi (Thừa Thiên- Huế) qua kết quả điều tra khảo cổ học. *Tạp chí Nghiên cứu và Phát triển, 4 (130)*, 57-69.

Noriko, N. (2017). An Introduction to Dr. Nishimura Masanari's Research on the Lung Khe Citadel. *Asian Review of World Histories, 5*(2), 11-27. https://doi.org/https://doi.org/10.1163/22879811-12340003

O'Harrow, S. (1979). From Co-loa to the Trung Sisters' revolt: Viet-Nam as the Chinese found it. *Asian perspectives., 22*(2), 140-164.

O'Harrow, S. (1986). Men of Hu, Men of Han, Men of the hundred man. *Bulletin de l'Ecole française d'Extrême-Orient*, 249-266. https://www.persee.fr/doc/befeo_0336-1519_1986_num_75_1_1707

Oey, G. P., & Luce, G. H. (1961). *The Man shu*. Department of Far Eastern Studies Cornell University.

Osborne, M. Professor George Coedes, 1866-1969: A Memoir. https://www.cambridge.org/core/services/aop-cambridge-core/content/view/433ec6ca2e601bb57a87d96d8616a30c/s0022463400000035a.pdf/professor-george-coedes-1866-1969-a-memoir.pdf

ourworldindata.org. (2021). *World population from 10,000 BC to today*. https://ourworldindata.org/world-population-growth

Papin, P. (2001). *Histoire de Hanoi*. Fayard.

Parmentier, H. (1909). *Inventaire descriptif des monuments Cams de l'Annam* (Vol. Planches). de l'École française d'Extrême-Orient, Ernest Leroux.

Parmentier, H. (1909a). *Inventaire descriptif des monuments. Cams de l'Annam* (Vol. Tome Premier - Description des Monuments). de l'École française d'Extrême-Orient, Ernest Leroux.

Parmentier, H. (1909b). Relevé archéologique de la province de Tây-Ninh (Cochinchine). *Bulletin de l'Ecole française d'Extrême-Orient*, 739-756. https://www.persee.fr/doc/befeo_0336-1519_1909_num_9_1_1976

Peak Advisor. *Nanling Mountains*. https://peakvisor.com/range/nanling-mountains.html

Pelliot, P. (1903). Le Fou-nan. *Bulletin de l'Ecole française d'Extrême-Orient*, 248-303. https://www.persee.fr/doc/befeo_0336-1519_1903_num_3_1_1216

Pelliot, P. (1904). Deux itinéraires de Chine en Inde à la fin du VIIIe siècle. *Bulletin de l'Ecole française d'Extrême-Orient*, 131-413. https://www.persee.fr/doc/befeo_0336-1519_1904_num_4_1_1299

Phạm, H. Q. (2011). Những ghi chép liên quan đến biển Đông Việt Nam trong chính sử Trung Quốc. *Nghiên cứu Trung Quốc, 6 (118)*, 22-55.

Phạm, L. H. Khảo cứu lại khởi nghĩa Dương Thanh (819-820). *Tạp chí Nghiên cứu Lịch sử, 12.2012*.

Phạm, L. H. Một số thủ lĩnh An Nam thời thuộc Đường. *VNH3.TB1.543*.

Phạm, L. H. (2009). Về một số thủ lĩnh An Nam thời thuộc Đường. *Tạp chí Nghiên cứu Lịch sử, No. 9, 2009*, 46-58.

Phạm, L. H. (2012). Một vài suy nghĩ nhân sự kiện phát lộ các ngôi mộ cổ tại Đông Ngạc (Từ Liêm, Hà Nội). *Thông Báo Hán Nôm Học Năm 2010-2011 - Viện Khoa Học Xã Hội Viện Nam - Viện Nghiên Cứu Hán Nôm*, 704-712.

Phạm, L. H. (2017). A Reconsideration of the Leilou – Longbian Debate: A Continuation of Research by Nishimura Masanari. *Asian Review of World Histories*, 5(2), 28-52. https://doi.org/https://doi.org/10.1163/22879811-12340004

Pham, T. (2021). *The Bronze Drums and The Earrings* (Vol. 1). 315Kio Publishing.

Phan, H. L. (2009). Khởi nghĩa Mai Thúc Loan - Những vấn đề cần xác minh. *Nghiên Cứu Lịch Sử - Viện Sử Học, Vol. 2.2009*.

Phan, H. L. (2012). *Power centres in North Vietnam during the period of Chinese occupation - Những trung tâm quyền lực ở miền bắc Việt Nam thời kỳ Trung Hoa đô hộ*. Perspectives on the archaeology of Vietnam international colloquium, Hanoi 29th February - 2nd March 2012 = Toàn cảnh khảo cổ học Việt Nam, Hanoi, Vietnam.

Phan , H. L. (2012). Thăng Long-Hà Nội vị thế lịch sử và di sản văn hóa. *8.2012*.

Phan, H. L. (2018). *Di sản văn hóa Việt Nam dưới góc nhìn lịch sử*. NXB Đại Học Quốc Gia Hà Nội.

Phan , H. L. (2018). *Lịch sử và văn hóa Việt Nam tiếp cận bộ phận* (P. T. Phan, Ed. 4th ed.). NXB Đại Học Quốc Gia Hà Nội.

Phan, K. (1967). *Việt Sử: Xứ Đàng Trong 1558-1777 - Cuộc Nam Tiến của Dân Tộc Việt Nam*. Nhà Sách Khai Trí.

Phan, L. H. (2015). Phép thuật Cao Biền tại An Nam-Từ ảo tưởng đến chân tướng. *Tạp Chí Nghiên Cứu Tôn Giáo, 17, no. 3(141), March 2015*, 105-132.

Proposed inscriptions for the permanent exhibition. HTTPS://WWW.EFEO.FR/CIK/DOCUMENTS/INSCRIPTIONSMNPP/SELECTIONEXPOPERMANENTE5.HTM

Quách, T. (2002). *Xứ Trầm Hương*. Hội Văn Học Nghệ Thuật Khánh Hòa.

Quang Nam Province. HTTPS://EN-US.TOPOGRAPHIC-MAP.COM/MAPS/9DDA/QUANG-NAM-PROVINCE/

Quốc Sử Quán Triều Nguyễn, Viện Khoa Học Xã Hội Việt Nam, & Viện Sử Học. (2006). *Đại Nam Nhất Thống Chí* (T. Đ. Phạm & D. A. Đào, Trans.). NXB Thuận Hóa.

Quốc Sử Quán Triều Nguyễn, & Viện Sử Học. (1998). *Khâm Định Việt Sử Thông Giám Cương Mục* (Hoa Bằng, Phạm Trọng Điềm, & Trần Văn Giáp (1957), Trans.). Giáo dục.

Real Chinese - Mini-guides - Chinese characters. (2014). HTTPS://WWW.BBC.CO.UK/LANGUAGES/CHINESE/REAL_CHINESE/MINI_GUIDES/CHARACTERS/CHARACTERS_HOWMANY.SHTML#:~:TEXT=HOW%20MANY%20CHARACTERS%20ARE%20THERE,ABLE%20TO%20READ%20A%20NEWSPAPER.

Rivers, P. J. (2004). Monsoon rhythms and trade patterns: ancient times east of Suez. *Journal of the Malaysian Branch of the Royal Asiatic Society, 77*(2 (287)), 59-93. HTTP://WWW.JSTOR.ORG/STABLE/41493525

Sabanski, C. *The Sundial Primer*. HTTPS://WWW.MYSUNDIAL.CA/TSP/GNOMON_HEIGHT.HTML

Sadalmelik - Public domain. (2007). *Topographic map of Vietnam. Created with GMT from publicly released GLOBE data*. HTTPS://COMMONS.WIKIMEDIA.ORG/WIKI/FILE:VIETNAM_TOPOGRAPHY.PNG

Schinz, A. (1996). *The Magic Square: Cities in Ancient China*. Edition Axel Menges.

Schweyer, A.-V. (2019). *The Birth of Champa*.

Seidenfaden, E. (1922). Complément à l'Inventaire descriptif des monuments du Cambodge pour les quatre provinces du Siam Oriental. *Bulletin de l'Ecole française d'Extrême-Orient*, 55-99. HTTPS://WWW.PERSEE.FR/DOC/BEFEO_0336-1519_1922_NUM_22_1_2912

Selections from Mouzi›s Disposing of Error (Lihou Lun). HTTP://AFE.EASIA.COLUMBIA.EDU/PS/CUP/MOUZI_DISPOSING_ERROR.PDF

Siddham the Asia inscriptions database. (2020). *Vat Thlen stele with an inscription (K.1) in Old Khmer*. HTTPS://SIDDHAM.NETWORK/OBJECT/OBJECTK1/

Silian, Y. (635). *Book of Liang (Liang shu)-Volume 3: Emperor Wu 3*. HTTP://CHINESENOTES.COM/LIANGSHU/LIANGSHU003.HTML#?HIGHLIGHT=%E6%9D%8E%E8%B3%81

Sima, Q., & Chan, C. M. (2016). *The Grand Scribe's Records, Volume X : Volume X: The Memoirs of Han China, Part III* [Book]. Indiana University Press.

Sima Qian, & translated by Phan Ngọc. (2018). *Sử ký Tư Mã Thiên : (trọn bộ hai tập)* (Vol. 1, 2). Văn học.

SLK. (5 February 2009). *The history of Cambodia from 1st century to 20th century [5] Why did Chinese call Cambodia «Chenla»?* HTTPS://SOKHEOUNNEWS.FILES.WORDPRESS.COM/2010/05/5-WHY-DID-CHINESE-CALL-CAMBODIA-CHENLA.PDF

Smith, C. R. U. S. M. C. H., & Museums, D. (1988). *U.S. Marines in Vietnam: high mobility and stand down, 1969*.

Southworth, W. A. (2001). *The origins of Campa in Central Vietnam: a preliminary review* /z-wcorg/. HTTP://CATALOG.HATHITRUST.ORG/API/VOLUMES/OCLC/57480138.HTML

Southworth, W. A. (2004). The coastal states of Champa. In B. P. IGlover I (Ed.), *Southeast Asia: from prehistory to history*. (pp. 209-233). Routledge Curzon.

Soutif, D., & Chollet, C. (2017). *Inventaire CIK des inscriptions Khmères (Corpus of Khmer Inscriptions)*. Siem Reap EFEO Center HTTPS://CIK.EFEO.FR/WP-CONTENT/UPLOADS/2017/04/INVENTAIRE-CIK-09042017.PDF

SS. (3 July 2017). *Map of Later Tang, one of Five Dynasties*

SS, CC BY-SA 4.0 <https://creativecommons.org/licenses/by-sa/4.0>, *via Wikimedia Commons*. HTTPS://COMMONS.WIKIMEDIA.ORG/WIKI/FILE:LATER_TANG.PNG

Stark, M. (2006). From Funan to Angkor Collapse and Regeneration in Ancient Cambodia. In (pp. 144-167).

Stefan Fussan / CC BY-SA (HTTPS://CREATIVECOMMONS.ORG/LICENSES/BY-SA/3.0). (20 December 2011). Trấn Quốc Pagoda, Hanoi, Vietnam. HTTPS://UPLOAD.WIKIMEDIA.ORG/WIKIPEDIA/COMMONS/3/3D/HANOI_-_TRAN-QUOC-PAGODE_0002.JPG

SY CC BY-SA 4.0 <HTTPS://CREATIVECOMMONS.ORG/LICENSES/BY-SA/4.0> via Wikimedia Commons. (7 July 2017). *Warlords in the End of the Han Dynasty*. HTTPS://COMMONS.WIKIMEDIA.ORG/WIKI/FILE:END_OF_HAN_DYNASTY_WARLORDS.PNG

Tana, L. (2002). *Nguyễn Cochinchina: Southern Vietnam in the seventeenth and eighteenth centuries* (Second ed.). Southeast Asia Program Publications.

Tana, L. (2019). The changing landscape of the former Linyi in the provinces of Quảng Trị and Thừa Thiên -Huế. In *Yusof Ishak Institute Nalanda-Sriwijaya Centre working paper series* (pp. 1-16). Yusof Ishak Institute Nalanda-Sriwijaya Centre.

«Tang Hui Yao» Volume Ninety-eight. Foreign countries: Uyghurs, Xicuan, Mikun, Linyi , Zhenla, Baigou Qiang, Caoguo, Shuna, Bayegu, Xi, Tanguts. HTTP://GUOXUE.HTTPCN.COM/HTML/BOOK/CQAZUYRN/UYPWUYKOUY.SHTML

Taylor, K. W. (1983). *The Birth of Vietnam*. Berkeley: University of California Press.

Team Wanderlust. (10 February 2017). *10 incredibly beautiful pagodas from around the world*. https://www.wanderlust.co.uk/content/10-incredible-pagodas-from-around-the-world/

Thái, V. C. (2009). *Nghiên cứu chữ viết cổ trên bia ký ở Đông Dương*. NXB Khoa Học Xã Hội.

Thakur, U. (1986). *Some aspects of Asian history and culture*. Abhinav publications.

The Metropolitan Museum of Art. *Buddha in Meditation, 8th–9th century, Southern Vietnam*. https://www.metmuseum.org/art/collection/search/77598

Thế Từ Đại Lý. (2018). *Goddess of (Lightning) Flash statue. Located in Trí Quả Buddhist Temple, Thuan Thanh, Bac Ninh, Viet Nam. Taken without usual decorative clothes. Public domain via Wikimedia Commons*. https://upload.wikimedia.org/wikipedia/commons/0/0c/t%c6%b0%e1%bb%a3ng_ph%c3%a1p_%c4%90i%e1%bb%87n_khi_ch%c6%b0a_phong_y_%c3%a1o.jpg

Theobald, U. (12 July 2010). *Manshu*. http://www.chinaknowledge.de/literature/historiography/manshu.html

Theobald, U. (2016). *duliangheng* 度量衡, *weights and measures*. http://www.chinaknowledge.de/history/terms/duliangheng.html

Thich, N. H. (1998). *The Three Doors of Liberation - The Heart of the Buddha's Teachings*. http://www.mpcmontreal.org/sites/pleineconscience.org/files/the%20three%20doors%20of%20liberation-%20emptiness.pdf

Thuydaonguyen CC BY-SA 3.0. Bàn thờ chính trong chùa Linh Sơn, núi Ba Thê, huyện Thoại Sơn, An Giang, Việt Nam. https://upload.wikimedia.org/wikipedia/commons/6/6d/b%c3%a0n_th%e1%bb%9d_ch%c3%adnh_trong_ch%c3%b9a_linh_s%c6%a1n.jpg

Tingley, N., with essays by Andreas Reinecke, Pierre-Yves Manguin, Kerry Nguyen-Long, & Nguyen Dinh Chien. (2009). *Arts of Ancient Viet Nam: From River Plain to Open Sea*. Asia Society; The Museum of Fine Arts; Yale University Press [distr.].

Tổng Cục Thống Kê - General Statistics Ofice. (2020). *Kết quả toàn bộ tổng điều tra dân số và nhà ở - Completed results of the 2019 Vietnam population and housing census*. Nhà xuất bản Thống Kê 2020. Statistical Publishing House 2020.

Tống, T. T. (2012). *Contributions to the Structure of the Thăng Long Citadel - Đóng góp vào việc nghiên cứu cấu trúc kinh thành Thăng Long* Perspectives on the archaeology of Vietnam international colloquium, Hanoi 29th February - 2nd March 2012 = Toàn cảnh khảo cổ học Việt Nam, Hanoi, Vietnam.

Tống , T. T. (2012). *A general outline on the history of archeology in Vietnam - Vài nét về lịch sử khảo cổ học Việt Nam*. Perspectives on the archaeology of Vietnam International Colloquium, Hanoi 29th February - 2nd March 2012 = Toàn cảnh khảo cổ học Việt Nam, Hanoi, Vietnam.

Tourism, M. o. C.-S. a., & BẢO TÀNG LỊCH SỬ QUỐC GIA VIETNAM NATIONAL MUSEUM OF HISTORY. (8 July 2010). *Từ Luy Lâu - Long Biên đến Thăng Long - Hà Nội (I)*. http://baotanglichsuquocgia.vn/vi/articles/2001/65224/tu-luy-lau-long-bien-djen-thang-long-ha-noi-i.html

Trần, B. Đ., Mạc, Đ., Tô, B. G., Phan, V. H., Lê, V. N., Nguyễn, N., & Tôn, N. Q. T. (2005). *Lịch Sử Việt Nam (Từ Đầu Đến Năm 938) - Tập 2* (V. G. Trần, B. Đ. Trần, & Đ. Mạc, Eds.). NXB Trẻ.

Trần, K. P. (2009). The Architecture of the Temple-Towers of Ancient Champa (Central Vietnam) - Chapter 6. In A. C. M. Z. P. Hardy (Ed.), *Champa and the archaeology of Mỹ Sơn (Vietnam)*. NUS Press.

Trần, Q. V. (2001). Vị thế Luy Lâu. *Nghiên Cứu Lịch Sử - Viện Sử Học, 315*, 3-7. https://repository.vnu.edu.vn/handle/vnu_123/71090

Trần, Q. V., & Vũ, T. S. (2004). *Hà Nội Nghìn Xưa*. NXB Quân Đội Nhân Dân.

Trần, T. D. (2019). *Việt Nam Thế Kỷ X: Những Mảnh Vỡ Lịch Sử*. Nhà Xuất Bản Đại Học Sư Phạm.

Trần, T. K. (1999). *Việt Nam Sử Lược*. Văn Hóa Thông Tin. (1921)

Trần, T. P. (2011). *Lĩnh nam chích quái* (restored and edited by Vũ Quỳnh and Kiều Phú, Đinh Gia Khánh, Nguyễn Ngọc San, Trans.). NXB Trẻ; Hồng Bàng. (1492)

Trần, V. G. (1932). X Le bouddhisme en Annam, des origines au XIIIe siècle. *Bulletin de l'Ecole française d'Extrême-Orient*, 191-268. https://www.persee.fr/doc/befeo_0336-1519_1932_num_32_1_4554

Trần, V. G. (1966). Sách «Vĩnh-Lạc đại điền bản Giao-Châu ký» mới bị phát hiện là một ngụy thư (sách giả tạo). *Tạp chí Nghiên cứu Lịch sử, Số 84 (Tháng 3)*, 26-28. (Viện Khoa học Xã hội Việt Nam)

Trần, V. G., & Tuệ Sỹ. (1968). *Phật Giáo Việt Nam từ khởi nguyên đến thế kỷ XIII - Le Bouddhisme en Annam* (T. Sỹ, Trans.). Ban Tu Thư Viện Đại Học Vạn Hạnh 1968.

The Trimurti. https://iskconeducationalservices.org/hoh/practice/worship/the-trimurti/

Tropic of Cancer. (2021). https://en.wikipedia.org/wiki/tropic_of_cancer

Trương, Đ. C. (2018). *Các nhóm mộ táng tại di tích Giồng Lớn (Bà Rịa - Vũng Tàu)*. https://baotanglichsu.vn/vi/articles/3127/68782/cac-nhom-mo-tang-tai-di-tich-giong-lon-ba-ria-vung-tau.html

Trương, T. D. (2018). *Khảo chứng tiền sử Việt Nam - Researching of Vietnam prehistory*. NXB Tổng Hợp Thành Phố Hồ Chí Minh.

Tứ Pháp. (2020). https://vi.wikipedia.org/wiki/t%e1%bb%a9_ph%c3%a1p

United States Office of Geography United States Board on Geographic Names. (1961). *Southern Vietnam and the South China Sea; Official Standard Names Approved by the United States Board on Geographic Names*. U.S. Government Printing Office.

unknown. (19th century). *King Lý Nam Đế and his Queen*. https://www.vnfam.vn/en/artifact/5af2af3d4e501e0026539520

Unknown, translated by Trần Quốc Vượng (1959), & compared and corrected by Đinh Khắc Thuân. (2005). *Việt Sử Lược*. Thuận Hóa. (1377)

V. Thanh. (6 June 2014). *Về sông Dâu*. http://www.dongky.bacninh.com/xem-tin-tuc/68721/ve-song-dau.html

Vallerin, M., & Manguin, P.-Y. (1997). Việt Nam. La mission « Archéologie du delta du Mékong ». *Bulletin de l'Ecole française d'Extrême-Orient*, 408-414. https://www.persee.fr/doc/befeo_0336-1519_1997_num_84_1_2495

Văn phòng Nôm Na (Hà Nội). (1993). *Phiên bản Alpha, Đại Việt Sử Ký Toàn Thư, Bản in Nội các quan bản, Mộc bản khắc năm Chính Hoà thứ 18 (1697)*. HTTP://WWW.NOMFOUNDATION.ORG/NOM-PROJECT/HISTORY-OF-GREATER-VIETNAM/PREFACE?UILANG=VN

Về các loại hình văn hóa Chămpa ở Quảng Trị. (11 December 2011). HTTPS://GIOITHIEU.QUANGTRI.GOV.VN/INDEX.PHP?LANGUAGE=VI&NV=NEWS&OP=LICH-SU-VAN-HOA/VE-CAC-LOAI-HINH-VAN-HOA-CHAMPA-O-QUANG-TRI-34

Verellen, F. (2015). *Prince Gao›s occupation of Annan and the rise of regional autonomy under the late Tang*. Hong Kong University Press.

Vĩ, A. L. (2016). *Sự kiện người Arab (Đại Thực) tấn công An Nam đô hộ phủ giữa thế kỉ VII (2014)*. HTTPS://WWW.ACADEMIA.EDU/19954557/S%E1%BB%B1_KI%E1%BB%87N_NG%C6%B0%E1%BB%9DI_ARAB_%C4%90%E1%BA%A1I_TH%E1%BB%B1C_T%E1%BA%A5N_C%C3%B4NG_AN_NAM_%C4%91%C3%B4_H%E1%BB%99_PH%E1%BB%A7_GI%E1%BB%AFA_TH%E1%BA%BF_K%E1%BB%89_VII

Vickery, M. (1994). What and Where was Chenla? *Recherches nouvelles sur le Cambodge*, 197-212. (Publiées sous la direction de F. Bizot. École française d›Extrême-Orient, Paris)

Vickery, M. (2000). Coedès› Histories of Cambodia. *Silpakorn University International Journal (Bangkok)*, *1*, *Number 1*(January-June 2000), 61-108.

Vickery, M. (2003). Funan Reviewed: Deconstructing the Ancients. *Bulletin de l›Ecole française d›Extrême-Orient*, 101-143. HTTPS://WWW.PERSEE.FR/DOC/BEFEO_0336-1519_2003_NUM_90_1_3609

Vickery, M. (2005). Champa revised.

Việt Nữ. (2018). *Những con đường rợp bóng cây cổ thụ ở Sài Gòn*. HTTPS://TUOITRE.VN/NHUNG-CON-DUONG-ROP-BONG-CAY-CO-THU-O-SAI-GON-20180120200829412.HTM

VNA. (9 February 2021). *Ethnic cultures, national treasures on display at An Giang Museum*. HTTPS://EN.QDND.VN/CULTURE-SPORTS/CULTURE/ETHNIC-CULTURES-NATIONAL-TREASURES-ON-DISPLAY-AT-AN-GIANG-MUSEUM-526838

Vu, H. L., & Sharrock, P. D. (2014). *Descending dragon, rising tiger: a history of Vietnam*.

Vuving, A. L. (2001). The References of Vietnamese States and the Mechanisms of World Formation. *ASIEN (Journal of the German Association for Asian Studies)*, no. 79 (April 2001), 62-86.

Wang Pu. (961). *Tang huiyao, «Institutional history of the Tang dynasty»*. HTTP://WWW.CHINAKNOWLEDGE.DE/LITERATURE/HISTORIOGRAPHY/TANGHUIYAO.HTML

Wang, Y., Sastra, L., & Boonsom, Y. (2018). Pearl Raising in Guangxi Province and Its Importance to the Local Economy. *International Journal of East Asia Studies*, *22(1)*, 20-41.

Wei Zheng, Shigu, Y., Yingda, K., & Wuji, Z. (636). *Book of Sui* HTTP://CHINESENOTES.COM/SUISHU.HTML

Wei Zheng, Yan Shigu, Kong Yingda, & Zhangsun Wuji. (636). *Book of Sui* HTTP://CHINESENOTES.COM/SUISHU.HTML

Wei Zheng, Yan Shigu, Kong Yingda , & Zhangsun Wuji. (636). *Book of Sui - Volume 56 Biographies 21: Lu Kai, Ling Huxi, Xue Zhou, Yu Wenbi, Zhang Heng, Yang Wang* HTTP://CHINESENOTES.COM/SUISHU/SUISHU056.HTML

Wheatley, P. (1956). *Tun-Sun* (頓 遜). *Journal of the Royal Asiatic Society of Great Britain and Ireland*(1/2), 17-30. http://www.jstor.org/stable/25222785

Wikipedia *Book of Han*. https://en.wikipedia.org/wiki/book_of_han

Wikipedia. *Historical Records of the Five Dynasties*. https://en.wikipedia.org/wiki/historical_records_of_the_five_dynasties

Wikipedia. *Tongdian*. https://en.wikipedia.org/wiki/tongdian

Wikipedia. *Varman (surname)*. https://en.wikipedia.org/wiki/varman_(surname)

Wikipedia. *Zizhi Tongjian*. https://en.wikipedia.org/wiki/zizhi_tongjian

Wikipedia. (2015). *Loaded march*. https://en.wikipedia.org/wiki/loaded_march

Wikipedia. (-e). *Book of Chen (Chen shu)*. https://en.wikipedia.org/wiki/book_of_chen

Wikipedia. (-f). *Book of Liang (Liang shu)*. https://en.wikipedia.org/wiki/book_of_liang

Wikipedia. (-g). *Book of Song*. https://en.wikipedia.org/wiki/book_of_song

Wikipedia. (-h). *Book of Sui*. https://en.wikipedia.org/wiki/book_of_sui

Wikipedia. (-i). *Book of Jin (Jin shu)* https://en.wikipedia.org/wiki/book_of_jin

Wikipedia. (-j). *Book of Qi*. https://en.wikipedia.org/wiki/book_of_qi

Wikipedia. (-k). *Book of the Later Han*. https://en.wikipedia.org/wiki/book_of_the_later_han

Wikipedia. (-l). *Commentary on the Water Classic*. https://en.wikipedia.org/wiki/commentary_on_the_water_classic

Wikipedia. (-m). *Funan*. https://en.wikipedia.org/wiki/funan

Wikipedia. (-n). *Mengzi City*. https://en.wikipedia.org/wiki/mengzi_city

Wikipedia. (-o). *New Book of Tang (Xin Tang shu)*. https://en.wikipedia.org/wiki/new_book_of_tang

Wikipedia. (-p). *Old Book of Tang (Jiu Tang shu)*. https://en.wikipedia.org/wiki/old_book_of_tang

Wikipedia. (-q). *Records of the Three Kingdoms*. https://en.wikipedia.org/wiki/records_of_the_three_kingdoms

Wikipedia. (-r). *Shi Xie*. https://en.wikipedia.org/wiki/shi_xie

Worcester, G. R. (2020). *Junks and Sampans of the Yangtze*. NAVAL INSTITUTE PRESS.

World Heritage List. https://whc.unesco.org/en/list/&order=country#alpham

Xiao Zixian. (489-537). *Book of Southern Qi*. http://chinesenotes.com/nanqishu.html

Xiao Zixian. (537). *Book of Southern Qi - Qi Shu*. http://chinesenotes.com/nanqishu.html

Xiao Zixian (537). *Book of Southern Qi - Volume 58, Biographies 39: Other Peoples from the Southeast*. http://chinesenotes.com/nanqishu/nanqishu058.html

Xiu, O., & Davis, R. L. (2004). *Historical Records of the Five Dynasties*. Columbia University Press.

Xiu, O., Qi, S., & Fan, Z. (1060). *New Book of Tang (Xin Tang shu) - Volume 222c Biographies 147c: Southern Man 3*. http://chinesenotes.com/xintangshu/xintangshu222c.html

Yao Silian (635). *Book of Liang (Liang shu)*. http://chinesenotes.com/liangshu/liangshu054.html

Yao Silian. (635). *Book of Liang (Liang shu) - Volume 54 - The Various Barbarians* HTTP://CHINESENOTES.COM/LIANGSHU/LIANGSHU054.HTML

Yao Silian. (636). *Book of Chen (Chen Shu), Volume 1: Emperor Wu 1.* HTTP://CHINESENOTES.COM/CHENSHU/CHENSHU001.HTML

Ye Myint Swe, Cho Cho Aye, & Khin Zaw. (2017). Chapter 25 Gold deposits of Myanmar. *Geological Society, London, Memoirs, 48*(1), 557-572. HTTPS://DOI.ORG/10.1144/M48.25

Yprpyqp. (27 February 2018). *A shieldbearer in the Dali Kingdom of Yunnan.* HTTPS://COMMONS.WIKIMEDIA.ORG/WIKI/FILE:DALI_SHIELD.JPG

Yuan Fang. (May 2017). *The favorite animal: the horse as mingqi in Han tombs* Cornell University]. HTTPS://ECOMMONS.CORNELL.EDU/BITSTREAM/HANDLE/1813/51570/FANG_CORNELL_0058O_10102.PDF?SEQUENCE=1&ISALLOWED=Y

Yue, S. (492-493). *Book of Song (Song shu).* HTTP://CHINESENOTES.COM/SONGSHU.HTML

Yue , S. (492-493). *Book of Song (Song shu)-Volume 38 Treatises 28: Administrative Districts 4.* HTTP://CHINESENOTES.COM/SONGSHU/SONGSHU038.HTML

Yue , S. (492-493). *Book of Song (Song shu)-Volume 92 Biographies 52: Liang Li* HTTP://CHINESENOTES.COM/SONGSHU/SONGSHU092.HTML

Yue , S. (492-493). *Book of Song (Song shu) -Volume 76 Biographies 36: Zhu Xiuzhi, Zong Que, Wang Xuanmo.* HTTP://CHINESENOTES.COM/SONGSHU/SONGSHU076.HTML

Yuqing Yang. (June 2008). *The role of Nanzhao history in the formation of Bai identity* University of Oregon].

Zhao Ying , Liu Xu, Zhang Zhao, Jia Wei, & Zhao Xi. (941-945). *Old Book of Tang (Jiu Tang shu).* HTTPS://CTEXT.ORG/WIKI.PL?IF=GB&RES=456206

Zhao Ying, Liu Xu, Zhang Zhao, Jia Wei, & Zhao Xi. (941-945). *Old Book of Tang , (Jiu Tang shu), Volume 35 Treatises 15: Astronomy 1.* HTTP://CHINESENOTES.COM/JIUTANGSHU/JIUTANGSHU039.HTML

Zheng, W., Shigu, Y., Yingda, K., & Wuji, Z. (636). *Book of Sui - Volume 2 Annals 2: Gaozu 2.* HTTP://CHINESENOTES.COM/SUISHU/SUISHU002.HTML
2512, 2712

www.ingramcontent.com/pod-product-compliance
Lightning Source LLC
Chambersburg PA
CBHW082336300426
44109CB00045B/2360